The Cosmic V

THE COSMIC VIEWPOINT

A *Study of Seneca's* Natural
Questions

GARETH D. WILLIAMS

OXFORD
UNIVERSITY PRESS

Library of Congress Cataloging-in-Publication Data
Williams, Gareth D.
The cosmic viewpoint : a study of Seneca's Natural questions / Gareth Williams.
p. cm.
Includes bibliographical references and index.
ISBN 978-0-19-973158-9 (acid-free paper)
1. Seneca, Lucius Annaeus, ca. 4 B.C.–65 A.D. Naturales quaestiones.
2. Science, Ancient—Historiography. 3. Meteorology—Historiography. I. Title.
PA6661.N3W55 2012
500—dc23   2011022209

1 3 5 7 9 8 6 4 2

Printed in the United States of America
on acid-free paper

For Bryley

Preface

This study aims to contribute to the modern reassessment of Seneca's *Natural Questions* as a meteorological work of considerable literary sophistication and importance—a highly original production in comparison with what survives of the larger Greco-Roman meteorological tradition. Initial studies of different aspects of the work (Williams [2005a], [2005b], [2006a], [2007], [2008a] and [2008b]) were not systematically planned as coordinated pieces. This study supplants those writings by attempting to take stock of the *Natural Questions* as a whole; although I have drawn extensively in this volume on my previous articles, they have undergone very significant modification, correction, revision, rearrangement and refashioning into the sequence of chapters that is presented here, and much new material has been added.

For permission to draw on previously published material I am grateful to *Ramus*, the *Cambridge Classical Journal*, the *American Journal of Philology* and the *Journal of Roman Studies*. Material from Williams (2008b) ©The Classical Association, published by the Cambridge University Press, is reproduced with permission, as is material from Williams (2005a) ©2005 The University of Chicago. I thank Claudia Heilbrunn, James Uden, Katharina Volk and James Zetzel for much practical help and advice; John Henderson for illumination on many points when the manuscript was taking final shape; Margaret Graver and Harry Hine for valuable criticism and guidance as readers for Oxford University Press; Thomas Finnegan for his excellent copy-editing, and Saladi Gunabala and Natalie Johnson for managing the production process so well; and Stefan Vranka for both his general encouragement of the project and his expertise in seeing it through the press. I am also grateful to Columbia's Stanwood Cockey Lodge Fund for a subvention toward the costs of production. All citations of the text of the *Natural Questions* follow Hine (1996a) unless otherwise stated; translations are my own.

Contents

Abbreviations

CIL   *Corpus Inscriptionum Latinarum.* Berlin, 1863–.

DG   H. Diels, ed. *Doxographi Graeci.* Berlin, 1879.

D-K   H. Diels and W. Kranz, eds. *Die Fragmente der Vorsokratiker.* 3 vols. 6th ed. Berlin, 1952.

E-K   L. Edelstein and I. G. Kidd, eds. *Posidonius, I: The Fragments.* 2nd ed. Cambridge Classical Texts and Commentaries 13. Cambridge, 1989.

FGH   F. Jacoby, ed. *Die Fragmente der griechischen Historiker.* Leiden, 1923–1958.

L-S   A. A. Long and D. N. Sedley, eds. *The Hellenistic Philosophers.* 2 vols. Cambridge, 1987.

LSJ   H. G. Liddell and R. Scott, eds., revised by H. Stuart Jones and R. McKenzie. *A Greek-English Lexicon.* 9th ed. Oxford, 1968.

OED   *Oxford English Dictionary.* 2nd ed. Oxford, 1989.

OLD   P. W. Glare, ed. *Oxford Latin Dictionary.* Oxford, 1968–1982.

PIR   *Prosopographia Imperii Romani saec. I. II. III.* 2nd ed. Berlin and Leipzig, 1933–1999.

RE   A. F. von Pauly, ed., rev. G. Wissowa et al. *Realencyclopädie der classischen Altertumswissenschaft.* Stuttgart, 1893–.

SVF   H. von Arnim, ed. *Stoicorum Veterum Fragmenta.* Leipzig, 1903–1924.

TLL   *Thesaurus Linguae Latinae.* Leipzig, 1900–.

Introduction

quid est praecipuum? erigere animum supra minas et prom-
issa fortunae, nil dignum putare quod speres...quid est prae-
cipuum? posse laeto animo aduersa tolerare, quidquid
acciderit sic ferre quasi uolueris tibi accidere...quid est prae-
cipuum? animus contra calamitates fortis et contumax, luxu-
riae non auersus tantum sed infestus, nec auidus periculi nec
fugax...quid est praecipuum? non admittere in animo mala
consilia, puras ad caelum manus tollere, nullum bonum petere
quod ut ad te transeat aliquis dare debet aliquis amit-
tere...quid est praecipuum? altos supra fortuita spiritus tol-
lere, hominis meminisse ut, siue felix eris, scias hoc non
futurum diu, siue infelix, scias hoc te non esse si non putes...

Ad hoc proderit nobis rerum inspicere naturam: primum dis-
cedemus a sordidis; deinde animum ipsum, quo summo mag-
noque opus est, seducemus a corpore; deinde in occultis
exercitata subtilitas non erit in aperta deterior. nihil est autem
apertius his salutaribus quae contra nequitiam nostram fu-
roremque discuntur, quae damnamus nec ponimus.

NATURAL QUESTIONS 3 PREF. 11–15, 18

What is most important? Raising your mind above the threats
and promises of fortune, and considering nothing worth
hoping for....What is most important? To be able to endure
adversity with a glad mind, and to experience whatever hap-
pens to you as if you wanted it to happen....What is most im-
portant? A mind that is bold and confident in the face of
calamity, not just averse to luxury but hostile to it, neither
courting danger nor fleeing from it....What is most impor-
tant? Not to admit bad intentions into your mind, to raise
pure hands to heaven, to seek no good thing which, for it to
pass to you, someone must give, someone must lose....What is
most important? To raise your spirits high above chance occur-
rences; to be mindful of being human, so that, if you are fortu-
nate, you know that this will not last long, and if unfortunate,
you know that you are not so if you do not think so...

> *For these reasons the study of nature will be helpful to us: first,*
> *we shall leave behind what is sordid. Second, we shall separate*
> *the mind, which needs to be elevated and great, from the body.*
> *Third, when we have exercised our intellect on hidden obscuri-*
> *ties, it will be no less effective in dealing with matters that are*
> *in plain view. But nothing is more visible than these salutary*
> *lessons that we are taught in order to combat our own wicked-*
> *ness and follies, which we condemn but fail to renounce.*

The study of nature as characterized here, and as conducted throughout the eight surviving books of Lucius Annaeus Seneca's *Naturales Quaestiones* (parts of two of them, Books 4a and 4b, are now lost),[1] is no narrowly focused exercise in purely technical exegesis. The weight of precedent in the Greek meteorological tradition naturally influences both Seneca's choice of topics and his commitment to the rational explanation of natural phenomena in this late work, on which he embarked in the early 60s CE, some four years before his forced suicide in April 65.[2] His range of subject matter is impressive: lights in the sky in Book 1; lightning and thunder in Book 2; terrestrial waters in Book 3; the Nile in Book 4a; clouds, rain, hail and snow in Book 4b;[3] wind in Book 5; earthquakes in Book 6; and comets in Book 7. But the technical thrust of his coverage of these various phenomena is inseparable from the ethical drive that guides his entire undertaking in the *Natural Questions*. Although Stoic physics provides a coordinating framework for the eight books, that physics is itself part of a Stoic philosophical holism that fundamentally shapes the *Natural Questions*—the holism, that is, among the parts of philosophy, ethics, physics and logic,[4] the first

---

1. The title, so attested in the manuscript tradition, may be assumed to be Seneca's own, but definitive proof is lacking; for the wording cf. also *cum uentum est ad naturales quaestiones* (*Letters* 88.24). On its equivalence to the Greek Προβλήματα φυσικά or Ζητήματα φυσικά (cf. *SVF* 3 App. II LX p. 205.6–13), and firmly against any possibility that Seneca derived the title from Asclepiodotus, see Hine (1981) 24–29, especially 24–27 on *N.Q.* 6.17.3, with Vottero (1989) 19–20.

2. Further on the dating, n. 26 below.

3. Only hail and snow are treated in the surviving fragment, but references there and elsewhere in the *Natural Questions* indicate that clouds and rain had been discussed in the lost portion; see Hine (1996a) 189.5–7 with Vottero (1989) 506.

4. On this holism, Hadot (1998) 77–80 and now Boeri (2009) 174–75; in general on the relationship of physics and ethics in Seneca's *Natural Questions* and beyond, Limburg (2007) 56–83.

two of which are inextricably intertwined in Seneca's tour of the natural world in his eight books.

A (perhaps *the*) dominating principle in the *Natural Questions* is that the study of nature is inseparable from reflection on human nature. For Seneca, by studying nature we free the mind from the restrictions and involvements of this life, liberating it to observe, and luxuriate in, the undifferentiated cosmic wholeness that is so distant from the fragmentations and disruptions of our everyday existence. So, in the contemporaneous *Moral Letters*, the *sapiens* is described thus:

> adhaeret quidem in corpore suo, sed optima sui parte abest et cogitationes suas ad sublimia intendit...interdicis mihi inspectione rerum naturae, a toto abductum redigis in partem?
>
> *Letters* 65.18–19

> He is bound closely to his body, but he is an absentee in the best part of himself, and concentrates his thoughts on lofty matters....Do you forbid me to contemplate the universe? Do you force me to withdraw from the whole and to be restricted to only a part of it?

By reaching for perception of this *totum*, we move toward a completeness of self-realization:

> Virtus enim ista quam adfectamus magnifica est non quia per se beatum est malo caruisse, sed quia animum laxat et praeparat ad cognitionem caelestium, dignumque efficit qui in consortium <cum> deo ueniat. tunc consummatum habet plenumque bonum sortis humanae cum calcato omni malo petît altum et in interiorem naturae sinum uenit.
>
> *N.Q.* 1 pref. 6–7

> The virtue to which we aspire is magnificent not because freedom from evil is itself so marvelous, but because it releases the mind, prepares it for knowledge of the celestial, and makes it worthy to enter into partnership with god. It possesses the full and complete benefit of human existence when it has spurned all evil, it has sought the heights and it has entered the inner recesses of nature.

This release brings with it the truest gratification and delight (cf. 1 pref. 3; *iuuat*, 7). It brings contempt for the literal and figurative narrowness of space and thought that the liberated mind has left behind, soaring as it does high above the pettiness of conventional values and vices at ground level (cf. 1 pref.

8–13). Above all, through knowledge of nature, it brings knowledge of god, who *is* nature:

illic demum discit quod diu quaesît, illic incipit deum nosse.

1 pref. 13[5]

There [sc. in the measureless space of the heavenly region where the *animus* roams free] the mind at last learns what it has long sought; there it begins to know god.

In *Dialogue* 8, *De otio*, Seneca portrays mankind as born to contemplate nature, to marvel at her wonders, to probe into her secrets and finally to unleash our investigative instinct so that "our thought bursts through the ramparts of the sky" (*Dial.* 8.5.6). Beyond the ethical imperative sampled just above, this innate disposition to inquire into nature is the second of two Senecan motives for studying physics that Brad Inwood neatly summarizes as follows: "Studying physics provides direct instrumental support to what we might call the enterprise of ethics, but it also fulfils something very important and fundamental in our natures, the built-in drive for contemplation of nature."[6]

The physics of the *Natural Questions*, then, is inseparable from ethical self-development. This book explores the artistic strategies by which Seneca develops and complicates this dynamic fusion of the physical and ethical components across his eight books. More particularly, my objective is to show that the *Natural Questions* is not so much about the natural world as an active form of engagement *with* nature: far from treating his diverse topics in the books with a steady, objective detachment, Seneca, I argue, constructs an eventful, often highly dramatized mode of discourse that not only brings the natural world to colorful life within the text but also activates the reader to be more than just the passive recipient of Seneca's researches; to be truly moved and transported by the figurative mind travels that the eight books instigate and enact; and to find in that energized state that the *Natural Questions* itself amounts to a form of literary participation in nature. The two objects of study, *natura ipsa* and the Senecan text, are in a way commensurate: the arduous and gradual task of probing nature's secrets (*secre-*

5. God as nature: cf. 2.45.2 with Hine (1981) 398 and Chaumartin (1996) 183. On "this equation of physical investigation with the contemplation of god" see Setaioli (2007), especially 334, 338–39, with Inwood (2000), especially 23–26; (2002), especially 119–25 = (2005) 157–65; (2009b) 215–22; Parroni (2000a), especially 437–38. Cf. also n. 7 below.

6. (2009b) 214–15.

tiora, 1 pref. 3) is replicated in Seneca's patient textual probings and doxographical surveillance across the books; but replicated also, perhaps, in the reader's task of probing and interpreting the artistic contours and subtleties of Senecan nature as drawn in the *Natural Questions*. On this approach, Seneca's meteorological theme, although traditional in one way, offers scope for real innovation in another: by focusing on *sublimia*, or atmospheric phenomena in the intermediate zone between the terrestrial and celestial regions (cf. 2.1.1), he raises our gaze above the level of what might be termed terrestrial perception. As we strive to understand such phenomena as rainbows and comets, the nature of winds and the cause of earthquakes, visual observation carries us only so far before the mind's eye becomes our guide in the formulation of conjecture and hypothesis at the intermediate, meteorological level of study. Within the overall framework of Stoic physics, the meteorological theme conveniently lends itself to a conceptual structure that differentiates between lower and higher forms of knowledge—a metaphysical distinction, if you will, not un-Platonic in character[7]—in the imaginative world of the *Natural Questions*.

The cognitive associations of Seneca's meteorological theme will be explored in detail in due course. But my insistence thus far on the hybrid status of the *Natural Questions* as a work that inextricably conjoins the physical and ethical strands immediately raises two basic questions. First, how does this vision of the *Natural Questions* as a hybrid physico-ethical production relate to the meteorological tradition that precedes it? Second, how does my own approach to the physico-ethical fusion in the *Natural Questions* relate to the directions taken in the existing scholarship? These questions are addressed in the next two subsections.

The Natural Questions and the Meteorological Tradition

Beyond Seneca's contribution to the founding of a meteorological literature in Latin, just how enterprising or novel a project is his *Natural Questions* when

---

7. On the Platonic aspect, Stahl (1964) 438–40 = Maurach (1975) 283–85; Donini (1979); Natali (1994); Chaumartin (1996) 180–81, 186–88; Setaioli (2007) 342–47; Limburg (2007) 401–11; and now Reydams-Schils (2010) with Hine (2010c) 58–61. True, an immanent Stoic god would seem to be incompatible with a transcendent, Platonizing image of god (see Limburg 401 with Natali 433); but my interest in the Platonic dimension in this book is to suggest only that Seneca experimentally appropriates within his Stoic worldview, and in his world picture in the *Natural Questions*, aspects of a metaphysical, Platonizing structure of thought— aspects that nevertheless hardly compromise his basic commitment to Stoic monism. Cf. in sum Natali 447 for Seneca as "uno 'stoico platoneggiante'" while always remaining fundamentally "very far from becoming a Platonist."

viewed against the other surviving remnants of the ancient meteorological tradition? Certainly, at least three interrelated factors underline his conformity to inherited practices.

First, there is the deep conservativeness of the meteorological tradition in general[8]: although the attempt to explain fearsome meteorological phenomena by appeal to reason rather than divine intervention extends back to the Pre-Socratics, Aristotle's demarcation of meteorology as a particular branch of knowledge in his *Meteorologica* was profoundly influential on his successors in the field, from Theophrastus onward.[9] Seneca is no exception. The range of topics covered in the *Meteorologica* is very similar to that on offer in the *Natural Questions*, as well as that "of every other meteorological work whose contents are known to us."[10] In several passages Seneca draws explicitly on Aristotle, although it is by no means certain that he knew the *Meteorologica* at first hand.[11] In sum, as Roger French puts it, "in understanding the natural world Seneca goes back principally to Aristotle."[12]

Second, in an important article Inwood fully acknowledges the imprint of tradition on the *Natural Questions*, but he plays down the ultimate significance of the meteorological component in Seneca:

> I will argue…that Seneca presents his readers with the fruits of serious thought about the relationship between god and man, and would like to suggest (though proof is not possible) that *Seneca's most important concern in the book as a whole is not the overt theme* (explanations of traditionally problematic natural phenomena) but the subterranean theme of the relationship between god and man, and most particularly the epistemic limitations of human nature.[13]

But, counters Margaret Graver, epistemological and theological reflections of the sort that Inwood attributes to Seneca are already present in the earlier

8. On this feature, Mourelatos (2005) 285.

9. Concisely on the Pre-Socratic contribution, Taub (2003) 72–76 with Frisinger (1971); succinctly on Aristotle's contribution and influence, Taub 77–115 with Frisinger (1973). Conveniently on the entire tradition down to Seneca, Frisinger (1977) 1–30, albeit with (for my purposes) unhelpful final judgment on the *Natural Questions*: "In the early development of meteorology the importance of Seneca's *Quaestiones Naturales* was its compilation of ancient Greek meteorological theories" (p. 30).

10. Graver (2000) 48–49.

11. Conveniently, Hine (2010b) 5.

12. French (1994) 170; cf. for this standard line e.g., Grant (2007) 96.

13. (2002) 125 = (2005) 164–65, and cf. (2000) 26; my emphasis.

meteorological tradition from the Pre-Socratics onward.[14] On the epistemological front, the limits of knowledge are tested in this tradition by the challenge of explaining phenomena that lie beyond our everyday observation and experience. On the theological front, naturalistic explanation supersedes the religious or magical interpretation of phenomena. Hence Graver finds "reason to believe that the meteorological project was in fact driven, all along, by concerns about the limits of our knowledge and about our relation to the divine"[15]; and hence a significant qualification to Inwood's thesis, with the further thought that Seneca was perhaps not the first Stoic to experiment with the epistemological and theological ramifications of meteorology.[16]

Third, there is the Epicurean tradition. "In turning to the meteorology of Seneca,...we should be aware," Graver urges, "that its emphases on the nature of divinity and on the limits of human knowledge are not his alone, and, further, that by the time of his writing this approach to meteorology had acquired a distinctly Epicurean flavor."[17] In his *Letter to Pythocles* (= Diogenes Laertius 10.85) Epicurus broaches his treatment of phenomena of the sky (τὰ μετέωρα) as follows:

> In the first place, remember that, as in the case of everything else, knowledge of phenomena of the sky, whether taken along with other things or in isolation, has no end in view other than peace of mind and firm conviction (ἀταραξίαν καὶ πίστιν βέβαιον).

In *De rerum natura* 6, Lucretius naturally follows this rationalizing path in his own extended treatment of meteorological phenomena—a treatment interrupted when he embarks on a digression (6.703–11) on the principle of the plurality of causation, that "hallmark of Epicurus' approach" in his *Letter to Pythocles*.[18] Seneca, too, deploys this technique in the *Natural Questions*, not least in his account of the Epicurean theory of earthquakes at 6.20.5–7. Even though multiplicity of causation is in fact, as Mourelatos duly stresses, "the standard and almost commonplace methodological tenet in many contexts of ancient natural philosophy,"[19] Graver presses its Epicurean associations hard in

---

14. Graver (2000), especially 45, 51.

15. Graver (2000) 45.

16. Graver (2000) 51.

17. (2000) 51.

18. Taub (2003) 130.

19. (2005) 284.

arguing for the larger Epicurean impact on the *Natural Questions* generally. The Epicurean flavor she detects in Seneca's reflections on the nature of divinity and the limits of human knowledge suggests, she writes, that "Seneca is consciously adapting a hallmark of the competing system."[20] Again, this Epicurean presence contributes significantly to Graver's broader critique of Inwood's thesis: in calling for that thesis to be fully contextualized within the meteorological tradition as a whole, she persuasively locates the *Natural Questions* within a larger community of thought, and Seneca's originality is qualified accordingly. In terms purely of its meteorological substance, and in terms of its many inherited strategies of procedure and argument, the *Natural Questions* marks no significant departure within the tradition.

Conformity to tradition on various fronts, then; but Seneca's fusion of the scientific[21] and artistic outlooks—his creation of a highly self-conscious mode of *literary*-scientific investigation—is another matter entirely. A central claim of this book is that the *Natural Questions* reveals a spirit of creative ambition and adventure that quite sets it apart from the meteorological tradition, at least as it survives on the prose side (we shall turn momentarily to the meteorological component of Lucretius' *De rerum natura* 6). The literary strategies of engagement with nature that we shall monitor in detail in the ensuing chapters are themselves richly diverse, as if the different faces of nature are matched in the *Natural Questions* by restless variations of artistic angle and approach; and yet those variations are coordinated by Seneca's overall promotion of what might be called cosmic consciousness, or the attainment of "seeing the all" (cf. *animo omne*

---

20. Graver (2000) 51.

21. About my use of "scientific": certain investigative techniques that Seneca uses in the *Natural Questions* may reasonably be so described, at least in their conformity with familiar ancient procedures of analysis and argument. Beyond his basic quest to explain phenomena in purely naturalistic terms, among these features are his frequent argumentation by analogy, his critical engagement with the ideas of earlier theorists, his judicious weighing of competing possibilities and his stress on the unreliability of the senses and the need instead for inferential speculation; see conveniently on these features Hine (2010b) 7–9, and cf. for the positive projection of Seneca as scientist Cailleux (1971). From a modern perspective, however, the *Natural Questions* must (*pace* Cailleux) in many ways appear un-, or at least pre-, scientific; and even from an ancient perspective, the prominent moralizing component, Seneca's eye for artistic elaboration, and his powers of imaginative reconstruction (e.g., of the cataclysm at the end of Book 3) surely complicate any straightforward generic designation of it as "a work of science," even in comparison with other works that in some ways challenge the definition, such as Pliny's *Natural History* (see now Doody [2010] 14–23 on "Science and Encyclopedism: The Nature of Pliny's Scholarship," and cf. Taub [2008] 12–13 on "What Is 'Scientific?'"). In the following chapters, therefore, the word is used sparingly of the *Natural Questions*, and then only advisedly. Cf. Hine (1995) 204 n. 1 on his use in that study of "the word 'scientific' to describe the subject-matter of Seneca's work—which falls within the sphere of several of our modern-day natural sciences—and not to imply anything about Seneca's methodology."

uidisse, 3 pref. 10)—the liberation of mind that, as we saw above, is the ultimate Senecan/Stoic goal of studying nature.

This cosmic consciousness suggests another important facet of Senecan originality, especially in relation to Lucretius' demystification of meteorological phenomena in *De rerum natura* 6. If in that great poem Lucretius offers his own highly original response to the meteorological tradition, naturally extending to such phenomena as thunder, lightning and earthquakes, etc., the fortifying reach of Epicurean *ratio*, then the *Natural Questions* can profitably be viewed as a Stoic response to the Lucretian undertaking.[22] On this approach, the Epicurean flavor that Graver discerns in the *Natural Questions* is indeed a profoundly significant presence: on the one hand, Seneca follows Epicurus/Lucretius in striving to assert a rhetoric of reason over that of wonder and to provide fortification in the face of awesome nature; on the other hand, Seneca's version of cosmic consciousness supersedes Epicurean *ratio* in the nonatomic and animated, Stoic world structure of the *Natural Questions*. In stressing the creativity of his response to Lucretius in particular, I also credit Seneca with a freedom of maneuver that surely tells against any subservient or dutifully mechanical reliance on his sources for the meteorological substance of his work. The belief that he relied on a single source, whether Posidonius or Asclepiodotus, his pupil, or a doxographical collection, has long given way to a more flexible approach that stresses the need to proceed cautiously, on a case-by-case basis, with alertness to the possibility that Seneca draws on a wide plurality of sources.[23] Above all, this study is committed to the view that he controls his sources rather than being controlled by them; as we shall see, the *Natural Questions* is a work of such diverse range and inventive literary design in and across the books that it is surely unlikely to have been slavishly reliant on its sources, let alone a single master source.

While Lucretius offers one antimodel for the Senecan worldview on offer in the *Natural Questions*, the elder Pliny (23–79 CE) offers another useful point of contrast in his *Natural History*, that massive feat of encyclopedic world collection in thirty-seven books: Lucretius and Pliny adopt distinctive approaches to rationalizing the world, whether through atomist explication or exhaustive cataloguing of facts, but Seneca brings the world to order through his own highly creative systematization in the *Natural Questions*. Further, the comparison with Lucretius and

---

22. On this line see Baldacci (1981) 587–88; Weber (1995) 91–92; Parroni (2002) xxxiv and (2004) 315.

23. See for succinct review of the whole question Vottero (1989) 24–39 with Parroni (2002) xxii–xxvi. The latter (p. xxiii) underscores the benefits of the case-by-case approach, with acknowledgment of the important advances made in this respect by Setaioli (1988) 375–452 and, on the plurality of sources, by Gross (1989); cf. in commendation of Gross' thesis Parroni (1992a) and (2000a) 434.

Pliny, both branches of which will be treated in greater detail later in this study,[24] contextualizes Seneca's project within a broader Roman interest in rationalizing, mapping and classifying the physical world in the late Republic and early Empire. The times matter: writing in the darkness of the later Neronian years, Seneca promotes cosmic consciousness in the *Natural Questions* not just, I propose, as an intellectual experiment whose timing is unimportant, or as a purely literary/theoretical response to Lucretius and the larger meteorological tradition, but as a work fundamentally shaped by the sociopolitical context in which it was written.[25] By personalizing the study of nature, as if giving the reader a sense of participation in a world far greater than the world of Rome; by constantly reinforcing the guiding principle that there *is* a governing *ratio* to things; by moving us toward the serenity of the detached, cosmic viewpoint—in these ways and more, the *Natural Questions* is no narrowly defined project of a forbidding, technical kind, but a work of very practical, therapeutic value. The detachment it fosters coincides all too suggestively, of course, with Seneca's literal detachment from the Neronian court after 62 CE[26], a turning point that might cause us to detect in the work a vision of expansive, uncontaminated nature that is implicitly contrasted by all the symbolic unnaturalness and claustrophobia of Nero's Rome.

---

24. For Lucretius, Chapter Six, Section III; Pliny, Chapter One, Section IV.

25. Further, Chapter One, Section V.

26. Much has been made in this respect of Tac. *Ann.* 14.52–6, but cf. Hine (2006) 71: "One might argue that we should not be too fixated on Tacitus' account of the interview between Seneca and Nero in A.D. 62 as a turning point, for the change in Seneca's influence and standing in the court, and in the balance he struck between court duties and philosophy, may have been more gradual." The work appears to have been well advanced—and perhaps concluded— by late 64, if not (considerably?) sooner, for in Book 7 Seneca mentions the Neronian comet of 60 (7.6.1, 17.2, 21.3–4, 23.1, 28.3, 29.2–3) but makes no allusion to that of May–July (or autumn?) 64 (see Plin. *Nat.* 2.92, Tac. *Ann.* 15.47.1, Suet. *Ner.* 36.1 with Ramsey [2006] 40, 146–48 and [2007] 181). Attempts to gauge the rate of composition around, and after, Seneca's *de facto* withdrawal in 62 are complicated by the problem of determining in which year, 62 or 63, the "recent" Campanian earthquake (6.1.1–3) is located. Seneca's text as we have it dates the earthquake to February 5, 63, in the consulship of C. Memmius Regulus and L. Verginius Rufus (*Regulo et Verginio consulibus*, 6.1.2). Wallace-Hadrill (2003) inclines to 63 (so p. 190: "An earthquake in February 63 allows a far more comfortable chronology for composition over a matter of months in 62–63, with the news arriving in mid composition"; cf. also Parroni [2002] 573). But see now Hine 68–72 for a judicious reevaluation of the whole question, with a cautious preference for 62 (so Tac. *Ann.* 15.22.2), the phrase *Regulo et Verginio consulibus* then being adjudged an interpolation (further, Hine [1984] with Vottero [1989] 178–79 for additional bibliography). Without reference to Wallace-Hadrill, 62 is now also defended by Gauly (2004) 22–24. The position taken in this book is that the earthquake happened in 62; and, on the basis of an original ordering of the books in the sequence 3, 4a, 4b, 5, 6, 7, 1 and 2 (see below in this Introduction on "The Addressee, and the Original Order of the Eight Books"), that the work was already at an advanced stage of progress by the end of that year/ early 63 (cf. Vottero 20–21).

The Moralizing Component in the Natural Questions, and the Relation of This Study to Existing Scholarship

Many aspects of that unnaturalness are colorfully condemned in the moralizing prefaces, digressions and epilogues that are strewn across the eight books. In keeping with my emphasis above on the holistic fusion of physics and ethics in the *Natural Questions*, the direction taken in this book is that these moralizing passages are no mere interludes detachable from Seneca's main scientific project, and that they are not designed merely to offer relief or distraction from the drier, more technical portions of the work; nor, on the other hand, are they to be viewed as the main focus of the work, the scientific portions secondary to Seneca's ethical thrust. On the balanced approach offered here,[27] the challenge, taken up in Chapter Two in particular, is to show in point of detail how the moralizing passages are fully integrated with their surrounding material; the normative functioning of nature in the scientific portions will be seen to be consistently contrasted with the abnormal disruptions to natural appetite, limit and process in the moralizing sections.

This integrating approach is certainly not unprecedented in the existing scholarship, but the detailed readings I offer are no mere reproductions of established interpretation. Above all, we shall trace the emergence in the *Natural Questions* of a community of related deviants across the eight books—a community exerting a gravitational force, as it were, that pulls downward even as Seneca impels his reader to look upward, to transcend ordinary life at ground level, to reach for cosmic consciousness. Senecan doxography contributes importantly to the tension that exists between this upward momentum and that downward drag: the deviants we encounter are contrasted by "the community of scholars" who are assembled via that doxography,[28] a community that strives in an enlightened Senecan direction while the deviants lose their way in the moral darkness. Through these contending forces the text is set profoundly in tension with itself, and there is arguably no easy winner by the work's conclusion. The delinquent counterculture of the *Natural Questions* grounds Seneca's promotion of cosmic consciousness in the grit of "real" life and vice, thereby defining the path of virtue through graphic representation of its opposite. But the deviants who infest the work amount to a formidable, perhaps even an overwhelming, body of opposition to

---

27. Similarly, Hine (2010b) 12–13. Key items in the recent bibliography are Codoñer (1989), especially 1803–1822; Salanitro (1990); Scott (1999); Berno (2003); Gauly (2004); and Limburg (2007).

28. Hine (2006) 53; cf. p. 58 for "the virtual academy" constructed by Seneca, "a community of inquirers that stretches across the centuries, backwards as far as the Pre-Socratics, and far forwards into future generations."

the claims of the philosophical life, and Seneca himself concedes in moments that the struggle against vice is a lost cause (cf. 4b.13.1, 7.32). And can we also detect in his portrayal of at least certain vicious types, chief among them the loathsome Hostius Quadra who is featured late in Book 1, a blend of revulsion and yet fascination, as if the artistic eye is perversely drawn to, even galvanized by, the luridness that it condemns? Is there a disconcerting attractiveness to the vices Seneca inveighs against in passages of a quasi-ecphrastic attention to detail, as if he inscribes himself as an all-too-enthusiastic witness into the scene he deplores?[29] Yet after we have moved through his latest outburst of moral outrage, his continuing investigation into nature's secrets returns to its steady rhythm, detaching us once more from the vicious ways of the world; the moralizing interludes function as interferences that recurrently challenge the uplifting trajectory of the *Natural Questions*.

The Addressee, and the Original Order of the Eight Books

Beyond this contrast between base deviance and philosophical uplift, a different tension exists in the *Natural Questions* between author and addressee, Seneca and his friend Lucilius Iunior, to whom *Dialogue* 1 (*De prouidentia*) and the *Moral Letters* are also addressed.[30] Lucilius was younger than Seneca, but apparently not by much (*iuuenior es*, *Letters* 26.7; cf. 35.2). Of humble origin (*Letters* 19.5) in Campania, Pompeii seemingly his birthplace (*Letters* 49.1, 70.1), he rose to equestrian rank (*Letters* 44.2, 6). After varied military service outside Italy (cf. *Letters* 31.9), he eventually became procurator of Sicily in or around 62 CE—in fact, "not a very important post."[31] So, in *Natural Questions* 4a pref. 1, Lucilius is installed in Sicily, and apparently enjoying his new position and the leisure time it affords him (*Delectat te... Sicilia et officium procurationis otiosae*)—*otium* that Lucilius will use well, Seneca is sure, because "I know how disinclined you are to ambition, and how devoted to leisure and study" (4a pref. 1). As Lucilius embarks on his new role, however, Seneca is in a very different position. Announcing, in the preface to Book 3, his ambitious new task of surveying the universe (*mundum circumire*), he claims to have thrown off the encumbrances of the occupied life so as to devote himself exclusively to his new project, his mind entirely free for itself (cf. *sibi totus animus uacet*, 4a pref. 2). It is from this liberated viewpoint in 62 CE, or

---

29. Further, Chapter Two, Section V.

30. For Lucilius, *PIR*² 5.1 pp. 103–104 no. 388 with Delatte (1935) and now Hine (2010c) 31–32; succinctly, Griffin (1976) 91, 94 with Vottero (1989) 21–24.

31. Griffin (1976) 350 n. 2; further on Lucilius in Sicily, Grimal (1980).

perhaps a little before,[32] that he urges Lucilius to devote himself to leisured study as best he can during, or despite, his term of office in Sicily.

Lucilius is making his way in the world, then, just at the time when Seneca is withdrawing from it and embarking on the *Natural Questions*. But this storyline of divergent life paths takes on added force if we accept that the books were originally ordered in the sequence 3, 4a, 4b, 5, 6, 7, 1 and 2. All editions print the books in the sequence 1, 2, 3, 4a, 4b, 5, 6 and 7, which, idiosyncrasies apart, is one of three orders found in the manuscript tradition.[33] Of the other two orders, one diverges from that given above to yield 1, 2, 3, 4b, 5, 6, 7 and 4a. The other, the so-called *Grandinem* order (named after the first word of Book 4b), has the sequence 4b, 5, 6, 7, 1, 2, 3 and 4a. It was demonstrably the order of the archetype from which the extant manuscripts descend, and this order is still upheld by some scholars.[34] But the position taken here is that the case for an order of 3, 4a, 4b, 5, 6, 7, 1 and 2, first proposed independently by Carmen Codoñer Merino and Harry Hine, is overwhelming: the preface to Book 3 reads naturally as an introduction to the whole work, the displacement of Books 3 and 4a in the archetype is readily explained, and the internal evidence derived from cross-comparison of the books further consolidates the overall case for the 3, 4a, 4b, etc., ordering.[35] In a pioneering, and welcome, development, Hine's 2010 translation of the *Natural Questions* presents the books in this order, which is also accepted throughout this study, an acceptance that naturally influences my characterization of the interrelationship between the different books. But to anticipate any continuing resistance to this ordering: although I do suggest that the work as a whole yields an arc of meaning predicated on the 3, 4a, 4b, etc., sequence, my readings of the individual books in the chapters that follow are for the most part deliberately self-contained,[36] and in no case is the interpretation of a given book built entirely on, or guided solely by, the assumption that the Codoñer Merino/Hine ordering is correct.

---

32. See n. 26 above.

33. Here and later in this paragraph I rely on Hine (1981) 2–23, (1983) 376–78 and (1996a) xxii–xxv with Vottero (1989) 109–13, Parroni (2002) xlvii–l and Gauly (2004) 53–67.

34. See e.g. Gross (1989) 320, albeit with the further hypothesis of a lacuna before Book 4b, caused by the loss of two books in which Seneca treated *caelestia* in accordance with the agenda apparently set out in 2.1.1–2 (see also Gross 310 B on the history of scholarly acceptance of the *Grandinem* ordering); Vottero (1989) 109–13; Gigon (1991) 321–22; Marino (1996) 11–38.

35. See Codoñer Merino (1979) 1.xii–xxi; Hine (1981) 6–19, especially 16–17, and (1996a) xxiv. For approval of this ordering cf. Parroni (2002) xlix, Gauly (2004) 66–67 and Limburg (2007) 11–12; but for assembled bibliography on the whole question, now Hine (2010c) 28–31.

36. Individual chapters are dedicated to Books 4a, 4b, 5, 6, 7 and 2. Given their relevance to disparate parts of my study, however, my treatment of Books 1 and 3 is spread over parts of Chapters One, Two, Three and Seven.

By reading in the sequence 3, 4a, 4b, etc., we soon find Seneca's inner turning in the preface to Book 3 contrasted at the beginning of Book 4a by the *negotium* of Lucilius' calling in Sicily.[37] Seneca hopes that his friend can maintain at least a measure of detachment from the task in hand (4a pref. 1), but Lucilius evidently takes pride in his responsibilities as procurator of a place of such historical importance (cf. 4a pref. 21). Lucilius may have traveled far, but Seneca has traveled further as a cosmic voyager, with Sicily now but a relative speck (cf. *punctum*, 1 pref. 11) in the cosmic mindscape. Two further allusions to Sicily occur later in the *Natural Questions*, at 6.8.2 and 6.30.3 (cf. also 6.30.1), but no reference is made in either case to Lucilius' role on the island; after Book 4a, there is no further mention of Lucilius as *procurator* anywhere in the 3, 4a, 4b, 5, 6, 7, 1 and 2 ordering. The omission may be casual and insignificant. But if Seneca is credited with a more calculating agenda, he not only qualifies Lucilius' (self-)importance in his mere *procuratiuncula* (cf. *Letters* 31.9) in Sicily by transporting him to the truly awesome spectacle of the Nile in the main body of Book 4a. After that first departure from Sicily, we also lose sight of Lucilius' mission and standing on the island in the rest of the work, where the localized ministrations of the *procurator Siciliae* give way, as if forgotten, to Seneca's free-ranging movement through the cosmic whole (cf. 1 pref. 7–13). Moreover, the 3, 4a, 4b, etc., ordering allows a loose thematic pattern to be drawn across the books, the four elements providing structure:[38] Books 3 and 4a, on the Nile, form one grouping based on water; then 4b, 5 and 6 treat phenomena caused by or consisting of air; and fire links Books 7, 1 and 2.[39] By allowing us to glimpse the celestial level above atmospheric *sublimia* in Seneca's theory of comets in Book 7 (he holds that they are planetary bodies moving in unknown orbits), the work shows a rising trajectory from ground level in Books 3 and 4a—a form of transcendence[40] that replicates, in the work's structure, Seneca's increasing distance in the *Natural Questions* from the world of the here-and-now, from Lucilius' Sicily, from Neronian Rome.

---

37. The order of the books may still be contested in some quarters, but there is no doubt that "Book IVa follows directly after Book III" (Hine [1981] 9).

38. See Codoñer (1989) 1799–1800, and cf. Hine (1981) 31 ("There is no other obvious pattern in the work"). For a brief overview of opinion on the thematic arrangement of the books, Gauly (2004) 69–70. Despite the interest of the thematic book pairings proposed by Waiblinger (1977) in particular (1 and 2 on fire; 3 and 4a on water; 4b and 5 on air; but the elemental link breaks down in the case of 6 and 7), I cannot accept the 1–7 ordering on which his thesis is based.

39. This arrangement assumes that the *Natural Questions* was planned in eight books. Though it is conceivable that Seneca wrote or planned more books than actually survive, there is no evidence to take us beyond mere speculation (see Hine [1981] 32 with Limburg [2007] 14–15).

40. Codoñer (1989) 1800.

The Scope of This Book

In the first of the eight chapters that follow, I present what I identify as certain fundamental characteristics of Seneca's self-presentation and world outlook in the *Natural Questions*, an outlook defined partly through contrast with the world-views on display in Cicero and in Pliny's *Natural History*. Chapter One thus seeks to provide a foundation for our examination of each of the eight books in later chapters. In Chapter Two, however, our theme is general, and one much discussed in recent scholarship: how, and how successfully, does Seneca reconcile his moralizing passages in the *Natural Questions* with his scientific agenda? The sample cast of deviants whom we review in Chapter Two is drawn from Books 1, 3, 5 and 7; those deviants are the very embodiment of the sordidness that, Seneca proclaims (3 pref. 18), we transcend through the study of nature. But our focus late in Chapter Two is on the drama Seneca generates by pitting the claims of philosophical enlightenment against the allurements and trappings of vice. This ongoing struggle, I argue, accompanies Seneca's symbolic shaping of meteorology as an area of study that raises us from a terrestrial level of thought and being; in terms of the tripartite division of the world into *caelestia*, *sublimia* and *terrena* at 2.1.1, the study of meteorological *sublimia* figuratively marks an intermediate stage in our philosophical striving toward "knowledge of the celestial" (*ad cognitionem caelestium*) and "partnership with god" (*consortium <cum> deo*, 1 pref. 6).

In Chapter Three we move to Egypt, and to Seneca's treatment of the River Nile in Book 4a. In this chapter, the Nile flood is viewed in relation to the awesome cataclysm that Seneca recreates in his own tsunami of description at the end of Book 3: the artful juxtaposition of the two books coordinates both floods, Nilotic and cataclysmic, as related events in nature's great scheme, events that are very different in scale but still obedient to the same cosmic timetable. Then, in Chapter Four, the free-flowing waters of Books 3 and 4a give way to Seneca's treatment of snow and hail in what survives of Book 4b. In his testing of different theories of hail in particular, I argue, Seneca experiments with various techniques of scientific argument and persuasion; we might call this introspective turning in Book 4b a form of methodological stock taking at this still relatively early stage in the *Natural Questions*.

Our journey recommences in Chapter Five, on winds, with our coverage of Seneca's careful delineation of wind types early in Book 5. The winds are brought to life, I argue, in a personifying account that reaches its climax in the short-lived violence of the hurricane (ἐκνεφίας) of 5.12 and the whirlwind (*turbo*) of 5.13. Later, in 5.18, Seneca condemns man's exploitation of wind, that gift of nature, to set sail in search of war and conquest. Can a comparison be drawn between the human marauders of 5.18 and the hurricane and whirlwind of 5.12–13? Or a contrast between, on the one hand, Seneca's mapping of the winds, local and global, in generally regular and predictable motion and, on the other hand, the deviant, "un-natural" movements of the warmongers, those models of ethical misdirection, who take to their ships in 5.18? In addressing these questions, Chapter Five argues strenuously against any judgment that Book 5 constitutes, at least down to its mor-alizing conclusion in 5.18, "[o]ne of the driest discussions in the entire *Naturales Quaestiones*."[41] When we turn, in Chapter Six, to Seneca's treatment of earthquakes in Book 6, Lucretius comes to the fore: in responding to news of the catastrophic Campanian earthquake of February 62,[42] Seneca deploys consolatory strategies and techniques of rationalization that, I argue, are consciously Lucretian in color. More importantly, Seneca asserts a form of superiority over nature that corre-sponds to the Lucretian sublime—a method of controlling awesome nature that, I propose, is as relevant to Seneca's portrayal of the cataclysm at the end of Book 3 or the great spectacle of the Nile in Book 4a, the ominous appearance of a comet in Book 7 or the intimidating lightning flashes of Book 2, as it is to the earthquake of Book 6. My reading of the Senecan sublime in Chapter Six therefore has impli-cations for much of the *Natural Questions* beyond Book 6.

In Book 7 Seneca rises to new conceptual heights in the *Natural Questions*, going beyond the meteorological realm of *sublimia* to locate comets as planetary phenomena in the celestial region. In plotting Seneca's ascending path from sub-lunary to supralunary theories of comet in Chapter Seven, I argue that the impor-tance of Book 7 lies not just in the counterweight that it offers to Aristotle's influential, sublunary theory of comets; in its dynamic, upward movement toward this celestial climax, the book also serves as a symbolic enactment of progress toward the ultimate goal of liberated, cosmic vision. Finally, in Chapter Eight I turn to Book 2, on lightning and thunder, with particular attention to Seneca's extended treatment of divination from lightning at 2.32–51. In striving to recon-cile Etruscan belief and Greek/Stoic philosophical rationalization of divinatory practice, he is engaged, I argue, in but one aspect of a larger restructuring of Roman systems of knowledge in the late Republic and early Empire. By relating his chapters on divination to the model of cultural revolution recently proposed by Andrew Wallace-Hadrill,[43] I try to inscribe Book 2—and, by extension, the body of specialized knowledge that is the entire *Natural Questions*—in the chang-ing intellectual climate at Rome in the late first century and beyond. There, after a brief epilogue, my treatment of the *Natural Questions* ends, but not without stressing to the last the *artistic* impulse that drives and shapes Seneca's entire project—his world tour, if you will, meteorology his vehicle.

---

41. Inwood (2002) 137 = (2005) 178.

42. For the date, n. 26 above.

43. Wallace-Hadrill (1997) and (2008).

I

Interiority and Cosmic Consciousness in the Natural Questions

I: Seneca's Totalizing Worldview

What is the origin of the waters that flow continuously from river to sea? Why is the sea apparently not enlarged by the addition of those waters, the earth unaffected by their loss? How does the earth produce such vast quantities of water? After raising these well-worn questions early in Book 3, "On the waters of the earth" (*de terrestribus aquis*, 3.1.1), Seneca reviews five theories in a survey (3.5–10) that, as so often in Senecan doxography in the *Natural Questions*, is vague in its allusion to sources (so, e.g., *Quidam iudicant*, 3.5.1; *Quidam existimant*, 3.6.1, 8.1).[1] The first theory is that the porous earth receives back into it whatever water it emits into the sea via rivers (3.5). The second, that rivers are derived from rainfall (3.6), is immediately refuted by Seneca (3.7); his own experience of viticulture[2] ostentatiously supplies the counterargument (*inter alia*) that rainwater does not penetrate deeply enough into the earth to supply subterranean rivers with sufficient abundance. The third and fourth theories proceed by analogy, the third (3.8) asserting that great expanses of fresh water exist in the earth's interior as they do on its surface; the fourth relates atmospheric change into rain above the earth (*aëris mutatio imbrem facit*, 3.9.2) to a parallel process below, where permanently cold, dense air is transformed into water. The fifth theory develops Seneca's claim at the end of 3.9 that "we [sc. Stoics] are satisfied that the earth is subject to change," and that the dense subterranean exhalations it gives off are turned into moisture (3.9.3). Elaborating on this changefulness, Seneca posits in 3.10.1 the mutability of the elements one into another: "You can add the principle that everything is produced from everything

---

1. See on 3.5–10 Brutsaert (2005) 567–58 with Rossi (1991) 149–52 = (1992) 50–56. Conveniently on the origins of each theory, Gilbert (1907) 431–33; Vottero (1989) 392 n. 1 on 5.1; 393 n. 1 on 6.1; 395 n. 1 on 8.1; 396 n. 1 on 9.1; and 396 n. 3 on 9.3 with n. 1 on 10.1.

2. For which cf. *Letters* 104.6, 112.1–2 with Col. 3.3.3 (on high-yielding vineyards such as Seneca's, which apparently produced eight *cullei* per *iugerum*, or the equivalent of approximately 1,096 U.S. gallons; Jellinek [1976] 1724–25 and n. 17), Plin. *Nat.* 14.50–2; Griffin (1976) 289–90.

[*fiunt omnia ex omnibus*]: air from water, water from air, fire from air, air from fire. Why, then, not water from earth? If the earth can change into other elements, it can also change into water, or rather, most especially into water."[3]

If we accept, as we should, that the books of the *Natural Questions* were originally ordered in the sequence 3, 4a, 4b, 5, 6, 7, 1 and 2, this doxographical survey marks Seneca's first extended recourse in this new work to the theories of earlier investigators. His procedure has long prompted a familiar line of questioning in modern scholarship: How accurate is Seneca as a source for earlier meteorological thought? Can we identify his unnamed sources at 3.5–10, or does he transmit the imprecision that he himself found in his informants, doxographical handbooks presumably among them?[4] Does he rely on a single dominant model or a combination of models for the inspiration and architecture of Book 3 as a whole?[5] Beyond the challenges of source analysis, however, Seneca's doxography in these early chapters has a programmatic quality to it as a model exercise that sets a standard for the *Natural Questions* as a whole: on the one hand, he establishes his credentials as a fair-minded, seemingly objective reporter by apparently letting the facts speak for themselves, recording received opinion without comment or objection in e.g. 3.5 and 3.8; on the other hand, his extended critique in 3.7 of the rivers-caused-by-rainfall theory (3.6) redresses the balance, asserting his self-presentation as a critical respondent who is no passive transmitter of inherited theory.[6] More important for present purposes, however, is the overall tendency that permeates the different theories he presents. Whatever the merits or plausibility of individual theories, each in its own way projects an

---

3. But in Stoic theory elemental transformation follows a fixed order, for Chrysippus fire changing into air, then water and then earth (the same order also applies in reverse), as at *SVF* 2.413 p. 136.19–24; cf. 1.495 p. 111.6–8 (Cleanthes), and for further sources see Hine (1981) 312 on 2.26.2 with Wildberger (2006) 62 and 578–79 nn. 378–80.

4. See on this nexus of problems Setaioli (1988) 434 and n. 2048 for bibliography with Gross (1989) 122–26.

5. On the problem as traditionally framed—Asclepiodotus as the main source, or reliance on Posidonius as well as Asclepiodotus, his pupil?—see Setaioli (1988) 432–33.

6. Seneca's doxographical approach may be compared to (and possibly influenced by?) Aristotle's use of the so-called *endoxa* ("reputable opinions"; on this translation, Taub [2003] 94 and 211 n. 98). For Freeland (1990) 78–79, Aristotle's refutation of *endoxa* not only gives him "a kind of rhetorical advantage" as he presents and dismisses his predecessors' efforts, but it also serves two other related purposes: (1) the technique might "indicate a special way in which Aristotle sees science as a sort of cumulative group endeavour," with possible advantage and insight to be gained from seeing where an existing theory fails; and (2) his "surveys of *endoxa* reflect a picture of science as a problem-solving activity," with significant questions raised and framed by the theories he reviews/rejects. Both purposes might equally be discerned in Seneca's use of critical doxography throughout the *Natural Questions*.

integrating vision of nature's workings: in 3.5 the water that flows from land to sea is returned from sea to land in cyclical fashion, while in 3.6 rainfall is recycled via river flow. So too in 3.8 and 3.9 analogy forges a conveniently close connection between conditions at the earth's surface and in its interior, while this vision of correspondence gives way in 3.10 to fundamental interchangeability and balance at an elemental level:

> nihil deficit quod in se redit. omnium elementorum alterni recursus sunt: quidquid alteri perit in alterum transit, et natura partes suas uelut in ponderibus constitutas examinat, ne portionum aequitate turbata mundus praeponderet. omnia in omnibus sunt. non tantum aër in ignem transit sed numquam sine igne est: detrahe illi calorem, rigescet, stabit, durabitur; transit aër in umorem sed nihilominus non est sine umore; et aëra et aquam facit terra sed non magis umquam sine aqua est quam sine aëre. et ideo facilior est inuicem transitus quia illis in quae transeundum est iam mixta sunt. habet ergo terra umorem: hunc exprimit. habet aëra: hunc umbra inferni frigoris densat ut faciat umorem. ipsa quoque mutabilis est in umorem: natura sua utitur.

> 3.10.3–5

Nothing becomes deficient if it returns to itself. Among all the elements there are reciprocal exchanges: whatever is lost to one element passes into another element, and nature weighs its parts as if they were placed on scales, to ensure that the world does not lose its equilibrium because the balance of its proportions is disrupted. Everything is in everything. Air not only passes into fire, but it is never without fire. Remove its heat, and it will become stiff, solid and hard. Air passes into moisture, but it is nevertheless not without moisture. Earth produces both air and water, but it is never without water any more than it is without air. And so the reciprocal transformation of the elements is easier because they are already mixed with the elements into which they must pass. Therefore, the earth contains water, and it forces it out. It contains air, and the cold darkness below condenses it so that it forms moisture. The earth is itself also capable of changing into moisture; it draws on its own natural capacity.

The key emphasis on interchangeability here is neatly underscored by the tight analogical relation that Seneca draws between different elements when, at 3.10.2, nature's endless flow of water effortlessly finds a cognate in air: "You show surprise [*miraris*]…that there is always new water available for rivers. You might as well be surprised [*quid si mireris…?*] that, when the winds put the entire atmosphere in motion, there is no shortage of air ...." So, too, at 3.12.3, the different elements merge into each other through verbal correlation and overlap (*quomodo aër ... uentos et auras mouet, sic aqua riuos et flumina. si uentus est fluens aër,*[7] *et flumen est fluens aqua*); to investigate any one of the four irreducible elements is, in a sense, to interrogate all of them simultaneously,[8] with findings that are necessarily common to all ("You realize that whatever proceeds from an element cannot run out," 3.12.3). The elements are profoundly equivalent, even if Seneca is inclined to agree with Thales and with his fellow Stoics that water is the most powerful of the four (*ualentissimum elementum est,* 3.13.1).[9]

This concentration on elemental interchangeability so early in the *Natural Questions* sets the stage for, and lends an anticipatory or even programmatic form of coherence to, Seneca's tour through phenomena related to elemental fire, air, earth and water in the subsequent books; at this, our entry point in Book 3 into his literary-scientific world, his unifying approach also suggestively recreates at a narratival level the physical coherence effected by Stoic *sympatheia*.[10] For present purposes, however, this vision of oneness provides the starting point for what we shall see to be Seneca's construction in the *Natural Questions* of a unifying mindset that redirects our focus away from the ordinary fragmentations and interferences of life at ground level, as it were, toward the alleviating, integrating perspective of cosmic consciousness: as we move from partial sight toward fuller insight, and from local participation to a more complete form of cosmic belonging, we begin to see the world for itself, not for ourselves.[11] The rightness or wrongness of a given theory, Seneca's technical accuracy in rendering it, the particular identity of the sources implicated in formulations such as *Quidam existimant*: while evaluation of Seneca's inventory early in Book 3 may begin with controversies of this familiar stamp, an alternative approach stresses the *cumulative* effect of his doxographical collecting, and also the common enterprise to

---

7. Cf. 5.1.1 and Chapter Five, Section II.

8. Cf. 3.12.1: "So you ask me how water is produced? In reply, I'll ask how air or earth is produced."

9. For Thales, D-K 11A12 and Graham (2010) 1.28–9 and 39–40 on Text 15 with Vottero (1989) 404 n. 2 on 3.13.1. On the Stoic side, Seneca here massages the familiar (Chrysippan) conception of fire as the primordial element from which the others are formed, and into which they are eventually resolved at the end of the world cycle: see *SVF* 2.413 p. 136.11–14 with Parroni (2002) 536 and Setaioli (1988) 435.

10. I.e. (Sambursky [1959] 9), the elements "subsisting only in co-existence with the rest, and not able to exist if the organization as a whole disintegrates"; further, Wildberger (2006) 16–20.

11. Cf. Hadot (1995) 254.

which each theory individually contributes. This communal enterprise is not so much, or only, the collective striving of the "virtual academy" of inquirers across time that Seneca assembles in the *Natural Questions*.[12] The different cumulative effort to be stressed here is rather the integrating tendency that takes shape in and across the inventory; and, to anticipate the objection that this tendency is naturally embedded in the theories and sources on which Seneca draws, and that it is no specially drawn emphasis of his own, we shall soon see that his preface to Book 3 lays an idiosyncratic foundation for the distinctively Senecan world perspective projected in 3.5–10.

II: *The Senecan Worldview Defined by Contrast with Cicero*

Before we turn to this preface, however, an important Roman literary precedent further informs our integrating approach to the *Natural Questions* in general, and to Book 3 in particular. It was of course no innovation for Seneca to emphasize the interactive relationship between different world parts and phenomena; we need look no further than the Pre-Socratic use of analogy to find this relational emphasis already deeply embedded in such fields of Greek natural science as meteorology, astronomy, biology and medicine.[13] In terms of Stoic cosmic sympathy, however, the long account of Stoic theology that Cicero delivers in the voice of Balbus in *De natura deorum* 2 is predicated on "the sympathetic relationship, interconnection and affinity of things" (*tanta rerum consentiens conspirans continuata cognatio*, 2.19). Cicero anticipates a key feature of the *Natural Questions* in Balbus' creative reenactment of this "affinity of things," especially in his extended argument for the providential government of the world at 2.73–153. Exquisite details fill out Balbus' picture of the wonders of interactive nature, the cooperation of the planets, the anthropocentrism of the physical world, and the harmonious perfection of the world's workings—a perfection, he argues, that can only be attributed to divine intelligence. The overall picture is sufficiently alluring and persuasive to survive Cotta's Academic critique of Stoic theology in *De natura deorum* 3, at least in the sense that Cotta endorses Balbus' view of nature's wondrous regularity and interconnectedness even as he contests the divine cause of that perfection (3.28).

Predictably enough, many of Balbus' familiar Stoic themes find representation in Seneca's own integrating worldview in the *Natural Questions*, among

---

12. For this "virtual academy," Hine (2006) 58, and cf. Introduction n. 28.

13. Lloyd (1966), especially 304–83. Further on analogy specifically in the *Natural Questions*, Armisen-Marchetti (1989) 283–311 and (2001), and see also Chapters Four, Section IV (B); Six, Sections III and V (C); and Eight, Section III (B).

them—to glance back at *N.Q.* 3.10—Balbus' disquisition on "the continuum of the world's nature":

> et cum quattuor genera sint corporum, uicissitudine eorum mundi continuata natura est. nam ex terra aqua ex aqua oritur aër ex aëre aether, deinde retrorsum uicissim ex aethere aër, inde aqua, ex aqua terra infima. sic naturis his ex quibus omnia constant sursus deorsus ultro citro commeantibus mundi partium coniunctio continetur.
>
> *N.D.* 2.84

> And since there are four kinds of matter, the continuum of the world's nature is constituted by the cyclical changes of those four kinds. For earth turns into water, water into air, air into aether, and then the process is reversed: aether turns into air, air into water, water into earth, the lowest of the four. Thus the world parts are conjoined by the constant passage up and down and to and fro of these four elements, of which all things are composed.

For now, however, two particular features of Balbus' exposition serve usefully to illuminate foundational principles of Seneca's worldview. First there is the movement from literal seeing to mental insight. At 2.45 Balbus prefaces his discussion of the nature of the gods as follows:

> ...in quo nihil est difficilius quam a consuetudine oculorum aciem mentis abducere. ea difficultas induxit et uulgo imperitos et similes philosophos imperitorum ut nisi figuris hominum constitutis nihil possent de dis inmortalibus cogitare.
>
> ...on this subject nothing is more difficult than to divert the mind's eye from seeing as our eyes usually see. This difficulty has caused both the uneducated generally and those philosophers who resemble the uneducated to be unable to reflect upon the immortal gods without envisaging human forms.

Although his agenda evidently differs from Balbus' narrower theological motivation in *De natura deorum* 2, Seneca too strives to redirect our gaze from an ordinary way of seeing toward a higher, less literal form of sight and intuition. So in his preface to *Natural Questions* 1 he distinguishes two branches of philosophy, ethics and theology:

> altior est haec et animosior; multum permisit sibi; non fuit oculis contenta: maius esse quiddam suspicata est ac pulchrius quod extra conspectum natura posuisset.
>
> 1 pref. 1

The latter [sc. the theological branch] is loftier and more noble; it gives itself much freedom; it is not satisfied with what is seen with the eyes; it suspects that there is something greater and more beautiful that nature has placed beyond our vision.[14]

This philosophical branch "rises far above this gloom [*caliginem*] in which we wallow and, rescuing us from the darkness [*e tenebris*], it leads us to the source of illumination [*illo unde lucet*]," our vision at last unimpaired and clear (1 pref. 2). To seek insight into nature's mysteries is to aim in this uplifting direction, to free the mind to look serenely down from its cosmic viewpoint (cf. *secure spectat* [sc. *animus*], 1 pref. 12), and hence "to see the all" (cf. *animo omne uidisse*, 3 pref. 10). Any reversion from this elevated vantage point marks a return to impaired vision: "Whenever you withdraw from consorting with things divine and return to human affairs [*a diuinorum conuersatione quotiens ad humana reccideris*], you will be blinded, like people who turn their eyes from the bright sunlight to dark shade" (3 pref. 11).

Secondly, by structuring higher and lower ways of seeing, this vertical axis in Seneca represents an informal hierarchy of world perception. Within this hierarchical scheme, his meteorological theme in the *Natural Questions* takes on a suggestive significance as an intermediate object of focus: it symbolically elevates our gaze from ground level, but in our concentration on meteorological phenomena we focus on a region of often random happenings and sporadic events, as opposed to the serene regularity that prevails in the celestial realm. This distinction between the sublunary and celestial regions is helpfully illuminated by the contrast that Cicero's Balbus draws at *De natura deorum* 2.56 between celestial regularity and its opposite in the zones below:

nulla igitur *in caelo* nec fortuna nec temeritas nec erratio nec uanitas inest contraque omnis ordo ueritas ratio constantia, quaeque his uacant ementita et falsa plenaque erroris, ea *circum terras infra lunam*, quae omnium ultima est, *in terrisque* uersantur. caelestium ergo admirabilem ordinem incredibilemque constantiam, ex qua conseruatio et salus omnium omnis oritur, qui uacare mente putat is ipse mentis expers habendus est.

In the heavens, therefore, there is no chance happening or random event, no deviation from any path, and no empty illusion, but absolute

---

14. Cf. 7.30.3–4; the limits of human vision as portrayed there are pointedly reasserted at 1 pref. 1 if we presuppose a book order of 3, 4a, 4b, 5, 6, 7, 1 and 2.

order, exactitude, system and regularity. Whatever lacks these qualities and is deceptive, false and full of error belongs to *the region between the earth and the moon* (which is the last of all the heavenly bodies), and *on the earth*. Anyone therefore who thinks that there is no rational basis to the wonderful order and the incredible regularity of the heavenly bodies, which is the sole source of the preservation and well-being of all things, cannot himself be regarded as a rational being.

This Ciceronian argument for the divine operation of the heavenly bodies is unparalleled in Seneca, but the conventional tripartite division of the universe into *caelestia*, *sublimia* and *terrena* recurs at the beginning of *Natural Questions* 2—a Senecan classification without ancient parallel in its fullness and clarity.[15] There, the stately regularity of the planets is itself suggestively reflected in the steady measure and movement of Seneca's one-sentence description of the celestial level:

> prima pars naturam siderum scrutatur, et magnitudinem et formam ignium quibus mundus includitur, solidumne sit caelum ac firmae concretaeque materiae, an ex subtili tenuique nexum, agatur an agat, et infra se sidera habeat an in contextu sui fixa, quemdamodum anni uices seruet, solem retro flectat, cetera deinceps his similia.
>
> 2.1.1

The first division investigates the nature of the planets, and the size and shape of the fixed stars which enclose the universe;[16] whether the heavens are solid and made of firm and compact substance, or woven from matter that is delicate and fine; whether they are moved or impart motion,[17] and whether the stars are held beneath them or are embedded in their structure; how they maintain the seasons of the year, turn the sun back,[18] and all other questions of a similar kind.

The expansive beginning (*naturam... et magnitudinem et formam*), the complex elaboration, the three carefully balanced disjunctive questions[19] before "whether"

---

15. See Hine (1981) 125.

16. For *siderum* of planets, *ignium* of the fixed stars, Hine (1981) 129.

17. On the difficulties of interpretation here, Hine (1981) 129–30.

18. Of the solstices; Hine (1981) 131, (2010b) 212 n. 2.

19. Perhaps a recurrence of "the multiple disjunctive question as a stylistic device for stimulating *contemplatio*" (Williams [2003] 85 on *Dial.* 8.4.2).

gives way to "how" in a further round of questioning (*quemadmodum . . . similia*): in these ways this single sentence, open-ended in its closing allusion to *cetera . . . his similia*, itself projects in its ornate design and scale the dimensions and complexity of its elevated subject matter. Then to the intermediate level of *sublimia*:

> secunda pars tractat inter caelum terrasque uersantia. hic sunt nubila imbres niues,[20] 'et humanas motura tonitrua mentes', quaecumque aër facit patiturue.
>
> 2.1.2

The second division deals with phenomena that occur between the heavens and the earth. In this category are clouds, rain, snow "and thunder which will trouble the hearts of men" [Ovid, *Met.* 1.55], and whatever the atmosphere brings about or undergoes.

The volatility intrinsic to this zone is enacted in the unsettled gathering of shifting conditions (*nubila . . . tonitrua*), in Seneca's sudden movement from prose to verse quotation, and in the juxtaposition of atmospheric action and passivity in *facit patiturue*—a phrase lacking the smoother symmetry of *agatur an agat* at the celestial level.[21] In his quotation of *Metamorphoses* 1.55, Seneca perhaps injects a further hint of chaos—or of order emerging out of chaos, as in the universal systematization at *N.Q.* 2.1.1–2—by alluding to the moment in the Ovidian cosmogony when the air/atmosphere is first assigned to its position above the land (cf. 1.53–4: "It was there that the creator ordered the mists and the clouds to settle, / there that he assigned the thunder to trouble the hearts of men"); and it is surely no accident that "[i]n this quotation the passing allusion to the fears aroused by thunder and lightning anticipates the theme of ch. 59, the epilogue,"[22] in an understated form of ring composition. Finally, the terrestrial level, investigating "water, earth, trees, plants

---

20. Hine (1981) 69 and (1996a) 53.13–54.14 follows Gercke (1907) 42.10 and other editors in proposing a supplement—in Hine's case *uenti terrarum motus fulmina*—after *niues*, thereby filling out the lacuna apparently demanded by 2.1.3 *"Quomodo"* inquis *"de terrarum motu quaestionem eo posuisti loco quo de tonitribus fulminibusque dicturus es?"* (earthquakes and lightning bolts have seemingly been mentioned in Book 2 before 2.1.3). For full discussion of the case for and against a supplement, Hine (1981) 132–33. But (I owe these points to John Henderson) (1) what pressing need is there for supplementation when *quaecumque* can surely include the "missing" phenomena that Seneca goes on to mention? And (2) the more pertinent point in any case—one well made via the Ovidian quotation—is the disturbing *effect* of phenomena in this intermediate zone, not the enumeration of the phenomena themselves.

21. On Seneca's penchant for pairing the active and passive forms of the same verb, Hine (1981) 130.

22. Hine (1981) 133, adding "but this may be chance."

and—to use a legal term [*ut iurisconsultorum uerbo utar*]—everything that is connected to the soil [*quae solo continentur*]" (2.1.2): Seneca's legal terminology here[23] lends a suitably mundane pitch to his diction as he addresses *terrena*; and given that in law *quae solo continentur* ("real estate") stood in contrast to *res mobiles* ("personal or movable property"),[24] he perhaps plays wittily on volatile, shifting *sublimia* as an unconventional branch of "movable property."

The *Natural Questions* is, as Hine neatly puts it, "literally poised between earth and heaven, for its principal subject is meteorology, the study of the phenomena occurring in, or caused by, the air or atmosphere."[25] But we shall see that Seneca channels his particular focus on *sublimia* in a highly idiosyncratic and—at least in comparison to what survives of the earlier meteorological tradition—original way in the *Natural Questions*. This independence of outlook is conveniently illustrated by a brief glance at his argument in Book 1 that atmospheric lights such as rainbow, streaks and double suns are optical illusions. As so often in Senecan prose, a countervoice here dramatizes the proceedings by creating the illusion of energetic dialogic exchange and disagreement.[26] As soon as the many interlocutory interventions in the main body of Book 1 are granted to the same narrative voice, a consistent character emerges to provide formidable opposition to Seneca's argument for the reflection theory of rainbow in particular. This interlocutor is brought to life as no mere straw man for Seneca's "superior" position, but as a rounded *dramatis persona* in his own right, a literal-minded character, albeit capable of mordant wit and irony, who argues doggedly for a plainer interpretation of such phenomena as rainbow. This difference in outlook is summed up at 1.15.6–7:

> de prioribus quaeritur (de arcu dico et coronis) decipiant aciem et mendacio constent, an in illis quoque uerum sit quod apparet. nobis non placet in arcu aut corona subesse aliquid corporis certi, sed illam iudicamus speculi esse fallaciam alienum corpus nihil amplius quam mentientis.
>
> Concerning the phenomena discussed earlier (I mean rainbow and haloes), there is a question whether [as Seneca holds] they deceive our

---

23. On which Hine (1981) 134.

24. Cf. *OLD solum*¹ 4b, *res* 1d; Hine (1981) 134.

25. Hine (2006) 67–68.

26. There are many cases (e.g., *"Quomodo" inquis "tu mihi… ?,"* 1.3.9; *"Fulgores" inquis "quomodo fiunt… ?,"* 1.15.1) where *inquis* need not refer exclusively, or at all, to Lucilius, the recipient of the work, but to a third, imagined participant in the proceedings (cf. Vottero [1989] 23–24, 45)—a third party who allows Seneca to indulge in sharper exchanges (e.g., in 1.5–8) than if his Lucilius, *uirorum optimus* (cf. 1 pref. 1), were visualized as the interlocutor.

vision and consist of an illusion, or whether [as the interlocutor holds] what is visible in them is also real. We are not content with the theory that there is some real substance in a rainbow or halo, but consider that what occurs is the deception of a mirror, which simply projects the illusion of a separate body.

In the lively exchanges between these two protagonists, differing worldviews are set in contention, the one (Senecan) progressive, imaginative and open-minded, the other more blinkered, rigid and down-to-earth: to the interlocutor's literal eye, a rainbow is no illusion but evidently real in substance and color.[27]

A main objective of this study is to show how this all-too-literal viewpoint, this terrestrial mind-set, is challenged and dislodged by the uplifting epistemological significance that, I propose, Seneca attaches to the tripartite world structure of *caelestia*, *sublimia* and *terrena* in the *Natural Questions*. From the perspective of the progressing philosopher who seeks insight into nature's mysteries (cf. 1 pref. 3), Seneca views *sublimia* such as rainbows not with his interlocutor's brand of down-to-earth literalness ("If I can see it, it must have substance"), but with the higher insight that is figured in Book 1 as an eye for optical illusion. More broadly in the *Natural Questions*, Seneca centers the work on that intermediate zone (*sublimia*) where our eyes begin to fail us and we begin to rely for guidance on a combination of visual and mental discernment; we leave behind the foggy perception (cf. *caliginem*, *tenebris*, 1 pref. 2) that he associates with ordinary humanity at ground level.[28] In the imaginative world of Senecan natural philosophy, our striving to know *sublimia* thus raises us from a level of literal, terrestrial cognition to a higher plane of seeing, inferring and speculating, so that Seneca's debate with his interlocutor in Book 1 is not just, or perhaps even primarily, about the true cause of haloes, rainbows and so on, but also between different kinds of world perception. While Seneca aspires to the enlightened view from above,[29] his interlocutor embodies

---

27. This clash of perspectives is already implicit in Seneca's use of *apparet* at 1.15.6 *de prioribus quaeritur... an in illis quoque uerum sit quod apparet*: the interlocutory mind-set is predisposed to understand *apparet* in one way ("is plainly the case"; cf. *OLD* 10), Seneca in another ("is apparently the case"). Cf. 1.6.3: for the interlocutor the rainbow's color is real (*esse*), for Seneca only apparent (*uideri*). See further on these contrasting perceptions of rainbow Chapter Two, Section IV.

28. Cf. on the metaphysical front Rosenmeyer (2000) 107 ("...this train of thoughts...might well have been written by a Middle Platonist for whom visible things are paltry tokens of what really counts"), and see also for Seneca's cultivation of a "platonisch-dualistische Weltkonzeption" Stahl (1964) 438–41 = Maurach (1975) 282–85 with Gauly (2004) 164–90 ("Platonische Motive in nat. 1 pr."); for further bibliography, Introduction n. 7.

29. On this "perennial motif in ancient philosophic writing," Rutherford (1989) 155–61 with Hadot (1995) 238–50.

a view from below, and within this vertical structure *sublimia* function as the objects of our mental and visual discernment at an intermediate level not just of the sky, but also of our cognitive progress toward the steady and serene cosmic consciousness symbolized by *caelestia*. To put the point differently: if at the celestial level the planets move with exact mathematical precision, our preoccupation among *sublimia* is with the *à peu près* or "more or less" of sublunary physics,[30] a mode of investigation by trial and error that nevertheless represents a beneficial relaxation and retraining of the (overly) literal eye that operates at ground level.

Seneca's steering of his meteorological subject matter toward this emphasis on cognitive progress is perhaps one of the most original features of the *Natural Questions* in comparison with Aristotle's *Meteorologica* and the other extant remnants of the meteorological tradition.[31] The Senecan view from above, on the other hand, was hardly innovative in the Roman (let alone the Greek) tradition: already in Book 6 of his *De republica*, in the so-called *Somnium Scipionis* ("Dream of Scipio") sequence,[32] Cicero had memorably crafted his own version of the cosmic viewpoint when the dream figure of Scipio Africanus (Hannibal's conqueror) directs the gaze of his grandson, Scipio Aemilianus, from earth to the heavenly immensity:

> quam cum magis intuerer, 'quaeso' inquit Africanus 'quousque humi defixa tua mens erit? nonne aspicis quae in templa ueneris? nouem tibi orbibus uel potius globis conexa sunt omnia....'

> haec ego admirans referebam tamen oculos ad terram identidem. tum Africanus 'sentio' inquit 'te sedem etiam nunc hominum ac domum contemplari; quae si tibi parua ut est ita videtur, haec caelestia semper spectato, illa humana contemnito. tu enim quam celebritatem sermonis hominum, aut quam expetendam consequi gloriam potes?...'

> *Rep.* 6.17.1–2; 20.1–3

> And since I [sc. Scipio Aemilianus] kept looking more intently at the earth, Africanus said: 'How long, I ask you, will your thoughts be fixed on the ground? Do you not perceive the precinct into which you have come? Everything is connected, you see, in nine circles or rather spheres....'

---

30. Cf. Koyré (1948) = (1961) 311–29.

31. For Seneca's relation to which, see in my Introduction the section on "The *Natural Questions* and the Meteorological Tradition."

32. Discussed in connection with *N.Q.* 1 pref. by Weber (1995) 81–85 and now Armisen-Marchetti (2007).

Although I marveled at all this, I kept turning my eyes back towards the earth. Then Africanus said: 'I recognize that you are still gazing at the home and dwelling of men. But if it seems to you as insignificant as in fact it is, always look at these heavenly bodies and despise human concerns. For what fame can you achieve among men, or what glory can you achieve that is worth striving for?...'

In constructing this vision of abstraction from the everyday world, Cicero pursues an agenda in his *De republica* evidently very different from Seneca's in the *Natural Questions*.[33] In contrast to the heavenly reward that awaits the Ciceronian states-man after death liberates him, for Seneca the cosmic viewpoint offers equipment for life in the Senecan sense of freedom from mundane, terrestrial interference. The Ciceronian view from above in *De republica* 6 may yet directly influence Seneca's appropriation of the phenomenon, and lend *grauitas* to his promotion of a similar cosmic detachment; but the Senecan emphasis here remains on self-development, and not on public service as the highest form of moral action.

Despite its seemingly objective, external focus on meteorology, then, Seneca's undertaking is distinguished, I propose, from what remains of the earlier meteorological tradition by the epistemological, interiorizing potential that we have sampled in this section. So too in the case of Cicero's *De natura deorum* 2 we have seen that Cicero's Balbus offers a vision of Stoic oneness that usefully illuminates Seneca's parallel construction of a totalizing viewpoint in the *Natural Questions*. But in contrast to Balbus' external form of engagement with nature—his systematic description of the Stoic interdependence of all the world parts—Seneca's approach to the natural world begins *within* the viewer, preconditioning the self to a vision of *natura ipsa* that is unimpeded by blinkered, everyday ways of seeing. Hence the key programmatic importance of the preface to Book 3 as a rehearsal for the thought experiment—the Senecan process of induction toward cosmic consciousness—that is played out in the *Natural Questions* as a whole. Whereas Balbus carefully collects his evidence of Stoic world interpenetration on so many fronts, the Senecan viewer first collects *himself* before collecting the world, retraining his perspective so as to engage with the cosmic immensity.

III: Interiorization in the Preface to Book 3

This process of self-retrieval finds various manifestations in Seneca's oeuvre, notable among them his provocative injunction to Paulinus, his addressee in *Dialogue*

---

33. Cf. Zetzel (1995) 26: "The statesman and the universe, in both its physical and moral aspects, come together at last in the *Somnium*."

10 (*De breuitate uitae*), to withdraw to the philosophical life from his important position as overseer of the Roman grain supply, and thereby to retake possession of himself (cf. 18.1: "The greater part of your life, and certainly the better part, has been given to the state: take possession of some of your time for yourself as well");[34] and so also, in the first of his *Moral Letters*, his admonition to Lucilius to reclaim mastery over his own time (1.1: "…gather and guard your time, which until recently has been forced from you or stolen away, or has merely slipped through your hands…"). In a fresh turning in the preface to *Natural Questions* 3,[35] however, it is his own persona that now undergoes reclamation and change:

Pref. 1 Non praeterit me, Lucili uirorum optime, quam magnarum rerum fundamenta ponam senex, qui mundum circumire constitui et causas secretaque eius eruere atque aliis noscenda prodere. quando tam multa consequar, tam sparsa colligam, tam occulta perspiciam? 2 premit a tergo senectus et obicit annos inter uana studia consumptos. tanto magis urgeamus et damna aetatis male exemptae labor sarciat. nox ad diem accedat, occupationes recidantur, patrimonii longe a domino iacentis cura soluatur, sibi totus animus uacet, et ad contemplationem sui saltim in ipso fine respiciat. 3 faciet, ac sibi instabit, et cotidie breuitatem temporis metietur; quidquid amissum est, id diligenti usu praesentis uitae recolliget. fidelissimus est ad honesta ex paenitentia transitus.

> Libet igitur mihi exclamare illum poetae incluti uersum:
> tollimus ingentes animos et maxima paruo
> tempore molimur.

hoc dicerem si puer iuuenisque molirer (nullum enim non tam magnis rebus tempus angustum est); nunc uero ad rem seriam, grauem, inmensam postmeridianis horis accessimus. 4 faciamus quod in itinere fieri solet: qui tardius exierunt, uelocitate pensant moram. festinemus, et opus nescio an <in>superabile, magnum certe, sine aetatis excusatione tractemus. crescit animus quotiens coepti magnitudinem aspexit, et cogitat quantum proposito, non quantum sibi supersit.

Pref. 1 It does not escape me, Lucilius, best of men, how vast is the project whose foundations I am laying in my old age, now that I have resolved to survey the world and to bring to light its causes and secrets, and to present

---

34. On this provocation to self-examination, Williams (2003) 22–25.

35. See already on this preface Inwood (2000) 26–28 and (2002) 126–28 = (2005) 166–68; Reydams-Schils (2005) 40–42, with emphasis on "the relation between ethics and physics."

them for the knowledge of others. When will I investigate things so numerous, gather together such disparate items and gain insight into such mysteries? 2 Old age presses hard at my back and rebukes me for the years spent amid empty pursuits. But let us strive all the more, and let hard work make good the losses of my ill-spent life. Add night to day, cut back my other involvements, give up all concern for family estates that lie far from their owner; let the mind be entirely free for itself, and at the very end at least look back in contemplation of itself. 3 It will do so, it will drive itself on, and every day it will measure the shortness of time. Whatever has been lost the mind will recover through its careful use of life in the present. The surest transition to the good is that made from a state of regret.

I want, therefore, to give full voice to the well-known lines of the celebrated poet:

We arouse our minds to greatness and strive for the grandest accomplishment in but a short span of time.

I would say the same if I were undertaking this task in boyhood or in youth (for any amount of time is too short for so vast a study); now, in the afternoon of life, I have unquestionably started on a task that is serious, formidable and boundless. 4 Let me do what is often done on a journey: those who set out late make up for the delay by their speed of travel. Let us hurry and, with no excuse made on the grounds of age, let us get to grips with an undertaking which is perhaps insurmountable, certainly great. When my mind considers the scale of this enterprise, it grows in stature and reflects on how much remains for it to do, not on how much remains of its own lifetime.[36]

Of course, Seneca's *de facto* retirement from Nero's court in and after 62 presumably allowed him to devote himself to his new task in the *Natural Questions* with all or much of the freedom reclaimed in §2 above. But biographical considerations aside, Seneca approaches his ambitious task not just with the urgency that comes with advancing age, but also with a totality of commitment (cf. *sibi totus animus uacet*) that matches a new wholeness of cosmic viewpoint, an integrity realized by letting go of all the localized, fragmenting encumbrances of life (cf. *nox…soluatur*).

This movement in a seamless, universal direction finds important expression in Seneca's shifting perception of time in §§2–4. His remarks on the pressing effects of old age in §2—remarks suggestively echoing Varro's preface to his *Res*

---

36. On the "high density" of prefatory commonplaces in this passage, Limburg (2007) 113–28.

Rusticae (1.1.1)[37]—place the greatest value on time and life in a localized, restricted sense: in the years he has left, he will hurry on, everyday measuring the shortness of time (*cotidie... metietur*, §3). On one reading, his verse quotation in §3, possibly from the little-known Vagellius,[38] supports this emphasis on his time running out: "We arouse our minds to greatness and we strive for grand accomplishments *in the little time left*"[39] – a reading made all the more poignant if Vagellius' poem was on the Phaethon myth, and if, in the line's original context, the young Phaethon roused himself and his horses (hence the first-person plural *tollimus* and *molimur*) for his fateful journey in the solar chariot.[40] But then a sudden change of direction, with further irony if in *puer iuuenisque* Seneca gently revives our poetic memory of Phaethon in the preceding quotation: from the localized significance of *paruo tempore*, and from the narrowness of Seneca's last remaining years, we now move in *hoc... molirer* to the expanded narrowness of an entire but mere lifetime that is spent in contemplation of nature (cf. again *nullum enim non tam magnis rebus tempus angustum est*, §3); and when we revisit the verse quotation, the sense now amounts to: "We arouse our minds to greatness and strive for the grandest accomplishment *in the short mortal span as a whole*." We move from anxious measurement of time in the localized sense in *cotidie breuitatem temporis metietur* [sc. *animus*] (§3) to the fuller, more liberated perception of time, including figurative time (*postmeridianis horis*), that is better calibrated to the dimensions of his cosmically vast, measureless (*inmensam*) undertaking in the afternoon of life; we move toward a Senecan sublimity of thought.[41] This shifting significance of time in a universal direction amounts to a radical form of conversion that distances us from what Pierre Hadot characterizes as utilitarian perception:

---

37. Perhaps lending Varronian prestige to the Senecan persona; for the echo, Parroni (1992b) 169, (1997) 116 and (2002) xlviii–ix with Hine (2006) 48 and Limburg (2007) 126–27.

38. Vagellius fr. 2 Courtney (1993) 347; cf. 6.2.9 for a citation explicitly attributed to Vagellius (= fr. 1 Courtney 347), and see further Chapter Six, Section IV. Courtney 347 identifies this Vagellius with "the man known as consul suffect between AD 44 and 46...; he may or may not be identical with the Vagellius mentioned by Juvenal [cf. 13.119, 16.23]." But for other proposed ascriptions at 1 pref. 3, Hine (1996a) 109 on 21–22 with Vottero (1989) 378–79 n. 13.

39. So Corcoran (1971–72) 1.203; my emphasis.

40. See Mazzoli (1968) and (1970) 258 with Duret (1988) 141–42, and cf. Chapter Six, Section IV. Dahlmann (1977) makes no allusion to Mazzoli's thesis, but he detects in the two quotations in Books 1 and 6 the themes of an epic *exordium*. By *paruo tempore* Phaethon means "lo spazio d'un *dies*" (Mazzoli [1968] 365); Seneca is slower to seize the (figurative) day, embarking on his different flight path (cf. *mundum circumire*, §1) only *postmeridianis horis*. In quoting Ov. *Met.* 2.264 at 3.27.13, Seneca draws on the Ovidian Phaethon episode; does he thereby give Phaethon a subtle double presence at both the beginning and the end of Book 3 (cf. Berno [2003] 93–94 n. 103 and 261)?

41. See further on traces of the sublime in 3 pref. 3 Chapter Six, Section IV; concisely on the surge toward the sublime (cf. *crescit animus...*, §4) in the preface as a whole, Mazzoli (1991).

The utilitarian perception we have of the world, in everyday life, in fact hides us from the world qua world. Aesthetic and philosophical perceptions of the world are only possible by means of a complete transformation of our relationship to the world: we have to perceive it *for itself*, and no longer *for ourselves*.[42]

As Seneca rises to his task in §4, his persona effects a strikingly similar transformation in its new focus not on the time left to him, but on the scale of the task before him (...*cogitat* [sc. *animus*] *quantum proposito, non quantum sibi supersit*): he perceives his undertaking for itself, and no longer for himself.

We have seen that Cicero's Balbus in *De natura deorum* 2 exemplifies an external mode of engagement with nature that is contrasted by Seneca's internalized approach to world description and world collection. We now return briefly to that external mode, but on this occasion with our focus on Seneca's negative critique in §§5–6 of historical inquiry into "the actions of foreign kings [*acta regum externorum*] and the sufferings that nations have undergone or inflicted on others in turn."[43] After expressing regret at "years spent amid empty pursuits" (*annos inter uana studia consumptos*, §2), he turns here on another *uanum stadium* whose wasteful expenditure of effort is likened to his own lost years through the reverberation of *consumptos* in *Consumpsere se quidam*... in §5 ("Some writers have worn themselves out in recording the actions of foreign kings..."); and the externalizing habit of mind that he faults in these *historici*—"How much better it is to eliminate one's own evils [*sua mala*] than to report for posterity the evils of others [*aliena*]" (§5) – is itself partially mirrored in their subject matter of *externi reges*. Two *exempla* illustrate the shortcomings that Seneca attributes to (his loaded portrayal here of) historical study, the first featuring father and son, Philip II of Macedon and Alexander the Great:

> quanto potius deorum opera celebrare quam Philippi aut Alexandri latrocinia, ceterorumque qui exitio gentium clari non minores fuere pestes mortalium quam inundatio qua planum omne perfusum est, quam conflagratio qua magna pars animantium exarsit!
>
> 3 pref. 5

---

42. Hadot (1995) 254.

43. On this apparent turning against historiography late in Seneca's life, see Hine (2006) 49–50 with Galdi (1924), and cf. Chapters Four, Section IV (A), and n. 47 and Seven, Section V. Given the primacy of Book 3 in the original ordering of the books, the position of this attack takes on "a programmatic importance: effectively Seneca is himself rejecting historiography as a literary and intellectual pursuit in favour of philosophy" (Hine 50).

How much more important it is to extol the works of the gods than the robberies of a Philip or an Alexander, or of others who were famous for the destruction of whole peoples, and were no less a disaster for mankind than a flood that inundated every plain or a conflagration that burned up the majority of living creatures.

From one perspective, the excesses of Philip and Alexander are vastly aggrandized by comparison with the cataclysm and the conflagration, in Stoic (and broader Greek) thought those great forces of periodic world destruction.[44] From another perspective, however, the likes of Philip and Alexander are themselves inevitably overwhelmed by the cosmic forces to which they are compared. Whatever the extent of their conquests and the number of their victims, their exploits are as nothing in comparison with the destruction perpetrated by cataclysm or conflagration, their regal standing is of no account in nature's higher, equalizing scheme, and their brief span of life is of no consequence in comparison with the vast temporal cycles that coordinate cosmic dissolution and renewal. As soon as the cosmic dimension asserts itself to this diminishing effect in §5, the universalizing impulse that overcomes the narrowness of merely utilitarian perception in §§1–4 is revitalized, countering the historians' emphasis on significant *acta* with the cosmic *in*significance of any Philip or Alexander.

In contrast to the historians' external preoccupation with "recording the actions of foreign kings," what matters in the Senecan text is the internalization of those *acta* so that they become aids to self-inspection. So in §6, on historical writing about Hannibal:

> quemadmodum Hannibal Alpes superiecerit scribunt, quemadmodum confirmatum Hispaniae cladibus bellum Italiae inopinatus intulerit, fractisque rebus, etiam post Carthaginem *pertinax*, reges pererrauerit contra Romanos ducem promittens, exercitum petens, quemadmodum non desierit *omnibus angulis* bellum *senex* quaerere: adeo *sine patria pati poterat*, sine hoste non poterat!

They write of how Hannibal crossed the Alps, how he unexpectedly brought to Italy a war that had gathered strength from disasters in Spain;

---

44. On these forces, κατακλυσμός and ἐκπύρωσις, see Wildberger (2006) 56–58 with Vottero (1989) 440 n. 2 on 3.27.1; the two ends of Book 3 are loosely coordinated through the framing presence of inundation in the preface and its full-blown description in 3.27–30 (see Berno [2003] 87 n. 85). For Seneca's consistently negative treatment of Alexander in particular see Vottero 380 n. 22 (adding Coccia [1984]) and Berno 200–201 and n. 78 with Spencer (2002) 69–79, 89–94 and 97–112, and cf. Chapters Five, Section V and n. 150, and Six, Section VI.

how, after his fortunes were dashed, he remained obstinate even after Carthage's demise and wandered from one king to the next, promising to be a leader against the Romans and asking for an army; and how as an old man he did not stop looking for war in every corner of the world. He could put up with being without a country, but not without an enemy.

On one level, a concise enough summary of Hannibal's career down to and after his defeat at Zama in 202, perhaps with gentle parody of an essentially descriptive historical mode.[45] On a deeper level, however, this summary is also philosophically meaningful: despite his persistence (*pertinax*) amid his oscillating fortunes and prolonged wanderings, Hannibal hardly resembles the Stoic *sapiens*, for whom "every place is his homeland" (*Dial.* 12.9.7);[46] by contrast, the Carthaginian tellingly "puts up with" (cf. *pati*) his own loss of *patria*. The *sapiens* roams free in his cosmic mind travels. So of the liberated *animus* at 1 pref. 8–9:

> non potest ante contemnere porticus et lacunaria ebore fulgentia…quam totum circuît mundum, et terrarum orbem superne despiciens angustum ac magna ex parte opertum mari…sibi ipse dixit: 'hoc est illud punctum quod inter tot gentes ferro et igni diuiditur!'
> O quam ridiculi sunt mortalium termini!
> It cannot despise colonnades and ceilings gleaming with ivory…until it has surveyed the entire world and, looking down[47] upon the earth from above—the earth that is narrow and mostly covered by sea…, it has said to itself: 'This is that mere pinpoint which is divided among so many nations by sword and fire!'
> How ridiculous are the boundaries of mortals!

From this cosmic perspective Hannibal travels *in angusto* (cf. 1 pref. 10) in his movement from Carthage to Spain to Italy and beyond, and in his ceaseless search for war in every corner (*omnibus angulis*) he advances from one mere *punctum* to another in the boundary-defined world of localized power—or from one point to another in the mere *punctum* that *is* the world. In contrast to the unifying vision of the *sapiens*, this Hannibal seeks to unify by hard conquest and fails in

---

45. Cf. Vottero (1989) 381 n. 25 on *scribunt* in §6 (Seneca has in mind Polybius, Cornelius Nepos and Livy). For Seneca's harsh judgment of Hannibal, cf. *Dial.* 4.5.4, *Letters* 51.5, 7.

46. On the familiar philosophical/consolatory idea, Williams (2006b) 147 and n. 2, 158–59. For *pertinax* of a more Stoic persistence, cf. *Dial.* 1.3.14, *Letters* 24.7 (of the younger Cato in both cases).

47. With disdain implied in *despiciens*; cf. *OLD* 2.

the attempt, his restless energies persisting into old age (*senex*); yet Seneca, that other *senex* (3 pref. 1),[48] embarks on a very different strategy of viable conquest in the *Natural Questions*, seeking to survey the universe (*mundum circumire constitui*, 3 pref. 1) in the manner of the liberated *animus* in Book 1 (*totum circuit mundum* [sc. *animus*], 1 pref. 8).

In contrast to an external preoccupation with historical *acta*, then, Seneca treats Hannibal with a highly self-conscious, interior significance, defining his own cosmic awakening in the *Natural Questions* by implicit differentiation from the Carthaginian, and also from Philip and Alexander, in 3 pref. 5–6. A variation on this interior meaning of the *exempla* is offered by Seneca's subsequent disquisition on the fickleness of fortune (§§7–9), and then by the recalibration of perspective that he urges in §10:

> magna ista quia parui sumus credimus: multis rebus non ex natura sua sed ex humilitate nostra magnitudo est.
>
> Quid praecipuum in rebus humanis est? non classibus maria complesse, nec in Rubri maris litore signa fixisse…, sed animo omne uidisse et, qua maior nulla uictoria est, uitia domuisse. innumerabiles sunt qui populos, qui urbes habuerunt in potestate, paucissimi qui se.
>
> We believe that these [sc. kingdoms and empires, *regna* and *imperia*] are great because we are small; many things draw their importance not from their own true nature but from our lowliness.
>
> What is most important in human existence? Not to have filled the seas with ships or to have fixed a flag on the shore of the Red Sea…, but to have seen the all with your mind and—the greatest victory of all—to have conquered your vices. There are countless people who have mastered nations and cities, very few who have mastered themselves.

Within the preface as a whole Philip, Alexander and Hannibal are no localized, momentary presences in §§5–6, but *exempla* of a more embedded relevance, as if versatile illustrations-in-waiting for so much that follows down to §17: in their rise and fall from greatness they amply demonstrate the oscillating fortunes of one dynastic power after another (cf. §9), while their thirst for conquest wins a (brief) mastery over others that is unmatched by self-mastery. As we saw in the case of Philip and Alexander in §5,[49] their destructiveness, however extreme in

---

48. With a play in *senex* on his own name, in pleasing contrast to his addressee, Lucilius *Iunior* (cf. 3.1.1, 4a pref. 9); see Ker (2009) 13, 105, 153.

49. See above in this section and n. 44.

one way, is as nothing in comparison with the universal forces of cataclysm and conflagration—a recalibration of their significance that anticipates Seneca's transition from a human to a cosmic criterion of measurement in §10 above ("We believe...lowliness"). It is from this cosmic vantage point that Seneca's mantra-like repetition of "What is most important in human existence?" (*quid prae-cipuum in rebus humanis est?*, §10; cf. §§11, 12, 13, etc.) works to fortify us in §§10–17 against the vagaries and impurities (*sordidis*, §18) of everyday life—"the threats and promises of fortune" (§11), for example, or sudden adversity (§12), the seductions of luxury (§13) or the temptations of evil scheming (§14), all of them thwarted by a higher detachment (cf. *erigere animum supra minas et promissa for-tunae*, §11; *altos supra fortuita spiritus tollere*, §15) that the likes of Seneca's Alexander and Hannibal signally lack in their tumultuous lives. If fundamental characteristics of the *sapiens* are delineated in §§10–17,[50] the likes of Alexander inevitably emerge as antitypes of the *sapiens*, misguided as they are in their obsession with earthly, military glory.[51]

The *exempla* of §§5–6 thus have a far-reaching significance that is deeply interiorized in the preface as a whole; and while Seneca's writers of history concern themselves with *acta* in §5, his is a more searching, interior approach to the *exempla* supplying those *acta*. This interiorizing process is itself symptomatic of his key emphasis in the preface on self-transformation as he begins to engage with the physical world in the *Natural Questions*. His is no purely objective inquiry, but a highly subjective, personally involving (even transforming) engagement with *natura ipsa*. In his more external approach to capturing nature's oneness, Cicero's Balbus offers one illuminating counterpoint to this Senecan interiority; but for different illumination we now turn to the counterpoint offered by the elder Pliny's *Natural History*.

IV: *The Differing World Outlooks of Seneca and Pliny*

Responding in *Letter* 3.5 to a request from his addressee, Baebius Macer, that he give a full account of all the books written by the elder Pliny (23–79 CE), the younger Pliny embarks on a chronological survey of his uncle's copious output. The diverse list ranges *inter alia* from an early work on military instruction (*Throw-ing the javelin from horseback*) to a twenty-volume history of *Wars in Germany*, and from a two-volume life of his friend and patron, the distinguished general and tragic poet P. Pomponius Secundus (cos. suff. 44 CE), to a three-book rhetorical

---

50. So Vottero (1989) 384–85 n. 47; see also Limburg (2007) 138–40.

51. On this contrast "between earthly glory and the pursuit of philosophy," Hine (2006) 46.

handbook, divided into six volumes because of its length;[52] in effect, the list amounts to an informal work of biography in its own right, capturing the elder Pliny's multifaceted accomplishments and rounded character before culminating in that "final explosion of universal text,"[53] the *Natural History* in thirty-seven books. After surveying these works (3.5.3–6), the nephew turns the focus of wonder away from this extraordinary output and on to the elder Pliny himself: How did he write so much? Here, after all, was an erstwhile advocate and a busy man of affairs who held a series of procuratorships in the seventies under Vespasian before dying during the Vesuvian eruption of 79 CE at fifty-five while in charge of the Roman fleet at Misenum.[54] The fact is, Pliny claims (3.5.8), that his uncle combined "a sharp intellect with unbelievable powers of concentration and the ability to manage with the minimum of sleep [*summa uigilantia*]." The elder Pliny himself claims in the dedicatory preface to his *Natural History* that he has consulted around two thousand volumes and included some twenty thousand facts drawn from a hundred authors (§17).[55] Apologizing for any omission (we can only hope with irony), he pleads the excuse that he is only human (*homines enim sumus et occupati officiis*, §18). He pursues his researches daily after his official duties are done, limiting his sleep so as to live longer; for "to live is to be awake" (*uita uigilia est*, §18).[56] No moment is to be lost: the more time spent on reading and excerpting (cf. *Ep.* 3.5.10), the more facts are collected and the more documented about the world in this Plinian response to that more widespread "anxiety of encyclopedic systematization"[57] in the early Empire. In his description of the elder Pliny's busy daily routine both "in the midst of his public duties and city-bustle" and in his country retreat (3.5.14), the nephew portrays a ceaseless hyperactivity divided between his uncle's public and private vocations—a picture pointedly contrasted by

---

52. For full coverage of his works, Sherwin-White (1966) 216–19 with Healy (1999) 31–35 and Henderson (2002).

53. Henderson (2002) 281; cf. now on the significant placement of the *Natural History* in the younger Pliny's listing Gibson (2011).

54. His career: Sherwin-White (1966) 219–21 with Beagon (1992) 1–6 and (2005) 1–5; Healy (1999) 1–30.

55. According to Gudger (1924) 269, in fact 473 authors, 146 Roman and 327 Greek.

56. On the tone of the preface more generally, with its telling Vespasianic traits, see Hoffer (1999) 169 ("Vespasianic traits seem...to be echoed in [the *Natural History*'s] unpretentious, practical outlook..., its almost financial approach to collecting and saving facts..., the diligent work required..., and the time-saving table of contents").

57. Conte (1994) 68. For encyclopedic writing claimed as "a Roman innovation," Murphy (2004) 194–95, and on Roman encyclopedic literature in general, Grimal (1965) 463–82. But cf. now the qualifications entered by Doody (2009) (so, e.g., p. 3: "There was no ancient genre of encyclopedia that ancient writers and readers understood as such").

Pliny's admiring portrait in *Ep.* 3.1 of the aged Spurinna's leisurely routine in retirement. Whereas Spurinna takes his time, the elder Pliny *applies* it meticulously: mediation between their contrasting outlooks is perhaps to be found in the younger Pliny's implicit projection for himself of an ideal *modus uiuendi* that strikes a balance between casualness and urgency, between using time and indulging it.[58] In *Ep.* 6.16, Pliny's celebrated response to Tacitus' request for a description of the elder Pliny's death during the Vesuvian eruption, his uncle is again typically quick to seize the moment, first climbing to a vantage point from which he can best examine the emerging volcanic cloud, and then summoning a boat for closer inspection of the phenomenon (§§5–7). His versatility in combining his public and private vocations in *Ep.* 3.5 here gives way to a different flexibility when, in answer to a neighbor's distress call, "he changed his plan, and what he had begun in a spirit of inquiry [*studioso animo*] he completed as a hero [*maximo animo*]," 6.16.9). As the letter continues, the humanitarian and scientific aspects of his motivation are blended in a picture of courageous devotion that is humbling in its implications for the younger Pliny: the uncle sets a standard for heroic action that the nephew cannot begin to meet.[59]

If Spurinna in particular offers one alternative to the elder Pliny's model of unremitting action and *doing*, then Seneca's self-projection in the preface to *Natural Questions* 3 offers a different alternative: doing in a more internalized sense (*faciet* [sc. *animus*], *ac sibi instabit*..., 3 pref. 3). The Plinian division of life between public and private callings, *occupatio* and *studium*, disappears in Seneca's emphasis on *studium* to the exclusion of all *occupatio*: "Add night to day, cut back my other involvements...; let the mind be left entirely free for itself..." (3 pref. 2). "Add night to day," he enjoins, as if sharing Pliny's tireless *uigilantia*,[60] but not his partitioned existence: the study of the all (cf. *animo omne uidisse*, 3 pref. 10) presupposes a seamless devotion (cf. *sibi totus animus uacet*, 3 pref. 2) that is made possible only by a radical turning away from all official duties such as Seneca himself performed before his alienation from the Neronian court in and after 62.[61] Beyond the external, public aspect of Pliny's partitioned life, his collection process

58. Cf. Henderson (2002) 265: "the styles of life that [the elder Pliny and Spurinna] profile help Pliny feel, and find, his way between their chalk-and-cheese polarity."

59. For the approach, Jones (2001); on the pairing of 6.16 and 6.20 (both to Tacitus on the elder Pliny's death), now Marchesi (2008) 171–89.

60. On the general "culture of *lucubratio*," or study by lamplight, to which Seneca and Pliny both contribute, Ker (2004), especially 229–36.

61. For comparison of the two prefaces, cf. Citroni Marchetti (1991) 19–21, setting Seneca's complete estrangement from the Neronian court against Pliny's collaborative relationship with the Flavian house. For general comparison of the Senecan and Plinian scientific/philosophical outlooks, Capponi (1996) 104–26.

in the *Natural History* might itself (at the risk of crude generalization) be termed external, in that the Plinian world lies out there to be gathered in, catalogued and controlled in his textual museum—a process very different from the self-engagement, the inner conversion, that preconditions Seneca's engagement with the cosmic immensity in the *Natural Questions*.

It is this inner conversion that crucially distinguishes Seneca's project from Pliny's, the encyclopedic exercise that tacitly promises "completeness, reliability, and authority" as "the authorized version of knowledge."[62] In the vast scale of its thirty-seven books (the table of contents that orients the entire *opus* in Book 1 itself presents an appearance of completeness even before we embark on the work proper), the *Natural History* exudes a sense of comprehensiveness as "a universal Latin text, a book patterned after the vast empire that has made the universe available for knowing."[63] Far outstripping all Roman encyclopedic precedents in its universal ambition, the work suggestively replicates the external world in its own grand design—a system that suitably begins in Book 2 with a description of the *mundus* before it describes the world's geographical divisions (Books 3–6) and then locates man at the top (Book 7) of a descending scale of nature (man, other animals, birds, fish, etc.); an anthropocentric vision of nature fundamentally conditions the whole enterprise. Pliny's description of the world at 2.2 offers a tempting commentary on the world as text:

> sacer est [sc. mundus], aeternus, inmensus, totus in toto, immo uero ipse totum, infinitus ac finito similis, omnium rerum certus et similis incerto, extra intra cuncta conplexus in se, idemque rerum naturae opus et rerum ipsa natura.
>
> The world is sacred, eternal, measureless, self-contained, or, rather, complete in itself, infinite yet resembling the finite, of all things certain yet resembling the uncertain, embracing in itself all things within and without. The world is at once the work of nature and the embodiment of nature herself.

If, with Sorcha Carey, we detect in the possible collusion here of nature's work and Pliny's *opus* an "equation of external reality and internal representation,"[64] the *Natural History* constitutes a literary mirroring of Roman imperial domination, as if the challenge of Roman world organization has been fully met by the later

---

62. Murphy (2004) 14.

63. Murphy (2004) 2.

64. (2003) 20.

first century CE and all that remains is the task of registration. Hence the mechanical feel to Pliny's process of collection: his appears to be an "impersonal concept of knowledge, which excludes individual originality"[65] as it systematically catalogues the world in down-to-earth fashion.[66]

By contrast, Seneca's is a highly personal concept of knowledge, and individual development is the function of knowledge acquisition. Serial comprehensiveness of the objective, Plinian kind is far removed from the expansiveness of cosmic vision that Seneca promotes, and the totalizing perspective that is gradually assembled through assiduous, fact-by-fact accumulation in Pliny differs fundamentally from the wholeness of viewpoint shaped in Seneca's ascending journey from terrestrial perception in the *Natural Questions*. It follows that the two works are centered on very different physical locales. Pliny's *Natural History* finds its center in Rome, it "arranges and classifies the world as unequivocally Roman,"[67] and in its ethnographical sections Roman life is the implicit yardstick by which other peoples and cultures are measured.[68] The work is dedicated to the future emperor Titus, but in his own way Pliny exercises supreme power over the world he surveys and controls in his master text—even if he tactfully plays down his quasi-imperializing credentials out of deference to his distinguished dedicatee. In his hostility to Greek culture[69] he also constructs a form of "nationalistic encyclopedia,"[70] even though a glance at his table of contents in Book 1 reveals his heavy debt to Greek sources; but there too his division of his sources into "authors" (*ex auctoribus*) and "foreign authors" (*externis*) reveals his nationalistic leaning, which itself reflects a broader Roman suspicion of Greek scholarship in the early

---

65. Calvino (1986) 318.

66. But for a different claim to Plinian originality despite the mechanical feel, cf. Doody (2010) 23: "Pliny's achievement is a conceptualisation of knowledge that privileges information over theory, movable facts over abstract ideas. For Pliny, knowing about *rerum natura* is not dependent on discussing a particular theoretical or philosophical position, as Lucretius or Seneca would have it.... This vision of a nature that can be broken into sections and catalogued, fact by fact, name by name, item by item, until all of it is listed, represents *a new idea about what it is to know about the nature of things*. In the *Natural History*, nature becomes exactly the sum of its parts, a catalogue of details that anyone can grasp, but *that only Pliny has contained and organized*" (my emphasis). For this vision of Pliny's down-to-earth conceptualization of knowledge cf. now Beagon (2011) 75 for Plinian "terrestrial curiosity" set against "the Senecan model of celestial curiosity."

67. Carey (2003) 33.

68. Murphy (2004) 94.

69. See Howe (1985) 570; Wallace-Hadrill (1990) 92–96; Beagon (1992) 18–20; French (1994) 218–19; Carey (2003) 23–25.

70. Howe (1985) 571.

Empire, and widespread belief in the moral inferiority of Greek culture in general (cf. 7.130: "The one race that is most outstanding in virtue in the whole world is undoubtedly the Roman").[71] In Seneca, on the other hand, there is no structuring principle based on any strong distinction between Roman and non-Roman sources, and "no trace of the anti-Greek prejudice that is so plain in Pliny."[72] Instead, he builds a more seamless community of Greco-Roman inquirers[73] into nature's workings, with a greater emphasis on the causal explanation of phenomena; and while the *Natural Questions* is in one sense evidently rooted in the Roman world through abundant geographical and historical allusion to places, people and events in the Roman past and present, Rome itself is conspicuously marginalized in the work as a whole. The name *Roma* occurs only once in the *Natural Questions* (4a pref. 21), the adjective *Romanus* only six times, whereas in Pliny they each occur some two hundred times—a striking disproportion even when the differing scales of the two works are taken into account.[74] When Seneca looks down from a cosmic perspective on the boundaries that distinguish this earthly power from that (cf. "How ridiculous are the boundaries of mortals!" 1 pref. 9), he surveys the *termini* separating Rome from her neighbors (e.g., Germans, Dacians and Sarmatians) and dividing different provinces (Gallic and Spanish) within the Roman empire; but Roman *imperium* is itself tacitly implicated in this disparagement of conventional geopolitical distinctions at ground level. So in Seneca's vision of the wholesale destruction caused by the cataclysm at the end of Book 3 ("A single day will bury the human race," 3.29.9), Rome herself is necessarily vulnerable to the same catastrophe,[75] her immense power of no account in the cosmic scale of things. However fanciful the prospect of Rome's demise may have seemed to the early imperial observer, the precariousness of fortune that is illustrated by the rise and fall of empires at 3 pref. 9 can allow no exceptions to the general rule, Roman *imperium* included.

In contrast to Pliny's Rome-centered world vision, then, the cosmic perspective promoted by Seneca inevitably realigns our view of Roman global (self-) importance—a realignment underscored by the contrast between Pliny's prefatory dedication of the *Natural History* to Titus and the more private trajectory that Seneca affects in addressing the *Natural Questions* to his old friend, Lucilius

---

71. On these points, Carey (2003) 24–25 with Beagon (2005) 328 on 7.130.

72. Hine (2006) 59.

73. And still others: cf. Hine (2006) 58 and n. 67 for Egyptians (3.14.2, 7.3.2–3) and Chaldeans (7.4.1, 28.1).

74. On these and later points in this paragraph, Hine (2006) 43.

75. Murphy (2004) 187 on 3.29.9.

Iunior. Whereas Pliny places his work "at the centre of the imperial world, and intends it to help, but not impede [cf. Pref. 33], Titus and others who are in public service,"[76] Seneca's new enterprise occupies more marginal territory, as if detached from the imperial center: even (or especially) after Lucilius becomes procurator of Sicily, the philosophical focus remains paramount when Seneca urges him in the preface to *Natural Questions* 4a to keep his official tasks within bounds so as to cultivate the all-important interior life (4a pref. 1).[77] Moreover, a central emphasis in Book 4a is that, for all the Nile's seeming marvels (cf. *miracula fluminis*, 4a.2.6), most obvious among them its summer flooding, the river is no less susceptible to rational explanation than every other part of Stoic nature's scheme. In this respect, the late Hellenistic and Roman preoccupation with *mirabilia* and miracle literature[78] is fundamentally resisted by Seneca's rationalizing discourse in the *Natural Questions*. But for Pliny the existence of *mirabilia*, whether at the periphery of the Roman world or in Italy and in the metropolis itself, provides confirmation of Rome's importance as *the* global center—a "second sun and second parent to the world and thus a second nature."[79] From a centrifugal perspective, Pliny's cataloguing of wonders and monstrosities on the margins of empire surrounds "the kingdom of certain knowledge"[80] with an uncertain periphery where chaotic *mirabilia* merely confirm the solidity of the center. Yet, from a centripetal viewpoint, the flow of war booty from the conquered world parts was accompanied by an influx of natural curiosities, exotic animals notable among them, for public display at Rome. Such display "symbolized the power and uniqueness of both Rome and her emperor," itself conferring wonder status on both city and ruler;[81] and this wondrous effect is further enhanced by the

---

76. Hine (2006) 48.

77. Cf. Scott (1999) 63, speculating that in the lost portion of Book 4a "Seneca went on to say that Lucilius' powerful position—or that of any man—is feeble and insignificant when compared to the awesome power and mystery of the Nile."

78. See Beagon (1992) 8–11, (2005) 18–19 and (2007) with Murphy (2004) 18–22, Healy (1999) 63–70 and, with emphasis on the Augustan era, Hardie (2009b); extensive background in Schepens and Delcroix (1996). Specifically on the Nile—and on aspects of Seneca's broader treatment of terrestrial waters in Book 3—related to the literature of *mirabilia aquarum*, see Callebat (1988), especially 156–57.

79. Beagon (2007) 20 on 27.3 and 37.201. Further on the positive Plinian/Roman significance of *mirabilia* in the *Natural History*, see now Naas (2011) and Beagon (2011), especially p. 82: "wonder, rather than paralyzing or disorienting, kick-starts reason into life. Pliny's frequent use of a wide range of terms connected with wonder... is intended to grab the readers' attention and to make them look harder at the world around them."

80. Murphy (2004) 20.

81. Beagon (2007) 31.

indigenous *mirabilia* that Pliny finds in Italy and at Rome.[82] Rome collects the world, but in her own wondrous diversity Rome/Italy too rivals the ingenuity of *natura ipsa*. For all his insistence that his work "has no place for digressions, speeches, discourses, miraculous events or motley occurrences [*casus mirabilis uel euentus uarios*], although such matters might have been pleasant for me to relate or entertaining to read" (Pref. 12), nature's capacity to amaze necessarily gives the miraculous a privileged place in Pliny's text: for all his emphasis on mechanistic regularity, (Roman) nature's ingenuity outruns the task of normative registration.

For Seneca, however, *mirabilia* and the rhetoric of *mirum* give way to a plainer rhetoric of necessity[83] in nature's functioning, and we move away from Rome as the triumphant, centralized showcase of amassed *mirabilia* to a cosmically revisionist view of Rome's relative (un)importance as a mere temporal and spatial *punctum* (cf. 1 pref. 11). From this Senecan perspective, Pliny's method of composition also stands in contrast to the unifying mind-set that integrates the literary as well as the physical world of the *Natural Questions*. As old age presses, Seneca hurries to his new task in the *Natural Questions* (cf. *tanto magis urgeamus*, 3 pref. 2; *festinemus*, 3 pref. 4) as a matter of urgency, not just (or so much) because his own time is running out, but because he views time in relation to the cosmic immensity of the subject.[84] Pliny too rushes, but seemingly without this higher perspective on time and the cosmic totality that dignifies Seneca's haste. Pliny projects the scale of his own totalizing task through a breathless striving for completeness that forces the pace, as at 3.42[85]:

> nimirum id quod in caeli mentione fecimus hac quoque in parte faciendum est, ut notas quasdam et pauca sidera attingamus. legentes tantum quaeso meminerint ad singula toto orbe edissertanda festinari.
>
> In this section I must again do what I did in discussing the sky, namely touch on some particular points and a few stars. I only ask my readers to bear in mind that I am rushing ahead in order to set out the details of the whole world.

At a stylistic level, Pliny's urgency of movement is also conveyed through loose sentence structure, abrupt and asymmetrical clausal arrangement, sudden changes

82. Beagon (2007) 26–32.

83. For this rhetoric see Conte (1994) 21 (on Lucretius) and 151 n. 47; Chapter Six, Section III.

84. See Section III above in this chapter.

85. Cited by Carey (2003) 21.

of grammatical subject, verbal compression that sometimes approaches unintelligibility, and tightly packed listings of given phenomena; all of these features contribute to "the impression of the half-finished work of a writer pressed for time," as if "in a hurry toward plenitude. Pliny sees himself confronting the world's knowledge in a narrow window of opportunity, defined on one edge by the expansion of Roman power, and on the other by the inexorable decay of knowledge."[86] For Seneca, by contrast, that "narrow window of opportunity" is defined by the shortness of even the longest life. Whereas the preface to *Natural Questions* 3 promotes attunement to the cosmic now as a goal in and of itself, detaching us from the anxious rush of life,[87] for Pliny time's value is measured in terms of the amount of excerpting achieved and the number of facts gathered in; or so the younger Pliny indicates in describing his uncle's extreme fixation with wasting not a moment (cf. *parsimonia temporis, Ep.* 3.5.13), to the extent of having books read aloud to him at dinner while he took running notes (3.5.11), or scolding his nephew for walking when he could have been carried by litter, thereby devoting his precious travel time to yet more study (3.5.16).

The daunting challenge of cataloguing nature's totality confers on the *Natural History* a unity of purpose that is reinforced by secondary modes of totality: as Mary Beagon remarks, Pliny's "interest in preserving past as well as present knowledge has the effect of giving [the work] a *temporal* totality," while "the totality of [Pliny's] enterprise has an important *spatial* aspect, in that the work reflects a contemporary vision of Roman imperial expansion."[88] Moreover, if "the central organizing principle of the encyclopedia is to divide things into categories by contrast,"[89] affinities across categories create balance and correspondence between different parts of the *Natural History*, while for G. B. Conte the work contains "an implicit organicity" that is not systematic but based on an authorial attitude yielding, perhaps despite itself, a unity in "the capacity to be astonished and the will to astonish."[90] Andrew Wallace-Hadrill similarly points to "a coherence,

---

86. Murphy (2004) 35, 69. But for an attempted reconstruction of Pliny's working method in the *Natural History*, and for system despite Murphy's "impression of the half-finished work of a writer pressed for time," see Naas (1996).

87. Cf. 3 pref. 17: "Enslavement to oneself is the most oppressive kind of slavery, but it is easy to shake off...if you keep before your eyes your nature and your age, even if you are still young, and you say to yourself: 'Why am I a fool? Why do I pant breathlessly? Why am I sweating?...I don't need much, and only for a short time'."

88. Beagon (2005) 22–23; my emphasis.

89. Murphy (2004) 29.

90. Conte (1994) 103–104. The case for a fundamental organicity is powerfully made by Henderson (2011), pointing to "a no-fail catena of interconnectedness" (p. 142): so, e.g., "*HN* self-proclaims an achieved, emphatically completed, *organic* structure, 'job done'" (p. 143;

indeed a passionate single-mindedness of purpose, that is reminiscent of, and parallel to, that of Lucretius."[91] On the premise of nature's providential beneficence, Pliny's vast assemblage of facts derives overall meaning from "their persuasive value: they prove that the world was built with a purpose";[92] and, like Seneca's comparable expressions of moral outrage in the *Natural Questions*, his sporadic outbursts against luxury are no awkward appendages but "an essential part of the argument, the underpinning and justification for his scientific labors."[93] Yet despite these unifying tendencies at the macro level, the *Natural History* was not so much written as assembled, a many-voiced, collage-like gathering of cuttings from diverse sources as opposed to a seamless construction with a consistent authorial voice.[94] In this "aesthetic flirtation with chaos,"[95] classification by contrast privileges the individual fact (or category of fact) and reduces sequential reading to a system of encounters with "detail juxtaposed with detail, parataxis, particularity, multiplicity, and self-contradiction."[96] In contrast to the integrated wholeness of Seneca's approach in the *Natural Questions*, Pliny's more fragmentary aesthetic of notecard and excerpt is preoccupied with limit and boundary in ways well captured by Conte:

> Whoever classifies—the naturalist—aspires to distinguish and to demarcate; *nature, in its teleology, proceeds without interruptions,* 'makes no leaps,' and loves to display this volition in borderline cases....
>
> The fact is that [Pliny's] archivistic commitment, his impetus to hoard the data individually and in continuous accumulation, his classification and division by categories and notecards, make the interest for the particular prevail in the text of the *Naturalis historia*, attract attention to the unusualness of things individually worth mentioning, privilege the con-

cf. *etenim peractis omnibus naturae operibus*, 37.201); "Seamless permeation rules, across the chasm of language" (p. 145); "...the hypertextuality should bring home to *readers* that this project could not have been launched without the implementation of a fully formulated and thoroughly internalised flexi-system, sturdy enough to sustain onslaught from assiduous successive addition and alteration to stock, but imperious enough to command enduring commitment to the scheme, come what may...." (p. 150).

91. Wallace-Hadrill (1990) 81.

92. Wallace-Hadrill (1990) 85.

93. Wallace-Hadrill (1990) 89.

94. Murphy (2004) 9–10. To the objection that the collage effect itself constitutes a consistent Plinian voice: this is but a secondary mode of "consistency," which is at one remove from the fundamental inconsistency—the many-voiced disjunctiveness—well captured by Murphy.

95. Murphy (2004) 49.

96. Murphy (2004) 30.

crete discontinuity of events and phenomena, and thus obscure the idea of the qualitative continuity of being. *The idea of the encyclopedia as a summation of positive facts prevails over an image of knowledge structured organically and motivated by a unified epistemological principle.*[97]

Conte makes no allusion to Seneca,[98] but he might have done, not least because of the important contrasts between the two that are implicit in the words above. Whereas Pliny collects his data with an earthy pragmatism and "the fascination of the archive,"[99] Seneca ventures forth in the preface to *Natural Questions* 3 by constructing an integrated vision that informs the entire work as (to modify Conte's phrasing) an organic structuring of knowledge that is motivated by a unified epistemological principle. Conte continues:

> [It] is not as though one could not recognize in Pliny the influence of the thought of Posidonius, in whom too the aspiration somehow to restore Aristotelian encyclopedism was alive. But the divorce between philosophy and science was already complete. The sage has become the *curiosus* scholar, *a compiler and distiller of an enormous library of auctoritates reduced to tiny pieces*. Now those ordered systems disintegrate into the fine dust of individual data, ready to use and of practical utility.[100]

True, in his doxographical reports Seneca may partially meet Conte's characterization of "the *curiosus* scholar" as "a compiler and distiller" of received ideas; but far from reducing that legacy to "tiny pieces," or crushing ordered systems of inherited knowledge "into the fine dust of individual data, ready to use and of practical utility," our Seneca shares the totalizing aspiration that Conte attributes to Posidonius. Yet he shares that aspiration not in the Aristotelian-Posidonian encyclopedic sense, but through an alternative literary construction of the totality. His different way of articulating the interactive unity of the all begins with the formative training of outlook—the movement toward cosmic consciousness—that takes place in the preface to *Natural Questions* 3. Conte detects in Pliny evidence that "the divorce between philosophy and science was already complete," but Seneca offers suggestive evidence to the contrary: the "ordered system" and organic wholeness of vision on offer in the philosophical/scientific blend of the

97. Conte (1994) 102, 103; my emphasis.

98. But see already the brief though insightful remarks of Baldacci (1981) 592–93.

99. Conte (1994) 85.

100. Conte (1994) 103; my emphasis.

Natural Questions fundamentally resist the particularizing tendency that Conte identifies with the compilations and distillations of "the *curiosus* scholar," or of the Plinian archivist.

A final distinction between Seneca and Pliny hinges on their different applications of a related topos. Pliny's frequent use in the *Natural History* of the metaphor of "the view from on high" configures the world as "laid open, as it were, to a single outward-looking glance," a perspective that "renders the *orbis terrarum* interpretable in every particular to a single, overarching system of meaning: it is, in a word, imperial."[101] From the commanding Senecan vantage point of the view from above, by contrast, the liberated *animus* traverses the cosmos, looking down upon the literal and figurative narrowness of life at ground level (1 pref. 8). From the Senecan perspective, Pliny's Rome-centered view from on high is itself relatively narrow and localized in scope, at least in comparison with the cosmic reach of the *Natural Questions*; and so too the *Natural History* is, for all its universal ambition, a work of restriction and partiality, selection and exclusion, in contrast to the all-embracing wholeness of Seneca's very different thought-experiment.

V: *The* Natural Questions *in Sociopolitical Context*

This universalizing emphasis in the *Natural Questions* is not without a practical utility, in that the cosmic engagement that Seneca engenders creates at least the illusion of release at the local level, whether from uncertain political or social conditions, or from the unpredictability of life under an inscrutable emperor. In an age that witnessed a rise of interest in astrology, the black arts and other forms of superstition offering psychological comfort in uncertain times,[102] the Stoic could find in the providence of cosmic reason at least a measure of solace or protection against the vagaries of the world; and in contrast to the vulnerable subservience of life under a Claudius or a Nero, the Stoic correlation of human and cosmic reason gave him a dignifying place in the universal structure.[103] By changing the compass of our understanding so that we belong first and foremost to the cosmos, and only secondarily to the local community, the *Natural Questions* makes its own contribution to the fortifying appeal of Stoic ideas; and in other ways as well it suggestively offers important reflection on, and reaction to, a larger set of sociopolitical tensions and tendencies in the first century, four of which may be crudely sketched as follows.

---

101. Murphy (2004) 131, 132.

102. Liebeschuetz (1979) 119–39 with Williams (1978) 171–84.

103. Cf. Liebeschuetz (1979) 125.

First, much attention has been paid in recent scholarship to the supposed rise of individualism and of interest in self-scrutiny in the first and second centuries CE (allegedly "a kind of golden age in the cultivation of the self"),[104] and the interiorizing emphasis of Stoicism has been identified as an important manifestation of that tendency.[105] The causes claimed for the tendency run deep, and have been related (*inter alia*) to the alienating effects of Roman imperial expansion,[106] to the disruption of traditional relationships because social structures throughout the Empire were becoming more fluid,[107] and to a shift in individual motivation for and in public life after the arrival of the Principate.[108] In keeping with this tendency, the *Natural Questions* and the *Moral Letters*, both of them addressed to Lucilius, conveniently suggest an intensification in and after 62 CE of the self-scrutiny that is a central preoccupation of Seneca's prose writings generally. In the *Natural Questions* in particular, Lucilius encounters a Seneca who, by distancing himself from his former *occupationes* in the preface to Book 3, has taken a decisive step in his own (persona's) progress through what Foucault terms "the practices of the self" toward the goal of "conversion to self."[109] We should proceed with caution at this point: the stress that Foucault places on "the practices of the self" as an increasingly marked phenomenon in the early imperial age risks distorting, or at least underestimating, the influence of the ethical-therapeutic strain in philosophy from the Hellenistic age onward; the brand of "egocentric Stoicism"[110] and "self-saturated Seneca"[111] that Foucault prioritizes may severely overestimate the novelty of Seneca's techniques of self-shaping and self-assertion.[112] Yet if, despite this qualification of Foucault's position, we still detect in the early imperial period an age of heightened anxiety and insecurity, Seneca's radical turning *in se*

---

104. Foucault (1986) 45.

105. See especially Foucault (1986) 39–68, 81–95; Edwards (1997); Bartsch (2006), especially 188–208.

106. Cf. Williams (1978) 176 on philosophy having become "totally preoccupied with the moral and religious problems of the individual, conceived as a lonely soul in an alien world"; 177 on "the individual as isolated in a more or less hostile world."

107. Edwards (1997) 27.

108. Cf. Liebeschuetz (1979) 109 ("Senators could no longer feel that they were serving their own state"), 112 ("Actions are judged less by success or public approval and more by the voice of conscience").

109. Foucault (1986) 64.

110. Veyne (2003) ix.

111. Inwood (2005) 326 = (2009a) 42.

112. Cf. in general Inwood (2005) 326–27 = (2009a) 42–43.

in the *Natural Questions* keenly reflects, and models a form of relief from, that oppressive climate. The work thus takes on a practical dimension that belies its seemingly detached and esoteric subject matter: it offers at least the illusion of release from confinement in the here-and-now, an illusion that extends to signs of defiance if we detect implied criticisms of Nero.[113]

Secondly, the *Natural Questions* is implicated in a broader pattern of Senecan response to the Principate as an all-encompassing system of power. By centering our focus not on Rome but on the cosmic whole, the work gently undermines imperial Roman self-assurance. But our focus for now is on a different challenge to imperial authority—a challenge unrelated to (the now largely discredited theory of) any formal "Stoic opposition" under Nero,[114] or to any simple nostalgia for Republican principles of government. The Senecan challenge lies rather in his advocacy of Stoicism as a source of empowerment for an aristocratic class that had lost privilege and prestige under the Principate. Matthew Roller summarizes his own larger argument to this effect as follows:

> ...Seneca puts forth Stoic ethics, which locates moral value in mental dispositions, in a way that systematically engages with traditional, received aristocratic ethics, which locates moral value primarily in observed actions. Seneca urges his audience to accept the former in place of the latter, a move that (I argue) addresses specific, concrete social and cultural dislocations experienced by elite Romans in the face of the emperor's power— for example, a reduction of the opportunities and rewards for displaying military prowess, and a perceived aggravation of certain problems associated with flattery. In addressing these issues as he does, Senecan ethics offers a way of reestablishing aristocratic power and prestige, albeit in a transfigured form, in the new order.[115]

On the military point, Roller draws one illustration of Seneca's grounding of virtue in mental disposition, not in action, from the preface to *Natural Questions* 3. There, Philip, Alexander and Hannibal (§§5–6) are "presented not as positive *exempla* on account of victories won, but as negative *exempla* for the scale of their murder and plundering";[116] while their military success partly betokens virtue in the traditional

---

113. For the possibility of such criticism, see, e.g., Sørensen (1984) 218–20, 226, Berno (2003) 327–35 and Gauly (2004), especially 193–207. But for a more cautious line (which I share) on the evaluation of subversive innuendo, Hine (2006) 63–64.

114. For the theory examined, Griffin (1976) 363–66 and (1984) 171–77.

115. Roller (2001) 11.

116. Roller (2001) 102.

sense, their "vicious mental dispositions"[117] here take priority, in contrast to the virtue of the Stoic disposition. On flattery, Roller draws (*inter alia*) on Seneca's elaborate discourse in the preface to *Natural Questions* 4a on the dangers of flattery that Lucilius now faces in his new role as procurator in Sicily.[118] In addressing his friend, Seneca also speaks to an age in which flattery is fundamentally encoded in aristocratic relations with the emperor on the one hand, their own social inferiors on the other: "on Seneca's account, philosophy (especially Stoicism) seems to offer an island of evaluative stability in a sea of ethical discourse roiled by flattery."[119] While Roller's argument may warrant qualification,[120] the use that he makes of the *Natural Questions* nevertheless points helpfully to its potential as a partial critique of its times. Beyond asserting the Stoic mental disposition against the erosion of tradition aristocratic privilege, the cosmic viewpoint it promotes creates an evaluative distance from the imperial regime—a form of detachment that empowers by preserving, even celebrating, individual integrity within (and despite) the all-controlling power system of the Principate.[121]

Thirdly, the *Natural Questions* potentially takes on a personal, restorative significance in the light of Seneca's long-standing presence in, and his late alienation from, the Neronian court. This aspect of the work is conveniently illuminated by the interesting comparison that Catharine Edwards draws between Seneca's role at court and that of Thomas More in the court of Henry VIII.[122] More, eventually executed on July 6, 1535, because he refused to take the Oath of Supremacy that recognized Henry as head of the Church of England, exhibits in his writings a profound tension between his public persona and his inner life—a tension articulated by Stephen Greenblatt as "the complex interplay in More's life and writings of self-fashioning and self-cancellation, the crafting of a public role and the profound desire to escape from the identity so

---

117. Roller (2001) 102.

118. See Chapter Three, Sections II and III.

119. Roller (2001) 119.

120. In particular, the negative treatment of Alexander and Hannibal constitutes a stereotype in and of itself (cf., e.g., 5.18.10, 6.23.2–3 with Vottero (1989) 380–81 nn. 22 and 26 on 3 pref. 5 and 6). That stereotypical aspect arguably limits the special, topical emphasis that Roller attributes to these *exempla* as part of Seneca's effort (in Roller's formulation, p. 102) to diminish "the worth of traditional Roman military valor relative to other kinds of achievement."

121. For another, and not incompatible, mode of detachment or evaluative distance from the imperial control-system, see Bartsch (2006) 183–208 with my Chapter Two, Section VII.

122. Edwards (1997) 35.

crafted."[123] A similar tension may also be discerned in Seneca's immersion in court politics even as he cultivated an inner life in his writings in the years between his return from Corsican exile in 49 CE and his *de facto* retirement in 62. If in More's case "his engagement in the world involved precisely the maintaining of a calculated distance between his public persona and his inner self,"[124] Seneca too maintains a similar distance until his *conuersio ad se* in the *Moral Letters*, and still more in the *Natural Questions*, marks a decisive form of self-cancellation—or perhaps rather of self-*affirmation*, as his complete turning away from his former *occupationes* (cf. again *N.Q.* 3 pref. 2) finally liberates his "true" self. Moreover, Seneca's prolonged influence in the Neronian court suggests that he was indeed the exponent of self-concealment that Tacitus portrays, his *dissimulatio* (the hiding of true feeling by a display of false sentiment) serving in one way as a necessary prerequisite for political success and even physical survival, in another as a distancing mechanism that heeded the voice of conscience.[125] In contrast to this strategic elusiveness of identity, the self-scrutiny of the *Moral Letters* suggestively marks a reversion from the dissimulating self in practical life toward the recovery and investigation of a more "authentic" self—a process expressed still more radically in the complete emancipation and self-reconciliation envisaged in the preface to *Natural Questions* 3.

    Fourthly, much light has been shed in recent scholarship on the textual and other symbolic forms of mapping and controlling Roman imperial space in the early Principate, whether through geography, chorography, cartography, numismatic imaging and monumental architecture, etc., or through bureaucratic systems such as census taking, tax collection and land registration.[126] These latter systems were of course hardly new, but the fresh Augustan impetus toward charting Roman power is well illustrated by Strabo's *Geography*, for example, its world "based on a unity centered on the present power of Rome, to which each place was bound, both conceptually and by the real flow of resources";[127] by the famous global map of Agrippa that, after his death in 12 BCE, was completed by Augustus and displayed in the Porticus Vipsania;[128] or by Augustus' own *Res Gestae*,

---

123. Greenblatt (1980) 12–13; for this appeal to Greenblatt, see already Edwards (1997) 35 and 38 n. 36.

124. Greenblatt (1980) 45.

125. On Seneca as *dissimulator*, Rudich (1993) 9–14.

126. See especially Nicolet (1991); Clarke (1999).

127. Clarke (1999) 314.

128. On which Nicolet (1991) 95–122.

whose long listing of peoples and regions subjugated in chapters 25–33 amounts to "a lesson in political and military geography" that supports his projection of the empire as "a world, almost a new world which had been discovered, explored, and mastered."[129] From the universal viewpoint of the *Natural Questions*, however, this imperial achievement is necessarily limited and partial, at least in comparison with the different mastery of "seeing the all with the mind" (cf. 3 pref. 10). For all his commitment to withdrawal from the practical business of the world in the preface to Book 3, Seneca may yet engage with his times in this new work by offering a different, cosmically informed perspective on Roman imperial self-confidence in the early first century. What matters is our *inner* victory, our different form of universal dominion (cf. 1 pref. 7–8), as Roman global measurement now gives way to measurement by a still higher standard: as Seneca puts it at 1 pref. 17, "I shall know that all else is petty when I have measured god" (*sciam omnia angusta esse mensus deum*).

129. Nicolet (1991) 19–20, 24; now Cooley (2009) 36–37.

2

Seneca's Moralizing Interludes

I: The Problem

We have already touched in the Introduction on the holistic fusion of the physical and ethical strains in the *Natural Questions*. But in terms of the work's literary
coherence, how (if at all) are Seneca's moralizing prefaces, epilogues and digressions to be reconciled with his focus on the physical world? This question, much
debated in recent scholarship, has drawn a variety of responses, ranging from positing complex systems of interaction between the technical and the moralizing
sections to stressing the disjunctive nature of digressions that relieve the alleged
aridity of so much of the *Natural Questions*. Most recently, the works of F. R.
Berno, B. M. Gauly and F. J. G. Limburg in particular have made valuable advances in this area,[1] albeit with very different approaches and emphases. For
Berno, intricate verbal and thematic linkages fully integrate the moralizing passages within their respective contexts. For Gauly, the tension that exists between
the moralizing and the technical components sets the two in productive dialogue
with each other, producing the hybrid effect of a Greek scientific mode interact-
ing with Roman moralizing discourse. For Limburg, on the other hand, the quest
for complex systems of integration obscures the plainer but no less effective form
of completeness that she discerns across the divide between the moralizing and
the technical portions: "the prefaces and epilogues may be regarded and studied
as separate pieces treating moral themes related to the study of nature."[2]

This chapter will argue for the integrating position; in method, if not results,
my approach most closely resembles Berno's, with emphasis on tight thematic
and verbal linkage between Seneca's moralizing passages and their surrounding
contexts. We shall focus in this chapter on a selection of passages drawn from
Books 1, 3, 5 and 7. Our findings there will in turn inform our reading in later
chapters of Seneca's moralizing interludes elsewhere (notably in the preface to
Book 4a and in the epilogues to Books 4b and 5); for the moral deviants on

---

1. Berno (2003); Gauly (2004); Limburg (2007), with an important theoretical grounding
(pp. 16–46) on "Prefaces, epilogues, digressions and transitions."

2. Limburg (2007) 298.

display in this chapter represent the larger population of related *uitiosi* that is strewn across the books, as if forming a counterculture that weighs the work down even as Seneca strives to raise us to cosmic consciousness.

One figure in particular, the vile Hostius Quadra of Book 1, will be a recurrent presence in this chapter:[3] we shall see that he epitomizes to an exquisite degree many of the vices on display elsewhere in the work. In Section II below, Hostius is formally introduced, his eye for deviance related to Seneca's broader interest in the *Natural Questions* in manifold ways and qualities of seeing or perceiving the physical world. Hostius' narrowness in this respect is related, in Section III, to the wholeness of cosmic vision that Seneca promotes more generally in the work. Hostius' blinkered or fragmented vision is then connected, in Section IV, with the limitations that similarly inhibit the world outlook of Seneca's imaginary interlocutor in Book 1. We descend, in Section V, to the figurative depths of those slaves to luxury who, in Book 3, relish the sight of the mullet as it expires on the dinner plate before their very eyes, showing a wondrous variety of colorations as it breathes its last. We remain below in Section VI, where we encounter the adventurers of Book 5 who, Seneca claims via Asclepiodotus, were sent underground by Philip II of Macedon in search of precious metals. These depths of corruption are matched above ground by our coverage, also in Section VI, of those *delicati* who, at the end of Book 7, restlessly explore every possible feminization of their traditional Roman maleness. On these various fronts Seneca gives graphic expression to the vices he features before fervently denouncing them. He thus moves to contain the rampant plague; yet in Section VII we shall consider the possibility that his containment efforts may simultaneously be challenged, even undermined, by the verve of his own descriptive powers. Hostius is ultimately killed off in the Senecan text, as if an exterminated abomination; but does he nevertheless arouse a certain fascination in the galvanized readership of Book 1? For all his vileness, is there a certain attractiveness to his freedom from all moral scruple and Senecan stricture at this late stage in the *Natural Questions*? *This* is the multifaceted, potentially disconcerting Hostius who waits to confront us at this chapter's close.

II: *Hostius Quadra as the Anti-*Sapiens[4]

If, at 3 pref. 18, two of the main benefits of studying nature are that "we shall leave behind what is sordid" (*discedemus a sordidis*) and "separate the mind...from the

---

3. See also Chapter Seven, Section II.

4. Cf. Berno (2002) 221–24 and (2003) 46–50; Limburg (2007) 273–74.

body" (*animum…seducemus a corpore*), the deviants we encounter in the *Natural Questions* are themselves intrusive impurities (*sordidi*) for whom mind cultivation runs distantly second to bodily indulgence. In contrast to the progressive community of scholars that Seneca constructs through his accumulation of sources throughout the *Natural Questions*, these *sordidi* represent a regressive community of squalor—a counterforce that negates and, at least from one angle, therefore vindicates the disciplined scientific direction of the *Natural Questions* by exhibiting *mis*direction of a spectacular kind. In contrast to the boundaries that the pioneering inquirers seek to cross as they probe nature's mysteries (*secretiora*, 1 pref. 3), these deviants are negative transgressors on their own boundary-breaking paths of exploration—a contrast neatly encapsulated when Philip II of Macedon's excavators at 5.15 are seen to dig deep in a symbolically transgressive way, the researcher to excavate in a higher, more figured way late in Book 7: "Let us not be surprised that things which lie hidden away so deeply are dug out [*erui*] so slowly" (7.30.2).[5] Within the dramatic framework of the *Natural Questions*, this deviant community offers a model of self-absorption, or of seeing the world for ourselves, which is countered by the Senecan mission to rise from ground level so as to see the world for itself.[6] Deviant focalization of this Senecan kind thus lends graphic degradation to the work as a way of ennobling yet further its higher mission—unless, that is, we find in these interludes throughout the *Natural Questions* a chorus-like return to the regrettable inevitabilities of life-at-ground-level, with Seneca continuously fighting a (losing?) battle against base passion.[7]

An extreme low point is reached late in the work when, near the end of Book 1, we first encounter Hostius Quadra.[8] After completing his account of atmospheric lights such as meteors, halo and rainbow in the main body of the book, Seneca steers his proceedings in a different direction in 1.16, where he suddenly embarks on a story concerning this Hostius. Seneca is our only source of information on this spectacular sexual deviant who apparently delighted in indulging

---

5. Cf. *OLD eruo* 2: "(fig.) To unearth…, search out…."

6. Cf. Hadot (1995) 254.

7. See Section VII below in this chapter.

8. *RE* 8 2.2517 Hostius 5; *PIR*[2] 4 p. 102 no. 230; Jory (1970) 234–36 (on the basis of inscriptional evidence, Quadra identified as "*magister* of a private college of *scribae librarii*"). For a convenient summary of scholarly interpretation of the Hostius episode, see Thomsen (1979–80) 183–97 (with rich footnotes) and Berno (2002) 214–16 and (2003) 33–35, adding Walters (1998) 361–62 on Quadra's "turning 'nature' upside down in many aspects: social power and gender, as well as the sexual activity which, for Romans, at least in public discourse, combined and symbolized these two social statuses"; Bartsch (2000) 82–87 and (2006) 103–114; Gauly (2004) 115–34; and Limburg (2007) 265–98 and (2008).

himself (and others) before distorting mirrors that reflected not just his every act from every angle but also his vile inner character.[9] In Hostius' mirror image we may further see an exaggerated textual reflection of early imperial decadence, as if a counterimage of Augustan propriety; hence perhaps the fitting significance of Seneca's claim that, after Hostius was killed by his own slaves, Augustus himself "virtually declared that he was seen to have been rightfully murdered" (1.16.1). In keeping with the (for Seneca) morally perverse images reflected back on him in his house of mirrors, Hostius' cruelty thus rebounds on him in death, with Seneca delivering the final blow at 1.16.9: "A shocking outrage! [*facinus indignum!*] Perhaps he was killed too quickly, before he could see it; he should have been sacrificed before his own mirror [*ad speculum suum inmolandus fuit*]." He should have been murdered before the mirror so that he could directly witness the fate he merited, feel real pain, not sweet sexual agony, and watch his sudden transformation from predator to victim, Hostius to *hostia*; this beast of a man deserved to die, Seneca implies, like a sacrificial animal.[10]

How is this sordid tale to be related to the rest of *Natural Questions* 1?[11] A superficial link between the Hostius episode and what precedes it is supplied by the theme of mirror-like distortion in nature. Holding that such phenomena as rainbow and halo are the products of *speculi fallacia* (1.15.7), Seneca characterizes them as *simulacra* and "the insubstantial imitation of real bodies" (1.15.8), the objects themselves being reflected *in prauum* just as distortion takes place in our trick mirrors (1.5.14). Hostius applies this phenomenon to shocking effect: "He had mirrors made…which gave off greatly magnified images, and in which a

---

9. Indirect evidence possibly in Suetonius' life of Horace (p. 47.13–15 Reifferscheid); for "[i]t is generally agreed that the story [Suetonius] relates…about the poet having mirrors arranged round his bedroom rests on…a confusion between the similar-looking names HORATIUS and HOSTIUS" (Wilkinson [1949] 47). On the nature, material and properties of ancient mirrors, see McCarty (1989) 165–71 with Jónsson (1995) 21–61 and Taylor (2008) 9–14. On the language of seeing intensified in the unfolding Hostius scene, as if obsessively sharpening its focus to match Hostius' ever closer inspection, Solimano (1991) 77–78.

10. A possible nexus of Senecan plays, with Hosti(u)s the enemy as well as (via *inmolandus*) ritual *hostia* (cf. Ov. *Fast.* 1.336 *hostibus a domitis hostia nomen habet* with Maltby [1991] 284 *hostia*; *TLL* 6.3 3045.34–41); cf. Berno (2002) 227 n. 82 = (2003) 60 n. 103: "Seneca potrebbe leggere *Hostius* come *nomen-omen* correlato con *hostia*." The phrase *facinus indignum!* may play tricks of its own, looking both backward and forward (cf. Shackleton Bailey [1979] 450: "The exclamation refers to what follows, not, as Oltramare and Corcoran,…to what precedes"): given Augustus' reluctance to avenge the vile Hostius' death, which is the true(r) *facinus* here, the slaves' or Quadra's, the latter just described with relish in his own reported voice (1.16.7–9)? For slaves murdering masters cf. Tac. *Ann.* 14.42–5, Plin. *Ep.* 3.14.1–5, 8.14.12, with Sherwin-White (1966) 246–47 ("Cases were sufficiently rare to merit attention").

11. For a useful survey of recent theories, Limburg (2007) 289–98.

finger exceeded the size and thickness of an arm" (1.16.2). As David Leitão observes, the "ever greater distortions in man's physical and moral universe" as portrayed earlier in *Natural Questions* 1 culminate in "the catoptric distortions of
Hostius' boudoir."[12] The book opens with a glimpse of the perfect celestial light to
which theology (cf. *hanc* [sc. *partem philosophiae*] *quae ad deos pertinet*, 1 pref. 1)
guides us by raising us above "this gloom in which we wallow" (1 pref. 2). As we
descend from this celestial place to the region of *sublimia*, that perfect light gives
way to "[t]he distorted reflections characteristic of haloes and other atmospheric
lights [which] are both a by-product [because of our impaired vision] and an
emblem of the human condition."[13] As we proceed through Seneca's account of
haloes (1.2), rainbow (1.3–8), streaks (1.9–1.11.1), double suns (1.11.2–1.13) and
finally other atmospheric fires (e.g. shooting stars, flashes; 1.14–15), we move
through stages of increasing distortion:

> [I]f streaks, because they have no curvature [1.9.1], are imperfect rainbows,
> then they are even more distorted reflections of the sun than rainbows are.
> Thus, they are further removed from the perfect light of the sun. Seneca
> sums up the relation between haloes, rainbows and streaks in this way:
> *coronam si diuiseris, arcus erit; si direxeris, uirga* (1.10).... The perfect
> circle is at the top of the hierarchy, and progressively greater distortions of
> the circle are progressively lower on the hierarchy.[14]

For Leitão, then, the Quadra episode is no mere appendage to the technical portion of *Natural Questions* 1 but integral to Seneca's imaginative, hybrid form of
physico-moral investigation here. For present purposes, however, Leitão's argument takes an important turn when he compares the preface to Book 1[15] with the
Quadra episode and finds in Hostius something beyond "our paradigmatic bestial man";[16] for "[a]ll these echoes [sc. between the preface and 1.16] assimilate
Hostius to some degree to the philosopher who strives to know god, but there are
also echoes which make Hostius look like god himself."[17] While the study of theology gives the philosopher access to "what nature has placed beyond our vision

12. (1998) 136.

13. Leitão (1998) 132.

14. Leitão (1998) 133.

15. For useful analysis of which, see Flammini (1992) 643–59 and especially Weber (1995).

16. Leitão (1998) 141.

17. Leitão (1998) 145.

[*extra conspectum*]" (1 pref. 1), Hostius' mirrors provide their own form of access to sexual acts "which our bodily structure has placed out of sight [*a conspectu*]" (1.16.7). While the philosopher penetrates nature's mysteries (*secretiora*, 1 pref. 3), Hostius investigates *secreta* of a baser kind (1.16.3). While the philosopher, too, is a vigilant observer of self (cf. *animus…speculator sui, Dial.* 5.36.2), Hostius reduces the focus of that vigilance to carnal inspection (*ipse flagitiorum suorum spectator*, 1.16.3). And while the philosophical mind that roves the heavens is "an attentive observer" that "scrutinizes individual details and investigates them" (*curiosus spectator excutit singula et quaerit*, 1 pref. 12), Hostius is a *curiosus spectator* of a sordid, albeit no less attentive and exacting, kind.

Leitão concedes that these echoes between the preface and 1.16 may demonstrate a pattern, but not necessarily "a completely conscious one."[18] In his effort to portray Hostius as a convergence of god and the beast, his body "an emblem of cosmic dissolution, and of natural philosophy's promise of regeneration,"[19] Leitão must deny that the echoes are deliberate, ironic and antithetical, setting the godlike *sapiens* wholly against the bestial Hostius. But is it really possible *not* to detect a conscious pattern of irony between the preface and 1.16? Is it credible that Seneca, so adept an ironist in so many other works, prose and verse, would so lack control of these conspicuous echoes in *Natural Questions* 1? No: through these contrasts Hostius is surely cast in 1.16 as a grotesque distortion of the philosopher as pictured in the preface; or rather—the ultimate irony—as a false reflection, or a reverse mirror image, at one end of the book of the philosopher at the other. But to what effect does Seneca fashion this contrast? On two fronts, Hostius, this anti-*sapiens*, contravenes fundamental principles that are connected to the Senecan wholeness of cosmic perspective drawn in the last chapter. First, we shall see that the totalizing consciousness of the *sapiens* that is glimpsed in the preface to Book 1 finds its opposite in Hostius' blinkered mind-set, one that sees in a partial and fragmented way in his mirror chamber, extending to the personal level the more general obsession with limit and territorial demarcation that Seneca decries from the cosmic viewpoint of 1 pref. 9 ("How ridiculous are the boundaries of mortals!"). Second, and in paradoxical modification of this first point, the mind-set that craves ever more extreme stimuli in 1.16 knows no limit to its transgressive energies, as if an antitype of the *sapiens* in its different form of

---

18. (1998) 146.

19. Leitão (1998) 152. A different emphasis, closer but not identical to my own, in Bartsch (2006) 108 (cf. [2000] 84): "Seneca's discourse on celestial distorting mirrors as a model for the flawed quality of human ways of knowing might predispose us to see Hostius as a sort of Everyman: we too live among the distorting mirrors of the phenomenal world, and his is but an extreme case."

self-liberation. In both cases—this restrictive form of myopia on the one side, this eye for unrestricted indulgence on the other—Hostius functions as an enemy within, or as a negation of the worldview propagated thus far in the *Natural Questions*. The full effects of this negative force will soon be addressed, but first a reprise of Seneca's integrating world vision, at least as manifested in Book 1 and early in Book 2.

III: *The Unified World as Drawn in Books 1 and 2.1–11*

After his classification of the universe into *caelestia*, *sublimia* and *terrena* at 2.1.1–2, Seneca's subsequent explanation of why earthquakes are included among *sublimia*, not *terrena* (2.1.3), reflects a broader imprecision in antiquity over the boundary between the meteorological and the terrestrial categories.[20] Earthquakes are elsewhere located among *terrena*, but the Senecan classification of them as meteorological on the grounds that they are caused by the violent motion of air was also well established, as Aristotle for one attests (cf. *Mete.* 1.1 338b25–339a2).[21] But then Seneca adds "a still greater surprise" in announcing that certain inquiries about *terrena* will fall into the celestial category (2.1.4). "This is scarcely as strange as he pretends," Hine observes,[22] "for all he means is that questions concerning the earth's relation to the heavens will be dealt with under *caelestia* rather than *terrena*, a sensible enough procedure (adopted e.g. by Arist. *Cael.* 2.13–4)." Finding no parallel for this section, Hine "would readily suppose that the idea is S[eneca]'s own, dressed up to round off the chapter with a vigorous flourish."[23] Perhaps; but of greater interest for now is a different possibility. After the boundary between *terrena* and *sublimia* is blurred through the ambiguous placement of earthquakes in 2.1.3, Seneca ostentatiously introduces ("a still greater surprise…") a second example of overlap between the categories as the earth becomes associated with both the terrestrial and celestial zones, its intrinsic properties the focus of attention in the terrestrial category (2.1.4), its relation to the other stars and planets the focus in the celestial category (2.1.5). After the demarcation of *caelestia*, *sublimia* and *terrena* at 2.1.1–2, that division is immediately qualified, partly to explain Seneca's favored interpretation of the boundary between *sublimia* and *terrena*, but perhaps also for another reason: the unifying mind-set that is forged in the *Natural Questions* as a whole focuses not on separa-

---

20. In general, Hine (1981) 124–27, and see Chapter Eight, Section III (A).

21. See Hine (1981) 126–27.

22. (1981) 127.

23. (1981) 127.

tion and difference between the world parts but on their interaction and mutual implication, a *modus uidendi* that is suggestively glimpsed in the eye for overlap between the universal categories at 2.1.3–5. And at this late stage in the *Natural Questions*, this eye for overlap not only applies a central lesson of the work as a whole but also looks ahead: it prepares us for the advanced lesson in the internal unity of air, and also its cosmically unifying significance, to which we now turn in 2.2–11.

Seneca's introductory account of the nature of air delays until 2.12.1 his discussion of his subject matter proper in Book 2, on lightning and thunder. After stating at 2.2.1 that *aër* (spanning plain "air" and "atmosphere")[24] has *unitas*, he develops the point by distinguishing at 2.2.2 the continuous (*continuum*) from the composite (*commissum*). Severe problems of text and interpretation later in 2.2.2–3 obscure the precise relationship among *continuatio*, *commissura* and *unitas* here,[25] but the illustrations that Seneca goes on to use in 2.2.3 clarify at least this much: "continuity" is "the uninterrupted joining of parts to each other" (*partium inter se non intermissa coniunctio*); hence, in contrast to things that are accumulated or assembled from parts (*composita* such as a rope, a heap of grain or a ship), a tree and a rock are "continuous" noncomposites that possess "a unity of substance" (*unitatem corporum*, 2.2.3).[26] By such unity Seneca refers "to the characteristic of an object that is held coherently together by its own oneness and not by external help" (*ad naturam corporis nulla ope externa sed unitate sua cohaerentis*, 2.2.4); air is a case in point. In proceeding to describe the place and function of air in the cosmic whole (2.3.1–6.1), its tension (2.6.2–9.4, with a timely attack on the atomists' theory of tensionless air in void) and then the nature of the atmosphere before finally making his transition to his main theme (2.11.3), Seneca offers "a vivid series of descriptions" of the character of *aër/spiritus* that relies for its persuasive effect not on "a straightforward, logical chain of reasoning" but "on the creation of a cumulative set of vividly drawn pictures of the power and importance of air."[27] But beneath this superficial vividness lies the passage's symbolic potential. In this last book of

---

24. Hine (1981) 122–23.

25. Full discussion in Hine (1981) 151–61; Wildberger (2006) 9–11.

26. In contrasting *continua* and *composita* here, Seneca distinguishes only two parts of the traditional Stoic tripartite classification of bodies, the third being aggregates *ex distantibus* (τὰ ἐκ διεστώτων), "of which each member still remains separate, like an army, a populace or a senate" (*Letters* 102.6): for Seneca's immediate purposes at 2.2.1–3 "there is no need to mention" this third category (Hine [1981] 149, with detailed discussion on pp. 143–49 of the tripartite division, which is "certainly Stoic in origin" and "probably... as old as Chrysippus").

27. Hine (1981) 124.

the extant *Natural Questions*, this disquisition on air assumes a suggestive retro-spective relevance in providing a foundation of sorts, or perhaps rather a capstone, for the cosmic unity pictured in earlier books; for Seneca's treatment of the inter-nal coherence of air makes oneness fundamental to the world at a primary, elemen-tal level, setting in a real, physical base his vision of cosmic coherence at more speculative and artistically intuitive levels in the work. On this approach, the tri-partite division with which the book begins gives way to a looser, more flexible vision of world integration; and the section on the tension of air at 2.6.2–9.4 is no mere "digression within the description of the atmosphere which occupies 6.1 and 10–11,"[28] but symbolically important for the vitality that the air thus acquires as a literal mover and shaker (cf. 2.8), as a transmitter of light and sound (2.9.1) or as the reason objects float in water and the voice can penetrate walls, etc. (2.9.3–4): the air is brought to life here as an activating and integrating force of nature.[29]

So also air as *materia* in Book 2. A unity in itself, the air is cast as both part and material of the universe (2.3.1–4.1), *materia* in the sense that, like blood in the human body (2.3.2), it is essential to the overall functioning of the cosmic body.[30] Seneca's account of how the air joins and mediates between the universal parts immediately offers a suggestive model of cosmic interaction:

> hic [sc. aër] est enim qui caelum terramque conectit, qui ima ac summa sic separat ut tamen iungat: separat quia medius interuenit; iungit quia utrique per hunc inter se consensus est; supra se dat quidquid accepit a terris, rursus uim siderum in terrena transfundit.
>
> 2.4.1

> For this air is what connects the heavens and earth and separates the lowest and the highest levels in such a way that it nevertheless joins them: it sepa-rates them because it comes between them as an intervening presence; it joins them because through it the two can communicate with each other. It delivers to the upper region whatever it receives from the earth; and, con-versely, it transfers energy from the heavenly bodies to things on earth.

---

28. Hine (1981) 185.

29. On the air's lively animation, see further Chapter Five, Sections II and III, and Chapter Six, Section V (D).

30. On the Pre-Socratic origins of the world-body analogy, Lloyd (1966) 232–72. For the anal-ogy in the *Natural Questions*, see, e.g., 3.15.1–2, 5, 16.2, 29.2–3; 5.4.2; 6.3.1, 14.2, 18.6, 24.2–4 Further, Hine (1981) 141–42 on 2.1.4; Taub (2003) 143–44, 147, 151–52; Wildberger (2006) 20 and 495 n. 135 (on the Stoic theory); Kullmann (2010) 70–74; and especially Althoff (1997).

The vertical axis that is drawn here in the harmonious picture of the air connecting and mediating between *caelestia* and *terrena* recurs in 2.10, where three atmospheric layers are distinguished. At the top the air is hot, dry and thin because of its proximity to the heavenly bodies in the celestial region. The bottom layer, near to the earth, is dense and dark[31] because it receives the terrestrial exhalations, which also contribute to its warming. The middle layer is more temperate in terms of dryness and thinness (2.10.2), but also colder than the top and bottom layers; "for air is by nature cold" (2.10.4). If "[t]he main elements of S[eneca]'s picture ultimately come from Aristotle,"[32] then Seneca's tripartite structure not only simplifies the complex Aristotelian picture; he also develops a very different emphasis that finds partial illumination in a passage of Pliny (*Nat.* 2.103–4) that describes the effect the heavenly bodies have on conditions below them in the sky, including the (literal) ups and downs of the weather:

> terrena in caelum tendentia deprimit siderum uis, eademque quae sponte non subeant ad se trahit. decidunt imbres, nebulae subeunt, siccantur amnes, ruunt grandines, torrent radii et terram in medio mundi undique inpellunt, iidem infracti resiliunt et quae potuere auferunt secum…tot animalium haustus spiritum e sublimi trahit, at ille contra nititur, tellusque ut inani caelo spiritum fundit. sic ultro citro conmeante natura ut tormento aliquo mundi celeritate discordia accenditur.
>
> The power of the stars forces down earthly objects that reach for the sky, and draws to itself things that cannot go up by their own agency. Rains fall, clouds rise upwards, rivers are dried up, hail crashes down, the sun's rays scorch and everywhere beat upon the earth in the center of the universe, and, broken, those same rays bounce back and carry off with them all that they can…. So many living things on earth draw their breath from on high, but that air strives in the opposite direction, and the earth pours the air back to the sky as if it were a void. Thus, as nature goes to and fro like a kind of catapult, discord is stirred up by the speed of the world's motion.

Our main point of interest here lies in Pliny's portrayal of the contested region between the heavens and earth as a layer of oscillation and exchange, departure and return, separation and reconnection; the discord stirred by these movements is a

---

31. *pars…densa et caliginosa*, 2.10.2; cf. 1 pref. 2 for "the gloom in which we wallow," *hanc in qua uolutamur caliginem*.

32. Hine (1981) 213, with bibliography.

consequence (or function) of the unity of the Plinian world order (cf. *Nat.* 2.1–2).[33] In distinguishing and conjoining the three atmospheric layers at *N.Q.* 2.10–11, Seneca offers his own creative vision of the vital connection between parts on a vertical axis.[34] When we seek analogies for this axis as a Senecan symbol of cosmic unity elsewhere in the *Natural Questions*, Book 1 at once yields significant samples, an overlap that may or may not coincide with the broader structural symmetry Hine detects between Books 1 and 2.[35] For present purposes, however, our turning to Book 1 also prepares the way for our closer treatment in Section IV below of Hostius Quadra.

At 1.14.1 Seneca moves to complete his account of lights in the sky by progressing from the visual illusions of 1.2–13 (halo, rainbow, streaks, parhelia) to phenomena showing real fire (*certa... substantia*, 1.15.6), including the lights that "the Greeks call σέλα" (= flashes, 1.15.1).[36] After his earlier emphasis in the cases of rainbow, streaks and parhelia on the necessary positioning of sun and cloud in relation to each other,[37] these flashes are distinguished in their Senecan choreography by their flexible occurrence in different zones. Conventional boundaries again count for little: at the level of *caelestia*, "the high heat of the heavens" (1.15.1) sometimes causes ignition by seizing on suitable elements below (*inferiora aliquando, si sunt idonea accendi, corripit* [sc. *ignis*]), while Seneca also orchestrates movement in both directions by having the motion of the stars send fire downward (*ignem... in subiecta transmittere*), the atmosphere below drive "the essence of fire" upward (*non potest fieri ut aër uim igneam usque in aethera elidat...?*). While some of these flashes are stationary, others move with a versatility that again symbolically connects the different cosmic levels from the celestial to cloud level (*quaedam in nubibus apparent*, 1.15.2), and from above the clouds (*quaedam supra nubes*, 1.15.2) to ground level when flashes of brief duration come to earth like lightning bolts (1.15.3).[38] When Seneca ends with the phenomenon of the sky

---

33. Cf. at the elemental level Beagon (1992) 200: "Overall,... *dimicatio naturae* results in a balance.... There is an interdependence of the elements designed by *Natura artifex* (2.166, cf. 2.10–12)."

34. An elaboration of the vertical axis first sampled in Chapter One, Section II.

35. (1981) 37–40; already, e.g., Waiblinger (1977) 33–34.

36. Hemsing (1913) 22–23 connects 1.14–15 with 1.1 (on meteors), presuming in 1.14–15 Seneca's reliance on Aristotle via Posidonius; his convenient schema (p. 23) separates these real fires into *ignes aerii* (1.1), *ignes aerii uarii coloris* (1.14), and *ignes aetherii* (= σέλα) (1.15).

37. On rainbow, 1.3.11, 1.4.1, 1.8.6–7; streak, 1.9.2; parhelia, 1.11.3.

38. At 1.15.1–3 interesting overlaps are discernible (Vottero [1989] 270 n. 1) with the pseudo-Aristotelian *De mundo* (395b3–10), attributed by some to Posidonius (with many challengers: Reale and Bos [1995] 29–37). We might speculate about Seneca's possible debt to the "early and Peripatetic" (cf. Barnes [1977] 41) *De mundo*, or to the tradition to which it belongs; but at 395b3–10 there is nothing like the elaborate Senecan choreography just described.

appearing to be on fire, the glow that ranges from high to low and draws our gaze up and down[39] offers a final illustration of the vertical axis in unifying action; hence perhaps the notable schematic clarity of this closing example.

When we look back on Book 1 from the integrating perspective of 1.15, we can begin to find traces of this oneness in seemingly incidental details or elaborations within Seneca's scientific mode, and in areas of his project that might at first appear to be more dutifully methodical (e.g., doxographical reporting, the sifting of competing rainbow theories, etc.) than "literary" or symbolic. So already in his treatment of Aristotelian theory in 1.1;[40] and then, for further example, in his report at 1.3.3 of the theory, possibly derived from Anaximenes,[41] that a rainbow is formed from the combination of brightness and shadow that results because some moisture drops in a cloud transmit sunlight, while others do not. The theory is immediately contested at 1.3.4: How then to account for the fact that a rainbow shows not just two colors, light and dark, but several? The objection, apparently endorsed by Seneca, is straightforward enough, and it allows him quickly to pass on to the (Aristotelian) mirror theory of rainbow at 1.3.5. But in a move that may at first appear more indulgent than necessary, he embellishes the objection with a quotation from Ovid's account of Minerva's weaving contest with Arachne in *Metamorphoses* 6. The colors are so finely worked by both contestants that they merge into each other like the different shades in a rainbow, in which (6.65–7)

> diuersi niteant cum mille colores,
> transitus ipse tamen spectantia lumina fallit:
> usque adeo quod tangit idem est, tamen ultima distant.

---

39. 1.15.5: "sometimes the burning is so high that it seems to be among the very stars, sometimes so low that it looks as if something is on fire in the distance [at ground level]."

40. In Seneca's report of the Aristotelian theory of exhalations (1.1.7–9) to explain meteors and shooting stars, his initial portrayal (1.1.7) of several kinds of exhalation from the earth, some wet, some dry, some hot, some flammable, is "just recognizable as a paraphrase of Aristotle's exhalation theory" (Hall [1977] 413). But in relating the varied hues of different stars and planets (the Dog Star, Mars, Jupiter) to different kinds of exhalation, and in having the earth expel a vast quantity of particles *in superiorem...partem*, some of which reach the clouds as "nutriments of fire" (*alimenta ignium*) so as to give rise to meteors, etc. (1.1.8–9), Seneca offers "more a theory of his own, based on Aristotle's, than Aristotle's theory itself" (Hall 414; see also Setaioli [1988] 444). If artistic considerations are allowed to infringe on his scientific agenda here, he molds and modifies the Aristotelian theory to derive from it a prototype, as it were, of the unifying vertical axis that he draws elsewhere in the *Natural Questions*, the exhalations supplying the vital connection between *caelestia* (the Dog Star, Mars, Jupiter), *sublimia* (clouds), and *terrena* (cf. *copia corpusculorum quae terrae eiectant*, 1.1.8).

41. Hemsing (1913) 14; D-K 13A18 and Graham (2010) 86–87 and 93 on Texts 32–33 with Guthrie (1962) 139 and 393 n. 1.

Although a thousand different shades shine forth,
the very transition between them eludes the watching eye:
so indistinguishable are they where they touch, and yet
so different where furthest apart.

The seamlessness of the transition between colors in line 66[42] is subsequently re-
stated by Seneca: "the join [*commissura*] is deceptive, to the extent that, by nature's wonderful handiwork, what begins from the extremely similar ends in the
extremely different" (1.3.4).[43] Why this further elaboration when the straightforward point of the objection is that multiple colors can be seen in a rainbow? As
so often in the *Natural Questions*, the verse quotation here lends diverting color
to his disquisition. But in their seemingly incidental way, the invisible transitions
between the rainbow's colors also reproduce and exemplify the seamlessness that
Seneca associates with the cosmic whole. Here is but one symbol of a unifying
principle that fundamentally conditions the entire *Natural Questions*; and the
passage will soon prove to have important implications for our analysis of 3.17–18
below.[44]

    Other modes of contact and correspondence support the general interactive
effect in Book 1 (and far beyond) as the text ingrains in us the habit of seeing diverse phenomena in relation to each other, frequently (and conventionally
enough) through analogy.[45] So, at the most basic level, the Greeks call haloes
"threshing floors" (*areas*, 1.2.3) because of their roundness.[46] At 1.2.4 the halo
effect is reproduced in the baths ("In the baths, too, a certain shape of this sort is
frequently seen around a lamp"). At 1.2.5 those apparently unrelated phenomena,
halo and wind, are linked by Seneca's claim that sailors expect wind from the direction where the circle of a halo has broken. At 1.3.2 the launderer who lightly
sprays water on the clothes stretched out before him reproduces in the spray the
multicolor of a rainbow. At 1.5.12 dyes that show their color better from a distance
illustrate a parallel phenomenon in cloud color. At 1.5.14 our distorting mirrors
illustrate by analogy the same effect in cloud ("Why, therefore, is it surprising

---

42. A symbol also of the artistic oneness of Arachne and Minerva despite their differences of
status, taste, and subject matter? Cf. Feeney (1991) 192 n. 18.

43. Cf. Parroni (2002) 489 for *commissura* as a technical term denoting, in painting, the "gra-
dation of tints in transition" (*LSJ* ἁρμογή 6; cf. Plin. *Nat.* 35.29).

44. See Section V below in this chapter.

45. Further on analogy in particular, Chapters One, Section II; Four, Section IV (B); Six, Sections III and V (C); and Eight, Section III (B).

46. Cf. *LSJ* ἅλως I.

that a mirror of this sort also occurs in cloud...?"). At 1.12.2 the sun and moon are said to be reflected in the atmosphere just as they are in oil- or pitch-filled basins on earth (*quemadmodum...in terris..., ita in aëre*). Of course, the appeal to everyday experience to elucidate the obscure is hardly exceptional in ancient scientific practice; but the cumulative *artistic* effect of the linkages that Seneca draws in the examples above is to create the illusion of an integrated whole, a co-operative system of mirrorings and reflections that find an especially suggestive example at 1.13.1, on multiple parhelia or double suns.[47] What is there, Seneca asks, to prevent any number of such parhelia being produced by any number of reflecting clouds? Consider our own mirrors:

> nam apud nos quoque cum plura specula disposita sunt ita ut alteri sit conspectus alterius, omnia implentur, et una imago a uero est, ceterae imaginum effigies sunt. nihil enim refert quid sit quod speculo ostendatur: quidquid uidet, reddit.
>
> 1.13.1

For, even in our own experience, when various mirrors are so positioned that one has sight of another, all of them are filled with images, and one image reflects the original object, while the others are copies of images. For it doesn't matter what is shown to a mirror: it reflects whatever it sees.

While the parhelion phenomenon is matched in our everyday mirrors, we might also detect a further reflection here: that of Hostius Quadra, his eyes feeding not just on the image of the real thing (cf. *a uero*) but perhaps also on images of the images that we visualize on all sides around him (1.16.8). On this approach, the mirror analogy at 1.13.1 *itself* functions as a versatile textual connector: it reflects and mediates between different parts of the book to connect Quadra's delusions in his hall of mirrors with optical illusion at the level of *sublimia*.

IV: *Hostius Quadra and Seneca's Interlocutor in Book 1*

From the outset Hostius is pictured as all image, a man who seemingly shows no signs of any reflective inner life in the sexual philosophy that he espouses in his

---

47. For which, see Kidd (1988) 466–70 on fr. 121. For Waiblinger (1977) 65–66, the parhelion marks the fullest perfection of mirror imaging in nature, in contrast to Quadra's distortions. But cf. more adroitly Leitão (1998) 134–35 for a Platonic emphasis on parhelia as copies (even copies of copies) far removed, in the conceptual hierarchy that he detects in *Natural Questions* 1, from the true light of the sun.

own voice at 1.16.7–9. For him the mirror has no edifying function beyond en-
abling him to know himself sexually: "By contrivance [*arte*]," he declares at 1.16.7,
"let even the things which our bodily structure has placed out of sight be brought
into view, so that no one supposes that I don't know what I'm doing."[48] The language that first describes him reflects in its own mirrorings and distortions the
confusion of image and reality that *is* Hostius:

> Hostius fuit Quadra obscenitatis in scaenam usque perductae. hunc di-
> uitem auarum, sestertii milies seruum, diuus Augustus indignum uindicta
> iudicauit cum a seruis occisus esset....
>
> 1.16.1

> There was a certain Hostius Quadra whose obscene behavior was brought
> right out into public display. This man, rich, greedy, and a slave to his own
> hundred millions, the deified Augustus judged not worth avenging after
> he had been killed by his slaves....

His *obscenitas* is appropriately (mis)reflected in *scaenam*.[49] The echo of *diuitem* in
diuus falsely aligns Augustus and Hostius, the divine and the bestial, and the shift
from figurative *seruum* ("the slave to money") to literal *seruis* creates another illusion—Hostius a slave but no slave—while also mimicking the broader movement
between object and reflection in Hostius' mirrors. But while verbal effects of this
sort reproduce the superficial distortions of his mirrors, Hostius feeds on the
images as if they have true substance: "If I could, I would make these images real;
because I cannot, I shall feast on the illusion [*mendacio pascar*]" (1.16.9).[50] The

---

48. But "Mirrors were invented so that man could know himself" (1.17.4): see Myerowitz
(1992) 150 for the hint of deliberate parody of the γνῶθι σαυτόν theme in Hostius' words at
1.16.7–9; for the Socratic tradition underlying 1.17.4, Vottero (1989) 282 n. 8 with Berno (2002)
220 n. 34 = (2003) 43 n. 37 and Bartsch (2000) 71–72, (2006) 108–109.

49. So Corcoran (1971–72) 1.83 n. 1; Hine (1996b) 32 cites Var. *Ling.* 7.96 ("*obscaenum*
['foul'] is said from *scaena* ['stage'];...anything repulsive is called *obscaenum*, because it ought
not to be said openly except on the *scaena*"), albeit in qualification of Corcoran's play. Hine 32
inclines to a metaphorical interpretation of *scaenam*, to the effect that Hostius "made a show
of his immorality instead of keeping it private" (cf. Hine [2010b] 159: "There was a certain
Hostius Quadra who turned his obscenity into a dramatic spectacle"). But if *scaenam* is taken
literally, see Vottero (1989) 276 n. 6 for the licentiousness of the mime show, presumably Seneca's point of allusion (further, Berno [2002] 224–25 = [2003] 53–55). But for *scaenam*
emended away, in my view too hastily, Watt (2000) 623, proposing *in summam* for *in scaenam*, to the effect of "Obscenity carried right to extremes."

50. *pascar* is perhaps sexual in connotation (Adams [1982] 138 cites Mart. 12.75.3 *pastas glande natis*
["buttocks that feed on the acorn/penis"] *habet Secundus*), and possibly accompanied by a faint
echo of *mentula* in *mendacio* (for Seneca's license in such plays cf. *mensura...mendaciis...mundi-
tiarum*, 1.16.3), especially if we trace *mentula* to *menta* (*TLL* 8 782.38–40, but cf. Adams 9–10).

metaphor of eating here supports the illusion that the distorted image is real and tangible, his eyes as full as his mouth literally is with his partners' enlarged *membra*: "he presented [his enormities] not just to his mouth but to his eyes as well" (1.16.3). At 1.16.2 the stallion (*admissarius*) positioned behind him lives out the metaphor by rising to superhuman size in the mirror; the only reality that Hostius sees in facing the mirror is the reflected image, so that "he delighted in the false size of his partner's member as if it really were so big" (*ipsius membri falsa magnitudine tamquam uera gaudebat*). In revealing to his gaze those sexual acts that are hidden from view by our body's arrangement (1.16.7), the mirror *is* his eye;[51] however distorted, the images he sees are true enough in this regard—his only means of access—so that his eyes are no less directly engaged in (making) the action than any other part of his body. Hence the literal truth of this extreme Narcissus'[52] wish that his "eyes, too, share in the lust and become witnesses and inspectors of it" (1.16.7).

We have seen that this Hostius is cast as the philosophical opposite of the *sapiens*; but another figure now emerges to complicate this duality. Already in the last chapter we briefly encountered Seneca's imaginary, literal-minded interlocutor early in Book 1.[53] If Hostius stands at the very bottom of the philosophical ladder of ascent informally shaped through the Quadra-*sapiens* contrast, this interlocutor clearly commands a higher place; yet he too shares something of Hostius' flawed vision, or his overly literal eye, in his own resistance to the possibility that such phenomena as rainbow are optical illusions. On this approach, the Hostius episode is potentially connected to the main body of Book 1 by representing an intensification of the literalist mind-set already manifested by the interlocutor, to whom we now turn.

The part of Book 1 that concerns us for now is Seneca's treatment of rainbow at 1.3–8, and in particular the sequence of argument running from 1.3 to 1.5. Three stages of argument can be conveniently distinguished as follows:

1. After an initial survey of rainbow theories (1.3.1–10),[54] Seneca pronounces a rainbow to be a reflection of the sun in a moist, hollow cloud (1.3.11). The

---

51. Cf. of the "seeing" mirror 1.6.2, 13.1 *quidquid uidet* [sc. *speculum*], *reddit.*

52. Cf. Citroni Marchetti (1991) 157 ("un cupo, mostruoso Narciso"); Berno (2002) 224 and n. 59, and (2003) 46 and n. 43.

53. Chapter One, Section II.

54. For ancient theory on rainbow, Gilbert (1907) 604–616 with Kidd (1988) 499–502 on fr. 134 and, conveniently, Boyer (1987) 33–65; from the perspective of modern science, Boyer 269–322 with Lee and Fraser (2001) 100–111, and cf. n. 61 below in this section. On Seneca's treatment of rainbow, now Bradley (2009) 38–45, albeit with an approach very different from my own.

image is reflected in the manner of a mirror (1.4.1)—for Artemidorus of Parium,[55] a concave mirror resembling a ball cut in half (1.4.3). He apparently held that a round, hollow cloud, when viewed from its side, produced a like effect (1.4.4).

2. 1.5.1–9: the interlocutor's objections to the mirror theory.[56]

3. A counterobjection drawn from Posidonius (1.5.10) and then itself qualified (1.5.11–12) before Seneca agrees (1.5.13) with the Posidonian view that a rainbow is shaped "by a cloud formed like a concave, round mirror, the shape of which is a section cut out of a ball";[57] a rainbow is indeed (cf. 1.4.3–4) produced by a principle of mirror distortion (1.5.14).

It is not hard to trace the many sharp thrusts in the interlocutor's argument that challenge, often with sly irony, specific points made by Seneca in (1) above. Given Seneca's emphasis on our defective vision and on mirror distortion,[58] the interlocutor shows a dogged literal mindedness in still objecting at 1.5.2 (cf. already 1.3.9) that the sun and a rainbow look so different: "What is as much unlike as the sun and a rainbow, in which neither the sun's shape is to be seen, nor its color, nor its size?" And so how can a rainbow be a mirror image of the sun? How can clouds function like mirrors when the two are evidently so different in nature and texture (1.5.3, 8)? Even after Seneca's rebuttal in (3) above, the interlocutor persists in his literal-minded attitude,[59] only for Seneca to point once more to distortion in mirrors (1.6.2). As if trapped in his own tunnel vision, the interlocutor presses on yet further (1.6.5: "But a rainbow is considerably larger than the sun"), his

---

55. He is usually assumed to be the Artemidorus attacked for his theory of comets at 7.13; possibly a contemporary of Seneca (see Gauly [2004] 149), but much uncertainty remains (see Parroni [2002] 491 with Hine [2006] 61 and n. 81; also Chapter Seven, Section V).

56. The position taken here is that Hine, in his Teubner text ([1996a] 23.447–26.514), rightly attributes 1.5.1 *de speculis*-1.5.9 *ictus* to the same notional interlocutor, with the sole exception of parenthetical *inquit* twice at 1.5.9. At 1.5.4 *"Singula stillicidia singula specula sunt"* (cf. 1.3.5) and 1.5.6 *"Quid ergo?" inquit* [sc. Seneca] *"non...solet?"* (cf. 1.3.2), it is crucial to recognize (with Oltramare [1929] 1.27 n. 1) that the interlocutor is "quoting" Seneca back at him, summarizing the latter's earlier points before answering each with interest.

57. Further on the Posidonian theory, Kidd (1988) 124 on fr. 15 and 501–502 on fr. 134, with the important clarification (p. 501) that "Posidonius differs from Aristotle [*N.Q.* 1.3.7–8] in taking the cloud *as a whole* as the reflector instead of the individual moisture drops in it" (my emphasis; the point will matter momentarily).

58. Cf. 1.3.9 "... I ought to say this: nothing is more deceptive than our vision"; 1.4.1 for a rainbow as "an image of the sun, imperfectly reflected because of the defectiveness and shape of the mirror."

59. Cf. 1.6.2: "But if the rainbow is a reflection of the sun, why does it appear far larger than the sun itself?"

stubborn fixity of view underscored by the hint of impatience in Seneca's response: "I have just said that there are mirrors made which magnify every object they reflect." For present purposes, however, two particular objections that the interlocutor raises in 1.5 warrant close scrutiny because of the further insight that they reveal into his mind-set.

The First Objection

"Singula stillicidia singula specula sunt" (1.5.4): with these words the interlocutor targets Seneca's earlier coverage of the theory that each raindrop forms a mirror, all of them individually reflecting the sun; a rainbow is a fusion of many such images. Seneca associates this position with Aristotle (1.3.7),[60] but with the difference that, for Aristotle, the individual raindrops are too small to reflect the sun's shape; they reflect only its color (1.3.8), the individual images again merging to form a unity.[61] But how, the interlocutor objects (1.3.9), can Seneca claim there are thousands of images where "I see none" (*ubi ego nullam* [sc. *imaginem*] *uideo*)— "none" in the literal sense that *his* rainbow is no mere reflection/*imago* but has real color? The interlocutor returns to the point, albeit from a different angle, at 1.5.4, now conceding that "individual raindrops are individual mirrors." But then two qualifications: first, clouds contain only the elements from which raindrops can be formed, not the drops themselves (1.5.4); this acutely to deny from the outset that a rainbow can be formed by the reflection of the sun *in cloud* (Seneca's position at 1.3.11). But second, suppose the clouds contained raindrops that *did* reflect the sun (1.5.5): even then, no rainbow would be formed because "all the drops [*guttae*] together would not give off a single image [*unam faciem*], but individual drops would give individual images." After all, when mirrors are joined together, they show individual images, not a unified whole; if you place *unum... hominem* (Hostius?) before a composite mirror, "a crowd appears" (*populus apparet*, 1.5.5). But a rainbow is clearly a unity; so how can individual raindrop reflections possibly merge to form such a coherent image?

For now our main point of interest here is not so much the true science (or optics) of raindrop reflection but the attitude revealed in the interlocutor's

---

60. Cf. *Mete.* 3.4 373a35–b28 with Gilbert (1907) 608–609, and see Hall (1977) 412–13 for analysis of the debt to Aristotle here (p. 413: 1.3.7–8 and 2.12.4–6 "create a presumption that Seneca had read *Mete.*; if he had not, the source he was using must have been a very good one").

61. Aristotle attributes the rainbow to reflection, not to refraction as well, their combination in fact supplying the true explanation: the so-called primary bow is formed when sunlight is refracted upon entering individual raindrops, reflected on their rear surface, and then refracted again when it exits (see further Lee and Fraser [2001] 321–22).

resistance to the fused-image theory. The evidence directly before him—mirror images cannot merge—is straightforwardly transposed to the region of *sublimia*, where he makes no effort, or recognizes no need, to adjust his vision to a different level of visual reality or possibility. And so he sees all too *precisely*: a rainbow is no composite but a single image (*una totius est facies*, 1.5.5), its color real and substantial. For Seneca, on the other hand, our sight is less infallible:[62]

> nihil refert quam exiguus sit umor aut lacus: si modo determinatus est, speculum est. ergo stillicidia illa infinita quae imber cadens defert totidem specula sunt, totidem solis facies habent. hae contra intuenti perturbatae apparent, nec dispiciuntur interualla quibus singulae distant, spatio prohibente discerni. deinde pro singulis apparet una facies turbida ex omnibus.
>
> 1.3.6

It makes no difference how small the amount of water or a pool is: if it has boundaries, it is a mirror. Accordingly, the countless drops carried down by the falling rain are so many mirrors and contain so many images of the sun. To the observer facing them these images appear confused, and the spaces between individual reflections cannot be discerned, since distance prevents them from being told apart. As a result, instead of individual images a single, confused image is visible from all of them.

Central to the imaginative Senecan vision here is that the optical illusions he identifies at the level of *sublimia* mark a symbolic transition point in our cognition: our terrestrial eye for the literal and the particular loses its precision, and we begin instead to see in a rainbow a natural fusion of things, a new unity,[63] the rainbow's different shades obviously distinct but merging into each other seamlessly.[64] In contrast to this integrating perspective, however, the interlocutor persists in his terrestrial focus on the particular, sharply segregating each mirror image and raindrop reflection and showing signs in the process of a divide-and-separate mentality that is fundamentally at odds with the one-world philosophy

---

62. The following words are attributed by Hine (1996a) 18.345–19.360 not to Seneca himself but to the quoted voice of those ("Some people think…," 1.3.5) who accept (Seneca of course among them) the rainbow-as-reflection theory.

63. Cf. 1.14.3–4: the speed of shooting stars is so great that we see not the stages (*partes*) of their flight but only the sum total (*summa*) of their movement; in the case of lightning we see only the unity (*uniuersum*) of the space through which it flashes.

64. Cf. 1.3.4, discussed in Section III above in this chapter.

permeating the *Natural Questions*. While the cosmopolitan *animus* "plunges into the totality of the world and directs its contemplating gaze on all its movements" (*Letters* 66.6), in the Senecan vision our everyday perception is fragmented and partial, our local involvements and localized mind-set dividing and separating the totality. If the *sapiens* alone can ascend to perfect comprehension of that totality, we nevertheless make progress by experimenting with a form of merged perception at 1.3.6 and 1.3.8; but the interlocutor is too entrenched in his literal, terrestrial way of seeing to rise from ground level.

Of course, the tendency to divide and separate phenomena is shared, albeit very differently manifested, by Hostius, whose mirrors are carefully positioned around him so that every act is caught in detail: "he surrounded himself with mirrors in which he could separate out his shocking acts and arrange them in order [*diuideret disponeretque*]" (1.16.4, where the mirrors that surround him also symbolically imprison him).[65] In his multiple reflections he offers his own distinct demonstration of the interlocutor's point that different mirrors, even if set close together (*coniuncta et simul conlocata*, 1.5.5), project separate images and "make from one man a crowd" (*ex uno quidem turbam efficiunt*). And so, in their different ways, the interlocutor and Hostius both exemplify the obsession with limits and fine distinctions that Seneca deplores at 1 pref. 9 ("How ridiculous are the boundaries of mortals!"), and that Leitão sharply observes "even in the mosaic floors [*pauimenta*, 1 pref. 7], composed as they are of countless small stones juxtaposed, each with its boundaries intact."[66] The liberated mind leaves all narrowness (*angustias*, 1 pref. 13) behind as it graduates to the cosmic viewpoint and takes the true measure of god. It is to *this* higher measurement that Seneca aspires ("I shall know that all else is petty [*angusta*] when I have measured god," 1 pref. 17)—in contrast to the false magnifications that so delight the self-worshipping Hostius.

The Second Objection

The interlocutor's second objection that warrants scrutiny in 1.5 arises from his insistence that the color in cloud is real and substantial. At 1.5.6, in a gesture that perhaps answers Seneca's quotation from Ovid early in his own statement on rainbows (1.3.4), the interlocutor introduces his new argument by quoting a line from Nero: *colla Cytheriacae splendent agitata columbae* ("the neck of the dove

---

65. Cf. Parroni (2002) 500 for *diuideret disponeretque* adapted from military language (e.g., Caes. *B. Gall.* 7.34.1), and also applied by Seneca to the division of philosophy into its parts at *Letters* 89.1; contrast Hostius' very different process of collection and division.

66. Leitão (1998) 143.

of Venus gleams when it moves");[67] then the further example of the peacock, possibly with Lucretian color: "the neck of the peacock gleams with many colors whenever it turns one way or another" (1.5.6).[68] These variations on "the pigeon's neck," that stock example of optical illusion that was worked especially hard by the skeptical tradition in its criticisms of dogmatism,[69] allow the interlocutor easily to score an initial point here: of course the feathers do not function as reflecting mirrors. In some animals, such as chameleons, the color is changed from within them (*ex ipsis*). In others, such as doves and peacocks, their plumage takes on this hue or that according to the position of the light, direct or oblique. In either case, color is intrinsic to the animal; and so too apparently in the case of a cloud, which is no more like a mirror than is any of the animals that he has mentioned (1.5.7).

For now there are two main points of interest here, the first of them another suggestive similarity between the interlocutor and Hostius Quadra. After 1.8.1 the interlocutor's objections to Seneca's argument that a rainbow is an illusion peter out, his case for seeing real color in a rainbow effectively lost. If Hostius "feeds on the lie" (cf. *mendacio pascar*, 1.16.9) that the images he sees in his mirrors are real, in his different way the interlocutor equally misconstrues image as reality, a rainbow's color as real; for, from the winning Senecan standpoint, "there is no actual substance in that reflecting cloud; it is no material body but an apparition, a likeness without reality" (1.6.4). Second, and to develop this first point, his appeal to "the pigeon's neck" at 1.5.6 is *itself* an optical illusion of sorts: the correspondence that he draws between the clouds and the doves, peacocks "and certain animals whose color changes" (1.5.7) is clearly, from the Senecan standpoint, a false correlation—as false as the correspondence that the interlocutor tries to enforce between mirrors and raindrops at 1.5.5 (i.e., multiple mirror images cannot merge; so how can multiple rainbow reflections merge to form a rainbow?). These false correspondences add another dimension to his blinkered and literal world vision, in that they show him to be forcing (mis)connections between phenomena to support his favored theories. In contrast to this forced use of analogy and comparison, the cosmopolitan *sapiens* who "never ceases to

---

67. Fr. 2 Courtney (1993) 357, itself with Ovidian color: *Cytheriacus* is not found before *Fast.* 4.15 and *Her.* 7.60 (cf. also *Cythereiadasque columbas, Met.* 15.386). Nero's presence here may lend a (perhaps ominous) shadow of authority to the interlocutor's case.

68. *uariis coloribus pauonum ceruix, quotiens aliquo deflectitur, nitet*; cf. Lucr. 2.799–809 for the dove (*pluma columbarum*, 801) and peacock (*cauda...pauonis*, 806) illustrating color change caused by the varying impact, direct or oblique, of light.

69. See Foss (1973) with Vottero (1989) 248–49 n. 10, citing Cic. *Luc.* 79, etc.

have the whole constantly present to mind"[70] never loses sight of the true interactive dynamic that operates throughout the totality.[71]

V: Of Subterranean Fish and Degenerate Diners in 3.17–18

At 3.16.4,[72] at roughly the midpoint of the book, Seneca takes us underground, arguing for the existence of subterranean marshes and lakes (3.16.5) and of "a great body of water that teems with fish which are repulsive because of their inertness" (3.19.1); for "beneath the earth, too, there are laws of nature that are less known to us, but no less firmly established. Believe that there exists below whatever you see above [*crede infra quidquid uides supra*]" (3.16.4). He subsequently expatiates on life forms in the subterranean waters:

> animalia quoque illis innascuntur, sed tarda et informia ut in aëre caeco pinguique concepta et aquis torpentibus situ, pleraque ex his caeca ut talpae et subterranei mures, quibus deest lumen quia superuacuum est; inde, ut Theophrastus adfirmat, pisces quibusdam locis eruuntur.
>
> 3.16.5

---

70. Hadot (1995) 273.

71. A third point of interest, often overlooked (but cf. Oltramare [1929] 1.33 n. 3; Vottero [1989] 256 n. 2), arises at 1.7.2, where Seneca meets another of the interlocutor's increasingly strained efforts to deny that a rainbow reflects the sun's shape (cf. 1.6.2, 5). Since the ridges on a striated glass rod receive the sun at an oblique angle, they appear to reflect only its color, not its image (1.7.1); the implication is that a rainbow might reproduce only the sun's color, not its shape. Seneca effortlessly counters the objection by explaining that the rod's irregular form prevents it from reflecting the sun's shape (1.7.3). But he also hits back by revisiting his interlocutor's contention, already answered to Seneca's full satisfaction (1.5.13–14), that a rainbow has real color: "it is obvious that in the case of a rainbow no actual color is formed, but only the appearance of illusory color, the sort which, as I have already said (*ut dixi*), the neck of a pigeon takes on or gives up whenever it changes position. This is also the case in a mirror, which assumes no actual color, but only a kind of copy of the color of something else" (1.7.2). In the strict sense it was not, of course, *Seneca* (cf. *ut dixi*) who mentioned the dove's neck earlier (1.5.6), but his interlocutor. Perhaps a simple misattribution on Seneca's part, or a rare loss of control over a subordinate narrative voice; or a conscious fusing of voices to the effect that (1.7.2) "a rainbow shows the same illusory color as ['as I said' through the interlocutor at 1.5.6] the dove's neck that changes its hues in the light"? Yet Seneca's *ut dixi* returns us to 1.5.6 only for us to be struck by the *difference* between the two contexts: whereas the interlocutor uses the optical illusion of the plumage as part of an elaborate argument that a rainbow has real color, Seneca applies it in the opposite direction at 1.7.2. On this approach, *ut dixi* draws yet further, and useful, attention to the fundamental ideological contrast between Seneca and his interlocutor.

72. In general on this section, Citroni Marchetti (1991) 161–67; Torre (1997) 384–87, 394–95; Berno (2003) 65–110; Gauly (2004) 96–104.

Living creatures arise in them as well, but they are slow and deformed because they were generated in dark, thick air and in waters that are lifeless
with stagnation. Many of these creatures are blind, like moles and subterranean mice, which have no vision because it is not needed. That is why, according to Theophrastus, fish are dug up from the depths in certain places.

The report here attributed to Theophrastus[73] is corroborated by the elder Pliny,
who cites Theophrastus as his source for the wondrous kinds of fish (*piscium
genera...mira*) he surveys at *Nat.* 9.175–8, among them those dug up from the
ground (§178). Other ancient allusions to these underground fish stress this wondrous element, casting them as *mira* or, worse, as implausible fictions.[74] We shall
return later to Seneca's initial description of these "fish dug up" at 3.16.5, but important for now is their status as wonders (cf. *re incredibili*, 3.17.1;[75] *incredibiliora*,
3.17.2). The melodramatic response that Seneca puts into Lucilius' mouth in reaction to this report of fish being extracted from the ground (3.17.1: "To imagine
someone going fishing not with nets or hooks but with a pickaxe!") sets the tone
for Seneca's vitriolic condemnation of luxury in 3.17–18.[76] The natural wonder of
fish dug from the earth is here superseded by the still greater *un*natural wonder of
luxury in full flow: What could be more truly incredible than the fashion not just
for dining on gourmet fish that are transferred from tank to table for the ultimate
in guaranteed freshness, but also for enclosing the prized mullet in a glass jar so
that the diners can relish the "shifting kaleidoscopic play of color, gradually
fading, that is fascinating to watch"[77] as the fish expires (3.17.2–3)?[78]

---

73. Fr. 217 Fortenbaugh et al. (1992) 390–93; cf. Theophr. fr. 171.7 Wimmer (1866) 456.50–457.5,
fr. 171 very possibly an extract from the work "On animals which live on dry land" (Περὶ τῶν ἐν
ξηρῷ διαμενόντων) cited by Diogenes Laertius (5.43; cf. Setaioli [1988] 436 n. 2060).

74. For sources, see Vottero (1989) 412 n. 9, and for the wondrous element, Strab. 4.1.7
παράδοξον, Plin. *Nat.* 9.178 (cf. also Ael. *N.A.* 5.27: Θεόφραστος δὲ δαιμονιώτατα λέγει "Theophrastus has the most amazing statement ..."). For the purely fictional element, cf. Mela 2.83.

75. Deleted as a gloss on *fabula* by Hine, who plausibly reads...*quae urbane <ut> in* [*re incredibili*] *fabula dicas*: (1996a) 131.418–19 with (1996b) 51–52, and cf. now (2009) 290 on
3.17.1.

76. On the force of Seneca's use of *fabula* of "going fishing with a pickaxe", see Berno (2003)
68 with p. 23 n. 25.

77. Andrews (1949) 187; cf. also Plin. *Nat.* 9.66, with Alexander (1955).

78. By *mullus* Seneca presumably means the *mullus surmuletus* as opposed to the smaller
mullus barbatus, as larger *mulli* were the more prized because of their taste. On this and other
characteristics of the *mullus*, Higginbotham (1997) 48–50; for the "incredibly high prices"
paid for surmullets weighing over two pounds, Corcoran (1963) 100.

The intrusiveness of this outburst in the midst of Seneca's technical enquiries in Book 3 is underscored by the digression abruptly announced at 3.18.1 ("Let me set aside my subject for a short while and castigate luxury"), and then by his sudden return to his main theme at 3.19.1 ("But to revert to the subject..."). In this, what I take to be the first book of the *Natural Questions* in its original ordering, so abrupt a change of direction in 3.18.1 intensifies his seemingly unstoppable outrage; but it may also be programmatic in function, starkly confronting his newly initiated reader with the special concoction of physicomoral investigation in this fresh undertaking. As we saw in the Introduction, the Senecan/Stoic study of nature inevitably implicates ethics, not least because the physical world of the *Natural Questions* supplies a vision of natural process and normative/rational behavior that is overturned in the moral excesses and irrationality that Seneca condemns at the human level.[79] So, at 3.17–18, those who delight in the shifting hues of the dying mullet act unnaturally from the Senecan viewpoint, not just in their luxury appetites of both eye and stomach but also in their perverse interest in death as play or theater, a form of entertainment for early imperial palates jaded by the familiar spectacle of gladiatorial combat and other institutionalized modes of cruelty; fascinated by this vaudeville of death,[80] they are heartlessly unmoved by ordinary death within the family (cf. 3.18.6). Their lack of all limit and restraint is itself suitably matched by Seneca's inability to temper his outrage ("At times I can't stop myself from using words rashly and exceeding the bounds of propriety," 3.18.7), but symbolic punishment nevertheless awaits within the text: the degeneration they exemplify is implicated in the cleansing physics of the world when, at 3.27–30, the cataclysm that rages there brings one world cycle to an end, destroying mankind before the new cosmic beginning ushers in another age of innocence (3.29.5).[81]

Within the broad community of deviants assembled in the *Natural Questions*, the degenerate diners of 3.17–18 are closely related to, and, given the primacy of Book 3, an important antecedent of, Hostius Quadra in 1.16. While he feasts on the illusory images he sees in his mirrors (cf. *mendacio pascar*, 1.16.9), they, too, are gluttonous observers (*oculis quoque gulosi sunt*, 3.18.7), the fish satisfying their eyes before it reaches their gullet (*oculos ante quam gulam pauit* [sc. *piscis*], 3.17.3).[82] If, in contrast to the unifying expansiveness of Senecan cosmic consciousness,

---

79. Cf. Rosenmeyer (2000) 105: "If physics is the science of how the world behaves, then ethics must be its mandatory junior or perhaps even senior partner."

80. Cf. Barton (1993) 60. Yet for the diner, not the food, as the real spectacle here cf. Richardson-Hay (2009) 86.

81. On the cataclysm, Chapter Three, Section IV.

82. On the link with Quadra, Berno (2003) 73.

Hostius' obsessive attention to every singular detail projected on each of his mirrors reflects a compartmentalized way of thinking and viewing, then the diners of 3.17–18 show a similar concentration of viewpoint—that particularization of emphasis—as they focus on the changing colors of the dying mullet:

'nihil est' inquis 'mullo exspirante illo formosius. ipsa conluctatione animam adficienti rubor primum, deinde pallor suffunditur, squamaeque uariantur, et <in> incertas facies inter uitam ac mortem coloris est uagatio....'
    ubi multum diuque laudatus est, ex illo perlucido uiuario extrahitur. tunc, ut quisque peritior est, monstrat: 'uide quomodo exarserit rubor omni acrior minio! uide quas per latera uenas agat! ecce sanguineum putes uentrem! quam lucidum quiddam caeruleumque sub ipso tempore efful- sit! iam porrigitur et pallet et in unum colorem componitur.'

3.18.1, 4–5

"There's nothing," you say, "more beautiful than that dying mullet. As it weakens its breathing in the very struggle for breath, first a shade of red and then a yellowish tinge spreads over it, its scales change hue, and shifts of color lead to differences of appearance between life and death."
    When the fish has been much admired for a long time, it is taken from its transparent aquarium. Then, each person, according to his expertise, points: "See how the redness has flared up and is more intense than any vermilion! Look at the veins that pulse throughout its sides! Look! You'd think that its belly was full of blood! What a brilliant white shade of col- oring, and of blue, flashed out just at the moment of death![83] Now it's stretching out, growing pale and settling into a single coloration."

We have already seen how the colors of the rainbow merge into each other at 1.3.4, where the seamless transitions between them are artfully conveyed through Seneca's appropriation of Ovid's rainbow description in *Metamorphoses* 6.[84] If that seamlessness offers one symbolic illustration of the harmonious interactions of the Senecan physical world, then a different tendency is revealed in the

---

83. Corcoran (1971–72) 1.245 renders *sub ipso tempore* "under its brow" (cf. *OLD tempus*² 1a, of animals); so others (e.g., Vottero [1989] 417 "sotto le branchie"; Parroni [2002] 205 "sotto la tempia"; Hine [2010b] 37 "below its forehead"), but Corcoran also recognizes (1.244 n. 1) the possibility of "just before death" (cf. *OLD sub* 8; for *tempus* of the "due time" of death cf., e.g., Cic. *Tusc.* 1.93, 103)—surely the more forceful sense here, bringing the brilliant spectacle to its climax just as the fish approaches its last breath (cf. Oltramare [1929] 1.135: "au moment où il va expirer").

84. See Section III above in this chapter.

separating out of colors as the degenerate diners watch the dying mullet. While Hostius gazes into his mirrors, they too watch minutely, their focus becoming ever more intense as they look ("See...vermilion!") and then look still more closely ("Look...coloration") for each new change of shade. The appeal here is to an eye for fine difference between colorations, not for seamless continuity between them; when colors *do* merge into oneness (cf. *in unum colorem componitur*), they do so only in death, the resulting pallor so different from the vibrant fusions that we experience in a rainbow. In contrast to the natural beauty that Seneca associates with the cosmic whole (cf. 1 pref. 14: "this world, than which *nothing is more beautiful* [*formosius*] or better organized or more reliable"), the mullet watchers find "nothing more beautiful" than the dying fish (3.18.1; cf. 18.4, 6).[85] From a cosmic perspective, they show a Quadra-like myopia in their closed field of vision, and in their perverse fixation on the details of death by controlled suffocation they themselves are seemingly constricted in their own narrow confinement. In their different way, their own condition is figuratively reflected in the slow exhaustion of life that so galvanizes their eyes.

Beyond distancing us from base matters (*sordidis*) and freeing us *a corpore*, the study of nature, Seneca asserts at 3 pref. 18, hones our powers of thought: "when we have exercised our intellect [*subtilitas*] on hidden obscurities, it will be no less effective in dealing with matters that are in plain view." In the luxury diners' quest for ever more exotic stimuli for their jaded senses, however, the positive connotation of *subtilitas* at 3 pref. 18 is lost in the decadent times of 3.18.3: "and despising anything ordinary, our madness every day contrives something so much more intricate [*subtilius*] and more refined."[86] Moreover, given our starting point at 3.16.4–5 literally below ground, amid the dead atmospherics where Seneca locates great stretches of stagnant water, can the mullet watchers escape comparison with the slow and deformed (*tarda et informia*) creatures born in that infernal darkness, creatures that are blind (*caeca*) and without vision "because it is not needed"? In their figurative way the diners, such keen observers in one way, are themselves blind, as if incapable of seeing any benefit to the ascent from darkness to light: to revert to 3 pref. 11 and 1 pref. 2,[87] the study of philosophy raises us from the gloom (*caligo*) and darkness (*tenebrae*) of ordinary existence, leading us to true illumination (*illo unde lucet*). If we press this comparison between the gourmet diners of 3.17–18 and the blind *animalia* below ground in 3.16,[88] an exquisite

---

85. On this contrast, Berno (2003) 77.

86. On this point, Berno (2003) 88–89.

87. Cited already in Chapter One, Section II.

88. See already Torre (1997) 395.

irony results: here is proof of Seneca's insistence at 3.16.4 that there does indeed exist below whatever you see above (*crede infra quidquid uides supra*).

VI: Further Transgressions in 5.15 and 7.31–32

In contrast to the uplifting vision of "consorting with things divine" (3 pref. 11), then, our gaze is lowered into the moral darkness in 3.17–18. This downward movement offers an important connecting motif across certain other moralizing interludes, among them Seneca's account in 1.17, directly after the Quadra episode, of how mankind has lost sight of the mirror's original *raison d'être* ("Mirrors were invented so that man could know himself," 1.17.4) for it now to become merely an accoutrement of luxury: "No, there's no vice for which it has not become essential" (1.17.10). Modern man is cast in 1.17 as a distorted reflection of his forebears of a simpler age (§5), ungroomed but nevertheless uncorrupted (§7).[89] The path of that descent is traced in Seneca's adaptation of the familiar sequence-of-ages theme at 1.17.6:

> primo faciem suam cuique casus ostendit; deinde cum insitus sui mortalibus amor dulcem aspectum formae suae faceret, saepius ea *despexere* in quibus effigies suas uiderant. postquam deterior populus ipsas subît terras effossurus obruenda, ferrum primum in usu fuit (et id impune homines eruerant si solum eruissent), tunc deinde alia terrae mala....
>
> At first, chance revealed to man his own face. Then, when the self-love that is intrinsic in mortals made the sight of their own appearance pleasing, they looked down more often at the things in which they had seen their own reflections. After a worse people went down into the earth itself to dig out what should lie buried, iron was first put to use (and they would have come to no harm by digging it out, if they had dug out iron alone). But then came other evils of the earth....[90]

In contrast to the liberated *animus* that looks down (*despiciens*, 1 pref. 8) from its cosmic vantage point on the narrowness of everyday existence at ground level, the

---

89. On 1.17, now Limburg (2007) 276–89, with an important critique (pp. 284–85) of Gauly's argument ([2004] 125) that Seneca portrays the *simplicitas* of the primeval age as only relative, with "natural" mirroring (e.g., in "a clear spring or a small rock" in 1.17.5) already a sign of vanity in that *aetas simplicior*.

90. Seneca here goes against the prevailing view that "the use of bronze was known before iron" (Lucr. 5.1287; further, Vottero [1989] 284 n. 12); he thus modifies the sequence-of-ages tradition by casting bronze *for mirroring* as a worse evil than (mere) iron (cf. Limburg [2007] 282–83).

reflection seekers who here look down (*despexere*) do so in a more confining, self-absorbed way.[91] If nature designed humans to behold and admire her own beauty,[92] this new preoccupation with their own reflected image represents an unnatural turning away from the true focus of their spectatorship—a form of alienation from *natura ipsa* that hardens in *ipsas subît terras* into their physical plundering of the earth, that familiar topos in ancient literary depictions of the Iron Age,[93] and one Seneca has already skillfully exploited in a related moralizing aside of downward direction, both literal and figurative, in Book 5, on wind.

In 5.14 Seneca takes up his earlier explanation at 5.4.1 of one possible cause of winds, namely that they are sometimes produced "from caves and recesses in the inner part of the earth" (5.14.1; for these recesses cf. 3.16.4–5). He posits that rivers and lakes exist in subterranean cavities just as they do above, the moisture-filled air exerting its pressure to stir wind underground (5.14.2–3). In 5.15[94] he finds anecdotal proof of the existence of these subterranean waters in a *fabula* that he tells of Philip of Macedon:[95]

> Nunc mihi permitte narrare fabulam. Asclepiodotus[96] auctor est demissos quam plurimos[97] a Philippo in metallum antiquum olim destitutum, ut explorarent quae ubertas eius esset, quis status, an aliquid futuris reliquisset uetus auaritia; descendisse illos cum multo lumine et multos duraturo dies, deinde longa uia fatigatos uidisse flumina ingentia et conceptus aquarum inertium uastos, pares nostris, ne compressos quidem terra superimminente, sed liberae laxitatis, non sine horrore uisos.
>
> 5.15.1

---

91. On the desire for mirrors in 1.17 as "a new aetiology for the sense of cultural decay represented by the Roman lament, *O tempora, O mores,*" Bartsch (2006) 32–35.

92. Cf. *Dial.* 8.5.3–4, quoted in Chapter Seven, Section II.

93. E.g., Ov. *Am.* 3.8.35–8, 53, *Met.* 1.138–42, [Sen.] *Oct.* 416–18 with Boyle (2008) 178–79. But for Stoic nature burying what harms us, cf. *Ben.* 7.10.2, *Letters* 94.56, 110.10.

94. In general on 5.15, Berno (2003) 179–207.

95. Surely Philip II, Alexander's father, who is regularly designated by plain *Philippus* elsewhere in Senecan prose (*Dial.* 5.23.2, 3, 24.1, *Letters* 94.62, *N.Q.* 3 pref. 5), but cf. *Philippus Macedonum rex, Ben.* 4.37.1 and *N.Q.* 5.15.3 (reading *ante Philippum Macedonum regem* with Hine [1996a] 218.290–1, *pace* Vottero [1989] 552 *Macedonum<que> reges*). For mining initiatives under Philip, Diod. 16.8.6–7.

96. Posidonius' pupil; cf. Chapter One, Section I n. 5.

97. *complures* Hine (1996a) 217.276, with MS Z in one main branch of the tradition; but *quam plurimos* in the Ψ branch (Hine [1980a], especially 217; [1981] 2–3; [1996a] vi–ix) better stresses Philip's *auaritia* (see immediately below).

Now let me tell a story. Asclepiodotus is my source that as many men as possible were sent by Philip down an old mine that was long abandoned, to find out how rich its deposits were, what its current condition was, and whether the greed of past ages had left anything for future generations. They descended with a great supply of torches that was sufficient to last them for many days. Then, when they were exhausted by the length of their journey, they came upon the sight of huge rivers and vast reservoirs of stagnant water, reservoirs no smaller than those above ground and not even pressed in by the earth that hung over them but with plenty of free space—a sight that caused them to shudder.

At one level the story lends the illusion of support to his intuition both here and at 3.16.4–5 that rivers and lakes like those above exist below. At a symbolic level, however, the mine, already old and long abandoned by Philip's time, bears witness to the antiquity of that *uetus auaritia* characterizing an Iron Age that apparently extends into Seneca's time (cf. 5.15.2). The great number of miners dispatched by Philip (*quam plurimos*), their large supply of torches and their exhaustion because of the length of their journey merely magnify the extent of this inherited *auaritia*: new adventurers have to dig ever further and deeper to find new veins to plunder. Moral transgressors in their quest for mineral wealth, these adventurers are also spatial transgressors as they gaze upon the seemingly Stygian waters of this Underworld in their brazen katabasis—a violation of the natural order that is suggestively underscored by evocations of Theseus' eyewitness account of the Underworld in Seneca's *Hercules Furens*.[98]

"I read this story with great pleasure" (5.15.2). The satisfaction that Seneca derives from the story lies partly in the canceling of one *fabula* by another: the myth that "those ancestors of ours whom we heap with praises" (5.15.2) were morally impeccable is exploded in his exaggerated surprise that "our age suffers not from new vices but from vices handed down all the way from antiquity."[99] If the

98. See Berno (2003) 203–206. Cf. also Citroni Marchetti (1991) 162 n. 126 for interesting parallels drawn between the Senecan expedition and the journey into darkness—Germanicus' disastrous expedition in 16 CE down the Ems into the North Sea—portrayed by Albinovanus Pedo ap. Sen. *Suas.* 1.15 (= Courtney [1993] 315–19, Hollis [2007] 373–81 fr. 228); further, Chapter Five, Section VI n. 153.

99. For the present age as no worse than the preceding, *Ben.* 1.10.1. But for the implicit emphasis at *N.Q.* 5.15.2 cf. *Letters* 97.1: "You are mistaken, my dear Lucilius, if you think that luxury…and other vices which everyone levels as a charge against his own age are the fault just of our own generation; they are the vices of human beings in general, not of the times (*hominum sunt ista, non temporum*). No era has ever been free from blame…" (further, Maso [1999] 50–54 with Limburg [2007] 220–24).

community of scholars that Seneca assembles through his gathering of sources in the *Natural Questions* places his own researches in the context of past achievement and striving, the modern corruption he condemns in his moralizing interludes is itself placed in quasi-historical context through this new emphasis on inherited vice. Yet by this stage in the work the moralizing dimension is not superimposed on Seneca's scientific agenda, or inserted as an intrusive interlude in the manner of 3.17–18. Rather, it deeply infiltrates his text, embedded as it is in the figurative potential of so much of his language, as when he asserts that by cutting into mountains our ancestors "stood over their source of profit but under the risk of collapse" (*supra lucrum sub ruina steterunt*, 5.15.2). Beyond the literal sense of *sub ruina*, the phrase's figurative connotation also directly, and etymologically, relates the ancestral digging for gold in 5.15.3 *ut erueret aurum* [sc. *homo*] to the subsequent (moral) collapse in *ruina*.[100] The earliest excavators lowered themselves in more ways than one when they descended into the darkness: "there were men who…, breathing upright and freely [*recto spiritu liberoque*], let themselves down [*se demitterent*] into those caves, where no distinction [*discrimen*] between light and day ever penetrated" (5.15.3).[101] Their upright, free breathing as they go underground perhaps extends symbolically to their upright, free being,[102] but the miners are soon bent over and imprisoned in their subterranean channels, where they resemble the dead in "leaving the light" (cf. *a tergo lucem relinquere*, 5.15.3), albeit in this case for live burial: "What powerful necessity…buried [*defodit*] man, and plunged [*mersit*] him into the very depths of the earth's interior?" (5.15.3).[103] They are buried by, and in, their greed (cf. *quos in imo…infodit* [sc. *auaritia*], 5.15.4), the earth with its alluring gold weighing more heavily on them than on the ordinary dead.[104] The poison that Virgil implants in the post-Saturnian age at *Georgics* 1.129—"Jupiter bestowed on black serpents their deadly venom [*malum uirus*]"—recurs in the "evil poison" of the precious metal that lies

---

100. For *ruina* lit. and fig., *OLD* 4 and 5 with Alexander (1948) 307 and Hine (2010b) 202 n. 21; etymology, Maltby (1991) 533.

101. *OLD demitto* 10b ("to abase oneself"); no *discrimen* also of a moral kind as they delve deeply but in a wrong, nonphilosophical direction.

102. Cf. *OLD spiritus* 4a; further on this word, Chapter Five, Section III.

103. Cf. *OLD lux* 6a (light extending to "life"). For *defodio* of live burial, Ov. *Fast.* 6.458, *Met.* 4.239, Plin. *Ep.* 4.11.6, and cf. Cato ap. Gell. *N.A.* 3.14.19. It is sharply ironic if the combination of *defodit* and *mersit* here reverses *Ben.* 7.10.2: "the earth has hidden [gold and silver] and buried them deep (*defodit et mersit*)…" (for the relative chronology of the two works, see Griffin [1976] 396 and 399–400 nn. G, H).

104. At 5.15.4 *ulli ergo mortuo tam grauis terra est quam istis…?* Seneca alludes ironically to the familiar inscription on epitaphs, *sit tibi terra leuis* (further, Vottero [1989] 554 n. 10).

concealed at 5.15.4 (*illud malum uirus latitat*), infecting the miners and so lending cause to the death analogy. "What powerful necessity bent man down [*incuruauit*] when he stood tall to face the stars [*hominem ad sidera erectum*]?" (5.15.3).
Man's upright stature is itself designed by divine teleology to elevate his gaze so
that he can contemplate *natura ipsa* in all her wonder.[105] But in their descent into
the dark depths the miners not only reverse this uplifting tendency toward celestial illumination; they also lose their moral as well as their physical uprightness (it
is bent crooked)[106] in their regression into an animal-like state in which they
crawl (cf. *reptauit*, 5.15.4) through their tunnels or burrowing holes (*cuniculos*) in
search of plunder/prey (*praedam*). The plunder they seek is "mud-smeared and
not sure to be found" (*praedam lutulentam incertamque*, 5.15.4)—*lutulentam* also
in the extended sense of being "morally polluted,"[107] *incertam* with the ominous
implication that such riches are fickle even when found; after all, gold is "no less
dangerous to seek than it is to possess" (5.15.3).[108]

The moral implications of much of Seneca's language at 5.15 contribute to the
complexity of a *fabula* that does much more than colorfully support his claim
that subterranean waters truly exist. In its portrayal of transgression at both the
physical and the moral levels, and in its adaptation of the familiar literary apparatus of the lost Golden Age, this *fabula* anticipates a major emphasis in Seneca's
crowning attack at the book's close (5.18) on man's abuse of that "great benefit
bestowed by nature" (5.18.4), the interaction (*commercium*) between different
peoples through wind-driven sea travel: as mankind delves deeply underground
in 5.15 and roves over the seas in search of ill-gotten gain in 5.18, the unnaturalness
(for Seneca) of that literal and figurative waywardness stands in contrast to the
settled character and natural motions of the winds that are differentiated and
described in Book 5 as a whole.[109] Further, the journey underground in 5.15 gives
literal expression to the symbolic moral descent we have plotted thus far in Books
1 and 3; but these various passages also yield more specific points of interconnection. In introducing his story at 5.15.1—*Nunc mihi permitte narrare fabulam*—
Seneca echoes the opening to his digression at 3.18 (*Permitte mihi paulum
quaestione seposita castigare luxuriam*) while also anticipating his introduction to

---

105. See on the topos Vottero (1989) 554 n. 9 with Dionigi (1983) 235–36 on *Dial.* 8.5.4.

106. Cf. again *incuruauit* at 5.15.3, with *OLD incuruo* 1c: "(fig.) to incline the mind of,
influence."

107. *OLD* 2.

108. Cf. for the idea *Dial.* 10.17.4, *Letters* 115.16.

109. This approach is developed in Chapter Five.

the Quadra episode at 1.16.1: *Hoc loco uolo tibi narrare fabellam.*[110] Then the likeness proposed earlier between the mullet watchers of 3.17–18 and the blind, deformed *animalia* born in the subterranean darkness at 3.16.5 is suggestively matched by the language—*cuniculos, praedam, reptauit*—that gently demotes the underground explorers of 5.15.4 to animal-like burrowers.[111] Quadra is a still more extreme monster (cf. *portentum*, 1.16.3; *monstrum*, 6), a beast destined to die like a sacrificial *hostia*.[112] In all three cases, animal comparison adds a dehumanizing dimension to the downward tendency that is contrasted by Seneca's uplifting drive toward cosmic consciousness in the *Natural Questions* generally; and if we accept that Book 1 occupied penultimate position in the original ordering of the collection, the animal comparison can itself be seen to descend to its nadir in the monstrous Quadra.

One other constituency remains to be added for now to our community of deviants in the *Natural Questions*, a constituency closely related to Quadra in particular, and housed late in the preceding Book 7, on comets. In contrast to Seneca's venturing into the cosmic darkness (*in occulta*, 7.29.3), and in contrast to the community of enquirers across time who, generation by generation, glimpse now one, now another of nature's secrets (cf. 7.30.6), this very different constituency is denounced at 7.31–2 for its devotion to (self-)discovery of a distinctly unphilosophical kind, vice perversely the discoverer:

> *inuenit* luxuria aliquid noui in quod insaniat, *inuenit* impudicitia nouam contumeliam sibi, *inuenit* deliciarum dissolutio et tabes aliquid adhuc tenerius molliusque quo pereat.
>
> 7.31.1[113]

> Luxury finds some new fad over which to act crazily. Sexual impurity finds a new indignity for itself. The loss of moral fiber and corruption of soft living find some still more sensuous and delicate means of ruination.

Our focus takes a distinctly limiting, self-absorbed turn here, with the body, not the firmament, now the center of attention. In contrast to the variety of colors that distinguish different comets earlier in Book 7 (17.3), all eyes are now on the

---

110. On these connections, Berno (2003) 181 and n. 5.

111. Already Berno (2003) 188 on *reptauit*.

112. See Section II above in this chapter.

113. On 7.31–2, Berno (2003) 291–321; Limburg (2007) 372–76.

"courtesan cosmetics" (*colores meretricios*, 7.31.2) that compromise gender[114] as men go beyond even "female concern for beauty treatments" (*muliebres mundi-tias*).[115] The sun "has as many steps [*gradus*],[116] so to speak, as there are days, and it defines the year by its own circuit" (7.1.3)—only one of the sun's wondrous characteristics that go unobserved in the regular order of things (7.1.4). The focus of modern man, however, is on a different kind of *gradus*, the delicate gait with which he steps lightly (*molli ingressu suspendimus gradum*, 7.31.2);[117] instead of contemplating the heavenly fires, he looks instead upon the gems that form an alternative constellation on his fingers (cf. 7.31.2).[118]

This turning away from *natura tota* and from apparently authentic maleness reaches its climax in the invention of ever new indignities for *uirilitas* at 7.31.3, where the exhilarating effects of releasing dynamic thought to "burst through the ramparts of the sky" (cf. *Dial.* 8.5.6) are reversed in modern man's voluntary submission to the ultimate in bodily degradation, self-castration and appearing in the gladiatorial arena as a net gladiator (*retiarius*).[119] Turning away from nature culminates in a turning against the self; or, as Carlin Barton puts it,

> Seneca imagines the climax of unchecked self-indulgence in men to take the form of a self-inflicted insult to their own virility.... The search for endless diversion ends with men either cutting off their genitals, like the *galli*, the devotees of Cybele, or entering the brothels of the *ludi* to serve the lusts of the gladiators.[120]

---

114. On the telltale signs of *mollitia* in 7.31, Edwards (1993) 68 and n.16; and for 7.31 mentioned in relation to the "urban subculture" of the pathic male, Taylor (1997) 338–49.

115. With a possible play on *mundus*, the physical world that no longer fascinates in 7.31–2. Cf. *OLD mundus*² ("The articles a woman uses to beautify herself") and *mundus*³; possible identification perhaps after the sense development of Gk. κόσμος (*LSJ* s.v. II, IV; cf. Cic. *Tim.* 35, Plin. *Nat.* 2.8). For another such play, cf. 1.17.10 (discussed in Section VII below in this chapter); in general, Puhvel (1976), especially 161–67.

116. *gradus* effectively "degrees"; cf. Man. 1.581, 3.268, 445 with Volk (2004) 43–44.

117. For this effeminate step, cf. *Dial.* 9.17.4, *Letters* 52.12, 114.3: "Do you not see that, if the mind has become enervated, his effeminacy is visible in his very gait (*in ipso incessu*)?"

118. For more than one ring as a "conventional sign of *mollitia*," Gibson (2003) 281 on Ov. *Ars* 3.446.

119. On this "lowest type of gladiator," Morton Braund (1996) 159 on Juv. 2.143–8; in the hierarchy of gladiators, the lightly armed and dressed *retiarius* "was regarded as particularly effeminate: the greater the exposure of the body, the greater the disgrace." Cf. also Juv. 6.O7–13, 8.199–208 with Housman (1904) = (1972) 619–22 and Cerutti and Richardson (1989); further bibliography in Berno (2003) 300–301 n. 29.

120. Barton (1993) 72–73.

Seneca's condemnation of these *delicati* in 7.31 is connected with the Quadra episode in 1.16 by a sequence of verbal and thematic overlaps[121] which include *morbus* used of sexual perversion in both cases (7.31.3; 1.16.8); *contumelia* of physical violation (7.31.1; 1.16.7); *inuenio* of lewd invention (7.31.1; 1.16.8); *exerceo* of sexual practice (7.31.3; 1.16.7); the gender divide crossed in the cosmetic effeminacy and castration featured in 7.31.2–3, and then when Quadra "submits to both man and woman" at 1.16.7 in an ambiguous mixture of passive and active performance[122]; and both passages share the quest for ever new refinement to bodily indulgence and pleasure, whether in the form of Quadra's mirrors or adornment added to adornment in 7.31.2 before the endlessly (un)satiated *delicati* resort to self-harm in 7.31.3. Again, Seneca's high-minded inquiry into the nature of comets in Book 7 rises loftily above the depravity he pictures at the low point of 7.31; and the cumulative effect of the linkages with the Quadra episode is perhaps to anticipate what might have happened if Hostius had lived long enough for his unchecked self-indulgence to exhaust itself in possible *ennui*. If we observe Hostius in his prime in 1.16, can we glimpse in the castrations and the gladiatorial brothel of 7.31.3 a plausible end, at least according to the Barton code as quoted above, for his vile typology?

VII: *The Textual Containment of Vice*

The deviants distributed across Seneca's moralizing interludes are no cast of lurid or bizarrely entertaining extras, as if colorful distractions from his technical material. Rather, the *uitiosi* we have considered above form a necessary counterforce to Seneca's promotion of cosmic consciousness—necessary because they embody the capacity for vice that is encoded in Stoic human nature. Mankind alone of all beings has the capacity to collaborate as an "ally" or "associate" of rational nature,[123] thus finding "perfection and fulfilment not just in rational behaviour, but in

---

121. Berno (2003) 298–99; further on linkage between Books 1 and 7, Chapter Seven, Sections II and VII.

122. At 1.16.7, passive with both sexes in *et uirum et feminam patior* (cf. *OLD patior* 2c; for the performance of oral sex on a female partner as passive, Williams [2010] 225); then active in *marem exerceo*, on which Housman (1931) 405–406 = (1972) 1178 (in Latin, but in English translation see Jayo [2001] 186–87). But for *marem exerceo* interpreted passively, Cardini (1985) 735–42; for a concise weighing of both sides of the controversy, Bartsch (2006) 107 nn. 163, 164.

123. Cf. *Letters* 92.30: "All this universe which encompasses us is one and it is god [*deus*]; we are associates of god, and his members [*et socii sumus eius et membra*]"; Wildberger (2006) 227–28.

behaviour as a member of a community of gods and men."[124] But given our capacity to act *not* in accord with nature's rationality, mankind is also a moral agent in its own right. Man is equipped by nature with "impulses to virtue," but the actual achievement of good character nevertheless relies on his arduous striving in that direction; virtue is the highest goal, but "[i]n order that virtue shall be attainable the potentiality for vice must also be granted."[125] This potentiality for vice finds extreme expression in Seneca's treatment of the likes of Hostius Quadra and the mullet watchers of 3.17–18, but it is also manifested in less spectacular failures of judgment and assent to passion, such as fear of death by lightning at 2.59, for example, or by earthquake at 6.1–3 and 6.32, or the vulnerability to flattery that is featured in the preface to Book 4a.

The *Natural Questions* strives to elevate us above these vicious tendencies, but, in David Leitão's neat formulation,

> [t]hat plan is constantly derailed, for Seneca finds himself again and again bogged down in distinctly terrestrial and atmospheric (as opposed to celestial) phenomena and in the moralizing that goes with an enquiry into this realm. Seneca finds it difficult, as we all do, to get out of this world; the more he aims upward, the more he seems to be dragged downward. Hostius Quadra exhibits this "gravitational pull" in its most extreme form; he represents a "bottoming out."[126]

On this approach our cast of deviants lends a necessary unifying tension to the *Natural Questions*, virtue set against vice. Or, to put the point differently, we might compare Seneca's condemnation of the contaminating crowd in the *Moral Letters* and elsewhere as a constant threat to individuality and to integrity of judgment: the crowd serves as a permanent background presence in and across the *Letters*, as if constantly testing Seneca's formation in Lucilius (and the reader) of self-reliance.[127] So in the *Natural Questions* the uplifting thrust toward cosmic consciousness requires for self-definition and validation a strong gravitational pull in the opposite direction. Like the *turba* of the *Letters*, the *uitiosi* stand condemned; yet they remain a powerful, even necessary, presence, educating the philosophical progressive (*proficiens*) through their negative example, and yet

---

124. Inwood (1999) 683.

125. Long (1986) 183.

126. Leitão (1998) 159–60.

127. Cf., e.g., 7.1–7, 8.1–2, 14.9–10, 68.1–7, 80.1–2, 103.1–2.

perhaps also testing his resolve by showing the passions in (darkly attractive?) release from all ethical stringency.

Quadra in particular perhaps commands a special fascination in his audience at 1.16. Why, we might wonder, does Seneca offer so elaborate a description of his vicious ways? For Limburg, the effect of this description is deterrent; and yet she too recognizes its enticing potential.[128] After all, the contrast drawn earlier between him and the *sapiens*,[129] vice and virtue, arguably underestimates the liberation of self that Quadra achieves before the mirrors. "Does he not, with his mirrors," asks Peter Toohey,[130] "display a remarkable level of self-awareness and, through this, a heightened sense of selfhood?" True, this self-awareness may nevertheless presuppose Quadra's alienation *from* himself, in that the self on which he gazes is obviously an illusion, at least to all but him.[131] Yet the sexual philosophy he espouses in the words that Seneca puts into his mouth at 1.16.7–9 shows a perversely principled rejection of conventional attitudes, an independence of outlook that, in his different way, the *sapiens* shares in his own detachment from popular opinion and values. If we accept that the passing of the Republic brought with it a collapse in "traditional forms of self-display, approbation, and censure"[132] and the emergence of an imperial monopoly on the nature and measurement of *uirtus*, a counterreaction can be discerned in the early imperial age—an impetus, as Shadi Bartsch puts it, "to negate the imperial eye, reinstall self-respect in the shamed senatorial class, and restore *libertas* to a group that had lost much of its former prerogatives."[133] Hence the intense gaze on the self on which Bartsch focuses in Seneca: the cultivation of virtue in isolation from the judgment and censure of the suspect imperial control system marks, in Seneca, the accentuation of a subjectivist form of ethics based on *self*-witnessing. The Senecan standard of individual virtue is

---

128. Limburg (2007) 267: "We must understand that the purpose of the description [of Quadra's depravity in 1.16] is to make one refrain from this vice.... Although it thus seems possible to speak of a moralizing intent for the passage, *its effect is less certain. Readers may well have been enticed rather than deterred by the vice described*, or scandalized by Seneca's graphic description" (my emphasis). Cf. for the titillating effect Richlin (1983) 221, Gross (1989) 59 and Gauly (2004) 128.

129. See Section II above in this chapter.

130. (2004) 262.

131. Toohey (2004) 262.

132. Bartsch (2006) 189.

133. Bartsch (2006) 191.

controlled and legitimated by obedience to Stoic principles; but does he nevertheless explore the fragility of subjectivist ethics by so graphically portraying Quadra's antiphilosophy of carnal self-scrutiny? Quadra takes delight, it seems, in parodying the familiar philosophical injunction to "know thyself" at 1.16.7;[134] and in this knowing action before his mirror, he so well exemplifies the basic problem Bartsch elegantly defines at the close of her study: the "problem of a philosophy that claims to have an answer to the human passions, but so precariously places its trust in the mirror of the self."[135] No one, that is, could be more assiduously "Stoic" in self-inspection, and yet no one less Stoic in maximizing his narcissistic self-indulgence before the mirror.

After the Quadra episode, Book 1 ends on a pessimistic note, with the luxury mirror grafted on to the familiar literary apparatus of the lost Golden Age at 1.17.4–10.[136] Luxury and vice, complains Seneca, have grown enormously, transgressing old boundaries:

> ...adeo...omnia indiscreta sunt diuersissimis artibus ut quidquid mundus muliebris uocabatur, sarcinae uiriles sint—omnes dico, etiam militares. iam speculum ornatus tantum causa adhibetur? nulli non uitio necessarium factum est.
>
> 1.17.10

> ...all distinctions are now so confused by all manner of contrivances that whatever used to be called female toiletries are now standard issue for men—all men, I mean, even soldiers. Is the mirror now used only for grooming? No, there's no vice for which it has not become essential.

While the *sapiens* contemplates the integrated *mundus*, what commands attention here is the very different *mundus muliebris*[137] in a world integrated (cf. *indiscreta*) by vice, not by a higher philosophy. Quadra lies dead, killed by his own slaves (1.16.1), but Roman mirrors continue to reflect his brand of self-regarding corruption. In at least this respect the values of Quadra win out at the book's close in Seneca's indictment of the contemporary moral climate. Could it be that

---

134. See Section IV n. 48 above in this chapter.

135. Bartsch (2006) 281.

136. On this passage cf. the beginning of Section VI above in this chapter.

137. For the wordplay cf. 7.31.2 and see Section VI n. 115 above in this chapter.

Quadra thus steals the show from the *sapiens*, and from the supposedly superior wisdom modeled earlier in the preface to Book 1? An intriguing possibility, but one Seneca perhaps anticipates by ensuring that we know from the outset that Quadra comes to a bad end (1.16.1), and that any ostensible triumph of his is as hollow as his mirror image. But despite this strategy of containment, we may yet detect in all the lurid details of the Quadra episode a descriptive energy and fascination that stretch Seneca's textual control over this star performer to breaking point. Seneca begins by asserting that he "wants to tell a little story" (*uolo tibi narrare fabellam*, 1.16.1); but after his narrative gathers pace and salacious interest, Quadra himself in a sense usurps control of the proceedings by coming to life in his own voice at 1.16.7–9, the climactic point in the episode where he defines his sexual philosophy in the confident, supremely self-aware rhetoric of a man on a mission. In response, Seneca abruptly closes the episode, suddenly killing off Quadra. Yet is this ending *truly* strong enough to countermand the impressive force of Quadra's preceding rhetoric, and to quell the transgressive energy already generated?[138]

In the various moralizing interludes that we have considered in Books 1, 3, 5 and 7, Seneca shows signs of the direct approach he attributes to his early mentor, Papirius Fabianus, who apparently held that "we must battle against the passions with a vigorous attack, not with nicety of argument; the enemy formation is to be turned by a full-frontal assault, not by tiny pinpricks; ... for vices are to be crushed, not merely nipped at" (*Dial.* 10.10.1).[139] Yet Seneca's moralizing task is daunting, and not just because of his bleak projection late in Book 7 that vice is relentlessly on the rise (7.32.1), the philosophy schools deserted (7.32.2–3). If we accept that Seneca struggles to contain the fascination his damning treatment of Quadra arouses, this struggle for closure suggestively carries over to his treatment of other deviants such as the mullet watchers of 3.17–18 and the *delicati* of 7.31–2. The

---

138. Senecan tragedy offers interesting *comparanda* for this transgressive energy, perhaps most obviously in the cases of Medea (see Hine [2000] 23–25 on "The triumph of evil") and, in the *Thyestes*, Atreus. On the latter cf. especially Schiesaro (2003) 117: "Atreus' power is doubly lethal, because it not only makes room for *nefas*, but also gives it an unquestionable aesthetic attractiveness. Atreus the poet is cunning, funny, articulate, simply irresistible. The destruction of any boundary to *nefas* and *decorum* is thus inextricably linked to his creative power, and we, the audience, must admit that one cannot exist without the other." So, too, Hostius' vile transgressiveness is inseparable from his creative power. In his own way cunning, funny, articulate, simply irresistible, Hostius might be said, like Atreus, to see his actions as "artistic achievements" (Schiesaro 59); he also approaches Atreus' "form of artistic and behavioural sublimity which transcends humanity and attracts the audience beyond and even against the purview of their ethical beliefs" (p. 127). See further for affinity between the Hostius episode and Senecan tragedy Berno (2003) 55–61.

139. On Fabianus and this passage, Williams (2003) 175–76.

paradoxical effect of his descriptive power is that he creates an underclass that actively challenges and disrupts the higher calling of the *Natural Questions*, thus setting the work in profound tension with itself. Cosmic consciousness is no easy winner here, as if soaring effortlessly above the forces of vice that represent the view from below: if it appears to be winning out at any given point in the text (and the *Natural Questions* is arguably centered on the struggle, not the result), the passions nevertheless always infect the work, as if a residual condition that continuously threatens a fresh outbreak and a new reverse.

3

The Cataclysm and the Nile

I: Introduction

Just as Seneca shifts our perspective by suddenly transporting us in the *Natural Questions* from one place (literal or conceptual) to another, from the local to the cosmic, from the limiting to the liberating, so we move in this chapter from the confines of Hostius Quadra's mirror chamber in Chapter Two to Egypt, and to the expansive wonders of the River Nile. What causes the Nile to flood in summer, that remarkable phenomenon that so challenged ancient investigators?[1] Seneca devotes a book of the *Natural Questions* to the topic, but his preferred theory (if he had one) remains elusive; for only the earlier part, perhaps a half or less, of Book 4a survives. John the Lydian offers some limited guidance in his *On the Months* as to the sources on which Seneca apparently drew in the lost portion of the book, but there is no supporting evidence for the shape and nature of the missing section.[2] A moralizing epilogue may have concluded 4a, after the pattern of the other books of the *Natural Questions*. But if we can only imagine how such an epilogue might have comple-mented the surviving preface, that preface stands as a complex minidrama in itself, and one that introduces Seneca's main subject in the book from a surprising angle.[3]

Seneca embarks here on a supplement of sorts to his dispatches to Lucilius in the contemporary *Moral Letters*:[4] the letter-like preface to Book 4a is bound for

1. For the tradition surveyed, Postl (1970) 36–89 with Frisinger (1965); concisely on the vari-ety of conjecture, Kidd (1988) 796–99 on fr. 222. For the true cause, see conveniently Lewis (1983) 108: "What really happened, as modern explorations have confirmed, was that each spring the snows melting in the mountains of Ethiopia poured billions of gallons of water into the Nile at its sources. The ensuing surge washed down the great north-south rift-valley of the African continent, entering Egypt in early June."

2. 4.107 (pp. 146.3–147.6 Wünsch); discussion in Gross (1989) 174–78.

3. In general on the preface, Berno (2003) 111–44; Gauly (2004) 210-14; Limburg (2007) 183–205.

4. Already Codoñer (1989) 1812; cf. Limburg (2007) 185–94. On the relative chronology of the *Natural Questions* and *Moral Letters*, Griffin (1976) 396, 399–400, but note p. 350 n. 3: "Unfortunately, the dates of neither work can be fixed so precisely as to make the temporal relation clear." The date of the Campanian earthquake featured in Book 6 (62 or 63 CE) is a major complication; see Introduction n. 26.

Sicily, where Lucilius is apparently now installed as procurator, in or around 62 CE.[5] The main topic of this preface is flattery:[6] Seneca expounds at length on the dangers to which a man of Lucilius' station is exposed because of false praise, that unnatural deceiver in the Senecan/Stoic sense that it diverts us from candid self-appraisal. How is this unlikely theme of flattery to be reconciled with Seneca's broader study of the physical world in the *Natural Questions*? A primary aim of this chapter is to try to identify this elusive "missing link,"[7] but as part of a larger undertaking: to suggest how key features of Seneca's philosophical project in the Nile book, and in the work more generally, are crucially conditioned by his treatment of terrestrial waters in Book 3, and especially by his celebrated account of the cataclysm that leads to periodic world destruction before renewal at 3.27–30. And it is important to stress at the outset that, even if an original book ordering of 3, 4a, 4b, 5, 6, 7, 1 and 2 should be contested, 4a demonstrably follows directly after 3.[8]

We begin in Section II with a preliminary analysis of Seneca's critique of flattery in the preface to Book 4a; then, in Section III, we consider Lucilius' own possible exposure to Senecan flattery in that preface. The implications of our reading of the preface will lead us back, in Section IV, to his depiction of the cataclysm at the end of Book 3. We then move forward in Section V to the main body of Book 4a, where our focus on the Nile will balance the preceding treatment of the cataclysm; we also touch on the moral implications of the cataclysm as a form of world catharsis in Section VI. In general, if insincerity prevails in the flatteries condemned in the preface to 4a, the guileless beneficence first of the Nile, then of nature more generally, will offer its own contrasting lesson on the unnaturalness of flattery, whether in Lucilius' Sicily or, by implication (and perhaps more to the

---

5. Griffin (1976) 91; on Lucilius in Sicily, Grimal (1980), and cf. the section on 'The Addressee, and the Original Order of the Eight Books' in my main Introduction.

6. On flattery, which of course commanded its own subfield of ancient analysis (see Diggle [2004] 181), cf. *Dial.* 4.21.7–8, 28.5, 9.1.16, *Ben.* 5.7.4, 6.30.3–6, *Letters* 45.7, 59.11, 13, 123.9 with Vottero (1989) 466 n. 13 on 4a pref. 3. See also the entertaining if slight coverage of Greco-Roman flattery in Stengel (2000) 89–108.

7. So Gauly (2004) 211, moving toward an answer based on rejection, under Nero, of the political life and withdrawal to philosophical *otium* and *contemplatio naturae*. For the core problem sharply defined, Rosenmeyer (2000) 106: "The extended harangue to Lucilius, longer than other prefaces, has nothing to do with the subject that follows, and much of it bears the stamp of Seneca wrestling with a problem that is really his own. Why he inserts it at this point is unclear; the avowed explanation—is it merely that a contemplation of the great river will turn Lucilius away from his self-absorption, or is there a putative identification of Lucilius' fancied presumption and the Nile's *tumescere*?—is too flimsy to persuade." For an interesting but perhaps overly subtle attempt to connect the Nile and flattery, Limburg (2007) 184–85.

8. See Hine (1981) 8–9.

point), in the Neronian court. After all, in his estrangement from the court after 62 CE, can Seneca fail to write from experience in detailing the devious workings and enticements of flattery?[9] Our efforts fully to contextualize the preface to 4a end, in Section VII, with an attempt to reconcile the earlier portions of the book with Seneca's incomplete critique, at the fragment's close, of earlier theories of why the Nile floods in summer.

II: *The Vice of Flattery*

That staple emphasis in ancient writing on friendship, the importance of telling apart flatterer and friend,[10] is duly invoked by Seneca at *Letters* 45.7: "Show me how I can see through this resemblance [sc. between flatterer and friend]." Without candor in friendship, the relationship can find no bedrock in truth.[11] Seneca himself asserts this candor as a *sine qua non* much earlier in his correspondence with Lucilius:

> sed si aliquem amicum existimas cui non tantundem credis quantum tibi, uehementer erras et non satis nosti uim uerae amicitiae. tu uero omnia cum amico delibera, sed de ipso prius: post amicitiam credendum est, ante amicitiam iudicandum…cum placuerit fieri, toto illum pectore admitte; tam audaciter cum illo loquere quam tecum…quid est quare ego ulla uerba coram amico meo retraham? quid est quare me coram illo non putem solum?
>
> *Letters* 3.2–3[12]

But if you consider anyone a friend whom you do not trust as much as you trust yourself, you are seriously mistaken and fail to understand sufficiently what true friendship means. Certainly, ponder everything with a friend, but first ponder about him. After a friendship is formed, you must trust; before it is formed, you must judge.…When you have decided to admit a friend, welcome him wholeheartedly. Speak as boldly with him as you do with yourself.…Why should I hold back any words in the presence of my friend? Why should I not regard myself as alone when in his company?

---

9. Cf. Vottero (1989) 466 n. 13 on Seneca's "esperienza diretta" of such flattery.

10. Also a familiar topic of the rhetorical schools; see conveniently Woodman (1977) 129 on Vell. 2.102.3.

11. Cf. for the familiar idea Cic. *Amic.* 92: "pretence [*simulatio*] is especially inimical to friendship; for it destroys truth, without which the word friendship cannot have meaning."

12. See on this passage Konstan (1996) 13–14.

The Senecan persona in the preface to *Natural Questions* 4a has a special claim to this candor—a claim based not just on his relationship with Lucilius as concurrently revealed or constructed in the *Moral Letters*, but also on the pledge of sincerity supplied by Seneca's self-presentation in his preface to *Natural Questions* 3. As we saw earlier,[13] the *conuersio ad se* enacted in that preface requires throwing off all the external encumbrances that interfere with his new undertaking in the *Natural Questions*. The self projected in Book 3 is liberated, authentic, true to itself; and this authenticity is carried into the preface to Book 4a, where it underwrites his persona as Lucilius' true and trustworthy intimate, the polar opposite of the flatterers against whom Seneca subsequently warns his friend (4a pref. 3–22). After Seneca's emancipation "to survey the world" (*mundum circumire*) in the preface to Book 3, we return to the specifics of localized place and preoccupation when, in the preface to Book 4a, Lucilius apparently relishes his own new turning:

> Delectat te, quemadmodum scribis, Lucili uirorum optime, Sicilia et officium procurationis otiosae, delectabitque si continere id intra fines suos uolueris, nec efficere imperium quod est procuratio.
>
> 4a pref. 1

> To judge by what you write, my excellent Lucilius, you take delight in Sicily and your office of procurator, with its leisure time; and you will continue to take delight if you are willing to keep all this within its own bounds, and not treat a procuratorship as supreme power.

Far from flattering Lucilius on his new position, Seneca views it all too candidly from the (belittling) perspective of his own new position in detachment from the world; and when he urges Lucilius to keep his duties *intra fines*, he perhaps evokes with nice irony the obsession with local limit and boundary that the cosmic mind-set ridicules elsewhere in the *Natural Questions*.[14] After Seneca's uncompromising *conuersio ad se*, Lucilius' divided existence between public service and private vocation marks an initial fracturing of that philosophical wholeness as we move away from the preface of Book 3. Lucilius may yet devote himself to philosophy in the time he has available (cf. 4a pref. 1: "I know how disinclined you are to ambition, and how devoted to leisure and study"). But the flatterers who surround him in Sicily symbolize in their insincerity our further alienation from that opening vision of complete integrity of self: as we progress from the cosmic

---

13. Chapter One, Section III.

14. Cf. 1 pref. 7–9, and see further Chapter One, Section III.

orientation of the preface to Book 3 to the particulars of Lucilius' posting to Sicily amid such "a hustle of people and things" (*turbam rerum hominumque*, 4a pref. 1), we descend from the divine to the mundanely human (cf. 3 pref. 11), from light to dark, from truth to dissimulation.

The flatterers of Book 4a thus form another, albeit less spectacular, constituency within the population of deviants who, as we saw in the last chapter, counter the uplifting thrust of the *Natural Questions* with their steady downdraft of corruption. If vices are "still making progress" (*adhuc in processu uitia sunt*, 7.31.1), flattery too hardens here from relative discreetness to a brazenness paradoxically relying on exposure for success:

> alius adulatione clam utetur, parce, alius ex aperto, palam, rusticitate simulata, quasi simplicitas illa, non ars sit. Plancus, artifex ante Vitellium maximus, aiebat non esse occulte nec ex dissimulato blandiendum.[15] 'perit' inquit 'procari si latet.' plurimum adulator cum deprensus est proficit, plus etiamnunc si obiurgatus est, si erubuit...
>
> Ita est, mi Iunior: quo apertior est adulatio, quo improbior, quo magis frontem suam perfricuit, cecidit alienam, hoc citius expugnat. eo enim iam dementiae uenimus ut qui parce adulatur pro maligno sit.
>
> 4a pref. 5–6, 9

> One person will use flattery secretly and sparingly, another openly and without disguise, with a feigned uncouthness, as if it were a case of guilelessness, not artifice. Plancus, the greatest practitioner of flattery before Vitellius, used to say that flattery must not be delivered furtively or with concealment. "Your wooing is wasted," he says, "if it is concealed." A flatterer achieves most when he is caught in the act, and even more if he is rebuked, if he blushes...
>
> So it is, my dear Iunior: the more open flattery is, the more shameless, the more it wipes the blushes from its own face and brings a blush to another, then the more quickly it wins out. For our madness has reached the point where someone who uses flattery sparingly is regarded as miserly.

---

15. Surely L. Munatius Plancus, cos. 42 BCE. So Vottero (1989) 467 n. 17, *pace* Oltramare (1929) 2.173 n. 2; the latter favors the son of our Plancus, cos. 13 CE, presumably (cf. Parroni [2002] 548) to find a nearer contemporary for Seneca. Velleius Paterculus in particular is harsh in his characterization of our Plancus: see Woodman (1983) 137 on 2.63.3, 216 on 2.83.1. For the words attributed to Plancus below as possibly drawn from a comic poet, and perhaps even "un frammento di senario," Grilli (1963) 102–103. For L. Vitellius, cos. 34, 43 and 47 and father of the future emperor Aulus Vitellius, cf. Tac. *Ann.* 6.32.4 ("through dread of Gaius Caesar and intimacy with Claudius, he shifted into a state of repulsive servility, and is regarded today as a model of obsequious ignominy"), 12.4.1, 14.49.1; further, Vottero (1989) 468 n. 18.

This shamelessness is in keeping with the lack of inhibition and the drive toward ever more explicit self-display elsewhere in the *Natural Questions*: in Quadra's fascination with his every further contortion before his mirrors in 1.16, for example, or in the re-finements that the *delicati* make to bodily ornamentation at 7.31. The element of spec-tacle—of being seen to approach the target with open flattery—is underscored by the language of gladiatorial combat,[16] which casts Lucilius as no match for expert oppo-nents who will inevitably find their target even "through his armor" (*per ornamenta*, 5); and Plancus, that larger-than-life Bernini of Blandishment (cf. *artifex*) who shame-lessly parades his manifesto of "brazen is best" (§5), contributes further to the theatri-cal feel of a section (§§5–7) in which Lucilius, in his role as governor, is dramatically cast amid "many a Plancus" in Sicily (*futuros multos in persona tua Plancos cogita*, 6).[17] Yet if we see dark humor in the powerful Lucilius' vulnerability here, Seneca quickly turns the tables on Plancus by introducing a very different class of character at §6:

> cogita...hoc non esse remedium tanti mali, nolle laudari. Crispus Passie-nus,[18] quo ego nil cognoui subtilius in omnibus quidem rebus, maxime in distinguendis et enarrandis uitiis, saepe dicebat adulationibus <nos> non cludere ostium sed operire, et quidem sic quemadmodum opponi amicae solet, quae si impulit grata est, gratior, si effregit.

> Realize that...reluctance to accept praise is no remedy against such a great evil. Crispus Passienus—I never knew anyone of greater shrewdness in all matters, but especially in telling apart and describing different kinds of fault—Crispus often used to say that we do not slam the door on flat-tery but close it gently, in the way it is usually closed on a mistress. If she pushes against it, we are pleased, and still more so if she breaks it down.

The comedic overtones of the *amica* at the door, that reversal of the more conven-tional "roistering male,"[19] contribute to the increasingly playful tenor of the pref-ace; and part of the playfulness lies in the decidedly unflattering juxtaposition of

---

16. Cf. Vottero (1989) 467 n. 16.

17. *in persona tua* effectively "in your case" (*OLD persona* 5c), but for the implication of "(dra-matic) role," *OLD* 2a. Hine (2010b) 54 translates: "Realize that *in your position* you will en-counter many Plancuses" (my emphasis); cf. already Scarpat Bellincioni (1986) 93 for *in persona tua* as "nei tuoi confronti," i.e., "toward you," with the implication of "given the posi-tion you occupy, the personage you are."

18. Cos. 27 and 44; via second marriage to Agrippina, stepfather to Nero until his death in 47, possibly through poisoning at Agrippina's instigation (further, Vottero [1989] 468 n. 20). He is plausibly the recipient of two epigrams attributed to Seneca, nos. 14 and 53 Dingel (2007) 54–55 and 82–83 with 22–23, 135–36 and 269–71.

19. Nisbet and Rudd (2004) 195 on Hor. *Carm.* 3.15.8–9.

crude Plancus and shrewd Crispus. Then the Cynic Demetrius takes center stage in §§7–8,[20] speaking in his own voice and offering his own sarcastic condemnation of the *ars blandiendi*. Seneca recalls him saying to "a certain powerful freedman [*cuidam libertino potenti*] that he [i.e., Demetrius] found an easy path to riches, on the day he came to think better of his high principles":

> 'nec inuidebo uobis' inquit 'hac arte; sed docebo eos quibus quaesito opus est... quemadmodum non solum facili sed etiam hilari uia pecuniam faciant gaudentisque despolient. te' inquit 'longiorem Fido Annaeo iurabo et Apollonio pycte, quamuis staturam habeas <pi>theci cum Thraece compositi. hominem quidem non esse ullum liberaliorem non mentiar, cum possis uideri omnibus donasse quidquid dereliquisti.'
>
> 4a pref. 7–8

> "I won't begrudge any of you this skill [sc. of flattery], but I'll teach those who need an income... how to make money and rob happy victims by a route that is not just easy but also enjoyable. You," he said, "I'll swear that you're taller than Annaeus Fidus and Apollonius the boxer, even though you have the build of a monkey paired with a Thracian gladiator.[21] Indeed, I'll not be lying when I say that no one is more generous than you; for you could be viewed as having gifted to everyone all that you've let them keep."

A witty speech that draws a fine line between tact and insult. If Seneca's Demetrius uses *te* in the nonspecific sense, he offers a harmless, hypothetical example of the bare-faced flattery that can apparently enrich one in an age of deafness to hyperbolical absurdity. But what if we identify "you" with the *libertinus potens* who is Demetrius' primary addressee? His words instantly take on added bite; yet Demetrius can always plead innocence by invoking the alibi of nonspecific *te*.

Demetrius' speech well illustrates the complexities of tonal manipulation and play extending throughout the preface. We shall soon find Lucilius himself teased and entrapped by this network, but first a crowning example of the ludic wit with which Seneca lightens his lecture on flattery, as if in keeping with the informal,

---

20. Seneca's admired friend (cf. *uirorum optimum*, *Letters* 62.3), for whom conveniently Goulet-Cazé (1996) 393 (there given as Demetrius of Corinth, not Sunium) with Kindstrand (1980).

21. Text as printed by Hine (1996a) 168.53–4; while there is no evidence for monkeys and Thracians paired in the arena, the point is rather "the contrast in size and the humorous improbability of the pairing" (Hine [1996b] 70). The gladiator (?) Annaeus Fidus (perhaps a freedman of Seneca? Cf. Vottero [1989] 470 n. 26) and Apollonius the athlete are otherwise unknown; in this context of insincere flattery, Demetrius' naming of Fidus ("faithful") is itself charged with irony (cf. Hine [2010b] 198 n. 8).

epistolary feel of this missive to Sicily. At §19 he turns to poetic quotation colorfully to reinforce his warning to Lucilius to be wary of flattery at every turn ("start
to be afraid of everyone, beginning with me"):

> Vergilianum illud exaudi, 'nusquam tuta fides,' aut Ouidianum, 'qua terra
> patet, fera regnat Erinys: in facinus iurasse putes,' aut illud Menandri (quis
> enim non in hoc ingenii sui magnitudinem concitauit, detestatus consen-
> sum generis humani tendentis ad uitia?): omnes ait malos uiuere, et in
> scaenam, uelut rusticus, poeta prosiluit; non senem excipit, non puerum,
> non feminam, non uirum, et adicit non singulos peccare nec paucos, sed
> iam <sceleri> scelus esse contextum.[22]
>
> Listen to this line of Virgil: "Nowhere can I safely place my trust"
> [*Aen.* 4.373]. Or of Ovid: "As far as the earth extends, the savage Erinys
> holds sway: you'd think that mankind had entered into a wicked conspir-
> acy" [*Met.* 1.241–2]. Or listen to Menander (for who has failed to rouse
> the full greatness of his abilities to address this topic, out of loathing for
> the human race's universal tendency towards vice?): he says that all live
> evil lives. The poet leaps on to the stage playing the rustic. Old man, young
> boy, woman, man: he makes no exceptions, and adds that it's not individu-
> als who sin, or a small number of people, but that crime is now enmeshed
> with crime.

Seneca neatly adduces Dido's anguished words after her faith in Aeneas is brutally
destroyed by his betrayal (cf. *perfide, Aen.* 4.366); but her outburst in line 373 is
also predicated on her loss of faith in Juno, her alleged protectress, and in Jupiter
himself in lines 371–2: "Now, now neither mighty Juno / nor the Saturnian father
looks on all this [that I am going through] with righteous eyes." If in Seneca we
recall that, for Dido, Jupiter has "forgotten all justice,"[23] the recollection quickly
gathers irony; for the words Seneca subsequently quotes from Ovid are spoken in
their original context by Jupiter himself, on the occasion of the divine assembly
that he calls in his outrage at the shocking impiety of Lycaon, king of Arcadia, in
Metamorphoses 1 (163–252). Lycaon pays for his offense against the god—testing
Jupiter's divinity by setting before him a feast of human flesh—by being transformed into a wolf (1.237). Could it be that, after the first quotation from *Aen.*
4.373, Seneca's Jupiter again "forgets all justice" in the Ovidian quotation, ruling

---

22. <sceleri> *scelus esse contextum* Hine (1996a) 172.136–7 after Watt (1994) 194, who compares *Dial.* 3.16.3 *animus . . . sceleribus scelera contexens* ("[the soul] weav[ing] its mesh of crimes,"
Cooper and Procopé [1995] 33).

23. Austin (1955) 116 on 371.

that the whole of mankind, and not just Lycaon, must be punished because of what the god perceives as universal wickedness?[24] If so, the irony can perhaps be pressed further: after sentencing the whole of humankind to destruction (albeit with the promise that a new race of beings will be created: 1.251–2), Ovid's Jupiter first plans to scorch the earth with his bolt but then changes his mind, opting instead to overwhelm the world by cataclysm (1.260–312). Before he proceeds to his account of the Nile's summer inundation, Seneca wittily evokes in the knowing reader the Ovidian flood of all floods; and he also returns us momentarily to the cataclysm that rages in 3.27–30, a passage that is itself drenched in Ovidian quotation from *Metamorphoses* 1, and which deploys the same moralizing emphasis (the cataclysm as punishment; cf. 3.29.5)[25] that underlies the Ovidian excerpt at 4a pref.19.

After Virgil, Ovid is the Roman poet most often cited in Senecan prose, with the great majority of borrowings drawn from the *Metamorphoses*.[26] On the Greek side, however, the only explicit and unambiguous naming of the comic poet Menander in the extant Senecan corpus is found here,[27] where Seneca's admiration for the Greek's strong moralizing capacities[28] may at least partly explain his inclusion alongside his two most favored Roman poetic sources. But two additional explanations may be hazarded. First, the allusion to Menander "leaping on to the stage playing the rustic [*uelut rusticus*]": if we assume that Menander here takes the stage figuratively and in a character of his creation,[29] the voice that melodramatically condemns the pandemic of human corruption projects in its rustic *simplicitas* a positive moral simplicity. Here, in this Senecan visit to the Menandrian theater, is a staged *rusticitas* of an upright, plain-speaking kind, in telling contrast to the *rusticitas simulata*, that pretence of gaucheness, with which the cynical

---

24. Cf. Habinek (2002) 51; already Ahl (1985) 79 ("We can make little case for justice").

25. See Section VI below in this chapter.

26. See Mazzoli (1970) 238–39, with pp. 231 and 240 for his statistical tabulations for Virgil and Ovid respectively. In his prose works, the great majority of Seneca's borrowings from the *Metamorphoses* occur in the *Natural Questions*—according to Mazzoli 240, eighteen citations = thirty-six verses, against twelve citations = thirty-one verses in the aggregate of the *Letters*, *Dialogues* and *On Favors*.

27. A Menander recurs at *Apoc.* 15.2, but suggestion that he is our Menander is for Eden (1984) 150 "pointless"; Mazzoli (1970) 178 n. 70 is more open-minded.

28. See Mazzoli (1970) 177.

29. *Pace* Sinko (1937), surely not the poet himself on stage in person: Mazzoli (1970) 177–78 and n. 69 with Setaioli (1988) 61 and n. 223 and Parroni (2002) 550. The comedy to which Seneca alludes (4a pref. 19 = fr. 931 p. 267 Körte-Thierfelder, 674 p. 338 Kassel-Austin) is unknown.

adulator deliberately overdoes his flattery for crudely transparent impact in §5. Second, and to develop this contrast between the Menandrian *rusticus* and the Senecan flatterer, can Seneca mention Menander without stirring recollection of the great powers of realism for which Menander was so lionized in antiquity? "O Menander and life, which of you imitated which?" So apparently asked Aristophanes of Byzantium;[30] and Menander is similarly hailed as the "mirror of life" in the later Roman tradition, with Quintilian for one a deep admirer: "So perfect is his whole representation of life [*omnem uitae imaginem*], so great is his store of invention and his power of expression, and so well does he adapt himself to every situation, character and emotion" (*Inst.* 10.1.69).[31] Does Menander's reputation for realism make its own subtle impact on the Senecan preface? The flatterers whom Seneca reviles are themselves skilled artists (cf. again Plancus as *artifex* at §5), so adept at role play. But if Seneca's rare, and therefore all the more striking, allusion to Menander in §19 triggers memory of his famed realism, those flatterers emerge in a still worse light; for quite apart from Menander's moral superiority here as a voice against vice, their methods and motivations are far beneath the higher art of character simulation in which the Greek apparently so excelled.

III: Lucilius in the Preface

The self-consciousness that the preface to Book 4a promotes in Lucilius (and us) not only works to qualify his own (self-)importance as procurator of Sicily by placing his new role in perspective (cf. *continere id intra fines suos*, 1), and to breed wariness of the potential flatterers who apparently surround him; it is also literary, in that irony and tonal shift complicate the superficial certainties of Seneca's ministrations against flattery. If one defense against *adulatores* is blunt dismissal of the sort sampled at 4a pref. 13—"When a flatterer approaches you, say: 'Why don't you take those words of yours…to someone who is willing to listen to whatever you say and to reply in kind?'"[32]—a more internalized approach is offered through the mode of self-praise rehearsed in §§14–17:

> cum cupieris bene laudari, quare hoc ulli debeas? ipse te lauda. dic: 'liberalibus me studîs tradidi. quamquam paupertas alia suaderet, et ingenium eo duceret ubi praesens studi pretium est, ad gratuita deflexi: ad carmina

---

30. Syrian. *In Hermog.* 2 p. 23.10–11 Rabe = Men. *Test.* 32 p. 7 Körte-Thierfelder = *Test.* 83 p. 25 Kassel-Austin.

31. Further on the Roman legacy, Peterson (1891) 64–65 on 10.1.69 with Mazzoli (1970) 177 n. 65.

32. Cf. for this direct approach *Letters* 59.13.

me et ad salutare philosophiae contuli studium.[33] ostendi in omne pectus
cadere uirtutem, et eluctatus natalium angustias, nec sorte me sed animo
mensus, par maximis steti.'

4a pref. 14–15

When you want to be suitably praised, why be indebted to anyone for it?
Praise yourself. Say: "I have devoted myself to liberal studies. Although
poverty urged me in other directions and tempted my talents toward a
career that brought immediate rewards for study, I turned aside to profit-
less pursuits: I devoted myself to poetry and to the beneficial study of philosophy. I have shown that virtue can find a place in every breast, and,
overcoming the limitations of my birth and measuring myself not by my
lot in life but by my intellect, I have stood equal to the greatest men."

At first sight the words that Seneca speaks in Lucilius' voice would seem to offer
a solid, unpretentious account of a life devoted to literature and philosophy, of an
impressive rise from relatively humble beginnings (§15), of personal loyalty out-
weighing the risks of dangerous associations in dark times under Gaius and Claudius (§§15–16),[34] and of an admirable resolve in refusing to seek refuge in suicide
amid the threat of torture and execution under Gaius (§17). When Seneca reverts
to his own voice in §18, he corroborates Lucilius' self-appraisal in §§14–17 by
bearing further witness to his friend's good character ("Add now that your mind
has not been won over by gifts"). But then a surprise:

post haec ipse te consule uerane an falsa memoraueris: si uera sunt, coram
magno teste laudatus es, si falsa, sine teste derisus es.
   Possum et ipse nunc uideri te aut *captare* aut experiri. utrumlibet crede
et omnes timere a me incipe.

4a pref. 18–19

After this, ask yourself whether what you've just said about yourself is true
or false. If it is true, you are praised in the presence of a great witness; if
false, no one is a witness to your being a laughingstock.

---

33. On the punctuation here (*ad gratuita deflexi: ad carmina...*), Hine (1996b) 70–71.

34. For details on associations (*in amicitia Gaetulici*, 15) and machinations (Messallina, Narcissus, 15), see Vottero (1989) 474 nn. 44–47 with Delatte (1935) 371, and cf. Griffin (1976)
52, 61 (Seneca quietly includes himself in describing Lucilius' loyalty to enemies of Messallina
and Narcissus?).

  I, too, can now seem to be either trapping you or testing you myself. Believe either option, and start to be afraid of everyone, beginning with me.

With this afterword Seneca wittily complicates the tone of his and Lucilius' (self-)
praises in §§14–18. In retrospect, does he write in §§14–17 in the manner of the
true friend who puts into Lucilius' mouth apparently candid (self-)praise without
embellishment? Or can we detect a hint of flattery (*captare*; cf. §3: "flatterers are
experts at courting their superiors," *ad captandos superiores*) in the way that he
indirectly praises Lucilius in the latter's assumed voice in §§14–17 and then offers
his own, seemingly independent corroboration in §18?

  Of course, the word *flattery* is itself problematic: if we follow a standard modern
definition of the term,[35] we might reasonably absolve Seneca of delivering blatantly
false praises in §§14–18. After all, his afterword in §§18–19 (quoted above) would then
lose all of its witty elusiveness and become transparently insulting, at least in the eyes
of those insiders among Seneca's contemporary readership (Lucilius himself of course
chief among them) who would all too clearly recognize the gross distortions in his
flatteries. If, on the other hand, flattery is more leniently interpreted as exaggerated
rather than straightforwardly insincere praise, we might suspect that Seneca flatters
through hyperbole in §§14–18, even though his tone may well appear no more excessive there than in many other passages delivering high praise to his loved ones elsewhere in his corpus.[36] True, Seneca was hardly incapable of what certain interpreters
have viewed as grotesque flattery: a notorious case in point is his high praise of Polybius, Claudius' powerful freedman, in his *Consolatio ad Polybium* (= *Dialogue* 11),
written in (probably) 43 CE ostensibly to comfort his addressee upon his brother's
death. It might be argued that Seneca's flattering tone to Polybius does nothing more
than reflect his attunement to the idiom of his times. Yet his portrayal of Claudius in
that same *Consolatio*, and especially the problematic tone of the invented speech that
Claudius delivers at 14.2–16.3,[37] also offer a compelling example of Seneca's interest in
the potential multivalence of (literary) flattery well before he experiments with the
phenomenon in the preface to *Natural Questions* 4a.

  For present purposes, however, it is not so much the degree of exaggeration or
untruth that is of interest in the preface, but rather how Seneca complicates his
tone—flattering or not, true or false?—through his manipulation of different narrative voices. Does Seneca test (*experiri*) Lucilius by challenging him, and us, to be
wary of the doublespeak in play in §§14–18, the delivery of indirect Senecan flattery

---

35. *OED* 1: "false or insincere praise."

36. So, e.g., *Dial.* 6.24.1–4 (Metilius), 12.16.2–7 (Helvia).

37. See Griffin (1976) 415–16 with Fantham (2007) 185–86.

in the guise of self-praise? Is Seneca's high praise made to appear more convincing to us, and less flattering, because it is expressed in Lucilius' "own" voice in §§14–17, not Seneca's? By provoking such questions, the text itself suggestively promotes wariness (cf. again *omnes timere a me incipe*) through the tonal ambivalences of Seneca's voice control;[38] and further difficulties are perhaps felt when Lucilius' (self-)portrayal in §§14–17 is compared with his characterization in the *Moral Letters*. As Miriam Griffin remarks, in *Natural Questions* 4a pref. 1 "Lucilius is *ambitioni alienus*, but in *Ep.* 19–22 he has to be cured of ambition."[39] As we saw above, at 4a pref. 14 Lucilius is said to have eschewed profitable career options to turn instead to unremunerative literature and philosophy, but in the *Letters* he appears more driven by gain and less ready to make sacrifices for the philosophical life: "I don't yet have enough: when I've reached the desired amount, then I shall devote myself completely to philosophy" (17.5). Of course, Lucilius' shifting characterization in *Natural Questions* 4a and in the *Moral Letters* respectively might at least partly be explained by differences of agenda in the two works. After all, Lucilius "is given a spiritual development of incredible rapidity" in the *Letters*,[40] a feature absent in the *Natural Questions*, and one that contributes to the "synthetic quality" that Griffin discerns more broadly in his characterization in the *Letters*.[41] But if we *do* grant Seneca license to create and exploit tensions between the two works, is the portrait in *Natural Questions* 4a consciously enhanced, even "un peu flatté"?[42] Does he signal this exaggeration in his invitation to Lucilius to consider "whether what you've just said about yourself is true or false" (§18)? And a further possibility: Does Seneca gently underscore his earlier message to Lucilius to keep his official duties in perspective (4a pref. 1) by saying little in praise of his performance in Sicily? "In the tribute to Lucilius' virtues" at 4a pref. 18, remarks Griffin, "those he would exercise as procurator come last and receive least elaboration: freedom from greed, frugality."[43] If we are troubled by the possible shades of flattery that may tinge Seneca's praises in §§14–18, the relative absence of high praise on a Sicilian front makes its own point in §18.

Another troubling aspect of the preface concerns Seneca's characterization of his brother, L. Junius Gallio Annaeanus, adopted by L. Junius Gallio, the

---

38. Cf. for this approach Citroni Marchetti (1994) 4573–74.

39. Griffin (1976) 350 n. 3 after Gercke (1895) 326–27; cf. also 1 pref. 6 for Lucilius credited with a lack of *ambitio*.

40. Griffin (1976) 351.

41. (1976) 350.

42. Delatte (1935) 372.

43. Griffin (1976) 239.

distinguished declaimer and senator, in his will.[44] In §§10–12 Seneca draws on
Gallio as an exemplary model for Lucilius to follow as one impervious to flattery;
and given the Greek reputation for flattery,[45] Gallio's experience as proconsul of
Achaea in 51–2 CE[46] perhaps gives him special relevance as a model for Lucilius
under siege in Sicily. Gallio is introduced as follows:

> solebam tibi dicere Gallionem, fratrem meum, quem nemo non parum amat,
> etiam qui amare plus non potest, alia uitia non nosse, hoc unum odisse. ab
> omni illum parte temptasti: ingenium suspicere coepisti omnium maximum
> et dignissimum, quod consecrari malles quam conteri—pedes abstulit.
>
> 4a pref. 10

> I used to tell you that my brother Gallio—who is not loved as much as he
> deserves even by those who couldn't love him more—knew nothing of other
> vices but loathed this one. You tried him on every side. You started to express
> admiration for his intellect as the greatest of all intellects, and fully deserving
> to be treated with reverence rather than contempt; he was gone.[47]

In an interesting note on *ab omni... temptasti*, T. H. Corcoran, the Loeb
editor, remarks that "[t]hroughout the rest of Sections 10, 11, 12 Seneca treats
Lucilius' attempts to flatter Gallio, and the results, as past facts. In English it
sounds better when treated as hypothetical."[48] If we adopt this (questionable)
hypothetical reading, Lucilius is only potentially a flatterer. But if we stand by
the straight perfect that delivers past facts, we confront the embarrassment
that Corcoran surely sought to avoid by his deft but desperate measure: Lucilius is an exponent of the very evil against which Seneca is striving to protect
him (cf. §3: "Keep yourself apart from the crowd as much as possible, so
that you expose no side of yourself to flatterers").[49] Seneca's, and indirectly

---

44. See Griffin (1976) 48 and n. 2 (the adoption "attested by 52").

45. See, e.g., Morton Braund (1996) 189 on Juv. 3.86–91 on this *adulandi gens prudentissima*.

46. Date: Griffin (1976) 83 and n. 5.

47. "[H]e ran away" (Hine [2010b] 54); for the idiom cf. *Dial.* 2.19.1.

48. Corcoran (1971–72) 2.9 n. 3. Cf. in criticism Winterbottom (1976) 47.

49. For Lucilius as flatterer, already Berno (2003) 119, 125–28. This despite Lucilius' characterization at 1 pref. 6: "You do not present a false front, nor do you shape your speech to suit
someone else's purpose." Or could it be that the "you" in play in most of 4a pref. 10 is not
necessarily Lucilius himself but another version of the impersonal *tu*, or of the fictional interlocutor, who appears so frequently in Senecan prose? Conceivably so; in which case Lucilius is
absolved from embarrassment. Yet if the "you" in §10 suddenly switches from Lucilius to some

Lucilius', stress in §11 on Gallio's unaffected charm (*comitatem et incompositam suauitatem*) merely draws implicit attention to the contrived nature of Lucilius' own *blanditiae*.

Gallio himself is made loosely to resemble the Stoic *sapiens* in his steady affability and honesty (§11), his wisdom and obduracy (*eius prudentiam et in euitando ineuitabili malo pertinaciam*, 12) and his imperviousness to flattery (*inexpugnabilem*, 11).[50] Confronted with this daunting model, Lucilius is again (in)directly cut down to size, his ego placed within bounds (cf. *intra fines*, 1). But in reporting Lucilius' flatteries, Seneca himself also elaborates on Gallio's virtues with an expansiveness that is surely redundant to his main point, that his brother was steadfast in his resistance:

> coepisti mirari comitatem et incompositam suauitatem, quae illos quoque quos transit abducit, gratuitum etiam in obuios meritum (nemo enim mortalium uni tam dulcis est quam hic omnibus, cum interim—tanta naturalis boni uis est, ubi artem simulationemque non redolet—nemo non imputari sibi bonitatem publicam patitur)—hoc quoque loco blanditiis tuis restitit....

> 4a pref. 11

> You proceeded to admire his friendliness and unaffected charm, which captivates even those whom it encounters in passing—a kindness freely given even to people he just chances to meet (for no mortal is as gracious to one person as he is to all people; and at the same time—such is the power of natural goodness when there is no whiff of guile or pretence—everyone lets his kindness, which he shows to all, be reckoned as a debt that they incur); at this point, too, he resisted your flattery....

If the whole section in "which captivates... a debt that they incur" is taken to render Lucilius' flatteries, Seneca offers a seemingly full and impressively candid record of events. And yet, from another perspective, why this potentially embarrassing attention to detail, this public listing of his friend's itemized *blanditiae*?

---

other anonymous party, that shift would seem to be uncommonly harsh in a preface whose epistolary appearance has developed a very specific sense of "you" from the outset (cf. *Delectat te, ...Lucili uirorum optime*, 4a pref. 1). Cf. also Citroni Marchetti (1994) 4573 for another deft, but surely strained, attempt to absolve Lucilius of flattery: his *blanditiae* were sincere, and yet he nevertheless risked *appearing* as a flatterer.

50. Cf. Vottero (1989) 472 n. 35 ("L'inespugnabilità è caratteristica del sapiente"; for *inexpugnabilis* of the *sapiens*, cf. Cic. *Tusc.* 5.41); Citroni Marchetti (1994) 4573.

Of course, one response is that the greater the elaboration, the more impressive is Gallio's resistance to any and all efforts to flatter him. But a further possibility, not necessarily incompatible with the first, is that these elaborations are Seneca's own: in reporting Lucilius' attempts on Gallio ("You tried him on every side," 10), Seneca himself goes on to embroider his own flattering picture of his brother—in which case Seneca succeeds where Lucilius fails, in that Gallio is powerless to cut short (cf. *prima statim uerba praecidit*, 10) the flow at least of *Seneca's* flattering words here.

When we look back on the preface as a whole, the tonal subtleties and the indirectness that complicate Seneca's possible flattery of Gallio in §§10–12 and of Lucilius himself in §§14–18 resemble the oblique approach outlined in §5, the approach that uses flattery "secretly and sparingly" (*clam* and *parce*), in contrast to the crudeness of Plancus' open and obvious assault (*ex aperto, palam*). While Seneca's overt message throughout the preface is to be wary of flattery, the text itself enjoins caution as we, with Lucilius, strive to tell apart and choose between the ambivalences, the flatteries and possibly also the ironic teasings of his written voice(s): the challenge before Lucilius lies partly in his reading of people, partly in how to read Seneca. And, in a further twist, despite the praises of Lucilius that Seneca delivers in Lucilius' "own" voice in §§13–17, the latter may detect a less-than-flattering subtext to the preface's conclusion in §§21–2:

> longe te ab ista prouincia abducam, ne forte magnam esse historiis fidem credas et placere tibi incipias quotiens cogitaueris: 'hanc ego habeo sub meo iure prouinciam quae maximarum urbium exercitus et sustinuit et fregit, cum inter Carthaginem et Romam ingentis belli praemium iacuit; quae quattuor Romanorum principum, id est totius imperi, uires contractas in unum locum uidit aluitque; <quae> Pompeii fortunam erexit, Caesaris fatigauit, Lepidi transtulit, omnium cepit; quae illi ingenti spectaculo interfuit ex quo liquere mortalibus posset quam uelox foret ad imum lapsus e summo, quamque diuersa uia magnam potentiam fortuna destrueret. uno enim tempore uidit Pompeium Lepidumque ex maximo fastigio aliter ad extrema deiectos, cum Pompeius alienum exercitum fugeret, Lepidus suum.'

> I shall draw you far away from that province of yours, in case you place great confidence in history and begin to be pleased with yourself whenever you think: "I have under my jurisdiction this province, which has both sustained and broken the armies of the greatest cities when it lay as the prize of the vast war between Carthage and Rome. It witnessed and nurtured the strength of four Roman generals—that is, the strength of the whole empire—condensed into one place. It elevated the fortunes of

Pompey, it wearied Caesar's, it transformed Lepidus' and had room for all of them.[51] Sicily was present at that great spectacle which made clear to mankind just how rapid the fall could be from the heights to the depths, and by what varied means fortune could destroy great power. For at one and the same time it saw Pompey and Lepidus thrown down from the highest pinnacle to the lowest depths, albeit in different ways: Pompey fled his enemy's army, Lepidus his own."

In contrast to Seneca's earlier injunction to Lucilius to keep his duties within bounds (*intra fines*, 1) and not to "treat a procuratorship as supreme power [*imperium*]," Lucilius' imagined words here show an opposite tendency: the world (cf. *totius imperi*) comes to Sicily, which is cast as a key battleground in the greatest Roman struggles from the first Punic War down to the thirties BCE,[52] when Sextus Pompey's grip on the island ("It elevated the fortunes of Pompey") was broken by the taxing (cf. *fatigauit*) but ultimately successful efforts of Octavian and Lepidus. Sicily now takes center stage as the place that has made or shattered the fortunes of Rome's leading players, and that oversaw Sextus' demise and Lepidus' eventual exclusion from triumviral power. In effect, the Lucilius imagined here (in)directly aggrandizes his stature as procurator by offering so grand a picture of Sicily's historical importance. We are returned by a form of ring composition to the beginning of the preface: Lucilius does indeed make an *imperium* of sorts of his procuratorship (§1) by writing himself ("I have under my jurisdiction this province") into his own formidable script both for the island's history and, we infer, for the large responsibility of its governor-in-charge. Hence the quasi-urgent need for the recalibration of perspective that Seneca announces in *longe te ab ista prouincia abducam* (§21).

But a further question beckons: Just how self-conscious is the Lucilius pictured in §§21–2? How alert is he to the possible relevance that his remarks on the vagaries of fortune might have for himself in his powerful position in Sicily? From the first in the *Natural Questions*, we have seen that the study of nature and of philosophy in general is presented as a form of escape from, and protection against, the flux and provisionality of the everyday world. So in the preface to Book 3 the refrain of *quid est praecipuum?* ("What is most important?") in §§10–16 finds one answer in rising above the claims of fortune: "What is most important? Raising your mind above the threats and promises of fortune... To raise your spirits high

---

51. *OLD capio* 25a, a nuance less contrived than "included decisively," i.e., effectively "decided" (sc. the fortunes of all four generals), in Alexander (1948) 298, where he also explains the absence of one of the *quattuor principum* ("no need to work in a mention of Antony").

52. Convenient elucidation in Vottero (1989) 480 nn. 72, 73.

above chance occurrences" (§§11, 15). The Lucilius found in imagined reflection at
4a pref. 21–2 proudly surveys Sicily's historical importance. We remember, however, that in the preface to Book 3 philosophy takes precedence over historical re-
portage and the recording of "the actions of foreign kings":

> Quanto satius est quid faciendum sit quam quid factum quaerere, ac
> docere eos qui sua permisere fortunae nihil stabile esse ab illa datum,
> munus eius omne aura fluere mobilius!
>
> 3 pref. 7

> It is far better to investigate what ought to be done rather than what was
> done, and to teach those who have entrusted their affairs to fortune that
> nothing given by fortune is secure, and that all her gifts flow away more
> rapidly than the breeze.

The enthusiastic procurator portrayed at the end of the preface to Book 4a discourses on the fickle fortunes of Sextus Pompey and Lepidus. But in the *Natural
Questions* more generally what matters is the *internalization* of the lesson that
such examples of fortune's fickleness offer; what matters is to apply the external
illustration to the process of one's own self-development toward indifference to
fortune. In this respect, the Lucilius drawn in §§21–2 apparently lacks the self-
conscious detachment Seneca also portrays as a necessary defense against flattery:
"So one must flee the world and withdraw into oneself; or even withdraw from
oneself" (*Fugiendum ergo et in se recedendum est, immo etiam a se recedendum*,
§20).[53] Will the real Lucilius addressed in Book 4a be alert to the reflexive significance of his alter ego's words on fortune in §§21–2? On this approach, the challenge set before him in §§21–2 is indeed *a se recedere*, or to withdraw from the self
as characterized there; and to escape by internalizing the life lesson that his alter
ego seems to leave external.

IV: *The Cataclysm of 3.27–30*

What, then, of the missing link that might connect this idiosyncratic preface to
Book 4a with the larger context of the *Natural Questions*? How to reconcile Seneca's disquisition on the dangers of flattery with his broader inquiry into the natural world? Certainly, within 4a itself the preface is neatly related to the rest of the
book by Seneca's method of transporting Lucilius to the Nile as a way of diverting

---

53. On the Platonizing associations of the idea here, Natali (1994) 440.

him from Sicily and his official preoccupations there. But what of any larger-scale integration within the work as a whole?

For present purposes, two factors draw important connections with the foundational Book 3, on terrestrial waters. First, if we accept that a network of ambivalence complicates the characterization of Lucilius in ways subtle and wittily ironic in the preface to 4a, the preface to 3 offers a study in contrast. As we saw earlier,[54] on offer there is a vision of enlightened detachment, a vantage point from which the ordinary interferences of life obscure our primary cosmic vision. This obscuring effect is couched in §11 in terms that have important implications for the preface to 4a:

> qui a diuinorum conuersatione quotiens ad humana reccideris, non aliter caligabis quam quorum oculi in densam umbram ex claro sole redierunt.[55]
>
> Whenever you withdraw from consorting with things divine and return to human affairs, you will be blinded, like people who turn their eyes from the bright sunlight to dark shade.

The new journey in the preface of 4a is not just to Sicily, or (by extension) to Egypt; it also constitutes a return, or a relapse after the preface to Book 3, *a diuinorum conuersatione ad humana*. The dangers of flattery, the practical burdens of being procurator of Sicily, the tonal difficulties that cast now Lucilius, now Seneca as deft flatterers in their own right, the shades of ambivalence that we monitored in Section III above: from the enlightened, god-like vision glimpsed in the preface to Book 3, our gaze is redirected to half-darkness in the new preface, where the challenge of teasing apart the ambiguities of Seneca's treatment itself reenacts, and wraps us up in, all the shadiness and provisionality that he associates with *conuersatio hominum* in the *Natural Questions* more generally.[56]

Second, in contrast to all the fine distinctions that we sampled in the preface to 4a in Sections II and III above, the cosmic viewpoint promoted in the preface to 3 is by definition total and complete, a form of integrity that leaves far behind

---

54. Chapter One, Section III.

55. For which see already Chapter One, Section II.

56. Cf. for this *conuersatio hominum* the confining effect of all the hubbub of everyday urban noise that Vottero (1998b) 292–96 hears in the *Letters* before turning (p. 296) to the intimidating sounds unleashed by the natural world in the *Natural Questions*; the serenity of the *sapiens* lies not least in his imperviousness to these different kinds of Senecan background noise.

the petty distinctions of this world.⁵⁷ Part gives way to whole: what is important is not "to have fixed a flag on the shore of the Red Sea" (3 pref. 10), to have traveled to this mere speck or that on the global map (cf. 1 pref. 11), or even to have served as procurator of Sicily, but rather "to see the all with your mind" (cf. *animo omne uidisse*, 3 pref. 10). From this cosmic perspective localized boundaries cease to matter, and the early allusion to the Red Sea in the preface to Book 3 is itself taken up in Seneca's climactic account (3.27–30) of the cataclysm that overwhelms the world and effaces all conventional distinctions as part of the process that leads to a new cosmic beginning:

> peribunt tot nomina, Caspium et Rubrum mare, Ambracii et Cretici sinus, Propontis et Pontus, cum <dilu>uies illa omnibus rebus unum aequor induxerit; peribit omne discrimen.
>
> 3.29.8

> So many names will pass away—the Caspian Sea and the Red Sea, the Ambracian Gulf and the Cretan Gulf, the Propontis and the Black Sea— when that deluge will spread a single sea over all parts. All distinctions will disappear.⁵⁸

Again, the fragmented, ambivalent tone of so much of the preface to 4a reasserts the partial, provisional human dimension in contrast to this larger Senecan emphasis in the *Natural Questions* on *undivided* oneness, the unity of the all. But the lack of candor on display in the preface to 4a also stands in contrast to nature's guilelessness as she steadily goes through her motions in 3.27–9. We shall consider in Section VI below how this guilelessness relates to a moralizing interpretation of nature's periodic destruction of mankind; but more pressing for now is the effect that Seneca's depiction of man's powerlessness in the face of the cataclysm has on his portrayal of Lucilius' self-importance, and the impression of importance that flattery projects, in the preface to 4a.⁵⁹

---

57. For the cosmic aspect of this integrity cf. the *sapiens* of *Letters* 59 who, rising above flattery (cf. §13) and all other enticements, knows always complete joy (§14), his mind reflecting the calm of the upper firmament: "Reflect, therefore, on this, that the result of wisdom is a joy that is steady and consistent. The mind of the wise man is like the supralunary firmament: there is always a state of calm there" (§16).

58. On this disintegration of boundaries in the cataclysm, heralding a return to primeval *unitas* (cf. 3.30.1), Murphy (2004) 184–88.

59. In general on the cataclysm, Hutchinson (1993) 128–31; Berno (2003) 93–102; Gauly (2004) 235–67; Wildberger (2006) 57 and 566 n. 345; Limburg (2007) 149–82.

For Brad Inwood, "[i]n the flood passage as a whole the anthropocentric nature of the deluge is prominent":[60] the sea assaults *us* (*nos*, 3.27.1), the rivers and seas all apply themselves "to the destruction of the human race" (3.27.1), agriculture fails us (3.27.4), our houses totter (3.27.6) until smaller dwellings are demolished by the torrent, then larger dwellings, and finally whole cities and peoples are swept away (3.27.7). For the few survivors who flee to the mountaintops, all "communication and travel" (*commercium ac transitus*, 3.27.11) are cut off; man's regression in 3.27 from a state of settled community to scattered desolation is complete. But while from one angle this passage (3.27) is evidently anthropocentric, from another angle the flood passage as a whole (3.27–9) reveals the opposite tendency, sweeping away humankind and all the trappings of organized society with a simple, brief flexing of cosmic muscle (cf. 3.27.2). Already in the preface to Book 3 mankind is cut down to size: "We believe that these [sc. kingdoms and empires] are great because we are small; many things draw their importance not from their own true nature but from our lowliness" (§10). What from a cosmic perspective appears tiny takes on a disproportionate scale and significance when viewed from the narrow perspective (cf. *angustias*, 1 pref. 13) of the localized mind-set, a tendency Seneca again assails at the end of Book 3, where the dynasties that rise and fall as *exempla* of shifting fortunes in the preface (§9) recur in "the kingdoms of great nations" destroyed in a mere cosmic moment at 3.29.9 ("A single day will bury the human race"). If the preface moves us toward a revised perspective on our place in the universal whole, the violence of Seneca's cataclysm does the same work more directly by shock effect, wiping away all misconceptions about our (self-) importance by simply wiping us off the map.

All the dramatic verve that Gregory Hutchinson well observes in the "successive waves" of Seneca's passage[61] thus reduces humankind to a stupefied spectator (cf. 3.27.12) of the cosmic process that will soon engulf all. The scientific eye imposes control on water at the beginning of the book, classifying types according to whether they are still, running or collected; bitter or sweet; clear or muddy, and so on (cf. 3.2–3), and carefully distinguishing different theories of how the earth generates the constant flow of waters (3.4–10). But as the waters merge together in the cataclysm, making a mockery of all such fine distinctions of water type, the controlling eye gives way at the book's close to helpless astonishment (cf. *mirantibus*, 3.27.12) at nature's matchless power. But another kind of spectator, serene and detached, also looks upon the events as if they are unfolding before his (and our) eyes. In depicting the cataclysm Seneca faces an obvious challenge: as

60. (2000) 30 = (2002) 130 = (2005) 170.

61. Hutchinson (1993) 130.

Inwood puts it, he "has to work against the implausibility of such an event, which is inevitably beyond the experience of human observers."[62] Inwood's response is to point to Seneca's own emphasis on "the unimaginable power of nature": Seneca attempts "to make such a unique event plausible" by stressing that "nothing is hard for nature" (cf. 3.27.2, 30.1).[63] And yet the implausibility of the details of the scene is arguably beside the point. What matters is Seneca's imaginative construction of a cosmic mind-set here, a form of consciousness that ranges unfettered over all ages and territories in the manner of the liberated *animus* portrayed at *Dial.* 12.11.7, for example: "its thought moves around the entire heavens [*circa omne caelum it*] and is granted access to the whole of time, past and future." So also at 12.20.2:

> terras primum situmque earum quaerit [sc. the exiled Seneca's *animus*, taking wing in its own form of philosophical liberation on Corsica], deinde condicionem circumfusi maris cursusque eius alternos et recursus; tunc quidquid inter caelum terrasque plenum formidinis interiacet perspicit et hoc tonitribus fulminibus uentorum flatibus ac nimborum niuisque et grandinis iactu tumultuosum spatium; tum peragratis humilioribus ad summa perrumpit et pulcherrimo diuinorum spectaculo fruitur, aeternitatis suae memor in omne quod fuit futurumque est uadit omnibus saeculis.
>
> My mind first seeks to know about the lands and their position, and then the nature of the sea that surrounds them, and its alternating ebb and flow. Then it investigates the expanse, full of frightening phenomena, that lies between the heavens and earth—this near space that is turbulent with thunder, lightning, wind blasts and downfalls of rain and snow and hail. Finally, after traversing the lower reaches, it breaks through to the heights above and delights in the most beautiful sight of things divine, and, mindful of its own immortality, it moves freely over all that has been and will be in every age across time.[64]

Like Inwood, T. H. Corcoran is troubled by the implausibility of the Senecan cataclysm, and he explains Seneca's marked use of the present tense as more than a device that lends vivid effect: "Seneca's treatment of the universal catastrophe as if occurring in his time may be caused by the idea that it recurs; and thus can be

---

62. (2000) 30 = (2002) 130 = (2005) 171.

63. (2000) 30 = (2002) 130 = (2005) 171.

64. Cf. for this temporal reach *Dial.* 6.26.4–5, 10.14.1, 15.5.

thought of as a permanent feature of the universe. Hence his present tenses."[65] But Corcoran's special pleading here makes no allowance for the fact that the cosmic consciousness through which Seneca focalizes our gaze in 3.27–30 can *only* see in the (timeless) present, or in a permanent condition of full ownership of all times past, present and future. His choice of tense is no stylistic affectation but contributes to the portrayal of a mind-set that attains a form of sublimity[66]— a revelatory departure from the smallness of everyday perception, and attunement instead to the rhythms of cosmic decay and rebirth.[67]

Important attention has recently been drawn to the significance in the *Moral Letters* of where author and addressee are physically located at different points in their correspondence.[68] When in *Letters* 51, for example, we find Seneca on the move, writing from Campania (cf. 49.1) to Lucilius in Sicily, that sudden change of scene shifts the terms of their epistolary (and philosophical) engagement; "[a]s precedent," *Letters* 51 "establishes the constant possibility that epistolary relations between writer and addressee (the axiom of mutual 'present absence' that motivates correspondence) may be plotted in terms of their *loci* in the Roman empire."[69] So too perhaps in the *Natural Questions*: as the preface to Book 4a opens, we find Lucilius in Sicily, exposed on all sides to the insidious flatteries that confirm the pejorative Senecan connotations elsewhere of *conuersatio hominum*.[70] Where is Seneca (or the Senecan persona) at this narrative point? We find him estranged

---

65. Corcoran (1971–72) 1.271 n. 2.

66. On Senecan experimentation with the sublime, Chapter Six, especially Section III.

67. Seneca reverts briefly to the past tense in his account of survivors clinging to mountaintops at 3.27.12: "The remnants of the human race clung (*adhaerebant*) to each of the highest peaks"; "this alone brought them solace (*hoc unum solacio fuit*)"; "in their astonishment they had no room for fear (*non uacabat timere*)." Down to 3.27.15 we witness only the first phase of the deluge, or what Seneca himself portrays as a mere prelude at 3.28.3 (*cum per ista prolusum est*). As he rouses the waters to still more awesome heights in his second narratival wave (3.28.3–7), the mountaintops are engulfed, and the few human survivors—presumably those who clung to the peaks at 3.27.12—are finally destroyed (3.28.4). Why, then, does Seneca use the past tense at 3.27.12, if he writes there *in anticipation of* the disaster that strikes only at 3.28.4? His confusion of narrative time may create its own pertinent effect in this "timeless," universal vision; and allowance should also be made for tense variation as a familiar feature of Senecan prose (see Hine [1981] 326–27 on 2.27.3; 417–18 on 2.52.2; and 446–47 on 2.59.10). But a more poignant possibility: the tenses that describe the survivors' plight at 3.27.12 already spell disaster by effectively regulating them to the past ("they did cling on, *but to no avail*") even before the waters finally engulf them at 3.28.4.

68. See Henderson (2003) 32–39, especially 32–33.

69. Henderson (2003) 33.

70. As opposed to *diuinorum conuersatio* at 3 pref. 11. For the pejorative aspect, see especially *Letters* 7, 103 and 123 (so, e.g., *inimica est multorum conuersatio*, 7.2; *ab homine homini cotidianum periculum*, 103.1).

from Nero's court and Rome after 62 CE; and at the opening of the *Natural Questions* we find him in a new turning to "surveying the world" (*mundum circumire*, 3 pref. 1; cf. *circa omne caelum it* [sc. *cogitatio animi*] at *Dial.* 12.11.7, quoted above) and detached from the ordinary business of life (cf. 3 pref. 2). Later in the preface to Book 3 the idealized place to which Seneca aspires is the elevated plane above the ordinary *sordida* of life where we "consort with god" (§11; cf. *consortium <cum> deo*, 1 pref. 6). It is from a similar vantage point or place of sublime detachment, I suggest, that we are to imagine Seneca surveying the cataclysm at 3.27–30. True liberation and contempt for earthly luxury, he asserts at 1 pref. 8, are only possible when the mind "courses round the entire universe [cf. *totum circuit mundum*]" and looks down on the narrowness of ordinary spatial and value distinctions at ground level. The narrative eye that witnesses nature's vast operations unfolding in "real" time in the cataclysm occupies a similar viewing position, as if the Senecan persona timelessly courses round the universe (cf. again *mundum circumire*, 3 pref. 1) in full philosophical freedom, carrying the reader along as a passenger, or perhaps even as an enlightened fellow traveler.

On this approach, the transition to Lucilius in Sicily at the opening of Book 4a indeed brings us down to earth as we return from the sublime to the mundane. Book closure and book opening are here used to highly creative effect in the juxtaposition of two such different philosophical locales in 3 and 4a, even if the return to *conuersatio hominum* in the preface to 4a is perhaps softened by the "unexalted gloom"[71] that already descends in the last words of Book 3. There, after the anticipated rebirth of a new age of innocence, Seneca is resigned to the eventual return of vice ("Wickedness quickly insinuates itself:…vices are learned even without a teacher," 3.30.8), a convenient point of transition into the corruptions of flattery as we read on into Book 4a.

V: Into Egypt

The wonders of Sicily (*mirabilia*, 4a.1.1) are trumped by those of Egypt (cf. *miracula*, 4a.2.6) in Seneca's treatment of the sublime Nile,[72] that "noblest of rivers" (4a.2.1). Before he turns to his formal critique of theories of why the Nile floods in summer (4a.2.17), he touches briefly on the fabled mystery of its source (4a.2.3), but without offering a theory of his own; rather, he takes us on an entertaining tour of the Nile, tracing its course and, with a hint of Herodotean color and

---

71. Hutchinson (1993) 131.

72. For the sublime aspect see [Longinus] as cited in Chapter Six, Section III. For the Nile's prominent role in the literature of *mirabilia aquarum*, Callebat (1988) 156–57 with Le Blay (2007) 122–23.

Herodotus' taste for θώματα,[73] introducing us en route to the peoples, places and animal life that exist by the river. Seneca himself visited Egypt in or before 31 CE,[74] he composed a work *On the geography and religious rites of the Egyptians* (*De situ et sacris Aegyptiorum*),[75] he may have been a driving force behind an expedition sent by Nero to investigate the source of the Nile[76] and he himself acquired extensive estates in Egypt, probably by Nero's gift.[77] Hence the possibility that a special interest in the alluvial richness of the Nile valley, and even firsthand observation of the region, inform *Natural Questions* 4a;[78] and the picturesque quality of his description down to 4a.2.15 may also reflect the popularity of Nilotic landscape art from the second century BCE onward—part of the more general Egyptomania that was especially marked in the early first century CE.[79] The famous Nile mosaic from Praeneste (modern Palestrina), dating to *ca.* 100 BCE,[80] already shows in its narratival selectivity, its panoramic bird's-eye view and its triumphalist connotations certain overlaps with later literary depictions of the Nile, Seneca's among them;[81] and by incorporating anecdotes of the Egyptian natives

---

73. On which Lloyd (1975) 141–47.

74. At *Dial.* 12.19.2 Seneca writes that he was nursed through illness *per longum tempus* by his aunt, the wife of C. Galerius, prefect of Egypt from 16 to 31 CE (canonical dates in modern scholarship, but for the question of the dates/duration of Galerius' prefectorship revisited, see Kavanagh [2001], especially 381–82); hence apparently the *terminus ante quem* of 31 for his Egyptian visit, the duration of which remains unclear (further, Griffin [1976] 43; Vottero [1998a] 20). Further on his direct experience of Egypt, Faider (1930) with Cesaretti (1989) 54.

75. Fr. VII (12) Haase = T19 Vottero (1998a) 130–31, with pp. 19–21 and 233–36; of uncertain date (Griffin [1976] 47 n. 2), but for the claims of 17–19 CE, Vottero 20.

76. See 6.8.3–4 and Chapter Six, Section V (B), with Hine (2006) 63.

77. See Griffin (1976) 287 and nn. 6 and 7 with André (2003) 174–76. But for speculation on Seneca's acquisition of Egyptian assets already by *ca.* 30 CE, Faider (1930) 86.

78. See French (1994) 177 and André (2003) 176, but Griffin (1976) 43 remains more skeptical (his Nile excursus in Book 4a "need not embody much personal observation").

79. In general on the Egyptomania phenomenon, Swetnam-Burland (2007) with Le Blay (2007) 122–26. But see also André (2003) 183 on the popularity of the Nilotic theme in Campania, which Seneca apparently visited in 63 and 64; and now the catalogue of 131 items in the *Corpus figurarum Niloticarum* assembled by Versluys (2002) 39–236 (pp. 90–170 for items from Campania).

80. 120–110 BCE: Versluys (2002) 52 after Meyboom (1995) 19. For the dating controversy conveniently surveyed, Meyboom 16–19, and cf. now Schrijvers (2007a) 233 and 234–39, favoring a post-Actium dating in the 20s BCE ("more ingenious than persuasive," Merrills [2009] 563). Since the lower section of the mosaic reveals a familiarity with Egypt and Egyptian life different from that in generic Nilotic scenes, "either the designer of the mosaic had first-hand knowledge of Egypt, or it must be an accurate copy of an Egyptian model" (Dunbabin [1999] 51).

81. Now Schrijvers (2007a), especially 225–29.

daringly shooting the Nile's rapids, or of river crocodiles battling dolphins from the sea, Seneca arguably colors his account with topoi—representations of people and fauna—familiar in the Campana reliefs (terracotta plaques with figurative representations, produced between *ca.* 50 BCE and 150 CE) which peaked in popularity in the first quarter of the first century CE.[82] Beyond this suggestive artistic dimension, however, Seneca also writes in the tradition of Greek rationalism that sought purely physical explanations for such wonders as the Nile's summer flooding presented: if "for the Egyptians the Nile was above all providential and divine... the Greek philosophers were bringing to the phenomena of the river's flooding very much their own style of explanation."[83] So at 4a.2.7 Seneca describes a ritual in which priests and prefects cast gifts of gold into the river near the so-called Veins of the Nile:[84] for J.-M. André, the *sollemne sacrum* of the *Nili uenae* is here evoked purely as spectacle—an example of how the summer flood, that jewel in the crown of Egyptian *mirabilia*, is for André wholly divested of religious significance in Seneca's account.[85]

But of special relevance for now is the harmonious relationship that Seneca portrays in 4a.2.1–15 between the Egyptians and the Nile. In contrast to the lack of candor (that epidemic of flattery) on display in the preface to 4a, a seemingly pristine and natural candor prevails in the sympathetic interactions between man and nature in the main body of the book. The Nile gives Egypt life,[86] and the river is itself suggestively brought to life in Seneca's personifying description of it. Whereas "[t]here is a striking lack of personifications of waterways or stretches of water in the Egyptian pantheon," and the Nile as such was not in fact deified,[87] in

---

82. Rauch (1999) 5; Versluys (2002) 87–90.

83. French (1994) 112.

84. On the "cultic and historical character" of this *sollemne sacrum*, Hannestad (1944).

85. André (2003) 181 ("le phénomène de la crue d'été... se trouve totalement désacralisé"). On this rationalist approach Seneca reacts against the multilayered associations of the Nile and its flood with myth, magic and ritual, on which see Bonneau (1964) 243–73 ("La crue dans le mythe osirien"), 275–314 ("La magie et la crue du Nil"), 315–60 ("Le Nil, dieu gréco-romain de la crue"), 361–420 ("Les fêtes de la crue du Nil"); also Schama (1995) 252–63.

86. For convenient background on the agricultural practicalities, Lewis (1983) 107–15.

87. For the quote above, Hornung (1982) 77; then Watterson (1984) 30 (instead of deification, the river "was represented by Hapy, the Spirit or Essence of the Nile"). But for the inundation itself depicted in the Egyptian tradition as "an apparently androgynous being with a male face, pendulous breasts, and an obese body, painted green or blue (the colors of vegetation and water)"—not strictly a god, but rather "a creative power of life"—Dunand and Zivie-Coche (2004) 270, with p. 271 for Osiris associated "at an early date... with the water of the Nile, whose fertilizing power he incarnated; they were the 'humors' that emerged from his body. But this idea was not translated into images prior to the first century of our own era."

the Greco-Roman tradition personified Neilos first comes to life in the catalogue
of children born to Oceanus and Tethys in the Hesiodic *Theogony* (338). On the
Roman side the river is a familiar personification;[88] but the dimensions of Seneca's more ambitious and extended personification find their closest parallel in the
tenth book of Lucan's *Civil War*, where Julius Caesar, now finally triumphant
over Pompey, succumbs to the seductive charms of Cleopatra at Alexandria. After
a luxurious dinner, Caesar enters into conversation with the enigmatic Egyptian
priest, Acoreus, from whom he seeks to learn about the country in general
(10.176–81), and about one matter in particular:

> sed, cum tanta meo uiuat sub pectore uirtus,
> tantus amor ueri, nihil est quod noscere malim
> quam fluuii causas per saecula tanta latentis
> ignotumque caput: spes sit mihi certa uidendi
> Niliacos fontes, bellum ciuile relinquam.
>
> 10.188–92

> But, even though such intellectual vigor is so alive in my breast,
> and such love of truth, there is nothing I would rather learn
> than the causes, hidden through long ages, that account for the Nile,
> and the secret of its origin. Give me some sure hope of seeing
> the headwaters of the Nile, and I shall abandon civil war.

As if the truer master of the situation, Acoreus responds with a suitably serpentine[89] account in three main sections, the first (10.199–218) describing astral and
planetary influences on the Nile; the second (10.219–67) refutes various theories
of the Nile's flood; and, after a (none too) subtly pointed digression on reckless
leaders who sought to uncover the Nile's secrets before Caesar (10.268–85), the
third (10.285–331) describes the Nile's course and traces its flow "through both
hemispheres" (10.301) to its obscure source in the southern hemisphere. In its way,
Acoreus' entire speech is as elusive as the river that it describes, and with a cultivated air of mystery: his "much-heralded 'secret' [sc. about the source] amounts to
little more than a rehash of the Eudoxan theory, but with high rhetorical color
added…to lend mystique to its otherwise predictable contents."[90] That mysteri-

---

88. So, e.g., Virg. *Aen.* 8.711–13; Hor. *Carm.* 4.14.46; Ov. *Met.* 1.728, 2.254–6.

89. Cf. Schama (1995) 262 (Acoreus "as serpentine as Caesar is direct"); on Acoreus' "dubious
character" and "duplicitous quality," now Barrenechea (2010) 273–80.

90. Romm (1992) 154 with p. 150 for Eudoxus. Cf. Schama (1995) 262 on Acoreus' "vexing
mixture of commonplaces and esoteric casuistry."

ous quality helps to disguise the subtext that may lurk in Acoreus' speech, which arguably challenges Caesar's invincibility by gently exposing the limits of his knowledge and dominion: the Nile remains unconquered (cf. 10.295: "Nature has revealed to no one [the Nile's] hidden source"), not least by Caesar himself.[91] For present purposes, however, a key feature of the high rhetorical color of Acoreus' speech is his personifying, second-person address to the river (10.282, 286, 296, 317, 328), with the implication that Acoreus, as an Egyptian, can claim a special affinity to the Nile that the foreign Caesar cannot. The river's human-like character is fleshed our further in its daring (*ausus*, 10.288), its anger (*iras*, 10.316) and its indignation and violence (*indignaris, lacessis*, 10.320).[92]

A second, looser but still pertinent parallel for the Nile's personification is to be found in Pliny's *Natural History*.[93] There, in accordance with Pliny's teleological and providential nature, the river colludes with human interests,[94] even "playing the part of a farmer" through its periodic flooding at 18.167 (*Nilus ibi coloni uice fungens euagari incipit*). More generally in Pliny, observes Trevor Murphy,

> [w]ith rivers, geographical description approaches biography.... From a practical point of view, of course, the progress of a river is the *Natural History*'s primary means of surveying a country's interior and listing the places it passes and the frontiers it defines. But rivers also deserve to have their life-stories told—they possess individual characters, they acquire property, and they exchange things with humanity.[95]

Pliny offers an illuminating parallel for the interactive relationship between man and nature (the Nile) that we shall momentarily consider in Seneca's case. But given that Lucan was directly acquainted with Seneca's Nile book,[96] the

---

91. With possible implications for Nero: Berti (2000) 213.

92. Further, Berti (2000) 239–40 on 316; 241 on 320; 248 on *moribus...receptis*, 329.

93. Cf. 36.58 with Carey (2003) 92 for Vespasian's reported dedication in his Temple of Peace of a statue (according to Pliny, the largest example of the Ethiopian marble known as *basanites*) of the Nile surrounded by sixteen children, each of them representing one cubit of the river's maximum growth during the flood.

94. So, e.g., 5.52: "Poured forth from this lake, [the Nile] resents [*indignatur*] flowing through sandy and barren territory, and hides itself away by its course for several days; later it bursts forth from another, larger lake...and searches, as it were, for association with humans [*hominum coetus ueluti circumspicit*]"; Beagon (1996) 290.

95. (2004) 142, 144.

96. For 4a as Lucan's main, but not his only, source, Holmes (1989) 337—part of an important reassessment (pp. 321–38) of the arguments of Diels (1886) = Burkert (1969) 379–408 for Lucan's close dependence on Seneca.

personifying features of Lucan's Nile arguably build on what he recognized as a key and conspicuous Senecan emphasis; and so, aided by this possible Lucanian insight, we now turn to the Nile's early beginnings and upbringing as recounted in Seneca's narrative.

At 4a.2.3 the language of listless spread—*peruagatus, diffusus, sparsus*—characterizes the river in its pre-state, as it were, as if a kind of primary matter,[97] before it is gathered into shape in the words *circa Philas primum ex uago et errante colligitur* ("after uncertain wandering it comes together for first time in the vicinity of Philae"). Then a factual error:

> Philae insula est aspera et undique praerupta. duobus in unum coituris amnibus cingitur, qui Nilo mutantur et eius nomen ferunt. urbem tota complectitur.
>
> 4a.2.3

The island of Philae is rugged and precipitous on all sides. It is surrounded by two rivers that are on the point of merging into one; they are changed into the Nile, and they take its name. The whole island encompasses a large town.

Seneca here confuses Philae, located just above the First Cataract,[98] with Meroe, which lay on the Nile's east bank between the Fifth and Sixth Cataracts.[99] Perhaps an innocent slip; but accidental or not, Seneca's error has the convenient effect of collecting the Nile at the acknowledged "gate of the Egyptian kingdom" (cf. *regni claustra Philae*, Luc. 10.313), which here serves as a symbolic threshold of Egyptian civilization. The possible etymological significance of Philae-Amicae as a place of "reconciliation"[100] may also bode well, at this entry point into Egypt, for Seneca's

---

97. Cf. the primordial *informis unitas* of 3.30.1.

98. For Philae, properly speaking two small islands (hence the plural name) south of Syene (modern Aswan), Jackson (2002) 118–23 with Holmes (1989) 224 on Luc. 10.313–22.

99. The confusion has long been recognized: see on previous scholarship Pfligersdorffer (1959) 374, and cf. Vitr. 8.2.6, Mela 1.50, Plin. *Nat.* 5.53 and especially Luc. 10.302–3 ("Meroe is surrounded by your widely parted waters") with Holmes (1989) 222 on 307–13.

100. So Servius *ad Aen.* 6.154 (Thilo-Hagen 2.34.1–4) on Seneca's *On the geography and religious rites of the Egyptians* (*De situ et sacris Aegyptiorum* fr. VII [12] Haase = T19 Vottero [1998a] 130–31): Philae so named because "there Isis was placated by the Egyptians," who had incurred her wrath when she could not yet find for proper burial the limbs of her husband, Osiris, who was killed by his brother, Typhon. But Vottero 234 n. 3 also refers to a scholion on Luc. 10.313 (= Endt [1909] 407.19–22), which explains the name by allusion to the cessation of hostilities between the Ethiopians and Egyptians, whence Philae from the peace concluded there (ἀπὸ τῆς φιλίας).

subsequent emphasis on the Egyptians' oneness with their natural environment. Surrounding the city with its two streams at this inception point (*duobus... cingitur* above), Seneca's Nile symbolically cradles civilization—a detail that anticipates the constructive interactions of man and river further downstream in Seneca's narrative.

In its growth toward maturity, the Nile meets its first real test when it encounters the great Cataracts (*excipiunt eum Cataractae*, 4a.2.4).[101] There, *dissimilis sibi* ("unlike itself," 4a.2.5), or transformed from its muddy, heavy self thus far, it is roughed up by the jagged rocks and narrows, and tossed, thrown and distilled (as it were) into the stream that flows from this transition point. Experience colors the waters and adds character (4a.2.5: "its color comes not from its own properties but from the rough treatment it receives in that place"); the Nile comes of age when, "at length struggling past obstacles, it is suddenly left hanging [*destitutus*] and falls down a vast height" toward taking final form in the waters below. Man, too, here gains from experience when it is his turn to shoot the rapids in the diverting, and apparently unique,[102] anecdote that Seneca reports at 4a.2.6. The locals take to their tiny craft (*paruula nauigia*) in pairs, their boats so small in comparison with the river's immense torrent. To the horror of onlookers, they are as if catapulted (cf. *tormenti modo*, 4a.2.6) downstream by the force of the rapids, death an apparent certainty. But these daredevils know the river, its mood and its personality. As one man controls direction and the other bails (*alter nauem regit, alter exhaurit*), they work together to work the rapids until the wave they ride delivers them to smooth waters. Their adventure is no mere digression here, pleasant[103] but irrelevant to Seneca's main purpose: his portrayal of the daredevils' harmonious interaction with nature discreetly foreshadows how man marshals the waters to more constructive effect when, near Seneca's Memphis just above the Delta (cf. 4a.2.12), the Nile finally begins to flood the surrounding lands (4a.2.8). At 4a.2.6 our daredevil joyriders find the narrowest channels (*tenuissimos canales*) through which to negotiate the rapids. The right channels are again exploited at 4a.2.8, albeit now in the sense that the Nile's waters are carefully distributed so as to spread their benefit far and wide: "canals are constructed by hand (*manu... canalibus factis*) to control the Egyptians' capacity to distribute the waters, and the Nile runs over all Egypt." At first distributed in pockets that gradually coalesce (cf. *continuatis aquis*, 4a.2.8),

---

101. Presumably, after Philae (4a.2.3), only the First Cataract, as at Luc. 10.313–22 (with Holmes [1989] 224), where Lucan follows Seneca in using plural for singular.

102. So Parroni (2002) 552.

103. Cf. André (2003) 183 n. 93: "IVa.2.6: *narratio* très étoffée, conforme à la règle du *delectare*." Can we glimpse in these daredevils in their tiny (*paruula*) craft shades of the pygmies/dwarfs so often seen performing in Nilotic pictorial art? For this Nilotic feature, see Versluys (2002) 275–77 with Meyboom and Versluys (2007).

the flood waters settle down to form a single expanse "with the appearance of a wide and muddy sea" (*in faciem lati ac turbidi maris*), as if an ironic counterreflection of the formless waters that we witnessed before the Nile took initial shape in 4a.2.3; and the process of the pockets of water coming together may itself symbolize the unifying function that Seneca's Nile serves for Egypt.

All of the power (cf. *nouarum uirium*, 4a.2.8) that the Nile has built up in Seneca's staged description of its growth is now channeled into its beneficence to Egypt. Its waters irrigate the land, its alluvial deposits make it fertile by binding the sandy soil (4a.2.10): the Nile flows and pulses with, even *as*, the country's life blood. But Seneca's description of the Nile's animal life adds another important dimension to the integrated relationship of man, river and natural environment that is drawn in Book 4a. He relies on an eminent source, Claudius Balbillus, prefect of Egypt from 55 to 59 CE,[104] for his account at 4a.2.13–14 of a battle that Balbillus apparently witnessed in the Nile Delta between dolphins from the sea and crocodiles from the Nile. The elder Pliny offers a similar report (*Nat.* 8.91),[105] but what distinguishes the Senecan account is its greater emphasis on the human-like properties of the battle and its protagonists, especially the dolphins. The language of ordinary battle description—*occurrere, agmen, proelium, acies*— is here transposed to the animals; and, true to their reputation for being closely related to man,[106] the dolphins approach the human in their intelligent cunning (*astu*, Plin. *Nat.* 8.91). Swimming under the crocodiles, they use their fins to cut them in their soft underbellies before dividing the enemy through a frontal assault. In turn, the natives of Tentyra resemble the dolphins, that *animal audacissimum* (cf. 4a.2.14), in their own plucky, even reckless, contempt for the crocodiles (*contemptu et temeritate*, 4a.2.15) and in the sheer nerve (*praesens animus*; cf. *praesentia animi*, Plin. *Nat.* 8.92) that makes for survival against so dangerous an enemy. In instinct and character the natives and the dolphins are

---

104. For whom Vottero (1989) 490 n. 38 with Cesaretti (1989) 54–55 and then Hine (2006) 61 and (2010b) 199 n. 29 (our Balbillus to be identified with the Julio-Claudian astrologer Ti. Claudius Balbillus?).

105. Cf. also Ammian. 22.15.20, possibly in imitation of Seneca (Parroni [2002] xxxvi–vii). Given that Pliny, like Seneca (4a.2.15), immediately goes on to recount how the natives of Tentyra are exceptional in their brave hostility to crocodiles (*Nat.* 8.92; cf. 28.31), it is possible that Pliny and Seneca share the same source (Balbillus: Le Blay [2007] 121); but for differences of emphasis in their respective treatments, Le Blay 121–22 with Ernout (1952) 134–35 n. 2 on 8.91–2.

106. So, e.g., Plin. *Nat.* 9.23, 24, 33, Ael. *N.A.* 1.18, 5.6, 8.3, 10.8, Opp. *Hal.* 1.649–53, 5.416–47 (βασιλεῦσιν, "kings of the sea," at 441) with Toynbee (1973) 206–7. Crocodiles, too, show human traits, albeit for Aelian at *N.A.* 5.23 "innate wickedness and villainy" (κακίας...καὶ πανουργίας κροκοδίλων συμφυοῦς).

truly related to each other in Seneca's narrative. Moreover, as Mary Beagon observes, Pliny often depicts nature as "deliberately staging *spectacula* in the form of duels between one kind of animal and another"—duels that "serve to uphold the balance of nature; thus the crocodile has more than one natural enemy because it is so great a pest (8.91)."[107] A similar balance of nature is upheld in the crocodiles' struggles against the dolphins and then man at 4a.2.13–15; and it also realistically accommodates natural strife within Seneca's unifying picture of environmental integrity on the Nile.

For all the diverting color of this Senecan staging of battle between the dolphins and the crocodiles,[108] the humanizing component contributes importantly to the overall emphasis in 4a.2.3–16 on Egypt as a fully interactive ecosystem of sorts, a balanced unity in which the true wonder is perhaps not the Nile per se, but the integrated vision of life that Seneca constructs around that main artery. In this uplifting form of *conuersatio naturae*, as it were, we have travelled far from the engrossments of *conuersatio hominum* in the preface to 4a—albeit with a crowning irony if Seneca is seen to flatter Egypt in his idealized Nile portrait.

VI: The Nile, the Cataclysm and Ovid

Many contrasts are easily drawn between Seneca's portrayal of the Nile on the one hand and the cataclysm of 3.27–30 on the other. Whereas the latter washes away crops, pasturage, houses and all the other trappings of civilization (3.27.4–7), the Nile brings not just fertility to Egypt but even the land itself (4a.2.10). Whereas the rivers that burst their banks at 3.27.8 (the Rhine, Rhone and Danube) run to the anarchic timetable of nature in disarray, the Nile floods reliably from one year to the next, freeing framers from excessive anxiety about each coming season ("Not one of the farmers gazes at the sky," 4a.2.2; cf. 4a.2.9). As in the case of the cataclysm, the Nile flood separates communities from each other: "towns stand out like islands, and for people living in the interior there is no communication [*commercium*] except by boat" (4a.2.11; cf. 3.27.11: "communication [*commercium*] and travel have been cut off among the wretched survivors"). But whereas for the Egyptians the flood is a beautiful sight[109] and a source of joy (4a.2.11), the

---

107. Beagon (1996) 298; cf. also (1992) 151–52.

108. Interestingly read by Le Blay (2007), especially 126–30, as an allegory for the Battle of Actium.

109. Well corroborated by Bonneau (1964) 88–89. Cf. the colorful account in Antes (1800) 72 (written in reminiscence of his twelve years as a missionary in Egypt after his ordination in 1769): "When the river is at its greatest height, the villages, which are commonly surrounded with a grove of date, and other fruit trees, appear as so many islands in an extensive sea, which is in some places broader than the eye can reach: this is a delightful prospect."

cataclysm brings fear and helplessness to those not killed by the initial onslaught (cf. 3.27.12).

These and other points of contrast are conveniently assembled by F. P. Waiblinger, who finds in 4a.2 a face or aspect of nature wholly different from that in Book 3: whereas benign nature gives abundance through the waters of 4a, in 3 she appears intent on the annihilation of humankind.[110] But while nature is in one sense obviously more benign in 4a, in a broader sense she is *always* benign. So A. A. Long on the Stoic conflagration (*ekpyrosis*) that returns the world, at the end of its periodic cycle, to its original fiery state out of which the cosmogonic process will begin again:

> …the conflagration explains why the present world, as observation and physical theory suggest, will not endure for ever. But it is not, for that reason, an event to be feared. Given the physical constitution of things, the conflagration is the necessary counter-phase to the condensed state which originally produced the present world. These physical processes, moreover, are not laws of an undesigning, uncaring, or lifeless nature. On the contrary, they are quite literally acts of god, *who works with a rational and beneficent plan for the good of the whole.* The world at present is the object of that plan. But any such world can be of only finite duration. Therefore, *to ensure the continuity of cosmic goodness*, the present world is everlastingly recreated.[111]

On this approach the Senecan cataclysm, which is seemingly cast at 3.27–30 as an agent of destruction "parallel and analogous" to the conflagration,[112] is no less

---

110. Waiblinger (1977) 55–58, especially 56; similarly, Schönberger (1990) 212.

111. (1985) 25; my emphasis.

112. Mader (1983) 64, citing the equation of fire and water at 3 pref. 5, 28.7, 29.2 and 30.6, and also the Babylonian astrologer Berosos' claim (3.29.1) that the conflagration occurs when all the planets converge in the sign of Cancer, the deluge when they converge in Capricorn. But while in these cases "the two forms of destruction are related and parallel phenomena" (Mader 64), elsewhere Seneca *does* apparently distinguish the cataclysm from cosmic *conflagratio/ekpyrosis*. So at *Dial.* 6.26.6 ("And when the time will come for the universe [*mundus*] to be obliterated for it to renew itself,…stars will clash with stars and all the fiery matter that now shines in ordered formation will burn in a common conflagration"), the stellar chaos signals that "the ἐκπύρωσις is envisaged as a phenomenon of cosmic, and not simply global dimensions (cf. *QNat* 6.32.4)" (Mader 63); the *inundationes…et ignes uasti* to which Seneca alludes earlier in *Dial.* 6.26.6 then refer to partial catastrophes as opposed to the final ἐκπύρωσις (Mader 63). Against this background, Long (1985) 33 n. 35 rightly asserts that "[w]hat Seneca describes in *Nat. quaest.* 3.27–8 is the 'fated day' of a deluge that will overwhelm most of the earth; i.e. *it occurs within a world-period*" (my emphasis; see also Wildberger [2006] 57 and 566 n. 344). Further on the whole question, Gauly (2004) 237–45 and Limburg (2007) 151–55; and for further Senecan allusions to *ekpyrosis*, Ferri (2003) 235 on [Sen.] *Oct.* 391–93.

part of nature's beneficent plan than is the annual flooding of the Nile. True, in
the dark mood that prevails at the end of Book 3 no effort is made to find cold or
contrived comfort in this beneficence. In contrast to the warm benevolence of 4a,
in 3 the actions of god/nature just *are*, and are inevitably just, as if part of the ge-
netic coding of a given world cycle:

> Sunt omnia, ut dixi, facilia naturae, utique <quae> a primo facere consti-
> tuit, ad quae non subito sed ex denuntiato uenit. iam autem a primo die
> mundi, cum in hunc habitum ex informi unitate discederet, quando merg-
> erentur terrena decretum est.
>
> 3.30.1

All things are easy for nature, as I have said [3.27.2], especially the things
that she has determined to do from the beginning, and to which she comes
not suddenly but after due warning. But already, from the first day of the
universe when it separated from its shapeless uniformity into the appearance it now has, it was decreed when all things on earth would be
engulfed.[113]

As soon as we recognize god's greater plan, the Nile itself is put in its place as but
one part of nature's scheme, its good works but a distant memory when it too
presumably joins the Rhone, Rhine and Danube (3.27.8–9) in that single vast
confluence when the day of the deluge dawns; like the Caspian and the Red Seas,
its name too will pass away into irrelevance (cf. *peribunt tot nomina*, 3.29.8), just
as the Tiber will disappear along with Rome and Roman *imperium*. In this respect, Book 4a can itself now be folded into Book 3: the annual flood cycle of the
Nile represents a microcosmic function of seasonal time within the cosmic time
cycle that coordinates the cataclysm at 3.27–30. Earlier in Book 3 Seneca relates
the fixed time cycles of springs that now flow fully and now dry up to the bodily
time cycles of gout, quartan fever and menstruation (3.16.2): like the body, water
has its own cycles/intervals (*interualla*), but "some intervals are shorter, and
therefore noticeable, others longer but no less fixed." By analogy, the Nile has a
relatively brief and noticeable annual flood cycle, while the cataclysm is equally

---

113. For nature's/god's plan cf. *fatalis diluuii dies*, 3.27.1; *illa necessitas temporis* and *fata*, 27.3;
mutari…humanum genus placuit, 28.2; *utrumque* [sc. conflagration and deluge] *fit cum deo
uisum est ordiri meliora, uetera finiri*, 28.7; *naturae constituta*, 29.4 with Kullmann (1995) 72–76
and (virtually identical) (2010) 70–73. Given my focus on the cataclysm as (merely) a part of
the impersonal and recurrent cosmic process, I doubt the very topical significance that Gauly
(2004) 256–64 detects in it, seeing it as a metaphor for political disaster and collapse under
Nero.

part of a fixed but much vaster cycle. Both cycles simultaneously operate within, and are complementary components of, a unified world plan, and also a tightly coordinated *literary* plan in Books 3 and 4a.

For the early Stoics, observes Gottfried Mader, the conflagration seems to have been regarded "primarily as a physical process, and only secondarily in moral terms as a catharsis. There is no evidence that the ἐκπύρωσις was thought of as a divinely inflicted *punishment* for man's moral degeneracy."[114] In the Senecan cataclysm, however, the moral dimension that is implicit from the outset in nature's exertions toward "the destruction of the human race" (3.27.1) is finally made explicit at 3.29.5:

> Ergo quandoque erit terminus rebus humanis, cum partes eius interire debuerint abolerique funditus totae, ut de integro rudes \<homines\> innoxiique[115] generentur nec supersit in deteriora praeceptor, plus umoris quam semper fuit fiet.
>
> Therefore, whenever the end beckons for human affairs, and when the world parts must pass away and be utterly destroyed in their entirety so that mankind can be generated from the beginning again, new and innocent, with no tutor of vice surviving, there will be more water than there has ever been before.

Two factors importantly complicate this moral emphasis in the cataclysm,[116] the first of them related to Seneca's familiar appropriation in the *Natural Questions* of the (Stoic) conception of the world as a living organism.[117] At 3.26.5 Seneca claims that certain springs cleanse themselves of impurities at fixed intervals of time. The Arethusa in Sicily is invoked as a case in point,[118] and also a spring in the Rhodian Chersonese (3.26.6), and then the sea (3.26.7). He then explains:

> omnis aquarum stantium clusarumque natura se purgat. nam in his quibus cursus est, non possunt *uitia* consistere, quae secunda uis defert et exportat.

---

114. Mader (1983) 62; his emphasis.

115. For \<homines\>, and also –*iique* with the Z branch of the MSS, Hine (1996b) 66.

116. Generally on the deluge as divine punishment in ancient thought, Caduff (1986) 205–16. Cf. Limburg (2007) 157, explaining the punishment element in Seneca as deriving possibly "from his personal concerns. But it could also have been caused by an evolution in Stoic thought."

117. See already Chapter Two, Section III n. 30.

118. And it is itself suitably personified at 3.26.6 by Seneca's quotation of Virg. *Ecl.* 10.4–5 (*a Vergilio, qui adloquitur Arethusam: "sic tibi…"*).

illae quae non emittunt quidquid insedit, magis minusue *aestuant*. mare
uero cadauera instrumentaque et naufragiorum reliquias alias ex intimo
trahit, nec tantum tempestate fluctuque, sed tranquillum quoque
placidumque *purgatur*.

3.26.8

All standing and enclosed water naturally purges itself. For in waters that
have a current, impurities cannot settle; the force of the current carries
them along and takes them away. Waters that do not eject whatever settles
in them are set in more or less violent motion. As for the sea, it draws up
from the depths dead bodies, equipment and other such debris of ship-
wrecks, and it is cleansed of them not just by storms and waves, but also
when it is tranquil and calm.

If the familiar world-body analogy is recalled at this point, this vision of natural
self-cleansing in 3.26 offers a suggestive reflection of human bodily function.[119]
Seneca immediately proceeds in 3.27.1 to the cataclysm: "But this subject reminds
me to ask how most of the earth will be covered by water when the fated day of
the deluge arrives." After the self-cleansing on display in 3.26, the cataclysm itself
now begins to resemble a form of world-bodily catharsis before renewal. The
body analogy is explicit at 3.30.4:

quemadmodum corpora nostra deiectu uenter exhaurit, quemadmodum
in sudorem eunt uires, ita tellus liquefiet et, aliis causis quiescentibus, intra
se quo mergatur inueniet.

    Just as the stomach drains our bodies through diarrhea, and just as our
energy goes off in sweat, so the earth will become liquid and, with no
other contributory causes, it will find within itself the means of its own
inundation.

Nature activates the destruction (cf. 3.27.2, 29.4, 30.1), but as an ordaining moral
as well as physical principle[120] when mankind meets its end at 3.29.5 in advance of
its "new and innocent" rebirth. It is *this* portrait of nature as an all-powerful,
guileless and beneficent agent of physical/moral change that collides with the
version of human nature (self-interested, partial and potentially guileful) that is
featured in the preface to 4a.

---

119. And a ready analogy for moral conditioning if the human/moral connotations of *uitia*,
aestuo (*OLD* 5a) and *purgo* (*OLD* 7a, 8a) are activated.

120. See on this "moral aspect to the disaster" Volk (2006) 192.

Second, Ovid: Seneca characteristically intersperses his account of the cataclysm with colorful verse quotations, all of them drawn from the *Metamorphoses*. The first describes the peaks that overtop the floodwaters:

ergo insularum modo eminent 'montes et sparsas Cycladas augent', ut ait ille poetarum ingeniosissimus egregie....

3.27.13; cf. Met. 2.264

So the mountains stick out like islands, and add to the number of the scattered Cyclades, as that most ingenious of poets says admirably....

In their original context in the Phaethon episode, the Ovidian words in fact refer to the effects when the sea is dried up after Phaethon crashes his father's solar chariot upon the earth. Given Seneca's cataclysmic theme, the Ovidian presence appears incongruous at first sight, and arguably a lapse of memory on Seneca's part[121]—unless he invokes the Ovidian conflagration scene partly with irony, partly as a subtle means of signaling that the cataclysm and conflagration are parallel agents of destruction.[122] Then a series of lines from the flood with which, as we saw earlier in connection with 4a pref. 19,[123] Jupiter punishes human wickedness in *Metamorphoses* 1:

...sicut illud pro magnitudine rei dixit, 'omnia pontus erat, deerant quoque litora ponto', ni tantum impetum ingenii et materiae ad pueriles ineptias reduxisset: 'nat lupus inter oues, fuluos uehit unda leones.' non est res satis sobria lasciuire deuorato orbe terrarum. dixit ingentia et tantae confusionis imaginem cepit cum dixit:exspatiata ruunt per apertos flumina campos,

> cumque satis arbusta simul pecudesque uirosque
> tectaque cumque suis rapiunt penetralia templis.
> si qua domus mansit, culmen tamen altior huius
> unda tegit, pressaeque labant[124] sub gurgite turres.

---

121. See Setaioli (1985) 828 n. 292 = (2000) 178 n. 318; Degl'Innocenti Pierini (1984) 144; Timpanaro (1984) 174.

122. Cf. on this point Degl'Innocenti Pierini (1984) 144, but see also n. 112 above in this section.

123. See Section II above in this chapter.

124. *latent* Ovid; but for Seneca's misquotation traced to Virg. *Aen.* 2.460 and 463, Solodow (1989) 120–21.

magnifice haec, si non curauerit quid oues et lupi faciant. natari autem in
diluuio et in illa rapina potest? aut non eodem impetu pecus omne quo
raptum erat mersum est? concepisti imaginem quantam debebas obrutis
omnibus terris, caelo ipso in terram ruente. perfer: scies quid deceat, si
cogitaueris orbem terrarum natare.

3.27.13–15

... just as [the previous quotation continues] it is appropriate to the grandeur of his theme when he writes: 'All was sea, and the sea had no shores'
[*Met.* 1.292]—had he not then reduced that great impetus of his inventiveness and of his theme to schoolboy silliness: 'The wolf swims among the
sheep, the water carries tawny lions' [*Met.* 1.304]. It shows a lack of serious-
mindedness to make fun when the world has been engulfed. He wrote
grandly and captured the image of such vast confusion in stating:

Breaking their bounds, the rivers rushed through the open plains
and swept away plantations along with their crops, and cattle and people,
and houses and shrines together with their temples.
If any house remained, its high roof was still covered by a higher wave,
and towers were overwhelmed and tottered under the flood.

[*Met.* 1.285–88 *mansit*, 289 *culmen*–290]

Magnificently said, if only he were not worried about what the sheep and
wolves are doing. Could anything be swimming in that cataclysm and that
destruction? Was every animal not drowned by the same great force that
carried it off? You've grasped the necessary scale of the picture, with all
lands submerged and the sky itself rushing to earth. Keep it up: you'll
know what is fitting if you bear in mind that the world is swimming.

Well before the moral connotations of the cataclysm are finally made explicit at
3.29.5, the evocations in 3.27 of the Ovidian flood and, by extension, of Jupiter's
"just" punishment of mankind already tinge the Senecan proceedings with an
understated moralizing color.[125] The delicacy of this maneuver allows Seneca
gently to impute to nature the role of moral arbiter without compromising his
rationalizing focus in the *Natural Questions* on nature's purely physical workings.

---

125. On this point, already Gauly (2004) 248–51; and cf. also 3.28.2 for *Met.* 1.272–3 quoted to
similar moralizing effect. Of course, Ovid's *Metamorphoses* is also a sympathetic presence here
because of Seneca's explicit emphasis on change (*mutatio*, 3.27.3; *mutari...humanum genus placuit*, 28.2; *quibus mutarentur terrena*, 29.3).

But why the seemingly intrusive critique of Ovid's "silliness" in portraying the wolf swimming among the sheep, the lion carried by the waters?

An initial answer is supplied by Gregory Hutchinson's observation that Seneca is here "using criticism of Ovid to bring out his own seriousness, and the greatness of his subject and his conception of it; this ending [3.27.14–15] boldly sets the lightness of Ovid's wit against the weightiness and, in his prose, the purposefulness of Seneca's."[126] But Aldo Setaioli digs deeper in exploring the tension between the modern and classical sympathies within Seneca himself: Seneca admires, as did his father (cf. *Contr.* 2.2.9, 12), the brilliance of thought and expression that both associate with *ingenium/ingeniosus*, but this sympathy for modern tendencies is tempered by the classical influence that weighs on Seneca *fils*. In particular, the classical doctrines of τὸ πρέπον and *conuenientia* (cf. *scies quid deceat*, 3.27.15) are transgressed in Ovid's unlikely portrayal of *any* animal surviving long enough to swim amid the deluge.[127] There remain intriguing, and not necessarily incompatible, alternatives to Setaioli's interpretation;[128] but of special interest for now is Ovid's broader reputation in antiquity for a lack of restraint. So the elder Seneca: "It is clear that what was lacking in this man of the greatest talent was not the judgment but the will to curb the license of his poetry" (*Contr.* 2.2.12; cf. 9.5.17: "Ovid does not know how to leave well alone"). The license that Seneca chastises also draws comment in Quintilian's characterization of Ovid as "lacking seriousness [*lasciuus*] even when he writes hexametrical verse" and as "too much an admirer of his own ability" (*nimium amator ingenii sui, Inst.* 10.1.88).[129] It is indeed ironic[130] that Quintilian faults Seneca himself at *Inst.* 10.1.130 for a lack of restraint similar to Ovid's:

> uelles eum suo ingenio dixisse, alieno iudicio: nam si aliqua contempsisset, ... si non omnia sua amasset, ... consensu potius eruditorum quam puerorum amore comprobaretur.

---

126. (1993) 129. I take it that the digression that ends at 3.27.15 (cf. 3.28.1: "Now let us return to the discussion") begins in 3.27.13, when Seneca turns to Ovid; so Vottero (1989) 450 n. 1 (Gross [1989] 143 declares 3.27.4–15 as a whole an excursus).

127. Setaioli (1985) 828–29 = (2000) 177–79.

128. So Mazzoli (1970) 245–47 (Senecan protest against "la poetica edonistica" and Ovid's excessive *lasciuia*). Degl'Innocenti Pierini (1984) 143–52 interestingly associates *lasciuire* (3.27.14) with the lighter lyric and erotic poetic modes: despite praise of Ovid on other fronts, Seneca takes him to task in *lasciuire* not just for an excessive exuberance, but also for infecting his *Metamorphoses* with a stylistic register more attuned to lyric (pp. 149–50).

129. Further, Peterson (1891) 84 on 10.1.88 *lasciuus*; Elliott (1985), especially 10–11.

130. Cf. Mazzoli (1970) 247.

You would wish that he had spoken with his own abilities, but with someone else's judgment; for if he had only despised certain expressions and…if he had not had such admiration for all that was his own,…he would have won the approval of learned men rather than the affection of mere boys.

But if Seneca poses a dangerous influence because of his *uitia*,[131] what of Ovid at *N.Q.* 3.27.14? If his *lasciuia* is there interpreted as a degenerate stylistic feature, a decadent abandonment of classical restraint, Seneca's rebuke takes on another suggestive dimension: even as evocations of the flood in *Metamorphoses* 1 lend significant dramatic and moralizing color to the Senecan cataclysm, could it be that Seneca here shows a playfulness of his own in loosely combining literary and moral criticism? Could it be that Ovid here symbolizes a form of literary corruption that runs parallel to the moral corruption (cf. *uitia*, 3.30.8) cleansed in the cataclysm? On this approach, part can again profitably be viewed in relation to whole: as Seneca rounds on Ovidian license, so the deluge punishes human *licentia* more generally.

VII: *The Missing Link, and Other Theories of the Nile Flood*

We finally return to the challenge of identifying the missing link that connects the preface to 4a to its larger context within the book, and also to the *Natural Questions* as a whole. "What a contemptible thing man is, unless he rises above his human concerns!" (1 pref. 5): we have seen that Seneca's disquisition on flattery in the preface reenacts in all its ambiguities and tonal enticements the entanglements of everyday human involvement. In the tumultuous climax of Book 3 and during our tour of the Nile in Book 4a, however, we rise above these *sordida*, as if liberated in the manner of the *animus* that roams freely across cosmic space at 1 pref. 7–13. On this approach, the preface to 4a amounts to a revisiting of *angustiae*, and it offers a highly creative counterfoil to the enlargement process toward cosmic vision that encompasses the cataclysm at 3.27–30 and then the Nile excursus in Book 4a. In the latter, so rich a picture is offered of candid and easy interaction between man and his environment—truly a vision distant from Sicily and Lucilius' procuratorship there, and from the distinctly *un*candid flow of flattery in the preface.

In the remaining portions of what survives of Book 4a, Seneca turns from the Nile's marvels (4a.2.1–16) to review four theories of why the Nile floods in

131. Cf. Quint. *Inst.* 10.1.129: "his style is for the most part corrupt and most harmful for the very reason that it abounds in vices that are so attractive" (further, Peterson [1891] 120 on 10.1.125).

summer.[132] We can only speculate, with John the Lydian's assistance,[133] on the course taken by the book after the surviving fragment's end, and any attempt to identify a guiding strategy or pattern of argument in Seneca's presentation of the different flood theories faces obvious difficulties because of the fragmentary nature of the evidence. But the process that we have witnessed thus far in Books 3 and 4a, releasing us from the narrowness of everyday vision, is also related to important aspects of Seneca's critical procedure at 4a.2.17–30. There, his method naturally reflects the rationalist tendency of so many treatments of the Nile problem in the Greco-Roman tradition,[134] and in this respect Herodotus' markedly scientific approach to the problem[135] is instructive. At 2.19–34 he reviews four theories (§§20–3) before stating (§24), and then elaborating upon (§§25–7), his preferred explanation. The third theory he reports attributes the flood to the melting in the summer of snow accumulated in winter on the high mountains of Ethiopia (2.22). This theory, derived from Anaxagoras,[136] is also the first reported by Seneca, at 4a.2.17. The fact that Herodotus reserves for this theory his most extensive refutation may be a measure of its popularity in the fifth century BCE, especially at Athens (cf. 4a.2.17: "All of antiquity was of the same opinion; Aeschylus, Sophocles and Euripides report it").[137]

Seneca, too, treats the theory at length (4a.2.17–21), dismissing it because (4a.2.18) (1) the Ethiopians' dark color is but one of several indications of the extreme heat of the place; (2) the south wind that blows from that region is "the hottest of winds"; and (3) snow never falls even as (relatively) far north as Alexandria, and not even rain further south. How, in sum, could snow sufficient to feed the Nile originate from a place as hot and rainless as Ethiopia? In any case, adds Seneca, if the flood originated from melting snow, it would be fullest in early summer when the volume of the snow is highest—whereas in the four months of its flood the Nile's waters remain constant (4a.2.21).

Herodotus adduces the first three of these arguments (2.22), specious though they in fact are because "they are based on a false premise, viz. the conviction of contemporary geography that Ethiopia had a hot climate because it lay on the

---

132. On Seneca's sources here, Setaioli (1988) 375–85 casts a doxographical net that extends beyond Posidonius, the traditional favorite (p. 376 and n. 1752).

133. See Section I n. 2 above in this chapter.

134. For the treatments usefully compiled, Postl (1970) 74–86.

135. On this point, Lloyd (1975) 160 and 161 on 2.22 with (1976) 93; Graham (2003).

136. D-K 59A42 (5) = Graham (2010) 1.296–7 Text 38 (5); further, Bonneau (1964) 161–69.

137. See Lloyd (1976) 101–102 with Bonneau (1964) 163, 168, and cf. Graham (2010) 1.304–5 and 321 on Texts 54–56.

edge of the world and, therefore, received the full blast of the sun's rays as it rose and set."[138] What matters for present purposes, however, is the enlarged perspective in which Seneca, like Herodotus, grounds his objections to the snow theory: when we take the broader view and, in addition to the three initial objections reviewed above, we compare the effect of melting ice on the Rhine, say, or the Rhone, the Lower Danube or the Cayster in Lydia, none of which nevertheless floods in summer (4a.2.20), the snow theory itself soon melts away. So to Thales, who held that the Etesian (summer north or northwesterly) winds check the flow of the Nile toward the sea, thus causing the river to run back on itself and accumulate before flooding (4a.2.22).[139] But the theory falls as soon as it is tested against the fuller picture drawn at 4a.2.23: How (for one thing) can the flood be caused by the Etesians if it begins before them and lasts after them? Oenopides of Chios, Anaxagoras' younger contemporary, explained the paradox of summer flooding by portraying the Nile as fundamentally no different from other rivers:[140] in winter, the earth's internal heat dries up subterranean veins of water (4a.2.26), but, for rivers in parts other than Egypt, winter rain more than compensates for this loss. In summer, when the earth's interior is colder and there is no loss of water through heat, the Nile reverts to its normal level; no longer swollen by rain, the waters of other rivers are meanwhile reduced in the summer. Again, in response, a fuller perspective: if Oenopides were correct, "in summer all rivers would grow, and all wells would have abundant water in summer" (4a.2.27).[141] Diogenes of Apollonia, also a younger contemporary of Anaxagoras, apparently

---

138. Lloyd (1976) 103.

139. D-K 11A16, including Hdt. 2.20 (cf. Graham [2010] 1.30–3 and 40–41 on Texts 21–23). On Hdt. 2.20 see also Lloyd (1976) 98–99; further, Bonneau (1964) 151–59 and Hall (1977) 435–36. For the Etesians cf. 5.10–11 and see Chapter Five, Section III. At 4a.2.22 Seneca adds dramatic color by having the sixth-century explorer Euthymenes of Massilia (*RE* 6.1 1509–11) give testimony, in his quoted voice, that the Nile flows from the Atlantic coast of Africa, and that the Etesians blow waves into this river, causing it to flood further downstream; see Bonneau (1964) 145–46 with Lloyd (1976) 99 and Graham (2003) 295 n. 14. By appeal to countertestimony at 4a.2.24, however, and by dismissal of falsehood (*tunc erat mendacio locus*), Seneca takes advantage of Euthymenes' presence here not least to establish his own (superior) scientific credentials.

140. D-K 41A11, but see now Bodnár (2007) 28–33 on Text 11 with Bonneau (1964) 182–84. Herodotus' preferred explanation (2.25), based on evaporation (Bonneau 188–93), similarly casts the Nile's behavior as fundamentally like that of other rivers (further, Lloyd [1976] 104–105 on §§24–26 in general; 106 on §25); but for Herodotus himself made vulnerable to the very objection that he levels against the other theorists he reviews, see Graham (2003) 297 ("why do the same causes not have the same effects in all cases?").

141. Seneca seems to presuppose that volume *gained* in summer from no more loss to the earth's winter internal heat would always more than adequately compensate for volume *lost* after the cessation of winter rainfall.

held a theory based on evaporation, which he associated especially with the southern regions where the sun is harshest. All lands are perforated with communicating passages that allow dry parts of the earth to draw from the moist parts; the Nile flood is derived from the flow of water from north to south to compensate for the evaporation effect in Egypt (4a.2.28–9).[142] But why then, objects Seneca (4a.2.30), is any part of the earth without water if all lands are connected by perforations? The theory offers but a partial viewpoint that cannot explain *all* of the observed phenomena.

Seneca's rationalist approach in testing these four theories may be traditional enough. Given his lack of original theorizing elsewhere in the *Natural Questions*, moreover, it is hardly likely that in the lost portion of Book 4a he ventured a strikingly original explanation of the Nile's summer flood. But while from this one angle his treatment of the Nile may contain few surprises, his collective response to Anaxagoras, Thales, Oenopides and Diogenes in 4a usefully illustrates a key feature of his creative approach to the doing of science in the *Natural Questions* more generally. By beginning analysis from the perspective of the broader viewpoint, the cosmic picture, Seneca's investigative method at 4a.2.17–30 fully conforms to that dominant emphasis throughout the work, and throughout this study: to enlarge our thinking so as to bring us closer to the primary goal of "seeing the all" (cf. 3 pref. 10). It is by recognition of this fuller perspective that the *angustiae* of the preface to 4a become all the more confining and repressive, as if narrows that separate the great waters and forces of nature on display in Books 3 and 4a.

---

142. D-K 64A18 (including *N.Q.* 4a.2.28–9 = Graham [2010] 1.446–7 Text 26); see Bonneau (1964) 180–82, and cf. also Hommel (1951), especially 321–22, for the rightness of Seneca's interpretation of Diogenes' theory set again the apparent misunderstanding in Aristoph. *Nu.* 272.

4

The Rhetoric of Science

Yonder the harvest of cold months laid up,
Gives a fresh coolness to the Royal Cup;
There Ice, like Crystal, firm and never lost,
Tempers hot July with December's frost;
Winter's dark prison, whence he cannot flie,
Though the warm Spring, his enemy, grows nigh.
Strange! that extremes should thus preserve the snow,
High on the Alps, or in deep Caves below!

EDMUND WALLER (1606–1687)[1]

I: Introduction

The surviving half-book (or less) of *Natural Questions* 4b, on hail and snow, can conveniently be analyzed in three parts: (1) on the nature and causes of hail (4b.3–7); (2) the argument that snow is formed in the lower atmosphere (4b.8–12); and (3) in a sudden shift of direction, Seneca's moralizing condemnation of the luxurious, high-priced excesses—notably the preserving of snow and ice for consumption in all seasons as a cooling draft—to which man applies water, that priceless gift of nature (4b.13). As Oltramare perceives,[2] Seneca's argument in (2) above indicates that at some point in the missing portion of the book he derived hail from the higher atmosphere, in contradistinction to snow from the lower atmosphere. It appears certain that the book as a whole encompassed the causes of dew and frost as well as of hail and snow, and likely that it also treated clouds and rain.[3]

---

1. From *A Poem on St. James's Park as Lately Improved by His Majesty*, published in 1661. The passage celebrates the completion, in 1660, of an icehouse built in Upper St. James's Park at the instigation of Charles II; see Wheatley (1891) 2.290 on October 22nd, 1660 with Taylor (2006) 232 s.v. Icehouse. For Waller's lines contextualized within interpretation of the whole poem, Chambers (1991) 57–73, especially 67–69.

2. (1929) 2.193–94.

3. *De nubibus* was possibly the original title (cf. Hine [1996a] 189.4 app. and 203.275 app.), the book then treating clouds *per se* and related phenomena (cf. 4b.3.6, 13.2 for dew and frost in addition to snow and hail) in line with the earlier meteorological tradition; Vottero (1989) 506 with Gilbert (1907) 488–510, Oltramare (1929) 2.193 and Kidd (1988) 510.

Of course, any coherent reading of the surviving fragment is necessarily provisional, the development of his entire argument in the book *in toto* now irrecoverable. Yet this cautionary point can itself be too restrictive, discouraging experimental engagement with what remains of Seneca's argument; and while the reading offered in this chapter is in one sense obviously incomplete, we shall see that the later part of the fragment in particular (4b.8–13) reveals an internal logic that at least partially offsets the problem of incompleteness.

We return in this chapter to a familiar challenge already raised by the moralizing interludes that we considered in Chapter Two: to what extent, and how, can Seneca's outburst in 4b.13 be reconciled with his earlier disquisition on hail and snow? In Section II we explore possible ways of integrating 4b.13 with what precedes. Those arguments for integration give way in Section III to our first sampling of what might loosely be termed Seneca's "rhetoric of scientific inquiry" in the technical portions of the fragment down to the end of 4b.12. In Section IV I attempt to distinguish five categories, or modes, of argumentation that are deployed in Seneca's survey of theories of hail and snow in 4b.3–7. Our focus then turns in Section V to his experimentation in 4b.8–12 with what, I argue, is an example of the "rhetoric of scientific inquiry" in rather more positive and persuasive—even model—Senecan action. In Section VI we finally take stock of Book 4b in the context of the *Natural Questions* as a whole, with emphasis on Seneca's highly self-conscious testing of the nature, and the potential frailties, of "the rhetoric of science" as manifested in the surviving fragment. We begin, however, with a brief preparatory glance at the *Moral Letters*.

II: 4b.13 in Context

Letters 109 is apparently prompted by Lucilius' wish to know "whether a wise man can be of help to a wise man" (*An sapiens sapienti prosit*, 1). After exploring the question, Seneca nevertheless casts it as the sort of enquiry that exercises our wit (*acumen*) but lacks the deeper engagement that his persona craves in its conversation-with-self in §§17–18, a conversation that itself enacts the introspective dynamic, or the stimulus to self-interrogation, that he finds so lacking in Lucilius' original enquiry:

> cogita quod soleo frequenter tibi dicere, in istis nos nihil aliud quam
> acumen exercere. totiens enim illo reuertor: quid ista me res iuuat?... quid
> me poscis scientiam inutilem? magna promisisti: exhibe fidem. dicebas
> intrepidum fore etiam si circa me gladii micarent, etiam si mucro tangeret

iugulum…: hanc mihi praesta curam, ut uoluptatem, ut gloriam con-
temnam. postea docebis inplicta soluere, ambigua distinguere, obscura
perspicere: nunc doce quod necesse est. uale.

Reflect, as I'm accustomed to telling you often, that in such topics we
do nothing but exercise our wits. For I repeatedly go to the same thought:
"What good does this do me?…Why do you ask of me knowledge that is
useless? You promised great things: show that you could be trusted. You
said that I would be unperturbed even if swords were flashing around me,
and even if the blade point were touching my throat….Provide me with
such a course of treatment, so that I despise pleasure and glory. Afterwards,
you'll teach me to work out intricate problems, to settle doubtful points,
to see through what is unclear. But for now teach me what I *need* to know."
Farewell.

Seneca's sudden shift from addressing Lucilius to conversing with himself, with
no reversion to Lucilius before the letter abruptly ends in "Farewell," offers but
one, albeit striking, example of his repeated emphasis in the *Moral Letters* on the
need for philosophy to dig deep, to penetrate the self, to move beyond the super-
ficiality that he associates at *Letters* 45.5 with philosophical quibbling about
words (*uerborum cauillatio*) and sophistical argumentation that exercises the
intellect to no purpose (*captiosae disputationes quae acumen inritum exercent*).[4]
We find a related phenomenon when, in a sudden turn in *Natural Questions* 4b,
the "trivialities" (*ineptiae*) of Seneca's technical researches are contrasted with the
serious business of moral instruction:

'Quid istas' inquis 'ineptias, quibus litteratior est quisque, non melior, tam
operose persequeris? quomodo fiant niues dicis, cum multo magis ad nos
pertineat dici a te quare emendae non sint.' iubes me litem cum luxuria
litigare? cotidianum istud et sine effectu iurgium est. litigemus tamen;
etiamsi superior futura est, pugnantis ac reluctantis uincat.

                                                                    4b.13.1

---

4. Cf. the kind of philosophical *superuacua* rejected at *Letters* 106.11 ("Our fine edge is dulled
amid such superfluous pursuits; these make men learned, but not good"), or the syllogistic
intricacies characterized at 117.18 ("All such matters are in the vicinity of wisdom, not in wisdom
itself. But our dwelling-place should be in wisdom itself"). See further Cooper (2006) 49–51
(especially p. 50: in such disparagement Seneca reveals "an inadequate and weak grasp of the
real value for the moral life of the study of logic") with Limburg (2007) 207–12, and cf. 2.59.1
and Chapter Eight, Section V. Further on the Senecan technique of "talking to oneself" at *Letters* 109.17–18 and elsewhere, see Hine (2010a) 209–10.

"Why," you say, "do you so painstakingly pursue these trivialities, which make a person more learned, not of better character? You tell us how snow is formed, though it's far more relevant to us to be told by you why snow shouldn't be bought." You bid me to fight it out in court with luxury? That dispute is waged daily, and to no effect. But let us nevertheless bring the case; even if luxury is going to win, let it defeat us while we are fighting and continuing the struggle.

The interlocutor enlivens the proceedings in 4b in several ways. First, if the "you" here is identified with Lucilius, Seneca shows a witty self-deprecation in subjecting himself, via the interlocutory voice, to the very criticism of philosophical fashion—the lack of deep personal engagement and relevance—that he himself levels, as we have just seen, against others in his correspondence with Lucilius in the contemporary *Moral Letters*. Second (a point related to the first), this Lucilius draws Seneca back into the dominant conceptual space of the *Letters*, as if diverting Seneca from physical investigation to the mode of philosophical self-development to which Lucilius has become habituated in his epistolary exchanges with Seneca. Third, by impatiently interrupting the Senecan master voice and demanding a change of direction, the interlocutor (whether or not identified with Lucilius) refreshingly varies how Seneca introduces his moralizing interludes across the *Natural Questions*; and we shall see that the humorous overtones of the interlocutor's intrusiveness here are typical of a broader playfulness that characterizes Book 4b. Fourth, Seneca paradoxically uses division and objection in 4b.13.1 as a way of harmonizing the technical and moralizing strands of the fragment as a whole. Whereas the interlocutor presents "becoming more learned" and "becoming of better character" as scarcely reconcilable alternatives, there is a middle way: for all their overt differences, we shall see that the two sections, 4b.3–12 and 4b.13, are mutually informing and tightly bound together, and that in combination they also reflect broader thematic currents in the *Natural Questions*.

At the most superficial level, the excursus of 4b.13[5] is connected to what precedes by Seneca's insistence that he *does* meet the interlocutor's preference for being told not how snow is formed, but "why snow shouldn't be bought" (13.1): by establishing that snow has more air than water in it, does he not bring reproach on those who not only pay for water but also compound that disgrace by getting

---

5. In general on 4b.13 Citroni Marchetti (1991) 168–70; Berno (2003) 145–77; Gauly (2004) 104–15; Limburg (2007) 206–42.

mostly air for their money (13.2)? Beyond this contrived linkage, however, as if Seneca playfully answers the interlocutor by straining for self-justification, there are at least three further, stronger and more intricate ties:

(1) The *uitiosi* pictured in 4b.13 offer a counter-reflection of the natural cold conditions portrayed in 4b.3–12: in the unbalanced microclimate of their own debauchery, they find no medium between the extremes of hot and cold.[6] Jaded appetites seek added spice: if a healthy stomach is easily refreshed and a healthy thirst easily quenched (cf. *sanus...stomachus*, 13.5; *sitim sanam*, 13.10), the increasingly scorching effects (cf. *perustus* [sc. *stomachus*], 13.5) of ever more elaborate consumption look for ever colder forms of relief. Hence the *luxuriosi* drink snow in summer as well as winter (13.5), but as their vicious ways harden and their senses grow numb through their excesses (a condition reflected in their insensitivity to seasonal difference, summer or winter), they progress from snow to ice. The medicinal practice of drinking water derived from snow or ice is first attested at Rome in the lifetime of the physician Asclepiades of Bithynia:[7] according to Celsus (writing on diarrhea at 4.26.4), Asclepiades "affirmed, against the opinion of earlier writers, that the drink [to be given to relieve diarrhea] should be kept constantly cold, and in fact as cold as possible."[8] Celsus reserves judgment on this recommendation (4.26.4: "I myself think that each should trust his own experiences as to whether hot rather than cold drink be used"), and although he too elsewhere endorses cooled drinks for a variety of ailments and conditions, such methods were by no means universally accepted.[9] It was in the first century CE, however, that the luxurious consumption of snow water became fashionable and notorious, as the many allusions to the practice elsewhere in Seneca and, notably, in Juvenal and Martial attest;[10] Nero himself is credited by the

---

6. For linkage between Seneca's condemnation of *luxus mensae* here and Roman satire, Limburg (2007) 224 and 235–36 with Richardson-Hay (2009).

7. For his death located in or recently before 91 BCE and not (as often supposed) later in the first century, Rawson (1982).

8. Cited by De Planhol (1995) 158.

9. See De Planhol (1995) 217–18.

10. Cf. *Dial.* 1.3.13 (with Lanzarone [2008] 259), 4.25.4, *Letters* 78.23, 95.21, 25, 119.3; Mart. 5.64.2, 12.17.6, 14.116–18; Juv. 5.49–50. Further, Geer (1935), Turcan-Deleani (1964) 691–93 and Gauly (2004) 106–108, with Dickson (1972) 17 for the origins of modern ices and ice cream traced back to the Neronian age ("...the emperor's dessert was obviously the forerunner of the modern fruit ice"; but cf. then Clarke [2004] 4: "A typical 'history' [sc. of ice cream] begins with...Nero," but on the basis of "little real evidence"). On the larger history of the practice and industry of using/distributing snow and ice for the cooling of drinks, see De Planhol (1995), with Senecan glances on pp. 159–60 and 162; David (1994), especially xii–xiii, 1–2; and Gosnell (2005), especially 369–80.

elder Pliny with inventing the restorative *decocta* [sc. *aqua*], or water boiled and then chilled by the vessel's immersion in snow.[11] Beyond the luxury of the cooled water itself, the storage of ice and snow (cf. 4b.13.8) to provide cold refreshment out of season further distorts the Senecan natural order here—an implication not without parallel in the more modern history of the icehouse.[12]

As F. R. Berno points out,[13] the language of natural balance and moderation at, e.g., 4b.13.5 *naturalibus fomentis contentus* (of the stomach "satisfied with natural remedies") is overthrown by endless disproportion and yearning in *non contenti* (13.3) and *ne niue quidem contenti sunt* ("they are not satisfied even with snow," 13.8), or by "a longing for something ever colder" in 13.6 *desiderium semper noui rigoris*. The physical and moral health associated with the balanced life gives way to sickness that is both literal and figurative,[14] as "the stomach that is healthy and receptive to wholesome food" (13.5) is countered by that which is "weak and en-feebled by its own burning" (13.7). The Tantalus-like shades[15] who are tormented by their hunger for ever more scalding food, and by their thirst for ever colder drink, are models of self-contradiction in their opposite obsessions, hot and cold. The irrationality of their behavior is further manifested through paradox (cf. 13.5: "the remedies only intensify the illness") and through the perverse economics of the thriving trade in water (13.3); after all, "the things that we need for our exis-tence are either freely given or cheap: nature craves only bread and water" (*Letters* 25.4; cf. 110.18). Beyond these internal linkages and verbal plays within 4b.13 itself, however, Berno also finds important thematic connections between the

---

11. *Nat.* 31.40; cf. Suet. *Ner.* 48.3 with De Planhol (1995) 159. For Nero suggestively implicated in 4b.13, Berno (2003) 330–31 and Gauly (2004) 109–11.

12. Cf. in eulogistic wonder Waller as cited at the beginning of this chapter. But against un-natural transgression see, e.g., the report in Funderburg (1995) 41–42 of the following remark passed in one history of Boston on an eighteenth-century Cambridge landowner wealthy enough to possess both a greenhouse and an icehouse: "Some thought a judgment would befall one who would thus attempt to thwart the designs of Providence by raising flowers under glass in winter, and keeping ice underground to cool the heat of summer." Cf. Buxbaum (2002) 4–5, including (p. 4): "Despite the popularity of the Grand Tour of Europe, an icehouse was still regarded as a luxury in 1755, 'the envy of the indolent who have no claim to temples, grottos, bridges, rocks, exotic pines and ice in summer'" (with quotation from Henry Hoare, 1705–1785, second-generation owner of the Stourhead estate in Wiltshire, writing to his nephew).

13. (2003) 150.

14. For Seneca's appropriation of the medical language of "Alcolismo e dispepsia," Migliorini (1997) 41–43.

15. See Berno (2003) 171–74 for stimulating remarks on "Analogie con le tragedie," especially *Thyestes*; and cf. p. 331 for the *luxuriosi* drawn with shades of the mere *graeculi* of comedy (with a possible jab at Nero, that renowned philhellene?).

excursus and 4b.3–12,[16] prominent among them the transition that Seneca makes from one kind of *lis* to another: at 5.1 different physical theories "go to law" (*litigant*), while at 13.1 Seneca takes on luxury (*cum luxuria litigare*). Another transition is from one set of *ineptiae* (Stoic absurdities at 6.1, on hail prediction) to another in the interlocutor's dismissal of the hail and snow theories covered down to 4b.12 as mere trivialities (13.1). And we also move from one kind of searching to another when the language of scientific investigation in the earlier part of the fragment (e.g. *quaestione, quaeritur*, 4.1; *Rationem . . . quaerunt*, 7.1) is reapplied to corrupt ends in the excursus (cf. *excogitatum est quemadmodum . . .*, 13.4; *quaeritur, quaerit*, 13.5, 7; *exquirunt*, 13.8). After the high-minded exertions of 4b.3–12, a very different kind of ingenuity exerts itself to pernicious effect in "luxury's inventiveness to its own detriment" at 13.4 *contra se ingeniosa luxuria*.[17]

(2) Just as luxury is "an invincible malady that progresses from being soft and fluid to hard and enduring" (*inuictum malum et ex molli fluidoque durum atque patiens*, 13.11), so plain, restorative water hardens first into snow (13.5) and then into ice at 13.7–8:

> . . . ita uiscera istorum uitiis torpentia nihil sentiunt, nisi frigore illa uehementiore percusseris.[18] inde est, inquam, quod ne niue quidem contenti sunt, sed glaciem, uelut certior illi ex solido rigor sit, exquirunt. . . .
>
> . . . so the internal organs of these people are numbed by their vices and feel nothing unless you shock them with still more intense cold. This is why, I say, they are not satisfied even with snow but look for ice, as if it had a more reliable coldness because of its density. . . .[19]

---

16. (2003) 165–71.

17. The delineation here of the *luxuriosi* of 4b.13 as a perverse reflection of the scientific investigators earlier in the fragment arguably contributes to the vein of irony that Berno (2003) 169 detects as another significant element spanning the two sections. The antithetical pairings of warm-cold and hard-soft that she explores in the excursus (pp. 167–69) are also loosely relatable to comparable pairings in, e.g., 3.4–5 and 5.3 (hard-soft in both cases) and 4.1–3 (icy hail prevalent in warm spring); and if we accept the parallel that she draws between *natura-luxuria* in the excursus and truth-falsehood earlier in 4b (cf. *mentior*, 3.1, 5.4; *incredibile*, 6.2; *mendacium et fabula*, 7.2; *falsum*, 11.5), she plausibly detects in both parts (p. 167) "una notevole preponderanza del secondo termine rispetto al primo, il che conferma la sua 'vittoria'": *luxuria* and *mendacium* triumph over nature and truth.

18. So *percusseris* Hine (1996a) 201.245. But *perusseris* (also in the manuscripts), though rhythmically less apt (Hine 201.245 app.), is perhaps not to be discarded too lightly: the irrationality of the debauched *modus uiuendi* would then be further reflected in *peruro* used paradoxically of scorching indigestion at 4b.13.5, here of intense cold (cf. *OLD* 3c).

19. Can we detect in this appetite for ice a resemblance to the obsessive syndrome now known as pagophagia? For medical writing warning against excessive consumption of cold or iced water already in antiquity, Parry-Jones (1992).

The different degrees of hardness and coldness that distinguish snow and hail in the earlier part of the fragment—snow is less solid (3.5) and, formed closer to the earth, "less compact than hail because it is condensed by less cold" (12.1)—now give way to gradations culminating in the moral freeze of 13.11, where mere snow is not enough: "Keep searching for something still colder than snow, because cold to which you've adjusted is nothing." On the assumption that Book 4b was positioned third in the original ordering of the *Natural Questions*, water flows freely in the early books as we move (*inter alia*) from the endlessness of its elemental production (3.10–13) to the cataclysm that rages in 3.27–30 before the Nile's flood brings annual relief to Egypt in Book 4a. In Book 4b that free flow gives way to a congealing process (cf. *coactis aquis*, 12.1) that itself lends stoppage and closure to the water sequence before Seneca moves to the study of wind in Book 5. In contrast to the limitless superabundance of all the floodwaters in Books 3 and 4a, no amount of plain water can ease the scorched palate in 4b.13 (cf. 13.5: "I shall explain how we reached the point that no flowing water seemed sufficiently cold to us"), and the focus now turns from nature's vastness to the microlevel of individual obsession and the small degrees of alleviation brought by each sip of snow and bite of ice (cf. 13.10). After our experience in Chapter One of the integrating vision of oneness that fundamentally conditions the *Natural Questions*, Seneca's outrage at the trade in water in 4b.13 targets another fragmentation of nature, as if the latter is reducible to commodities that are subject to individual grades of valuation:

> hoc quod illa [sc. natura] fluere et patere omnibus uoluit, cuius haustum uitae publicum fecit, hoc quod tam homini quam feris auibusque et *inertissimis animalibus* in usum large ac beate profudit, contra se ingeniosa luxuria redegit ad pretium. adeo nihil illi potest placere nisi carum.
>
> 4b.13.4

> This water, which nature wanted to flow for everyone and to be available to all, and the drinking of which she made common to life everywhere; this water, which she has generously poured forth in abundance as much for the use of mankind as for animals and birds and the idlest of creatures; on this water, luxury, inventive to its own detriment, has put a price. So true is it that nothing can please luxury unless it is expensive.

Beyond its integration within Book 4b as a whole, Seneca's excursus offers another instance of the divide-and-separate mentality that we have already observed in the mullet watchers of Book 3, say, or Hostius Quadra in Book 1.[20] The merchants who trade in water impose distinctions of price on the undivided wholeness,[21] while the *luxuriosi* who pay those high prices live fractured, uneven lives in their oscillations between indigestion and relief, between hot mouthfuls and ever colder drafts (13.10). In their different way they too are the idlest of creatures (*inertissima animalia*), but also self-imposed exiles from nature's unified compact; for they exist as if in isolation from the reassuring commonality of man and animal as pictured in 4b.13.4 above.

(3)   In contrast to the extremes of heat and cold that battle each other in 4b.13, Seneca's preceding argument (4b.8–12) that snow is formed in the nearer atmosphere asserts a balance in nature that is then overthrown in the excursus. Snow itself acquires a median status in 12.1 as a phenomenon formed from congealed water "in this moderate and not-too-intense cold" (*hoc medio frigore non nimis intento*); and clausal symmetry suitably reinforces this balanced picture, as snow is produced when "the adjacent atmosphere both has too much cold to be changed into rainwater, and too little to be hardened into hail" (*uicinus aër et plus habet frigoris quam ut in aquam imbremque transeat, et minus quam ut duretur in grandinem*, 12.1). But this elegant conclusion completes an argument that is carefully balanced and controlled *in its entirety*, as we shall see in Section V below; and this balance and control offset the picture of imbalance in 4b.13. The ramifications of this argument in 4b.8–12 extend backward as well as forward, however: the strategies of persuasion that Seneca here deploys project a confidence and plausibility, I contend, unmatched in his earlier treatment of hail down to 4b.7. And so to Seneca's testing of the "rhetoric of science" in 4b.3–7.

III: The Rhetoric of Science

A familiar controversy in modern science centers on the problematic relationship between the rhetoric and the rationality of scientific argument. "From the dawn of modern science," writes Philip Kitcher,[22] "strenuous announcements have advocated that thinkers are not to be diverted from the conclusions that they ought to

---

20. Can we fleetingly glimpse this mentality in the sorting and storage of luxury wines at 4b.13.3: "[We store snow,] not content as we are with bottling [*diffundere*] our wines and arranging [*disponere*] our cellars by taste and vintage"?

21. 4b.13.8: "water does not even have a uniform price but has dealers and—for shame!—a variable market-value"; cf. Plin. *Nat.* 19.55: "different kinds of water, too, are distinguished, and nature's elements are themselves differentiated by their price."

22. (1995) 47–48.

reach by the enchantments of language used to clothe a chain of reasoning. Hence the need for a restrained idiom that will 'let the facts speak for themselves'. Science is to be a rhetoric-free zone." Kitcher here describes, rather than endorses, an objectivist position extending back to Enlightenment philosophy's "proclamation of the triumph of scientific knowledge (*episteme*) over mere belief (*doxa*)"[23]—a position fundamentally challenged in the last five or so decades by the rhetoric-of-science movement, which relegates scientific inquiry from a privileged source or class of sure knowledge to another form of persuasion. Few scholars would now accept that scientific writing can ever truly exclude rhetoric by deploying a disciplined objectivity, or by affecting "a style of non-style";[24] for present purposes, however, our concern is not with the broader debate on science as a rhetorical activity, but with the rhetorical quality of Seneca's own scientific argumentation.

The term *rhetorical* is itself evidently problematic in its possible range of applications and meanings in scientific (and of course other) contexts, and the full scale of its complexity can only be hinted at here: so, for example, in its neutral sense as the practice of persuasion, rhetoric is itself a general term for a great repertoire of techniques or emphases that can go into the making of a given case (e.g., "rhetoric as invention, as argumentation, as figuration, as stylistics,"[25] etc.); rhetoric of a conventionally accepted, generic kind shapes the format and persuasive wording of the research paper, for example, or the grant application;[26] rhetoric as mere rhetoric implies the ascendancy of style over substance (or worse) and contrasts with the hard scientific rhetoric that, as Marcello Pera puts it, is "the set of those persuasive, argumentative techniques scientists use in order to reach their conclusions, not the modes of expression, or the ornament, or the style that may accompany those arguments";[27] and the rhetoric of accommodation,[28] which

---

23. Simons (1990a) 2.

24. So Gusfield (1976) 17, characterizing (in his own highly stylized and playful mode of analysis in this paper) "The literary style of Science": "The writer must persuade the audience that the results of the research are *not* literature, are *not* a product of the style of presentation. The style of non-style is itself the style of science. There is a literary art involved in scientific presentation."

25. Simons (1990a) 5.

26. Further, Simons (1990a), 5–6, and cf. for the generic emphasis (1980) 123: "Rhetorically speaking [scientific professions] are required to recruit and indoctrinate new members, justify their claims to special expertise before accrediting agencies, plead for freedom from political regulations or other such pressures, mold and reinforce the sense of collective identity among individual members, and, in general, legitimate the profession and its activities before outsiders and insiders."

27. (1991) 35.

28. See Fahnestock (1986).

translates the scientific idea from its specialist point of origin to a broader audience (we might think here of the elucidating techniques that Seneca builds into his extensive doxographical reporting), potentially casts the idea as more certain than it really is by presenting it in a format that irons out its more involved complexities.

We shall see that, in his idiosyncratic way, Seneca touches on certain of these categories of rhetoric in his survey of hail theories at 4b.3–7. But our approach to this survey takes its start from Stephen Toulmin's stimulating remarks on communication in science:

> In the last resort, can we dissociate the justification of scientific concepts and beliefs entirely from issues of communication in science? Can we talk in real life of "carrying the rational tasks of science through to completion" while ignoring questions about communication? Or do the rational and rhetorical aspects of science legitimately and inescapably overlap? *Surely the persuasiveness, and even the "probativeness," of a scientific argument requires us to present it in terms that carry conviction with its audience.* Judging the rational merits of a theoretical novelty in, say, electrodynamics, we do well to consider the rhetorical power with which it "speaks to the condition of" the scientists concerned. From this point of view, the rhetoric of communication and the rationality of discovery are no longer separate, as they were before 1960; instead, they now share common ground.[29]

If in modern science "[t]he manner in which an argument is presented ('Was it convincing, or only heartwarming?'; 'Did it hit the point, or go over their heads?') is…as relevant to its intellectual merits as the intrinsic solidity of the case,"[30] issues of persuasive methodology and presentation are still more pressing in a Greco-Roman context, where the practical limitations of experimentation and observation into so many physical phenomena make definitive explanation so elusive.[31] Well before Aristotle undertook his systematic analysis of reasoning and

---

29. Toulmin (1995) 4; my emphasis.

30. Cf. Toulmin (1995) 6.

31. Conveniently, Rihll (1999) 12–13. Cf. the distinction drawn already by the author of *On Ancient Medicine* between medicine and those studies (e.g., "on things in the sky or under the earth") that rely on ὑποθέσεις or "postulates" (ch. 1 = 1.572 Littré, cited by Lloyd [1979] 135): "In such matters, medicine differs from subjects like astronomy and geology, of which a man might know the truth and lecture on it without either he or his audience being able to judge whether it were the truth or not, because there is no sure criterion" (trans. J. Chadwick and W. N. Mann).

of modes/techniques of valid-invalid argumentation,[32] the Pre-Socratics had already pioneered the use of rational techniques of persuasion such as analogy, deductive reasoning, careful observation of patterns in nature, appeal to abstract argument as opposed to reliance on the senses, and so on.[33] Many of these techniques recur in the *Natural Questions*, whether in Seneca's own seemingly independent speculations about given phenomena or in his extensive doxographical coverage of the "virtual academy"[34] of Greco-Roman researchers who, spanning the centuries, lend their own form of internal scientific chronology to the work. Of special interest for now, however, is not so much Seneca's redeployment of inherited modes of argumentation, but rather his reflection in Book 4b on the inseparability of "the rhetoric of scientific communication" on the one hand, "the logic of scientific justification" on the other.[35]

Quite apart from the restrictions that the book's incomplete state obviously imposes on any full, contextualized reading of its surviving part, two further considerations importantly condition our analysis of Seneca's testing of rhetorical/scientific argument in Book 4b. First, our preoccupation is not with the more general Stoic theory of rhetoric as a branch of logic along with dialectic, and not with any significant Senecan contribution in Book 4b to Stoic reflection on the technical parts and divisions of rhetoric.[36] Nor is our preoccupation with the broader, longstanding tension in antiquity between natural science/philosophy on the one hand, rhetoric on the other as a lurking enemy of rationality. If Plato's *Gorgias* classically frames the terms of that debate,[37] the Socratic/Platonic incompatibility of philosophy and rhetoric nevertheless left much room for ambiguity and irony in the eyes of later interpreters. Cicero for one, in his *De oratore*, has his Crassus blame Socrates for "the truly absurd, unprofitable and reprehensible rift between the tongue and the brain, leading to our having one set of professors to teach us to think, another to speak" (3.61); yet Cicero's Socrates is himself cast as rhetorically adept,[38] and in mocking other orators Plato himself "seemed to be the consummate orator" (1.47; cf. *Or.* 62, *Off.* 1.4). Cicero declares it his brief to reconcile the professions of philosophy and rhetoric, which had long been at

32. Lloyd (1979) 62–66; Warner (1989) 41–54.

33. Lloyd (1979) 66–79 on "Early philosophical argumentation."

34. Hine (2006) 58–59. Cf. Introduction n. 28.

35. Toulmin's terms: (1995) 3–4.

36. Conveniently, Schenkeveld (1999) 216–19.

37. Succinctly, Warner (1989) 32–33, in connection with the *Phaedrus*; Smith (1995) 304–305.

38. Cf. 3.60 with Long (1995) 51.

loggerheads[39]—a mediating tendency that is well illustrated by Crassus' argument in *De oratore* 1 that science and philosophy find important assistance in oratory: "your[40] natural science and mathematics...are matters of expert knowledge [*scientiae*] for those who teach them, but if anyone should want to give luster to those arts in speech, his first recourse would be to oratorical skill [*ad oratoris...facultatem*]" (1.61). But whereas Cicero rises in his *De oratore* and elsewhere to the great challenge of resolving the complex history of antagonism between rhetoric and philosophy, Seneca's focus in *Natural Questions* 4b is much narrower. We shall see that, by testing the strengths and weaknesses of particular strategies of argument, he consolidates his own self-projection in the *Natural Questions* as a highly self-conscious researcher who engages not just with the *res ipsa*, the natural world as external object-of-study, but also with pressing internal issues of methodology and critical orientation.

Second, the objection awaits that the coherent methodological subplot reconstructed in Section IV below is not explicitly signaled or announced by Seneca: Why this silence if the methodological introspection claimed for him in what follows is so important to the evolution of the *Natural Questions* as a whole? Of course, it is possible that the lost portion of Book 4b contained a programmatic allusion of this sort. Yet the absence of any such formal announcement would not be atypical of Seneca's understated artistic procedure elsewhere in the work, where the subtlety of his *literary*-scientific mode so often lies precisely in his power of suggestion rather than in explicit textual signaling. In contrast to any more formal undertaking, this implicit approach in Book 4b arguably allows greater room for maneuver and creative risk taking; and it is also in keeping with Seneca's oblique and playful manner throughout the surviving fragment. After all, in contrast to the drier, insistently methodical procedure of (say) Aristotle's *Meteorologica*, Book 4b is notably shot through with shafts of humor and ironic commentary[41] that develop in another direction the highly idiosyncratic researcher-persona that Seneca has cultivated from the outset of the *Natural Questions*. In Book 4b itself the serious work of testing different modes of argument is

---

39. See Long (1995) 55 with Kennedy (1963) 321–30, MacKendrick (1989) 31–35 and Warner (1989) 55 ("To this thesis, that the two arts [sc. wisdom and eloquence] are separable but each can benefit the other, Cicero was committed throughout his life").

40. I.e., Q. Mucius Scaevola, Crassus' father-in-law, representing in *De oratore* 1 the view that Crassus overestimates the political/social influence of orators; often incapable of dealing with intricate questions of law, religion, science and philosophy, they belong only in the law courts or political debate (1.35–44).

41. In general on this tendency, Waiblinger (1977) 78–79; Hine (1980b); Gross (1989) 195; Vottero (1989) 508 n. 10, 512 n. 6, etc.; Parroni (2002) xxxi; Berno (2003) 169–71; Taub (2003) 144 ("often...deliberately jocular").

gently alleviated by this witty presence, as if our investigator plays down any hint of lofty pretension by cultivating a ludic mode of treatment. Hence, perhaps, his informal and often colloquial tone,[42] and his notable use of ordinary legal language and metaphor, as at 4b.5.1: "Very few theories pass unopposed; the others, even if they win through, still have to go to law [*litigant*]."[43] Seneca's opinionated coverage of these litigants suggestively casts him as a free-ranging arbiter of sorts in 4b, albeit with a shift of emphasis in 4b.8–12. There, as we shall see in Section V below, he serves as an advocate for his favored theory that snow is formed in the near atmosphere; but first his coverage of the various theories on display in 4b.3–7.

IV: Strategies of Argument in 4b.3–7

The modern reader can turn to the assured rhetoric of the textbook to learn the true cause of hail and snowflakes:

> A cloud is an assembly of tiny droplets usually numbering several hundred per cubic centimeter.... Precipitation develops when the cloud population becomes unstable, and some drops grow at the expense of others. There are two mechanisms whereby a cloud microstructure may become unstable. The first is the direct collision and coalescence (sticking) of water droplets and may be important in any cloud. The second mechanism requires the interaction between water droplets and ice crystals and is confined to those clouds whose tops extend to temperatures colder than 0°C.
>
> ... When an ice crystal exists in the presence of a large number of supercooled water droplets the situation is immediately unstable. The equilibrium

---

42. So, e.g., 4.1 *bene mensum dabo* with Vottero (1989) 53; 4.1 *coepi tibi molestus esse* with Berno (2003) 169 n. 113; 4.1 *ut fallar tibi* with Vottero 53 (but *ut fatear tibi*...Hine [1996a] 192.54; cf. Section IV (D) n. 80 below in this chapter); 6.2 *paenulas* and *scorteas* with Bourgery (1922) 213; 6.3 *bene acuto* with Setaioli (1981) 24–25 n. 6 = (2000) 70 n. 464; 6.3 *agello* with Vottero 514 n. 6 (the diminutive "tipico dello stile diatribico"); 7.3 *tam palam est* with Hofmann (1951) 203; 13.3 *nempe* and 13.10 *dii boni* with Summers (1910) l; the markedly diatribic tone of 4b.13 in particular yields numerous other examples (so, e.g., 13.10 *boletos* and *focali* with Bourgery 211). Proverbial phrases (Vottero 51; Berno 169 and n. 113): variations at 3.4 on the idea *gutta cauat lapidem*, with Otto (1890) 156–57 no. 774; 5.3 *in Care experiaris* with Otto 75 no. 348; 7.1 *quamuis munera et deos uincant* with Otto 233 no. 1165; 11.5 *pilus pilo crassior* with Otto 279 no. 1420.

43. Cf. 3.1 *testibus* and *spondere*, 4.1 *Poteram me peracta quaestione dimittere* with Hine (2006) 55 and nn. 50–52; 7.1 *paciscatur* with Armisen-Marchetti (1989) 108; 13.1 *cum luxuria litigare* with Berno (2003) 147 and n. 10 (cf. also *Letters* 51.13: *satis diu cum Bais litigauimus, numquam satis cum uitiis*).

vapor pressure over ice is less than that over water at the same temperature and consequently the ice crystal grows by diffusion of vapor and the drops evaporate to compensate for this....

Once the ice crystal has grown by diffusion to a size appreciably larger than the water droplets, it begins to fall relative to them and collisions become possible. If the collisions are mainly with other ice crystals snow-flakes form; if water droplets are collected graupel or hail may form. Once the particle falls below the 0°C level melting can occur, and the particle may emerge from cloud base as a raindrop indistinguishable from one formed by coalescence. In cold weather, or when large hailstones are formed, the particle may of course reach the ground unmelted.[44]

If the steady, dispassionate tone and the impersonal style here are generically conditioned by the protocols of modern textbook rhetoric, Seneca's playful and often ironic tone in Book 4b gives his voice a more personal character; and that characterful effect lies partly in his opinionated engagement with the strengths, and especially the weaknesses, of the theories he reviews. Down to 4b.7.3 five categories of argument and explanation may be distinguished as follows.

(A) Reliance on Influential Authority

The first category sampled by Seneca relies on what Toulmin characterizes as "the extrinsic probability of a belief," i.e., "the support lent it by people who speak about the matter with authority (e.g. 'learned teachers of the subject generally agree')."[45] So Posidonius at 4b.3.1–2, for Kidd "a baffling fragment" in which Seneca writes with "kittenish playfulness":[46]

[3.1]...grandinem hoc modo fieri si tibi adfirmauero quo apud nos glacies fit, gelata nube tota, nimis audacem rem fecero. itaque ex his me testibus numera secundae notae, qui uidisse quidem se negant. aut quod historici faciunt et ipse faciam: illi cum multa mentiti sunt ad suum arbitrium, unam aliquam rem nolunt spondere, sed adiciunt: 'penes auctores fides erit'.[47] [3.2] ergo si mihi parum credis, Posidonius tibi auctoritatem prom-

---

44. Rogers and Yau (1989) 82–84.

45. Toulmin (1995) 6–7.

46. Kidd (1988) 510 on fr. 136.

47. For this phrase cf., e.g., Sall. *Jug.* 17.7 with Vottero (1989) 507 n. 7; Eden (1984) 82 on *Apoc.* 5.1, where Seneca's amusing allusion to "relying on his informant" for his account of

ittet tam in illo quod praeterît quam in hoc quod secuturum est. grandinem
enim fieri ex nube aquosa iam et in umorem uersa sic adfirmabit tamquam
interfuerit.

[3.1] If I assured you that hail is formed in the same way as ice is with
us, except that an entire cloud is frozen, I would be making too bold a
claim. So consider me as one of those second-grade witnesses who state
that they themselves were not direct observers. Or I may follow the practice of historians: after they have told a lot of lies to their satisfaction, they
are unwilling to pledge the truth of a given point, but add: 'Verification
will be found in my sources'. [3.2] So, if you lack faith in me, Posidonius
will pledge you his authority, on both what has passed and what follows.
For he will assure you, as if he'd been there to see it, that hail comes from a
cloud that is full of water and has just changed to liquid.

According to Diogenes Laertius (7.153), "hail is frozen cloud, crumbled by wind;
while snow is moisture from a cloud that has frozen: so Posidonius in the eighth
book of his *Natural Philosophy*." If the hail theory *as well as* the snow theory is
here taken to be Posidonian,[48] Diogenes helpfully illuminates the different components of Posidonius' theory as represented by Seneca: (1) 3.1 *grandinem... tota*:
hail is formed when a whole cloud has frozen; (2) 3.2 *grandinem enim... uersa*:
the cloud later begins to melt, and so breaks apart into ice-drops. On this interpretation, the phrase *tam in illo quod praeterît quam in hoc quod secuturum est*
(3.2) hardly amounts to T. H. Corcoran's "Posidonius guarantees you his authority both *on the point he omitted* and on what follows [i.e., *grandinem... uersa*]."[49]
In *quod praeterît* Corcoran detects "[a] reference to some lost section of the
book"[50]—by which he presumably means a Senecan allusion in the missing part
of 4b to a point that Posidonius apparently passed over in silence; yet how could
Posidonius "guarantee his authority" on a point that he had passed over?[51] The
more natural complement to "what follows" is to interpret *praeterît* in the sense

---

the proceedings in heaven after Claudius' death again shows him (in Eden's words) "scepti-
cal of this cliché of 'historians.'" For Seneca's hostility to *historici* elsewhere (albeit Callisthenes a notable exception at 6.23.2–4), see Chapters One, Section III and n. 43, and Seven,
Section V.

48. Kidd (1988) 513 is cautious. Cf. Vottero (1989) 508 n. 9: Diogenes attributes the Stoic hail
theory "to no one in particular; it belongs to the Stoic school generally."

49. Corcoran (1971–72) 2.47; my emphasis.

50. (1971–72) 2.47 n. 3.

51. So Parroni (1992a) 357 and (2002) 558, objecting to the interpretations of Oltramare
(1929) 2.195 and Vottero (1989) 509.

of Seneca's "past statement," i.e. the first part of the Posidonian theory that he has just rendered in 3.1 *grandinem...tota*;[52] or, more enterprisingly, to see in the contrast between *quod praeterit* and *quod secuturum est* the process of becoming (cf. *fieri*, 3.2) in the different stages of hail formation, to the effect that the movement from "what has passed" to "what follows" tracks (1) hail originally formed when a cloud is frozen, and (2) hail eventually released when the cloud melts.[53]

Writing of rhetorical conventions of scientific presentation that serve at a basic level to establish confidence in a given author's proficiency, Philip Kitcher focuses first on proactively drawing attention to factors that could potentially weaken or contaminate the findings reached, and then on locating a given experiment in a reassuring context of established techniques.[54] These conventions are characterized by Kitcher as a form of "dead rhetoric,"[55] as if mandated by the research-paper genre; and in his different way Seneca rounds on a comparable phenomenon in his treatment of Posidonius. Kidd expresses puzzlement at Seneca's maneuvers in 3.1 *grandinem...fecero* ("Why does Seneca protest that the first statement on hail is bold or shocking?") and *itaque...fides erit* ("Why the elaboration of Seneca's claim that he is only a hearsay witness? And it is elaborate"), and he finds "a very laboured joke" if Seneca effectively asserts merely that "*I* have never seen a frozen cloud."[56] Yet Seneca's arch tone, his histrionic condemnation of the "tribe" of historians (cf. *natio*, 7.16.2), the extravagant gesture with which he invokes Posidonius as his guarantor of the scientific truth (cf. *tibi auctoritatem promittet*, 3.2), as if Posidonius had himself been up there amid the clouds (*tamquam interfuerit*, 3.2): all these features contribute to the jocular, and ironically self-implicating (Seneca himself relies on Posidonius...), critique that he builds here (1) of the limits of firsthand scientific observation, perhaps with "a general quip at Posidonius' stress on autopsy";[57] and (2) of what might be termed

---

52. Kidd (1999) 195, after (1988) 512; cf. now, in the same vein, Hine (2010b) 65: "Posidonius will guarantee you his authority both *for what has been said* and *for what is to follow*" (my emphasis). Parroni (1992a) 357 and (2002) 558 hesitates to render *quod praeterit* "ciò che precede" because "questo significato non è documentato per *praetereo*," but cf. *OLD* 4b, incl. Cic. *Diu.* 1.126: fate is "the eternal cause of things, the reason why things past [*ea quae praeterierunt*] happened, why things present happen, and why things to come [*quae sequuntur*] will happen." Emendation to *praeiit* (Garrod [1915] 45) or *praeterii* (Gross [1989] 191–93, to the effect that Seneca has just "passed over" the Posidonian affinity of hail and ice in 3.1 *grandinem...glacies fit* without going into details) is unnecessary.

53. Suggested to me by John Henderson.

54. Kitcher (1995) 55–56.

55. Kitcher (1995) 56.

56. Kidd (1988) 510, 511, 512.

57. Kidd (1988) 512.

"secondary science," or the attempt to persuade by relying on the "authoritative scaffolding"[58] of an imposing source—an inherently fragile technique that, in cynical operation (cf. *illi...fides erit*, 3.1), potentially amounts to an illusionist's exploitation of the Kitcher brand of "dead rhetoric."

(B) Argument by Analogy

This category is based on simple observation (4b.3.3–4), no teacher necessary (cf. *sine magistro*, 3.3): hail is round because any and all liquid drops are globular. Moisture collected on mirrors, drops scattered on cups and globules clinging to leaves all illustrate as much, but these pleasing images cannot disguise at least two difficulties: (1) to state that hail is round because it is like any liquid droplet is merely descriptive and fails to address the why of the roundness itself;[59] and (2), if Seneca accepts the Posidonian theory of hail produced by liquefaction in or of cloud (cf. *ex nube aquosa iam et in umorem uersa*, 3.2), how were the round moisture drops falling from cloud (re)frozen to form hail?[60] Perhaps Posidonius suggested that the shape of the hailstones "was determined by the process of liquefaction in the cloud having started, and so round ice drops are produced before they start to fall";[61] but Seneca seems to speak of *complete* liquefaction (cf. again *in umorem uersa*, 3.2), and so to presuppose refreezing by some unclear means. The point matters because of Seneca's subsequent maneuver in 3.5: "Moreover, *even if hail was not originally so shaped*, it could be rounded when it fell," the friction of its fall through thick air wearing it into globular shape.[62] Does

---

58. Gross (1990) 13. Gross's analysis of "the structure of scientific authority" has implications for Seneca's own impressive appeal in the *Natural Questions* to the authority of the "virtual academy" (Hine [2006] 58–59) of researchers before him; for (Gross 13) "All scientific papers...are embedded in a network of authority relationships: publication in a respected journal; behind that publication, a series of grants given to scientists connected with a well-respected research institution; within the text, a trail of citations highlighting the paper as the latest result of a vital and ongoing research program. Without this authoritative scaffolding, the innovative core of these papers—their sections on results, and their discussions—would be devoid of significance." In his different way Seneca, too, relies upon, and draws part of his investigative credibility from, the "network of authority relationships" that his "virtual academy" provides.

59. Cf. Oltramare (1929) 2.196 n. 1.

60. Cf. Kidd (1988) 514 ("how was this 'rain' subsequently frozen?").

61. Kidd (1988) 513.

62. Roundness through falling: cf. Anaxagoras in Section IV (C) below in this chapter; Antiphon the Sophist, D-K 87B29 = fr. 29 Pendrick (2002) 148 with 298–99, and cf. Graham (2010) 2.806–7 and 835 on Text 43; Aristot. *Mete.* 1.12 348a30–6; Epic. *Ep. Pyth.* 107, with Aet. *Plac.* 3.4.5 (*DG* p. 371).

he conveniently evade the difficulty just sketched in (2) above by now circumventing the Posidonian process of liquefaction-in-cloud? Or does he neatly account for all possibilities by now explaining the shape of hail as a consequence of its fall, not of its origin in cloud?

A further difficulty arises in 3.4:

> quid magis est saxo durum? quid mollius unda?
> dura tamen molli saxa *cauantur* aqua.

aut ut alius poeta ait, 'stillicidi casus lapidem *cauat.*' haec ipsa excauatio rotunda fit, ex quo apparet illud quoque huic simile esse quod cauat: locum enim sibi ad formam et habitum sui exsculpit.

> What is harder than rock? What softer than water?
> Yet hard rocks are hollowed out by soft water.

> [Ovid, *Ars* 1.475–76]

Or, as another poet says [Lucretius 1.313], 'The fall of dripping water hollows out a stone'. This hollow is itself round, and from this it is clear that the shape in the rock resembles that which causes the hollow; for it hollows out a spot corresponding to its own shape and character.

True to his penchant for topical verse quotation throughout the *Natural Questions*, Seneca's borrowings from Ovid and Lucretius offer a colorful, if somewhat redundant, variation on the analogies that he has already adduced—moisture on mirrors, etc.—for the roundness of hail (what pressing need is there for yet further illustration?). But if we detect a hint of overdecorous superfluity to the Ovidian/Lucretian presence here, does Seneca also gently test the limits of persuasive analogical argument? After all, his impressive rhetoric barely disguises the slickness of his logic, to the effect that water causes round hollows in rock, *and therefore* (cf. *ex quo apparet*) the droplets are themselves round—a transition as smooth as it is suspect. And something more: in its original context the celebrated Ovidian couplet illustrates the attritional effects of time, and the impact that a lover can gradually make on his beloved through his patient and persistent attentions; and the Lucretian verse is one of a series of *exempla* illustrating material attrition through atomic loss, again with emphasis on the slow passage of time (cf. *multis solis redeuntibus annis*, 1.311). If at 4b.3.4 we recall the contexts of these familiar verses (quotations too famous to need attribution to their authors),[63] Seneca's

---

63. See Mazzoli (1970) 208; on the lines' proverbial quality, cf. Section III n. 42 above in this chapter. That the Ovidian couplet was itself proverbial by Seneca's time is indicated by its (mis-)quotation among the Pompeian graffiti (*CIL* 4.1895; further, Mazzoli 239 n. 68).

distortion of their original illustrative point is immediately striking: it is the shape of the attrition, not the time it takes or the atomic depletion that it causes, that now matters above all, with Ovid's *cauantur* and Lucretius' *cauat* suddenly promoted to a significance that they signally lack in their home texts.[64] The verse quotations are adduced, we remember, to support the case for the roundness of hail. But the poetic memory in play here is so selective, even distorting, in the emphasis it prioritizes in Ovid and Lucretius that the analogical function of the quotations appears strained to the knowing reader— a factor that, in combination with Seneca's slick logic, threatens to make the poetic presence more of a liability than an asset to his main argument, especially if we are in any case disconcerted by his "straight" application of an Ovidian couplet that masquerades as offering serious instruction in its original, erotic context.

(C) Argument by Bold Inference

This category of argument here takes its start from Anaxagoras:

> Quare non et ego mihi idem permittam quod Anaxagoras? inter nullos magis quam inter philosophos esse debet aequa libertas.
>
> 4b.3.6

> Why shouldn't I allow myself the same liberties that Anaxagoras takes? There should be equal freedom among no group more than among philosophers.

It may be that in *Quare...Anaxagoras?* Seneca takes up an allusion to Anaxagoras in the lost portion of Book 4b,[65] now claiming for himself something of the imaginative license that had presumably characterized Anaxagoras in that earlier reference. Perhaps the allusion was to Anaxagoras' paradoxical theory of the blackness of snow[66]—a theory mocked by Cicero, and perhaps similarly treated by Seneca

---

64. For the familiar topos, Smith (1913) 269 on Tib. 1.4.18. That Seneca means to give *cauo -are* special prominence is signaled by his avoidance of the still more striking Lucretian application of the topos at 4.1286–7, where water drops "beat a way through" (*pertundere*) the stone—but where *cauo -are* does not feature. For other Ovidian instances of the topos with *cauo*, cf. *Pont.* 1.1.70, 2.7.40, 4.10.5.

65. So, e.g., Oltramare (1929) 2.196 n. 6; Corcoran (1971–72) 2.49 n. 4; Hall (1977) 432 and n. 1; Gross (1989) 195; Hine (1980b) and (2010b) 200 n. 4.

66. So Hine (1980b); Gross (1989) 195; Parroni (1992a) 358 and (2002) 558–59. For the theory, D-K 59A97 with Guthrie (1965) 286 and n. 2; Kirk et al. (1983) 371.

as an example of extreme *libertas*.[67] Alternatively, the theory just reported at 3.5—hailstones are made round by the friction of their fall—has been connected via Aetius with Anaxagoras' theory of hail, to the effect that "hail is formed when some parts are thrown downwards towards the ground from the frozen clouds—parts which, chilled by their descent, are made round in shape."[68] If we accept that Anaxagoras is indeed present in 3.5,[69] the Senecan allusion at 3.6 *Quare... Anaxagoras?* need not be to the lost portion of 4b but simply to the preceding paragraph. But wherever we locate any backward reference to Anaxagoras (and, on balance, it is perhaps more tempting to suspect a colorful allusion to the "black snow" theory), the important point for now is that Seneca's subsequent argument is better taken to be Anaxagoran in the liberties it takes, and not necessarily as an Anaxagoran theory in itself:[70]

> grando nihil aliud est quam suspensa glacies, nix pruina pendens. illud enim iam diximus, quod inter rorem et aquam interest, hoc inter pruinam et glaciem, nec non inter niuem et grandinem interesse.
>
> 4b.3.6

Hail is nothing other than ice held in suspension, snow is suspended frost. For we have already said [sc. in the lost part of 4b] that the difference between frost and ice, and also that between snow and hail, corresponds to that between dew and water.

The precise nature of the three-way correlation worked in *quod... interesse* between dew and water, frost and ice and snow and hail appears to lie in the presumption that "dew, frost and snow all have a large admixture of air, whereas water, ice and hail contain no air."[71] From the descriptive use of analogy in 4b.3.4

---

67. Cf. Cic. *Luc.* 72, 100, *Q. fr.* 2.12.1. For the humor of the Senecan treatment, Hine (1980b) and (1996a) 189.7–190.10; but for "a serious edge" cf. also Hine (2006) 60: "'Equal freedom' was a political slogan of the late Republic, but Seneca finds it in philosophy rather than politics."

68. So Aet. *Plac.* 3.4.2 as given at D-K 59A85 (cf. *DG* p. 371).

69. So inclines Vottero (1989) 509–10 n. 19; already Setaioli (1988) 449.

70. Rightly Parroni (2002) 559: "Quel che segue [sc. *grando...pendens*] non ha dunque nulla a che vedere con il pensiero di Anassagora"; contrast Setaioli (1988) 449, and cf. D-K 2 p. 420.15–18.

71. Hine (1996b) 78, adducing 4b.13.2: "When we investigate how snow is formed, and we say that it is similar in nature to frost (*pruinae*), that there is more air than water in it...." He rightly rejects Gross's superficially attractive but unnecessary rewriting to effect a contrast between phenomena formed on the ground and those formed in the atmosphere ([1989] 195–96):...*hoc inter pruinam et niuem nec non inter glaciem et grandinem interesse*, accepted by Parroni (1992a) 357–58, (2002) 282.31–2, 559.

we now progress to analogy as an incisive tool, an inferential principle that leads from the known to the unknown, raising our vision from here (frost and ice at ground level) to yield speculative insight there (snow and hail as frost and ice in suspension).[72] Seneca's apparent satisfaction with the theory allows him to draw a provisional close to his investigation ("I could stop now, since the inquiry is complete…" 4.1), but the objection remains: the license (cf. *libertas*) that he indulges in 3.6 makes for a daring leap of logic that relies to no small extent on neat rhetorical packaging (*grando…pendens*) for its air of conviction and its enticing effect. Here is a good example of inferential speculation transformed by "the enchantments of language"[73] into seemingly plausible fact.

(D) Competing Arguments

This category offers a miniature case study of sorts in the weighing of different arguments; at issue is why hail tends to fall not in winter but in spring, after the cold is broken (4b.4.1). Aristotle for one had already grappled with the problem of why hail, although ice, is commonest in spring and autumn, rather less common in summer, and apparently rare in winter (*Mete.* 1.12 347b37–348a2). He attributed the cause to the mutual reaction of heat and cold on one another (ἀντιπερίστασις), whereby cold compressed in warmer seasons may produce heavy rain or, if the compression is greater and the refrigeration process quick, hail.[74] Of the two theories offered by Seneca, *the first* stresses spring warming (4.2–3): whereas the stiff atmosphere in winter produces snow but only sluggish and thin rains, the warming effect causes larger drops to form and occasions greater turbulence in the now-loosened atmosphere. The movement from stiff winter to looser spring is suggestively replicated at a textual level in the eventual emergence of *uer* in *nondum in aquam uertitur* [sc. *aër*]…*cum uer coepit* (4.2), in the growth and development signified by Seneca's marked sequence of comparative adjectives (*maior, calidiore, maiora, uehementior*), and in the sudden shift of register from prose to verse when he quotes *Georgics* 1.313 *ideo, ut ait Vergilius noster, "cum ruit imbriferum uer"*…("So, as our Virgil says, 'when rain-bearing spring rushes in…'"). After this emphasis on hail caused by atmospheric warming, however, *the second*, apparently Stoic, argument[75] featured by Seneca at 5.2–4 effectively

---

72. For this bold use of analogy, cf. especially Chapter Six, Sections III and V (C).

73. Kitcher (1995) 48.

74. *Mete.* 1.12 348b2–18. On ἀντιπερίστασις, Lee (1952) 82–83 n. *b* with Hine (1981) 193–95 (a different sort of ἀντιπερίστασις or *circumstantia* at *N.Q.* 2.7).

75. Cf. *Rem a nostris positam* (5.1) with Wildberger (2006) 506 n. 157.

asserts the opposite position: when the icy grip of winter is loosened by the arrival of spring in Scythia and the Black Sea region, cold air arises from those northern parts and condenses the warming and moist atmosphere in the southern regions, thus converting rain into hail.

After spring warming as the cause of hail in 4b.4, then, a sudden cold front develops in 4b.5. The second, Stoic argument has been interpreted as anecdotal and diverting in flavor, as if Seneca here briefly applies a lighter touch to his proceedings.[76] Considered together, however, I propose (1) that the two arguments in 4b.4–5 function as juxtaposed opposites, to the effect that the original question—why hail in spring (4.1)?—is made relative and answerable from diametrically contrasting positions; (2) that the two theories are effectively in deadlock, neither of them intrinsically more probable or persuasive than the other, at least when the two expositions (4.2–3, 5.2–4) are removed from their context and measured directly against each other; and (3) that Seneca's brief introductory remarks (4.1, 5.1) before he sets out each of the two theories nevertheless crucially condition our response to both of them, as if a mini-demonstration of how rhetorical casting manipulates and affects the plausibility of a given, neutral theory (i.e., one that neither persuades nor dissuades on its own merits). Seneca's playful tone throughout 4b.4–5 is well suited to what is itself an informal, ludic testing of scientific neutrality on the one hand, the power of rhetorical shaping and shading on the other.

At 4b.5.1 Seneca conveniently establishes his credentials as an independent-minded and apparently fair investigator by resisting the theory of "our" Stoics and yet still presenting it, despite the weaknesses he alleges, for Lucilius' own inspection:

> Rem a nostris positam nec dicere audeo quia infirma uidetur, nec praeterire. quid enim mali est aliquid et faciliori iudici scribere? immo si omnia argumenta ad obrussam coeperimus exigere, silentium indicetur. pauca enim admodum sunt sine aduersario, cetera, etsi uincunt, litigant.
>
> I hesitate, because it seems weak, to mention a theory advanced by our Stoic[77] friends, but hesitate also to overlook it. For what harm is there in writing something for a more lenient judge as well? After all, if we start to subject every argument to testing by fire, we'll be compelled to silence. For very few theories pass unopposed; the others, even if they win through, still have to go to law.

---

76. Cf. Vottero (1989) 512 n. 1.

77. See n. 75 above in this section.

Positioned as it is between the two arguments set out in 4b.4 and 4b.5, this passage implicates both as competing litigants and adversaries before Lucilius as adjudicator.[78] Yet for all his pose of evenhandedness, Seneca's reluctance to omit the Stoic theory is perhaps more backhanded in its claim to objective coverage. From the outset *infirma* surely tilts the balance against this second litigant; and given his distinctly negative subcommentary on the theory ("If, then, they are not liars...," 5.4), certain features within his recounting of it at 5.2–4 take on a sharper edge. It is hard, for example, to read an inflection such as "It is therefore conceivable" (*credibile est ergo*, 5.2) without irony, and hard not to detect a hint of trivialization in Seneca's witty refusal ("Rather you than me")[79] to test the Stoic claim that feet feel less cold when they tread on hard and solid rather than soft and slushy snow. Yet despite this gentle undermining of the Stoic theory in 4b.5, Seneca's earlier argument in 4b.4 struggles to overcome difficulties of its own:

> ...quoniam coepi tibi molestus esse, quidquid in hoc loco quaeritur dicam. quaeritur autem quare hieme ninguat, non grandinet, uere iam frigore infracto cadat grando. nam ut fallar tibi, uerum mihi quidem persuadetur,[80] qui me usque ad mendacia haec leuiora, in quibus os percidi non oculi erui solent, credulum praesto.

4b.4.1

> ...since I've begun to make a nuisance of myself to you, I'll set out everything asked about this question [sc. phenomena such as snow and hail]. (And in fact a common question is why there is snow in winter but no hail, and why in spring, when the cold is broken, hail falls.) For although I may be mistaken in your eyes, I myself at any rate am persuaded of the truth—a man who shows himself credulous up to the limit of these less

---

78. Perhaps with gentle irony in *faciliori*: is Lucilius too accommodating, even a somewhat impressionable judge (cf. *OLD* 9a)?

79. My paraphrase for *tu quoque, censeo, si uolueris uerum exquirere, niuem in Care experiaris* (5.3, with Gronovius' *Care*), "You also, I think, if you want to discover the truth, should test the snow on a Carian." For the proverbial *in Care experiaris* (cf. Pl. *Laches* 187b, Cic. *Flacc.* 65), to the effect that a Carian slave is sufficiently worthless to be risked in any experiment, or that the Carians supplied the first mercenaries, Vottero (1989) 512–13 n. 7, and cf. Otto (1890) as cited in Section III n. 42 above in this chapter.

80. *nam ut fatear tibi uerum, mihi quidem <facile> persuadetur* Hine (1996a) 192.54–5, perhaps rightly (*facile* Shackleton Bailey [1979] 453); *fatear*, conjectured by F. Skutsch, and in a single manuscript (Hine [1996a] 192.54 app.) is already accepted by Gercke (1907) 162.11, but for the text as given here stoutly defended, cf. Alexander (1948) 301–302 with Vottero (1989) 171. For the force of *nam* felt in relation to *quidquid...dicam*, Alexander 301 after Oltramare (1929) 2.197 n. 2.

serious lies, for which you usually get your face slapped, not your eyes gouged out.[81]

The truth of which Seneca is persuaded naturally extends to the theory that he recounts in 4b.4.2–3, and which is then opposed to the "weak" (*infirma*) Stoic theory in 4b.5. But just how reassuring are the words preceding that first argument (4b.4.1)? After all, if in 5.1 Seneca works to affirm his credentials as an objective investigator, in 4.1 he appears much more subjective in his sureness of mind (*nam...persuadetur*: "You may think I'm wrong, but I'm sure I'm right"); and the self-deprecating irony with which he admits his impressionability ("a man who shows himself credulous...") also threatens to work against him. Even as his ensuing argument speaks for itself in 4.2–3, the immediate background to it in 4.1 wittily tests our confidence in Seneca's investigatory credentials: if the Stoics are effectively branded as liars at 5.4 (*si non mentiuntur*, with heavy irony), does Seneca's self-positioning in 4.1 ironically compromise the plausibility of the argument that he presents in 4.2–3? Is that argument cast from the outset as potentially another trivial falsehood (cf. *mendacia haec leuiora*, 4.1) that impresses itself upon his credulous persona? The task before Lucilius as *iudex* is perhaps to judge not just the two arguments/theories *per se* in 4b.4–5, but also the nuances and vulnerabilities that Seneca's framing rhetoric (4.1, 5.1) gently imposes on each of them. The bare hypothesis is one thing (4.2–3, 5.3–4), its enhancement (or otherwise) through its mode of presentation quite another.

(E) Superstition in Contention with Reason

After his initial critique of Stoic opinion (cf. 4b.5.1), Seneca continues in a seemingly impromptu vein, jauntily asserting in 4b.6.1 that he "cannot refrain [*Non tempero mihi*][82] from mentioning all the absurdities [*omnis...ineptias*] of our Stoic friends."[83] In the event, after *omnis*, he comes up with just one such "absurdity," which here functions as a humorous interlude within his treatment of hail and snow; his target is the apparently Stoic assertion that experts can predict hail by observing, from experience (*usu*), the telling coloration of cloud. Given his acceptance elsewhere of the Stoic chain of causation (cf. 2.32.4: "Whatever happens is a sign of something that will happen"), and given the impressive weight of

---

81. "These less serious...gouged out": from Hine (1996b) 78; cf. (2010b) 66.

82. The *non tempero mihi quominus/quin* formulation recurs in the *Natural Questions* only at 3.18.7; for acute comparison of the usages/contexts, Berno (2003) 84–85.

83. For *nostrorum* here of the Stoics, Wildberger (2006) 506 n. 157.

the ancient tradition of meteorological prediction by signs,⁸⁴ the exact nature of Seneca's objection to the Stoic position here is less than clear—unless his target is not so much the Stoic claim that these experts exist,⁸⁵ but rather the strange fact (cf. *illud incredibile*, 6.2) that at Cleonae in the Argolid hail guards (χαλαζοφύλακες) were employed at public expense to avert hail by sacrifice.⁸⁶ "Rain has never caused problems to men without prior warning": so Virgil at *Georgics* 1.373–4 *numquam imprudentibus imber/obfuit*, in a passage on weather signs in which the value of forecasting brings but limited comfort: "Man...can learn...of impending disaster, but still that disaster always occurs, and occurs completely, *in spite of* the signs that tell of its coming."⁸⁷ From Seneca's rationalizing standpoint (cf. 7.1), and from this grimly realist Virgilian perspective, the people at Cleonae who, alerted by the hail watchers, try to avert the imminent shower by sacrificing a lamb or a chicken or (to save expense) by offering a pinprick of their own blood, are entrapped in superstition (cf. *mendacium et fabula est*, 7.2). Here is an easy target for Seneca to exploit in the name of reason (cf. 6.3: "Are you laughing at this? Here's something to make you laugh even more");⁸⁸ the "modern" age collides with uneducated antiquity (*rudis adhuc antiquitas*, 7.3),⁸⁹ and the educated who reject all possibility of bargaining with hail or buying off a storm are pointedly, even acidly, juxtaposed (*alteri...alteri*, 7.1; again the illusion of evenhanded-

---

84. Conveniently, Taub (2003) 15–69, 96–98 and (on Seneca) 157–59.

85. Cf. Inwood (2002) 135–36 = (2005) 176: "Evidently some members of his own school had tried to justify such antiquated and superstitious religious practices." Yet, in defense of the Stoics apparently attacked by Seneca, it might also be noted that in other areas of the predictive sciences, especially divination, philosophical supporters of such practices had well-established arguments to justify continuing belief in the practice despite failure in the particular instance of it; cf. Chapter Eight, Section III (C).

86. Cf. Paus. 2.34.3–4 with Frazer (1898) 3.289–90 for other "equally absurd modes of averting a hail-storm" in antiquity (further, Frazer 83 on Cleonae at 2.15.1); Plin. *Nat.* 28.77, Plut. *Quaest. conuiu.* 7.2 = *Mor.* 700e. See also Graver (2000) 46 on the hail watchers of 4b.6–7 implicated among "elements of Greek religion" which "provide us with a glimpse of the kind of power that can be wielded by those who are in a position to explain what to most people is both inexplicable and, in a farming society, genuinely threatening....The natural anxiety to understand and, if possible, control such events can easily be exploited to maintain the status of one or another group of persons. Most often these will be the priests...offering explanations in terms of divine agency, and directing remediations as they see fit, to serve their own interests or further their own aims."

87. Thomas (1988) 1.128; his emphasis.

88. Cf. Inwood (2002) 136 = (2005) 177 on "this nugatory point" about hail guards "as a foil. Seneca is self-consciously presenting himself as a thoughtful and methodologically careful author, unlike so many even of his own school" (cf. *nostrorum*, 6.1).

89. For this collision cf. 2.42, 3.14.1–2, 4a.2.24, but Seneca shows greater indulgence at 6.5.2–3 (see Chapter Six, Section V (A)).

ness) with investigators who apparently *do* suspect that blood has some force in it powerful enough to repel clouds.

The people of Cleonae take the hail guards to task when, because of the latter's alleged negligence, a hail shower is not averted and crops are flattened. Their continuing belief, even after such failures, that hail can be averted by sacrifice focuses attention not so much on the fact of their superstition as on their failure to move beyond it; the issue, that is, is not so much "How on earth can such people believe in naïve superstition?" but rather "Can people with inefficient [superstitious] beliefs come to be critical of them, under what conditions and to what extent?"[90] Seneca's Rome, however, has made different progress over time. As if balancing out the unscientific Greek experience at Cleonae with Roman superstition, he invokes the injunction in the Twelve Tables "that no one may use magical enchantment against another's crops" (7.2).[91] This Roman example of *rudis antiquitas* again offsets the "modern" rationalism that Seneca champions; the implication is that Rome has moved far beyond the naïve form of belief illustrated first in the case of Cleonae, then in this sample from the Twelve Tables.

V: The Better Argument

In 4b.3–7 as a whole we have sampled different approaches to articulating experience of the physical world, approaches ranging from the seemingly naïve and superstitious (4b.6–7) to ones that are more probing in their strategies of argument (4b.3–5), albeit with significant procedural weaknesses of their own, as we have seen. How, after all, to find words adequately to explain meteorological phenomena that challenge our understanding and tax the imagination? In this respect, the structural mechanics of argument and the persuasiveness of its rhetoric crucially aid and abet, and even in a sense amount to, the (Senecan) doing of science; and thus far in what remains of Book 4b Seneca has tested this "rhetoric of science" with a witty and playful detachment, his lightness of touch lending an entertaining air to the proceedings. This ludic aspect takes a different turn, however, in his new sequence of argument in 4b.8–12, a sequence prefaced by his confident claim that Lucilius "will be glad both to approve and applaud" Seneca's elaboration of the proposition that "snow is formed in that part of the atmosphere which is close to the earth" (8.1). After the vulnerabilities of approach and argument that we have detected down to 4b.7, I propose that this confident beginning ushers in a new *lusus*: a pilot demonstration, as it were, of "the rhetoric of scientific

---

90. Cf. Jarvie and Agassi (1967) 71 = Wilson (1970) 193, cited by Lloyd (1979) 7.

91. Bruns (1909) 30 *tab*. viii, fr. 8a; Crawford (1996) 2.682–4 *tab*. viii, 4.

communication"[92] in rather more successful, persuasive action—a success implicitly signaled from the outset by Seneca's anticipation of Lucilius' approval.

The argument is divisible into three sections that form a complex whole, creating the appearance of a well-controlled train of reasoning from beginning to end. For present purposes, the third section—Seneca's neat rounding out of his entire argument with the summation (4b.12) that "for the reasons I've given, most authorities are of the view that snow is formed in the part of the atmosphere which is near the earth"—concerns us least. We begin with Seneca's demonstration in the first section of argument (4b.8–10) that atmospheric warmth is commensurate to proximity to the earth "for four reasons" (8.1). Within this assured, systematic framework (cf. *una* [sc. *causa*]...*altera*... *tertia causa*, 8.1), Seneca anchors the argument by drawing first (*una*) on Aristotle's exhalation theory, to the effect that dry exhalation from the earth "is hotter the more recently it has been formed" (8.1); then (*altera*) the sun's rays rebound off the earth, twice impacting the near atmosphere (8.1)—a theory also closely combined, as here, with the Aristotelian exhalation theory at 2.10.3,[93] as if a tight grouping of safe, conventional argument in both places. Next (*tertia causa*), the near atmosphere is warmer because the lower regions are less wind-blown than the upper regions (8.1), an argument apparently at odds with Seneca's position at 2.11.1 (the atmosphere "is especially variable, inconstant and changeable in its *lowest* part"). In applying the wind argument in 4b.8, Seneca also overlooks the third argument for the warmth of the near atmosphere that he will go on to deploy at 2.10.3 (after the exhalation and *duplicatio radiorum* theories): the lower air is warmed by the breath from animals, trees and plants. In 2.10 does he offer correction of, or mere variation upon, the position taken in 4b.8, now replacing the *tertia causa* offered in 4b (the wind argument) with a newly favored alternative? Does he merely resort in 4b.8 to a source not used at 2.10.3? Either is conceivable, but for present purposes a third possibility holds special interest: is one of the ludic qualities of his procedure in 4b.8 precisely to use in a rhetorically persuasive frame (*una* [sc. *causa*]...*altera*... *tertia causa*) a third argument that (our broader experience of the *Natural Questions* tells us) is provisional and open to adjustment, and not especially favored by Seneca himself?

The fourth *causa* is more elaborate in its construction, its foundations laid in the Democritean theory that Seneca voices in Democritus' apparently quoted words in 4b.9.[94] By his presence here in his own reported voice, this Democritus

---

92. Toulmin (1995) 3.

93. On the Aristotelian impact on 2.10–11 in general (the nature of the atmosphere), Hine (1981) 213.

94. Not in D-K, and apparently not corroborated elsewhere for Democritus (but cf. Vottero [1989] 518 n. 2). But Seneca's various accounts of Democritean (*inter alia*) theories reported

lends a certain *grauitas* and rhetorical color to the proceedings, but more important for now is the impressive, systematic method on display in his three stages of argument. First, his proposition (*omne…seruat*): the more solid an object, the more quickly it absorbs heat and the longer it retains it. Second, empirical evidence to support the proposition (*itaque…haerebit*): if a bronze vessel, one of glass and one of silver are placed in the sun, "heat will enter the bronze one more quickly and will cling to it longer."[95] Third, his proposed explanation (*adicit deinde quare hoc existimet fieri*): the harder and more compact a given body, the smaller its openings ("too small for the eye to see"), and the air is thinner in each opening; in contrast to the more spacious openings in less compact bodies, these small openings feel heat more quickly and more slowly lose the heat they receive. This third stage is clinical in its organization, the rhetoric of necessity (*necesse est*)[96] generating an inference (*sequitur ut*) that is then consolidated by a carefully controlled analogy that transports us from the visible to the invisible, sight to insight; the balanced structure of the analogy (*quemadmodum…sic*) itself contributes to the judicious air of Democritus' entire approach in 4b.9. Here is no overdeveloped digression from Seneca's main line of argument, or mere background preparation for his eventual point at 10.1: "But it has already been demonstrated [sc. in 4b.9, via Democritus] that, the thicker and more solid the material substance of things, the more persistently they all [the near atmosphere included] retain the heat they receive." If we credit Democritus with a mini-demonstration of model rationalist technique here, his rhetoric is quoted and appropriated as *Senecan* rhetoric; the Democritean method becomes Seneca's own persuasive method.

In contrast to Seneca's pose of defensiveness or diffidence earlier in 4b (e.g., 4.1: "although I may be mistaken in your eyes, I myself at any rate am persuaded of the truth"; 5.1: "I hesitate…to mention a theory advanced by our Stoic friends, but hesitate also to overlook it"), his different persona in 4b.8–12 is much more assured in its control of argument and sense of direction (cf. 4b.9: "This long

---

nowhere else are accepted as "at least roughly correct" by Hall (1977) 432 on 4b.9, 5.2 and 7.3.2; see also Setaioli (1988) 450 and n. 2123 ("un fondamento di verità" in Seneca's account).

95. Hine (1996a) 196.135 reads *aeneum uas et uitreum et argenteum*, but *et argenteum* is deleted by Gercke (1907) 165.23–4; for given what follows ("heat will…cling to [the bronze] longer"), can Democritus really have assigned to bronze a specific gravity greater than that of silver (cf. Oltramare [1929] 2.341 on p. 201 n. 4)? Yet if *et argenteum* is retained with the manuscripts, Seneca presumably imputes to Democritus a contrast between metal (whether bronze or silver) on the one hand, glass on the other; bronze alone then serves as the featured metal when he continues with "heat will enter the bronze one more quickly."

96. On which Conte (1994) 21. Cf. Chapter Six, Section III.

preamble leads up to the point of the present discussion"). So, in 4b.10, the Democritean theory presented in 4b.9 is effortlessly recast as proof (*iam autem probatum est…*) that denser objects better retain their heat—a proof now deployed in a well-worked argument, syllogistic in resemblance, that finally supplies our fourth *causa* for why the lower part of the atmosphere is warmer. As if following the Democritean lead in 4b.9 (*quemadmodum…sic*), Seneca uses analogy in 4b.10 (*quemadmodum…ita*) to assert that, just as the dregs settle at the bottom of liquids, so the closer the air is to the earth, the thicker it is. Then (*autem*)[97] the secondary premise based on Democritean "proof"—denser objects better keep their heat—leads to the conclusion that the thicker, lower atmosphere must be warmer than the higher, thinner atmosphere that does not retain the sun's heat. But our wider experience of the *Natural Questions* again discloses an inconsistency between Seneca's argument here and the position he takes elsewhere on the relative warmth of the upper and lower atmosphere. In contrast to 4b.10 (the upper atmosphere less warm than the lower), at 2.10.2 the upper region is "extremely dry and hot [*siccissima calidissimaque*], and also for that reason very rarified because of the proximity of the eternal fires…"; at 2.10.3 both the upper *and* the lower regions are warm, albeit through different causes. In retrospect, does Seneca pursue an argument at 4b.10 (the lower atmosphere warmer than the upper) that is highly rhetorical in its plausible presentation here of but one side of a double-edged coin, the other side of which is favored in Book 2? This shift of position could be explained as a simple inconsistency; as a consequence of Seneca's reliance on conflicting sources in 4b.10 and 2.10.2–3 respectively; or perhaps as a Senecan adjustment to meet the differing needs of divergent contexts. But whether by accident or by design, the effect of the inconsistency between 4b.10 and 2.10.2–3 is to underscore (as in 4b.8) the pliancy of Seneca's scientific rhetoric as a changeful commodity, a force for persuasion according to the needs of the moment.

Seneca's next maneuver, in the second stage (4b.11) of his overall argument in 4b.8–12, indirectly consolidates his own case—the lower atmosphere is warmer—by refutation of the counterclaim[98] that greater elevation brings greater warmth: "the peaks of mountains must be warmer the closer they are to the sun" (11.1). His strategy is of interest for much more than the two specific arguments that he makes here. The first concerns a matter of perspective: the mountains that seem so high from our lowly human vantage point are, from a cosmic perspective, so

---

97. Cf. *OLD* 5b ("spec. introducing the minor premiss of a syllogism").

98. Stoic, if with Vottero (1989) 520 n. 1 we accept that, when Seneca uses indefinite terms of reference (e.g., *quidam aiunt*, 11.1), he usually means Stoic philosophers.

lowly themselves, and no more disruptive to the rounded complexion of the world than are the seams and chinks of a hand-stitched ball used in games (*lusoria pila*, 11.3).[99] If Seneca's allusion to that *lusoria pila* is already playful, that ludic quality hardens into ridicule through destructive analogy: if a higher mountain must be warmer because it is closer to the sun, will a tall man be warmed more quickly than a short man, and his head more quickly than his feet (11.4)? Second, an additional argument is deftly implanted in Seneca's summary of his first argument: "Those mountains we look up at, *and whose tops are always covered in snow*, are nevertheless of very low standing" (11.5): why eternal snow on those peaks if they are so much warmer than lower altitudes through closer proximity to the sun?[100] After the ball analogy in 11.3, *pila* gives way to *pilus* as Seneca rounds on hair splitting in 11.5:[101] from a cosmic viewpoint, a mountain is closer to the sun than a plain or valley is in the same way as one hair is thicker than another (*quomodo est pilus pilo crassior*),[102] with perhaps a further play on *pilus* in the earthbound *pusilla* that include even the highest peaks: "between small things [*inter pusilla*] there can be no great difference, except when they are compared among themselves" (11.5).

As part of his overall argument in 4b.8–12, then, Seneca works to enhance his own persuasive case by demolishing the opposition that he conveniently ranges against himself in 4b.11. But his appeal to the cosmic perspective in 4b.11 also revives a central preoccupation in the *Natural Questions* generally. So, at 11.4, no one who "judges the world by its own measure [*mensura sua*] and recognizes that the earth occupies but the space of a pinprick [*puncti locum*]" will be under any illusion that anything on earth can be in close proximity to the heavenly bodies (*caelestia*) above. Such is the mind-set promoted in the preface to Book 3, looking beyond the boundaries and distinctions of this world to contemplate the seamless totality of the all—to measure the world by its scale, not ours.[103] From this cosmic viewpoint, the highest mountains appear small:

---

99. For *pila* of the earth's globe, cf. 2.1.4; *TLL* 10.1 2133.21–9, and cf. 47–60.

100. Yet Seneca fails to explain the cause of *this* snow. Are we to connect it in some way with the cooler temperatures that he associates with greater elevation in 4b.10, the purer air there not retaining the sun's heat but transmitting it as if through a vacuum (cf. Oltramare [1929] 2.203 n. 1)?

101. It is tempting to detect a Senecan play on *pila/pilus*, with added punch if the popular etymology later given in Isidore is traditional (*pila proprie dicitur quod sit pilis plena*, *Orig.* 18.69.1 = Maltby [1991] 475 *pila*³).

102. For the proverbial quality, Section III n. 42 above in this chapter.

103. Cf. Hadot (1995) 254, and see my Chapter One, Section III.

excelsa sunt ista [sc. cacumina montium] quamdiu nobis comparantur; at uero ubi ad uniuersum respexeris, manifesta omnium est humilitas. inter se uincuntur et uincunt, ceterum nihil in tantum attollitur ut in collatione totius ulla sit uel maximis portio.

4b.11.2

These mountain tops are high so long as they are compared to us; but when you turn your gaze to the universe, the lowness of all of them is evident. They are surpassing, or are surpassed, in relation to each other, but none rises high enough for even the greatest of them to have any significance in comparison with the universal whole.[104]

In the remains of Book 4b, however, a different kind of competition is also envisaged, on this occasion between rival meteorological theories: for "very few theories pass unopposed; the others, even if they win through [*uincunt*], still have to go to law [*litigant*]" (5.1). We have seen that the alternative theories given at 4b.4–5 of why hail is prevalent in spring—the one theory emphasizing spring warmth, the other cold air from the north—suggestively act out this process of pleading on both sides before Lucilius as presiding judge (*iudici*, 5.1). From a cosmic perspective, the mountains that vie against each other in 4b.11 offer a tempting analogy for the physical theories that compete for acceptance earlier in the fragment. The several theories we have tested implement different rhetorical or methodological strategies of argumentation, all of them superior (because of their rationalizing intent) to the superstition derided in 4b.6–7, but none of them without its own logical or procedural frailties. In contrast to these theories, provisional and partial as they are in their unverifiable projections, the cosmic consciousness that comes into focus in 4b.11 rises serenely above the infirmities of scientific argument at ground level. Assured and complete, it reasserts the importance of taking a whole view of nature before we turn our eye to the relatively petty and myopic distinctions that prevail *apud nos* (cf. again *inter se uincuntur* [sc. *cacumina montium*] *et uincunt*). It reasserts the all as an alleviating counterpoint even as we descend into, and become embroiled in, the contentious claims of this argument or that about the specific workings of now one branch of nature (e.g., hail and snow in Book 4b), now another (e.g., winds in Book 5).

Within the carefully controlled, even model argument presented in 4b.8–12, then, I propose that Seneca also offers self-conscious commentary on his own

104. Cf. 3 pref. 10: "We believe that these [sc. kingdoms and empires, *regna* and *imperia*] are great because we are small; many things draw their importance not from their true nature but from our lowliness."

exploratory mode in Book 4b and beyond. The theories surveyed in 4b.3–12 as a whole are speculations cast in that relative darkness in which we wallow (*hanc in qua uolutamur caliginem*, 1 pref. 2); as we grope for the correct explanation of each given phenomenon, these speculations are at best approximations to the truth that is owned by the all-seeing cosmic viewpoint, as if they constitute (in Platonic terms) a form of *doxa* that aspires to *episteme*. The speculative science that dominates so much of the *Natural Questions* strives to climb above the darkness, and it may do so by offering plausible, rhetorically impressive explication. But full illumination necessarily remains elusive, so that the *Natural Questions* is cast as a work fundamentally *in* and *of* progress,[105] and but one contribution to the collective human inquiry into nature that, for Seneca, is itself always in progress.

VI: Book 4b in Context

When the interlocutor protests at Seneca's pursuit of "these trivialities [*ineptias*], which make a person more learned, not of better character" (13.1), it is perhaps important not to underestimate the sophistication of the interlocutor's case against these *ineptiae*. If we imagine that this (Lucilius?) figure has been in attendance with us throughout the varieties of argument that we have experienced in 4b.3–12, his objection might run as follows: any secure notion of scientific truth and objectivity has been eroded by the relativities of argument and the ascendancy of rhetorical craft down to 4b.12; and yet, if the cumulative effect of Seneca's enquiries is to undermine the very exercise of striving for sure meteorological knowledge, his own relativist critique is itself vulnerable to "the checkmate of rhetoric"[106]—the charge that it, too, is as much a rhetorical exercise as the theories that it exposes as fundamentally, and compromisingly, rhetorical. On this approach, the interlocutor's objection might be said to resemble that against "postmodern discourse-analytic approaches generally" which, as H. W. Simons puts it, "are vulnerable to the criticism that they shift attention from ideas to words, and that in doing so they end up in endless quibbling [cf. Seneca's *ineptias*], or in verbal seductions leading to false consciousness, or in aesthetic preoccupations."[107] In contrast to such involved controversies, the interlocutor's call for change in a moralizing direction replaces the rhetorical flux with a demand for fixity, or for the unambiguous language of censure and judgment in 4b.13.

---

105. Further, Chapter Seven, Section II.

106. For which Gergen (1990).

107. Simons (1990a) 15.

Yet two factors counter this interlocutory criticism of Seneca's procedure in 4b.3–12. First, whatever the shortcomings of the "rhetoric of science" as tested earlier in the fragment, that investigative effort is vindicated by contrast with the vice-ridden excesses of the *luxuriosi* in 4b.13. In contrast to the depths of the latter's depravity in 4.13, the physical speculations in 4b.3–12 strive in an elevating direction despite their fragilities and flaws. The fight against luxury may already be lost, at least according to 13.1: "That dispute is waged daily, and to no effect." For all its shortcomings, however, the investigative striving down to the end of 4b.12 is itself morally improving despite the interlocutor's insistence to the contrary: by consorting speculatively with nature, we far distance ourselves from the kind of sordidness so graphically visualized in 4b.13, thereby following the prescription at 3 pref. 18 that "the study of nature will be helpful to us" because "we shall leave behind what is sordid" and "separate the mind...from the body."

Second, and more important for present purposes: on the assumption that Book 4b was third in the original ordering of the books, Seneca's testing of argument in 4b.3–12 is significantly placed within the *Natural Questions* as a whole. After two books of physical inquiry-in-action in Books 3 and 4a, I propose that what survives of Book 4b (or, we might conjecture, the whole of the original book) represents a theoretical pause of sorts, or a form of methodological stock-taking even as Seneca ostensibly proceeds with business as usual in examining the causes of snow and hail. He advances the work to a stage of maturity where it interrogates its own procedure, raising "fundamental issues—including particularly second-order questions concerning the nature of the inquiries themselves."[108] On this approach, the Senecan effort in 4b.3–12 is directed not at rejecting *tout court* the attainability of scientific truth, or at enthusiastically promoting a relativist "rhetoric of science," but at a more neutral goal. What matters centrally in 4b.3–12 is not the truthfulness (or falsity) of any given theory of hail or snow; to borrow K. J. Gergen's incisive formulation, the point in Book 4b is "to invite readers into linguistic space that, once understood, enables them *to transcend the ontology into which they were previously locked.*"[109] Seneca's initial mode of exposition in Books 3 and 4a, that is, has yet to turn introspectively upon itself, testing the strengths and weaknesses of its own methodology and articulation. But we then pass in the remains of Book 4b into a new linguistic space that transcends, or better, challenges, the initial mode—the safe ontology, as it were—by questioning the foundations and authority of Seneca's sample strategies of argument; and this inner

---

108. To extend to Seneca "the claim to be critical" that Lloyd (1979) 234 attributes to Greek philosophy, science and medicine.

109. Gergen (1990) 297; my emphasis.

turning has important side effects for his self-positioning in the *Natural Questions* more generally.[110] He projects the sincerity of his continuing task by pledging through his introspective exercises in 4b to pay close and "honest" attention to the techniques of persuasion that deliver his science, and so to preserve the integrity of his operation through this self-critical diligence; a contrasting lack of self-discipline is perhaps targeted in his allusion to "all the absurdities [*ineptias*] of our Stoic friends" at 4b.6.1. At the same time, the self-consciousness on display in 4b guards against any relapse into the impersonal objectification of science in the *Natural Questions*, and away from his idiosyncratic combination of physico-ethical analysis; for Seneca's show of self-scrutiny in 4b is itself, along with his notable touches of humor, part of the expressive personality that drives the entire work.

We can only speculate on the extent to which the above reading captures tendencies that were also present in the lost portion of Book 4b. The loss naturally challenges any coherent reading of the surviving fragment, and I remain acutely conscious of the risks of distortion and decontextualization that my analysis of 4b.3–13 incurs. The approach taken in this chapter thus offers its own illustration of "the rhetorical turn"[111] in potentially dangerous action: given the partial state of the evidence, this very reading of 4b will itself perhaps activate a truly Senecan vigilance about the fragility of argument.

---

110. I am indebted to John Henderson for the formulations that follow.

111. Simons (1990b).

5

Seneca on Winds

I: Introduction

Seneca's extended treatment of wind in Book 5, surveying its cause(s), types and regional and seasonal variations, builds on the earlier anemology tradition conveniently to bring to order a phenomenon that, in ordinary experience, must so often be associated with disorder. The different winds, that is, fall into their neat Senecan classifications, and fearsome phenomena such as cloudbursts are plausibly explained (5.12), whirlwinds rationalized (5.13); yet still the winds can surprise and overwhelm us, so that our understanding of their workings offers but cold comfort at the stage of damage assessment after the storm has passed. On this approach, perhaps, one lesson of Book 5—with significant implications for Seneca's broader enterprise in the *Natural Questions*—is that nature so often eludes our best efforts fully to capture her: when we brace for the tornado or hurricane, our technical understanding of such events counts for so little.

Yet Seneca can still offer a comforting vision of systematization and order in the carefully delineated stages of his disquisition on wind:

5.1: definition of wind

5.2–6: theories of its cause

5.7–13: individual types of wind

   5.14: elaboration on his initial coverage (cf. 5.4) of the subterranean origin of wind, to the effect that the underground air, laden with moisture, stirs wind through the pressure exerted by that moisture (5.14.3)

   5.15: from Seneca's recounting (via Asclepiodotus[1]) of an expedition sent underground by Philip of Macedon to assess "whether the greed of past ages had left anything for future generations" to mine for (5.15.1),[2] anecdotal evidence of the existence of caverns and lakes under the earth supports the argument of 5.14

---

1. For whom cf. Chapter One, Section I n. 5.

2. On 5.15, Chapter Two, Section VI.

5.16–17: classification of major winds by compass-card arrangement (5.16) and by position within the twelve-sector scheme of global division drawn in 5.17 before Seneca turns his focus to purely local winds at 5.17.5.

5.18: protest against mankind's abuse of the wind, the gift of nature that, after the birth of navigation, "made communication possible between all peoples" and enabled us "to know distant parts" (5.18.4, 14)—a gift thoroughly corrupted by all the warmongers whom high-minded Seneca condemns in this spirited climax to the book.

At a superficial level, the moralizing component in 5.15 and 5.18 fits seamlessly enough within this schematic summary of Book 5. At a deeper level, however, the central objective of this chapter is to argue for the complex interplay of 5.15 and 5.18 in a bookwide experiment or (better) prose drama that contrasts the steady and normative tendencies of *natura ipsa* with human aberration. As mankind goes underground in search of precious metals in 5.15 and roves voraciously over the seas in his warships in 5.18, those movements conspicuously distort what we saw earlier to be the uplifting impetus of the *Natural Questions* toward "consorting with things divine" (3 pref. 11).[3] If the triad of mining, shipping and warmongering evokes the literary Iron Age in 5.15 and 5.18,[4] we reach another low point here in comparison with the highest goal in the *Natural Questions*, that of "seeing the all" (cf. *animo omne uidisse*, 3 pref. 10); from cosmic illumination we descend into literal and figurative darkness (cf. *a tergo lucem relinquere*, 5.15.3; *inuolutos nubilo dies et nimbis ac tonitribus horridas noctes*, 5.18.7). As we rise above the distractions of the everyday world, what is important is not "to have filled the seas with ships...or *to have wandered over the ocean in search of the unknown* when the land has been exhausted for wrongdoing" (3 pref. 10). As the enlightened mind wanders among the stars at 1 pref. 7, it delights in laughing (*ridere*) at the luxuries so prized in ordinary life, including "the mosaic floors of the rich and the whole earth with all its gold—I mean not just the gold that the earth has already yielded and given over to be struck for coinage, but also *all that it keeps hidden for the greed of future generations*"—generations emulating the likes of Philip's adventurers in 5.15,[5] or the greedy M. Licinius Crassus who is pictured in

3. For 3 pref. 11 see already Chapters One, Section II, and Three, Section IV.

4. Cf. Tib. 1.3.37–40, 47–50 with Smith (1913) 245–47, 251; Ov. *Am.* 3.8.35–38, 43–44, 47–50, 53–54, *Met.* 1.132–34, 137–43; Sen. *Phaed.* 527–28, 530–36, 544–52, [Sen.] *Oct.* 416–21, 425–26. But for due qualification of the Iron Age significance here, see Section V below in this chapter.

5. Cf. 5.15.3: "What powerful necessity...plunged man into the very depths of the earth's interior, in order to dig out gold [*ut erueret aurum*]?"

5.18 en route to his disastrous defeat at the hands of the Parthians at Carrhae in
53 BCE.[6] From the elevated perspective of 3 pref. 10 and 1 pref. 7, we inevitably
look down on the lowly proceedings in 5.15 and 5.18; and in contrast to the familiar character, pattern and direction of the winds as represented more generally in
Book 5, Seneca's focus on human *mis*direction and transgression in those chapters
counters that broader vision of nature in normative action. True, the cloudburst
and whirlwind that break out in 5.12–13 are themselves chaotic, transgressive
presences within the natural order. But we shall see that they too take on important symbolic meaning as a paradigm for, or perhaps rather as a counterpoint to,
the "unnatural" violence unleashed when man takes to the seas in his warships in
5.18, or when Xerxes and Alexander the Great disregard all boundaries in their
whirlwind progress toward limitless conquest at 5.18.10. All winds, from the
benign to the violent, follow the Plinian principle of obedience to "a law of nature
[*legem naturae*] which is not unknown even if it is not yet fully known" (*Nat.*
2.116).[7] In their transgressiveness, Seneca's Xerxes and Alexander exemplify a negative extreme, or perhaps rather an extreme perversion, of the *lex naturae* implicitly drawn in *Natural Questions* 5.

For present purposes, then, what crucially separates the Senecan approach
from its surviving antecedents in the anemology tradition, most notable among
them the extended treatments in Aristotle's *Meteorologica* and Theophrastus' *On
winds*,[8] is the human dimension: Seneca's priority in Book 5, I propose, is not so
much the *res ipsa*—the study of wind for its own sake—but rather the advancing
of his own physico-ethical agenda. Basic to that agenda is his exploitation of the
familiar correlation drawn in Greco-Roman literature between the wind and aspects of human character. The wind as a symbol of fickleness in love or friendship;[9]
the wind metaphorically cast as a storm force in life, or as an agency affecting our
course for good as well as ill;[10] the wind as a personified being, raging as if with

---

6. Cf. 5.18.10: "He will journey for gold [*ad aurum ibitur*] despite the anger of men and
gods."

7. On this law, Beagon (1992) 179; Taub (2003) 181.

8. On the tradition in general, Gilbert (1907) 511–84 with *RE* 8A 2.2211–2387. For Theophrastus'
On winds in relation to Aristotle, Coutant and Eichenlaub (1974) and (1975) xxxvi–xlix with Gross
(1989) 209–11 and French (1994) 90. But for Theophrastus' treatment of wind in a different work,
no longer extant in Greek but partially preserved in one Syriac and two Arabic versions—his *Meteorology*, also known as the *Metarsiology* (cf. D. L. 5.44)—see Daiber (1992) with Taub (2003) 116 and
120–21 (*On winds* the later work; Taub 121 after Daiber 286). For reports/sources on Theophrastus
on wind in later antiquity, Fortenbaugh et al. (1992) 356–61 nos. 186A–89.

9. See for examples Otto (1890) 364 no. 1863 *uentus* 1 with Häussler (1968) 81, 223, 246;
OLD uentosus 5 and *aura* 2b with Nisbet and Hubbard (1970) 77 on Hor. *Carm.* 1.5.11.

10. See conveniently the figurative examples at *OLD uentus* 1d and 2a, b; *aura* 3a, b.

human feeling¹¹—this multivalent symbolism of the winds is well represented else-where in Seneca's writings,¹² a fact that itself gives *a priori* reason to suspect similar enterprise in the *Natural Questions*.¹³ But in the Senecan/Stoic living cosmos¹⁴ we might in any case reasonably expect this animating dimension, which is already discernible at the book's opening: even before we encounter the wind types and personalities that populate Seneca's treatment from 5.7 onward, we shall see that the air is brought to life as a vital elemental force, as if the rude substance out of which the winds take shape later in the growth pattern of the book.

We begin in Section II with these vital signs in the book's opening chapters (5.1–6), signs that will provide the foundation for our subsequent tracing of the winds' life course through the rest of Book 5. In Section III we monitor Seneca's careful arrangement of individual wind types in 5.7–13: in his progression from the relatively weak and benign predawn breezes (5.7) to the explosive cloudburst and then whirlwind of 5.12–13, we shall find a finely worked analogy for norma-tive and then transgressive conduct at the human level. After the chaotic whirl-wind of 5.13, order is restored in 5.16–17: in Section IV our focus turns to Seneca's mapping there of the winds by natural global or local position. But this vision of natural place and self-restriction is then contrasted, in Section V, by Seneca's pic-turing of the human storm force that rampages across the seas in 5.18. From the detached perspective of Senecan cosmic consciousness in 5.18, the real world—the pragmatics of Roman military, economic and social governance in Italy and overseas in the early Empire—is (it seems) effortlessly elided in his condemnation of the corruptions wrought by seafaring, and by his highly idealized, even senti-mental, vision of the munificence with which the winds were originally gifted to the world by divine providence. In Section VI, however, we explore the implica-tions that this detached viewpoint in 5.18 may yet have for Roman imperial power and self-perception in the first century CE.

II: *Pre-Stoic and Stoic Theories of Wind*

Seneca embarks on his task with an impressive appearance of methodological rigor as he scrupulously defines wind (5.1) and reviews theories (5.2–6) of its

---

11. So, e.g., Ovid's Eurus, Zephyr, Boreas and Auster are confined to their different world sec-tors at *Met.* 1.61–6 so as to prevent them from tearing the world to pieces through their broth-erly strife (cf. *tanta est discordia fratrum*, 60). On Seneca's quotation of *Met.* 1.61–6 at 5.16.1 see Section IV (A) below in this chapter.

12. Examples in Armisen-Marchetti (1989) 127–28.

13. *Pace* Limburg (2007) 245 n. 106 and 421, strongly resisting the human-wind comparison in Book 5.

14. For which see Chapter Two, Section III n. 30.

cause.[15] Here alone in the extant *Natural Questions* he dispenses with a preface, a change of procedure that beneficially juxtaposes fixity and flow: after the ice shards that cool feverish appetites in the stifling atmosphere of 4b.13, the wind that flows at 5.1.1 *Ventus est fluens aër* brings new movement and fresh air, as it were, as we progress to the next book. For all the methodological rigor of his opening, however, our concern for now is with the *artistic* effect of his ordering of material in 5.1–6 as a whole, and especially in his arrangement of causal theories of wind at 5.4–6. The definition of wind as air in motion[16] can be traced back to Anaximander, for whom wind is "a flowing of air (ῥύσιν ἀέρος), occurring when the finest [and most moist] parts of it are set in motion [or liquefied] by the sun."[17] Similar early definitions are attributed to Anaximenes and found in the Hippocratic corpus,[18] but for Aristotle the concept of wind as air in motion is a gross oversimplification:

> There are some[19] who say that wind is simply a moving current of what we call air, while cloud and water are the same air condensed; they thus assume that water and wind are of the same nature, and define wind as air in motion. And for this reason some people, wishing to be clever, say that all the winds are one [the sea-of-air concept], on the ground that the air which moves is in fact one and the same whole, and only seems to differ, without differing in reality, because of the various places from which the current comes on different occasions: which is like supposing that all rivers are but one river.
>
> *Mete.* 1.13 349a16–26; trans. H. D. P. Lee

---

15. In general on the history of anemology in antiquity and beyond, DeBlieu (1998) 30–33; Huler (2004), especially 62–64, 81–92; De Villiers (2006) 34–69.

16. Cf. already 3.12.3 *si uentus est fluens aër, et flumen est fluens aqua.* In fact, "[w]inds, whether global or local, are produced when pockets of air move around in their attempts to equalize the temperature and pressure differences caused by the uneven spread of sunlight over the earth" (Hamblyn [2001] 189).

17. D-K 12A24 = Aet. *Plac.* 3.7.1 (*DG* p. 374) = Graham (2010) 1.60–1 Text 32 (see also p. 69 on Texts 30–33); cf. D-K 12A11 (7) = Hippol. *Ref.* 1.6.7 (*DG* p. 560.8–9) = Graham 1.58–9 Text 20 (7). Square brackets because (Guthrie [1962] 105) Aetius' brief note about Anaximander "seems to have conflated Theophrastus's reports of his explanation of winds on the one hand and rain on the other."

18. For Anaximenes, D-K 13A7 (7) = Hippol. *Ref.* 1.7.7 (*DG* p. 561.12–13), but see now the different reading in Graham (2010) 1.80–1 Text 12 (7). Cf. [Hippocr.] *Flat.* 3 with Hine (1981) 137 on *N.Q.* 2.1.3 for more citations, and see also Bailey (1947) 1656 in discussion of Lucr. 6.685 *uentus enim fit, ubi est agitando percitus aer.*

19. Presumably including Anaximander and Hippocrates; cf. Lee (1952) 89n.

For Aristotle, wind is derived from that crucial material cause of phenomena in his *Meteorologica*, exhalation (ἀναθυμίασις) from the earth.[20] Of the two exhalations he posited, the one cool and moist (from water in and on the earth; cf. 1.4 341b9–10), the other warm and dry (from the sun's drying and heating of the earth itself), wind is produced by the latter. The sun's heat draws up the moist exhalation, but when the sun recedes, the raised-up vapor is condensed by the resulting cold to form rain (2.4 360a1–2). The warm exhalation, by contrast, "is the origin and the natural substance of winds" (2.4 360a13); but, since the exhalation rises vertically, the winds' horizontal movement is caused by the motion of the celestial sphere (2.4 361a23–5). But if the warm-dry exhalation is the cause of wind, how is the existence of cold and moist winds to be explained? If the winds' horizontal motion is caused by the turning of the celestial sphere, how to explain the origin of west winds? While problems such as these already challenge Aristotle's attempt at a fully unified theory of wind based on the exhalations,[21] Theophrastus shows a greater willingness to contemplate a multiplicity of causes, conspicuously demoting the importance of the Aristotelian warm-dry exhalation.[22] In his *On winds*, the exhalations (or exhalation, as he uses only the singular ἀναθυμίασις) occur only twice, in §§15 and 23, and the sun now "becomes increasingly important" and "is mentioned 20 times, in no slighting fashion."[23] So at §15:

> If the generation of all winds is the same and caused by the same factors (by taking on some material), the sun is the agent. Perhaps this is not correct taken universally, but rather the exhalation is the cause, while the sun assists. But the sun by rising seems both to set the winds in motion and to halt them. Therefore the winds augment and die down frequently.[24]

Theophrastus' most striking departure from Aristotle in his *On winds* lies in his statement that "the movement of air is wind" (ἡ δὲ τούτου [sc. ἀέρος] κίνησις ἄνεμος, 29)—a position that not only compromises the primacy of the Aristotelian warm-dry exhalation but also allows the horizontal movement of wind through the

---

20. On the Aristotelian exhalation theory, cf. Chapters Two, Section III n. 40 and Six, Section V (C) n. 102.

21. See Coutant and Eichenlaub (1974) 1456 and (1975) xxxix.

22. Cf. Taub (2003) 123 on Theophrastus' *Meteorology/Metarsiology*: "Theophrastus does, to some extent, incorporate Aristotle's exhalations into his meteorological explanations. Fine vapour forms winds, while clouds arise from moist vapour.... However, for Theophrastus, the exhalations typically provide only one of several possible causes for any given phenomenon."

23. Coutant and Eichenlaub (1975) xlv.

24. Trans. Coutant and Eichenlaub (1975) 15–17.

immanent nature of air, without Aristotle's recourse to the motion of the celestial sphere.[25] Theophrastus retains significant aspects of Aristotelian theory, including a firm insistence on the individualism of winds and resistance to the Pre-Socratic sea-of-air theory. But the *On Winds* also shows important signs of innovation as well as a more empirical outlook: "The relegation, mostly by omission, of the Aristotelian warm-dry exhalation to a minor role in his etiology allows Theophrastus to redirect his anemology to the Presocratic concept of wind as air in motion, whereas Aristotle's renunciation of this idea had directed the understanding of winds a step backward into speculative metaphysics."[26]

The Stoics accepted the definition of wind as "a flowing of air" (ἀέρος ῥύσις);[27] the cause of this flowing is "the sun through the evaporation of the clouds (τὸν ἥλιον ἐξατμίζοντα τὰ νέφη)"[28]—a process akin to the "separating out" of the vapor that the sun draws up, after water is separated from earth, to form the atmosphere in Anaximander's cosmogonic system.[29] Otto Gilbert associates this theory of wind's origin in evaporation *from cloud* with the old Stoa, distinguishing it from the theory of exhalation *from earth* that he associates with the later Stoa;[30] he goes on to infer a compromise between the two positions—wind derived indirectly from clouds, and then directly from the earth—from the distinction evidenced between ἄνεμος and αὔρα by the probably third-century CE astronomer Achilles Tatius:

> Anaximander therefore called the wind a flowing of air, but some called it an exhalation of air. Others say that wind [ἄνεμος] differs from breeze [αὔρα]; for wind is a flowing of air [ῥύσιν ἀέρος], breeze an exhalation from earth [ἀναθυμίασιν].[31]

For present purposes, the compromise that Gilbert detects here between different Stoic emphases—wind as flowing air (caused by evaporation from cloud) and wind

---

25. See Coutant and Eichenlaub (1974) 1455–56, (1975) xl, xliv–xlv.

26. Coutant and Eichenlaub (1975) xlviii.

27. *SVF* 2.697 p. 202.17 = Aet. *Plac.* 3.7.2 (*DG* p. 374).

28. *SVF* 2.698 p. 202.24–5 = D. L. 7.152.

29. See for Anaximander Section II n. 17 above in this chapter, and cf. Guthrie (1962) 105: "This [sc. vapour] in its turn, as the 'separating-out' continues, divides into two substances, a lighter (finer, drier) and a heavier (wetter). The former is set in motion as wind, the latter precipitated as rain."

30. Gilbert (1907) 536–37.

31. Achilles *Isagoge* 33 = Maass (1958) 68.11–14.

derived from terrestrial exhalation—conveniently introduces Seneca's own inte-grating technique in his survey of different, potentially multiple causes at 5.4–5.

Four theories are weighed here, the first two of them distributed over the whole of 5.4:

> *4.1* 'Quomodo ergo' inquis 'uenti fiunt, quoniam hoc negas fieri?' non uno modo: alias enim terra ipsa magnam uim aëris eicit et ex abdito spirat; alias cum magna et continua e summo euaporatio in altum egit quae emiserat, luctatio ipsa halitus mixti in uentum uertitur. *4.2* illud enim nec ut credam persuaderi mihi potest, nec ut taceam: quomodo in nostris cor-poribus cibo fit inflatio, quae non sine magna narium iniuria emittitur, et uentrem interdum cum sono exonerat, interdum secretius, sic putant et hanc magnam rerum naturam alimenta mutantem emittere spiritum. bene nobiscum agitur quod semper concoquit; alioquin inmundius aliquid timeremus. *4.3* numquid ergo hoc uerius est dicere, multa ex omni parte terrarum et adsidua ferri corpuscula? quae cum coaceruata sunt, deinde extenuari sole coeperunt, quia omne quod in angusto dilatatur spatium maius desiderat, uentus existit.

> *4.1* "How, then," you ask, "do winds come about, since you deny that this [sc. Democritus' atomic theory of wind[32]] is true?" In more ways than one. For [*Theory I*] sometimes the earth itself ejects a great quantity of air, breathing it out from the hidden depths. [*Theory II*] Sometimes, when the great and continuous evaporation from the earth's surface has driven into the high atmosphere the earth's emissions, the struggles of these mixed exhalations themselves turn into wind. *4.2* [*Elaboration of Theory I*] Here is a theory that I cannot be persuaded either to believe or to pass over in silence: just as in our bodies flatulence is caused by food and is emitted not without great offence to our sense of smell (sometimes it relieves the bowels noisily, and sometimes more discreetly), so people think[33] that this great natural system, too, gives off air when it digests its nourishment. It's lucky for us that the earth always has good digestion; otherwise, we'd have something quite foul to fear. *4.3* [*Elaboration of Theories I and II com-bined*] Surely, then, it is truer to say this, that many particles are constantly given off from all parts of the earth? When they are accumulated in a mass and then begin to be thinned out by the sun, wind develops because every-thing which expands in a confined space wants more space.

---

32. For which see the end of Section II and n. 51 below in this chapter.

33. Vottero (1989) 534–35 n. 6 detects a probable allusion to Epicurean doctrine on thunder.

Theory I both presupposes the existence of underground caverns and recesses as outlined at 3.16.4–5 and anticipates Seneca's return to the theme of wind's subterranean origin in 5.14. If the evaporation from below in Theory I loosely corresponds to the warm-dry Aristotelian exhalation,[34] the transmitted text of Theory II as printed by some modern editors—*cum magna et continua ex imo euaporatio in altum egit*—appears pleonastic in the replication of *ex abdito* in *ex imo*. Hence Axelson's proposal of *e summo* as a natural foil for *ex abdito* earlier:[35] Theory II then plausibly incorporates the *other* Aristotelian exhalation from moisture "within and upon the earth,"[36] and Axelson's *luctatio*[37] represents the mixture and contention between the different exhalations, warm-dry and cool-moist, that produce wind in the post-Aristotelian tradition.[38] Seneca returns to the exhalation theory in 4.3, where his emphasis on *multa ex omni parte terrarum . . . corpuscula* surely accommodates exhalations from both below and on the earth's surface, *ex abdito* and *e summo*. As the massed particles carried up from the earth are thinned out by the sun to cause wind, the theory gains plausibility (*numquid ergo hoc uerius est dicere . . . ?*) by contrast with the outlandish theory that lends pungent wit to Seneca's proceedings in 5.4.2.[39] There, the analogy with human flatulence adds another dimension to his emerging portrait of the living cosmos in the *Natural Questions*;[40] but within the sequence of argument in 5.4 as a whole, it amounts to a parenthetical development of the subterranean emissions posited in Theory I.

Of the two further theories that Seneca goes on to add in 5.5–6, Theory III (his most favored of the four) is given special prominence by his commendation of it at 5.5.1:

---

34. Cf. for this warm-dry Senecan exhalation from below (*siccus ille terrarum uapor unde uentis origo est*, 2.12.5) *Mete.* 1.4 341b8–10: "one [sc. of the two exhalations] is more vaporous in character, the other more windy, the vapour arising *from the water within and upon the earth* (τοῦ ἐν τῇ γῇ καὶ ἐπὶ τῇ γῇ ὑγροῦ), while the exhalations *from the earth itself, which is dry* (αὐτῆς τῆς γῆς οὔσης ξηρᾶς), are more like smoke" (trans. H. D. P. Lee; my emphasis).

35. (1939) 230–31; the conjecture is accepted by Hine (1996a) 206.65.

36. *Mete.* 1.4 341b8–10, as given in n. 34 above.

37. (1939) 232; so Hine (1996a) 206.66.

38. Cf. Strohm (1977) 319 for this combination of "die klassische Anathymiasenlehre . . . mit der nacharistotelischen Pointierung"; the post-Aristotelian emphasis lies in wind's production *not* from the dry exhalation only (further, Gross [1989] 212).

39. Cf. Armisen-Marchetti (2001) 171 on Seneca's air of skepticism and also "un sentiment mêlé de scandale et d'amusement"; also Althoff (1997) 104.

40. See Chapter Two, Section III n. 30.

Quid ergo? hanc solam esse causam uenti existimo, aquarum terrarumque
euaporationes? ex his grauitatem aëris fieri, deinde <solis> solui impetu,[41]
cum quae densa steterant, ut est necesse, extenuata nituntur in ampliorem
locum? ego uero et hanc iudico; ceterum illa est longe ualentior ueriorque,
habere aëra naturalem uim mouendi se, nec aliunde concipere sed inesse
illi ut aliarum rerum ita huius potentiam.

What then? Do I think that this alone is the cause of wind, namely evaporation from water and land? Do I think that the air derives its heaviness
from these exhalations, and that it is then rarified by the sun's force, when
all that was tightly packed together is inevitably thinned out and struggles
toward a roomier place? I certainly think that this is one explanation; but
the far stronger and truer explanation is that the air has a natural capacity
for self-motion. It derives this capacity not from elsewhere; just as it has
other capacities within itself, so it has this power of self-movement.

In claiming (Theory III) that air has this capacity for self-motion, Seneca exploits
the old Stoic theory of vital heat, which, in his extended treatment of the Stoic
world soul in *De natura deorum* 2, Cicero associates with Cleanthes.[42] Like Zeno,
Cleanthes accepted that the living cosmos has a soul; but new, for David Hahm,
is Cleanthes' proof for this doctrine.[43] According to the Ciceronian evidence,
Cleanthes' proof for the existence of the world soul relied fundamentally on analogy with a living animal: just as no living thing can be nurtured without the self-
moving capacity of vital heat, so heat constitutes a vital force extending throughout
the cosmos (*uim... uitalem per omnem mundum pertinentem*, 2.24). The inference that the cosmic whole is sustained by heat finds support in the demonstration (2.25) that the cosmic parts are themselves all supported and sustained by
heat: heat pervades the earth (cf. *in terrena natura*, 2.25), water (2.26) and air,
which is "by nature the coldest of the elements but by no means entirely without
heat" (2.26).[44] So also, in Seneca, the self-motion that is the world's vitalizing

---

41. Already *solui <solis> impetu* Reinhardt (1921) 152 n. 1, but cf. Hine (1996b) 83.

42. See especially 2.23–32, and for background, cf. 2.24 (= *SVF* 1.513 p. 115.4–7 = L-S [1987]
1.47C (2)) with Sambursky (1959) 3–4 and especially Hahm (1977) 140–53. For Cleanthes
probably as Cicero's original source at 2.23–32, see Solmsen (1961) with Hahm 175 n. 8; the
latter adjudicates decisively against Mansfeld's attempted refutation ([1971] 93–97) of Solmsen in favor of Posidonius as Cicero's point of reference.

43. See Hahm (1977) 140.

44. On the Zenonian basis for this Cleanthean argument at *N.D.* 2.24–8 as a whole ("If the
world-parts are sustained by heat, then the whole is also sustained by heat"), Hahm (1977)
141–42.

force[45] is attributed to air at *N.Q.* 5.5.1 *habere aëra naturalem uim mouendi se*, and then also to water (5.5.2) and to fire (5.6) before he circles back to air (*habet ergo aliquam uim <ui>talem aër*, 5.6). Wind arises from this elemental "principle of life" (cf. *aliquid... uitale*, 5.5.2)—a theory for which Seneca shows special favor by elaborating on it at relative length before turning finally, and briefly, to Theory IV at the end of 5.6: the exhalations have no role to play in this vision, related by Steinmetz and Gross to Theophrastus,[46] of the sun sometimes as the direct cause of wind through the heating and expansion of the dense, compressed air.

Despite Seneca's enthusiastic preference for Theory III, it is strikingly absent from his broader argumentation in Book 5, as Strohm and Gross have remarked.[47] A strange omission; yet, from a different perspective, the theory's ramifications are powerfully felt throughout the book, at least if we accept that the air is brought to life in 5.5–6 in readiness for Seneca's personifying treatment of wind from 5.7 onward. We shall soon trace those vital signs. But first a glance back at 5.1, where Seneca makes much of what might at first appear a slight distinction, as he himself acknowledges:

> Ventus est fluens aër. quidam ita definierunt: uentus est aër in unam fluens partem. haec definitio uidetur diligentior, quia numquam aër tam inmobilis est ut non in aliqua sit agitatione...
>
> scio quid responderi pro definitione altera possit: 'quid necesse est adicere te "in unam partem fluens aer"? utique enim quod fluit in unam fluit partem. nemo aquam fluere dicit si tantum intra se mouetur, sed si aliquo fertur. potest ergo aliquid moueri et non fluere, et e contrario non potest fluere nisi in unam partem.' sed siue haec breuitas satis a calumnia tuta est, hac utamur, siue aliquis circumspectior est, uerbo non parcat cuius adiectio cauillationem omnem poterit excludere. nunc ad ipsam rem accedamus, quoniam satis de formula disputatum est.
>
> 5.1.1, 4–5

> Wind is flowing air. Certain authorities have defined it in this way: wind is air flowing in one direction. This definition seems more careful, because air is never so immobile that it is not is not in some kind of motion...
>
> I know the reply that can be made in favor of the first definition [sc. wind is flowing air]: "Why is it necessary for you to add 'air flowing in one

---

45. Cf. Cic. *N.D.* 2.23: "everything that is of a hot and fiery nature provides its own source of motion and activity [*cietur et agitur motu suo*]."

46. Steinmetz (1964) 70; Gross (1989) 216.

47. Strohm (1953) 291; Gross (1989) 216.

direction'? For surely anything that flows does so in one direction. No one
says that water flows if its motion is simply internal, but only if it is carried
in some direction. Something can therefore be subject to motion and yet
not flow; on the other hand, nothing can flow except in a given direction."
But if this short definition [sc. wind is flowing air] is safe enough from
carping criticism, let us use it. But the more cautious sort of person should
not avoid a phrase if, by its addition [i.e., wind is air flowing *in one direction*], all quibbling can be excluded. Let us now get to the subject itself,
since there has been enough discussion about the form of words.[48]

For Gross, the distinction drawn in 5.1.1 between wind as flowing air and wind as
air that flows in one direction differentiates a Theophrastan from a Posidonian
position; Seneca shows an exemplary rigor in demarcating the two positions.[49]
But while the elaboration *in unam partem* reaffirms his careful attention to detail
in his researches,[50] why make *so* much of the distinction in 5.1 as a whole? One
answer is that, by focusing at this early stage on the intrinsic movement (*agitatio*)
of air and water, he prepares the way for his later confrontation with atomic
theory when, at 5.2–3, he confounds the Democritean explanation of wind.[51]
How can wind result from packed atoms (*corpuscula, quae ille* [sc. Democritus]
atomos uocat, 5.2) pushing against each other in a small space? After all, experience shows (5.3) that there is little or no wind when the atmosphere is heavy with
cloud, wind when the sun thins the morning air; so how can wind be related to
the jostling of packed atoms? Already at 5.1.2 Seneca concedes the movement of
tiny particles even in still air:

> quod ex hoc intellegas licet: cum sol in aliquem clusum locum infusus est,
> uidemus corpuscula minima in diuersum ferri, alia sursum alia deorsum
> uarie concursantia.
>
> That the air is always in motion you may deduce from the following:
> when the sun pours into any enclosed space, we see very tiny particles
> moving in different directions, some upwards, some downwards, and ran-
> domly running into each other.

---

48. On the legal overtones of *formula* here, Hine (2010b) 201 n. 2.

49. Gross (1989) 208.

50. Over and above the fact that in 5.1 Seneca's "concern with definition is reminiscent of
Aristotle's and Theophrastus' approach to explanation" (Taub [2003] 146).

51. *N.Q.* 5.2 = D-K 68A93a = Graham (2010) 1.560–1 Text 80; see also Guthrie (1965) 425
with Gilbert (1907) 519–20 and Gross (1989) 210–11.

This appeal to dust particles to illustrate the internal motion of air was no Senecan novelty. Lucretius had already used the analogy of the movement of motes in a sunbeam to illustrate the random behavior of atoms (2.114–22)[52]—a precedent Seneca appears to echo directly,[53] ironically redeploying the Lucretian analogy to a nonatomic, distinctly un-Lucretian end. When the word *corpuscula* recurs in 5.2, now in reference to Democritean atoms, Seneca's opening amendment to define wind as air flowing *in unam partem* (5.1.1) no longer appears incidental: by turning attention *from the outset* to the (nonatomic) internal motion of air, his opening amendment functions as the first in a series of steps leading up to his anti-Democritean argument in 5.2–3; and that argument itself anticipates his extended demonstration at 2.6.2–9.4 of the (Stoic) tension of air,[54] including his necessary rebuttal once more of atomic theory (2.6.2–7.2).

For present purposes, however, the more important effect of Seneca's early amendment *in unam partem* is already, from the book's very opening, to give the quasi-animate air impetus and direction. Already, in 5.1, Seneca's emphasis on air's intrinsic vitality importantly anticipates his later, Stoically refined focus (5.5–6) on its natural capacity for self-motion. By bringing the air to life in this embryonic phase down to 5.6, Seneca prepares the way for his animated and animating, even personifying, account of specific wind types and their distinctive characteristics, locales and habits in 5.7–13, to which we now turn.

III: Seneca's Typology of Winds

One of the features distinguishing Seneca's great storm scene in his *Agamemnon* (431–578) as "the most rhetorical of all" such episodes in Roman literature[55] is the prolonged buildup to the whirlwind (*turbo*) that finally erupts in line 478. The herald Eurybates recounts to Clytemnestra the disaster that befell the Greek fleet on its homeward voyage after Troy's fall. Even though "[t]he topic is usually passed over with brief and general comment,"[56] Seneca dwells at notable length

---

52. The illustration "appears to have been traditional in atomism" (Bailey [1947] 821 on 2.112–24, with sources; see also Vottero [1989] 531 n. 4).

53. See Parroni (1992b) 172 and (2002) 562: Seneca's *corpuscula minima* recalls Lucretius' *minuta corpora* (2.116–17); for Seneca's *infundo* of the sun's penetrating rays, cf. Lucretius' *fundunt* (2.115); and for Seneca's *alia sursum, alia deorsum*, cf. Lucretius' *nunc huc nunc illuc in cunctas undique partis* (2.131).

54. On 2.6.2–9.4 cf. Chapter Two, Section III.

55. Morford (1967) 36 after De Saint-Denis (1935) 404–406 (p. 404: "C'est un exercice de rhétorique"), 419–20.

56. Tarrant (1976) 256.

on the period of calm before the storm: at first, a gentle breeze (*aura... lenis*, 431) assists the rowers as the ships depart from Troy with sails up; when they reach the open sea, a stronger breeze (*aura...fortior*, 442) fills the sails, the oars are laid aside, and "the ship is entrusted to the wind" (*credita est uento ratis*, 443); Troy is left far behind until the smoke arising from its ruins is visible as but a distant speck (458–9). But then the evening sky shows an ominous coloration (462–4): the falling winds (cf. *iacent / deserta uento uela*, 465–6) are but one of a sequence of storm signals that bode ill for the fleet as the waves gradually gather momentum, lashed as they are by the rising winds (cf. *agitata uentis unda uenturis tumet*, 469). The storm finally erupts with all the suddenness (*subito*, 470) which is so traditional a motif in such episodes:[57] in the darkness the cardinal winds rage from every direction (*undique*, 474), all blasting the waters so that "a whirlwind churns the sea" (cf. *turbo conuoluit mare*, 478). The storm of storms that rages thereafter in Eurybates' account is fueled by "the most exaggerated hyperbole,"[58] as "[w]hat in the early part of the speech has been style becomes mannerism"[59] through what Richard Tarrant characterizes as Seneca's "comprehensive but uninspired manipulation of familiar topics."[60] Of special relevance for now, however, is Eurybates' building of dramatic tension before the storm finally erupts:[61] in the movement from *aura lenis* (431) to *aura fortior* (442) and then, after the ominous lull in the winds (465–66), from *agitata uentis unda uenturis* (469) to the raging *turbo* (478), I propose that Seneca deploys a narrative structure analogous to that which shapes his treatment of the different wind types that he analyzes in *N.Q.* 5.7–13. My contention is not, of course, that he necessarily or directly evokes the *Agamemnon* in this section of the *Natural Questions*. Rather, our sampling of the prolonged buildup to the main event in Eurybates' speech conveniently illuminates a similar phenomenon—an acute eye for dramatic development—beneath the technical façade and surface aridity[62] of his book on winds.

A loose structuring principle in 5.7–13 is supplied not just by Seneca's official program at 5.7.1 ("It will perhaps be clear how winds are formed if it is first clarified where they come from, and when"), but also by his five-stage progress from predawn breezes (*antelucani flatus*, 5.7) to the livelier gulf breeze (ἐγκολπίας

---

57. Tarrant (1976) 262.

58. Huxley (1952) 121.

59. Henry and Walker (1963) 6.

60. Tarrant (1976) 249.

61. On this "progressing series of events leading to a climax," Henry and Walker (1963) 6.

62. Cf. Inwood (2002) 137 = (2005) 178 ("One of the driest discussions in the entire *Naturales Quaestiones*").

[sc. ἄνεμος], 5.8.1–10.1) and then to the Etesians (5.10.2–11.2) before violent cloud-burst (ἐκνεφίας [sc. ἄνεμος], 5.12) finally gives way to climactic whirlwind (*turbo*, 5.13). At the embryonic stage (5.7.1) of this increasingly lively gathering of winds, Seneca begins with a modest sample: the predawn breezes are brief in their daily span, they are low in elevation and they extend from spring to no later than summer's end (5.7.2). These breezes soon expire, giving way to Seneca's lengthier treatment of the stronger gulf breeze,[63] whose greater force is immediately signaled by the amount of accumulated exhalations that give rise to it:

> quidquid ex se paludes et flumina remittunt (id autem et multum est et adsiduum) per diem solis alimentum est, nocte non exhauritur, et monti-bus inclusum in unam regionem colligitur.
>
> 5.8.1

All the exhalations from swamps and rivers (they are considerable and constant) provide nourishment for the sun through the day. At night they are not drawn off in their entirety, and when they are closed in by mountains, they build up in one spot.

The theory that this compressed accumulation eventually forms a breeze by streaming into open space (5.8.2) pointedly modifies in a nonatomic direction the Democritean theory (5.2) of massed *corpuscula* colliding and jostling with each other to cause wind.[64] Already, through the impact of its first light,[65] the emerging sun stimulates this accumulation to help form the gulf breeze; the breeze is eventually dispelled when the sun's full heat of day either draws up or dissipates the exhalations (5.8.3). After the predawn breeze of 5.7, Seneca's hardier gulf breeze advances the narrative clock toward late morning before its stronger gusts subside around noon ("they slacken off around midday, and in fact the breeze never lasts right up till noon," 5.8.3).[66] In contrast to the predawn breeze's limited seasonal duration (5.7.2), the gulf breeze lasts throughout the year, albeit blowing most strongly in spring and summer (5.9.1).

---

63. For discussion alongside the predawn breezes, Gilbert (1907) 566–67 with Gross (1989) 217–19.

64. See Section II and n. 51 above in this chapter.

65. "For even before the sun appears, its light is strong" (5.8.2; cf. 5.9.3).

66. Seneca simplifies this narrative clock by restricting himself (as Vottero [1989] 540 n. 5 observes) to morning winds and by excluding evening risings; cf., e.g., Theophr. *On winds* 18 ("the winds begin at dawn or sunset"), 31, Plin. *Nat.* 2.129.

If Seneca's predawn breeze cannot compete with the gulf breeze, we soon encounter a wind made of still sterner stuff: the Etesians begin to blow in summer
"when the day grows longer and the sun's rays are directed straight upon us" (5.10.2).[67]
The Etesians are introduced in a difficult sequence of argument where severe textual
problems complicate yet further Seneca's already challenging train of thought:

9.1: Why are such winds as the gulf breezes stronger in spring and summer? In
spring, because greater moisture creates a larger amount of exhalation.

9.2: But why do they blow as strongly in summer? After sunset, the day's
heat lingers longer, lasting most of the night. This lingering heat continues to draw out exhalations from below, but eventually loses the strength
to absorb those exhalations.

9.3: Sunrise causes wind by the impact of first light; for, *ut dixi* ("as I have
said"; cf. 5.8.2), the light that precedes the full force of the sun "does not
yet warm the air but only strikes it; but when the air is struck it moves
sideways."

9.4: The light thus separates and rarifies the massed spring/summer exhalations [it thereby causes the predawn and gulf breezes].

9.5–10.1: Heat naturally dispels and repels cloud. The sun does the same; hence
the belief in some quarters that the wind blows only from the direction
of the sun. But, insists Seneca, that belief is demonstrably wrong: ships
can sail in all directions, including *toward* the sunrise—an impossibility
if wind comes always from the sun.

10.2: *Etesiae quoque, qui in argumentum a quibusdam aduocantur, non nimis
propositum adiuuant* ("The Etesians, too, which are brought into the
discussion by certain authorities, do not help their thesis too much").
What precisely is the *argumentum* here, what the *propositum*? I take it
that Seneca refers primarily *not* to 9.5–10.1, and that the Etesians are *not*
invoked only in connection with the (just discredited) claim that wind
blows from the direction of the sun. The matter at hand (*argumentum*)
and the point of discussion (*propositum*) remain the larger question
(9.1) of why winds such as the gulf breezes are stronger in spring
and summer. Seneca distances himself from the constituency whose

---

67. Regular (ἐτησίαι [sc. ἄνεμοι] lit. "annual") northerly or northeasterly winds occurring between May and October, and most frequent in July and August (Coutant and Eichenlaub
[1975] xxi–ii, xxx–xxxi; further, Gilbert [1907] 570–72 with *RE* 8A 2.2212–14, Pease [1955–58]
890–91 on Cic. *N.D.* 2.131 and Gross [1989] 219–20). Seneca, or perhaps rather his notional
opponents in argument here, apparently fails to acknowledge the existence of Etesians blowing
from the south in winter (*"etesiae" inquiunt "hieme non sunt,"* 5.10.2; cf. Aristot. *Mete.* 2.5
362a11–20, Theophr. *On winds* 11).

"quoted" voice describes the Etesians in 10.2 ("I shall first tell you what their opinion is, and then why I disagree"). That opposing voice takes its cue from 9.1, explicitly framing its response in terms of the initial question: "The Etesians," they say, "do not exist in winter...They begin to blow in summer" (10.2); cf. 9.1 "Yet why are winds of this sort stronger in spring and summer?"

10.3–4: Still the opposing voice on the Etesians. In contrast to the short days of winter, when the sunshine ends before the snows of the northern region can begin to melt, the longer spring/summer days produce large amounts of exhalation from the snow. The Etesians get their start from the movement of these exhalations toward "the regions that are lower and warmer [*loca...submissiora ac tepidiora*]"; they allegedly blow from the summer solstice and remain strong beyond the rising of Sirius in July.[68] The southern motion of the sun itself assists the movement of the Etesians: "they have already been shifting air from the cold north to the hot south, and now the sun too pushes along [*impellit*] the air to the south of it, and continues to attract [*alteram partem aëris attrahit*] air from the north as before (cf. §3)."[69] Flowing from/in the direction of the south-moving sun, the Etesians arguably gesture in favor of the (discredited) proposition of 5.9.5, *inde flatus est unde sol*; but the primary point of reference in the Etesian section as a whole remains the initial question posed in 9.1. For:

11.1: *Nunc quod promisi dicendum est, quare etesiae nos non adiuuent, nec quicquam huic conferant causae* ("Now, as promised [cf. 5.10.2], I must state why the Etesians do not help us, and contribute nothing to the matter in hand"). Back to the main subject (*causa*) broached in 9.1: unlike the breezes of 5.7–8, the Etesians are not stirred by the light at sunrise or soon dissipated by the sun's full rays, but "begin to emerge at about the time when even the longer-lasting breezes have abated." In effect, the "sleepy" and "lazy" Etesians (they "are called *somniculosi* and *delicati* by sailors because, as Gallio says,[70] 'They don't know how to get up in the

---

68. Reading *ultraque ortum Caniculae* †non† *ualent* with Hine (1996a) 212.171 and (1996b) 84–86 (cf. [2010b] 201 n. 10). For the rising of the Dog Star, Beaujeu (1950) 203 on Plin. *Nat.* 2.123 (according to Pliny, July 18th).

69. Hine (1996b) 86—part of his extended, and convincing, elucidation of this vexed passage (see also [2010b] 201 n. 11).

70. Presumably the Gallio praised at 4a pref. 10–12—Seneca's elder brother, adopted by L. Junius Gallio (see Chapter Three, Section III); so Oltramare (1929) 2.224 n.1, Corcoran (1971–72) 2.90 n. 1 and Hine (1996a) 327 in *Index nominum* s.v. *(Iunius) Gallio*, but Vottero (1989) 544–45 n. 3 after Gercke (1907) 179.22 and p. 272 inclines toward the other Gallio, while Parroni (2002) 564 is noncommital.

morning,'"[71] 5.11.1) do nothing to advance Seneca's specific argument because—in terms of the original question in 9.1 *Quare tamen tales uenti uere et aestate validiores sunt?*—those late risers are evidently different from the early-rising and fast-abating predawn and gulf breezes. Hence they are ultimately irrelevant to Seneca's discussion.

For present purposes, the detailed controversies that complicate this summary of Seneca's argument in 5.9–11 do not affect our main point of interest: Seneca's personifying characterization of the Etesians as late sleepers who emerge after lesser winds have succumbed to the summer heat. Time again progresses in this Senecan account of the winds: the Etesians' late appearance advances the narrative clock further into the day after the morning breezes have come and gone before noon in 5.7–8; the Etesians prove their greater strength by breaking, not succumbing to, the sun's heat (5.10.4).[72] But while they surpass the predawn and gulf breezes on Seneca's ascending scale of robustness here, all three wind types nevertheless share a similar consistency of character in their regular seasonal recurrence, their reliable daily schedule in season, their familiar association with place, and their measured force—a picture of consistency that is shattered when the cloudburst (ἐκνεφίας) explodes with sudden violence in 5.12.[73]

Seneca's colorful explanation of cloudbursts is possibly at least partially his own, combining two components: first, the dry and the moist Aristotelian exhalations in contention with each other; and, second, from that discord, the formation of certain hollow clouds. Thin air is trapped in the tubular pockets that form within (or between?) these hollow clouds;[74] the cloudburst is apparently caused

---

71. For the late rising, cf. Plin. *Nat.* 2.127 *Etesiae...a tertia diei hora oriuntur*, with Beaujeu (1950) 207.

72. For this cooling effect, see Vottero (1989) 544 n. 5 with Pease (1955–58) 890–91 on Cic. *N.D.* 2.131, and cf. Watson (1984) 43: "despite a clear sky, [the Etesians] whip the blue Aegean into a stormy froth and keep old women in their island villages knitting thick winter sweaters for astonished and grateful summer tourists. Along the Turkish coast, they call these winds *melteme*, the 'bad tempered' ones."

73. On ἐκνεφίας (= *procella*), Plin. *Nat.* 2.131 with Beaujeu (1950) 211; Gilbert (1907) 558–63 (with τυφῶν, as in the pairing at *N.Q.* 5.12–13) with *RE* 8A 2.2295; Gross (1989) 221–23; and Vottero (1989) 546 n. 1 for sources concisely collected.

74. At 5.12.1 *interualla inter illas* [sc. *nubes*] *relinqui*, *inter* is taken to mean "between clouds" by, e.g., Vottero (1989) 547 ("fra nube e nube") and Hine (2010b) 78 ("gaps are left between them"). But "inside" the clouds is favored by Corcoran (1971–72) 2.93, Gross (1989) 221 and Parroni (2002) 317; *inter* of "inside," "within" is rare but far from unprecedented: cf. *Dial.* 10.18.6 and see *TLL* 7.1 2127.28–57 with Brink (1982) 335–36 on Hor. *Ep.* 2.2.114 *inter penetralia Vestae.*

by the internal motion and the heating and expansion of the trapped air (5.12.2), which eventually erupts from its confined space. Dramatic considerations shape if not Seneca's entire theory then at least his mode of exposition in this tumultuous passage. In contrast to the consistent and tamer winds that precede it in Seneca's narrative, the cloudburst is born of and to violence, as if its origins in the discord within cloud (cf. *ex tanta discordia corporum inter se pugnantium*, 5.12.1) predispose it to explode as a short-lived ("Usually this is a brief blast," 5.12.2) and uncontrolled force. The vitalizing effect here is supported by two factors, the first Seneca's use in 5.12.2 of personifying language that gives the air feeling (cf. *desiderat*) and warms it figuratively as well as literally when, "restricted in its movement, it is buffeted and becomes heated [*incaluit*]";[75] when the cloudburst finally erupts, its character (*uehemens et acer*) is itself defined by human-like struggle and exertion (*laborat et iter sibi ui ac pugna parat*).

Secondly, the term *spiritus*. On the assumption that the books of the *Natural Questions* were originally ordered in the sequence 3, 4a, 4b, 5, 6, 7, 1 and 2, it is notable that *spiritus* occurs relatively infrequently down to Book 6, on earthquakes, where it is found some fifty-five times;[76] thereafter, it occurs only four times in Book 7, never in Book 1, but then some fifty times in Book 2, on lightning and thunder. The word is used thirteen times in Book 3, never in what survives of Book 4a, only four times in what survives of Book 4b, and then nine times in Book 5. Beyond its relative scarcity down to Book 6, however,[77] what matters for present purposes is its range of Senecan meaning. So Harry Hine on 2.1–11, on the nature of air:

> [Apart from *aer*] S. also uses the word *spiritus*, which at any rate never means "atmosphere" [as *aer* can], but which has ambiguities of its own. Thus sometimes it means simply "air," and is interchangeable with *aer*...; sometimes it may mean "wind"...; and sometimes it represents the technical Stoic concept of pneuma.... S. does not consistently observe any distinction between *spiritus*, in the technical sense, and *aer*; a relaxing of the strict doctrine of the early Stoa.[78]

---

75. Cf. *OLD incalesco* 2a, "of persons, their passions, etc."

76. This and the following figures are based on the listings in Busa and Zampolli (1975) 1274–75; see also the parallel tabulation in Bravo Díaz (1991) 20.

77. Seneca's choice of subject matter in the preceding books may, of course, partly explain this scarcity. Yet it is notable that *aer does* occur before Book 6 far more frequently than *spiritus*: according to the tabulation of Bravo Díaz (1991) 20, *aer* is found twenty-three times in Book 3, twice in 4a, thirteen times in 4b and thirty-one times in 5, and then twenty times in Book 6, twenty-two times in 7, thirty-five times in 1 and forty-nine times in 2.

78. Hine (1981) 123; cf. his p. 139 on 2.1.3.

In the great majority of occurrences down to the end of Book 4b, *spiritus* means simply "air" and is interchangeable with *aer*.[79] At 3.15.1, however, Seneca uses *spiritus* of both the human and the cosmic body:

> placet natura regi terram, et quidem ad nostrorum corporum exemplar, in quibus et uenae sunt et arteriae, illae sanguinis hae spiritus receptacula. in terra quoque sunt alia itinera per quae aqua, alia per quae spiritus currit; adeoque ad similitudinem illa humanorum corporum natura formauit ut maiores quoque nostri aquarum appellauerint uenas.
>
> I like the idea that the earth is governed by nature, and in fact after the model of our own bodies, which have veins and arteries—the former as containers of blood, the latter as containers of air. In the earth, too, there are some passages through which water runs, others through which air passes; and nature formed those passages with such a resemblance to the human body that our ancestors too called them "veins" of water.

The earth-body analogy here not only introduces Stoic vitalism as fundamental to the Senecan worldview constructed in this, the foundational book of the *Natural Questions* as a whole;[80] it also gently exploits the technical connotation of *spiritus* as Stoic pneuma, the mixture of air and fire that was "the active agent par excellence in [the Stoic] cosmos."[81] The earth-body analogy recurs in Book 5, albeit in the witty comparison of human flatulence to emissions of *spiritus* from earth at 5.4.2: "just as in our bodies flatulence is caused by food…, so people think that this great natural system, too, gives off air [*spiritum*] when it digests its nourishment." When Seneca turns to cloudbursts in 5.12, he suddenly redeploys *spiritus*, using it three times of the raging air:[82] Why this striking preference for

---

79. So ten of seventeen overall occurrences: 3.9.1; 3.10.2; 3.15.8; 3.16.5; 3.20.1; 3.24.3; 4b.5.2; 4b.9; 4b.13.2; 4b.13.3. Seven exceptions remain, two at 3.15.1, on which I focus immediately below. The other five: 3 pref. 15 *spiritus attollere* ("elevate one's consciousness"); 3.3, of wind (cf. Hine [2010b] 195 n. 17); 3.17.2, of the laboring breath (*luctante spiritu*) of a dying mullet; 3.20.2, of "the disagreeable exhalation/odor" of certain water (cf. *OLD spiritus* 10); and 3.30.2, of "floods bursting forth with great wind [*magno spiritu*]."

80. On 3.15–16 in relation to the vitalist tradition, Gross (1989) 131–34, and cf. Chapter Two, Section III n. 30.

81. Sambursky (1959) 4. A pervasive Senecan theme: "much of the *Naturales quaestiones* is taken up with explanation of the behaviour of *spiritus*" (Lapidge [1989] 1399).

82. Overall distribution of the nine occurrences of *spiritus* in Book 5: 5.4.2; then absent until the triad at 5.12.2, 4 and 5; then a second cluster of three at 5.13.4 before two further appearances at 5.14.4 and 5.15.3 respectively (see immediately below for these five occurrences after 5.12).

the term *here* in the sequence of 5.7–13 as a whole? The new word appropriately accompanies the other personifying signs in 5.12.2[83] because, I propose, it now carries a special, animated meaning, to the dramatizing effect of "wind with heightened personality."[84] True, Seneca draws a relatively banal distinction between *spiritus* and *uentus* on the one hand, and between *spiritus* and *aer* on the other, at 5.13.4:

> spiritum a uento modus separat: uehementior enim spiritus uentus est, inuicem spiritus leniter fluens aër.
>
> *spiritus* differs from wind in degree: more violently moving *spiritus* is wind; in turn, *spiritus* is gently flowing air.

But already here *spiritus* is invested with a liveliness that *aër* lacks; and in every other occurrence of *spiritus* in Book 5 beyond the flatulence of 5.4.2, it denotes an energetic, vitalized force, whether in the personified form of the subterranean air that "seeks a way out" at 5.14.4 (*per haec loca... se exitum quaerens spiritus torsit*), or in the form of human breath/spirit at 5.15.3, where underground excavation symbolically compromises the upright, free breathing (*recto spiritu liberoque*) of the miners.[85] So in 5.12: as the winds from 5.7 onward rise with increasing robustness, we progress toward the "higher" *spiritus* of ἐκνεφίας before reaching the climactic whirlwind (*turbo*) of 5.13. The special force that I claim for *spiritus* at 5.12.2 in particular adds a fourth category—air or wind as a truly spirited entity, full of dramatic animation—to the three meanings of *spiritus* that are distinguished by Hine in his comments, quoted above,[86] on 2.1–11.

We saw in Chapter One that the principles of interaction and merging that are fundamental to Senecan nature's integrated oneness in the *Natural Questions* are powerfully emblematized by the interchangeability of the four elements as portrayed in 3.10.[87] Analogical correspondence between the elements contributes to sustaining that interactive principle after Book 3, as when Seneca compares the merging effect of multiple winds to that of multiple rivers at 5.12.3–4: just as rivers

---

83. See above in this section and n. 75.

84. See already Bravo Díaz (1991) for *spiritus* in the *Natural Questions* markedly (albeit not exclusively) denoting a heightened force, an agency that tends to be associated with action verbs such as *premere, elidere, dimouere,* etc. (p. 17) and is favored over *aer* "when the context implies the idea of action and energy" (p. 20).

85. See Chapter Two, Section VI.

86. Hine (1981) 123.

87. Chapter One, Section I.

of immoderate size result when individual streams of modest size combine their currents, so with wind storms (*procellae*) that are of but brief duration as long as they occur singly; "but when they have united their forces and the air [*spiritus*], driven from the different parts of the sky, has merged in the same direction, the storms increase in both violence and duration" (5.12.4). On our ascending scale of winds, this conglomerated storm force builds yet further momentum before the climactic whirlwind finally erupts in 5.13; and the transition to whirlwind is eased by Seneca's continuation in 5.13 of the river analogy of 5.12.3–4. But in 5.13 the analogy serves to illustrate an idiosyncratic theory that departs radically from the influential Aristotelian view (*Mete.* 3.1 370b17–371a3) that a whirlwind is caused when the wind within a cloud meets resistance and forms an eddy; when the hurricane (ἐκνεφίας) that has thus been produced in cloud is unable to free itself from the cloud, it spirals to earth together with the cloud, so forming the whirlwind or τυφῶν (*Mete.* 3.1 371a9–12).[88] At 5.13.1–2 *uertex* of both water and air[89] seals the analogy as rivers that meet an obstacle are turned back on themselves "in such a way that they are swirled about and swallowed up in themselves and form a whirlpool" (5.13.1); so the wind, obstructed by a promontory or collected in a narrow canyon, revolves upon itself to form its own strong eddy (*uerticem*, 5.13.2), a phenomenon that is perhaps of interesting symbolic value in light of developments later in Book 5.[90] As in the case of the cloudburst, the whirlwind shows personifying traits: the obstructed air flow becomes increasingly excited (cf. *se ipsa uertigine concitans turbo*, 5.13.3) until, inflamed in its increasing violence (*pugnacior...inflammatur*),[91] it may evolve into the fiery *turbo* "which the Greeks call a prester" (*quem* πρηστῆρα *Graeci uocant*).[92] Our drama is now complete: from their modest origin in the meek predawn breezes of 5.7, the rising Senecan winds culminate in this spectacular fire storm.

   Seneca's wind coverage in 5.7–13 as a whole, moving from samples that are relatively weak, benign and consistent in their regularity to blasts that are dangerously random and violent, has important paradigmatic implications for our reading of the later part of Book 5, and especially for developments in 5.18. There, we shall discern a similar ascending movement from initial calm to violent *furor* of a

---

88. On Seneca's departure from the Aristotelian line see Gilbert (1907) 563 with Gross (1989) 222.

89. Cf. *OLD* 1a, 1b.

90. See Section V n. 152 below in this chapter.

91. For *concito* of exciting feelings, etc., *OLD* 5; *pugnax* of natural forces, *OLD* 1c; *inflammo* of the passions, *OLD* 2a, b.

92. On which see *RE* 8A 2.2318–19 with Vottero (1989) 548–49 n. 4.

figurative kind, as man launches his warships on voyages of blind aggression, not enlightened discovery, as if a raging storm force himself. First, however, Seneca's classification of the winds by compass point and celestial region in 5.16–17 will importantly condition our approach to 5.18.

IV: Mapping the Winds

The human waywardness featured in the story that Seneca recounts in 5.15 of Philip's adventurers going deep underground in search of precious metals[93] is perhaps matched by a form of narratival drift: in this digressive interlude, Seneca's main line of argument momentarily loses its way until it is retrieved at 5.16.1 *Sed ut ad id de quo agitur reuertar…* ("But to return to the subject under discussion…"). In contrast to the waywardness portrayed in 5.15, Seneca's charting of the winds by place and direction in 5.16–17 represents a mapping of the natural world in more normative action. This vision of timeless regularity, universal in scale (most obviously in Seneca's zonal division of the skies in 5.17), offers a comforting counterpoise (1) to the aberrational ways that he traces across time at 5.15.2 ("our age suffers not from new vices but from vices handed down all the way from antiquity")[94] and (2) to the unfettered war voyaging—and, more generally, man's transgressive wanderings far from his "natural" place on dry land—that he condemns in 5.18. Seneca's mapping of the winds is carefully structured in four phases in 5.16–17.

(A) The Cardinal Winds in Ovid

In Ovid's account of the cosmogony in *Metamorphoses* 1, the creator assigns the four cardinal winds to their different regions to thwart their danger:

> his quoque non passim mundi fabricator habendum
> aera permisit. (uix nunc obsistitur illis,
> cum sua quisque regant diuerso flamina tractu,
> quin lanient mundum; tanta est discordia fratrum.)

1.57–60

Nor did the world creator allow the winds to have the air at their disposal everywhere. (As it is, they are scarcely held from pulling the world to pieces,

---

93. See Chapter Two, Section VI.

94. On the latter passage, Chapter Two, Section VI.

even though each controls his own blasts in a different region;
such is the discord between brothers.)

Seneca's ostensible motive for quoting *Met.* 1.61–6 at 5.16.1 is to set up a basic
four-point wind compass[95] that he goes on to refine (as we shall see) by appeal to
Varro in 5.16.3–4. But Ovid also gives graphic expression to Seneca's broader emphasis in 5.16–17 on the winds as fixed by region according to cosmic design, their
influence naturally limited to their given sectors, in stark contrast to the human
transgressors of 5.15 and 5.18:

> Sed ut ad id de quo agitur reuertar, uenti quattuor sunt, in ortum occasum
> meridiem septemtrionemque diuisi. ceteri, quos uariis nominibus appella-
> mus, his adplicantur.

> *eurus* ad auroram Nabataeaque regna recessit
> Persidaque et radiis iuga subdita matutinis.
> uesper et occiduo quae litora sole tepescunt
> proxima sunt *zephyris*. Scythiam septemque triones
> horrifer inuasit *boreas*; contraria tellus
> nubibus adsiduis pluuioque madescit ab *austro*.[96]

5.16.1

But to return to the subject under discussion, there are four winds, divided
into the east, west, south and north. The other winds, which we call by
various names, are associated with these winds.
   The east wind's retreat is toward the dawn and the realms of the Arabian
Nabataeans, and Persia and the mountains that gleam in the morning rays.
The evening and the shores that are warmed by the setting sun are closest
to *the west wind*. Scythia and the northerly reaches have been seized by *the
chilling north wind*; the opposite region lies wet from constant cloudiness
and *the rainy south wind*.

As if in replication of their different sectors, each of the four cardinal winds in
Ovid occupies its own metrical *sedes*—a cardinal point, as it were—within its

---

95. Cf. Barchiesi (2005) 158 on Seneca's appeal to these verses as a "canonical representation"
of the geographical distribution of the winds.

96. *zephyris* in the Senecan manuscripts replaces *-o* in the Ovidian tradition; for *pluuio* at *Met.*
1.66 Anderson (1982) 3 prints *-a* (cf. [1996] 46 and 159), conjectured by Gilbert (1896) 11: "Sic
enim v. 66 puto scribendum: *pluuiaque* (adsidua) uel *pluuiisque*, non *pluuioque* (ab austro)."

line.[97] The east wind (*eurus*) is separated as far as Ovid's syntax allows from the west wind (*zephyris*), the north wind (*boreas*) as far as possible from *zephyris*, the south wind (*austro*) as far as possible from *boreas*; harsh juxtaposition also underscores the winds' incompatibility (*matutinis/uesper*, 62–3; *zephyris/Scythiam septemque triones*, 64; *boreas/contraria tellus*, 65). But after this positive demonstration of the winds' fixed sectors, Seneca draws on the great Virgilian storm in *Aeneid* 1 to make the same point from a negative direction:

uel si breuius illos [sc. uentos] complecti mauis, in unam tempestatem, *quod fieri nullo modo potest*, congregentur:

una eurusque notusque ruunt creberque procellis
africus,
et, qui locum in illa rixa non habuit, aquilo.

5.16.2

Or if you prefer to capture those winds more concisely, let them be gathered into a single storm (an impossible occurrence under any circumstances):
Both the east wind and the south wind rush together, and the west wind thick with squalls [*Aen.* 1.85–6],
and the north wind, which had no place in that famous [Virgilian] conflict.

After *quod fieri nullo modo potest*, Seneca creates a virtual litotes out of *congregentur* and Virgil's *una*: the language of gathering merely stresses the impossibility of congregation. The northern *aquilo* appears later in the Virgilian storm: "As Aeneas hurls forth such words, a gale, shrieking from the north [*stridens aquilone procella*], strikes full on his sail" (1.102–3). But Seneca's seemingly innocent notice of its absence at *Aen.* 1.85–6 (*qui... non habuit*) merely reaffirms the fact that the cardinal winds *cannot* converge, even in the realm of Virgilian fiction.[98] They are thus put in their place before Varro enters (5.16.3) to complicate the Senecan mapping process.

(B) The Varronian Compass Card

The different wind-rose or compass-card systems that oriented the winds in the Greek anemological tradition varied widely in the number of their compass points.

---

97. Barchiesi (2005) 159.

98. But cf. Hom. *Od.* 5.295–6, and Senecan fiction too is another matter (cf. *Agam.* 475–84). On the familiar ἀνέμων στάσις, Tarrant (1976) 265 on *Agam.* 476.

So, of the authorities apparently recognized by Posidonius (fr. 137a10–12 E-K), Aristotle "operated basically on an 8-point system with two additional northerly winds (NNW Thrascias, and NNE Meses); a system which he saw as reducible to 4 and even further to 2 (northerly and southerly winds)";[99] Timosthenes of Rhodes (third century BCE), according to Pliny (*Nat.* 6.183) an admiral under Ptolemy II Philadelphus,[100] "used a regular 12-point card."[101] Apart from Seneca, Vitruvius (1.6.4–10), Manilius (4.589–94), Pliny (*Nat.* 2.119–22), Gellius (2.22), Suetonius (ap. Isid. *De rerum nat.* 37) and Vegetius (*Epit.* 4.38) all bear witness to the strong influence that the Greek tradition had on Roman thinking in this regard.[102] But a foundational figure in Romanizing the Greek wind-rose is Varro,[103] whose twelve-point system Seneca emulates at 5.16.3–6, its basic structure as follows: within the fourfold division of east, west, north and south, each quarter is itself divided into three, with each main wind accompanied by two subsidiaries.

Varro's apparently pioneering Roman organization of the winds on his compass card developed in another direction the project of Roman (self-)definition and systematization discernible in so much of his oeuvre, most obviously his *Antiquitates rerum humanarum et diuinarum* in forty-one books, that foundational work that "brought the Romans home" by collecting and ordering the Roman cultural past.[104] The Varronian card also contributed to stabilizing the winds' Latin nomenclature relative to the Greek, a linguistic dimension that eases the transition to Seneca's striking analogy at 5.17.1 (with suggestive relevance to Varro, given the latter's *De lingua latina*): the twelve-wind system is said to be favored "not because there are that many winds everywhere…, but because there are

---

99. Kidd (1988) 518; cf. *Mete.* 2.6 363a21–364a5, and see further Thompson (1918) 49–50 and *RE* 8A 2.2344–50 with Coutant and Eichenlaub (1975) l–liii.

100. Further, Harley and Woodward (1987) 152–53 with Healy (1999) 45 and n. 22.

101. Kidd (1988) 518; further, *RE* 8A 2.2351–6 with Nielsen (1945) 41–46. Nothing is known of the wind system of Bion, apparently Posidonius' other authority (cf. fr. 137a11–12 E-K Βίωνα τὸν ἀστρολόγον), for whom Kidd 518.

102. Vitruvius, etc., are thoroughly surveyed by Nielsen (1945) 73–107; conveniently, Obrist (1997) 38–41.

103. On this point, Nielsen (1945) 72. The relevant Varronian works are his *Ephemeris naualis* and especially *De ora maritima*, which is sometimes identified with the *Ephemeris naualis*: see Gilbert (1907) 553 n. 2 with *RE* 8A 2.2372; Rawson (1985) 288–89; and Salvadore (1999) 48–52 *De ora maritima* fr. 6 (= *N.Q.* 5.16.3–6).

104. Cf. Cic. *Acad.* 1.9: "we were traveling about like foreigners and wandering like visitors in our own city, and your books brought us back home, so to speak, so that we could at last recognize who and where we were. You have revealed the age of our native city, the chronology of its history, the laws of its religious rites and its priesthoods, its civil and its military institutions, the topography of its districts and sites, the terminology, types, duties and origins of all our religious and secular institutions… ."; Rawson (1985) 236–37, 312–16.

nowhere more than twelve winds. Just so, we say that there are six cases, not because every noun takes all six, but because no noun has more than six."[105] The
analogy is of interest not least because it implies the ownership and rationalization of "our" winds on the model of "our language," that foundation of our self-
identity; and the emphasis on Roman identity is already signaled when, at 5.16.3,
Seneca assigns two *subpraefecti* to each cardinal wind, as if those auxiliary winds
are extended components of the Roman bureaucracy.[106]

After Varro, Roman writers still customarily coordinated the Latin wind
names with their Greek counterparts. So e.g., Pliny at *Nat.* 2.119: "Accordingly,
there are two winds in each quarter of the sky, from the equinoctial rising point
the *subsolanus*, from the winter solstitial rising the *uolturnus*; the Greeks call the
former *apheliotes*, the latter *eurus*…" Or Gellius (2.22.8): "The *eurus* is given another name by the Greeks, *apheliotes*, and called *subsolanus* by Roman sailors."
But in Seneca's Varronian wind compass the naming of the winds is a more
charged affair, their Latin identity primary, Greece no longer the epicenter of
their coverage culturally and linguistically. Hence the priority given to "our"
names (albeit names that themselves often represent regionalisms from different
parts of Italy and beyond)[107] in Seneca's listing of the twelve winds (Figure 1): (1)
the wind rising from the equinoctial sunrise (E) "is called *subsolanus* by us, while
the Greeks call it *apheliotes*" (5.16.4).[108] (2) The *eurus* from ESE (winter solstitial
rising) is pointedly presented as a naturalized Latin word ("but *eurus*, too, has
now been granted citizenship, and is no foreigner when it occurs in our language,"
5.16.4); but Seneca also reports that "our people" (*nostri*) use *uolturnus* of the
same wind, Livy in his account of Hannibal's defeat of the Romans at Cannae
in Apulia in 216 BCE (22.43.10).[109] Seneca's excursus on the battle (5.16.4) gives

---

105. Cf. Varro on the cases at *L.* 8.16, 63, 9.50–2, etc.

106. The term *subpraefectus* is conspicuous here for its technical valence; for its appearance
elsewhere on inscriptions, see *OLD* 1a, with examples from public administration, the army
and the navy (further, Vottero [1989] 557 n. 9 with Cervellera [1992] 114 on what she claims
as "un neologismo della sfera politica").

107. See Adams (2007) 224–30.

108. *subsolanus* not found before Cels. 2.1.3 (= *solanus*, Vitr. 1.6.4); further, Nielsen (1945) 86
with Vottero (1989) 558 n. 13 for sources.

109. See Adams (2007) 228–29 on Col. 5.5.15 for *uolturnus* also located in Baetica in Spain
("The name must have been transported to Spain by southern Italian colonists"). But for the
Italian diffusion of the name, p. 229 n. 117: "here [5.16.4] *nostri* refers to Romans as distinct
from Greeks, and implies a knowledge of the word within Italy beyond Apulia." Cf. also Silius'
colorful picture of *Volturnus* personified at 9.491–523 (during Silius' representation of
Cannae). The name is possibly derived from *uultur*, the vulture (wind) related to the eagle
(northern *aquilo*) as "oiseaux d'augure" (Nielsen [1945] 82; cf. p. 77); or from *Vultur*, the
mountain in Apulia (*RE* 8A 2.2323).

historical depth to his Romanizing strategy here by evoking a key moment when Rome faced disaster from Hannibal, only finally to win by crushing the transgressive, external threat; in its different way the foreign *eurus*, Hannibal's ally,[110] is itself tamed, as if made Roman through naturalization into the Latin mainstream. (3) From the equinoctial sunset (W) comes Latin *fauonius*, "which even those who cannot speak Greek will tell you is *zephyrus*" (5.16.5);[111] (4) from the summer solstitial setting (WNW) comes the Latin *corus*, "which is called *argestes* by some" (5.16.5);[112] (5) from the winter solstitial setting (WSW), *africus*, "furious and rushing, is called *lips* among the Greeks."[113] But while in these cases the Latin name takes precedence, those instances where the Greek prevails in Seneca's inventory partially restore the balance of Greco-Roman cultural negotiation. So (6) at the summer solstitial rising (ENE), *kaikias* "has no name in our language" (5.16.4); (7) for *thraikias* (NNW) "there is no equivalent term in our language" (5.16.6); so also (8) *euronotus* (SSE) and (9) *leukonotus* (SSW),[114] the latter two separated in 5.16.6 by the entry (10) "then *notus*, in Latin *auster*" (S).[115] Despite the prominent Greek presence in 5.16.6, however, Seneca sustains his Romanizing emphasis here by arraying the north winds - (11) *aquilo* (NNE) and (12) *septemtrio* (north) in addition to *thraikias* (7 above); *aquilo* is the highest (*summus*), *septemtrio* in the middle (*medius*), *thraikias* the lowest (*imus*)[116] - after the arrangement of places (*summus, medius, imus*) on a couch in the Roman dining room.[117]

---

110. For Hannibal winning "with the help of the wind and the glare that dazzled the enemies' eyes" (5.16.4), cf. Liv. 22.43.10–11, V. Max. 7.4 ext. 2, Sil. 9.501–12, Flor. *Epit.* 1.22.16.

111. *fauonius* already Plautine and in Cato's *De agri cultura* (cf. *OLD* 1a, b); traditionally identified with ζέφυρος by Latin writers (Nielsen [1945] 80–81; *RE* 8A 2.2296–97).

112. *corus/caurus* is not attested before Lucr. 6.135 but it is frequent thereafter (Nielsen [1945] 81–82; *RE* 8A 2.2294). For the identification with *argestes* cf., e.g., Plin. *Nat.* 2.119, 18.338, Gell. *N.A.* 2.22.12; further, Vottero (1989) 559 n. 20, with useful remarks (p. 560 n. 21) mitigating Seneca's unconventional characterization of *argestes* as "usually gentle" (*fere mollis*).

113. λίψ from Λιβύη, Λίβυς by popular etymology, whence Latin *africus* in Cicero, Caesar and later (Nielsen [1945] 19, 85; *RE* 8A 2.2288–89); a common identification (Vottero [1989] 560 n. 22).

114. *kaikias*: Nielsen (1945) 29, 33–34; *thraikias*: Nielsen 38–39; *euronotus*: Nielsen 42–43; *leukonotus*: Nielsen 43, 98 (further, Vottero [1989] 558 n. 18, 561 nn. 26–27, 29).

115. *auster* is already in Ennius and Plautus (*OLD* 1); on the common identification, Nielsen (1945) 79–80 with Vottero (1989) 561 n. 28.

116. For *thraikias*, n. 114 above. *aquilo* is often used of the north wind generally from Ennius on (*OLD* 1a) until it is more precisely identified as NNE or NE wind in the post-Varronian tradition (see Vottero [1989] 560–61 n. 24 with Nielsen [1945] 76–78, 90–91, and cf. n. 109 above).

117. *OLD summus* 2a, i.e., "Furthest to the left on a couch (from the viewpoint of those eating)"; *imus* 2d; Vottero (1989) 560 n. 23, including Sen. *Dial.* 2.10.2.

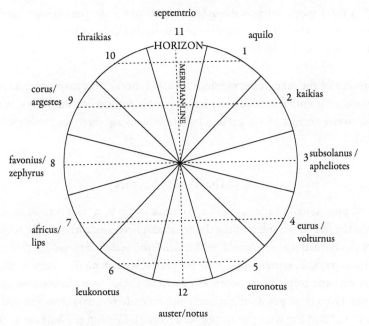

FIGURE I. Seneca's Twelve Winds.

Note: the numeration of the winds seen here differs from the numerical order in which they are discussed in the text.

Source: adapted from a similar illustration in Vottero (1989) 560–61.

This emphasis on the *Roman* systematization of the winds will have important implications for our reading of Seneca's moralizing conclusion to the book: To what extent is Roman "ownership" of the winds symptomatic of a world outlook—a striving for conquest and control, whether intellectual, military, economic or sociopolitical—that potentially finds far more troubling expression in 5.18?[118] Rome goes unnamed there, but can we fail to detect traces of her imperializing war craft in the marauding excesses condemned in 5.18? From a cosmic perspective, however, even the strongest imperial power must appear minuscule:

> punctum est istud in quo nauigatis, in quo bellatis, in quo regna disponitis, minima etiam cum illis utrimque oceanus occurrit.
>
> I pref. 11

---

118. See Section VI below in this chapter.

A mere speck—that is the area in which you make your voyages and wage war, and where you organize kingdoms that are tiny, even when they are met on both sides by ocean.[119]

In advance of the marauding warships of 5.18, Seneca's next mapping maneuver (5.17) asserts a similar cosmic perspective, on this occasion through his charting of the twelve sectors of sky posited by "those who say there are twelve winds" (5.17.2).

(C) The Twelve Sectors

Seneca's procedure at 5.17.1–4, brisk and elusive as it is in certain details, amounts to this: the five circles subdividing the celestial sphere (*caelum*) into five zones— the circles termed *septemtrionalis*, *solstitialis*, *aequinoctialis*, *brumalis* and *contrarius septemtrionali*, corresponding to (respectively) our arctic circle, tropic of cancer, equator, tropic of capricorn and antarctic circle[120] – are intersected by the horizon. From these points of intersection, Seneca derives ten *partes*, five east (*ab ortu*, 5.17.4) and five west (*ab occasu*; see Figure 1). Cutting the horizon at right angles, the meridian line adds two further points, north and south, to Seneca's scheme (11 and 12 in Figure 1), allowing him to contrive two additional sectors (*regiones*). By establishing twelve sectors for twelve winds, Seneca expands the symbolic point of the Varronian compass card by drawing a still larger map of natural zonal "ownership" and restriction, a map that is filled out by his sudden reversion from the macro picture of the twelve zones to the micro level of local winds (5.17.5).

(D) Local Winds

These winds are introduced here conventionally enough after the main winds, as they are in e.g., Vitruvius (1.6.10), Pliny (*Nat.* 2.120) and Gellius (2.22.19):[121] "*atabulus* infests Apulia, *iapyx* Calabria, *sciron* Athens, *crageus* Pamphylia, *circius* Gaul." Local derivation gives these winds distinctive names and quasi-ethnicity:

---

119. I.e., (Hine [2010b] 208 n. 8), "even if your kingdoms stretch from one side of the inhabited world to the other" (the ocean was thought to surround the entire landmass of the known world; cf. *OLD Oceanus* 2a).

120. For background on the familiar subdivision into five celestial zones, extending back to the Pre-Socratics, see Vottero (1989) 562 n. 3 with Kidd (1988) 747–49 on fr. 209 E-K; Gross (1989) 228–34; Volk (2009) 41–42.

121. Further, Vottero (1989) 564 n. 10 with Beaujeu (1950) 199.

so, in Horace, *atabulus* "in an appropriate context underlines his [Apulian] origin" (cf. *Sat.* 1.5.78);[122] *iapyx* from Ἰαπυγία/Iapygia in the heel of southeast Italy;[123] *crageus* apparently from Mount Cragos in Lycia;[124] *circius* possibly of Celtic origin, given its attestation in the Iberian peninsula as well as Gaul;[125] and *sciron* from the Scironic rocks between Megara and Corinth, themselves taking their name from the infamous brigand destroyed by Theseus.[126] This derivation from the monstrous Sciron strengthens the hint of personification already latent in *infestat*,[127] while the aggression of these winds, *circius* in particular,[128] becomes symbolically suggestive if this picture of local *uenti* is centered on Rome and the superficially unifying imperial project is seen to be challenged by relentless regional difference and idiosyncrasy: local character is set powerfully against centralized standardization. Hence the possible irony when Seneca reports that *diuus Augustus* dedicated a temple to *circius* "when he spent time in Gaul" (*cum in Gallia moraretur*, 5.17.5): in contrast to the Augustan visitation, *circius* is a permanent resident in Gaul—truly a telling difference if we find Augustus' centralized authority challenged by the Gauls' devotion to the wind that more directly affects their daily existence (cf. 5.17.5: "When *circius* makes their buildings shake, the local inhabitants nevertheless give thanks in the belief that they owe to it the healthfulness of their climate"). This implicit challenge to imperial authority is underscored by Seneca's closing flourish in 5.17: by raising to epic proportions the task of surveying all such local winds—"It would be an endless task [*infinitum est...*] if I wanted to discuss each and every wind" (5.17.5)[129]—he vastly enlarges

---

122. Adams (2007) 225; the word is "possibly of African origin, the name of an Ethiopian tribe (Plin. *Nat.* 6.189), in which case the wind would have derived its name from a region thought to be its source."

123. From WNW, favorable for voyages to Greece and Egypt (cf. Hor. *Carm.* 1.3.4 with Nisbet and Hubbard [1970] 47; Virg. *Aen.* 8.710, of Cleopatra after Actium); see Nielsen (1945) 545 with *RE* 8A 2.2299–304.

124. A SW wind, not otherwise known (Vottero [1989] 565 n. 14); for Cragos, cf. Nisbet and Hubbard (1970) 258 on Hor. *Carm.* 1.21.8.

125. Adams (2007) 225–28, disputing the Greek origin that has also been suggested for *circius* (cf. Nielsen [1945] 43–44, 93–94). This strong wind is identifiable with the Mistral; see Vottero (1989) 565 n. 15, and for its strength, cf. n. 128 below.

126. For this NW wind, Nielsen (1945) 35–36 with *RE* 8A 2.2320.

127. Cf. *OLD infesto* 1: of human action (1a), then (1b) of diseases, etc., before (1c) "of Fortune, circumstances."

128. Cf. Plin. *Nat.* 2.121 ("inferior to none in violence"), Suet. *Claud.* 17.2 with Hurley (2001) 136, Gell. *N.A.* 2.22.20, 29; Nielsen (1945) 93.

129. For the familiar idiom, *OLD infinitus* 4b with Williams (2003) 198 on *Dial.* 10.13.1 *Persequi singulos longum est*.

the story of regional difference and idiosyncrasy far from the imperial center. For present purposes, however, this flourish also provides our point of departure for 5.18 by associating the winds once more with set places and patterns of movement ("For there is almost no place that does not have some wind that rises in it and subsides in its vicinity," 5.17.5), a picture of natural regularity that is soon disrupted by man's waywardness in 5.18.

V: Wind Direction, Human Misdirection

Book 5 arguably shows a lack of finish, at least in comparison with other books of the *Natural Questions*: there is no introductory prologue, the book has been faulted for the harshness of its transitions from one thematic part to another, and it compares unfavorably with other books in the frequency and control of its clausulae.[130] As we have seen, however, the abruptness of Seneca's opening is offset by artful juxtaposition with the end of Book 4b;[131] and, more important, the tight artistic coordination which will now be claimed for Book 5 as a whole will challenge the second criticism (i.e., the alleged harshness of Seneca's transitions), albeit with our focus not on localized transition but on overarching coherence. Two central threads have been distinguished thus far: (1) Seneca's survey of wind types and personalities, culminating in the raging whirlwind of 5.13; and (2) his schematization of the winds by fixed place or direction in 5.16–17. These two threads will now be seen to merge in our treatment of 5.18.

Shipbuilding and seafaring are but two of the many capabilities that Balbus, Cicero's spokesman for Stoic theology in *De natura deorum* 2, represents as gifts of Stoic providence:[132]

> magnos uero usus adfert [sc. arborum consectio et materia] ad nauigia fa-
> cienda, quorum cursibus subpeditantur omnes undique ad uitam copiae;
> quasque res uiolentissimas natura genuit earum moderationem nos soli
> habemus, maris atque uentorum, propter nauticarum rerum scientiam,
> plurimisque maritimis rebus fruimur atque utimur.
>
> 2.152

> Tree-felling/timber, moreover, is of great value for the building of ships,
> whose voyages supply all manner of sustenance from all parts of the earth;
> and, thanks to our knowledge of navigation, we alone have the capacity to

---

130. See Waiblinger (1977) 77.

131. See the beginning of Section II above in this chapter.

132. On the following two Ciceronian passages, 2.152 and 131, see Limburg (2007) 254.

control the most violent of nature's offspring, the sea and winds; and we use and enjoy very many products of the sea.

The winds are equally a gift:

> quam tempestiuos autem dedit [sc. benignitas naturae], quam salutares non modo hominum sed etiam pecudum generi, iis denique omnibus quae oriuntur e terra, uentos etesias; quorum flatu nimii temperantur calores, ab isdem etiam maritimi cursus celeres et certi diriguntur.
>
> 2.131

> How seasonable and wholesome not just for mankind but also for animals and for everything that grows from the earth is nature's gift of the Etesians! Their breath moderates extremes of heat, and they also guide our ships across the sea on a swift and certain course.

In contrast to the familiar literary portrayal of the folly of navigation, especially in contexts lamenting the demise of the Golden Age,[133] this Stoic/Ciceronian association of navigation with human progress offers one important precedent for Seneca's own positive picture in *Natural Questions* 5.18. True, negative features are undeniable, as when Seneca's condemnation of voyaging for war and conquest causes him to denounce seafaring itself: "Why do we disturb the seas? Evidently, the land does not extend widely enough for our deaths" (5.18.8). True also, different elements converge in 5.18 to evoke the literary Iron Age.[134] Seafaring, war, greedy acquisitiveness (cf. *uela uentis damus bellum petituri*, 5.18.6; *ad aurum ibitur*, 10): "one sin begot another,"[135] all of them merging into a single storm force of corruption that might remind us of the collected winds at 5.12.3: "These winds are much more powerful and longer lasting if they have also gathered up other gusts that are rushing along from the same cause, and if the several winds have flowed together into one" (cf. 5.12.4, 13.4). But despite Seneca's negative emphasis in these moments, his broader treatment of navigation in 5.18 characterizes it not as an intrinsic evil, or unambiguously as a permanent and universal bane for mankind;[136]

---

133. See Smith (1913) 245–47 on Tib. 1.3.37–40 with Heydenreich (1970) 15–19, 25–27, and now Limburg (2007) 249–55.

134. Cf. Section I and n. 4 above in this chapter.

135. Smith (1913) 246.

136. Rhetorical effect may explain (even dictate) Seneca's harsher pronouncements here against sea travel. Cf. Limburg (2007) 260, attributing such complaints to "the nature of Seneca's moralizing text, not [to] the philosopher's most profound convictions. It is in the nature of the moralizing *uituperatio* to lead to such strongly negative statements."

fundamentally at fault is man's abuse of this gift of nature, not the gift itself (cf. 5.18.4).[137] So, too, the elder Pliny, himself prefect of the Roman fleet at Misenum at the time of his death in 79 CE, rises to occasional attacks on seafaring, casting the sea as "the most savage area of Nature" (*per fluctus, saeuissimam rerum naturae partem, Nat.* 36.2), while "*benignitas naturae* manifests itself exclusively in *Terra.*"[138] The *real* objection in Pliny, Mary Beagon observes,[139] is not to navigation or sea commerce per se, but to unnecessary risk taking and reckless cupidity—a balanced picture that Beagon relates to the Senecan representation in 5.18: "The [Senecan] idea is broadly similar to those of Pliny on the use and abuse of *ratio* in connection with seafaring…[Seneca] seems to be trying deliberately to combat simplistic ideas of 'impiety' or of 'unfriendly elements'. It seems right to see here the influence of increased confidence at sea in the first century."[140]

Between the two extremes on display in 5.18—excessive vice on the one hand provokes Seneca's moments of extreme negativity about seafaring on the other—a balanced moderation characterizes his initial portrait of *prouidentia* inventing the winds for the good of mankind (5.18.1–4). They bring orderly proportion to the world, whether by supplying rain while yet holding excessive rains in check, or by regulating cloud movement "so that precipitation can be distributed all over the world" (5.18.2). This emphasis on the winds as an instrument that helps to keep the world in balance is repeated as if in summary at 5.18.13: "God gave the winds to preserve the temperateness of the sky and the earth, to cause waters to flow and also to hold them in check, to nurture the fruit of crops and trees." In contrast to the balancing effect of the winds, however, the marauders who sail the seas in search of war are Senecan models of *im*balance, disproportion and madness (cf. *furor*, 5.18.4; *dementia*, 6; *insaniam*, 9; *prauitate*, 15), as if, like the cloudburst and whirlwind of 5.12–13, they are themselves a storm force of random direction and violence. The animating characteristics that bring Seneca's treatment of the different winds to life in 5.7–13 now provide a crucial analogy for developments at the book's close: just as we progress in 5.7–13 from weaker to stronger winds, and from those that are consistent in their daily or seasonal movements to cloudbursts and whirlwinds of a much more fierce, unstable character, so we progress in 5.18 from the providentially ordained winds in measured and beneficent motion to the storming warships that, like an impersonal force of nature, bring random destruction to innocent victims (cf. 5.18.9). Before we press

---

137. On this emphasis, Heinonen (2000) 73–74 and now Limburg (2007) 251–52, 255–60.

138. Beagon (1992) 160.

139. (1992) 179; cf. also Citroni Marchetti (1991) 171.

140. Beagon (1992) 183.

the wind analogy further, however, can it be shown to be explicitly grounded in the text of 5.18?

The clearest evidence lies in the correlation drawn between man and wind at 5.18.4:

> nunc quod de C. Mario uulgo dictum est, et a Tito Liuio positum,[141] in incerto esse utrum illum magis nasci an non nasci ex re publica fuerit, dici etiam de uentis potest. adeo quidquid ex illis utile et necessarium est, non potest his repensari quae in perniciem suam generis humani dementia excogitat.

> As matters stand, it could be said of winds what was commonly said of Gaius Marius, and was stated by Titus Livius, that it is uncertain whether it was better for the state for Marius to be born or not to be born. Likewise, whatever is useful and essential from the winds cannot compensate for the things that the madness of the human race devises to its own ruination.

Of course, Seneca hardly implies that the winds can be judged by the moral or sociopolitical criteria that apply in Marius' case, or that they are complicit in the guilt of those who exploit them for harmful ends (cf. 5.18.5: "But if they do harm through the wrongdoing of malefactors who misuse them, their benefits do not on that account cease to be intrinsically good"). In this respect the Marius comparison is obviously loose, even facile. But it remains *direct* nonetheless, thereby opening the way to Seneca's more daring experimentation with the man-wind analogy later in 5.18. Subtler is the correlation drawn, or perhaps rather implied, at 5.18.11:

> Ergo non inmerito quis dixerit rerum naturam melius acturam fuisse nobiscum, si uentos flare uetuisset et inhibito discursu furentium in sua quemque terra stare iussisset.

To whom does *furentium* refer? Most translators interpret the subject of the participle as the "frenzied voyagers" who are subsequently confined to their native

---

141. Liv. Bk 80 (cf. *Per.* 80); cf. fr. 58 Weissenborn and Müller (1965) 179, fr. 20 Jal (1979) 214 (with pp. 253–56). *de Caesare maiori* (= Julius Caesar) Haase (1852) 2.267, Gercke (1907) 189.5–6; *de Caesare maiore* Oltramare (1929) 2.234 (but cf. 2.342 on p. 234 n. 3 and [1921] 30 for appraisal of the claims of MS Z *de G marior*), Corcoran (1971–72) 2.114. But for the superior case for *C. Marius, uir in bello hostibus, in otio ciuibus infestissimus* (Vell. 2.23.1; cf. 2.11.1 *quantum bello optimus, tantum pace pessimus*), Vottero (1989) 177 with Hine (1978) and now Parroni (2002) 570–71, convincingly countering Canfora (2000) 175–76 n. 12.

land in *in sua… iussisset*. So Thomas Lodge in his 1614 rendering: "It were therefore some reason, to say that Nature had greatly favoured us, if she had forbidden
the winds to blow, to the end *to bridle the forces of humane furie*, by staying every
one in his own countrie."[142] T. H. Corcoran, however, translates as follows: "Accordingly, someone sensibly said that nature would have done better for us if she
had forbidden the winds to blow and, by restraining *the varied extent of their
raging*, had arranged that each man stay in his own land."[143] Does *furentium* refer
to the winds, as Corcoran's version implies, or to "[each of] the raging voyagers"?[144] If we accept the ambiguity, the man-wind analogy is neatly encased in the
participle; and yet, even if *furentium* is taken to refer unambiguously to the voyagers, their storming progress is still cast in the metaphorical language of winds
that are out of control[145]—a phenomenon that extends to other parts of 5.18.

The rage for war in 5.18 (cf. *uela uentis damus bellum petituri*, 6) is itself cast as
furor and further characterized by the associated language of (wind-like) madness
and violence. So, at 5.18.4, the communication made possible between peoples by
the winds constitutes "a great benefit bestowed by nature, if the madness [*furor*]
of mankind did not turn it to his own detriment." And at 5.18.9:

hoc uero quid aliud quis dixerit quam *insaniam*, circumferre pericula et
ruere in ignotos, *iratum* sine iniuria occurrentia deuastantem, ac ferarum
more occidere quem non oderis?

What else would anyone call it than sheer madness, to carry danger
around with you and to rush against peoples who are unknown to you, to

---

142. (1614) 856; my emphasis.

143. Corcoran (1971–72) 2.121; my emphasis.

144. Cf. Oltramare (1929) 2.236: "la terre aurait mieux agi à notre égard, si…, *empêchant
l'homme de courir partout en furieux*, elle avait obligé chacun de rester en son pays." Vottero
(1989) 573: "la natura avrebbe agito meglio nei nostri confronti, se…, *proibendo le scorrerie dei
pazzi*, avesse costretto ciascuno a restare nella propria terra." Parroni (2002) 337: "la natura si
sarebbe comportata meglio con noi se…, *posto un limite alla frenesia umana*, avesse ordinato a
ciascuno di non muoversi dal suo paese." Hine (2010b) 85: "nature would have treated us
better if she had banned the winds from blowing, *had prevented madmen from rushing off in all
directions*, and had ordered everyone to stay in his own land." None of these translators appears
to doubt that *quemque* refers to the voyagers encased in *furentium*. In the linear movement of
the sentence, however, can we avoid the invitation or allure, however momentary or beguiling,
of perceiving the genitive *furentium* as dependent on *discursu*, and of relating *uentos* and *furentium*? On this approach, the participle floats in sense until its meaning is fixed only by eventual
coordination with *quemque*. The coordination between "no winds" and "no travel" is in any
case neatly underscored by the conceit of *flare uetuisset* balanced by *stare iussisset*.

145. For *furo* of winds, see *OLD* 6a, adding, e.g., *Phaed.* 937, *Dial.* 10.7.10, *N.Q.* 6.14.4. Cf.
*OLD furor*² 5, adding, e.g., *Agam.* 576, Ov. *Tr.* 2.150; *OLD furibundus* 2, including *N.Q.* 5.16.5
africus furibundus.

resort to anger without cause and to destroy all that you encounter, killing those you do not hate, as wild animals do?[146]

At 5.18.10, the carefully regulated winds of 5.16–17 give way to the literary language of winds raging where they will:

quousque nos mala nostra *rapuerunt*? parum est intra orbem suum *furere*. sic Persarum rex stolidissimus in Graeciam traiciet, quam exercitus non uincet cum impleuerit. sic Alexander ulteriora Bactris et Indis uolet, quaeretque quid sit ultra magnum mare, et *indignabitur* esse aliquid ultimum sibi. sic Crassum auaritia Parthis dabit; non horrebit reuocantis diras tribuni, non tempestates longissimi maris, non circa Euphraten praesaga fulmina et deos resistentes: per hominum et deorum iras ad aurum ibitur.

How far have our evils carried us? It's not enough to rage in our own part of the world. Hence that most brutish king of the Persians will cross into Greece; his army will not conquer the country when it has filled it. Hence Alexander will want to possess territories beyond Bactria and India[147] and will seek to know what lies beyond the great sea; and he will be angered to encounter any furthest limit to his progress. Hence greed will deliver Crassus to the Parthians; he will not tremble at the curses of a tribune calling him back,[148] or at the storms on the very long sea voyage, or at the ominous lightning and the hostile gods around the Euphrates; he will journey for gold despite the anger of men and gods.

Seneca's various strategies of wind mapping in 5.16–17 now give way to a more chaotic picture of transgression at the human level.[149] Not content to rage (*furere*) only in their own part of the world (*intra orbem suum*; cf. 5.17.4 *orbes*, of the five zonal regions), Xerxes and Alexander violate the model of a fixed world order in

---

146. For *insania* of natural forces, see *OLD* 4, and cf. *insanus* 4a, adding, e.g., *Phaed.* 736, 1130, *Phoen.* 420, 429; *insanio* 3 with Nisbet and Rudd (2004) 66 on Hor. *Carm.* 3.4.30. For *ruere*, *OLD* 1b, adding, e.g., *N.Q.* 5.12.3, 16.5. For *iratus*, *OLD* 1d, and cf. *ira* 3.

147. On *ulteriora...uolet*, Hine (1996b) 89.

148. Cf. Flor. *Epit.* 1.46.2–3: "Both gods and men were defied by the greed of the consul Crassus, in coveting the gold of Parthia, and in punishment eleven legions were slaughtered, his own life lost. For Metellus, the tribune of the people, had called down terrible curses on the general as he was leaving Rome [in late 55 BCE]." For further sources, Vottero (1989) 571 n. 28.

149. For *rapio* of winds, see *OLD* 9a, adding, e.g., *Phoen.* 430, *Letters* 109.18, *N.Q.* 5.13.3, 7.8.3. For *furo*, n. 145 above. For *indignor*, *OLD* 2a.

5.17 by storming their way into Greece and beyond Bactria and India,[150] their *furor* fully unleashed;[151] and Crassus speeds forth on his own overambitious Parthian venture, only for all three of these whirlwinds soon to expire. For, to invoke the helpful analogy of 5.12.4, storms are "of but brief duration as long as they occur singly." Or, at 7.9.3:

> nulla autem tempestas magna perdurat: procellae quanto plus habent uirium tanto minus temporis; uenti cum ad summum uenerunt, remittuntur; omnia uiolenta necesse est ipsa concitatione in exitum sui tendant. nemo itaque turbinem toto die uidit, ne hora quidem. mira uelocitas eius et mira breuitas est.

> A violent storm never lasts long: the more strength gales have, the shorter their duration. When they have reached their peak [the play in *uenti/uenerunt* reenacts that buildup], the winds abate; *all violence necessarily tends by its very tumultuousness towards its own extinction.* So no one has observed a whirlwind for a whole day, or even for an hour; its speed is astonishing, and so also its brevity.

By projecting his three *exempla* of Xerxes, Alexander and Crassus into the future (*traiciet, uolet, indignabitur,* etc.), Seneca creates the illusion that their arrogant excesses precipitate an all-too-predictable outcome.[152] In the narrative movement of 5.18 as a whole, they merge, perhaps not unlike the merging cloudbursts of 5.12.3, to bring to an explosive climax the picture of mounting *insania* that loosely replicates the ascending sequence of wind violence in 5.7–13. It was for man's enlightenment that the providential maker had apparently sanctioned travel

---

150. For transgressive Xerxes, *Dial.* 10.17.2, 18.5, *Ben.* 6.31; for Alexander (here suitably chosen to follow the transgressive Philip of 5.15), *Ben.* 1.13.3 ("a robber from his boyhood and a ravager of nations"), 2.16.1, 5.6.1, 7.2.5–3.1, *Letters* 91.17, 94.62–63, 113.29, 119.7 with Vottero (1989) 380 n. 22 on *N.Q.* 3 pref. 5. For Alexander as a negative embodiment of the compulsive traveler (so Montiglio [2006] 569–70), cf. also Chapters One, Section III and n. 44, and Six, Section VI.

151. Cf. *furiosi…regis,* of Xerxes at *Dial.* 10.18.5; *agebat infelicem Alexandrum furor aliena uastandi, Letters* 94.62.

152. For the effect, cf. Williams (2003) 234 on *Dial.* 10.17.6: "Quinctius Cincinnatus hastens to get through his dictatorship, but he will be recalled [*reuocabitur*] from the plow. Scipio will march against the Carthaginians [*ibit in Poenos*]…." Given Crassus' failure to heed all opposition to his venture (*non horrebit reuocantis diras tribuni*), does his fate remind us of how the free-flowing wind is said to form a violent but brief whirlwind at 5.13.1–3? The wind meets an obstacle (cf. *deos resistentes,* 5.18.10) and forms an eddy so that, "driven in circles and going round the same spot and stirring itself up by its own rapid motion, it is a whirlwind" (5.13.3). In his own way, does Seneca's Crassus, too, stir himself up to a comparable form of (ultimately self-)destructive violence by persevering with his expedition despite the gods' opposition?

between peoples (5.18.14). But Seneca's marauders progress only in their *dementia* (5.18.6), as if they were whirlwinds that differ from their natural counterparts in one crucial respect: whereas the whirlwind is an insentient force, willing no harm to anyone, our figurative whirlwinds destroy with brutal intent, even relish.

VI: The Roman Dimension

It is hard to exempt Roman imperial operations from this *insania* and *dementia* (5.18.4, 6, 9) that Seneca condemns as mankind sets sail in search of war;[153] or to forget that Aeneas for one, after Troy's fall, embarks on a voyage that culminates in dangers strongly resembling those forecast at 5.18.7:

> …quis erit huius laboris ac metus fructus, quis nos fessos tot malis portus excipiet? bellum scilicet et obuius in litore hostis et trucidandae gentes tracturaeque magna ex parte uictorem et antiquarum urbium flamma.
>
> …what reward will there be for this hardship and fear, what port will take us in, wearied by so many adversities? Surely war will meet us, and an enemy waiting for us on the shore; and peoples who are destined to be slaughtered while dragging most of their conquerors down with them; and the burning of ancient cities.[154]

If the spatial dimensions of Roman *imperium* are reduced to a mere pinpoint (*punctum*) from the cosmic perspective of the *Natural Questions*,[155] the very process of Roman imperial expansion recedes by implication into a wider, and troubling, historical context in 5.18. Greed (*auaritia*) motivates Crassus on his disastrous Parthian expedition at 5.18.10; in his distant rampages through Bactria, India and beyond (5.18.10), Alexander "pushed his arms beyond nature's limits" and "through reckless greed [*auiditate caeca*] plunged headlong into an unexplored and boundless sea" (*Ben.* 7.2.6); and Xerxes, too, of course offers another model of similar excess (cf. *Ben.* 7.3.1: "Consider Cyrus, Cambyses and the whole royal line of Persia: whom will you find among them who was satisfied with the limits of his empire?"). Given these *exempla*, is Roman imperial ambition to be

---

153. Cf. for this implied critique Citroni Marchetti (1991) 171. For suggestive contact between 5.18 and Albinovanus Pedo's portrayal of Germanicus' disastrous North Sea expedition of 16 CE (as cited in Chapter Two, Section VI n. 98), see Tandoi (1964) 165–66.

154. Hence, perhaps, a telling echo of *Aen.* 2.20 (Aeneas describing the Trojan horse) *uterum…armato milite complent* at 5.18.5 *ut nos classes…compleremus milite armato* (cf. Vottero [1989] 568 n. 10 for this "Probabile reminiscenza virgiliana").

155. Cf. Chapter One, Section III.

viewed as an exception to the Senecan rule implicitly constructed through Crassus, Alexander and Xerxes? Or as further evidence of that same reckless tendency?

When we look back on the Varronian compass card's Roman systematization of the winds (5.16), and on the clinical division of the skies in 5.17 into twelve zones, each with its fixed wind, we find a loose but suggestive blueprint, or analogy, for the rationalizing structure of Roman *imperium*. After the transgressions pictured in 5.18, however, a darker implication of 5.16–17 is that the (self-)regulation of the winds stands in stark contrast to the unrestrained impetus of Roman *imperium*, its expansion through the *insania* of war engaging Rome (like Xerxes and Alexander) beyond her "natural" place and limit. Crassus softens the implication by representing Rome's checkered past, as if the danger is no more, the hard lesson learnt; but the future tense (*sic Crassum auaritia Parthis dabit*; ... *ad aurum ibitur*, 5.18.10) is still potentially disconcerting, "predicting" Crassus' demise as if on the principle that he manifests an all-too-repeatable tendency. It may well be that, on purely pragmatic grounds, Seneca the politician favored the idea and practice of empire, at least with certain caveats.[156] On the approach taken here, however, he takes a more critical line in *Natural Questions* 5, offering an oblique, artistically contrived commentary on the folly of military expansion that is driven by ambition of the Pompeian kind at *Letters* 94.64–5:

> ne Gnaeo quidem Pompeio externa bella ac domestica uirtus aut ratio suadebat, sed insanus amor magnitudinis falsae ... quid illum in Africam, quid in septemtrionem ... traxit? infinita scilicet cupido crescendi, cum sibi uni parum magnus uideretur.
>
> Not even Gnaeus Pompey was persuaded by virtue and reason to take part in foreign and civil wars, but by a mad passion for an illusory kind of greatness.... What drew him into Africa, what drew him to the north ...? It was evidently his boundless desire to grow bigger, for only in his own eyes was he not great enough.

Seneca's analysis of wind action thus targets human action to chastening effect; but Roman power and self-perception are also qualified in another way if, with Sandra Citroni Marchetti,[157] we detect a certain insecurity in Seneca's vision of possible danger lurking across the seas at 5.18.12:

---

156. Cf. Griffin (1976) 223: "Seneca never doubts that the Empire was acquired through Roman virtue and is worth preserving.... But after victory, though full control should remain with the victors, *ira* must change to *amicitia*."

157. (1991) 171–73.

nulla terra tam longe remota est, quae non emittere aliquod suum malum possit. unde scio an nunc aliquis magnae gentis in abdito dominus, fortunae indulgentia tumens, non contineat intra terminos arma, an paret classes ignota moliens? unde scio hic mihi an ille uentus bellum inuehat? magna pars erat pacis humanae maria praecludi.

No land is so distantly remote that it cannot export some evil of its own. How do I know if, at the present moment, some ruler of a great nation in some abstruse place—a ruler puffed up by fortune's favor—is not containing his armies within his own territory, or is readying his fleets for his launching of unknown plans? How do I know if this wind or that is bringing me war? The fact that the seas were once closed made a major contribution to human peace.

For Citroni Marchetti, the elder Pliny, writing in the changed climate of Vespasianic Rome, finds in the sea a state of nature fundamentally known and demarcated, tamed and made subject to exploitation by the *pax Romana*. For Seneca, on the other hand, from the detached perspective of his *de facto* retirement from the Neronian court after 62 CE, there is no such secure confidence in *pax Romana*, but rather anxiety and "a restless projection of aggression."[158]

From the utilitarian perspective of the everyday world, the *simplicitas* that Seneca envisages (5.18.1–4) before mankind began to abuse the winds, or his sweeping denunciation of sea travel in 5.18.16 ("Different people have different reasons for setting sail, but no one has a good reason"), must seem all too remote from the practical concerns of running the empire by trade- and troopship in the first century CE. But in those moments when he evokes a world without warships (even *any* ships; cf. 5.18.11), or a post-Golden Age world in which sea travel nevertheless brings enlightened benefit to mankind by facilitating communication between peoples (5.18.4, 14), Seneca aggressively reasserts, I propose, the cosmic consciousness that distances us from the claims of the everyday world in the *Natural Questions* more generally. From this cosmic perspective, our primary focus in Book 5 is on the macro movements of "the works of providence" (5.18.1), on the winds as a healthful force of climatic balance and proportion in the world, and on the one-world connectivity to which navigation contributes: balanced wholeness is all. In contrast to this macro focus, the empire building of a Xerxes or an Alexander, however impressive in one way, represents a reversion to the micro level of limit and division, of conflict and fragmentation *in rebus humanis*; here we lose sight of the larger oneness, just as we do in all the descriptive detail of the

---

158. Citroni Marchetti (1991) 173.

storm-tossed voyage to war at 5.18.7, say, or in all the name places and events
through which Seneca hurries us in recounting his three historical *exempla* at
5.18.10. Given this cosmic dimension, he draws to a close all too fittingly, and
ironically, with a philosophical borrowing that acts out to the last his persona's
detachment from the ways of the world at large: "Plato made the excellent
remark…that it is the most trivial things that people buy with their lives"
(5.18.16).[159] Yet, despite Plato, Seneca has the last word, wittily identifying with
the very crowd from which detachment is all:

> immo, Lucili carissime, si bene illorum furorem aestimaueris, *id est nos-*
> *trum* (in eadem enim turba uolutamur), magis ridebis cum cogitaueris
> uitae parari in quae uita consumitur.
>
> 5.18.16

> Yes, my dear Lucilius, if you've rightly judged the madness of those
> people—*our* madness, that is (for we wallow in the same crowd)—you'll
> laugh all the more when you consider that we acquire for our lives the very
> things on which life is squandered.[160]

Seneca may be one of us, but he stands typically aloof (*magis ridebis…*) while
the majority in 5.18 remains all at sea (*uitae…consumitur*). In a book that so
carefully charts the "correct" and natural direction of the winds (5.16–17), the
people-at-large are thus implicated in the misguidedness that manifests itself
most starkly, and literally, in the subterranean adventures of 5.15 and the war
voyages of 5.18—scenes of misdirection that divert us from the higher philosophical journey that the rest of the book promotes.

---

159. The Platonic passage is unknown (Setaioli [1988] 123, 450–51), but Hall (1977) 423 nevertheless relates Seneca's words to such passages as *Rep.* 520c, 586a–b, finding "a rhetorical re-
statement of a view Plato held."

160. I.e., life is squandered on luxuries, or on trying to import them by sea. *uitae* dat. (*OLD
paro* 1a; cf. also Chaumartin [1993] 110–11), *pace* Alexander's strained "genitive of indefinite
value" ([1948] 309), to the effect of "at cost of life is won that whereon life wastes itself." Hine
(2010b) 86 takes *uitae* as dative, but cf. his p. 203 n. 43 for the attractive suggestion that *uita*
(abl.) *parari* be read, to the effect of "reflect that people pay with their lives for the acquisition
of things on which life is wasted."

6

Earthquakes, Consolation and the
Senecan Sublime

I: Introduction

*In an instant the men lost touch of each other. This is the
disintegrating power of a great wind: it isolates one from one's
kind. An earthquake, a landslip, an avalanche, overtake a
man incidentally, as it were—without passion. A furious gale
attacks him like a personal enemy, tries to grasp his limbs,
fastens upon his mind, seeks to rout his very spirit out of him.*

FROM JOSEPH CONRAD, *Typhoon*[1]

After the animated properties and personalities of the wind types that Seneca
brings to life in 5.7–13, the earthquake that devastated Pompeii and surrounding
parts of Campania in 62 CE[2] strikes without passion in *Natural Questions 6 De
terrae motu*, as if a vast, impersonal force that overtakes Pompeii incidentally, as it
were. Book 6 takes its starting point from this event, which Seneca describes with
a concentration on localized detail and on the earthquake's apparently singular
effects (6.1.1–3) that runs counter to the wider, alleviating vision of seismological
process that the rest of the book promotes. In this respect, the sheer length of
Seneca's patient and impressively wide-ranging review of theories of earthquake in
6.4–26 is itself reassuring: despite his own preference for a pneumatic explanation
(6.21.1), his coverage of alternative theories (cf. 6.5.1: "Some have thought that the
cause of earthquakes lies in water, others in fire, others in the earth itself, others in
air, others in several of them, others in all of them") is based on the bedrock assumption that the phenomenon is systematic in its causation. If a rare event such as an

---

1. Here cited from Kirschner (1990) 84.

2. For the date in connection with 6.1.2 *Nonis Februariis hic fuit motus* [*Regulo et Verginio
consulibus*], see Introduction n. 26. For sources, inscriptional evidence and bibliography on the
Campanian earthquake, Guidoboni et al. (1994) 196–210 with Waldherr (1997) 71–72; as a
precursor of the Vesuvian eruption of 79, Sigurdsson (2002) 33–35.

earthquake or an eclipse leaves the popular imagination awestruck and causes us to reach for a supernatural or divine explanation, Seneca campaigns in the opposite direction, privileging *ratio* over *religio*: whereas an eclipse, say, too often "fills minds with awe" (*religionem incutit mentibus*, 6.3.3), reason has the opposite effect (*ratio terrorem prudentibus excutit*, 6.2.1). The Senecan treatment of earthquake thus promises to steady the mind that has experienced its own secondary form of collapse (cf. *motae... mentis*, 6.1.3);[3] for what Seneca envisages at 6.1.5 as the literal shaking of the *fundamentum mundi* is inseparable in his narrative from the destabilizing of (as it were) the *fundamentum mentis*.

"Comfort [*solacia*] must be found for people in distress, and their great fear removed" (6.1.4): the consolation that Seneca offers for the Campanian earthquake of 62 lies partly in his reliance on technical explanation of such phenomena in 6.4–26, and partly in the fortification of mind that is his goal in the book's opening and closing sections, 6.1–3 and 6.27–32. In this combination of seismological exegesis on the one hand, mental fortification through *praemeditatio futurorum malorum*[4] on the other, familiar elements of the literary *consolatio* are integrated within the world of Senecan physical *explicatio*—a fusion that extends in a different way Seneca's generic experimentation in his earlier *consolationes* to Marcia, to Polybius and to his mother Helvia (*Dialogues* 6, 11 and 12 respectively), and also in certain of his *Letters*. We shall monitor this consolatory presence in Book 6 in due course; but a more urgent priority in this chapter is to argue for the fundamental influence of Lucretius on Seneca's treatment of earthquakes. Although important headway in assessing the Lucretian impact on *Natural Questions* 6 has been made by Arturo De Vivo in particular,[5] our concern here is with an aspect of Lucretian influence less visible in De Vivo's study: Seneca's emulation (or, better, his adaptation) of the Lucretian sublime[6] in his own emboldened approach to nature—an approach that treats phenomena such as earthquakes not

3. Cf. *moueo* of earthquakes at, e.g., 6.4.1, 18.1, 26.4; *OLD motus* 1c. For *inmotus/inmobilis* of the (philosophically) becalmed mind-set, cf. *Dial.* 2.5.4, 9.3; 4.12.6; 7.4.5, 16.1; 12.2.3; *Letters* 71.32.

4. On the importance of this therapeutic exercise in Seneca generally, Armisen-Marchetti (1986), especially 189 on its relevance to *N.Q.* 6.32.

5. De Vivo (1992a), especially 82–89, 91–93, 96–98, 104–105; cf. Berno (2003) 258–60 and, more generally, Althoff (2005). For Seneca's special regard for Lucretius elsewhere, cf. *Letters* 58.12 (Lucretius aligned with such luminaries as Cato and Cicero) with Mazzoli (1970) 206–9.

6. For the latter, see now Porter (2007) with Hardie (2009a) 7–8 and 153–228 (Chapters Five and Six) on, respectively, Horatian and Virgilian responses to the Lucretian sublime. Senecan prose is but one barely touched area in (Hardie, p. 7) the "rather understudied category" and the "still incomplete history of the sublime in Latin literature." But for enticing remarks on the influence of nature's sublimity in late Republican and early Imperial literature generally, Schrijvers (2005), especially 31 and n. 22, and (2006), especially 97–101.

with a passive awe and helplessness, but with an active, controlling grasp of all phenomena as normative parts of nature's scheme. Doctrinal difference between Lucretius and Seneca, Epicurean and Stoic, fails to diminish the commonality that we shall observe between them as artists who, as James Porter puts it *à propos* of the Kantian sublime,

> rise up proudly and assertively against the natural world, discovering within [themselves] a power to assess the world independently of its allures and threats, and ultimately to discover within [themselves] a superiority...over nature...not a real superiority over nature, to be sure, which cannot be verified in any objective way, but rather an *a priori* one.[7]

While emulating this Lucretian superiority in *Natural Questions* 6, Seneca reinforces it by applying familiar consolatory strategies that are briefly sampled in Section II below. Our focus then turns, in Section III, to Lucretius and the Lucretian sublime as a paradigm for strikingly similar features in Seneca's own response to awesome nature in Book 6. In Section IV we pause to consider his complex elaboration of the sublimity theme in his two notable verse quotations at 6.2.2 and 6.2.9 respectively. We then progress, in Section V, to the "superior" control over nature that he exerts in his survey of theories of earthquake in 6.4–26, an assertion of control that is subsequently related, in Section VI, to Seneca's "whole" grasp of the universal *totum* late in his treatment of earthquakes. We finally take stock, in Section VII, of his overall consolatory strategy in Book 6.

II: *Consolatory Amplification Before Reduction*[8]

In *Letters* 91[9] Seneca reports to Lucilius that "our friend Liberalis[10] is now in a mood of mourning; for he has just heard of the fire that has wiped out the colony of Lugdunum [Lyons]" (91.1). Liberalis is perhaps to be imagined as doubly vulnerable: the city he loves (cf. *hominem patriae suae amantissimum*, 91.1) has suffered disaster, and, absent as he is from the disaster zone, we might suppose that he is pained not just by the events themselves but by his absence from them, his imagination potentially aggrandizing a catastrophe that he cannot witness for

---

7. Porter (2007) 179.

8. On the consolatory theme in *Natural Questions* 2 as well as 6, Limburg (2007) 299–342, and see also Berno (2003) 277–79 ("Analogie con le *Consolationes*").

9. Already well treated in connection with *Natural Questions* 6 by Limburg (2007) 306–7.

10. Presumably the dedicatee of *On Favors*; on the identity question, Griffin (1976) 254, 455–56 with Viti (1997) 397–99.

himself. Seneca does nothing to bridle this maximizing tendency, at least at the letter's opening, where the fire, which can be plausibly dated to the late summer or early autumn of 64 CE,[11] is portrayed as a disaster of singular proportions (*sine exemplo*, 91.1). Many cities had hitherto been damaged by fire, he asserts, but none annihilated in the manner of Lugdunum (91.1), which is depicted as a place of singular beauty and distinction ("pride of Gaul," 91.2;[12] "jewel of the provinces," 91.10). The frequency of intensifiers such as *tam*, *tot* and *tantus* in 91.1–2, Seneca's emphasis on the unprecedented scale of the catastrophe, the astonishing suddenness of Lugdunum's demise ("A single night elapsed between the city at its greatest and its reduction to nothing," 91.2), the possible evocations of Troy's fall and of the familiar Augustan poetic topos of "the death of the city": as Viti observes,[13] all of these features and more suggestively contribute to the dramatic inflation of an event whose magnitude in Seneca finds no supporting evidence, archaeological or otherwise.[14] For present purposes, this augmentation of the disaster in 91.1–2 conveniently illustrates a familiar Senecan *modus consolandi*. So in *Dialogue* 12, for example, his *Consolation to his mother Helvia*, written to comfort her after the loss of her son to exile on Corsica in 41 CE, he begins by offering no gentle prescription for healing her wounds but readies her for major surgery with cautery and the knife (*urere ac secare*, 2.2), directly confronting her with all the grief that he works to overcome (2.1–2). The change of outlook that he promotes in Helvia does not admit of half-measures but amounts to a deracination of sorts, an exercise that begins by maximizing the source of grief in order then to remove it at root;[15] and the same technique of amplification before reduction finds various other Senecan applications[16] before he redeploys it in *Letters* 91.

After the initial stress on singularity and unexpectedness (cf. *nouitas*, 91.3), the shock of the new is absorbed and resolved in *Letters* 91 by argumentation that

---

11. See Decourt and Lucas (1993) 43 with Viti (1997) 400–402, and cf. Koestermann (1968) 360 on Tac. *Ann.* 16.13.3.

12. *Lugdunum, quod ostendebatur in Gallia*; on the nuance of *ostendebatur*, Viti (1997) 404 n. 28.

13. (1997) 404–406; on the theme of "la morte delle città," Labate (1991).

14. The dearth of evidence: Viti (1997) 403–404 with Bedon (1991); Limburg (2007) 307.

15. On *Helu.* 2.1–2, Williams (2006b) 162–63; Limburg (2007) 307–8.

16. See on the technique Armisen-Marchetti (1986) 189, and now Limburg (2007) 306–9. Cf. Seneca's confrontational approach in the consolations to Marcia (especially *Dial.* 6.1.5–8) and to Polybius (especially *Dial.* 11.4–5, on the futility of excessive grieving); and *Dial.* 10.10.1 for his approval of Fabianus' direct approach to combating vice ("we must battle against the passions with a vigorous attack, not with nicety of argument").

"normalizes" the experience through a broadening of perspective. Hence Seneca's characteristic defense against *fortuna* by urging forethought on any and all possible eventualities (91.4); and hence also his adducing of multiple parallels for such disaster from a wide diversity of places and times. When we begin to locate Lugdunum in the context of all those cities that have succumbed to natural disaster over the ages (so, e.g., the many towns of Asia and Achaea, Syria and Macedonia, etc., that are destroyed by earthquake at 91.9), it recedes into relative insignificance as no exception to the general rule: cities "stand but to fall" (91.12). Singularity thus gives way to multiplicity and commonality as we gain distance from *this* disaster's epicenter at 91.1–2 and move with Liberalis through the methodical procedures of Senecan consolation (cf. *Haec ergo atque eiusmodi solacia admoueo Liberali nostro...*, 91.13).

So, too, in *Natural Questions* 6 Seneca begins with the localized viewpoint, as if writing *in angusto* (cf. 1 pref. 10):

> Pompeios, celebrem Campaniae urbem, in quam ab altera parte Surrentinum Stabianumque litus, ab altera Herculanense conueniunt, et mare ex aperto reductum amoeno sinu cingunt, consedisse terrae motu uexatis quaecumque adiacebant regionibus, Lucili uirorum optime, audiuimus, et quidem hibernis diebus, quos uacare a tali periculo maiores nostri solebant promittere. Nonis Februariis hic fuit motus [Regulo et Verginio consulibus][17] qui Campaniam, numquam securam huius mali, indemnem tamen et totiens defunctam metu, totam magna strage uastauit.
>
> 6.1.1–2

> Lucilius, best of men, we have just heard that Pompeii, the populous Campanian city, has been overwhelmed by an earthquake, which also ravaged all the regions adjacent to it. On one side the coasts of Surrentum and Stabiae, and on the other side the coast of Herculaneum, converge upon the city and encircle the sea, which is set back from the open water, with a charming bay. Moreover, it happened in the winter season, which, our forebears used to assure us, was free from such danger. This earthquake was on the Nones of February [in the consulship of Regulus and Verginius]; it brought great devastation and destruction to the whole of Campania, which had always been uneasy about this danger, but it had nevertheless remained undamaged and had so often got off with a fright.

---

17. On the (likely) interpolation, Introduction n. 26.

This early attention to the details of precisely where and when the earthquake struck reasserts Seneca's credentials as a careful investigator in the *Natural Questions* while also evoking a certain serenity that was shattered when the disaster happened: the profusion of local names in the opening sentence, and the luxuriant description of the bay that surrounds Pompeii (as if the town is protected by the shores that bound it), generate an atmosphere of safe familiarity, as if lulling us into a calm before the storm. But in this careful mapping process we witness not just the literal epicenter of the earthquake, but also a concentration on the particular—an epicenter of descriptive detail—that will gradually be resolved as we begin to view the Campanian disaster in the normalizing context that takes shape in the course of the book.

First, however, Seneca magnifies the singular terror of earthquakes, moving from the Campanian event to the shock and awe induced by all such events, and intensifying the intimidating effect by visualizing the danger as if through the eyes of the common man.[18] His profusion of rhetorical questions in 6.1.4–6 ("What can anyone regard as adequately safe if the world itself is shaken...?...What hiding place do we look to, what help, if the world itself begins to crack?") stages its own rush toward panic and hysteria, maximizing the danger by casting earthquakes in superlative terms as "the very worst kind of death," with plague and lightning relatively benign afflictions by comparison:

> nullum malum sine effugio est. numquam fulmina populos perusserunt; pestilens caelum exhausit urbes, non abstulit. hoc malum latissime patet, ineuitabile, auidum, publice noxium. non enim domos solum aut familias aut urbes singulas haurit: gentes totas regionesque submergit....
>
> 6.1.6–7

> No disaster is without a means of escape. Lightning bolts have never scorched entire peoples, and a plague season has depleted cities but not destroyed them. But the disaster of an earthquake extends to the widest possible degree and is inescapable, insatiable, deadly for whole communities. For it engulfs not just homes or households or individual cities; it buries entire peoples and regions....

By this aggrandizing technique, dangers quickly emerge on all sides (cf. *undique*, 6.2.1), only for Seneca to work toward neutralizing that Everywhere by later asserting a secondary form of ubiquitousness: in comparison with so many paral-

---

18. On this point, Berno (2003) 243–44. Like Limburg (2007) 323–24, I remain unconvinced by Gauly's argument ([2004] 224–35) for earthquake as a *prodigium* with symbolic political implications in Book 6.

lel and worse disasters elsewhere (cf. 6.1.13–15), the Campanian earthquake emerges as but an unexceptional example of a common global experience.

In terms of his overall consolatory method in *Natural Questions* 6, then, Seneca predictably conforms to the familiar, and therefore themselves reassuring, formulae of (1) amplification before reduction, and (2) reduction by locating the specific event within a normalizing context of cognate phenomena. From one perspective, Seneca may appear to urge solace through our passive submission to nature's way. From another perspective, however, he promotes a far more active mode of engagement with, and even superiority over, nature in Book 6; and here Lucretius enters.

III: Sublime Superiority over Nature

Lucretius' treatment of earthquakes at 6.535–607, a passage with which Seneca was surely directly acquainted,[19] contributes to his broader effort to banish *terrorem animi* (6.39) by allowing "the outer aspect and inner law of nature" (*naturae species ratioque*, 6.41) to prevail over superstition in our responses to thunder, lightning and other such occurrences. In leading us from blind reasoning (*caeca ratione*, 6.67) to *ratio uerissima* (6.80), he works to free us from fear of the gods, and so to prevent our reversion to old superstitions (*antiquas… religiones*, 6.62; cf. *N.Q.* 6.3.1: "It will also help to keep in mind that none of these occurrences is caused by the gods, and that neither heaven nor earth is shaken by divine anger"). For Lucretius, the task of rational explanation replaces "a rhetoric of *mirum*" with "a rhetoric of necessity,"[20] reducing our sense of wonder as apparently singular events become explicable as necessary parts of a mechanistic process; hence Lucretius' frequent recourse to such formulations as *necesse est.*[21] Seneca, too, records the apparently singular effects of the Campanian earthquake, including such marvels as a flock of hundreds of sheep killed in the vicinity of Pompeii (6.1.3, 27.1) and statues split apart (6.1.3, 30.1)—marvels that take their place in a rhetoric of *mirum*[22] that is countered by Seneca's voice of reason and necessity at, e.g.,

---

19. Cf. De Vivo (1992a) 92; Althoff (2005) 21.

20. For these rhetorics, Conte (1994) 21, and cf. Chapter One, Section IV and n. 83. For the significant presence of earthquakes in the Roman tradition of prodigy lists, see Traina (1985) 871–77 with De Vivo (1992a) 93, 98–99, Guidoboni et al. (1994) 17, 25–26 and Hine (2002) 64–65.

21. So, e.g., 1.579, 2.243, 526, 3.798, 4.216. So also *non est mirum* vel sim. at, e.g., 4.768, 814, 5.192, 799, 6.130; *non mirandum* at, e.g., 4.595, 858, 5.590; *non mirabile* vel sim. at, e.g., 2.308, 465, 4.256, 5.666. Further, Conte (1994) 21 and 151 n. 47.

22. Cf. 6.3.4: "We marvel [*miramur*] at none of these phenomena [sc. eclipses, comets, etc.] without fear"; 6.4.1: "An earthquake produces thousands of marvels [*miracula*]."

6.30.1 *Statuam diuisam non miror*, or 6.16.3–4 *fieri enim non potest ut non…*; *non est ergo dubium quin…*; *quod si uerum est, necesse est.…* The sole category of *mirum* that impresses Seneca is the intrinsic wonderment that rewards the philosophical study of nature herself: so at 6.4.2 "the study of this subject… is cultivated not for gain but for its marvellousness [*miraculo*]."

Another rationalizing technique that Seneca has in common with Lucretius, and that he perhaps deploys under Lucretian influence, may be termed the domesticating use of analogy.[23] So at 6.548–51, on earthquakes, the (Epicurean) theory that the earth's trembling results from subterranean collapse is illustrated by analogy (1) with the trembling effect that passing wagons even of no great weight have on nearby buildings (548–49), or (2) with the shaking effect when the wagons themselves are jolted by a stone on the road (550–51).[24] The wagon comparison, for Bailey "probably traditional,"[25] recurs in Seneca at *N.Q.* 6.22.1, on the jolting (as opposed to the tilting at 6.21.2) subterranean movement that causes an earthquake:

> si quando magna onera per uicos <ordine> uehiculorum plurium tracta sunt et rotae maiore nisu in salebras inciderunt, tecta concuti senties.[26]
>
> If heavy loads are ever drawn through the streets by a series of several wagons, and the wheels, because of the greater strain, slip into ruts in the road, you'll feel the buildings shaking.

For Conte, "often the grandiose pathos that accompanies the description of frightening phenomena" in Lucretius "is corrected by an exemplification belonging to a lower register, almost an attenuation of the sublime and its capacity to arouse *horror*."[27] After his initial description of an earthquake at 6.543–7, Lucretius thus "feels the necessity of a counterpoint in *diminuendo* [e.g., the wagon analogy]," so that

---

23. On this phenomenon, Schrijvers (1978), especially 98–101 = (2007b), especially 273–76, with Conte (1994) 152–53 n. 49 and Setaioli (2005), and cf. Chapter Two, Section III.

24. For 550–51 so construed, Bailey (1947) 1637 and (further reflections in his addenda) 1758.

25. (1947) 1637.

26. For *per uicos <ordine>*, Hine (1996b) 106. *tecta/ terram* MSS: if *tecta* with Hine (1996a) 263.665, a closer tie to Lucretian (1) above (cf. *tremescunt/ tecta*, 6.548–49); if *terram* (so, e.g., Vottero [1989] 632 and Corcoran [1971–72] 2.190), closer to (2) above.

27. Conte (1994) 152 n. 49.

[i]t seems that his argumentative intention prevails over the emotional effects; the need to diminish the frightening phenomena makes the reasoning cool down in a comparison with banal and controllable experiences.[28]

Seneca achieves a like effect, domesticating earthquake by reducing the phenomenon to everyday proportions. But this taming use of analogy has the further effect in the *Natural Questions* of relating different world parts and operations within a unifying Stoic whole[29]—an analogical technique that was of course hardly new, in that already among the Pre-Socratics Empedocles "had constantly kept in mind [via analogy] the unity of being, the totality of things as the solidarity of the elements, their subjection to simple principles, so that everything was also the image of something else."[30] For Conte, however, Lucretius' use of analogy modifies the Empedoclean model, in that, for Lucretius, analogy is

> not so much a rhetorical scheme (metaphorical transposition) useful for displaying the elements' original affinity, as it was for Empedocles; rather, *it is a cognitive principle integrated into a rational system.* It lets us overcome the dividing line that separates us from the intelligible; it is the path that leads from the known to what is still unknown, from the visible to the invisible.
>
>   In Lucretius, in short, analogy is *the structured form of thought that knows.*[31]

For present purposes, the greatest interest of Conte's remarks lies in the distinction that he draws between different analogical modes—analogy not just as a descriptive instrument but as an incisive tool, an experimental instrument by which the scientific eye looks intuitively to the other side, seeing here so as to infer and know there. The special empowerment that Lucretius asserts through this dynamic use of analogy (and not only through analogy) is paralleled, I

---

28. Conte (1994) 152 n. 49.

29. See already Chapter Two, Section III.

30. Conte (1994) 12. Further, Lloyd (1966) 325–36, especially 325 ("by far the most important evidence for the use of analogy in Presocratic philosophy comes from Empedocles"); and for the imprint of Empedoclean analogical method on Lucretius, see now Garani (2007), especially 18–25.

31. Conte (1994) 12–13; my emphasis. For the dramatic and dramatizing impact of metaphor on ancient seismological investigation in particular, Shute (1979), especially 59 ("Imaginative insight created new values by metaphoric formulations").

propose, by a similar self-privileging that Seneca exerts in *Natural Questions* 6: there, as elsewhere in the work, analogy functions as a bold, imaginative thrust, or as an unleashing of speculative energy that takes risks, experiments with connectivity and thereby defies conventional limits of thought.[32]

Lucretius' domesticating use of analogy is intimately connected to the Lucretian sublime. Although the concept of the sublime is in one sense modern, its history traceable to Nicolas Boileau-Despréaux's 1674 translation of [Longinus] Περὶ ὕψους and to his use of the French *sublime* for ὕψος,[33] the sublime that Conte claims for Lucretius is supported by explicit parallels with [Longinus] that, for James Porter, "seem to point to a literary dependency going beyond a simple affinity of mind or spirit."[34] So at 6.608–737 Lucretius demystifies three wonders of nature by explaining (1) the constant size of the sea (608–38); (2) volcanoes, with exclusive focus on Etna (639–702); and (3) the summer flooding of the Nile (712–37). Compare *On the Sublime* 35.2–5, the only other context in surviving ancient literature where, as Porter points out,[35] this same grouping occurs:

> What then was in the mind of those godlike authors who, aiming at the highest flights of composition, showed no respect for detailed accuracy? Among many other things this—that nature has adjudged us men to be creatures of no mean or ignoble quality. Rather, as though inviting us to some great festival, she has brought us into life, into the whole vast universe, there to be spectators of all that she has created and the keenest aspirants for renown; and thus from the first she has implanted in our souls an unconquerable passion for all that is great and for all that is more divine than ourselves. For this reason the entire universe does not satisfy the contemplation and thought that lie within the scope of human endeavour; our ideas often go beyond the boundaries by which we are circumscribed, and if we look at life from all sides, observing how in everything that concerns us the extraordinary, the great, and the beautiful play the leading part, we shall soon realize the purpose of our creation.

---

32. Cf. Armisen-Marchetti (2001) 172 on "the scientific imagination perceived [by Seneca] as a courageous passing of the barriers of everyday perception, as a courageous explorer which leads the human spirit beyond its ordinary condition all the way to the very depths of nature, i.e., all the way to the divine."

33. For convenient background, Shaw (2006) 4–6; Battersby (2007) 3–4; and Delehanty (2007), especially 236–37.

34. Porter (2007) 172. Cf. p. 174: "These parallels suggest a common source, possibly in meteorological doxography (Longinus is unlikely to have drawn directly on Lucretius)."

35. Porter (2007) 173.

This is why, by some sort of natural instinct, we admire, not, surely, the small streams, beautifully clear though they may be, and useful too, but the Nile, the Danube, the Rhine, and even more than these the Ocean. The little fire that we have kindled ourselves, clear and steady as its flame may be, does not strike us with as much awe as the heavenly fires, in spite of their often being shrouded in darkness; nor do we think it a greater marvel than the craters of Etna, whose eruptions throw up from their depths rocks and even whole mountains, and at times pour out rivers of that pure Titanian fire. In all such circumstances, I would say only this, that men hold cheap what is useful and necessary, and always reserve their admiration for what is out of the ordinary.

Trans. T. S. Dorsch

This passage finds various suggestive resonances in Seneca, for whom the cosmic viewpoint in the *Natural Questions* and elsewhere (e.g., *Dial.* 6.18; 8.5.3–8; 12.20) takes on a strikingly sublime aspect by carrying us "beyond the boundaries by which we are circumscribed" with a similar "unconquerable passion" and exhilaration.[36] Much the same impetus drives the Lucretian persona, for whom (as for [Longinus]) the sublime constitutes not just a stylistic mode but a whole way of being, not just a *genus scribendi* but a *genus uiuendi*.[37] So, for Conte, the Lucretian sublime

operates within the text as a form of perception and knowledge *even before it functions as a stylistic form*, and it is in intimate harmony with the poem's strong didacticism; Epicurus' hard and difficult doctrine can only act by educating a reader disposed toward the sublime.[38]

Confronted with nature's majesty and power, the sublime observer overcomes the intimidating impact of that encounter by transcending the passivity of ordinary experience; awe and terror give way to a superiority over nature that asserts itself in Lucretius' bold rationalization of her hidden workings.[39]

---

36. The effect by which our eye is drawn to the awesome—the observation in [Longinus] that "by some sort of natural instinct, we admire, not, surely, the small streams…but the Nile"—finds a particularly suggestive parallel in the way Seneca transports Lucilius in Book 4a (Chapter Three above) from his (relatively minor) procuratorship in Sicily, and from his confirmed interest there in the river Alpheus and the Arethusa myth (cf. 3.1.1), to the awesome spectacle of the Nile, "noblest of rivers" (4a.2.1).

37. Conte (1994) 19.

38. (1994) 23; my emphasis.

39. For cognate formulations of this Lucretian strategy, see now Hardie (2009a) 7 and especially 153.

This Lucretian superiority recurs in Seneca as part of a binary complex of positive and negative responses to awesome nature—a complex conveniently describable in the terms that Malcolm Budd uses to summarize the double-aspect emotion of the Kantian sublime:

> *The negative component* of the feeling of the sublime is an unpleasant awareness of the inadequacy of our sensory or physical power: the inadequacy of our sensory power to the perceptual comprehension of nature's immensity—our inability to construct an adequate aesthetic unit of measure, one that can be taken in in one intuition and is suitable for an estimation of the infinite—or the inadequacy of our physical power to resist the immense force of a natural object or phenomenon. The felt realization of this inadequacy, which is somewhat distressing, is forced upon us by confrontation with an appropriate natural phenomenon. *The positive component* is a feeling of elevation in judging our own worth, a feeling of our supremacy over the natural world, the compensatory realization that, in comparison with anything in the sensible world, however immense, even the entirety of the sensible world, and despite our physical vulnerability to the might of natural phenomena, "the rational vocation of our cognitive powers" [from *Critique of Judgement* §27] and the presence within us of the moral law that commands allegiance notwithstanding obstacles of sensibility, endow us with *an importance, a value, infinitely superior to that of nature.*[40]

This contrast of negative and positive components, and this emphasis on "the rational vocation of our cognitive powers," offer a loose but helpful analogue for the Lucretian—and, I propose, the Senecan—contrast between *religio* and *ratio*, or between awed submission to and exalted superiority over nature; and that superiority can itself be understood as a state of inner sublimity.[41] The commonalities to be drawn between Lucretius and Kant on the sublime are plain enough to suggest "a certain awareness on Kant's part that he is working in a Lucretian, or at the very least atomistic, tradition";[42] but could he also have

40. Budd (2002) 82; my emphasis.

41. Cf. *Critique of Judgment* §28 (= Bernard [1951] 104): "Sublimity, therefore, does not reside in anything of nature, but only in our mind, in so far as we can become conscious that we are superior to nature within, and therefore also to nature without us (so far as it influences us). Everything that excites this feeling in us, e.g., the might of nature which calls forth our forces, is called then (although improperly) sublime."

42. Porter (2007) 180.

been touched by a Senecan tradition? Certainly, Kant's writings show reminiscence of Seneca.[43] But even if no direct Kantian connection to *Natural Questions* 6 can be confirmed, it nevertheless remains tempting to speculate on the relevance of the Lucretian-Kantian sublime to Seneca's *De terrae motu* in light of the young Kant's fascination with, and his struggle to comprehend the vast dimensions of, the earthquake and tsunami that devastated Lisbon on November 1, 1755.[44]

On display in the trauma pictured early in Book 6, I propose, is a Senecan version of what might be termed the negative sublime—the passive submission to nature's power that is also glimpsed in the *stupor* of the awestruck remnants of humankind (cf. *mirantibus*, 3.27.12) who contemplate the cataclysm of 3.27–28.[45] While fear of death by earthquake apparently captivates so many (6.1.8), the Senecan response ("Death amounts to the same thing everywhere," 6.1.9) asserts a version of the positive Lucretian/Kantian aspect—a state "of *megalophrosyne*, of mental grandeur"[46] that Seneca, too, renders as "greatness of mind" at 6.1.10 *Proinde magnum sumamus animum aduersus istam cladem* ("Accordingly, let us face this disaster with great courage"). Straightforward points of contrast between, e.g., the impulse to emigrate from Campania and the broader perspective that sees such flight as futile (cf. 6.1.10: "For who promises them that this land or that stands on better foundations?") express the dualistic tension in 6.1–3 between these passive and active mind-sets; but subtler contrasts can also be discerned.

---

43. So, e.g., Bickel (1959) on reminiscence of *Letters* 64.6 (but cf. in response Kullmann [1995] 110–11 and Küppers [1996] 59–60), and for further suggestive points of contact, Baron (1995) 212 n. 35 and 222–26. According to Kuehn (2001) 49, "Seneca and perhaps somewhat surprisingly Lucretius and Horace" were favorites among the Latin authors whom Kant continued to read "throughout his life"; cf. Horn (2008) 1081 for Kant's understanding of Stoicism acquired especially through Cicero and Seneca. Despite its promise by title, Jackson (1881) sheds no light on specific contact between Kant and Seneca.

44. On the earthquake, Kendrick (1956) and now, conveniently, Zeilinga de Boer and Sanders (2005) 88–107. For its profound effect on Kant, Araujo (2006) 314–15 and Larsen (2006); for the series of three articles that he wrote on earthquakes thereafter, all published in 1756, see *Kants Werke I: Akademie Textausgabe. Band I: Vorkritische Schriften I (1747–1756)* (Berlin and New York, 1968) 417–27, 429–61 and 463–72 with Grünthal (2004) 634–35 and Guidoboni and Ebel (2009) 175–76, and also Reinhardt and Oldroyd (1983) for English translation of parts of those works, with emphasis (p. 252) on "those sections in which [Kant] presented his theoretical suggestions." The Lisbon earthquake is nowhere explicitly named in the *Critique of Judgment*, but for possible resonance of it, see Ray (2004) 9–10.

45. See Chapter Three, Section IV; there, Seneca's cosmic spectatorship of the cataclysm offers another version of the positive sublime that I claim for Book 6.

46. Conte (1994) 19.

IV: The Two Verse Quotations at 6.2.1–3 and 6.2.9

In the first of these two passages Seneca turns to Virgil:

> nego quicquam esse quietis aeternae; quod perire possit, et perdere. ego uero hoc ipsum solacii loco pono, et quidem ualentissimi, quoniam quidem sine remedio timor stultis <salutaris> est: ratio terrorem pruden- tibus excutit, imperitis magna fit ex desperatione securitas. hoc itaque generi humano dictum puta quod illis subita captiuitate inter ignes et hostem stupentibus dictum est: 'una salus uictis nullam sperare salutem'. si uultis nihil timere, cogitate omnia esse metuenda.
>
> 6.2.1–3

> I say that there is nothing which enjoys eternal calm; that that which can be destroyed can also destroy.[47] However, I put this very point as a solace (and in fact a very powerful solace), since fear without remedy is <helpful> for fools. Reason dispels terror from the wise, and the ignorant derive a great sense of calm from despair. And so consider that what was said to those dazed by their sudden entrapment amid fire and enemies was said to the human race: 'The conquered have this sole deliverance: to hope for none'. If you want to fear nothing, think that everything is to be feared.

Seneca cites Aeneas' words as he rallies his companions to a brave last stand in burning Troy. Now that the city's fate is decided (cf. *Aen.* 2.348–50), a courageous death is better than submission to the enemy: "Come, let us die, let us rush into the midst of arms. The conquered have this sole deliverance: to hope for none" (*Aen.* 2.353–54).[48] For Giancarlo Mazzoli, Seneca finds in the Virgilian citation "strong support for the Stoic doctrine of ἀπάθεια achieved by means of λόγος."[49] Through the universal appeal of *hoc itaque…dictum est*, however, Seneca also lends fortification to nonphilosophers (*imperitis*): after *ratio* is set in strong con- trast to the resigned calm that comes with the abandonment of all hope (*ex des- peratione securitas*), inferential *itaque* introduces the Virgilian line as an explicit illustration of that hopelessness before Seneca varies the idea of *ex desperatione securitas* in that of "Fear nothing by fearing everything!" On this approach, Virgil

---

47. Thus far, as construed and translated by Alexander (1948) 309.

48. For extensive analysis of the Virgilian citation, albeit with a focus different from my own, De Vivo (1992a) 20–33 = (1992b).

49. Mazzoli (1970) 226.

supplies a balm to the *imperiti*, but one that amounts—however unfairly to Aeneas' meaning in the original context—to a passive capitulation to one's fate. But to offer one important modification to this reading: Hine's proposed supplement of *salutaris* groups together the foolish and the ignorant, *stulti* and *imperiti*;[50] but a finer Senecan distinction is drawn if the supplement is rejected as needless and three constituencies are identified, *stulti*, *prudentes* and *imperiti*.[51] Whereas fear simply overwhelms the foolish (*stulti*), the ignorant (*imperiti*)—or, perhaps more precisely, "persons of good natural quality who have not, however, attained to anything near the insight of the sages, the *prudentes*"[52]—channel their despair toward the comfort of passive resignation.[53] Further, the distinction between the *ratio* of the *prudentes* on the one hand, the *securitas ex desperatione* of the *imperiti* on the other, arguably implies a division between different aspects of Seneca's therapeutic strategy in Book 6 as a whole. So, for Florence Limburg:

> Liberation from fear by means of the scientific discussion (for the wise ones) is sought in the main part of the book, and liberation from fear by means of an ethical lesson (for the less intelligent ones) is found in preface and epilogue.[54]

Yet despite their different proclivities, one active, one passive, both aspects have method and benefit—in contrast to the third way, or the *timor* to which the *stulti* mindlessly succumb at 6.2.1.

For all their (relative) merit, however, the *imperiti* remain resigned to their fate; and that passivity continues in Seneca's characterization in 6.2.3 of the mind-set that recognizes only its own vulnerability: "You'll soon realize that we are insignificant and weak little bodies [*nugatoria... et inbecilla corpuscula*], fleeting, and destined to

---

50. See Hine (1996b) 94–95; cf. for the same identification, albeit with different textual interventions, Axelson (1933) 76, Shackleton Bailey (1979) 453–54 and Watt (1994) 195.

51. So, powerfully, Alexander (1948) 309–11; also Parroni (2002) 575 and Limburg (2007) 313 n. 37. The objection that "elsewhere in S. the *imperiti* are normally indistinguishable from the *stulti*" (Hine [2005b] 546; cf. Chaumartin [1993] 111–13) does not automatically require conformity at 6.2.1—if, that is, we accept the *de facto* identification of *stulti* and *imperiti* in the first place (but cf. Alexander 310).

52. Alexander (1948) 310.

53. On this approach the second *quidem* in the passage quoted above yields not just "a strengthened *quoniam*, 'because indeed, in truth'" (Solodow [1978] 134), but introduces a μέν clause (Solodow 31) in contrast to the two-fold δέ counterpoise in *ratio... excutit* and *imperitis... securitas*. For this antithetical use of *quidem* without an explicit *sed* vel sim. cf. 2.10.4 *quoniam quidem sterile frigus est, calor gignit, Dial.* 10.15.4.

54. (2007) 314. Cf. Section VII n. 156 below in this chapter.

be destroyed with no great effort." But then, in 6.2.4, the man who fears lightning bolts, earthquakes, etc., is said "to esteem himself highly" (*magni se aestimat*), as if—in sudden contrast to 6.2.3—underestimating his vulnerability to smaller, more ordinary dangers such as heavy catarrh. This man, who "esteems himself highly" by fearing an earthquake before more everyday threats, forgets his basic human frailty (*inbecillitatis…suae*, 6.2.4), as if exalted above our common condition by a misguided sublimity of thought, or by a false superiority to ordinary nature. In contrast to this misguided sublimity, Seneca suggestively portrays a truer version when, in his vision of death by earthquake at 6.2.8–9, he draws comfort from coordinating human mortality with the mortality of the earth itself:

> quid habeo quod querar, si rerum natura me non uult iacere ignobili leto, si mihi inicit sui partem? egregie Vagellius[55] meus in illo *incluto carmine*, 'si cadendum est' inquit 'mihi, e caelo cecidisse uelim.' item[56] licet dicere, 'si cadendum est, cadam orbe concusso, non quia fas est optare publicam cladem, sed quia ingens mortis solacium est terram quoque uidere mortalem'.

> What do I have to complain about if nature does not want me to die an inglorious death, if she hurls a part of herself on me? My friend Vagellius expresses it admirably in that renowned poem of his: "If I must fall, I would want to have fallen from the heavens." Similarly, one might say: "If I must fall, let me fall with the world shattered, not because it is right to wish for a general disaster, but because a very great solace in dying is to see that the earth, too, is mortal."

Given that Seneca applies the epithet *inclutus* to a poet or his verses on only two occasions (he otherwise uses the adjective almost exclusively in his tragedies), Vagellius is surely also meant at *N.Q.* 3 pref. 3:

> Libet igitur mihi exclamare illum *poetae incluti* uersum:
>   tollimus ingentes animos et maxima paruo
>   tempore molimur.

> I want, therefore, to give full voice to the well-known lines of the celebrated poet:
>   We arouse our minds to greatness and strive for the grandest
>   accomplishment in but a short span of time.

---

55. For whom Chapter One, Section III and n. 38.

56. So, persuasively, Housman (1935) 168 = (1972) 1247–48 for MSS *idem*; endorsed by Hine (1996b) 95, albeit with fair objections to Housman's larger treatment of 6.2.9.

Giancarlo Mazzoli persuasively connects the two citations at 3 pref. 3 and 6.2.9, tracing both to a Vagellian poem on the (Ovidian) Phaethon myth and conjecturing that the words quoted in Book 6 are spoken by Phaethon himself as part of his effort to win his father's permission to drive the sun-chariot.[57] But Mazzoli then connects both citations with the sublime. So at 3 pref. 3 the (Vagellian) verses illustrate a heightening of inspiration and effort as Seneca rises to his forbidding task in the *Natural Questions* (cf. 3 pref. 4: "When my mind considers the scale of this enterprise, it grows in stature"). For Mazzoli, this projection of *magnanimitas* combines μεγαλοψυχία, moral virtue, and μεγαλοφροσύνη, or an inspired heightening of sensation—a mode of aesthetic virtue; in combination, these two qualities, *magnitudo animi* and *magnitudo ingenii*, "contribute to the same supreme ethico-aesthetic goal, the sublime."[58] The Vagellian citation in Book 6 again expresses a lofty *magnanimitas*—a spiritedness that Seneca himself acknowledges in his admiring portrayal of Phaethon as a model of high-minded *uirtus* in his *De prouidentia* (= *Dial.* 1.5.10):

> uide quam alte escendere debeat uirtus: scies illi non per secura uadendum...haec cum audisset ille generosus adulescens, 'placet' inquit 'uia, escendo; est tanti per ista ire casuro'.... humilis et inertis est tuta sectari: per alta uirtus it.
>
> See to what heights virtue must ascend: you will realize the dangers through which it must advance [Seneca then inserts *Met.* 2.63–9, Apollo to Phaethon on the terrifying heights to which the latter will rise on his ill-fated journey]. When he had heard these words [in Ovid], that noble-spirited youth said: "I like the road, and shall climb it; to travel through those regions is worth the price of falling...." To follow the safe path is the mark of a lowly lack of spirit; virtue takes the high road.

Despite the disastrous outcome of Phaethon's flight, his soaring *uirtus* here offers a tacit analogy for the ὕψος of the Stoic *sapiens*.[59] If we carry this positive represen-

---

57. (1968) 366 and (1970) 258, with considered endorsement in Duret (1988) 141–42; cf. also Chapter One, Section III and n. 40.

58. Mazzoli (1970) 48.

59. Cf. *SVF* 1.216 p. 52.34, 36 and p. 53.1 = 3.567 p. 150.6, 8, and see Mazzoli (1970) 48 for linkage to the literary sublime via reference to *On the Sublime* 9.2 ὕψος μεγαλοφροσύνης ἀπήχημα ("sublimity is the echo of a noble mind") and 36.1 τὸ δ'ὕψος ἐγγὺς αἴρει μεγαλοφροσύνης θεοῦ ("sublimity raises one up to proximity to the majestic mind of god").

tation of Phaethon[60] over to the *Natural Questions*, the sublime impulse of 3 pref. 3 is sustained in the Vagellian citation at 6.2.9; and that sublimity now collides with the passivity we detected in the Virgilian quotation at 6.2.2.

On this approach, the two verse citations in 6.2.2 and 6.2.9 respectively are hardly just casual occurrences, or isolated textual adornments that bear no relation to each other. In combination, they illustrate the larger tension that we have observed in 6.1–3 between positive and negative aspects of the Senecan sublime, or between passivity and self-assertion in confrontation with nature. In moving to Seneca's survey of theories of earthquake in 6.4–26, we shall see that this whole section builds on the momentum of the positive sublime—our superiority over nature—that has already been generated in parts of 6.1–3. In what follows, the rightness or wrongness of any or all of the theories reviewed in 6.4–26 matters less than the broader attitude to nature that Seneca asserts by activating an empowered mind-set throughout this section—a Senecan/Stoic variation on nature's subjugation to "superior" Lucretian *ratio*.

V: *Controlling Nature in the Senecan Inventory (6.4–26)*

What causes all the "strange things" (*miracula*) and all the great convulsions occasioned by an earthquake (6.4.1)? The question is large, but Seneca portrays the reward to be gained by such questioning as still larger: "knowledge of nature" (*nosse naturam*, 6.4.2). He therefore launches his enquiry ("Let us examine, then, the causes of these phenomena," 6.4.2), but in one sense he has *already* attained the goal of knowing nature: quite apart from the fact that he is no newcomer to the subject but had apparently written a work on earthquakes in his youth (6.4.2),[61] he projects an air of confident control over his subject matter in 6.4–26, as if he writes from the perspective of a preformed, whole grasp of the subject, as opposed to writing *toward* that full picture. His survey of earlier theories of earthquake[62] is loosely structured as follows: at 6.5.1 opinion is said to be divided between water, fire, earth and air or a combination of the four elements as the

60. Contrast the pejorative Ovidian/Horatian (cf. *Carm.* 4.11.25–6) and Silver strain: Duret (1988) 142–43 with La Penna (2001) 540–45 and Lanzarone (2008) 371–72. But for the positive interpretation connected to Nero's (self-)projection as Phaethon, Duret 143–49 with Champlin (2003) 134–35 and Berno (2003) 333 and n. 20.

61. For this work, perhaps dating to the first years of his Corsican exile (41 CE), Vottero (1998a) 31–33.

62. In general, Gilbert (1907) 293–324; See (1907) 232–67; Chatelain (1909) 87–101; *RE* 4A 344–74; Ringshausen (1929); Bollack (1978) 515–28; Gross (1989) 248–70; Oeser (1992); Guidoboni et al. (1994) 42–47; Waldherr (1997) 47–220; Guidoboni and Ebel (2009) 147–53.

possible cause of earthquakes; 6.6–8: water as the cause; 6.9: fire; 6.10: earth; 6.11: fire again; 6.12–19: different theories of air as the cause; 6.20: all or multiple elements as the combined cause; 6.21.1: Seneca's preferred emphasis on a pneumatic explanation, given that there is nothing in nature (he insists) more powerful than air; 6.21.2–23.4: classification of the different ways in which the earth is moved (by shaking from below, by inclination, by trembling); 6.24–6: how air accumulates under the earth, its motion leading to earthquake. If the elements are mutually interchangeable at a physical level (cf. 3.10.3–5), they here converge as interchangeable *causae* within doxographical history, albeit with Seneca's preference for a pneumatic cause. In his steady movement through the different theories ventured by different philosophical schools across the ages, and in his coverage of all four elements, whether individually or in combination with each other, Seneca's fullness of treatment is matched by the fluent authority with which he handles the natural parts. In this respect, the controlling perspective on display in 6.4–26 is directly relatable to the all-seeing viewpoint from which he surveys the great cataclysm at the end of Book 3.[63] His superiority over nature is expressed, I propose, through this panoptic mastery in 6.4–26; or, more particularly, through the following six aspects of that mastery.

(A)   Taking Stock of Earlier Seismological Investigation

To the modern scientific eye, so many of the theories reported by Seneca must seem hopelessly inadequate and procedurally flawed. From an ancient perspective, however, the very exercise of positing different natural explanations for earthquakes works to demystify the phenomenon by subjecting it to experimental reason and locating it within a reassuring world system. The *effort* to explain counts for so much: hence Seneca's indulgent attitude to past investigators,[64] their main contribution lying in their pioneering spirit (cf. 6.5.2); and hence his coverage even of theories with which he disagrees, theories that nonetheless contribute to the collaborative historical effort from the Pre-Socratics onward that Seneca represents and updates in 6.6–26. He follows a roughly chronological path in progressing from Thales in the sixth century (6.6.1) to Anaxagoras, Anaximenes and Archelaus, Anaxagoras' pupil, before turning (6.13.1–2) to Aristotle, Theophrastus and Strato of Lampsacus, head of the Peripatetic school after Theophrastus. Another (atomist) tradition is later traced in his coverage (6.19–20) of

---

63. See Chapter Three, Section IV.

64. Cf. 6.5.3: "And so the ancients must be listened to with indulgence." For *rudis antiquitas* (4b.7.3), see Chapter Four, Section IV (E) and n. 89.

Democritus, Metrodorus of Chios (fourth century BCE, of the Democritean school), and Epicurus; and then forward in time to Posidonius and Asclepiodotus[65] in 6.21.2 and 22.2 respectively. Yet this chronological linearity is accompanied by a different form of progress in Seneca's careful orchestration of his inventory. We shall see that he builds into his coverage of different earthquake theories a sub-plot of sorts that suggestively conditions his often idiosyncratic portrayal of the *opiniones* he surveys—a subplot of movement from visual perception of the world to an increasingly theoretical and abstract mode of engagement with its workings. However speculative in its probings, this eye for the nonvisual marks a crucial formative stage in Seneca's effort fully to capture the nature of earthquakes in Book 6.

(B) From Sight to Insight

The general movement *ex oculis ad rationem* is initiated by Seneca's treatment (6.6) of Thales' early theory of water as the cause of earthquake. Seneca appropriately begins his inventory with what Thales held to be the first principle (ἀρχή).[66] Aristotle corroborates the Senecan report (6.6.1) of Thales' theory that the earth floats on water,[67] but he makes no mention of the further idea that "when the earth is said to 'quake', it is tossed about by the movement of the water" (*N.Q.* 3.14.1; cf. 6.6.2).[68] Seneca's report of Thales' earthquake theory may be derived indirectly from Theophrastus;[69] but whatever his source, and even if we allow for a certain doxographical zeal as he embarks on his inventory, why does he go to such lengths in 6.6 to report and refute a theory that he has already dismissed at 3.14.1–2 as "silly" and "antiquated and unscholarly"? The theory is evidently false, he asserts at 6.6.3: if the earth floated on water, how could earthquakes be only

---

65. For whom see Chapter One, Section I n. 5.

66. ἀρχή in the sense of (Kirk et al. [1983] 90) "the original constituent material of things, which persists as a substratum and into which they will perish."

67. D-K 11A12 and 14 = Kirk et al. (1983) 88–89 frr. 84–85 = Graham (2010) 1.28–29 and 30–31 Texts 15 and 18. Given the possibility that Thales left few if any written works, Seneca's quotation at 6.6.1 (*'hac' inquit 'unda…'*) naturally invites suspicion of being either a Senecan fabrication or derived from an intermediary doxographical source; see Vottero (1989) 404 n. 2 on 3.13.1 with Setaioli (1988) 401.

68. Cf. Hall (1977) 433–35, concluding (p. 435) that it is "unlikely that Seneca has invented the earthquake theory…; he probably found it in his source," but "the chances are against its being genuinely Thales' theory"—the latter judgment at one with that of Diels (*DG* p. 225) on Aetius' claim (*Plac.* 3.15.1; *DG* p. 379) that Thales and Democritus attributed the cause of earthquake to water (further, Lapini [1995] 195–99).

69. So Lloyd (1966) 308 n. 2; Kirk et al. (1983) 93 n. 2.

occasional, and how could only a part of the earth be shaken, not its entirety? Aristotle himself raised obvious objections to the theory that the earth floats on water,[70] but G. E. R. Lloyd emphasizes the considerations that nevertheless reflect positively upon Thales' efforts. In contrast to "previous conceptions of the physical connection between different world-masses" (e.g., the Hesiodic myth of Atlas supporting the heavens in *Theog.* 517–20),

> Thales' idea…is a rational account, a λόγος, first in that it omits any reference to anthropomorphic gods or the supernatural, and secondly in that it is based on a certain positive analogy between the effect to be explained (why the earth is "held up") and an effect that is observed elsewhere (solid objects being "held up" when they float).[71]

Seneca, too, acknowledges a positive side in prefacing his inventory in Book 6 with a moderate judgment on his predecessors, praising them for their investigative instinct (cf. 6.5.2) even if he rejects their ideas; indeed, his extended treatment of Thales in 6.6 perhaps constitutes an initial, exemplary illustration of the *ueteres* in keen but "primitive" action (cf. *rudem*, 3.14.2; 6.5.2). But the ease with which he counters Thales' theory also exposes the fragility of the relatively uncomplicated, descriptive mode of analogy that is sampled and tested here, whereby A and B are straightforwardly related, with no acknowledgement made or account given of the stark differences between the two: "'The earth is supported by this water,' Thales says, 'just as some great ship weighs heavily on the waters on which it presses down'" (6.6.1). It is from this beginning that our Senecan ascent into higher modes of seismological conjecture begins.

In contrast to the descriptive mode of analogy on offer in 6.6, a more penetrating, inferential mode takes shape in Seneca's coverage (6.7) of theories that attribute earthquakes to the movement of subterranean water. If we think in terms of a hierarchical ascent from sensory to cognitive levels of awareness, this inferential mode occupies a middle place in positing the invisible from the visible, the plausible from the evident. So, at 6.7.1, in the voice of an interlocutor,[72] "many

---

70. See Lloyd (1966) 307.

71. Lloyd (1966) 308.

72. Hine (1996a) 241.261–244.304 assigns the whole of 6.7.1 *per omnem* to 7.6 *superstantium* to an interlocutor, a decision queried by Inwood (2000) 35 n. 20 and (2002) 140 n. 44 = (2005) 182 n. 43 on 6.7.5, perhaps rightly (cf. now Hine [2010a] 221–22 and [2010b] 203 n. 12): given the weight that will be attached below to Seneca's inferential/analogical procedures in 6.7.5 in particular, it matters for my purposes that the interlocutor falls silent (at the end of 6.7.4 at the latest?) so that the Senecan master voice resumes.

kinds of water" are said to run "over the whole earth"; then we go underground in
6.7.3 *omnis aquarum et intra terram natura faciesque est* ("Within the earth as well
there is every type and form of water"), where reasonable inference licenses the
transition from above to below:

> non est diu probandum ibi multas aquas esse unde omnes sunt: neque enim
> sufficeret tellus ad tot flumina edenda, nisi ex reposito multoque funderet.
>
> 6.7.3

> It does not take long to demonstrate that many waters exist in the place
> from which all waters come; for the earth would be incapable of produc-
> ing so many rivers unless it poured them out from a reservoir of ample
> proportions.

Of course, theories of subterranean water extended back to the Pre-Socratics,[73] a
tradition on which Seneca draws at 3.8–9 and also at 5.14.2.[74] In contrast to those
passages, however, Seneca's emphasis at 6.7.5 on the limits of human vision and
our failure to engage the mind's eye not only contributes to the larger construction of a hierarchy-of-seeing in the *Natural Questions* generally;[75] it also amounts
to a strong justification of the inferential mode itself:

> Iam uero nimis oculis permittit, nec ultra illos scit producere animum, qui
> non credit esse in abdito terrae sinus maris uasti. nec enim uideo quid
> prohibeat aut obstet, quominus habeat aliquod etiam in abdito litus et per
> occultos aditus receptum mare....
>
> 6.7.5

> Moreover, people who refuse to believe that there exist in the recesses of the
> earth the gulfs of a vast sea are too reliant on their eyesight, and they don't
> know how to extend the mind beyond it. For I see nothing to preclude or
> hamper the possibility that the earth has some sort of shore concealed
> within it as well, and that a sea is admitted through hidden channels....

---

73. So Anaxagoras, D-K 59A42 (4) and (5) = Graham (2010) 1.296–97 Text 38 (4) and (5);
Democritus, D-K 68A97, 98 = Graham 1.558–61 Texts 78–79.

74. At 5.14.2 in particular his justification of the subterranean theory may appear more facile
than convincing in its excessively neat, chiastic formulation: "For not even these [sc. clouds
and mist] above ground exist because they are seen, but they are seen because they exist [*ne haec
quidem supra terras quia uidentur sunt, sed quia sunt uidentur*]; there [sc. under the earth], too,
rivers do not exist any the less because they are not seen."

75. See Chapters One, Section II, and Two, Section IV.

The inferential method on display here is bolstered by the hard-driving rhetorics of "What is there to prevent...?" and "How [vel sim.] unless...?";[76] and the rhetoric of necessity also contributes at 6.8.5 ("For it must be—*oportet*—that the earth's interior parts contain moisture...scattered in many parts"). But Seneca rounds out this demonstration of analogical inference in action ("What is above the earth also exists below...") with a climactic display in 6.8 of the limits of visual investigation, the inevitability of inferential speculation.

What is the source of rivers if not the wetness inside the earth (6.8.1)? Seneca first appeals to the visual evidence of two famous cases in point ("When you see the Tigris interrupted...; when you see the Alpheus disappear underground in Achaea...", 6.8.2)[77] before turning to the Nile at 6.8.3: among the theories that explain the Nile's summer flooding, he reports, is that the river takes its volume *e terra* and *ex intimo*. Implicated here are presumably the theories of Oenopides of Chios and Diogenes of Apollonia, both of which are found to be flawed at 4a.2.26–30.[78] But whatever the detailed and disputed inner workings of the earth that produce the Nile's summer flood, Seneca seeks at 6.8.3–4 to prove that the Nile has a subterranean origin by citing the testimony of two centurions who were reportedly sent by Nero to investigate the river's source. Since the elder Pliny also mentions a Neronian mission to Ethiopia and the Upper Nile (*Nat.* 6.181, 184–86), a lively controversy has arisen as to whether or not Seneca and Pliny refer to the same expedition; and, if it is indeed the same mission (in 61 CE or later?),[79] how is Seneca's stress on its scientific motivation and on Nero's high-minded commitment to the truth (he is cast at 6.8.3 as that "very great lover of the other virtues, and especially of truth") to be reconciled with the military emphasis in Pliny?[80] Whatever the possible overlap with Pliny, however, Seneca would seem

---

76. For "what prevents...?" cf. 6.7.6 *quas* [sc. *undas*] *quid uetat illic fluctuare...?*; for "how unless...?," 6.7.3 *neque enim sufficeret tellus..., nisi,* 6.8.1 *unde enim ista prorepunt..., nisi...?,* 6.8.2 *quo illum* [sc. the Tigris] *putas abire nisi in obscura terrarum...?*

77. For the disappearing Tigris and Alpheus, 3.26.4–5 with Vottero (1989) 438–39 nn. 10–12 for sources, and cf. 3.1.1; Seneca again strives to demystify *mira* by tracing such rivers to their logical, underground course/origin.

78. See Chapter Three, Section VII.

79. See De Nardis (1989) 125–26 for a survey of opinion on two expeditions (p. 125 n. 11; add Cesaretti [1989] 60 and n. 81) as opposed to one (p. 126 n. 12; De Nardis' favored option, p. 129). Date: 61 CE, Lana in discussion (p. 342) after Gigon (1991); cf. Desanges (1988) 17 (one expedition between 61 and 63 CE), with De Vivo (1998) 165–81 and now Hine (2006) 63 and n. 88 for an overview of the question. For a concise account of pre-Neronian expeditions to the Upper Nile, Sheikh (1992) with Kirwan (1957).

80. Cf. *Nat.* 6.181 *Neroni...inter reliqua bella et Aethiopicum cogitanti.* See further Gauly (2004) 198–99 and n. 37 for the main issues and bibliography, with Hine (2006) 63–64 and n. 90 on implied criticism of Nero here and elsewhere in the *Natural Questions.*

to follow his own agenda in the colorful way in which he describes the limits of
the adventurers' investigations:

ego quidem centuriones duos, quos Nero Caesar…ad inuestigandum Nili
caput miserat, audiui narrantes longum ipsos iter peregisse, cum a rege
Aethiopiae instructi auxilio commendatique proximis regibus ad ulteriora
penetrassent. qui 'inde' aiebant 'peruenimus ad inmensas paludes, quarum
exitum nec incolae nouerant nec sperare quisquam potest: ita implicatae
aquis herbae sunt et <herbis> aquae, nec pediti eluctabiles nec nauigio,
quod nisi paruum et unius capax limosa et obsita palus non fert. ibi' inquit
'uidimus duas petras, ex quibus ingens uis fluminis excidebat'.

6.8.3–4

In fact, I have listened to two centurions whom Nero Caesar…had sent to
investigate the source of the Nile. They reported that, when they had been
provided with assistance by the king of the Ethiopians and had received intro-
ductions to neighboring kings, they had penetrated to the more distant parts
and completed a long journey. "Then," they said, "we came to vast swamps; the
natives didn't know where they ended; nor could anyone hope to know. So
enwrapped in the waters was the vegetation, the waters in the vegetation,[81] and
there was no way through either on foot or by boat; the muddy and overgrown
marsh takes only a small craft large enough for only one man. There," he said,
"we saw two rocks, from which a vast body of river water fell."

The intrusiveness of this anecdote within the scientific context that it interrupts[82] is
underscored by the tonal shift that occurs when Seneca reverts to direct quotation
and to a stylistic mode that is colloquial in feel and diction.[83] By allowing the centurions to speak in their apparently unadorned voice, Seneca may enhance the credibility of his account, even though there are distinct signs of careful construction here.
Describing the many kinds of surface water on the earth, Seneca includes among
them "the very wide lakes and expanses of water surrounded by peoples who are

---

81. The so called "sudd," or the periodic blocking of the river by floating vegetation. For Seneca's allusion related to modern exploration, see Anon. (1900), especially 235–36 (with interesting photographs), and for the Senecan emphasis on directionless disorientation, cf. Stanton
(1903) 376: "As you proceed along the twisting and narrow channel, constantly doubling back
on itself, and the sun sets in the west in the sea of reeds and swamp, a feeling of desolation and
utter loneliness comes over you."

82. On this "digressive and transgressive element," De Vivo (1998) 170.

83. See De Vivo (1998) 172 for analysis, and cf. Setaioli (1980) 9–10 n. 6 = (2000) 13 n. 20 on
the nonliterary character of *petras*.

unknown to each other, and swamps that a boat cannot get through [*ineluctabiles nauigio paludes*]" (6.7.2). Our centurions conveniently confirm as much in their report of *aquae nec pediti eluctabiles nec nauigio*,[84] while the sequence of negatives, the points of linguistic strangeness in their account, and the lack of any clear direction markers all contribute to the unsettling atmosphere of this lost place.[85] Then, at the end of our passage, the two rocks to which the Nile is ultimately traced back are perhaps the so-called "Veins of the Nile" at 4a.2.7,[86] from which its great force of water descends from parts unknown (*ibi…excidebat*). The anecdote takes us literally to the very limits of world investigation *per oculos*, limits that leave room for doubt and uncertainty ("But whether that [sc. great force of river water] is the source of the Nile or merely a tributary…"; 6.8.5), inference the only way ahead: "Surely you think that, whatever that force of water is, it ascends from a great lake under the earth?" (6.8.5). In effect, the anecdote is no mere colorful aside here, but is fully integrated into Seneca's continuing argument; for it offers from a different angle a crowning illustration of the need "to project the mind beyond the eyes" (cf. 6.7.5).

(C) From Analogical Inference to Abstract Speculation

As Seneca's inventory of causes gains momentum after 6.7, its roughly chronological sequence from the Pre-Socratics onward is matched by a movement first to analogical inference and then toward more abstract speculation, the mind's eye increasingly our sole guide as Seneca penetrates further into nature's secrets; he thus exerts a growing superiority over nature in his inventory. Two stages of operation are distinguishable in 6.7–13. In the first, the inferential technique championed at length in 6.7–8 (as in B above) is immediately reapplied without fanfare in Seneca's treatment of Anaxagoras' fire theory at 6.9.1:

> Anaxagoras…existimat simili paene ex causa et aëra concuti et terram: cum <in> inferiore parte spiritus crassum aëra et in nubes coactum eadem ui qua apud nos quoque nubila frangi solent rumpit, et ignis ex hoc conlisu nubium cursuque elisi aëris emicuit, hic ipse in obuia incurrit exitum quaerens, ac diuellit repugnantia….
>
> Anaxagoras…reckons that both the atmosphere and the earth are shaken by just about the same cause. Down below, air breaks through the

---

84. On the parallel with 6.7.2, De Nardis (1989) 134.

85. See De Vivo (1998) 173–74 for this "semantica dell'ignoto." Linguistic strangeness: *eluctabilis* is unprecedented, and the absolute use of *obsita* without an accompanying ablative a bold touch (De Vivo 173 and n. 27; 174 and n. 28).

86. So, e.g., Oltramare (1929) 2.262 n. 1.

atmosphere, which is thick and compacted into clouds;[87] it does so with
the same force with which clouds are usually broken open in our region
also. Fire flashes forth from this collision with clouds and from the rush of
air that is forced out; this fire, seeking an exit, runs against anything in its
path and tears apart anything that resists it....

Various efforts have been made in this particular case to reconcile Seneca's report
with earlier versions,[88] but he may yet rely on a divergent source that stressed fire
as the cause.[89] Or, if we allow a still greater independence of maneuver, does he
massage his reporting here in a particular direction, reaching for fire as the Anaxagoran cause in 6.9 and returning briefly to *ignis* in 6.11 to achieve a full representation of, and rough balance between, the four elements in his overall survey?

Despite these uncertainties, however, inference now serves as an accepted
foundation of argument in Book 6, our license to "project the mind beyond the
eyes" (cf. 6.7.5) firmly established and hence variously applied in the chapters that
follow. So in Seneca's report at 6.9.2–3 of another fire theory, that earthquakes are
caused by subterranean erosion, our experience above ground allegedly confirms
what happens below:

> alii in igne quidem causam esse, sed non ob hoc iudicant, sed quia pluribus
> obrutus locis ardeat et proxima quaeque consumat: quae si quando exesa
> ceciderunt, tunc sequi motum earum partium quae subiectis adminiculis
> destitutae labant donec corruerunt, nullo occurrente quod onus exci-
> peret...hoc apud nos quoque uidemus accidere quotiens incendio laborat
> pars ciuitatis. cum exustae trabes sunt aut corrupta quae superioribus fir-
> mamentum dabant, tunc diu agitata fastigia concidunt.

Other authorities[90] hold that the cause of earthquake is fire, but for a
different [i.e., non-Anaxagoran] reason: buried fire breaks out in many
places and burns up all that is near it.[91] If the parts that have been eroded

---

87. Dynamic *spiritus* here perhaps with a special charge, for which see Chapter Five, Section III.

88. See Traglia (1955) 740–42 with Guthrie (1965) 310–11. Much depends on Aristotle's derivation of the Anaxagoran cause from air (αἰθήρ) entrapped in hollows under the earth (*Mete.*
2.7 365a19–25): since Anaxagoras identified αἰθήρ with πῦρ (see Hall [1977] 428 and n. 4 for
references), Aristotle's αἰθήρ arguably corresponds to Anaxagoras' term for fire, in which case
(Hall 428–29) "Seneca's account in part agrees with Aristotle's."

89. Setaioli (1988) 403–4.

90. Perhaps extending to Epicurus (cf. 6.20.7), but for earlier traces of fire-as-cause, Vottero
(1989) 604 n. 3 with Gross (1989) 241.

91. For Hine (2010b) 204 n. 15, "A reference to volcanic fire within the earth"; for "allusions au
volcanisme" in Seneca's wider treatment of the fire theory in 6.9–11, see Dupraz (2004) 249–52.

fall, then an earthquake follows in those parts which have lost their underlying support; they totter until they collapse, because there is nothing
there to take the weight.... We, too, see this same thing happen before our
eyes whenever a part of the city is afflicted by fire. When beams are burned
to a cinder, or what gave support to the upper levels is damaged, then the
rooftops tremble for a long time before finally collapsing.

The mind's eye now begins to move easily between the visible and the invisible in
the Senecan text. His report of Anaximenes' theory of earth as the cause of earthquake again implicates the different elements (the dissolving effects of moisture
as the cause, then fire, then blasts of air) before he focuses on natural aging leading to eventual collapse;[92] that collapse is illustrated by the example of buildings
succumbing because of age,[93] the falling sections of earth rebounding "like a ball"
(6.10.2). These illustrations again serve to domesticate the phenomenon, a technique reapplied in Seneca's appeal in 6.11 to a homely analogy ("We see water
bubbling away when there is a fire beneath it") to support the fire theory: an
earthquake is caused by the pressure resulting from fire heating and vaporizing
enclosed water underground.[94] If we now glance back at Conte's characterization
of Empedoclean analogy as a unifying instrument that grasps the totality of
being,[95] the Senecan inferential process at work in these examples in 6.9–11 (as
often elsewhere in the *Natural Questions*) is itself a unifying mechanism, promoting similarity and continuity between separate orders. Yet the Senecan process is
not limited to intuitive leaps of an Empedoclean kind as characterized by Conte;[96]

---

92. 6.10.1. Cf. D-K 13A21 = Graham (2010) 1.86–87 Text 34 with Guthrie (1962) 139 n. 1 (overlap with Anaximander?). Seneca apparently offers an enlargement of Anaximenes' thought
(Traglia [1955] 743), perhaps following a source that diverges from the Aristotelian (and also
the doxographical) testimony in D-K above (cf. Setaioli [1988] 405). See also Hall (1977) 429:
the section down to 6.10.1 *ignis exederit* "is recognizable as a version of the theory given by
Aristotle and Aetius. The rest may conceivably be an alternative theory of Anaximenes', ignored by Aristotle; but much more likely it is another example of Seneca's habit of drifting
away from the author he has started to paraphrase" (hence a significant qualification in n. 93
below).

93. 6.10.2. For Guidoboni et al. (1994) 43, seemingly *Anaximenes'* original choice of comparison, but for possible Senecan interference, cf. n. 92 above. The point matters because of my
own emphasis on Seneca's artful structuring of, and full control over, *every* aspect of his inventory in *Natural Questions* 6 as a whole.

94. Attribution of the theory is uncertain, but for Empedocles tentatively discussed in relation to 6.11 *Quidam* (cf. 3.24.1–3), see Vottero (1989) 608 n. 1 after Ringshausen (1929) 38.

95. See Section III above in this chapter.

96. Conte (1994) 12–13.

rather, it constitutes "a logical procedure" in the Lucretian manner, a "structured form of thought" that, by this stage in *Natural Questions* 6, truly *knows*.[97]

After analogical inference, the second stage of operation that concerns us in 6.7–13 is Seneca's recourse to purely abstract speculation. The first of three samples of this movement in an abstract direction occurs in Seneca's report in 6.12 of the earthquake theory of Archelaus, Anaxagoras' pupil and allegedly Socrates' teacher.[98] His theory, that earthquakes are caused by air penetrating the earth from outside and then being compressed and pushed into movement by air that presses in on top of it,[99] finds empirical support in the observation that the atmosphere tends to be calm just before an earthquake, when the force of air that normally generates wind is instead located under the earth. In contrast to the inferential process that has prevailed thus far in the Senecan inventory, however, positing an analogical relationship between the visible and the invisible, Archelaus' approach as portrayed by Seneca is more liberated in its subterranean probing: the mind's eye reconstructs events below with only a tangential relation to events above ground (the prevailing calm before an earthquake).

Seneca's subsequent version (6.13.1) of Aristotle's and Theophrastus' theory of earthquake[100] amounts to "merely a rough paraphrase" of Aristotle's fuller account,[101] with Seneca taking up Aristotle's derivation of the cause from the latter's theory of exhalations (warm and dry or cold and moist) from the earth.[102] In

---

97. Conte (1994) 13.

98. For Archelaus, Guthrie (1965) 339–40. It is unfortunate that Seneca's own characterization at 6.12.1, *Archelaus* †*antiquitatis*† *diligens*, is beyond recovery; see further, Hine (1996b) 99, persuasively rejecting the defense of *antiquitatis diligens* mounted by Parroni (1994) 2.546–47 (cf. Parroni [2002] 368 and 580 for that reading adopted).

99. 6.12.1–2 = D-K 60A16a. The theory, unattested before Seneca, is ascribed by Ammian. 17.7.11 to Anaxagoras—itself perhaps a reflection and consequence of the latter's close association with Archelaus. For parallels between 6.12.3 (riposte to an objection to Archelaus' theory) and Aristot. *Mete.* 2.8 366a5–12, see Traglia (1955) 747; given Seneca's subsequent reversion (6.13.1) to Aristotle's theory, he arguably relies on a doxographical source that itself groups Archelaus and Aristotle in a similar fashion (cf. Setaioli [1988] 406–7).

100. Aristot. *Mete.* 2.8 365b21–369a9; *N.Q.* 6.13.1 = Theophr. no. 195 Fortenbaugh et al. (1992) 364–65; for earthquake included in Theophrastus' *Meteorology/Metarsiology*, that work no longer extant in Greek (cf. Chapter Five, Section I n. 8), see Daiber (1992) 271 with Taub (2003) 119. Further on the Aristotelian and Theophrastan theories, Gilbert (1907) 305–13 with Guidoboni et al. (1994) 44–45 and Waldherr (1997) 49–59.

101. Hall (1977) 413 (with n. 2: insufficient evidence "to show how accurately Seneca is reporting Theophrastus").

102. On the Aristotelian exhalations, cf. Chapters Two, Section III n. 40, and Five, Section II. The exact role of the Aristotelian exhalations in Seneca's formulation here is problematic, but for the issues well clarified, see Hall (1977) 413 n. 4: "Seneca does not state clearly *which* exhalation is cause; but nor, in this chapter [*Mete.* 2.8], does Aristotle. Theoretically, dry exhalation causes wind (360b 10ff. etc.), which causes earthquakes (366a 3f. etc.); but in 2.8 moisture is also involved in producing the exhalation to which earthquakes are due (365b 24–27, 366b 9f.)."

terms of methodology, however, Seneca extrapolates the Aristotelian cause from a postulate, the exhalation theory, which owes nothing to visual analogy. Then the theory of Strato of Lampsacus, Theophrastus' successor as head of the Peripatetic school: he derives earthquakes from the mutual exclusiveness and repulsion of heat and cold and from the resulting cycles of conflict between hot and cold air underground.[103] This theory presumably constitutes a Peripatetic development of the Aristotelian notion of ἀντιπερίστασις, or the mutual reaction of hot and cold to each other.[104] It apparently finds empirical support in the observation that in winter wells and caves are warm because heat gathers there in retreat from the cold above, while in summer the cold retreats.[105] Again, however, the theory itself is based on *a priori* principle (heat and cold in conflict), and it accordingly takes us further in a cognitive direction *ex oculis ad rationem* within Seneca's survey; but at this point a different development adds another important dimension to the inventory.

(D) The Living Cosmos

Another method by which Seneca moves to normalize earthquakes is to draw on the familiar ancient conception of the cosmos as a living organism.[106] Aristotle had already compared earthquakes with the tremors and throbbings of the human body, the effects in both cases caused by the pent-up force of wind (*pneuma*) within the earth (*Mete.* 2.8 366b14–22). Lucretius similarly compares the dispersal of earthquake-inducing wind under the earth to the effects of cold on the body (6.591–5);[107] the broader Lucretian influence on *Natural Questions* 6 may extend to Seneca's similar use of the body analogy as a way of domesticating earthquake. The comparison is introduced early ("these things [sc. the heavens and earth] rage not on command, but they are disturbed by certain defects, *just as our bodies are*," 6.3.1), and it recurs with a notable frequency throughout the book (cf. 6.10.2, 14.1–2, 18.6, 24.4); but it comes into its own after Seneca has led us through

---

103. *N.Q.* 6.13.2–4 = fr. 89 Wehrli (1950) 28–29; on the difficulty of determining where Strato's reported speech ends in the Senecan text, Hine (2010a) 222–23. As in the case of Archelaus in 6.12, Seneca is our sole authority for Strato's theory, whence Setaioli (1988) 408 infers that the theory is here derived not from the doxographical tradition, but from the principle source, now lost, on which Seneca drew in Book 6.

104. See Lee (1952) 82 n. *b* with Gilbert (1907) 196, and cf. Chapter Four, Section IV (D) n. 74.

105. Something of a commonplace in the ancient scientific tradition; cf. 4a.2.26 (of Oenopides of Chios) with Chapter Three, Section VII, Aristot. *Mete.* 1.12 348b2–8 with Vottero (1989) 611 n. 6.

106. See already Chapter Two, Section III n. 30.

107. On the linkage between Lucretius and Aristotle here, Garani (2007) 133–35.

the progressive stages, traced in sections (B) and (C) above, of our inferential journey *ex oculis ad rationem*. So, at 6.14.1, it is applied with impressive elaboration: there, Seneca attributes to an unnamed constituency (*Sunt qui existimant*...) that presumably includes the Stoics[108] the view that air and water function within the earth as blood and air do within a healthy body.[109] Any disruption to the regular flow of these properties in the earth or body leads to equivalent kinds of tremor; hence earthquake at 6.14.3–4. The analogy is not without weakness here,[110] but it nevertheless contributes to a familiar refrain in Book 6 as a whole. Against this background, the (Stoic) theory of vital air that Seneca accepts in 6.16–18 as *the* cause of earthquakes naturally complements, and gains impetus from, the book's broader presumption of a living cosmos.

At a literary level, the air has already begun to show signs of life earlier in Seneca's inventory—a development for which his vitalizing portrayal of air and wind in Book 5 has already prepared us. So at 6.9.1 fire rages as if with animate force (*hic ipse in obuia incurrit exitum quaerens, ac diuellit repugnantia*...),[111] while at 6.12.1–2 Seneca's account of Archelaus' theory (in Archelaus' reported voice) shows a poetic coloring that gives distinctive personality to the compressed air that rages below ground:

> uenti in *concaua* terrarum deferuntur. deinde, ubi omnia spatia iam plena sunt, et in quantum potuit aër *densatus est*, is qui superuenit spiritus priorem premit et *elidit*, ac frequentibus plagis primum cogit, deinde *proturbat*; tum ille *quaerens* locum omnes angustias dimouet, et *claustra* sua *conatur* effringere. sic euenit ut terrae spiritu *luctante* et *fugam quaerente* moueantur.

> Winds are carried down into cavities in the earth. Then, when all the spaces are full, and the air has been condensed to the fullest extent possible, the air which comes in on top of it compresses the air that was there first and moves it forcibly, first packing it together with repeated blows and then driving it forward. Then, seeking room, that air parts all the crowded spaces and tries to break out of its enclosure. So it happens that the earth quakes when the air struggles in its search for escape.

---

108. See Vottero (1989) 613 n. 1.

109. Cf. especially Chapter Five, Section III and n. 80.

110. If the analogy is pressed too closely, how to account for the fact that an earthquake is localized, the body's trembling total? Cf. Lloyd (1966) 362 on Aristot. *Mete.* 2.8 366b14–22 (one of Aristotle's "less happy" analogies); Althoff (1997) 102.

111. "This fire, seeking a way out, runs against anything in its path and tears apart anything that resists it." For *quaero* of natural forces, cf. 6.12.2 with *OLD* 1a, including Lucr. 5.519–20 *aetheris aestus/ quaerentes...uiam*.

Beyond the enlivening poetic language here,[112] such terms as *quaerens/-ente, conatur* and *luctante* of the wind contribute to a personifying trend that is still more explicit in Seneca's report of Strato's theory (6.13.4–5, heat and cold in mutual reaction to each other):

> fugiens ergo et omni modo *cupiens* excedere proxima quaeque remolitur ac iactat. ideoque antequam terra moueatur solet mugitus audiri, uentis in abdito tumultuantibus. (nec enim aliter posset, ut ait Vergilius noster, 'sub pedibus mugire solum et iuga celsa moueri', nisi hoc esset uentorum opus.)

> Therefore, the air in its flight [i.e., warm air retreating before cold, or vice versa], desiring to escape at all costs, pushes back and hurls aside all that is in its immediate vicinity. And so, before an earthquake happens, a rumbling sound is usually heard from winds that are causing a commotion underground (for, as our Virgil says, in no other way could "the ground rumble beneath our feet and the high ridges move," unless this were the work of the winds).

The personifying emphasis is most directly felt in *cupiens*, but it is present throughout the passage, where the various poetic resonances[113] culminate in a quotation from *Aeneid* 6[114] that is part of a broader Virgilian presence in *Natural Questions* 6.[115]

---

112. At the risk of oversimplifying the complexities of detecting or defining poeticism in Senecan prose (see now Hine [2005a]): so *concauus* of rocks, caves, etc. (cf. 6.20.1), Cic. *N.D.* 2.98 but then predominantly poetic (*TLL* 4 6.22–32); *denso* of air, etc., Livian and then found in Seneca, Columella and the elder Pliny but otherwise in verse (*TLL* 5.1 544.50–69); *elido* of natural phenomena, poetic and in Senecan prose and the elder Pliny (examples applied to μετέωρα, *terrena* and *liquida* at *TLL* 5.2 371.17–40); *proturbo* of inanimate things, only verse examples at *OLD* 1a; *quaero* of natural forces, apparently not before Lucr. 5.520 (cf. n. 111 above); *claustra* of winds in verse (*TLL* 3 1320.74–80); *luctor* of air/wind is Senecan after Virg. *Aen.* 1.53 (*TLL* 7.2 1733.9–20), as is *fuga* (cf. *Georg.* 3.201, *Aen.* 1.137; *TLL* 6.1 1467.77–81). Poetic allusion of this sort generates atmospheric sound, as if lending special aural effect to Seneca's treatment of the given physical phenomenon (cf. on this point Chapter Eight, Section III (B) n. 49).

113. So *fugio* of winds in verse before Seneca, *TLL* 6.1 1482.61–7; so also *cupio*, *TLL* 4 1434.73–1435.5; *mugitus* of inanimate things, Cic. *Diu.* 1.35 and then in verse before Seneca (*TLL* 8 1560.71–1561.7); for poetic *mugire*, *TLL* 8 1559.26–53 with De Vivo (1992a) 60 n. 41.

114. 6.256, in fact modified here, *celsa* for *coepta*, the change surely not due just to a lapse of memory (cf. Timpanaro [1984] 172 with De Vivo [1992a] 59), but designed to relate both infinitives, *mugire* and *moueri*, to *posset*. Seneca pointedly reapplies the Virgilian line to his own rationalistic ends, divesting it of all its mythopoetic significance in the original context, where Virgil anticipates the imminent arrival of Hecate (cf. *aduentante dea*, 6.258) before Aeneas descends to the underworld.

115. In general, De Vivo (1992a) 49–74.

So, at 6.17.1, the air that has been brought to life as a pervasive vital force in 6.16 is seen to rage, when its free movement is restricted, "like the 'river Araxes raging at its bridge'" (*non aliter quam ille "pontem indignatus Araxes"*; the quoted words are from *Aen.* 8.728). Seneca goes on to develop the river analogy in his extended description (6.17.2) of the parallel violence of water and air when the free flow of each is obstructed; if the analogy there offers its own suggestive re-enactment of the interchangeability of the Stoic elements,[116] it also supports the case made elsewhere in Book 6 for water and air as optional causes of earthquake (cf. 6.7.6, 20.1–2). More important for now, however, at 6.17.1 Seneca echoes not just a Virgilian line but also a Virgilian personification in its own right: on the Shield of Aeneas such peoples as the African *Nomades* and the Scythian *Geloni* and *Dahae* (8.724–5, 728) illustrate the extent of Augustus' global conquests—a picture varied by the equal submission of the Armenian Araxes, the Euphrates and the Rhine (8.726–8) and of the peoples they symbolically represent.[117] The enlivening effect of air compared to raging water at 6.17.1 is compounded by the personifying emphasis, surely recalled by Seneca, that is *already* in the Virgilian intertext—a subtlety of response to Virgil that is matched elsewhere in Book 6. So in 6.18 his appeal to the Aeolus scene in *Aeneid* 1 may seem innocent enough when (6.18.2) air entrapped under the earth is said to "rage around its prison with a mighty rumbling from the mountain" (*"magno cum murmure montis / circum claustra fremit"*).[118] But when Seneca revisits the Aeolus scene at 6.18.4–5, he strikes a rather different pose in gently "correcting" Virgil:

> spiritus uero inuicta res est: nihil erit quod
>   luctantes uentos tempestatesque sonoras
>   imperio premat ac uinclis et carcere frenet.
> sine dubio poetae hunc uoluerunt uideri carcerem in quo sub terra clusi laterent, sed hoc non intellexerunt, nec id quod clusum est esse adhuc uentum, nec id quod uentus est posse iam cludi.

> Moving air is indeed an unconquerable force. There will be nothing
>   to repress by command or restrain by chain or prison the winds
>   when they struggle and the storms when they resound.

---

116. Cf. Chapter One, Section I.

117. Cf. Quint. *Inst.* 8.6.11 on the bold sublimity of Virgil's personifying *indignatus*, with De Vivo (1992a) 56.

118. *Aen.* 1.55–6, albeit in fact *fremunt* [sc. *uenti*] in Virgil. On 6.18 in connection with the personification of winds in the *Aetna*, see Garani (2009) 108–11.

The poets doubtless wanted this place where the winds are shut in underground to be thought of as a prison. But they failed to realize that what is shut in is not yet a wind, and that which is wind cannot be shut in.

In quoting *Aeneid* 1.53–54 here, Seneca significantly modifies the mood and subject of the verbs *premo* and *freno* in the original, replacing Virgil's *Aeolus...premit ac...frenat* with *nihil erit quod...premat ac...frenet* and countering poetic fiction with (his version of) the prosaic, seismological reality. A rather contrived and indulgent assertion of his rigor as a researcher, perhaps, and of his unwavering commitment to *ratio*; but in "correcting" Virgil here, he nevertheless sustains his broader effort in 6.16–18 to bring the air fully to life, giving the wind a spiritedness that even Aeolus would be powerless to control.

　　Through his borrowings from the *Aeneid*, then, Seneca channels the Virgilian animation of air and wind into his own elaboration in 6.16–18 of the (Stoic) theory of air as a vital, and here notably vitalized, unifying principle at both the micro- and macrocosmic levels. At 6.16.1 the air gives unity and coherence to individual world parts through the tension that holds all things together, from the world as a whole to the tiniest object within it; and it also has a universal function as "a sustaining and invigorating force that nourishes everything" (*illo* [sc. *spiritu*]...*uitali et uegeto et alente omnia*), the subterranean air nurturing trees and plants (cf. Cic. *N.D.* 2.83) even as the earth's exhalations provide nourishment (*alimentum, pastus*) for the heavenly bodies in the firmament as a whole (*totum hoc caelum*, 6.16.2).[119] Seneca steers his specific argument here, that "it is obvious that the earth is not without air" (6.16.1), in this universal direction to convey the vastness of the amount of air that the earth must be able to generate and store within itself (6.16.3)—air whose restlessness causes earthquakes (6.16.4). But beyond his localized argument, his elaborations on air as a universal connector also support the integrated worldview that is promoted more generally in the *Natural Questions*. Our arrival at this unifying perspective—this *complete* grasp of nature, here enacting the positive aspect of the sublime that we witnessed earlier—marks the culmination point of our progress through stages of increasingly abstract argument that detach us from the visual shock and apparent inexplicability ("Why here? Why now? Why us?") of the Campanian disaster; for by colorfully bringing air to life[120] and by stressing its unifying pervasiveness, Seneca diverts our focus from the particular earthquake to the vast living system of which it is but a functional part and side effect.

---

119. For this holistic vision, cf. Chapter Two, Section III on *aer* as both part and sustaining material of the universe at 2.3–6.

120. Culminating in 6.16 in the personifying touch at the end of §4: "nothing is as restless as air, as shifting and delighting [*gaudens*] in its agitated movement" (*gaudeo* "poet., of things," *OLD* 2; further, De Vivo [1992a] 57).

(E) Elemental Interchangeability Revisited

As part of Seneca's strategy of indulgently reporting even those early theories of earthquake of which he disapproves (cf. 6.19.1), and perhaps implicitly as a measure of the broader Lucretian influence on Book 6 and of his own wide-ranging control over seismological theory generally, he advances his inventory in 6.19–20 by turning to the atomist tradition and to the theories of Metrodorus of Chios,[121] Democritus and Epicurus. This section offers a recapitulation of sorts of certain emphases that we have already witnessed earlier in the inventory. So, in 6.19.2, we return to inferential analogy of the sort sampled in 6.10–11: just as air in a jar vibrates from the action of sound upon it, so Metrodorus extrapolates the cause of earthquake from subterranean air agitated by the action of other air falling upon it from above.[122] Within Seneca's larger ordering of his inventory, this theory appears one-dimensional and unnecessarily restricted in scope, at least in comparison with the variable causes ascribed to Democritus, who "says that an earthquake is produced sometimes by air, sometimes by water, sometimes by both" (6.20.1). Seneca here departs from Aristotle, who limits the Democritean cause of earthquakes to water (*Mete.* 2.7 365b1–6; cf. *N.Q.* 6.20.2–3). True, the two positions, Senecan and Aristotelian, may not in fact be irreconcilable, given that "*N.Q.* 6.20.4 suggests that *spiritus* had but a subordinate part in Democritus' earthquake theory: if so, Aristotle may have thought it not worth mentioning."[123] But if we take it that Seneca rightly includes air in the Democritean theory, he may yet exaggerate the importance of that *spiritus*, and not just because he finesses his evidence in his desire to include thinkers who attribute earthquakes to multiple elemental causation (cf. 6.5.1, 20.2). A further possibility, I propose, is that, after the progress made earlier in Book 6 from the segregated analysis of individual elements toward the integrative, holistic viewpoint of 6.16, he briefly restages that integrating vision in 6.19–20. So, at 6.20.2, he smoothly relates air and water as cognate causes of earthquake ("We must yet speak of water in the way that we spoke about air"); and that dyad of air and water is significantly placed in his continuing argument, preparing the way as it does for his implication of all four elements in his coverage of the Epicurean theory of earthquake at 6.20.5–7.

---

121. Although a later follower of Democritus, Metrodorus is introduced at 6.19.1 before Democritus. For Metrodorus, see conveniently Brunschwig (1999) 237–39.

122. For Metrodorus' theory, cf. Aet. *Plac.* 3.15.6 (*DG* p. 380) = D-K 70A21—an account so distant from *N.Q.* 6.19 that, for Setaioli (1988) 409, Seneca can hardly have drawn on that doxographical tradition.

123. Hall (1977) 430. 6.20.1–4 = D-K 68A98 = Graham (2010) 1.558–61 Text 79.

But Seneca apparently misrepresents Epicurus in point of detail. Epicurus himself singles out air and earth among "many other" possible causes in his *Letter to Pythocles* (§§105–6), while Lucretius refers to water, earth and especially air but omits fire in his coverage of earthquakes at 6.535–607.[124] Seneca seemingly imports his own emphasis in embracing all four of the elements at 6.20.5–7,[125] a maneuver by which he restates in summary, as it were, the unifying equivalence of the elements as drawn earlier in the book. Despite this equalizing tendency, however, the Stoic and Epicurean schools are united (6.20.7–21.1) in giving priority to air as the primary cause. At 6.21.1 air is also characterized as the primary element, an agent that arouses fire, sets water in motion and moves the earth and is therefore an unsurpassed force of nature ("Nothing in nature is more powerful than air, nothing more vigorous"); and its special force is underscored by Seneca's marked use of *spiritus* for air in Book 6 generally. Here, the loaded connotation of *spiritus* that we observed in Book 5, to the effect of air as a specially vital and vitalizing force, comes into its own;[126] the word occurs some fifty-five times in Book 6, a frequency conspicuously greater than in any previous book and later rivaled only in Book 2.[127] At 6.21, this climactic point in Seneca's inventory, this vital *spiritus* stands alone not just as his preferred cause of earthquake but also as the supreme force of cosmic cohesion—the symbolic embodiment and connecting principle of the one-world viewpoint that has gradually taken shape from 6.4 onward.

(F) The Normalization of Seismic Experience

According to Seneca, Posidonius distinguished two kinds of earthquake,[128] one a jolting from beneath (*succussio*) as a consequence of the collapse of subterranean rock,[129] the other a tilt (*inclinatio*) that Seneca attributes to the pressure of air entrapped below ground.[130] In adding to the Posidonian scheme a third category,

---

124. Further, Bollack (1978) 328–35.

125. On this point, Setaioli (1988) 411–12.

126. Cf. Chapter Five, Section III.

127. For a full listing of occurrences, Chapter Five, Section III and n. 76.

128. 6.21.2 = fr. 230 E-K with Kidd (1988) 816–20; further, Gilbert (1907) 315–20; Traglia (1955) 748–49; Waldherr (1997) 59–63.

129. So at least Asclepiodotus, Posidonius' pupil, as reported at 6.22.2–4.

130. So 6.23.1. Cf. Posid. fr. 12 E-K (= D. L. 7.154) for a Posidonian classification of four kinds of earthquake, with Ringshausen (1929) 19–30 and Kidd (1988) 817–19 for discussion of the types. Kidd 817–18 identifies Diogenes'/Posidonius' βρασματίας with Seneca's *succussio*, κλιματίας with *inclinatio*. For Kidd 818, moreover, "Diogenes may preserve a combination of two classifications," one "based on distinguishing vertical and horizontal earthquakes"—a distinction seemingly reflected in Seneca's *succussio*/*inclinatio* (see already Steinmetz [1962] on the compatibility of Seneca's and Diogenes' reports).

that of vibration (*tremor*, 6.21.2), apparently his own contribution,[131] Seneca would seem to be making accommodation for the Campanian disaster, given that "Campania did stop experiencing continual tremors [*tremere*]" (6.31.1). For present purposes, however, his classification of types of earthquake is one of several normalizing techniques that he deploys late in Book 6 to portray the Campanian event as no exception to a standardized template for all such occurrences. So, at 6.1.13, he achieves a similar effect by visiting equal or worse disasters at Tyre and in Asia, Achaea and Macedonia,[132] all of which serve to generalize the singular Campanian experience. Our world tour later recommences with visits to Atalante and Sidon (6.24.6);[133] Chalcis and Aegium, Helice and Buris (6.25.4);[134] and Paphos and Nicopolis, Cyprus and Tyre (6.26.4).[135] But for now Egypt is our destination.

After our experience of Egypt's wonders in Book 4a, another apparently beckons in the tradition that Egypt is unaffected by earthquakes:

Poteram ad hoc probandum abuti auctoritate magnorum uirorum qui Aegypton numquam tremuisse tradunt.

6.26.1

To prove this [sc. that an earthquake extends over an area equal to the extent of a cavity below ground], I could have exploited the authority of distinguished men who report that Egypt has never had an earthquake.

---

131. Cf. Kidd (1988) 818. With *tremor* Seneca also revives the body analogy (cf. *corpora... tremunt*, 6.18.6; *nullus est tremor corpori*, 6.18.7; 24.4).

132. Cf. *Letters* 91.9. Further, Vottero (1989) 582–84 nn. 26 (Tyre), 27 (including Tac. *Ann.* 2.47.1–4 on Asia in 17 CE); Guidoboni et al. (1994) 180–85 for Asia in 17 CE (no. 79 in their catalogue) and p. 195 for Achaea (no. 93) and Macedonia (no. 94) in 61 CE.

133. Cf. Thuc. 3.89.3 (Guidoboni et al. [1994] 119–22 no. 14): in 426 BCE a tidal wave produced by an earthquake did limited damage at Atalante, far less than in Seneca's version. "Did he misremember, or take the reference from someone else?" (Kidd [1988] 823 on fr. 232 E-K); or did he dramatically enhance the given fact for effect? Sidon: after Atalante, Seneca's "Believe Posidonius that the same thing happened at Sidon" (6.24.6 = fr. 232.3 E-K) implies another tidal wave, but from Strab. 1.3.16 (= Posid. fr. 231 E-K) it appears that a genuine earthquake did indeed strike Sidon (in *ca.* 197 BCE?); see Kidd 821–22 with Guidoboni et al. 145 no. 39.

134. Chalcis (cf. 6.17.3), *ca.* 197 BCE(?): Vottero (1989) 620 n. 4 with Guidoboni et al. (1994) 145–47 no. 40. Aegium, 23 CE(?): Guidoboni et al. 186 no. 81. Helice and Buris (cf. 6.23.4, 26.3, 32.8, 7.5.3-4, 16.2), 373–72 BCE: Vottero 634–35 n. 8 with Guidoboni et al. 128–32 no. 24 and Lafond (1998).

135. Paphos on Cyprus (cf. *Letters* 91.9), 17 BCE: Guidoboni et al. (1994) 177 no. 74; given *iam* ("*already* familiar with this kind of disaster," so soon after its foundation), Nicopolis presumably of Epirus, founded by Octavian as a victory city after Actium (cf. Suet. *Aug.* 18.2). Cyprus generally: cf. for post-Senecan reports Guidoboni et al. 214 no. 101 (77 CE), 246, 247, 249 nos. 132, 136, 140 (earthquakes in Cyprian Salamis in 293–306 CE, 332, 342); 277 no. 157 (*ca.* 370 CE). For Tyre, 6.1.13 and n. 132 above in this chapter.

The rich, muddy soil that Egypt derived from the Nile was allegedly so compacted that no empty spaces could exist below ground (6.26.1; cf. 4a.2.9–10). Egypt would thus seem to support Seneca's argument that an earthquake presupposes the existence of a subterranean cavity—*if only it were actually true that Egypt had never experienced a quake* ("But Egypt does have earthquakes," 6.26.2).[136] Seneca partly reinforces his pose as a scrupulous researcher by manifestly not misusing (cf. *abuti*) the authority of his sources to advance his own agenda (i.e., exploiting the claim that Egypt has never had an earthquake to push the subterranean cavity theory). More importantly, however, by rejecting the tradition that Egypt was earthquake-free, Seneca reinforces the essential normalizing point that *no* place is not at risk: "All regions lie subject to the same laws, and nature has created nothing to be immobile" (6.1.12). There can be no exceptions to the generalizing rule, no *mira*: hence his resistance also to claims that Delos never experienced earthquakes.[137] In a *prosodion* to the island, Pindar casts Delos as "unmoved marvel of the broad earth" (χθονὸς εὐρεί/-ας ἀκίνητον τέρας),[138] a characterization seemingly shared by Virgil:

> Sed mouetur … Delos, quam Vergilius stare iussit: '*inmotam*que coli dedit et contemnere uentos'; hanc philosophi quoque, credula natio, dixerunt non moueri auctore Pindaro.
>
> 6.26.2

But Delos does have earthquakes—Delos, which Virgil ordered to stand motionless: "and he [sc. Apollo] arranged for it to be inhabited, *a land without earthquakes*, and to scorn the winds" [*Aen.* 3.77]. Philosophers, too, a credulous race, have said on Pindar's authority that Delos is free of earthquakes.

---

136. Cf. Plin. *Nat.* 2.195 *Galliae et Aegyptus minime quatiuntur*. For an overview of Egypt's confirmed seismicity, see Degg (1990), especially 300, with Guidoboni et al. (1994) 87–90 and Waldherr (1997) 44 ("Ägypten weist dagegen eine sehr niedrige Erdbebenfrequenz auf"). But there *is* an interesting spread of occurrences: according to Badawy (1999), of the eighty-three earthquakes reported for the period from 2200 BCE to 1899 CE, only seven belong to the period BCE; in his catalogue, Sieberg (1932) 187–89 lists fifty-five occurrences from 2200 BCE to 1926 CE, only six of them BCE. The historical record may be incomplete, but "[t]he absence of past seismicity in the Libyan desert, much of Egypt and the Sudan, as well as central Arabia, seems to be confirmed by the short-term instrumental record [based on twentieth-century data], suggesting it is not purely a function of a dearth of sources of information" (Ambraseys et al. [1994] 158).

137. For ancient allusions to Delos' alleged resistance to earthquakes, see Barchiesi (1994) 440–41 and n. 15; Lapini (1995) 183–84; Nishimura-Jensen (2000) 289 n. 6. But for collected testimony of earthquakes there, Guidoboni et al. (1994) 109–11 no. 4 (*ca.* 490 BCE), 117–18 no. 11 (shortly before 431 BCE), 128 no. 23 (shortly before 373 BCE), 171 no. 66 (*ca.* mid-first century BCE), 188–89 no. 86 (*ca.* 47 CE).

138. Fr. 33c 3–4 Snell-Maehler. But for ἀκίνητον τέρας interpreted figuratively as "fixed *star* of the earth," Lapini (1995) 194–95.

But whereas Seneca's Delos is here *inmota* in one sense ("without earthquakes"), a very different sense prevails in the original Virgilian *sedes*, where Apollo granted that Delos should no longer wander afloat but remain fixed (*inmotam*) in its location.[139] In wittily modifying the Virgilian sense at 6.26.2 and pointedly emphasizing Virgil's authorial will (*stare iussit*), Seneca again targets "la poesia mitologica"[140] as a source of unscientific misinformation that here stands in contrast to his own strivings, apparently free as they are from all fictional embellishment. Even before he turns to Thucydides and Callisthenes for countertestimony that Delos did indeed experience earthquakes,[141] the transparency of his Virgilian distortion surely signals to the knowing reader the fragility of the evidence for a quake-free Delos; and, for the reader who delves deeper, a similar ambiguity in ἀκίνητον ("no longer floating" as opposed to "not shaken by earthquake"?) may equally compromise the Pindaric testimony to which Seneca alludes.[142]

The tremors of Campania are gradually resolved ever further, then, into a normative macrofield of seismic activity. But what of the remaining peculiarities (*mira*) of the Campanian disaster, among them hundreds of sheep found dead (6.27.1, taking up an allusion to the same incident in 6.1.3)? In explaining this phenomenon Seneca again reverts to general principles, countering the rhetoric of *mirum* with "We have said [*diximus*] that a plague usually occurs after a great earthquake, *and this is not surprising*" (6.27.2).[143] But he perhaps achieves a further

---

139. Honor done, of course, because Delos sheltered Apollo when Leto bore him; for the legend, see, e.g., Hom. *H. Ap.* 14–18, Call. *Hymn* 4 (to Delos), especially 51–54, Ov. *Met.* 6.184–91, Stat. *Theb.* 8.197–98, Hygin. *Fab.* 53.2, 140.4 with Williams (1962) 70 on *Aen.* 3.75–6. On Seneca's distortion of Virgil here, Lapini (1995), especially 184–85, 199; cf. also *Ag.* 384–85 for Seneca "assert[ing] independence" (Mayer [1990] 404) by attributing the stabilization to Lucina/Diana, not Apollo.

140. See De Vivo (1992a) 50–53.

141. 6.26.2–3, where the juxtaposition of…*auctore Pindaro. Thucydides ait…*, fiction vs. "truth," is itself telling. At 6.26.3 Callisthenes' voice = *FGH* 124 fr. 19 Jacoby; further on this historian, Aristotle's nephew, see the discussion of 6.23.2–3 in Section VI below in this chapter with Kidd (1988) 797–98, and cf. 7.5.3–5. Thucydides reports at 2.8.3 that Delos first felt an earthquake a little before the outbreak of the Peloponnesian War in 431 BCE, but Herodotus claims at 6.98.1 that the only quake experienced at Delos "down to my time" occurred in 490 BCE. Perhaps a Thucydidean "correction" of Herodotus (so Momigliano [1930] 87–89), unless different earthquakes are contemplated; see for an overview of the problem Hornblower (1991) 245–46 ("I believe there is no factual inconsistency") with Guidoboni et al. (1994) 110 and especially 117–18, and Hine (2002) 63–64.

142. Cf. Sandys (1924) 563 n. 1: "This [sc. Delos no longer a floating island] seems better than the rendering 'unshaken by earthquake'", albeit ἀκίνητον of earthquake-free Delos also at Hdt. 6.98.3.

143. Despite *diximus*, no such statement is found in the extant text; see Hine (2010b) 205 n. 49.

effect in declaring no surprise (cf. *non miror*, 6.27.4) that the sheep were infected by poison from below: their heads close to the ground, the animals feel the full effect of the tainted air, as would humans if the pestilence were not cleared by the abundance of pure air above ground (6.28.2–3).[144] Seneca subsequently returns to the fear aroused by the Campanian earthquake, fear that "shatters minds" even when it is "confined to individuals and is modest," but whose worst effects are felt when it induces public panic (6.29.1). Can we detect in the spread of this contagious *metus* in 6.29 signs of a human pestilence to match that which erupts from below ground in 6.27–8? If the sheep are so vulnerable to the plague at 6.27.4 because their heads are so close to the ground, those most terrorized by panic at 6.29.2 are people of a blinkered, terrestrial mind-set, their lack of perspective and higher insight (such as Seneca aims to promote) making them so vulnerable to every shudder at ground level.

VI: *The* Totum *in Book 6*

When our focus is redirected from the particular to the general, the local effects of the Campanian (or any other) earthquake become inseparable from the universal process—a feature of Seneca's therapeutic repertoire well illustrated by his report of statues being split apart by the quake (6.1.3). He returns to the phenomenon at 6.30.1, using a comparison that may at first seem hyperbolical to an extreme:

Statuam diuisam non miror, cum dixerim montes a montibus recessisse, et ipsum diruptum esse ab imo solum:

> haec loca ui quondam et uasta conuolsa ruina
> (tantum aeui longinqua ualet mutare uetustas)
> dissiluisse ferunt, cum protinus utraque tellus
> una foret. uenit ingenti ui pontus et ingens
> Hesperium Siculo latus abscidit, aruaque et urbes
> aequore diductas angusto interluit aestu.

---

144. For suggestive shades in 6.27–28 of the Lucretian plague (6.1090–1286), again reflecting Lucretius' broader influence on *Natural Questions* 6, see De Vivo (1992a) 96–97; and on 6.27–28 as a *tour de force* of Senecan scientific observation/description, Pisi (1989) 81–93. For the emissions Seneca describes as a sign that "the [Vesuvian] volcano was returning back to life in A.D. 62 and that the earthquake was also related to the volcano," see Sigurdsson (2002) 35, continuing with: "Increased emission of volcanic gases commonly occurs before eruptions, including large quantities of carbon dioxide. Such gases are frequently lethal to livestock, and in Iceland, for example, flocks of sheep are often killed as they wander into pools of the invisible but suffocating carbon dioxide, which, because of its higher density, gathers in depressions and valleys."

I am not surprised that a statue was split apart, since I have described how mountains were detached from mountains, and the ground itself broken apart from the depths:

> These lands, they say, were once split apart, torn by force and vast upheaval
> (such great change can the long process of time effect),
> though from the first both countries were one unbroken stretch.
> The sea came with massive violence, and split the huge Hesperian coast
> from the coast of Sicily; in its narrow tideway it flows between
> the fields and cities that are divided by the sea.

The three modifications that Seneca introduces to *Aen.* 3.414–19 here—*ingenti* for *medio* (whence also the tense change in *uenit* from Virgil's perfect to Seneca's present) and *ingens* for *undis* in 417; *aequore* for *litore* in 419—have been explained on various grounds, among them the pitfalls of citation from memory.[145] But if we allow for a more calculating Senecan intervention here, the repetition of *ingens* in 417 dramatically enhances the already massive Virgilian force that causes the sea to separate Sicily from Italy. An impressive argument *ex maiori exemplo*: lands, cities, houses, statues—all are equally susceptible to the splitting action of earthquakes, a unifying vision underscored partly by the neat encapsulating effect that Seneca achieves by placing *statuam* as the first and last word in the chapter, and partly by his connecting of different world parts through careful verbal overlaps.[146] So, at 6.30.1, the ground is *diruptum...ab imo*, while at 6.30.4 the bronze statue is *diruptum*, at 6.30.5 severed *ab imo ad caput*; in the Virgilian extract at 6.30.1 the fields and cities of Italy/Sicily are separated (*diductas*) by the sea, while at 6.30.4 "we have seen buildings shaken and their corners pulled apart [*diductis...angulis*]"; Sicily is cut away from Italy (*resecta*, 6.30.3), the statue cut in two (*sectam*) at 6.30.5.[147]

145. So Vottero (1989) 650 n. 3; more broadly on the question, De Vivo (1992a) 72–73. *ingens* is a favored Virgilian word: for that predilection (the word occurs some 158 times in the *Aeneid*, or once every fifty-eight lines), see Mackail (1912) with Austin (1955) 49 on *Aen.* 4.89, and cf. the inimitable note in Henry (1881) 3.40: "Not only the whole body, the *integrum corpus*, but parts and sections of bodies, no matter whether of men or animals, no matter whether alive or dead, hands, horns, mouths, eyes, beards, breasts, ring the bell for *Ingens*, as 10.446." Through sonorous repetition of the word at 6.30.1, does Seneca draw attention, whether consciously or unconsciously, innocently or wittily, to the Virgilian predilection? Or might we detect through such repetition "[u]n caso...di 'Pathetisierung' inconscia" (Timpanaro [1984] 176–77)?

146. On the following overlaps, De Vivo (1992a) 71–72.

147. *resecta* Gercke (1907) 230.5 after Gronovius, and evidently accepted by De Vivo (1992a) 71; but the play with *secta* is lost if *reiecta* is read with Hine (1996a) 275.878 and most modern editors (further, Vottero [1989] 192).

We thus revert, partly through these verbal bindings, to the all-important *totum*. Already at 6.30.2 Seneca explains the astounding force of earthquakes by reference to the *totum*:

> quorum mira ut ex toto uis est: quamuis enim parte saeuiat, mundi tamen uiribus saeuit.
>
> Their strength is astonishing, since it comes from the whole universe; for although it rages only in one part, it nevertheless rages with the world's force.

The relation drawn here between *pars* and *totum* is emblematic of the mind-set that Seneca's broader treatment of earthquakes in Book 6 has inculcated in us; and it is this grasp of the totality, I propose, that contributes fundamentally to the strength of mind (*robur*) that Seneca claims to derive *a contemplatione naturae* in his closing chapter (6.32). It is this breadth of vision that represents true world possession, as opposed to the false ownership that characterizes Alexander the Great at 6.23.2–3. There, Seneca would seem to pay remarkable tribute to the historian Callisthenes:[148]

> fuit enim illi nobile ingenium et furibundi regis inpatiens. hic est Alexandri crimen aeternum, quod nulla uirtus, nulla bellorum felicitas redimet; nam quotiens quis dixerit, 'occidit Persarum multa milia,' opponetur ei Callisthenes;[149] quotiens dictum erit, 'occidit Darium, penes quem tunc maximum regnum erat,' opponetur ei Callisthenes; quotiens dictum erit, 'omnia oceano tenus uicit, ipsum quoque temptauit nouis classibus et imperium ex angulo Thraciae usque ad orientis terminos protulit,' dicetur, 'sed Callisthenem occidit'. omnia licet antiqua ducum regumque exempla transierit, ex his quae fecit nihil tam magnum erit quam <hoc>[150] scelus.
>
> For he had an outstanding intelligence that did not submit to the rage of his king. The murder of Callisthenes is an everlasting accusation against Alexander, for which no virtue, no success in war will atone. For whenever someone says "Alexander killed many thousands of Persians," Callisthenes

---

148. For whom see Section V n. 141 above in this chapter.

149. But *opponetur ei "et Callisthenen"* is read here and below by most modern editors before Hine with manuscripts in the δ branch (see Hine [1996a] xiii)—perhaps rightly if, with Parroni (2001) 153, Hine's reading is seen to reduce the dramatic effect of the passage (with possible autobiographical overtones; see n. 151 below).

150. For which Hine (1996b) 107, albeit there proposed with hesitation ("If we need a demonstrative with *scelus*"), and not printed at (1996a) 265.699.

will be raised in retort to him. Whenever it is said "Alexander killed Darius, who oversaw the greatest kingdom at that time," Callisthenes will be raised in retort to him. Whenever it is said "He conquered everything all the way to the ocean, and even made an attempt on the ocean itself with ships unknown to that water, and he extended his empire from a corner of Thrace right up to the furthest limits of the east," it will be said: "But he killed Callisthenes." Although he exceeded all the achievements in antiquity of generals and kings, of all that he did, nothing will be as great as this crime.

Why this sudden, extraordinary outburst of praise for Callisthenes, seemingly the only instance in the *Natural Questions* where Seneca embarks on a digressive eulogy of one of his author-sources? Hints of a coded anti-Neronian significance have been detected here,[151] while Alexander's portrayal as a predatory conqueror also reinforces his broader characterization in the *Natural Questions* and elsewhere in the Senecan corpus.[152] But given Callisthenes' historical investigations into the cause of the inundations that buried Helice and Buris (6.23.4; cf. 6.26.3), and given the nature and extent of his writings, including a ten-book *Hellenika* covering the period 386–356 BCE, his different form of world exploration and probing into nature is perhaps set in salutary contrast to Alexander's destructive grip on the world that (so briefly) submits to him. Moreover, in 327 BCE, in an incident that led to his being falsely implicated in a conspiracy against Alexander and subsequently executed, Callisthenes apparently resisted Alexander's efforts to impose on Macedonians and Greeks *proskynesis* (the prostration of an inferior before his superior) after the style of the Persian court: "The man's influential bearing and his ready outspokenness [*prompta libertas*] were hateful to the king, as if that man alone checked the Macedonians' willingness to show that kind of subservience" (Curt. 8.5.13).[153] If this reputation for brave independence is recalled at 6.23.2 *nobile ingenium et furibundi regis inpatiens*, his *libertas* offers an attractive paradigm for the fearless independence of outlook that achieves that ultimate goal and refuge in *Natural Questions* 6, contempt for life (cf. 6.32.4: "A man's life is an insignificant thing, but contempt for life an immense thing").

---

151. So Lana (1955) 15: Seneca's digression is explicable only if Seneca means to represent himself in Callisthenes, Nero in Alexander. Further, Wallace-Hadrill (2003) 188 and n. 26; Gauly (2004) 204–206; Hine (2006) 64.

152. Cf. Chapter One, Section III and n. 44; Chapter Five, Section V and n. 150.

153. Cf. 8.8.21, Arr. *Anab.* 4.12, D. L. 5.5, Justin. *Epit. Hist. Phil.* 15.3.3–7 with Spencer (2002) 136–37 and 238 n. 22.

VII: *The Campanian Earthquake in Perspective*

The radical shift of perspective that *Natural Questions* 6 has promoted thus far, fortifying us against trauma at the local level by centering our existence in the cosmic whole, culminates in Seneca's final, liberating revision of the significance of death: "Death itself is no great thing" (*ipsum perire non magnum est*, 6.32.5). In contrast to Alexander, that ephemeral conqueror, the enlightened mind achieves a world mastery that embraces all parts, sea, sky and earth, at 6.32.4:

> hanc [sc. animam] qui contempsit *securus* uidebit maria turbari, etiamsi illa omnes excitauerunt uenti, etiamsi aestus aliqua perturbatione mundi totum in terras uertet oceanum. *securus* aspiciet fulminantis caeli trucem atque horridam faciem, frangatur licet caelum et ignes suos in exitium omnium, in primis suum, misceat. *securus* aspiciet ruptis compagibus dehiscens solum, illa licet inferorum regna retegantur. stabit super illam uoraginem *intrepidus*, et fortasse quo debebit cadere desiliet.
>
> Anyone who regards life with contempt will look *with easy mind* on the seas in their disturbance, even if all the winds have stirred them up, and even if the tide turns the entire ocean against the land through some upheaval of the world order. *With easy mind* he will look upon the cruel, dreadful sight of the thundering heavens, even if the firmament is breaking apart and blending its own fires for the destruction of everything, beginning with itself. *With easy mind* he will look upon the ground gaping open with its framework broken, even if the realms of the dead are exposed to view. He will stand *undaunted* at the edge of that abyss, and perhaps he will leap in where he must inevitably fall.

Such a man, we might surmise, is Callisthenes. Such a man serenely embraces the rage of nature in the cataclysm at the end of Book 3, rather than succumbing to it with stupefied terror (cf. 3.27.12). Such a man achieves a *securitas* very different from that state of passive resignation—*ex desperatione securitas*—featured in 6.2.1. In his complete grasp of nature and his fearless superiority over all that she throws against him, such a man embodies the Lucretian/Senecan sublimity of thought that transports the mind beyond conventional human vulnerability: "[t]he sublime reader or spectator feels that he overcomes the limitations of his inert, passive forces by overcoming the discomfort of inferiority, by trying to adapt his consciousness to a greatness that transcends passive experience" so that he instead takes on "the agonistic attitude."[154] Given

---

154. Conte (1994) 23.

Lucretius' widespread presence elsewhere in Book 6, this sublimity of response to the Campanian earthquake may be markedly Lucretian in color; but Seneca elsewhere delineates a like mind-set without obvious connection to Lucretius. So in *Letters* 41, for example, on the effect of "the god within us" (cf. *prope est a te deus, tecum est, intus est*, 41.1), that divine presence inspires a sublime-like transcendence:

> si hominem uideris interritum periculis, intactum cupiditatibus, inter aduersa felicem, in mediis tempestatibus placidum, ex superiore loco homines uidentem, ex aequo deos, non subibit te ueneratio eius? non dices, 'ista res maior est altiorque quam ut credi similis huic in quo est corpusculo possit'? uis isto diuina descendit; animum excellentem, moderatum, omnia tamquam minora transeuntem, quidquid timemus optamusque ridentem, caelestis potentia agitat.
>
>   41.4–5

> If you see a man who is undaunted amid dangers, untouched by desires, happy in adversity and calm in the midst of storms, a man who looks down upon mankind from a higher elevation and views the gods on an equal footing, will not a feeling of reverence for him come upon you? Will you not say: "That quality is too great and too lofty to be thought of as resembling this petty body in which it resides." A divine power has descended on that man; a heavenly force stirs the soul that rises above the ordinary and, tempered, passes over all conventional experiences as if they were of little account, and laughs at whatever we fear or desire.

The transcendent perspective from which the Campanian disaster is normalized in *Natural Questions* 6 is no sudden innovation within the Senecan therapeutic armory, but another version of the *megalophrosyne*, the mental grandeur, that elevates the sublime *sapiens* across his corpus.

  If we finally look back on Seneca's therapeutic program in *Natural Questions* 6 as a whole, the book is perhaps concerned not so much with earthquakes *per se* but with traumatic experience more generally. True, "[e]arth tremors and earthquakes were a regular feature of life in the mainland and islands of Greece and Italy, and in Asia Minor: few adults in these regions can have been without some experience of at least minor tremors and minor damage."[155] But beyond this topical relevance of Book 6, the protections that Seneca offers against fear of earthquakes, normalizing such phenomena by casting them as but ordinary aspects of

---

155. Hine (2002) 58.

cosmic functioning, are themselves versatile in their applicability to so many other of life's stresses and tremors. And so as we progress in Book 6 *ex oculis ad rationem*, we might also find ourselves transported from a literal to a more nuanced and figurative view of earthquakes, which themselves offer a powerfully suggestive metaphor here for any significant disaster or affliction, public or private, physical or psychological, that destabilizes life: the normalizing techniques that Seneca uses to ease the particular trauma here are transferable to so many other aspects of our existence.

If, then, we approach Book 6 purely as an exercise in earthquake relief, we may indeed find in it "a peculiar comfort. Where (one might wonder) is the remedy in being told that dangers are actually more widespread than we might have thought (VI 2.1)?"[156] But as we begin to reconcile Book 6 with the mind-expanding process that gradually unfolds in the *Natural Questions* more generally, the point of "being told that dangers are actually more widespread than we might have thought" may strike us differently, especially if it causes us to turn our gaze from the aggravating *unum* and to focus instead on the alleviating *totum*.

---

156. Inwood (2000) 33, and then (2002) 138 = (2005) 179, adding in mitigation Stoic appeal "to a rational person" ([2002] 138 n. 41 = [2005] 179 n. 40), whence "Seneca is, I suspect, aware that this consideration will provide cold comfort to many." Inwood then mitigates that coldness of comfort by positing Seneca's recognition of "a dual audience: *prudentes* will be freed from fear by the use of reason, and the *imperiti*, those not trained in philosophy, will find comfort in the abandonment of (false) hopes" ([2000] 33 and [2002] 138 = [2005] 180). Cf. for this dual audience Limburg (2007) 314 as cited in Section IV above in this chapter.

Seneca on Comets and Ancient Cometary Theory

During many centuries [comets] gave rise to the direst superstition and fanaticism. The records of every nation are full of these. The Chaldeans alone among the ancient nations seem to have regarded comets without fear, and to have thought them bodies wandering as harmless as fishes in the sea; the Pythagoreans alone among philosophers seem to have had a vague idea of them as bodies returning at fixed periods of time; and in all antiquity, so far as is known, one man alone—Seneca—had the scientific instinct and prophetic inspiration to give this idea definite shape, and to declare that the time would come when comets would be found to move in accordance with natural law.[1]

I: Introduction

Seneca's focus on comets in *Natural Questions* 7 concentrates our attention on a phenomenon that is in a sense familiar and yet so distant, known but so unknown: they are obscurities that challenge us to project the mind's eye beyond the limits of our ordinary vision. Given this incitement to ever further inquiry into nature's secrets, the broad aim of this chapter is to locate Book 7 in the larger pattern of movement that we have plotted in previous chapters from one kind of world perception in the *Natural Questions* to another; to demonstrate, that is, that Seneca's treatment of comets shapes, and actively applies in inventive ways within the text, a mind-set moving restlessly from narrow, more literal and (as it were) terrestrial ways of reflecting upon the universe toward an unfettered mode of investigation that speculates boldly on what lies beyond the limits of the known. This adventurous mind-set proceeds by conjecture (cf. 7.29.3), but it nevertheless follows the approved Senecan path even in possible error: it reaches dynamically beyond

---

1. White (1887) 8.

conventional confines—in this case, the zodiac—to engage with the universal immensity, thereby fully aspiring to that main Senecan goal in the *Natural Questions* generally, "to see the all with the mind" (cf. *animo omne uidisse*, 3 pref. 10).

On this approach to Book 7, the psychological import of comets extends beyond their significance, in the popular Greco-Roman imagination, as portents of disaster, and, more rarely, also of good.[2] In reviewing various theories of their cause (7.6–21) before setting out his own opinion (7.22), Seneca counters the awe and fear commonly associated with these rarities with the same confidence in rational explanation, and the same assertion of superiority over nature, with which he counters the terrifying specter of earthquakes in Book 6;[3] the movement between Books 6 and 7 from below ground to the heights of *sublimia* and *caelestia* (we shall see that a key tension point in Book 7 centers on whether comets are to be counted as *sublimia* or *caelestia*, meteorological or astronomical) itself expresses his breadth of cosmic vision and the reach of *ratio* across the world parts. Despite this rationalizing effort, however, the more superstitious Roman viewer may yet look upon comets with apprehension; and Seneca himself comes close to drawing an explicit distinction between comets of good and bad imperial omen at 7.21.3–4:

> sex...mensibus hic, quem nos *Neronis principatu laetissimo* uidimus, spectandum se praebuit, in diuersum illi Claudiano circumactus. ille enim a septentrione in uerticem surgens orientem petiit semper *obscurior*, hic ab eadem parte coepit, sed in occidentem tendens ad meridiem flexit et ibi se subduxit oculis. uidelicet ille <illic>[4] *fumidiora* habuit et aptiora ignibus, quae persecutus est, huic rursus haec *uberior* fuit *et plenior regio*; huc itaque descendit, inuitante materia, non itinere. quod apparet duobus quos spectauimus fuisse diuersum, cum hic *in dextrum* motus sit, ille *in sinistrum*.

---

2. The comet that was apparently observed in 44 BCE (for which Ramsey and Licht [1997]; Ramsey [2006] 106–24) during the games that honored the late Julius Caesar was allegedly judged highly propitious (*admodum faustus*) by Octavian himself (cf. Plin. *Nat.* 2.93–94), and it later played an important role in Augustan ideology and iconography (see Gurval [1997] with Zanker [1988] 34–36); but interpretation was far from exclusively positive (see Ramsey and Licht 135–37 with Domenicucci [1996] 73–74). In a treatise on comets the Stoic Chaeremon, one of Nero's tutors, apparently gave an account of comets of good omen (Orig. *C. Cels.* 1.59 = fr. 3 Van der Horst [1984] 12; Hine [2006] 66), but possibly to flatter Nero, or to dispel suspicions aroused by cometary sightings of the Neronian era. Otherwise, positive interpretations are rare indeed (*RE* 11 1149.62–1150.38 with Ramsey and Licht 135–36 and Gurval 44–45); but as tokens of disaster, Schechner Genuth (1997) 20–26, 70–88 with Whipple (1985) 1–9, Domenicucci 72–79 and Daston and Park (2001) 50, 52–53, 181, 208, 334.

3. For this superiority, see Chapter Six, especially Section III.

4. For this supplement, see persuasively Hine (1996b) 119–20.

The comet that we have seen in the very happy principate of Nero remained visible for six months, moving in a direction opposite to the
comet of Claudius' time. The Claudian comet rose from the north
toward the zenith and moved east, always growing dimmer. The Neronian comet began in the same place, but as it started moving westward,
it turned south (cf. 7.29.3), and there disappeared from view. Evidently,
the Claudian comet found <in that region> smokier elements which
were better suited to its fires, and it followed those elements; the Neronian comet, on the other hand, found this richer and more plentiful
region, and so it descended to it, drawn by the fuel, not by the route. It
is apparent that the two comets we saw had opposite courses, since the
Neronian comet moved to the right (i.e., west), the Claudian one toward
the left (i.e., east).[5]

The Neronian comet to which Seneca refers here appeared in the latter half of 60
CE; the Claudian comet belongs to 54 CE.[6] On one level, Seneca adduces these
two comets to elaborate upon the atmospheric theory of comets attributed to the
Stoics at 7.21.1: the considerations (1) that a comet "follows its fuel in the way fire
does" (7.21.2), and (2) that its duration is dependent on the richness of its atmospheric nourishment, are apparently borne out in the different durations of the
Neronian and the Claudian occurrences. In plotting the Neronian comet's movement westward from its northern starting point, and then to the south, Seneca's
report coincides with Chinese reports[7]—corroboration that shows there is no
straightforward distortion of fact here in order to privilege a symbolic point. On
another level, however, in his finer description of both comets—the contrast between smokiness (*fumidiora*) and abundant richness (*uberior... et plenior regio*),
and most obviously between *in dextrum* and *in sinistrum*[8]—Seneca surely tailors
his account of the two occurrences toward a symbolic end: if, for the superstitious, the comet of 54 betokened Claudius' imminent demise,[9] the positive

---

5. Left and right are here predicated on the Roman practice of facing south to scan the skies in
taking the auspices (Ramsey [2006] 138 n. 188).

6. For the former, Ramsey (2006) 140–46 and (2007) 181 no. 34; for the latter, Ramsey
(2006) 136–40 and (2007) 181 no. 33.

7. See Ramsey (2006) 141.

8. With the plain connotation of right as "favorable," despite the Roman augural influence
here (above, n. 5), with its complication that according to Roman augural practice signs on the
left are favorable, according to Greek practice unfavorable (see Pease [1973] 76–77 on Cic.
Diu. 1.12 *a laeua* and 482–83 on 2.82 *laeuum*, and cf. *OLD sinister* 3).

9. Cf. Plin. *Nat.* 2.92, Suet. *Claud.* 46 with Hurley (2001) 242–43, Dio 60.35.1.

features of the Neronian comet at 7.21.3–4 tactfully (or all too transparently?) defy any such baleful interpretation.[10]

Seneca may not entirely ignore, then, the portentous significance of comets in the popular imagination. But a key proposition in this chapter is that he experiments in a highly imaginative way in Book 7 with a different mode of cometary symbolism. In rejecting theories that explain comets as atmospheric phenomena or as optical illusions, Seneca builds toward his preferred theory that they are celestial bodies moving in unknown orbits. As we progress in this chapter toward this celestial explanation, we shall see that Seneca configures comets as guiding lights that symbolically lead us from one level of world perception to another. In our movement from the atmospheric interpretation to testing the optical illusion theory, and ultimately to a celestial explanation of comets, we ascend to the liberated cosmic viewpoint from which the remotest cometary orbits become visible to the mind's eye. On this approach, the book's entire treatment of comets is symbolic in trajectory, and Seneca's arrangement of his subject matter is dictated by his artistic, as opposed to a purely technical/astronomical, agenda. By finding meaning in comets not just, or primarily, as portents of disaster or of good but as signs that can challenge and enlarge our worldview, he embarks on a hybrid form of astronomical and literary-philosophical investigation that is unparalleled among other surviving Greco-Roman analyses of comets and their causation;[11] and given the unusual frequency of comets in the Neronian years,[12] he apparently seizes the moment in writing against a backdrop of rich and timely evidence for his cause.

---

10. This comet is nevertheless associated with subsequent earthquakes, etc., at 7.28.3 (see Ramsey [2006] 143–44). Yet at 7.17.2 Seneca remarks that the same comet "did away with the bad reputation of comets," presumably because the prospect of a change of ruler in 60 CE failed to transpire (cf. Tac. *Ann.* 14.22.1 with Ramsey 141–42 and Boyle [2008] 144 on *Oct.* 231–32). Cf. Gurval (1997) 43–44: "The cynical reader might detect some irony in the philosopher's remark [sc. that the comet of 60 *cometis detraxit infamiam*]. Or disappointment: the comet appeared but Nero didn't die."

11. For these analyses surveyed, Gilbert (1907) 642–58 with *RE* 11 1164.12-1174.30; Hellman (1944) 13–44; Brandt and Chapman (2004) 2–5; Jervis (1985) 11–21; Whipple (1985) 10–16; Bailey et al. (1990) 41–66; Yeomans (1991) 1–17; Keyser (1994) 647–51; Schechner Genuth (1997) 17–26; Van Nouhuys (1998) 44–59; Fernández (2005) 1–7; Heidarzadeh (2008) 1–23. For ancient occurrences catalogued, see Barrett (1978) 86–106, and now Ramsey (2006) and (2007).

12. With the help of Chinese records, six comets in all by the count of Rogers (1953) 240. Of these, Seneca mentions only that of 60 CE. That of 64 may have appeared after he had put the finishing touches to *Natural Questions* 7 (see Rogers 241 with Ramsey [2006] 141). But why omit the occurrences in 55/56 and 61? Perhaps because he was not "a very keen observer; he was, rather, a bookish scholar; and the comets of 54 and 60 were for some reason the ones which held interest for him" (Rogers 241). Or he may have omitted them because he did not count them as comets (Ramsey 141 n. 191), but possibly as novas; so at least Bicknell (1969) 1075, but (Ramsey 141 n. 191) "the length and movement assigned to the one in 55/6" tell against the nova interpretation.

On the assumption that the *Natural Questions* was originally ordered in the sequence 3, 4a, 4b, 5, 6, 7, 1 and 2, Book 7 on comets and then Book 1 on lights in the sky and Book 2 on lightning and thunder form a triad loosely connected by elemental fire; and in its broader movement from water (Books 3–4a) to air (4b–6) and then fire (7–2), the work as a whole shows a rising trajectory, gradually elevating our gaze from ground level until it hovers on the borderline between *sublimia* and *caelestia* in Book 7 before we revert unambiguously to the intermediate zone of *sublimia* in Books 1 and 2.[13] Within the triad of Books 7, 1 and 2, we shall see that the first two, Books 7 and 1, show important linkages in their combined analysis of more and less elevated modes of world perception. Already in Chapters 1 and 2 we observed a differentiation between terrestrial vision and a higher, less literal form of sight and intuition in Book 1 in particular.[14] The vile Hostius Quadra of 1.16 offers an especially graphic merging of a *modus uidendi* with a *modus uiuendi*: his eye for every carnal detail as he pleasures himself before his mirrors itself reflects a debased fixation with physicality that is countered elsewhere in the *Natural Questions* by the Senecan stimulus toward a higher, more figured level of philosophical vision. Our treatment of Hostius in Chapter 2, however, focused primarily on integrating his story within the broader thematic context of Book 1, with emphasis on certain similarities between his overly literal eye and that of the imaginary interlocutor who stubbornly resists Seneca's argument that such phenomena as rainbows are optical illusions.[15] In this chapter, Hostius will again figure prominently, but now as a key source of connection between Books 7 and 1. Within this dyad, I argue, Hostius offers a counterpoint not just to the enlightened thrust of Book 1 (Seneca's retraining of terrestrial vision in a higher, nonliteral direction), but also to the progress that we make in Book 7 from "lower" to "higher" forms of cometary explanation.

In Section II below we approach the theme of vision in Book 7 from the starting point of Seneca's moralizing epilogue at 7.30–2,[16] a section whose emphasis on the Eleusinian-like experience of initiation into nature's secrets will yield important contrasts with the Hostius episode in 1.16. After we descend with Hostius to the lowest point of our hierarchy-of-seeing in Books 7 and 1, Sections III to VII then plot the stages of Seneca's exhilarating surge in Book 7 toward a very different form of liberated, cosmic vision. In this respect, Hostius offers a model of claustrophobic limita-

---

13. On this thematic arrangement of the books, see my main Introduction on "The Addressee, and the Original Order of the Eight Books."

14. See especially Chapters One, Section II, and Two, Section IV.

15. See especially Chapter Two, Section IV.

16. See already Chapter Two, Section VI.

tion, of myopic imprisonment, by which Seneca enhances yet further the allure of the cosmic mind-set that is shaped in the preceding Book 7. It remains another question, and one left open in this chapter, whether this Hostius, for all his limitations and vileness, retains the dangerous allure on which we lingered earlier.[17]

II: Seneca on Progress, on Hostius Quadra and on Nature's Mysteries

Natural Questions 7 is open-ended at its close, at least in the sense that Seneca's view of comets as astronomical bodies that move in remote orbits ("I say that they are not accidental fires but are interwoven in the world order; it causes them to appear only infrequently, and to move in ways that cannot be observed", 7.30.2) prompts him to elaborate on our ever-incomplete knowledge of nature:

> Quam multa praeter hos per secretum eunt numquam humanis oculis orientia!…Quam multa animalia hoc primum cognouimus saeculo, quam multa ne hoc quidem! multa uenientis aeui populus ignota nobis sciet, multa saeculis tunc futuris cum memoria nostri exoleuerit reseruantur.
>
> 7.30.3, 5

> How many other bodies apart from these [sc. comets] move in secret, never rising before human eyes!…How many animals we have learned about for the first time only in this age, and how many are unknown even now! The people of a future time will know much that is unknown to us, and many discoveries are held in reserve for generations to come, when memory of us will have died out.

This vision of knowledge gradually accumulated over time is qualified by Seneca's denunciation of the pervasiveness of vice (7.31) and what he presents as the concomitant dearth of interest in philosophy (7.32)—a cultural crisis maximized, and surely exaggerated, by the high rhetorical pitch of his outrage.[18]

---

17. See Chapter Two, Section VII.

18. On the exaggeration, see Limburg (2007) 373–75, and for the decline of philosophy as a trope of moralizing discourse, Vottero (1989) 732 n. 13 with Citroni Marchetti (1991) 34. In focusing on the lack of *successores* in the old and new Academy, the Pyrrhonists, the Pythagoreans and the Sextians (7.32.2), Seneca perhaps studiously omits those schools in ruder health (including the Stoic and Epicurean schools; Vottero 730 n. 3); but for the plausible fact of decline in at least the cases Seneca does mention, cf. Glucker (1978) 338–44.

Despite this pessimistic conclusion, however, Seneca's focus in 7.30 on the gradual, open-ended discovery of nature's secrets across generations has been invoked as important supporting evidence for the existence of a Greco-Roman
concept of human progress; this in revisionist challenge to the view that a linear
and progressive Christian notion of time differs fundamentally from the pagan
notion, whose nonlinear/nonprogressive character is apparently revealed in
embedded beliefs such as the myth of decline from the Golden Age and theories of cyclical world recurrence.[19] For Ludwig Edelstein, Seneca, along with
Manilius and the elder Pliny, bears reliable witness to the concept of progress as
it continued to evolve in the time of Panaetius and Posidonius; agreement
among Seneca, Manilius and Pliny "can hardly be fortuitous but must reflect
the common philosophy of the Middle Stoa."[20] Yet Seneca stands apart in Edelstein's judgment, giving "a clearer and more comprehensive picture of what the
ancients meant by progress than does any other author"; for Seneca, "the ideal
of progress was an expression of the highest aspirations of man and mankind."[21]
But what precisely constitutes "progressivism"?[22] If Edelstein's vagueness on
this point is symptomatic of a more general "feeling of imprecision"[23] in his
volume, E. R. Dodds takes a more measured line, finding that the idea of progress was not "wholly foreign" to antiquity but qualifying its prevalence with
acute sensitivity to the dangers of generalization.[24] So, in Seneca's case, he finds
inconsistency: "But the most confident pronouncements [sc. on progress]
come, to our surprise, from that same Seneca who predicted the early demise of

19. See Bury (1932) 7–20, also with the robust opinion (p. 14) that Seneca had not "the least
inkling of a doctrine of the Progress of humanity. Such a doctrine is sharply excluded by the
principles of his philosophy and his profoundly pessimistic view of human affairs....Yet, at
least, it may be said, Seneca believed in a progress of knowledge and recognised its value. Yes,
but the value which he attributed to it did not lie in any advantages which it would bring to the
general community of mankind....[The value of natural science] lay not in its results, but
simply in the intellectual activity; and therefore it concerned not mankind at large but a few
chosen individuals who, doomed to live in a miserable world, could thus deliver their souls
from slavery." But for the succinct weighing of counterreaction to Bury's influential view that
the idea of progress was alien to Greco-Roman thought, see Motto (1984) 225–26 = Motto and
Clark (1993) 21–22 with Blundell (1986) 165–68.

20. Edelstein (1967) 169.

21. Edelstein (1967) 169, 175; cf. Motto (1984) 226 = Motto and Clark (1993) 22 for the case
to be made "for Seneca's vital importance as apostle of progress." For bibliography on the
theme of progress in Seneca, conveniently Berno (2003) 293 n. 4 with Hine (2010c) 84–86.

22. Cf. Dodds (1968) 453–54, reviewing Edelstein (1967).

23. So Keller (1969) 89; cf. Dodds (1968) 454, 455 and Reno (1968). For a critique of Edelstein's relative inattention to Rome, Novara (1982) 1.31–32.

24. Dodds (1973), especially 24–25.

the present world [cf. *N.Q.* 3.27–30]."[25] And, more importantly, Dodds plausibly limits Seneca's enthusiasm for progress

> to pure science, whose aim is simply "the knowledge of Nature"; applied science he thinks positively harmful; the liberal arts he judges in the old Stoic manner as worthless save in so far as they conduce to moral improvement. And in his own day he sees only decadence: far from advancing, science and philosophy are actually on the retreat.[26]

For present purposes, however, and despite the interest and importance of Seneca's broader reflections on the concept of progress across his corpus, our focus on 7.30–2 is narrower: To what extent, and how, can that passage be seen to be *intimately* connected to Seneca's disquisition on comets in the main body of the book?

Our answer begins in the humility that Seneca projects as he contemplates the limitations that inevitably hinder the human investigator:

> ueniet tempus quo ista quae nunc latent in lucem dies extrahat et longioris aeui diligentia. *ad inquisitionem tantorum aetas una non sufficit, ut tota caelo uacet. quid quod tam paucos annos inter studia ac uitia non aequa portione diuidimus?* itaque per successiones ista longas explicabuntur. ueniet tempus illud quo posteri nostri tam aperta nos nescisse mirentur...
>
> quota pars operis tanti nobis committitur! ipse qui ista tractat, qui condidit, qui totum hoc fundauit deditque circa se, maiorque est pars sui operis ac melior, effugit oculos: cogitatione uisendus est. multa praeterea cognata numini summo et uicinam sortita potentiam obscura sunt, aut fortasse, quod

---

25. Dodds (1973) 23. Against the inconsistency, see Motto (1984) 232 = Motto and Clark (1993) 26: "Rather than regard the conflagration as total destruction, one should see it as a change, a revival of everything." But cf. then Dodds (1968) 454 n. 3: "As Edelstein points out…, the concept of Eternal Return does not exclude limited progress within a particular world period. But in its strict form, the doctrine of *identical* return held by Pythagoreans and Stoics, it excludes all genuine human initiative." Motto (1984) 232 = (1993) 26–27 fails to address this exclusion of human initiative in pressing a different (and overly fine?) point: Seneca "does not accept the earlier teaching of the Porch that the recreated world will be identical, an exact replica of the previous world. On the contrary, he hastens to assure us that a better world will replace the present one [cf. *N.Q.* 3.28.7 *cum deo uisum est ordiri meliora*]…. Thus he has, in effect, imposed a progressive interpretation upon the traditional Stoic theory of cycles." However, (1) each new world cycle will evidently improve upon the corrupted world it replaces (so *meliora* at 3.28.7); but how can each new world *beginning* itself be measurably or meaningfully better than the last beginning? And (2) the progress that Motto posits is in any case ordained by god (cf. again 3.28.7 *deo*), not achieved through human effort or development.

26. Dodds (1973) 23. Cf. Hadot (2006) 168–73, especially 168 on Seneca's hostility "to the idea of technical progress [cf. Dodds' "applied science"]. For him, the only true progress is progress in knowledge and in moral life."

magis mireris, oculos nostros et implent et effugiunt, siue *tanta illis subtilitas est quantam consequi acies humana non possit*, siue in sanctiore secessu maiestas tanta delituit, et regnum suum, id est se, tegit, nec ulli aditum dat nisi animo. quid sit hoc sine quo nihil est, scire non possumus; et miramur, si quos igniculos parum nouimus, cum maxima pars mundi, deus, lateat!

7.25.4–5; 7.30.3–4

The day will come when the passing of time and the careful researches of a longer stretch of years brings to light what now lies hidden. A single lifetime, even if it is wholly devoted to astronomy, is not enough for the investigation of so large a subject. And what of the fact that we divide our years, which are already so few in number, disproportionately between our studies and vices? And so this knowledge will only be revealed through the long succession of ages. The time will come when our descendants marvel that we did not know what is so plain to them…

How small a part of this immense creation is entrusted to us! The one who manages the universe, established it, laid the foundation of this totality and arrayed it around himself, and who is the greater and better part of his own creation—he has escaped our vision and must be perceived in thought. Moreover, many things that are related to the highest divine power and allotted a similar influence are imperfectly known. Or perhaps—this may cause you greater surprise—they both fill and escape our vision, whether because their fineness of operation is such that the human eye cannot comprehend it, or because such grandeur hides itself away in holier seclusion, concealing its kingdom—that is, itself—and granting admission to nothing except the mind. What this is, without which nothing exists, we cannot know. And yet we are surprised if we have an imperfect understanding of some mere fires, when the greatest part of the world—god—escapes our notice!

The former passage echoes and reverses a major emphasis in Seneca's authorial self-positioning at the beginning of the work, in his preface to Book 3: there, as at 7.25.4 *ad inquisitionem… uacet*, no lifetime, however extended, lasts long enough to allow us fully to penetrate nature's mysteries.[27] Seneca devotes himself fully to his new task of surveying the world (*mundum circumire*) with a totality of commitment (3 pref. 2–4) that excludes all such division of life as that portrayed in 7.25.4 *quid quod… diuidimus?* But not even this total devotion can compensate for the deficiency of human vision as portrayed in 7.30.3–4, where sight gives way to insight (cf. *cogitatio*), and a true mark of progress at the personal level suggestively lies in our ability to ad-

---

27. See Chapter One, Section III.

vance from *acies* of a conventional kind ("one's vision," *OLD* 2a) to the *acies* of mental discernment (*OLD* 5). Indeed, on the assumption that Book 7 held antepenultimate position in the original ordering of the *Natural Questions*, it is striking that the word *acies* appears only twice before Book 7, on both occasions in the sense of "battle line" (cf. 4a.2.14, 5.18.8). It then occurs five times in Book 7, all with reference to plain eyesight;[28] ten times in Book 1; and once in Book 2.[29] As we saw earlier,[30] Seneca centers our focus in Book 1 on *sublimia*, which, often as optical illusions, challenge our powers of perception, moving us from a literal, terrestrial level of vision to a higher plane of inference and speculation; just as the meteorological phenomena of Book 1 (meteors, rainbow, etc.) are located in the middle zone between the heavens and earth, so they "epistemologically require both observation of the material world and rational speculation that goes beyond the material."[31] Our powers of perception are similarly challenged in Book 7, as we shall see; and in the combination of Books 7 and 1 we shall also find a process of cognitive development that is still more complex in its artistic orchestration than the journey from sight to insight, *ex oculis ad rationem*, that we have already tracked in Book 6.[32] The facts (1) that *acies* itself spans both literal and mental forms of discernment, and (2) that Seneca first uses *acies* of human eyesight only in Books 7 and 1, conspire to suggest that the word carries a special loading at this late stage in the *Natural Questions*: as we strive to elevate our gaze above the level of terrestrial vision in Books 7 and 1, the literal and figurative multivalence of the word itself captures the essence of that striving.[33]

---

28. Apart from 7.30.4, cf. 7.11.3, 18.2, 20.1 and 26.1.

29. Cf. 1.3.7 (twice), 3.8, 3.9, 3.10, 5.1, 6.5, 13.2, 14.3, 15.6; 2.9.1, of eyesight in each of these cases. Further on Seneca's use of *acies* of physical/mental vision, Solimano (1991) 107–108.

30. Chapter One, Section II. Cf. Chapter Two, Section IV.

31. Hine (2006) 68.

32. See Chapter Six, Section V (A)–(C).

33. More generally, the journey that we traced in Chapter Six from literal to more intuitive ways of seeing in Book 6 apparently marks a fresh development in the *Natural Questions* as a whole. True, already at the outset, in the preface to Book 3, the limits of our terrestrial, everyday vision are contrasted with the limitlessness of cosmic vision—a contrast developed in the "false" ways of seeing that define the mullet watchers of 3.17–18. Thereafter, down to Book 6, this preoccupation with ways of seeing appears to subside. But then, after our speculative probing below ground in Book 6, our movement toward inner vision—*acies animi*, not just *acies oculorum*—is taken further, I argue in this chapter, in the next phase of visual experimentation in Book 7. In the Hostius episode of 1.16 the language of vision moves quickly from surface to depth, or from cursory seeing to close inspection (see on this point Solimano [1991] 77–78), but to distorting effect so late in the work: if our cosmic vision has been gradually awakened, trained and refined thus far in the *Natural Questions*, that progress is shockingly challenged, even reversed, in the spectacle of Hostius looking ever more deeply into mere surface reflection in his mirrors. For the implications of that challenge or reversal, see Chapter Two, Section VII, and also my Epilogue below.

The hard process of discovery as depicted in such passages as 7.25.4–5 and 7.30.3–4 also importantly qualifies the idea, embedded in early Greek thought, of the anthropocentrism of nature.[34] Seneca elsewhere subscribes to this idea conventionally enough;[35] and Gercke sought to preserve that orthodoxy by conjecturing *neque enim omnia deus homini <pate>fecit* at 7.30.3 ("For god has not revealed all to mankind"), thereby removing the implication that "god has not created everything for mankind."[36] Gercke's conjecture is needless, however, if we take it that the sense of *fecit* is rather that god, the all-provider, has not made all straightforwardly *available* for our understanding, as his full workings elude our vision and comprehension.[37] There is no departure here from Stoic orthodoxy; but the slow process of discovery, the inadequacy of our perceptual powers as we strain for insight into divine *subtilitas*, the awesome specter of that all-ordaining power we struggle to visualize—all of these factors nevertheless diminish mankind's (self-)importance at the center of nature's scheme in this Senecan display of anthropocentric humility, as it were. Yet a distorted form of anthropocentrism is also visible in Seneca's condemnation of Roman decadence and the neglect of philosophy in 7.31–32. As we saw earlier,[38] man there becomes the self-absorbed center of his own universe, his bodily polish and ornamentation now *the* captivating spectacle in a world where the investigative instinct turns in on the self, but without philosophical edification: bodily experimentation instead tests and erodes traditional Roman masculinity, with literal emasculation (cf. *alius genitalia excidit*, 7.31.3) serving as an extreme metaphor for a form of cultural introspection that feeds obsessively upon itself until it becomes literally self-harming.[39]

---

34. For Stoic development of the idea, Pease (1955–58) 949 on Cic. *N.D.* 2.154 with Dyck (2004) 136 on Cic. *Leg.* 1.25, and see in general Renehan (1981) with Verhagen (2008) 3–7. For Chrysippus as "the great champion, if not the originator, of this doctrine," De Lacy (1948) 16 (cf. *SVF* 2.1152–67 pp. 332.26–35.16).

35. Cf. especially *Dial.* 8.5.4–5 with Dionigi (1983) 235–36.

36. Gercke (1907) 264.23–4; cf. Gauly (2004) 163, seeing in 7.30.3 a cancellation of the doctrine of man as the world *telos*. But see against Gercke's proposal already Oltramare (1929) 2.339, Alexander (1948) 328 and Vottero (1989) 203. For the "god-has-not-made-all-for-mankind" theme extending back to Xenophanes of Colophon, see Inwood (2002) 147 = (2005) 189 (Xenophanes "seems to hover in the wings" at 7.30.3), with Tulin (1993) for helpful reassessment of D-K 21B18 = Kirk et al. (1983) 179 fr. 188 = Graham (2010) 1.126–27 Text 77: "Not from the beginning have the gods revealed all things to mortals, but in time by seeking they come upon what is better."

37. See *OLD facio* 14a. Cf. the different, but not irreconcilable, shading given by Alexander (1948) 328: "Gercke's *<pate>fecit* shows a failure to comprehend the idea. Many of the works of God are made by Him only for His own pleasure as planner and creator."

38. Chapter Two, Section VI.

39. Cf. Barton (1993) 72–73 on "self-denial" (such as the "self-inflicted insult to [one's] own virility" at 7.31.3) as "the culmination of the spiral of desire."

Nature may be imagined as highly seductive in the way she reveals her charms to mankind:

> curiosum nobis natura ingenium dedit et artis sibi ac pulchritudinis suae conscia spectatores nos tantis rerum spectaculis genuit, perditura fructum sui, si tam magna, tam clara, tam subtiliter ducta, tam nitida et non uno genere formosa solitudini ostenderet. ut scias illam spectari uoluisse, non tantum aspici, uide quem nobis locum dederit: in media nos sui parte constituit et circumspectum omnium nobis dedit;...deinde sena per diem, sena per noctem signa producens nullam non partem sui explicuit, ut per haec quae obtulerat oculis eius cupiditatem faceret etiam ceterorum.
>
> *Dial.* 8.5.3–4[40]

Nature granted us an inquisitive disposition.[41] Aware of her own skill and her beauty, she gave us life to be spectators of her great spectacle, since she would be sure to lose all pleasure in herself if she displayed her works, so vast, so distinct, so finely contrived, so bright and so beautiful in more ways than one, to an empty solitude. For you to understand that she wanted not just to be seen but to be closely observed, consider the place to which she assigned us: she positioned us at the center of her creation, and gave us a commanding view of the universe.... Then she caused six constellations to rise by day and six by night, and so revealed to view every single part of herself, to the effect that, through the wonders that she had presented to our gaze, she aroused keen interest in the others as well.

In contrast to the enticing display of nature's attractions here (partial revelation now stirs desire for further revelation later), the deviants of 7.31 hold nothing in reserve in their shameless exhibitionism, and also in their striving for ever-lewder discovery. The mysteries penetrated by these base initiates are countered by the quasi-Eleusinian experience of initiation into nature's *sacra* at 7.30.6:[42]

> non semel quaedam sacra traduntur: Eleusin seruat quod ostendat reuisentibus; rerum natura sacra sua non semel tradit. initiatos nos credimus?

---

40. For discussion of this and other passages, Senecan (*Ben.* 6.23.6) and otherwise (e.g., Man. 4.866–935), as comparanda for the quest for, and for the limits of, knowledge in 7.30, see Limburg (2007) 354–61.

41. For the positive connotation of *curiosus* here (but not always so), cf. *N.Q.* 7.25.5 and then 1 pref. 12 with Labhardt (1960) 212 and Joly (1961) 36–37.

42. On this "traditional metaphor in Stoicism," Hadot (2006) 170 (cf. also p. 96) with Boyancé (1962) 466–68, citing *SVF* 1.538 p. 123.6–10, and also 2.42 p. 17.1–2 for τελεταί of initiation into theology, the highest branch of physics.

in uestibulo eius haeremus. illa arcana non promiscue nec omnibus patent:
reducta et interiore sacrario clusa sunt, ex quibus aliud haec aetas, aliud
quae post nos subibit aspiciet.

Some sacred rites are not revealed all at once: Eleusis holds in reserve
something to show those who come back. Nature does not reveal her
sacred mysteries once and for all. Do we believe that we are nature's initiates? We linger in her forecourt. Those secrets are not made indiscrimi-
nately available to everyone; they are held back and locked up in the inner
sanctum. This generation will glimpse something of those secrets, and the
age which succeeds us will glimpse something else.

Variations on the Eleusinian comparison are found twice in the *Moral Letters*, at
90.28 and 95.64, but more relevant for now is a third comparandum: the preface
to Book 1.[43] There, as we saw earlier,[44] Seneca begins by heralding the benefits to
be derived from one of two parts of philosophy (ethics is the other): "[That
branch which deals with the gods] rises far above this gloom in which we wallow
and, rescuing us from the darkness, it leads us to the source of illumination [*illo
unde lucet*]" (1 pref. 2); hence Seneca's gratitude when he views nature "not just in
that aspect where she is open to everyone, but when I have penetrated her mysteries [*cum secretiora eius intraui*]" (1 pref. 3), as if a privileged initiate ("Were I not
admitted to these secrets, it would not have been worth it to be born," 1 pref. 4).
In this movement from darkness to light, this penetration of nature's secrets and
this aura of religiosity and divine privilege, the preface is delivered as if from the
mouth of a new initiate who has reached the other side—an initiate who translates the Eleusinian comparison at 7.30.6 into a seemingly lived reality in the next
book, Book 1, so that he begins to know nature with deeper insight, and not from
the limiting perspective of the ethical branch of philosophy that is ruled inferior
in 1 pref. 2: "In short, there is as much difference between the two branches of
philosophy [sc. ethics and theology] as there is between man and god: one teaches
what should be done on earth [*in terris*], the other what is done in the heavens [*in
caelo*]."

Sandra Citroni Marchetti offers important analysis of this linkage between
the striving for Eleusinian-like initiation into nature's secrets at 7.30.6 and Seneca's apparent admittance into the inner sanctuary in the preface to Book 1.[45]

---

43. See on these passages Limburg (2007) 369–70 and especially Citroni Marchetti (1991)
144–48.

44. Chapter One, Section II.

45. (1991) 147–48.

But a further connection between Books 7 and 1 is supplied by the affinity to be drawn between Hostius Quadra in 1.16 and the deviants of 7.31.[46] After the Eleusinian experience of 7.30.6, Hostius in particular now offers an alternative sanctum—his carefully arranged hall of mirrors—for initiation into his own sordid mysteries (cf. *secreta*, 1.16.3); the verb *admitto* has one meaning for Seneca (*nisi ad haec* [sc. nature's secrets] *admitterer*..., 1 pref. 4),[47] quite another for Hostius (cf. *spectabat admissos sibi... uiros*, 1.16.5); and while Seneca sees the light as if newly initiated into nature's mysteries at 1 pref. 2, Hostius brings to light spectacles "which no night is dark enough to conceal" (1.16.6). The ordaining force that "manages the universe, established it, laid the foundation of this totality and arrayed it around himself [*deditque circa se*]...has escaped our vision and must be perceived in thought" (7.30.3). But then Hostius: as if presiding over his own creation after surrounding himself with mirrors (cf. *specula sibi... circumdedit*, 1.16.4; *id genus speculorum circumponam mihi*, 1.16.8), he is all image, yearning to see and be seen and leaving nothing to the imagination, and certainly offering no stimulus to higher *cogitatio*. Whereas nature's truths are revealed slowly (7.30.6), Hostius rushes instantly to know all, to maximize his lewd images through magnification, to observe every arcane novelty in minute detail. Whereas succeeding generations build on the gradual accumulation of knowledge, Hostius deforms that process by striving singlehandedly for *complete* discovery in his own sexual lifetime, and by reveling in the contemplation not of lasting truth but of ephemeral mirror illusion. In every way Hostius is a model of maximization. In contrast to the discreet opaqueness of the Eleusinian experience, he all too enthusiastically reveals the mysteries of his mirror chamber in his own reported voice at 1.16.7–9. The philosophical initiate attains a breadth of vision (cf. 1 pref. 3: "when I learn what the material of the universe is, who its creator or guardian is...") that ultimately extends to our beginning "to know god" (*deum nosse*, 1 pref. 13); in his very different mode of panoramic vision, Hostius studies each sexual nuance from every angle in his mirrors, as if god-like in his ability to see all that no ordinary mortal can. He sees all, but hardly in the enlightened Senecan sense of seeing the all with the mind (cf. *animo omne uidisse*, 3 pref. 10).

As we look back upon Book 7 from the perspective of 1.16, then, the Eleusinian-like mystique of initiation into nature's secrets is rudely countered by Hostius' drive for limitless revelation in his very different rituals; and if we detect a touch of dark humor in Hostius' disruptive presence here, one that challenges the ambition

---

46. Cf. already Chapter Two, Section VI, for verbal linkage between the two passages.

47. On *admittere* here as a metaphor drawn from court etiquette (permission for an audience), Weber (1995) 78.

(or pretension) of any higher Senecan engagement with nature, Seneca arguably checks that intrusive effect by abruptly killing Hostius off at 1.16.9. But two further tendencies of Hostius usefully illuminate contrasting phenomena in Book 7. First, Hostius' overly literal eye, interpreting as true the false magnifications that it sees, concentrates intently on each new wonder in the mirrors.[48] In his search for the ultimate in visual/sexual fulfillment, satisfaction is always in prospect but never completely achieved (cf. 1.16.8: "I *shall* find a way of both deceiving and satisfying my sick appetites"). This eye for the sordidly spectacular represents an extreme version of the mind-set on display in 7.1. Overfamiliar with the daily wonders of the firmament, we scarcely notice their motions and workings:

> haec tamen non adnotamus quamdiu ordo seruatur; si quid turbatum est aut praeter consuetudinem emicuit, spectamus interrogamus ostendimus. adeo naturale est magis noua quam magna mirari.
>
> Idem in cometis fit....

7.1.4–5

> But we fail to register all this [sc. the daily wonders of the firmament] as long as the usual order of things is maintained. But if there's any disturbance or something unusual flashes forth, then we watch, we ask questions, we point it out. So natural is it to marvel at novelty rather than at greatness.
>
> The same thing happens in the case of comets....

For Seneca, the daily spectacle of the firmament should permanently impress, a *mirum* so striking that we repeatedly behold it as if for the first time.[49] But those awestruck by a comet observe it as if they are *spectatores noui* of a different stamp, or as viewers who have an eye *only* for singularity and difference in nature, and not for (the consistency of) her everyday splendor. In his deviant way Hostius, too, views each more extreme image as if a *spectator nouus* of this secondary kind, galvanized for the first time by every next novelty and fresh perversion of nature.

Second, for all his free license and the exhibitionism of his recruitment procedures at the public baths (1.16.3), Hostius is paradoxically a captive within his mirror chamber. The images that so excite him exist only in that enclosed theater; only there can he achieve his triumph over nature through careful mirror

---

48. Cf. *miretur* (1.16.9), significantly placed as the last word, and the word's only occurrence, in Hostius' entire reported speech at 1.16.7–9.

49. Cf. *Letters* 64.6 *mundum...saepe tamquam spectator nouus uideo* with Hadot (1995) 257–58, 261.

placement and by feeding on the illusory as real (cf. *mendacio pascar*, 1.16.9). His mirrors may enable him to achieve an ever more explicit viewpoint, but, beyond that brief heightening of stimulus, there is nothing truly *progressive* about his experiences in the chamber: each new perspective entrenches the same obsession. New discoveries similarly feed obsession in the case of the degenerates condemned in 7.31: "Luxury finds some new fad over which to act crazily" (7.31.1). But even though "vices are still making progress" (7.31.1), there is nothing progressive about the degenerates themselves apart from the intensification of their vicious ways. In contrast to this slavishness, however, a very different class of progress—what might be termed the emancipation of the cosmic mind-set—is found in Book 7 in the ascent that Seneca stages from lower to higher, or from terrestrial to celestial, explanation of the nature of comets. We now turn to that ascent in 7.4–29, our approach oriented by an important divergence between two main camps of Greco-Roman thought, one of which held that comets are astronomical in nature, the other meteorological.[50]

III: *Sub- and Supralunary Interpretation of Comets*

In asserting that a comet is not just "a sudden fire but one of the eternal works of nature" (7.22.1), Seneca departs fundamentally from the influential Aristotelian theory of comets, "one of the most widely accepted and long-lasting theories in the history of natural philosophy."[51] To echo Sara Schechner Genuth's brisk summation,

> In the *Meteorologica*, Aristotle judged that comets were sublunar meteors composed of hot, dry "windy" exhalations. They had two causes. The most common were formed when [1.7 344a8–33] a condensed mass of volatile exhalations ascended from the earth into the upper atmosphere, where it was ignited by revolutions of the contiguous heavenly sphere. Comets were also formed when [1.7 344a33–344b8] a star or planet gathered atmospheric exhalations into a stellar halo that appeared as the comet tail

---

50. Cf. Plin. *Nat.* 2.94 for his presentation "without serious scrutiny or discrimination [of] what must have been the two standard views on the origins of comets" (Gurval [1997] 43): "There are those who believe that even these stars are eternal and travel in their own orbits, but are not visible except when they are apart from the sun; but others believe that they arise from chance moisture and fiery force, and for that reason they are dissolved." See also the Manilian distinction drawn between the (Aristotelian) exhalation theory (1.817–66) and the celestial theory (1.867–73) with Volk (2009) 46; and for an attempt to clarify the finer nuances of the theory as given at 1.867–73, Montanari Caldini (1989) 4–17.

51. Heidarzadeh (2008) 16.

but was not attached to the star or planet. Unlike the first type of comet, which moved more slowly and erratically than the stellar sphere, the second type had the same motion as its generating star [1.7 344b8–12].[52]

In terms of Seneca's division of the universe into three regions (*caelestia, sublimia* and *terrena*) at the opening of Book 2, Aristotle's theory locates comets firmly among *sublimia*, i.e., *inter caelum terrasque* (2.1.2). For Seneca, on the other hand, comets are among *caelestia*; in refuting (7.4–10) Epigenes' argument for deriving comets from terrestrial exhalations, he in effect attacks what was "basically the theory of Aristotle and Posidonius."[53] Seneca was hardly the first to hold that comets were planetary or stellar bodies,[54] but the planetary theory was powerless to resist the influence of Aristotle. In a powerful convergence of forces for the shaping of the post-antique tradition, the Aristotelian theory, which can itself be traced back to the Pre-Socratics,[55] was adopted by Ptolemy, whose important role in the development of cometary astrology was also profoundly influential in later ages.[56] Aristotle's continuing preeminence in the Western world as the greatest scientist of antiquity, and the combined authority of Ptolemy as well as Aristotle on comets, partly explain the long predominance of the sublunary theory down to the Renaissance, but another important factor was the influence of the early and medieval Church: beyond the theory's compatibility with specific Biblical texts, the Church encouraged the view that comets were atmospheric phenomena sent as a divine message or warning by an angry God.[57] These factors slowed the serious study of comets in the West and did nothing to allay the culture of superstition attaching to them; but another consequence was that few careful observations of comets were recorded

---

52. Schechner Genuth (1997) 17; cf. pp. 92–93.

53. Kidd (1988) 494. Hine (2006) 61 stresses the "unusual feature" that in Book 7 Seneca focuses on "three virtual unknowns," Epigenes, Artemidorus and Apollonius of Myndus. Given his brusque critique later in the book of theories that differ from his own, Seneca perhaps tactfully avoids confrontation with more distinguished names; and yet Posidonius for one, arguably a key source (see n. 79 below in this section), still qualifies for attack at 7.20. Alternatively, Seneca possibly confines himself here to targeting contemporaries; but the dates of Epigenes, etc., are far from certain (see Hine 61–62).

54. See subcategory 3 below in this section, and Section VI below in this chapter.

55. See, e.g., Fernández (2005) 6 on Xenophanes of Colophon (D-K 21A44 = Graham [2010] 1.124–5 Text 70) with Guthrie (1962) 390–91.

56. Concise background in Hellman (1944) 39–41; Yeomans (1991) 14–16; Heidarzadeh (2008) 27–28.

57. On the Biblical aspect, Whipple (1985) 11–13; Schechner Genuth (1997) 31–45. On the portentous aspect, White (1887) 8–12; Yeomans (1991) 22–23, 48–49; Schechner Genuth 29–31, 217; Daston and Park (2001) 50.

before 1472[58], an embarrassment in comparison with Chinese achievement in particular.[59] At last, in the fifteenth and sixteenth centuries, the Aristotelian sublunary theory met serious challenge,[60] not least through the revival of Stoicism.[61] But it was not until the appearance of the nova of 1572 and the comet of 1577 that attitudes were fundamentally changed. This transformation is conventionally attributed to Tycho Brahe:[62] through his compilation of all the available observations (including his own measurements) of the 1572 nova and the 1577 comet, he determined them to be supralunary,[63] thereby directly countering the Aristotelian orthodoxy, even though many who accepted Brahe's conclusions still clung to the traditional view by dividing comets into two classes, sub- and supralunary.[64]

This fundamental divergence between two schools of thought—are comets above or below the moon?—conveniently introduces what we shall see to be the productive *artistic* tension in Book 7 between the categories of the celestial and the meteorological, *caelestia* and *sublimia*. By locating comets among *caelestia*, Seneca experiments enterprisingly with a conceptual hierarchy of a quasi-Platonic stamp: in contrast to the ephemeral and contingent nature of *sublimia* in the intermediate region of the atmosphere, I propose (1) that he here associates the permanence and regular movements of *caelestia* with a metaphysical level of fixity and sure knowledge; and (2) that by rejecting the sublunary theory of comets (thereby departing from Stoic orthodoxy; cf. 7.22.1), and by plotting his own idiosyncratic

---

58. So Whipple (1985) 13; on the great comet of 1472, Hellman (1944) 76–85 with Seargent (2009) 102–104 ("[w]idely recorded in the annals of many cultures," and set apart from other comets "primarily because of a very close approach to Earth, simultaneously coupled with a favorable location in the sky").

59. See Williams (1871), especially vii–viii, with (concisely) Yeomans (1991) 42–48 and now Ramsey (2006) 18–24 and (2007) 175–77.

60. See conveniently Marsden (1974) and Schechner Genuth (1997) 104–105 with Van Nouhuys (1998) 84–88 (on "Sixteenth-Century Heterodoxy"), 115, 569, but cf. p. 88: "The vast majority [sc. of scholars] still clung" to the Aristotelian view.

61. See Van Nouhuys (1998) 142–43, 569–70.

62. On Brahe's place in the astronomical culture of sixteenth-century Europe, now Mosley (2007).

63. The superlunary interpretation was far from his alone (see Hellman [1967] 50–52 with [1963] for the extent of his influence reassessed), and he was by no means the first to use parallax measurement of comets; yet "the fact remains that he was the first do so correctly, arriving at values that actually placed the comet above the moon" (Van Nouhuys [1998] 122).

64. See Schechner Genuth (1997) 261 n. 5, and cf. Van Nouhuys (1998) 143: "The comet of 1577 has often been credited with facilitating the break with Aristotle and the adoption of Copernicus"—for Van Nouhuys "a very oversimplified representation of historical reality." For one sample of the resilience of the Aristotelian tradition despite the modern sixteenth- and seventeenth-century challenge, see Ariew (1992), to the effect that "the Aristotelians seem…able to absorb and assimilate all invaders" (p. 355).

course toward a celestial explanation, he stages a philosophical ascent to that cosmic/metaphysical plane above *sublimia* where provisionality gives way to certainty, *doxa* to *episteme*.[65] In rising with Seneca to these heights, we are led on an experimental journey of sorts, a variation on the explicit metaphor of the heavenly journey and the flight-of-the-mind idea that are commonly found earlier in the Greco-Roman literary-philosophical tradition.[66] But Seneca offers no tired repetition of a familiar trope: beyond turning the study of cometary nature from a purely objective, exterior exercise into a spur to self-examination and interior development, Book 7 adds an important dimension to our larger itinerary in the *Natural Questions*; for by speculating on remote cometary orbits far beyond the zodiac, Seneca transports us here to the furthermost, and most liberating, limits of the cosmic mindscape that is mapped in the work as a whole.

Before setting out his preferred explanation of comets, Seneca reviews three theories:[67]

1. Comets are produced through whirlwinds in the atmosphere. So Epigenes at 7.4–10,[68] with similarities to Aristotle and Posidonius.[69]
2. Comets are optical illusions produced by planets in conjunction. So Democritus and Anaxagoras,[70] but Seneca attributes the theory only vaguely to *quibusdam antiquorum* at 7.12.1.

---

65. I here develop in a different way the symbolic potential of Book 7 that has already been well explored by Gauly (2004) 155–57 in his analysis of the contrast between serene order and detachment at the metaphorically higher and superior celestial level, restless instability at the lower, atmospheric level.

66. On the heavenly journey, Volk (2004) 36–37 with n. 5 for bibliography; on the flight of the mind, Volk (2001) 88 and n. 5.

67. Succinctly surveyed by Kidd (1988) 494 and Rossi (1992) 129–30, but see already Hartmann (1911) 16–26.

68. This student of astrology, who apparently studied among the Chaldeans (7.4.1), is not cited before Seneca, he is little heard of thereafter, and it remains unclear when he lived. He was possibly Seneca's contemporary, but the Senecan clues to that effect (*nuper*, 7.3.1; allusions to two comets "in our own lifetime" are perhaps, but not certainly, to be attributed to Epigenes' reported voice at 7.6.1) are far from conclusive: see Hine (2006) 61–62 and (2010a) 223 n. 25 with Gross (1989) 291–92 and Gauly (2004) 147–48, and cf. Keyser (1994) 648 ("He wrote, at a guess, *ca.* 120–100 BCE"). For Seneca, the Chaldean connection would seem to be unimpressive given his polemic elsewhere; cf. 2.32.7 with Vottero (1989) 334 n. 10.

69. See Kidd (1988) 492 A4 on frr. 131a 26–37 E-K, 131b 12–24. For ancient proponents of the atmospheric theory conveniently surveyed, see Jervis (1985) 20; Bailey et al. (1990) 57–62; Schechner Genuth (1997) 18.

70. See D-K 59A81 = Graham (2010) 1.302–3 Texts 48, 49, and cf. D-K 68A92 = Graham 1.556–57 Text 71; Posid. fr. 131a13–16 E-K. For other proponents of this theory conveniently listed, Jervis (1985) 20.

3. Comets are themselves planets. So Apollonius of Myndus at 7.17–18,[71] but the theory is attributed by Aristotle to "some of the so-called Pythagoreans," to Hippocrates of Chios and to Aeschylus, his pupil.[72] Seneca also attributes to Apollonius the claim (7.4.1) that "comets are included in the category of planets by the Chaldeans."[73]

When he reverts to Stoic theories of comets (7.19.1–21.2),[74] this tripartite structure recurs, albeit in a different order that suitably begins with the school's founder, Zeno, for whom comets are caused by planetary conjunction (7.19.1);[75] then (7.19.2) some Stoics are said to hold the planetary theory,[76] most (7.19.2–20.1) that comets are neither planets nor optical illusions but a brief, fiery efflorescence—Posidonius' theory.[77] In tabulated form:

7.4–10: atmospheric theory   7.19.1 Zeno (optical illusion)
7.11–12: optical illusion theory   7.19.2 *quidam ... exire* (planetary theory)
7.17–18: planetary theory   7.19.2 *quidam ... dissipantur* (atmospheric theory)

Seneca's double use of this tripartite structure indicates that "the three types of solution had become commonplace";[78] and it may be that he relies on Posidonius

---

71. The exact identity and date of this Apollonius are uncertain (this uncertainty is compounded by manuscript variations on *myndius*; see Gurval [1997] 42 and n. 12). He was perhaps a contemporary of Seneca, given his reported voice's allusion to the Neronian comet of 60 CE at 7.17.2; so Gauly (2004) 150 after Gross (1989) 295–97, unless (Hine [2006] 62 with [2010a] 223 n. 25) Seneca inserts into his account of Apollonius' views this reference to recent comets, an intervention arguably paralleled in Seneca's treatment of Epigenes as well (n. 68 above). Keyser (1994) 648 places him "after Hipparchos, and before Poseidonios..., so perhaps *ca.* 100 ± 20 BCE."

72. Aristot. *Mete.* 1.6 342b29–343a 20 (= D-K 42 5); for the Pythagorean attribution, cf. also Posid. frr. 131a1–12 E-K, 131b6–12, and on Hippocrates' and Aeschylus' theory, see further Heidarzadeh (2008) 10–11, 13.

73. Theophrastus as well may have held comets to be celestial, not atmospheric; so inclines Steinmetz (1964) 215–17, but Kidd (1992) 297–98 remains circumspect.

74. Posid. fr. 132 E-K with Kidd (1988) 494–96. On "The Stoic Outlook," Van Nouhuys (1998) 46–52.

75. 7.19.1 = *SVF* 1.122 p. 35.8–10.

76. So perhaps Diogenes of Babylon; Kidd (1988) 495, citing Aet. *Plac.* 3.2.8 (*DG* p. 367).

77. Also Panaetius' theory, given 7.30.2 (see Vottero [1989] 700 n. 5 on 7.19.2). Cf. *SVF* 2.692 p. 201.22–24 for Chrysippus (albeit Kidd [1988] 496: "The reference in D. L. vii.152, although printed in *SVF* ii.692 as Chrysippan, almost certainly derives from Posidonius"); 3.9 p. 267.6–7 for Boethus.

78. Kidd (1988) 493.

as his main informant for earlier cometary theory, albeit probably through an intermediary.[79] But whatever the extent of Seneca's debt to his Posidonian (and possible other) source(s), experience of his creative use of doxography elsewhere in the *Natural Questions*[80] might lead us to expect similar enterprise in his coverage of Epigenes at 7.4–10.

IV: The Whirlwind Theory

Seneca's treatment of Epigenes' theories here[81] is in two parts, the first (7.4–5) dealing with Epigenes' explanation of lights in the sky other than comets: lightning bolts and flashes (*fulmina, fulgurationes*), beams (*trabes*) and torches (*faces*). The second (7.6–10) deals with comets themselves, two types of which he distinguishes at 7.6.1, different in appearance and one moving, the other stationary. Two issues are of special interest for now: First, is it purely for reasons of comprehensiveness that Seneca embarks on his somewhat diversionary account of Epigenes' theories of other lights in the sky before he turns to comets? Second, why begin with the whirlwind theory of comets, as opposed to the planetary and optical illusion theories? What artistic considerations might influence the priority given here to Epigenes?

What Seneca provides in Epigenes' reported voice in 7.4.2–4 is a summary description of events in the intermediate zone of *sublimia*. True, in deriving thunder and lightning flashes (*fulgurationes*) from Saturn absorbing the sun's rays, and lightning bolts (*fulmina*) from Saturn absorbing the sun's rays while in conjunction with Mars, Epigenes apparently offers a celestial, planetary origin for phenomena that Seneca will go on to attribute (1.1.6) to more and less violent collisions between clouds. But Epigenes' theory takes on a lower, noncelestial dimension when he derives the material of *fulgurationes* from wet exhalations from the earth, that of *fulmina* from warmer, drier exhalations (7.4.3). At 1.1.5 Seneca will explain beams and torches as effects of atmospheric friction. Hence, presumably, his strong objection to Epigenes' derivation of those phenomena from whirlwinds (7.4.4): Given that a whirlwind is conceived, and rages, so close to the

79. See Setaioli (1988) 420–22, with basic acceptance of the influential case in Rehm (1921) for dependence on Posidonius; but for cautionary words against "the pan-Poseidonism [*sic*] of Rehm," cf. Keyser (1994) 648–49.

80. See Hine (2006) 56–58, especially 57 ("Seneca's use of [critical doxography] has distinctive features"), and cf. Chapters One, Section I; Four, Section IV; Five, Section III; and Six, Section V.

81. Detailed coverage in Hartmann (1911) 17–20; cf. Hellman (1944) 23–26, Jervis (1985) 15, Keyser (1994) 647–48.

earth (*circa terras*, 7.5.1) and "is generally lower than the clouds and certainly never higher," how can it possibly produce a beam in the higher part of the sky? How can beams be caused by a whirlwind when the latter is evidently so different in the rapidity of its circular motion (7.5.2)? Then a seeming digression: Seneca cites the report of one Charmander[82] that a large and long-lasting light the size of a beam was witnessed by Anaxagoras (7.5.3); and then also Callisthenes' alleged report that "a similar likeness of an extended fire" appeared before the Achaean cities of Helice and Buris were destroyed by earthquake and tsunami in 373–72 BCE (7.5.3; cf. 6.23.4).[83] Seneca implies that Callisthenes interpreted the phenomenon as a beam,[84] but he states explicitly that Aristotle identified it as a comet, not a beam (*Aristoteles ait non trabem illum* [sc. *ignem*] *sed cometen fuisse*, 7.5.4). In his *Meteorologica* Aristotle does indeed refer to a great comet (cf. ὁ... μέγας κομήτης, 1.6 343b 1) coinciding with the earthquake of 373–72; but he offers no straightforward identification of comets with beams (*trabes*/δοκοί), and there is nothing whatsoever in the Aristotelian passage to warrant Seneca's seemingly incredulous assertion at 7.5.5: "Is it really possible, then, that Aristotle believed that not only this beam but all beams are comets, with this difference, that beams have a continuous fire, comets a scattered fire?"[85] And so why this manipulation, if direct manipulation it is,[86] of Aristotle to associate comets so closely with beams? More generally, why, in 7.4–5, this impressively complete but seemingly circuitous preamble to Epigenes' theory of comets proper in 7.6–10?

Both questions find good answer, I propose, in Seneca's ascending structure of argument in the book as a whole. In the context of his evolving treatment of comets, we begin from the ground up: the whirlwind of 7.5.1 literally grounds

---

82. Otherwise unknown. He is identified by Gruppe (1887) 433–34 n. 2 (cf. also Oltramare [1929] 2.305 n. 2) with the Stoic Chaeremon, according to Origen *C. Cels.* 1.59 author of a book on comets (further, Hine [2006] 66; cf. also Section I n. 2 above in this chapter); but see firmly *contra* Van der Horst (1984) 53 on Chaer. fr. 3 with Vottero (1989) 674 n. 3 on 7.5.1. On the hypothetical possibility that Charmander is Seneca's intermediary source for Posidonius in Book 7, Setaioli (1988) 425.

83. *FGH* 124 fr. 21 Jacoby. For Helice and Buris cf. Chapter Six, Section V (F) and n. 134; for Callisthenes, Chapter Six, Section V (F) and n. 141 and Section VI).

84. Seneca's testimony finds support (Setaioli [1988] 425–26) in Diodorus Siculus' allusion to a "fiery beam" (πυρίνη δοκίς, 15.50.2).

85. Cf. Hall (1977) 414 (Seneca "a bad source for Aristotle's theory"). Dall'Olmo (1980) 19–20 too quickly concludes from 7.5.2–5 that *trabs* is "an ambiguous term" and "in some cases...may refer to a comet."

86. Cf. Setaioli (1988) 426 and n. 2003, positing Seneca's reliance on an intermediary source. Given the discrepancy between the Senecan and Aristotelian versions, it is for Setaioli (p. 426) "certain that Seneca did not have before him the text of Aristotle." Yet is it unthinkable that Seneca might *deliberately* have modified Aristotle's original emphasis?

(cf. *circa terras*) a discussion which rises to the level of *sublimia* (beams, torches, etc.), comets notionally among them at 7.5.5; and Seneca turns to Aristotle for an impressive endorsement of comets as *trabes*-like *sublimia*. Of the two kinds of comet distinguished at 7.6.1, one moving, one stationary, Epigenes' first type— "hair on all sides, motionless and generally low"—is attributed to the same causes as beams and torches: it is ultimately terrestrial in origin, produced as it is by "the intemperate state of disturbed air, which whirls round with it many dry and wet exhalations from the earth" (7.6.1).[87] After these lower comets in 7.6, Epigenes' second type of comet (type 2a for now) is derived from the same causes (cf. 7.7.2). But we now move to new heights, for our purposes symbolic as well as literal: this second type of comet differs from the first in elevation because the exhalations that produce it "carry with them many dry elements and make for a higher region [*celsiorem…partem*], and are driven by the north wind into the more elevated parts [*in editiora*] of the heavens" (7.7.2). Again, simple observation supplies Seneca with powerful counterarguments (7.7.3; cf. 7.7.1), but still Epigenes persists (as if a dogged antagonist in Seneca's carefully organized treatment) with another theory, to produce type 2b: whereas dry exhalations predominate in type 2a, dry and wet exhalations combine in discord at 7.8.1 to form a whirlwind that ignites and lifts *in altum* whatever is caught within it; a comet results from the fire powerfully ejected from the whirlwind.

Yet how can a comet be produced by a whirlwind when its steady motion more closely resembles planetary movement (cf. 7.8.3–4)? If lower comets cannot reach great elevation because they are weighed down by too much earthy substance (*plus terreni*, 7.9.1), how can the type 2 comets, "longer lasting and higher" as they are (7.9.1), bear the far greater weight of nourishment that they must necessarily carry? Central to the concluding arguments that Seneca ranges against the whirlwind theory in 7.9–10 is the inability of any whirlwind "to persist for very long or to rise above the moon or all the way up to the stellar region" (7.9.2). For present pur-

---

87. In Seneca's later summation of Epigenes' theory (7.6.3), comets are said to occur for the same reason as beams and torches at 7.4.4-5.1; so at 7.5.1 beams and torches are (according to Epigenes) "squeezed out by a whirlwind" (*exprimi turbine*), while at 7.6.3 such lights are "emitted by a whirlwind" (*ignes turbine eiecti*). But here a key difference between beams and torches on the one hand, comets on the other, importantly impinges upon a textual matter at 7.6.3: *illi turbine ex superiore parte in terras deprimuntur, hi de terra in superiora luctantur* ("those [sc. beams] are pushed downwards to earth from above by the effect of a whirlwind, while these [sc. comets] struggle up from the earth to the higher regions"). Hine (1996a) 289.151 rightly follows Parroni (1990) 112–15 (see also [2002] 426.17 and 596) in rejecting *turbines*; for if the latter is read with most editors, to the effect (Corcoran [1971–72] 2.241) of "*whirlwinds are pressed down to the earth* from the upper regions while comets struggle up from earth to the upper regions," how to reconcile the whirlwinds' *descent* with their formation and progress *circa terras* at 7.5.1 ("For a whirlwind is formed and carried along near to the earth")?

poses, these final arguments firmly locate the whirlwind theory at a terrestrial level of analysis, as it were; and it is this lowly significance, I suggest, that conditions Seneca's arrangement of his cometary theories so that he begins with Epigenes before moving to a higher theoretical plane at 7.12–16: comets as optical illusions.

V: *The Optical Illusion Theory*

Seneca rises to the celestial level in presenting the theory that comets are illusions created by planetary conjunction (7.12.1); but in his ensuing critique the grounds for the theory prove to be as illusory as the optical effect that it posits.[88] Three features of his treatment of the theory in 7.12–16 are of special relevance for now, the first his initial rebuttal at 7.12.2–8. There may be no great originality to the arguments that drive his powerful case here, notable among them the objection that, if a comet is an illusion caused by planetary conjunction, the appearance of comets *outside* the zodiac (7.12.8) is hard to explain.[89] Beyond the specifics of his critique, however, a secondary form of refutation works more stealthily in the subdrama played out in the interchanges between Seneca's narrative voice and that of his notional interlocutor introduced at 7.12.6. After Seneca's first round of objections to the conjunction theory (7.12.2–5), we are to imagine the interlocutor deftly shifting his ground:

> 'stellarum' inquit 'duarum lumen miscetur et praebet unius speciem, nempe sic quemadmodum rubicunda fit nubes solis incursu, quemadmodum matutina aut uespertina flauescunt, quemadmodum arcus alterue sol uisitur'.
>
> 7.12.6

> "The light of two stars," he says, "is blended and gives the appearance of a single star. In just the same way, a cloud is suffused with red by the impact

---

88. Seneca refers for this theory to "certain of the ancient scholars" (*Quibusdam antiquorum*, 7.12.1), Anaxagoras and Democritus among them (see Section III and n. 70 above in this chapter). But cf. Bailey et al. (1990) 52–53 for problematization of the term "conjunction" in connection with the Pre-Socratics: "it is quite possible that the kind of conjunction which Anaxagoras had in mind had very little to do with planets. For example, a rather similar idea for comets was also advocated by Diogenes of Apollonia (*ca.* 430 BC), who taught that stars were rocky bodies akin to pumice stone and that comets were chains of such stars.... This account again suggests that the connexion [*sic*] between comets and *planetary* conjunctions may be a later distortion, possibly based upon a misunderstanding as to the kind of conjunction which was observed. It is conceivable, in fact, that a comet may have been identified as a swarm of 'stars', suggesting in this context that the word 'star' should be understood to mean 'meteor' or 'fireball.'"

89. Cf. Posid. fr. 131a16–18 E-K with Kidd (1988) 491 on A (2) (a) and 492 on A (3) (a).

of the sun, in the same way the early morning or evening shows a golden coloration, in the same way a rainbow or a second sun is made visible."

From one angle, perhaps, a shrewd reply to Seneca that keeps the optical theory alive while no longer relying on planetary conjunction as posited in 7.12.1[90]—only for another devastating blow to be dealt in Seneca's second round of objections, including the crucial point that all these phenomena such as rainbow, etc., occur "below the moon [*infra lunam*], in the vicinity of the earth. The upper regions are pure and with no admixture, always retaining their own color" (7.12.7). For all his quick-wittedness, the interlocutor has in effect lowered (or been forced to lower) his sights, applying a meteorological explanation for the optical illusion that, he asserts, causes comets at the planetary level; the boundary between *caelestia* and *sublimia* (cf. 2.1.1–2) is too easily elided in the correspondence that he effortlessly draws (*nempe sic quemadmodum...quemadmodum...quemadmodum*) between the two distinct regions, as if the celestial planets can be straightforwardly grouped with the atmospheric *ignes* that will be featured in Book 1.

Second, Artemidorus, of whom virtually nothing is heard outside Seneca.[91] Introduced to resuscitate the planetary optical theory that Seneca's objections have left for dead at the end of 7.12, Artemidorus counters in his own reported voice with an argument of interest for more than Seneca's withering dismissal of it as but "a shameful falsehood" (7.13.2):

> Aduersus haec ab Artemidoro illa dicuntur: non has tantum stellas quinque discurrere, sed has solas obseruatas esse; ceterum innumerabiles ferri per occultum aut propter obscuritatem luminis nobis ignotas aut propter circulorum positionem talem, ut tunc demum cum ad extrema eorum uenere uisantur: 'ergo intercurrunt quaedam' ut ait 'stellae nobis nouae, quae lumen suum constantibus misceant et maiorem quam stellis mos est porrigant ignem'.
>
> 7.13.1

In response to these points [sc. the series of objections to the optical theory in 7.12.2–8],[92] Artemidorus offers the following arguments: it is not just

---

90. This interlocutor's emphasis on rainbow and second sun as optical illusions will indeed be borne out at 1.3–8 and 1.11.2–13.3, despite the overly literal objections in Book 1 of another imaginary interlocutor (cf. Chapters One, Section II, and Two, Section IV).

91. For Artemidorus, Chapter Two, Section IV and n. 55. On his theory, Hellman (1944) 26–27; Jervis (1985) 15; Bailey et al. (1990) 52–53; Keyser (1994) 649–50.

92. So *haec* with most modern editors, but *hoc*, also in the manuscript tradition (referring back only to 7.12.8 *stellis...exeant?*) is read by Hine (1996a) 297.319 and Parroni (2002) 440.1 on the analogy of 7.7.1 *Aduersus hoc multa dicuntur*.

these five planets that move about, but these are the only ones that have been observed. But countless planets move without being seen, and are unknown to us either because of the dimness of their light, or because the position of their orbits is such that they are visible only when they have reached the extremity of their circuits [i.e., at their point closest to earth]. "Therefore," he says, "certain planets that are new to us are mingled in with the regular planets and blend their light with them, projecting a larger fire than is usual in planets."

If Artemidorus truly held that "the highest region of the heavens is completely solid, 'hardened like a roof and of thick (*alti*)[93] and dense material, formed by a mass of accumulated atoms...'" (7.13.2), Seneca presumably responds with a basic Stoic antipathy to an atomic worldview.[94] Given the infinite void that stretches in all directions beyond the Stoic cosmos, he naturally rejects Artemidorus' vision of fires passing back and forth through "ventilators and windows, as it were" (7.13.3) in the hard outer wall of the cosmos. From a Stoic perspective that considers the earth to be immobile at the center of the closed cosmos, the cosmos immobile within the infinite void and everything within the enclosed cosmos to be held together in tension,[95] Artemidorus' theory is open to obvious objections: If in the external void there are evidently no cables to support the hard and presumably weighty cosmic roof, what infrastructure is there, what internal force operative from the center (*de medio*, 7.14.3), to hold it in place? When by rhetorical force of argument ("Again, no one will dare to say...," 7.14.3) Seneca excludes any additional possibility that the world itself, with its weighty and unsupported roof, is constantly falling in void, Artemidorus' theory itself goes into freefall. Again, Seneca's lengthy critique would appear to demonstrate a thoroughness that the theory itself barely warrants. Or is there more to his agenda here?

 If Artemidorus were right in his claim that there are innumerable other planets in the cosmos, how can that host of bodies produce so *few* comets by planetary conjunction (7.14.4)? How can comets possibly be so rare? A strong objection

---

93. For this nuance, Hine (1996b) 117; in this quotation I also follow the punctuation in Hine (1996a) 297.329–298.331 (cf. [2010b] 123).

94. For the skin or membrane surrounding the world according to the fifth-century atomists, D-K 67A1 (32) = Graham (2010) 1.542–43 Text 47 (32). But for this "inherited and deeply seated belief" (Guthrie [1965] 411), see further Anaximenes, D-K 13A14 = Graham 1.82–83 Text 17 ("the stars are fixed like nails to an ice-like surface so as to form designs [i.e., constellations]") with p. 92 on Texts 16–24. Parmenides, D-K 28A37 = Graham 1.222–23 Text 27; Empedocles, D-K 31A51 = Graham 1.370–71 Texts 71, 72, with p. 427 on Texts 69–72.

95. Conveniently, Furley (1999) 440–48.

that Seneca has perhaps held back thus far for maximum impact; but for all the frailties of Artemidorus' case, he takes on a suggestive relevance in Book 7 as a whole as more than a theorist whom Seneca easily dismisses with an entertaining sharpness of tone. We shall soon return to Seneca's own open-minded engagement in 7.24 with the possibility that planets may exist outside the zodiac.[96] Artemidorus' theory may signally fail, but he nevertheless shows a breadth of outlook, a spirit of inquiry beyond conventional limits of thought, that survives Seneca's devastating attack in 7.13–14 to reappear in a more positive guise later in the book.

Third, Seneca's adducing of historical evidence further to counter the planetary conjunction theory (7.15) before he turns in 7.16 on *historici*, Ephorus of Cyme (*c.* 405–330 BCE) in particular.[97] At one level, his argument in 7.15 is straightforward enough: between the death of Demetrius I Soter, king of Syria from 161 to 150 BCE, and shortly before the Achaean War of 146/5 (*paulo ante Achaicum bellum*, 7.15.1), and then during the reign of Attalus III of Pergamum (138–133), two comets appeared of such size that they intolerably strain the conjunction theory:[98] how many planets—hundreds, even a thousand?—would have to coincide to project such vast images?[99] By dating these comets through reference to historical markers, Seneca obliquely contrasts the timeless protocols of the universal workings with the ebb and flow of human fortunes as kings and kingdoms emerge and pass away; and he indirectly endorses the portentous significance of comets as soon as we relate the gradual waning of the comet of 147 to Achaea's fall to Roman rule in 146–45, and the comet of 135 to Attalus' bequeathing of his kingdom to Rome in 133. But the passage's fuller importance lies in another, albeit understated, argument that it yields against the conjunction theory. The comet of 147 rises and diminishes in gradual stages marked by *primo*,

---

96. See Section VII below in this chapter.

97. See Schepens (1977) and Pownall (2004) 113–42 on this *notissimus scriptor historiarum* (Macr. *Sat.* 5.18.6), author of (*inter alia*) a thirty-book universal history, and "characterized by ancient tradition as an historian of undeniable merit" (Schepens 95).

98. Given "shortly before the Achaean War," and in light of Chinese observation, the first comet is "almost certainly identical" with that recorded in China for 6–16 August 147 BCE (Ramsey [2006] 79–81; cf. [2007] 179 no. 17). The second belongs to 135 BCE, *not* 137, and is to be identified with that which Justin connects with the birth of Mithridates VI, king of Pontus (37.2.1–2; see Ramsey [1999] 200–13, 220–22; [2006] 83–88; [2007] 179 no. 19). The relative richness of the description of both comets in 7.15 indicates to Ramsey (2006) 80–81 that Seneca draws on a report by a careful second-century observer—possibly Hipparchus, perhaps via Posidonius.

99. Seneca may exaggerate for effect, but corroboration *is* to be found for the notable size and brightness of both comets; see Ramsey (1999) 221–22 and (2006) 79–80, 84.

deinde paulatim and *nouissime* (7.15.1); so, too, the comet of Attalus' time appears moderate at first (*initio*, 7.15.2) before then (*deinde*) "spreading out and extending as far as the equinoctial circle." Seneca has already objected to the conjunction theory on the grounds that, given the speed at which planets move, "if a planet made a comet by converging upon another planet, the comet would cease to exist in a moment" (7.12.4). But comets remain for months at a time, "which would not happen if they were caused by the conjunction of two planets" (7.12.4). In stating that the comet of 147 only *gradually* (*paulatim*) diminished in size and brightness (7.15.1), Seneca subtly reapplies his earlier objection: How can that or any other comet linger in its waning for so long if it is produced by planetary conjunction?

But the conjunction theory yet clings to life: Ephorus apparently reported that the comet preceding the destruction of Helice and Buris (cf. 7.5.3–4) "split into two stars [coming out of conjunction], a fact which [Seneca adds with barely concealed sarcasm] no one but he related" (7.16.2).[100] But, responds Seneca (7.16.3), who could witness that moment of division into two? After all, and again to invoke 7.12.4, such is the speed of the planets moving out of conjunction that their separation would be impossible to capture in the way Ephorus describes. It follows at one level that Seneca's attack on the distinguished Ephorus as "not a man of very scrupulous reliability" and "one who is often deceived and more often deceives" (7.16.2) is not merely gratuitous; from a Senecan standpoint, what Ephorus (and Ephorus alone) reports *cannot* correspond to any visible reality, even though the splitting effect has in fact been observed in other comets in other ages.[101] At another level, however, the broader contempt in which he holds *historici* generally at 7.16.1–2 is no colorful but otiose repetition of a familiar Senecan refrain.[102] Our seeker after truth admonishes first Artemidorus and then the *historici* for their respective lies (cf. *mendacium* at 7.13.2 and then 7.16.2); by in-

---

100. Ephorus, *FGH* 70 T14b and fr. 212 Jacoby. Seneca makes no allowance for Ephorus' possible prioritization of a moral, rather than a purely factual, point in this instance. Given that various authorities connect the destruction at Helice and Buris to sacrilege committed there, "it is reasonable to infer that Ephorus mentions the comet to point out the moral lesson provided by the disaster. A heavenly portent that twinned would provide a much clearer presage of the fate of the two cities and would also indicate it was heaven-sent, as a result of some misdeed committed by their inhabitants" (Pownall [2004] 126; cf. also Bosworth [2003] 169–70 on Seneca's "overkill" in his treatment of Ephorus and historians generally in 7.16, and already Galdi [1924] 42–43 after Hartmann [1911] 24 for qualification of the Senecan hard line).

101. So, e.g., Biela's comet, found in its 1846 appearance to have split (see Yeomans [1991] 183–88). For later reports, cf. Anon. (1929) and (1955) ("about once a decade") and Jayawardhana (1994). On the possibility that a split was indeed observed/recorded by Ephorus, Seargent (2009) 68–69; and cf. also Aristot. *Mete.* 1.6 343b26–28 for attribution to Democritus of the claim that "stars have been seen to appear at the dissolution of some comets."

102. Cf. 3 pref. 5, and see Chapters One, Section III and n. 43, and Four, Section IV (A) and n. 47.

veighing (however unfairly) against Ephorus in particular, he targets a writer re-
puted in antiquity for his *akribeia*,[103] thereby damning the *historici* in general by
discrediting one of their most eminent representatives. By this attack he reasserts
his commitment in the *Natural Questions* to a rhetoric of reason, as opposed to
the rhetoric of wonder that he attributes to the *historici*; and, as purveyors of *in-
credibilia* and *mira*, the latter are set in alignment with the public that shows such
appetite in 7.1 for spectacular irregularities in nature, and such blindness to her
everyday wonders. The *historici* "do not think that their works can win approval
and become popular unless they sprinkle them with lies [*mendacio*]" (7.16.2):
after Seneca's reading of the popular mood in 7.1, with its craving for sensational
singularity, his *historici* share that perception but respond to it differently, as if
serving rather than deploring the public appetite—a "low" literary trajectory that
is countered in Book 7 by Seneca's striving in a celestial direction.

VI: *The Planetary Theory*

After theories of causation first by whirlwind and then by optical illusion through
planetary conjunction, we rise in 7.17 to the planets themselves *in caelesti* with the
theory of Apollonius of Myndus:[104]

> 'non est' inquit 'species falsa nec duarum stellarum confinio ignis extentus,
> sed proprium sidus cometae est sicut solis ac lunae. talis illi forma est, non
> in rotundum restricta sed procerior et in longum producta. ceterum non
> est illi palam cursus: altiora mundi secat et tunc demum apparet cum in
> imum cursus sui uenit.
>
> 7.17.1–2

> "A comet," he says, "is no illusion or fire extending from the proximity of
> two planets, but a heavenly body in its own right, like the sun and the
> moon. Its shape is as it appears to be—not limited to a circle, but more
> extended and drawn out lengthwise. However, the path of its orbit is un-
> clear: it cuts through the upper regions of the world, and only becomes
> visible when it reaches the lowest point in its orbit."

In surveying Apollonius' planetary theory, Seneca continues on his rising trajectory toward unveiling (cf. 7.22.1) his own theory of comets as celestial bodies that

---

103. See Schepens (1977) 96 with Pownall (2004) 119–21.

104. For whom Section III and n. 71 above in this chapter. On his theory, Hellman (1944)
24–25; Jervis (1985) 14–15; Bailey et al. (1990) 62; Yeomans (1991) 8–9.

move in unknown orbits. As we move in this higher, more expansive direction, however, a countervoice operates within the text to restrict comets to the level of *sublimia*, as if representing a mind-set that cannot rise to the cosmic viewpoint that Seneca's master voice promotes. In its stubborn literal-mindedness, this counterforce is closely related to the interlocutory voice of Book 1 that, as we saw earlier, vehemently resists all possibility that such phenomena as rainbow are optical illusions.[105] Through the competition played out between these two voices in Book 7, Seneca's disquisition evolves into an animated clash of world perspectives, one liberated and searching, the other restricted and unimaginative. Two passages in the current section (7.17–21) conveniently illustrate the subtlety with which he controls these contending perspectives.

(1) Aduersus hoc protinus respondetur non idem accidere in cometis quod in ceteris.

7.18.1

Against this theory of Apollonius, an immediate response is that what happens in the case of comets differs from what happens in the case of other heavenly bodies.

The countervoice is about to raise three objections in 7.18 to Apollonius' planetary theory. Since Seneca's own favored theory agrees in essentials with Apollonius', he can hardly endorse the attack of 7.18; hence the impersonal *respondetur* crucially distances him from the counterarguments that he goes on to advance.[106] All three objections falter when we take the enlightened, broader view. So in answer to the first objection, that whereas planets grow in size the nearer they approach, comets are largest when they first appear (7.18.1): if we read this objection in the fuller context of Seneca's cometary coverage and thereby glance back at 7.15.2, the comet that appeared in Attalus' time already offers countertestimony in its *gradual* growth to extreme size. As for the second objection, that if a comet were a planet, it would necessarily move within the zodiac (7.18.1; cf. 7.12.8, 24.1): this claim reveals the narrow, terrestrial preoccupation with limit and boundary that is countered in the *Natural Questions* more generally by the unrestricted cosmic mind-set that allows Seneca sharply to ask at 7.24.1: Is it *really* so impossible to imagine that a planetary body could have an extrazodiacal orbit? As for the third objection, that a planet is never visible through another planet, but a

---

105. See Chapter Two, Section IV.

106. Rightly Parroni (2002) 599, and also Vottero (1989) 698 n. 1, with speculation as to who might be implicated—Epigenes and Posidonius among other possibilities?—in *respondetur*.

comet is transparent, and therefore no celestial body but a "faint, irregular fire" (7.18.2): Seneca later argues (7.26) that the core comet (*sidus ipsum*) is opaque, and only the scattered glow of its tail transparent. From the perspective of 7.26, what drives the objection of 7.18.2 is our fallible vision from below—a variation on the myopia that prevents Apollonius' imagined critics in the second objection from looking beyond the zodiac, and beyond their own *angustiae mentis*,[107] so as to speculate on possible planetary motion outside that fixed zone/mind-set.

> (2) Placet ergo nostris cometas, sicut faces sicut tubas trabesque et alia ostenta caeli, denso aëre creari. ideo circa septemtrionem frequentissime apparent, quia illi plurimum est aëris pigri. quare ergo non stat cometes sed procedit? *dicam.*
>
> 7.21.1

> Accordingly, our Stoics accept that comets, like torches, like trumpets and beams and other marvels of the sky, are formed from condensed air. For that reason they appear most frequently in the north, because the greatest quantity of slow-moving air is there. So why does a comet not stand still but moves forward? *I shall tell you.*

Seneca evidently speaks in *dicam*, but with a shading importantly supplied by Posidonius. After the familiar tripartite division of cometary causation is applied to the Stoics in 7.19, the atmospheric theory (i.e., that of Epigenes in 7.4–10) is presented by Seneca as prevalent among the Stoics (7.20.1).[108] Although there is no direct attribution of the theory to Posidonius in 7.19.2, the latter is soon introduced (7.20.2), albeit in circumstances where Seneca "uses him to deride the theory as pandering to the general love of the miraculous."[109] From a Senecan standpoint, Posidonius is doubly misguided: beyond subscribing to an atmospheric theory of comets, he here reveals, or is accorded, an interest in *miracula* (7.20.2) that loosely aligns him with the *historici* of 7.16; for both have an eye for the marvelous that is countered by Seneca's emphasis in 7.1 on regularity in nature, not exceptionality.

Posidonius remains an important subpresence when Seneca reports, in 7.21.1 as quoted above, that the Stoics derive comets from condensed air.[110] If we accept

---

107. Cf. 7.24.1: *quis in angustum diuina compellit?* ("Who is forcing the divine within narrow limits [i.e., orbiting planets *only* within the zodiac]?").

108. But cf. Kidd (1988) 495–96: the atmospheric theory "is undoubtedly that of Posidonius, and when Seneca says that most Stoics hold it, he must mean most Stoics of his own day. There is no sure trace of it before Posidonius in the Stoa."

109. Kidd (1988) 496.

110. Cf. Posid. fr. 131a31–33 E-K, 131b18–19.

that Stoic position, why, asks an imaginary interlocutor, would comets ever move from the thick air that is their source? *Dicam*: Seneca makes ready to reply, but in a voice that, we know in retrospect, cannot be fully his own, committed as he is to a celestial theory of comets (cf. 7.22.1); for in the rest of 7.21 he explores certain ramifications of the atmospheric theory as if he were temporarily an advocate for the other (Posidonian) side. Here is a form of literary ventriloquism different from the familiar presence in Senecan prose of an antagonistic interlocutory voice: in what might loosely be termed a Posidonian tone that supports the atmospheric theory, Seneca presents three arguments (7.21.2–4) that distinguish comets from planets and thereby resist the planetary theory (so, e.g., whereas comets, like fire, apparently follow their fuel source, planets do not). By allowing the Posidonian voice briefly to commandeer the text, Seneca sets up a powerful juxtaposition between the atmospheric theory (7.21) and the celestial corrective that he introduces when his "true" voice resumes in 7.22; and so to his own preferred theory.

VII: *The Senecan Theory*

The contrast between lower and higher explanations of comets is recast in temporal terms when Seneca distances himself from his school at 7.22.1: "I do not agree with our Stoics; for I do not consider a comet to be a sudden fire, but one of the eternal works of nature." The hierarchical distinction drawn here between permanence at the celestial level, ephemerality at the atmospheric level, is reinforced by each of the arguments that Seneca subsequently deploys in his point-by-point critique of the atmospheric (Posidonian) theory just sampled in 7.20–21.[111]

In this critique as a whole (7.22–23) the atmosphere emerges as a region of provisionality and accident, of directionless display and short-lived spectacle, whereas the celestial region is a place of systematic regularity. If we press this division further, the atmosphere from which most Stoics derive comets can itself be taken to represent a level of contingency, or of a quasi-Platonic *doxa*, that generates false opinion or half-truth; the Senecan "reality" about comets only comes into view when we rise to the epistemic level of *caelestia*. It is to these heights that we finally ascend late in Book 7, our eye trained on comets as no ordinary planets but rather as phenomena that challenge us to look beyond the familiar confines of the zodiac. From this superior vantage point we encounter the lowly objections of the localized mind-set represented by the stubborn imaginary interlocutor of

---

111. So, e.g., a comet follows its fuel in the way fire does (7.21.2). Not so (7.22.2): if fire clings to its fuel, it should always descend, because the atmosphere is thicker the closer it is to the earth; but a comet never descends to those lower atmospheric reaches.

7.24–27. "If a comet were a planet, it would be in the zodiac" (7.24.1): the series of open questions that Seneca launches in response to this reversion to familiar limit and convention—"Who lays down a single boundary for planets?...Indeed, these very planets which you believe are the only ones that move follow different orbits. Why, then, should there not be some planets that have moved away on their own path, separate from the others?" (7.24.1)—functions as a thought experiment of sorts that stretches the confines of the interlocutor's (and our) mind-set. Could it be that a comet may have so unusual an orbit that it enters the zodiac in only a portion of its orbital cycle? Perhaps, perhaps not (cf. *quod fieri non est necessarium, sed potest*, 7.24.2): what matters is not so much the objective truth here as the widening of the mind that engages with the universal immensity. In this respect, the Artemidorus we witness in 7.13–14 is hardly to be faulted at least for his spirit of intellectual adventure, even if we reject his cometary theory out of hand. Artemidorus looked beyond the conventional zodiac, and so too does Seneca in contemplating the possibility that comets move in orbits as yet unknown, and on principles yet to be fully understood (cf. 7.25.3). True Senecan liberation is achieved by this heterodoxy—by moving beyond an anthropocentric view of nature that tries to explain the unfamiliar *only* in terms of established knowledge, or to assume that the laws regulating comets exist only insofar as man knows them.[112] As new universalists, we begin instead under Seneca's tutelage to glimpse nature on her terms, not ours.[113]

This change of perspective presupposes a letting go, of which the interlocutor appears incapable. So in Seneca's account of recent progress in astronomical inquiry,[114] including a better understanding of the morning and evening risings of planets, their positions and "the time of their motion directly forwards, and why

---

112. So Oltramare (1929) 2.326 n. 2.

113. Cf. Hadot (1995) 254, quoted in Chapter One, Section III. This qualification late in Book 7 to the familiar (Stoic) anthropo- and geocentric vision of the cosmos arguably gives, in retrospect, a delayed significance to Seneca's passing allusion at 7.2.3 to heliocentric theorizing: "There have been people [presumably including Aristarchus of Samos in the early third century; see Vottero [1989] 668 n. 6 with Heath [1913] 299–316] who said that we are the ones whom nature causes to move without our knowing it, and that risings and settings happen not by the motion of the heavens, but we ourselves rise and set. The subject warrants study so that we may know what our status is—whether we occupy a very slow-moving or a very fast-moving abode, and *whether god causes all things to move around us, or causes us to move.*"

114. Specifically Roman progress (cf. *apud nos*, 7.25.3) in astronomy dates back at least to C. Sulpicius Galus (cos. 166), author of a book on the subject in the midsecond century. For this and later developments, Rawson (1985) 162–64, and on Galus, Powell (1988) 202–3 on Cic. *Sen.* 49 with Linderski (1990) 68 = (1995) 316. The lunar crater known as Sulpicius Gallus [*sic*] was named for our Galus by the eminent Italian astronomer Giovanni Battista Riccioli (1598–1671), for which see MacDonald (1967).

they move backwards" (7.25.5): if these developments represent an enlightened, modern approach, the interlocutory voice introduced at 7.25.6 is backward-looking in its all-too-unnuanced view of planetary movement:

> inuenti sunt qui nobis dicerent: 'erratis quod ullam stellam aut supprimere cursum iudicatis aut uertere. non licet stare caelestibus nec auerti: prodeunt omnia; ut semel missa sunt uadunt. idem erit illis cursus, qui sui, finis.
>
> People have been found who would tell us this: "You are misguided in thinking that any star either stops or alters its course. It is not possible for celestial bodies to stand still or to be diverted from their course; they all move forward, and they proceed just as they first began. Their motion will end only when they end."

This voice of bare literalism instantly cuts through, and shows no interest in, the illusory properties of planetary motion that Seneca goes on to explore in 7.25.7 ("Why is it, then, that some planets seem to move backwards?"); the interlocutor sees all too *precisely*,[115] and stubbornly persists in his literalist viewpoint still later into the book.[116] He may stand apart from the *luxuriosi* condemned in 7.31, but this interlocutor still contributes to a larger pattern of resistance in Book 7 not just to the celestial view of comets but also to the rise toward cosmic consciousness that, I propose, Seneca intimately associates with the celestial theory.

We saw earlier that the community of deviants that is strewn across the *Natural Questions* constitutes a counterweight of sorts to the uplifting tendency of Seneca's meteorological investigations.[117] So, in Book 7, his denunciation of the *luxuriosi* in 7.31 and of the demise of philosophy in 7.32 is no mere afterthought appended to his main treatment of comets, but a last assault on the forces that draw down the upward trajectory plotted in this chapter. Exaggeration and bombast lend entertaining color to this show of outrage,[118] but the deviants of 7.31 are only an extreme

---

115. Cf. for this tendency the interlocutor featured in Chapter Two, Section IV, under "The First Objection."

116. So in 7.26 the double distinction that the interlocutor draws between planets and comets—(1) "We cannot see through planets to objects on the other side, but our vision passes through comets" (cf. 7.18.2), and (2) "Planets are all round, comets extended"—is based on what Seneca casts as another blinkered, overly literal form of viewing that neither perceives nor allows for any material difference between the comet's tail and the *sidus ipsum* of the comet itself.

117. See Chapter Two, especially Section VII.

118. See Chapter Two, Section VI.

manifestation of a tendency shared by many other participants in the book: those who have an eye just for nature's seeming aberrations in 7.1; the *historici* of 7.16 who are charged with sprinkling their works with wonders and lies (*miraculo* and *mendacium*/-*io* at 7.16.1–2); investigators such as Artemidorus and Posidonius, their theories held to ridicule; the Stoics, committed as they are to an atmospheric explanation of comets (cf. 7.21.1, 22.1); and finally the various interlocutory interventions—all of these presences, in their own ways and to different degrees, resist, counter or slow Seneca's movement toward the celestial viewpoint, as if a gravitational force that pulls relentlessly in a downward direction (most spectacularly in 7.31–32) even after he has reached his celestial arrival point at 7.27.6:

> cometas non frequenter ostendit, attribuit illis alium locum, alia tempora, dissimiles ceteris motus: uoluit et his magnitudinem operis sui colere. quorum formosior facies est quam ut fortuitam putes, siue amplitudinem eorum consideres siue fulgorem, qui maior est ardentiorque quam ceteris. *facies uero habet insigne quiddam et singulare, non in angustum coniecta et artata, sed dimissa liberius et multarum stellarum amplexa regionem.*
>
> Nature does not often display comets. She has assigned them a different place, a different timetable, and movements unlike those of the other planets; through them, she also wanted to enhance the greatness of her own creation. The appearance of comets is too beautiful to be thought of as accidental, whether you contemplate their size or their brightness, which is greater and more brilliant than that of the other planets. In fact, their appearance has some exceptional and distinctive quality to it, constricted and limited as it is to no narrow confine, but freely sent forth and covering the territory of many stars.

The cometary appearance as pictured here bears a striking resemblance to the process of adventurous thought by which Seneca has risen to his celestial interpretation of comets. The liberated mind-set leaves behind the narrowness that defines the low-atmospheric levels of analysis that we sampled in the case of Epigenes' whirlwind theory of comets. As we ascend through the optical-illusion and planetary theories toward the extrazodiacal orbits that Seneca posits for comets, we move toward an unfettered vision that is itself freely sent forth and ranges boldly over the whole celestial region (cf. again *non in angustum coniecta et artata, sed dimissa liberius*). Whereas the interlocutor remains firmly grounded in his literalist mind-set, this suggestive dovetailing of form and subject matter—this correlation between the book's increasingly expansive conceptual journey and the expansive movement of comets in their far orbits—casts Book 7 as *fundamentally* progressive well before Seneca explicitly introduces the concept of progress in 7.30.

At this late stage in the book, the official concept of progress rounds out the acti-vated form of progress that *is* Seneca's entire discourse on comets.

It may appear that Book 7 closes on a profoundly pessimistic note when Seneca laments the seemingly irrepressible proliferation of vice and the terminal decline of philosophy (7.32.1, 4). But a more positive projection emerges when we make the transition from Book 7 to the preface of Book 1, and when Seneca's ascent to a celestial level of cometary interpretation is seen to give way to full habitation of the celestial plane in Book 1. He has arrived. As if a new initiate who has gained privileged admission to nature's mysteries, he speaks in the preface to Book 1 as one liberated by his elevation to new heights of consciousness:

> Virtus enim ista quam adfectamus magnifica est non quia per se beatum est malo caruisse, sed quia animum laxat et praeparat ad cognitionem caelestium, dignumque efficit qui in consortium <cum> deo ueniat.
>
> 1 pref. 6

For that special virtue to which we aspire is magnificent not because free-dom from evil is in itself a happy state, but because it unchains the mind and readies it for comprehension of the celestial, and makes it worthy of entering into association with god.

By unchaining the mind and readying it for the comprehension of comets as ce-lestial phenomena, Book 7 has already rehearsed, in its way, the rise *ad caelestia* that is heralded at 1 pref. 6. Book 7 has already raised us to the heights from which the enlightened mind looks down at 1 pref. 7: "Then, as the mind [*animum*] wan-ders among the very stars [*inter ipsa sidera uagantem*], it delights in laughing at the mosaic floors of the rich and at the whole earth with all its gold." By visualiz-ing the remote cometary orbits, Book 7 has already transported us up to and across the vastness of the heavens:

> Sursum ingentia spatia sunt, in quorum possessionem animus admittitur, <s>ed ita, si secum minimum ex corpore tulit, si sordidum omne detersit et expeditus leuisque ac se contentus emicuit. cum illa tetigit, alitur, crescit, uelut uinculis liberatus in originem redit.... nam secure spectat occasus siderum atque ortus et tam diuersas concordantium uias; obseruat ubi quaeque stella primum terris lumen ostendat, ubi columen eius sit, quousque descendat. curiosus spectator excutit singula et quaerit. quidni quaerat? scit illa ad se pertinere.
>
> Tunc contemnit domicilii prioris angustias.
>
> 1 pref. 11–13

The spaces of the heavens are immense. The mind is admitted to possession of them only if it retains as little as possible of the body, if it has wiped
away all impurity and, unencumbered and light and self-contained, it
flashes force. When the mind has reached those regions, it is nourished, it
grows and, as if freed from chains, it returns to its origin....For it looks
serenely upon the risings and settings of the stars, and their different but
harmoniously coordinated paths. It observes where each star first shows
its light to the earth, where its zenith is, and the point to which it descends.[119] A diligent observer, it scrutinizes and examines each detail. Of
course it does so: it knows that these things relate to itself.

Then it despises the restrictions of its former dwelling place.

As in the transition from Books 3 to 4a, the movement from Book 7 to Book 1 is
far from disjunctive, as if Seneca proceeds separatively from one topic to another.
The surge of development between the two books is all-important. Beyond the
close connection of Books 7 and 1, however, the former is significantly placed in
antepenultimate position in the *Natural Questions* for a larger reason. After our
movement from water in Books 3 and 4a to air in Books 4b-6, our ascent to the
celestial heights in Book 7 and then in the preface to Book 1 represents the figurative high point of the entire work, as if Seneca here rises to a clarity of viewpoint
from which he then lowers his gaze to focus on the atmospheric lights in the main
body of Book 1, thunder and lightning in Book 2.[120] True, if, as certain scholars
contend,[121] Book 7 occupies terminal place within the collection, the work might
be seen to rise to a fitting climax *in caelestibus*. But if we accept that Book 7 holds
antepenultimate position, Seneca's celestial comets shine forth as symbols of our
highest ambition as we try fully to penetrate nature's secrets in his company; and
the heightened perspective attained in Book 7 also betokens a sublimity of
thought that enables the Senecan *animus* not just to soar above the *sordidi* of
7.31-2, but also to survey from a controlling position the entire surrounding landscape, Books 3-6 and 1-2, of the *Natural Questions* as a whole.

---

119. I.e. (Hine [2010b] 208 n. 9), "the mind observes the point on the horizon at which the
star rises, the highest point of its course across the sky, and the point on the horizon at which it
sets."

120. For response to the possible objection that Books 1 and 2 amount to an anticlimax after
the literal and figurative heights reached in Book 7 and then in the preface to Book 1, see my
Epilogue below. The celestial/cosmic emphasis in the preface to Book 1 may also seem at odds
with the atmospheric subject matter in the main body of Book 1, at least at first sight; but for
the compatibility of these book parts, see the painstaking analysis of Weber (1995).

121. See conveniently Gross (1989) 310-11 F, G and L.

8

Seneca on Lightning and Divination

I: Introduction

Seneca's treatment of comets in Book 7, and of the other technical subjects (anemology, seismology, etc.) featured in Books 1–6, is conveniently relatable to the model of cultural revolution in Roman society that Andrew Wallace-Hadrill has recently associated with profound change in the control of knowledge in the late Republic and early Empire.[1] According to that model, the rise of Helleniza-tion and Rome's own universalizing aspirations contributed to the erosion of a traditional, localized structure of knowledge—knowledge hitherto safe-guarded by an elite that defined by its self-perpetuating authority the essentials of Roman identity in such areas as morality, language, law and religion. For Wallace-Hadrill, this elite had lost control and authority in these areas by the mid-first century BCE: "With the model of Hellenism, the discourse is trans-formed, and their authority passes to specialists who can master increasingly complex and technical fields of knowledge. The rupture is decisive."[2] Under the Empire, these specialists consolidated their authority through the emperor's reliance on their expertise. For Harry Hine, the *Natural Questions* offers one illustration of this restructuring of knowledge. A discourse of suspicion and belief about comets, for example, is replaced in Book 7 by Seneca's rationalizing discourse, a model that applies to much else in the work. For

> earthquakes, lightning strikes on public buildings, meteorite showers, and other unfamiliar lights in the sky, as well as comets, had all traditionally been treated by the Senate as prodigies requiring expiation by religious means; and thunder and lightning was treated as a sign of the gods' favour or disfavour both in the Roman augural system and in the lore of the Etruscan haruspices. Seneca offers a rational rather than a traditional reli-gious approach to these features of the natural world on which Roman religion focused much attention.[3]

---

1. Wallace-Hadrill (1997) and (2008).

2. Wallace-Hadrill (1997) 21; cf. (2008), especially 213–58.

3. Hine (2006) 67.

In our movement from comets in Book 7 to lightning and thunder in Book 2, this stress on the emergence of specialist knowledge and authority has important implications for our analysis of Seneca's extended treatment of divination from lightning in 2.32–51. What role does this involved, somewhat circuitous section play in his broader treatment of lightning and thunder? Much will depend, in answer, on two key themes that will be explored in detail in this chapter: first, the tension that exists in 2.32–51 between Etruscan fulgural divination on the one hand, Stoic rationalization of divinatory practice on the other; and, second, a certain narrowness of divinatory interpretation that is contrasted, as we shall see, with the Senecan/Stoic promotion, not just in Book 2 but in the *Natural Questions* more generally, of an undifferentiated wholeness of world outlook—what we have so far equated in this study with "seeing the all" (cf. 3 pref. 10). In our analysis of these two themes, my goal is not simply to assert the superiority of a *uox rationis* over a *uox religionis*, but to attribute to Seneca a more complex agenda: his exploration in Book 2 of the extent to which, and of the possible ways in which, different systems of thought, traditional and "modern," religious and philosophical (loosely to apply dichotomies that are overly schematic), are reconcilable amid this climate of change in knowledge control in the late Republic and early Empire.

The process of cultural negotiation that I identify in Book 2 offers an outstanding example of a tendency that permeates the entire *Natural Questions*, and that is implicit in each of my seven preceding chapters. But Book 2 is especially relevant to Wallace-Hadrill's model of cultural revolution because the first century BCE witnessed "the beginning of a progression to the isolation of 'religion' as an autonomous area of human activity, with its own rules, its own technical and professional discourse."[4] As we shall see, Cicero for one attests to this development in his *De diuinatione*, that complex investigation of the case both for and against the validity of Roman augury. Whether the reader is persuaded by the arguments on this side or that, Mary Beard plausibly argues that the larger importance of the work centers on the fact that such an enquiry into traditional practice was being staged *at all*.[5] Whether marshaled in defense of or in skeptical attack on traditional piety, Roman philosophy in the later first century BCE can be seen to exercise itself in a new way under Greek influence, with Greek theory deployed on "specifically *Roman* problems and practice, defining and differentiating new areas of recognizably *Roman* discourse."[6] In this period Roman

---

4. Beard et al. (1998) 1.150 after Beard (1992) 755–57; cf. Wallace-Hadrill (2008) 248–51.

5. Beard et al. (1998) 1.150–51.

6. Beard et al. (1998) 1.151.

philosophy thus comes of age as something more than a translation or rendering of Greek philosophy; it was "the first period to define 'religion' through (and as part of) such intellectual theorizing."[7]

My contention is that Seneca fully reflects this climate of theorizing in his treatment of divination in 2.32–51; but he hardly enforces a crude contrast between irrational belief and philosophical rationalization. After all, the divinatory practices on display in Book 2 themselves amount to a scientific discipline, at least in the sense that they rely on a systematic method of interpretation based on given categories of observation.[8] In probing certain logical weaknesses in aspects of that system in Book 2, Seneca hardly attacks divination per se, and naturally so: divination was of course of deep interest to the Stoics, committed as they were to the view that all occurrences are predetermined in accordance with the rule of fate.[9] We can also infer from Seneca's respectful portrayal of the ancient diviners (cf. *sapientissimi uiri*, 2.42.3; *altissimos uiros*, 2.44.2) that he "saw Etruscan religion as a valid and successful attempt to discover something of the workings of the universe and of god";[10] and it is not as if distinguished practitioners of the *disciplina Etrusca* were themselves unschooled in Latin rhetoric and Greek philosophy.[11] Far from seeking to discredit divinatory practice, Seneca searches for commonality as well as difference between the philosophical and religious positions (cf. 2.41.1: "The ideas up to this point are shared by the Etruscans and the philosophers"). We shall focus in detail below on this search for commonality; and we shall also see that this section of Book 2 is no self-enclosed digression of sorts within Seneca's broader examination of lightning and thunder, but that the two viewpoints on display here, Etruscan and Stoic, the one seemingly more restricted and inflexible, the other liberated and expansive, contribute importantly to that broader concern in the *Natural Questions* as a whole—the contrast that we have already observed in previous chapters between the narrowness of terrestrial vision and the breadth of the cosmic viewpoint.

---

7. Beard et al. (1998) 1.151.

8. On this point, Rasmussen (2003) 199–217, especially 201, and Hankinson (1988) 125, and cf. Hine (1981) 341 ("for S., Etruscan religion...is elevated to the level of a genuine, enlightened religion, grounded on true philosophy").

9. Background on the Stoics and divination: Cic. *Diu.* 1.6 with Wardle (2006) 115 on Panaetius' deviation from the more familiar Stoic line, for which Bouché-Leclercq (1879) 58–64 with Sambur+sky (1959) 65–71; further, Lévy (1997), Armisen-Marchetti (2000) 194–95, Kany-Turpin (2003) and Struck (2007), and cf. Vigourt (2001) 162–67 for Seneca and the elder Pliny treated under the rubric of "L'influence stoïcienne." For Seneca alone, Guillaumont (1995).

10. Hine (1981) 420.

11. Notably Aulus Caecina, for whom Hohti (1975) with Rawson (1978) 137–38 and (1985) 28. See also Sections IV (C) and (D) below in this chapter.

A brief summary of the structure of Book 2 will orientate our direction of argument.[12] After Seneca's *diuisio* in 2.1 of the universe into its three parts, the celestial, the meteorological and the terrestrial, and after his extended introductory section on the nature of air in 2.2–11, Book 2 is loosely symmetrical in structure: his extended treatment of the nature of lightning flashes, lightning bolts and thunder in 2.12–30 (doxography in 2.12–20, Seneca's apparently independent analysis of those phenomena in 2.21–30) is offset by a second, cognate section, much shorter but roughly similar in internal structure, at 2.54–58. Between these sections, his report of some of the marvels associated with lightning culminates in its importance as a source of Roman prophecy (2.32.1); hence his examination in 2.32–51 of staple features of Etruscan divination before he reverts, in 2.52–53, to other of the *mira* first introduced in 2.31 (e.g., silver coins fused together in boxes that are themselves undamaged by the lightning strike). After the second technical/doxographical section in 2.54–58, a consolatory epilogue concludes the book, as if Seneca belatedly offers practical counsel against fear of death by lightning (cf. 2.59.1: "I know what you've long wanted, and what you are demanding: 'I'd rather not be afraid of lightning bolts', you say, 'than understand them'"). The epilogue's similarity to the exhortation against fear of death by earthquake at the end of Book 6[13] itself offers a certain reassurance as we move from one order of danger to another and find essentially the same consolatory techniques in operation in both cases, as if another unifying factor within the integrated world(view) of the *Natural Questions*.

Within this schema of Book 2, we first focus in Section II on the two sequences on theories of lightning, 2.12–30 and 2.54–58. Despite certain frailties in Seneca's procedure here, the integrated mode of Greco-Roman discourse that we shall observe in these chapters (as elsewhere in the *Natural Questions*) will be set in contrast to the more problematic integration of the Etruscan/Stoic religious and philosophical strains in 2.32–51. Before we turn to the chapters on divination, however, we survey in Section III the techniques by which Seneca sustains in Book 2 the totalizing worldview that he promotes throughout the *Natural Questions*. In this respect, the initial treatment of 2.12–30 and 2.54–58 in Section II is supplemented by our closer inspection, in Section III, of certain unifying tendencies and emphases that Seneca builds into his technical argumentation in those two passages. The totalizing viewpoint is also contrasted, in Section III, with the relative blinkeredness of vision—the (over)limited circumscription of what is deemed relevant or valid ritual evidence—that Seneca associates with divinatory interpretation in 2.32–51. We then turn, in Section IV, from this clash of perspec-

---

12. After Hine (1981) 35–40; cf. (2010b) 21–22.

13. See Berno (2003) 242–49 with Limburg (2007) 339–42.

tives to our main focus of interest in 2.32–51: Seneca's contribution here to the larger challenge of (to borrow Mary Beard's neat formulation) "integrating the traditions of Roman state religion with a Hellenizing, 'scientific' approach."[14] Finally, in Section V, this challenge of integration in Book 2 is briefly related to the *Natural Questions* as a whole, with due weight given to Seneca's assertion of *Roman* achievement throughout the work: even as he draws fundamentally on the Greek meteorological tradition, he recenters that tradition on Rome. Yet the triumphalist connotations of this Roman emphasis are, for present purposes, of less interest than the process of cultural integration itself; in Book 2 (and far beyond), our Seneca is concerned first and foremost with the dynamics of cultural contestation, and only then with its positive implications for Rome's self-image.

II: Coordination Between 2.12–30 and 2.54–58

A notorious problem complicates the relationship between these two sections. "Now I shall return to Posidonius' view": so begins the second sequence (2.54.1), but where precisely has the *opinio Posidonii* figured down to 2.30? To what passage does Seneca return us at 2.54.1? A brief sketch of his entire argument in 2.12–30 will clarify our options:

12.1–2: initial separating out of lightning flashes (*fulgurationes*), lightning bolts (*fulmina*) and thunder (*tonitrus*); agreement that all of these phenomena occur in, and come from, clouds.[15]

12.3: two schools of thought, (A) that the fire giving rise to *fulgurationes* and *fulmina* preexists in the cloud before it is emitted as lightning; and (B) that the fire is created only at the moment when the lightning is ejected.

12.4–6: Aristotle's exhalation-based theory, along the lines of (B) above in 12.3; "very close" to *Mete.* 2.9.[16]

13–14: critique of the idea that fire is stored up in clouds; emphasis on the fact that, when fire is emitted from clouds, it does not fall but is carried downward, its natural movement being upward.

15: a Stoic theory, attributed to unspecified *quidam*. Lightning results from the fire that is produced by the self-motion of air; thunder is produced when the lightning dissipates cloud.

---

14. Beard (1986) 36.

15. For the modern scientific explanation of lightning and thunder conveniently recounted, see Friedman (2008) 101–4.

16. Kidd (1988) 504; cf. Hall (1977) 410–11 (2.12.4–6 "the most accurate" of Seneca's citations of Aristotle in the *Natural Questions*).

16: the difference between a lightning flash (*fulguratio*) and a lightning bolt (*fulmen*); "probably a continuation of the Stoic theory of ch. 15."[17]

17–20: Presocratic theories, from an unspecified *quidam* (17), Anaximenes (17), Anaximander (18),[18] Anaxagoras (19)[19] and Diogenes of Apollonia (20).

21.1: Seneca strikes out in a seemingly independent direction ("Now we dismiss our teachers and begin to proceed independently"); but he ultimately gives his own theory only in 2.57.

21.2–4: consensus that both lightning flashes and bolts consist of fire; the difference between *fulguratio* and *fulmen* again defined (cf. 12.1–2 and 12.16 above).

22–23: how fire is produced in or by clouds.

24–26: objections are answered. 24: how does a lightning bolt move to earth when fire's natural motion is upward? 25: how can fire be produced in moist cloud? In 26, the fire produced by underwater volcanic eruptions is invoked as evidence that it can be derived from water.

27–30: different types of thunder distinguished on the authority of unspecified *quidam* (27, including Posidonius?);[20] an objection answered (28: how to explain occasions when a cloud strikes a mountain with no resulting sound?); the cloud shape best suited to produce sound (29); and, in 30, thunder and lightning produced by the friction of dry bodies[21] colliding (bodies such as volcanic sand particles from Etna). The friction theory in 30 apparently coincides with the Senecan/Stoic view of the matter: "Such a view is not contrary to our own assumptions. For we have said [*diximus*] that the earth gives off two kinds of bodies," dry and moist (30.3). More strictly, however, he refers in *diximus* back to the *Aristotelian* exhalation theory at 2.12.4.

Posidonius is first mentioned in Book 2 at 2.26.4. The idea that fire can persist in, and despite, water apparently finds support in Posidonius' account of an underwater volcanic eruption that led to the creation of a new island in the Aegean, Hiera, in 197 BCE (2.26.4–5).[22] If at this point we turn again to 2.54.1, it is highly

---

17. Hine (1981) 265.

18. On the superiority of Seneca's report on Anaximenes and Anaximander here to that of Aet. *Plac.* 3.3.1–2 (*DG* pp. 367–68), Bicknell (1968) 182–83.

19. Anaxagoras by conjecture for the surely corrupt *Anaxandros*, which Hine (1996a) 70.338 nevertheless prints; for discussion, see Hine (1981) 281 and cf. (2010b) 213 n. 24.

20. Cf. Hine (1981) 36, 320 ("There is some reason to think that *quidam* might conceal Posidonius").

21. Reading *siccorum* with Hine (1996a) 80.520–21 after (1981) 336.

22. See Kidd (1988) 811–12. For the apparently corroborating case of another island emerging "in our time" (*nostra memoria*), presumably Thia in 46 CE, cf. 2.26.6 and 6.21.1 with Kidd 811 and 816 (but see Henry [1982] for a spirited challenge to the identification of Thia at 6.21.1).

improbable, if not impossible, that Seneca makes a simple but glaring error there, either (1) somehow falsely assuming that he has already referred to the Posidonian theory of thunder and lightning before 2.54, or (2) falsely recalling his mention of Posidonius at 2.26.4 as a full-blown reference to the Posidonian thunder-and-lightning theory, to which he eventually returns in 2.54. But if we exclude, as we surely should, so simple an error at 2.54.1, the presumption must be that Seneca has drawn on Posidonian theory before 2.54, but without direct ascription to Posidonius. On this approach, one passage, 2.12.4–6, has attracted special scrutiny: inaccuracies in Seneca's rendering of Aristotle's exhalation-based theory of lightning and thunder, and similarities between that passage and Posidonius' exhalation-based theory as given in 2.54, have prompted the proposal that Seneca relies in 2.12 on *Posidonius'* account of the Aristotelian theory; when Seneca announces his return to Posidonius at 2.54.1, he therefore refers back to 2.12.[23] Yet Hine details the convincing case against this hypothesis,[24] and he instead highlights parallels between 2.15 and 2.27 on the one hand, 2.54 on the other, to suggest that "in chs. 15 and 27 S. may be using Posidonius"—a debt that "may well extend further; perhaps to ch. 26 as a whole, for example."[25] Kidd similarly relates Posidonius on thunder in 2.54–55.3 to the earlier section on thunder in 2.26–30, but he holds it likely that "the whole of the unnamed theory from ch. 21–30 is then to be taken as derived from Posidonius (how accurately or faithfully is another matter)."[26] But how *then* to reconcile this putative Posidonian presence with Seneca's apparent dismissal of his teachers at 2.21.1? The fact remains that, despite his declaration of independence at 2.21.1, Seneca reports theories in 2.21–30 that are not his own; he delivers his own opinion only in 2.57. The most reasonable conclusion is perhaps that proposed by Kidd: down to 2.21, Seneca "has admitted doxographies from elsewhere.... Then, he operates a development or procedure of argument that is his own, but on a base of Posidonian theory (21–30)."[27] In effect, by dismissing his teachers at 2.21.1, Seneca asserts only a partial independence in 2.21–30; by his return to the view of Posidonius at 2.54.1, he refers back to the Posidonian basis for 2.21–30.

Yet wherever we locate the original *opinio Posidonii* to which Seneca reverts at 2.54.1, there is no continuation in 2.54 of a tight line of argument that is

---

23. Müller (1893) 16 n. 1, and then, e.g., Oltramare (1929) 1.99 n. 3 and Corcoran (1971–72) 1.185 n. 1; inaccuracies in Seneca's rendering of Aristotle even though this is "the most accurate" of Seneca's citations of Aristotle in the *Natural Questions* (see n. 16 above in this section).

24. (1981) 321.

25. (1981) 321–22.

26. Kidd (1988) 505.

27. (1988) 505–6.

interrupted by 2.31–53. Each of the two technical sections, 2.12–30 and 2.54–58, is for Hine "self-contained, and built on a similar pattern"[28]: after doxography (2.12.3–20; 2.54–56), Seneca's own view is given (2.21–23; 2.57), and then his treatment of objections and further problems (2.24–30; 2.58); he perhaps seeks a balance of eminences by beginning his first doxographical section with Aristotle (2.12.4), the second with Posidonius (2.54.1).[29] Despite these loose structural parallels, however, there is no discernible order by chronology or by theoretical content in his doxographical coverage in either 2.12–20 (where, if unspecified sources are excluded, he ranges from Anaxagoras to Aristotle, the Stoics and finally a clustering of Pre-Socratics) or in 2.54–56 (after Posidonius, Clidemus is featured at 54.4,[30] Heraclitus at 56.1). There are notable absences in his doxography: no mention of Theophrastus, for example, and no allusion to atomist theory,[31] although the latter omission might be explained as an aftereffect of Seneca's rebuttal of the atomist theory of air at 2.6.2–9.4. Vagueness in Seneca's exposition of some theories, and sudden transitions from one theory to the next, sometimes obscure or confuse his precise line of thought. Repetitions or inconsistencies in matters of substance are discernible within and across the two scientific sections: at 2.55.1, for example, Seneca denies that thunder is produced by two clouds colliding with each other; this apparently in contradiction of his stance at 2.27–28. At 2.55.2 thunder is derived from fire being extinguished in moist cloud—a theory already featured in 2.17. He explains the difference between lightning flashes (*fulgurationes*) and lightning bolts (*fulmina*) on several occasions (cf. 2.12.1; 2.16; 2.21; 2.57.3), perhaps to draw repeated attention to a Senecan distinction that was not necessarily universal—unless the repetition is simply accidental, and symptomatic of his loose compositional mode.[32] Then there is the impression that Seneca sometimes strains to include material that is peripheral or redundant to his main argument, such as when he inserts brief doxographical notices on Clidemus and Heraclitus at 2.55.4–56.1 before turning to two minor philological curiosities at 2.56.1–2. As if incidental material drawn

28. (1981) 37, with tabulation of the similarities.

29. See Hine (1981) 37.

30. For Clidemus, D-K 62 with Bicknell (1968) 184; presumably different from the fourth-century historian of Attica of the same name (see Guthrie [1965] 359 and n. 2 with Hine [1981] 426–28).

31. Hine (1981) 232.

32. See Hine (1981) 226, and cf. Section III (B) below in this chapter. In modern terms, *fulmen* corresponds to cloud-to-ground lightning, *fulgur/fulguratio* to intracloud discharges, or sheet lightning (Hine 225; [2010b] 213 n. 17).

from memory or index card,[33] such details divert Seneca from the main task at hand until he appears to collect himself at 2.57.1: "You ask what I think."

But the *cumulative* effect of Seneca's presentation is so different. His wide-ranging doxographical coverage; his attention to detail (not least in his repeated differentiations of *fulguratio* and *fulmen*); his orchestrating voice, which is heard early (cf. *dixi*, 2.12.5; *fateor*, 2.13.3) but asserts itself more forcefully as he progresses further into 2.12–30; his later detachment from the authorities on which he draws (cf. *Dimissis nunc praeceptoribus nostris*, 2.21.1) as he moves toward delivering his own judgment ultimately in 2.57; his emphasis on searching for fundamental principles as opposed to ad hoc explanations for seemingly aberrational or chance occurrences (cf. 2.55.3: "We are now looking for the natural and regular cause, not an uncommon, accidental one"); his frequent elaborations and extensions of argument in response to interlocutory queries or objections; above all, his commitment to a purely natural explanation of lightning and thunder, with no allowance made for divine intervention or popular superstition: in all of these ways, and as if in recapitulation of his *modus operandi* throughout the *Natural Questions*, Seneca's two sequences in 2.12–30 and 2.54–58 showcase a stringently rational[34] approach to physical explanation, in a medium that displays all the complexity and technical specialization that Wallace-Hadrill associates with a new structuring of Roman knowledge in the late Republic.[35] Strengths and weaknesses in specific points of argument matter less than this overall impression of assurance and control; and by interrupting the two sections with his treatment of divination in 2.32–51, I propose that Seneca aims for an encircling effect, surrounding those chapters with this demonstration of the Hellenized, scientific method in exemplary action.

III: *The Totalizing Worldview: Strategies of Unification in 2.1, 2.12–30 and 2.54–58*

Another important feature of 2.12–30 and 2.54–58, one that is directly relevant to Seneca's treatment of divination in 2.32–51, is anticipated in his *diuisio* of the three branches of the study of the universe in 2.1 and then in his discourse on the nature of air in 2.2–11. Once defined by reference to 2.1–11 in (A) below, this feature will deepen our analysis of 2.12–30 and 2.54–58 in (B) before we relate it, in (C), to a cognate phenomenon in 2.32–51.

---

33. Cf. Hine (1981) 425, 430.

34. Cf. Inwood (2000) 39; (2002) 152 = (2005) 195.

35. See Section I above in this chapter.

(A) 2.1–11

"The entire study of the universe is divided into the branches of the celestial, the meteorological and the terrestrial" (*in caelestia sublimia terrena*): after this division at the beginning of Book 2, and after Seneca's delineation of the properties of each of the three branches (2.1–2), the neat demarcation of categories is immediately qualified in two respects, as we saw earlier.[36] First, 2.1.3: Why, asks an imaginary interlocutor, has Seneca included earthquakes among *sublimia*? Earthquakes are classified among *terrena* by other ancient researchers, but, explains Seneca, he (like Aristotle) locates them among *sublimia* because their cause—air in motion—is meteorological. Secondly, 2.1.4–5: "I shall tell you something that will seem a still greater surprise: earth will have to be discussed [*de terra dicendum erit*] in the context of celestial phenomena." The surprise element here is in fact minimal: Seneca quite reasonably proposes to treat the earth's relation to the heavens in the category of *caelestia*, not *terrena*.[37] And so why does he draw special attention to this unremarkable overlap between *caelestia* and *terrena*? Why does he make so much of both footnotes to the original *diuisio*? We earlier explored the possibility that Seneca's blurring of boundaries in 2.1.3–5 gently reasserts the indivisibility of nature's parts after the tripartite division introduced in 2.1.[38] From the perspective of the Senecan oneness that we have experienced thus far in the *Natural Questions*, that division, while evidently valid in one sense, appears overly schematic and insensitive to ambiguity on the margins; it runs counter to the synthesizing tendency of the whole work.

After our initial sampling in Chapter Two of the elusiveness of rigid demarcation in nature, we observed a more ambitious assertion of Seneca's integrating perspective in his treatment of the unity of air (2.2); of its place and importance as a mediating presence in the universal scheme (2.3.1–6.1, especially 2.4.1: "air is a part of the world order, and an essential part. For this air is what connects the heavens and earth and separates the lowest and the highest levels in such a way that it nevertheless joins them"); of its tension (2.6.2–9.4, with a forceful rebuttal of atomic theory, by which air can have neither unity nor tension); and of the nature of the *aer*/atmosphere (2.10–11, especially 10.1: it is "more mobile, thinner and higher than the earth, and the waters too, but it is thicker and heavier than the aether, and is intrinsically cold and dark").[39] Seneca justifies his extended disquisition on air in 2.2–11 as follows:

---

36. See Chapter Two, Section III.

37. See Hine (1981) 127.

38. See Chapter Two, Section III.

39. See Chapter Two, Section III.

Haec necessarium fuit praeloqui dicturo de tonitru fulminibusque ac fulgurationibus. nam cum in aëre fiant, naturam eius explicari oportebat, quo facilius appareret quid facere aut pati posset.

2.11.3

It has been necessary for me to make these preliminary remarks before I go on to speak of thunder, lightning bolts and lightning flashes. For since they occur in the atmosphere, its nature had to be explained to make it more easily apparent what it could do or undergo.

A convenient transition to Seneca's main theme in Book 2; but, as Hine observes, the connection between 2.2–11 and what follows is "not so close as he makes out."[40] And, on the assumption that Book 2 was positioned last in the original ordering of the *Natural Questions*, why does Seneca expatiate only *here* on the properties of air? That element is fundamental to Seneca's treatment of winds in Book 5, of earthquakes in Book 6; why delay his discourse on air until the beginning of Book 2? Perhaps Seneca compensates in 2.1–11 for an earlier omission; yet "there is not a word in what [he] says to indicate such an intention."[41] Or should we revisit the problem of the books' original ordering? Unsurprisingly, the *diuisio* of 2.1 has been interpreted as programmatic in function, laying out a plan for the entire work. Hence the body of opinion that Book 2 was the first in the original ordering, or that the first chapter of Book 2 is to be relocated at the beginning of the work.[42] But quite apart from the impressive strength of the case for an original order of 3, 4a, 4b, 5, 6, 7, 1 and 2, the facts remain (1) that in 2.1 Seneca alludes to topics that are not treated in the extant work even as he omits topics that *are* treated; and (2) that even when allowance is made for the possible incompleteness of the work, and also for a certain imprecision in his programmatic forecast, his statements of intent in 2.1.4–5 (e.g., *ubi quaeretur quis terrae situs sit*) need amount to nothing more than generalizing futures of the sort that deliver only vague promises elsewhere in the *Natural Questions* and beyond.[43]

---

40. (1981) 224; cf. pp. 12–13 ("the tension of air, which bulks large in the first eleven chapters, is forgotten in the rest of the book").

41. Hine (1981) 13.

42. See Hine (1981) 13 with Gross (1989) 315–16. The programmatic interpretation of 2.1 extends back to Koeler (1819) 250–57, but Rehm (1907) 376–77 offers but one strong sample of the case against (further, Codóner [1989] 1787–91).

43. Cf. Section IV (A) and n. 113 below in this chapter on 2.38.3, and Section IV (C) and n. 136 on 2.46; see also Hine (1981) 195 on 2.7.2 *sed hoc alias*.

But if we therefore reject the theory that 2.1 constitutes a programmatic introduction to the whole work, and if we still hold that Book 2 was placed last in the
original collection,[44] how then to account for that initial *diuisio* and Seneca's subsequent disquisition on air? The proposal was made earlier that 2.1–11 *in toto* serves
an important retrospective function as a capstone demonstration, centered on air
as an essential connecting and unifying agent, of the oneness that has characterized
the Senecan cosmos throughout the preceding books; the initial *diuisio* of 2.1 is
supplanted by the exemplary, unifying emphasis that prevails in 2.2–11.[45] In this
chapter, however, our focus turns to the *prospective* significance of 2.1–11 within
Book 2: to what extent, and how, can the wholeness of world perspective as experienced in 2.1–11 be seen to inform and affect later developments in the book?

(B) 2.12–30 and 2.54–58

Two main tendencies sustain the unifying emphasis of 2.1–11 in these sections.
The first is argument by analogy: the marked frequency with which Seneca uses
the technique in 2.12–30 in particular[46] contributes significantly to the conjoining effect—the coordination of separate orders via analogy throughout the *Natural Questions*—that we have already observed in previous chapters.[47] The second
tendency concerns Seneca's general eye not for boundary, difference and limit in
nature, but for ambiguity, mixture and cohesion between the natural parts. Of
the various illustrations of this tendency that present themselves, the following
three cases nicely exemplify the subtlety with which Seneca privileges merger
over separation.

Consider first, at a relatively trivial level, Seneca's repeated explanations of the
difference between *fulgura/fulgurationes* and *fulmina*, lightning flashes and bolts
(cf. 2.12.1; 2.16; 2.21; 2.57.3)—a difference articulated in several ways in 2.21 alone
before Seneca comments self-consciously on his elaborations at 2.21.4:

> non ad exercendum uerba diutius hoc idem tracto, sed ut cognata esse ista
> et eiusdem notae ac naturae probem. fulguratio est paene fulmen. uerta-
> mus istud: fulmen est plus quiddam quam fulguratio.

---

44. True, "nothing in Book II indicates or acknowledges that it was the last book," and Seneca
may conceivably have written, or planned to write, more books than have survived (Hine
[1981] 32). Yet the work as we have it yields no clue to indicate that Book 2 was *not* terminal.

45. See Chapter Two, Section III.

46. So 2.12.5; 14.2; 15; 16; 17; 22.1–2 with Hine (1981) 292–93; 24.2; 27.3; 27.4; 28.1; 28.2; 29.
Cf. also 2.55.1; 55.2; 55.4; 56.1; 57.2.

47. See especially Chapters One, Section II and n. 13; Four, Section IV (B); and Six, Sections
III and V (C).

I deal with this same point at considerable length not just to play with words, but to prove that these phenomena are related and of the same kind and nature. A lightning flash is almost a lightning bolt. Let's turn the point around: a lightning bolt is something more than a lightning flash.

Seneca's self-justification here can indeed be read with "a grain of scepticism," as he does indeed seem to be "enjoying repeating the same idea in several different and unexpected ways."[48] But his attention to detail reinforces his credentials as a painstaking researcher; and, more important, the particular case in point—the relatedness of *fulguratio* and *fulmen*—is itself symptomatic of Seneca's wider habit in the *Natural Questions* of looking to correspondence and interconnection in nature. What matters in 2.21, perhaps, is not so much the correctness of the distinction that he draws between *fulguratio* and *fulmen*, but the unifying mindset that conditions his treatment of the particular case here: his eye is preconditioned, as it were, to see difference despite similarity, similarity amid difference.

Second, a deeper example of this merging tendency focuses on elemental interchangeability. So, in 2.15, Seneca reports the Stoic theory that thunder and lightning result from the spontaneous movement and self-ignition of air. That motion sparks lightning; thunder is produced when the fire dissipates clouds that have dense and compacted hollows.[49] Other surviving reports of the Stoic theory derive thunder and lightning from the kindling effect (ἔξαψις) of clouds that rub against each other or are torn asunder by wind; from the impact of wind (itself derived from cold exhalations from earth) when it enters a cloud and breaks up and scatters its thinnest portions very rapidly; or from dry exhalation from earth being enclosed in clouds and seeking exit.[50] As Hine points out, however, no other extant Stoic account explicitly mentions the self-ignition of air, while the friction or bursting of clouds that *does* feature prominently in the Stoic tradition plays but a subsidiary role in 2.15.[51] It may be that Seneca

---

48. Hine (1981) 291–92.

49. With possible resonances of Lucr. 6.279–80 *ipse* [sc. *uertex*] *sua cum/ mobilitate calescit et e contagibus ignis* at 2.15 *ipse* [sc. *aër*] *enim se mouendo accendit*, and of Virg. *Aen.* 5.434–35 *pectora uastos/ dant sonitus* (of the boxing match between Entellus and Dares) at 2.15 *uastum … reddit* [sc. *aër*] *sonum*. On these and other echoes, Parroni (2002) xxxiii–iv and 511; for the atmospheric sound that they contribute to Seneca's proceedings here, cf. Chapter Six, Section V (D) n. 112.

50. For the first, *SVF* 1.117 p. 33.33–34.2 and 2.704 p. 203.20–26 (D. L. 7.153 in both cases), and cf. 2.703 p. 203.11–13 and 2.705 p. 203.27–29. For the second, *SVF* 2.699 p. 202.26–31 (= Cic. *Diu.* 2.44). For the third (Posidonian), *N.Q.* 2.54 with Kidd (1988) 507–509, especially 509.

51. Hine (1981) 263–64.

preserves an emphasis on self-ignition that was traditional;[52] but, for now, the
interest of his theory lies less in the problem of its origin (can we rule out the
possibility that Seneca goes his own way here?) than in the elemental interchangeability that it presupposes. "Some of our people believe that, since air
can change into fire and water, it does not draw any new source of fire from
outside itself: the air ignites itself by its motion [*ipse…se mouendo accendit*]"
(2.15). The air is brought to life in 2.15 as it is at 5.5.1, where air is said to have "a
natural capacity for self-motion" (*naturalem uim mouendi se*)[53]; but the mutability of the elements is not restricted only to 2.15. So at 2.23.2, on the formation
of lightning from air, the air, which "can change into fire" (*aër mutabilis in
ignem*), is ignited when subjected to a great force of friction—including its own
force of friction (*uiribus…suis*) when it is changed into wind. Then, in 2.26,
Seneca answers the interlocutory objection (2.25) that clouds are moist, even
wet: How, then, can they produce fire by friction? Nothing prevents fire, he
asserts at 2.26.2, from being drawn from moisture; indeed, "some say that nothing can turn into fire without first changing into water." In this instance, the
Peripatetic view that fire is fueled by moisture has been invoked by commenta-
tors,[54] even though Seneca's emphasis on change *into* water evidently differs
from the Peripatetic position; and further difficulties beckon if we try to reconcile Seneca's statement with the Stoic theory that fire changes into the other elements in a fixed order (air, water, earth), the elements then changing back into
fire in reverse order.[55] Tracing the Senecan theory to its origins is evidently
problematic in this instance. But the mutability that his wording here clearly
assumes contributes to a broader series of allusions in 2.15, 23 and 26 to elemental transference between different material states. Seneca draws no special
attention to this changeability, in contrast to his quasi-programmatic disquisition on elemental mutability in 3.10.[56] At the other end of the extant work, in

52. Cf. Hine (1981) 264: other accounts of the Stoic theory do not necessarily represent a
theory different from that given by Seneca, "*for the doxographers may have left out the distinctive
details which [he] preserves*" (my emphasis).

53. See on 5.5.1 Chapter Five, Section II.

54. See Hine (1981) 311 for sources, including Theophr. *Ign.* 10: "It also happens that some
ceasing of it [sc. fire] occurs, since *the moisture of what was ignited earlier is being consumed*; and
the greater fire, when it is brought closer, destroys the lesser fire, either by taking away its food
or else by drying up its beginning and causing it to wither by overpowering it. For *nothing can
burn either without moist, or, when there is moist in it, if it does not have the power that will actually produce fire*" (so Van Raalte [2010] 97; my emphasis).

55. To begin with, Seneca mentions no intermediate step at 2.26.2 in the change from water
to fire; further, Hine (1981) 312, and for the Stoic theory, Chapter One, Section I n. 3.

56. See Chapter One, Section I.

Book 2, that mutability appears unremarkable, as if by now a long-accepted fact of the Senecan physical framework; hence its understated presence in 2.12–30 as a basic source of continuity and connection in the material substratum.

Our third, and perhaps the most interesting, example of the merging tendency takes us back to the Aristotelian theory of thunder and lightning as reported by Seneca at 2.12.4–6. If we momentarily revert to the Aristotelian original on which Seneca (or his source) draws, Aristotle summarizes the Empedoclean and Anaxagoran theories of fire's preexistence in cloud before it is ejected as lightning; he then offers four criticisms of those theories, two directed first at Anaxagoras, then two at Empedocles (*Mete.* 2.9 369b19–370a10). Seneca modifies the Aristotelian ordering, first introducing the Empedoclean and Anaxagoran theories at 2.12.3 (he names only Anaxagoras) and subsequently moving to Aristotle's exhalation-based theory (2.12.4–6); only *then*, in 2.13, does he offer his critique of the Empedoclean/Anaxagoran theory of fire's preexistence in cloud.[57] In 2.13 itself, Seneca reproduces only the first two of Aristotle's four criticisms, but in reverse order; "[t]he greater complexity of the latter two, and the weakness of the third, are possible explanations of the omission, whether it is due to S. or to his source."[58] So Aristotle:

> The enclosure of the fire [sc. in cloud] is difficult to account for on both [Empedoclean and Anaxagoran] views. The difficulty is greater on the [Anaxagoran] view that it is drawn down from the upper aether. For *we should be told the reason for the downward movement of something whose natural movement is upwards*, and further why this happens only when the sky is cloudy and not all the time, since it does not happen in clear weather.
>
> *Mete.* 2.9 369b19–24; trans. H. D. P. Lee (my emphasis)

Compare Seneca at 2.13.1:

> Falsam opinionem esse eorum qui ignem in nubibus seruant per multa colligi potest. si de caelo cadit, quomodo non cotidie fit, cum tantundem semper illic ardeat? *deinde nullam rationem reddiderunt quare ignis, quem natura susum uocat, defluat.*

---

57. For 2.12.3 "agree[ing] fairly well with *Mete.*, being evidently derived from it," Hall (1977) 428, adding that "[a]lmost certainly, 2.19 is another version of Anaxagoras' theory" (but cf. Section II n. 19 above in this chapter).

58. Hine (1981) 254.

That the theory of those who preserve fire in the clouds is incorrect can be deduced from many factors. If the fire falls from the heavens, why does it not happen daily, since it always blazes to the same degree there? *Then they've given no explanation of why fire, which is naturally summoned upwards, flows downwards.*

Seneca (or his source) conveniently simplifies the Aristotelian critique. But why, in marked contrast to Aristotle, does he make so very much of fire's natural motion upward?[59] From 2.13.1 down to the end of 2.14 he offers an extended, rhetorically charged justification of his case that fire cannot descend to the atmosphere from the heavens. Certainly, his initial critique at 2.13.1 is impressively, if unnecessarily, reinforced in 2.13–14 as a whole (yet Aristotle's pithy argument is surely no weaker for the absence of any such elaboration). But a side effect perhaps helps to explain the sheer length of that elaboration.

"Everything is set in order" (*ordo rerum est*, 2.13.4): in response to an imaginary interlocutor who asks "Are some fires not commonly brought down to the lower regions, as are these lightning bolts we are investigating?" (2.13.3), Seneca stresses that they are indeed carried downwards by a noncelestial force, rather than going by their own natural motion (*non eunt tamen sed feruntur; aliqua illos potentia deprimit, quae non est in aethere,* 2.13.3). In terms of Seneca's initial *diuisio* at 2.1.1–2, he forcefully demarcates the *ordo caelestium* at 2.13.4:

> ordo rerum est, et expurgatus ignis in custodia mundi summa sortitus oras operis pulcherrimi circumit; hinc descendere non potest, sed ne ab externo quidem comprimi, quia in aethere nulli incerto corpori locus est: certa et ordinata non pugnant.
>
> Everything is set in order, and the purified fire that has been assigned to the highest regions in protection of the world encircles the boundary of this most beautiful structure. It cannot descend from there, and it can't even be pressed down by any outside force, because there is no place in the aether for any unstable body: no conflict exists in things that are stable and ordered.

---

59. Beyond 2.13.1, cf. also 2.14.1 and 7.21.2, 23.1 with Galdi (1923) 120–21 on the fire-moves-upward theme as one example of "una particolare forma di ripetizione" in the *Natural Questions*, i.e., the marked recurrence of ideas that (for Galdi p. 119) appear "secondary and of meager value." In this case, as we shall see, I depart fundamentally from Galdi: the fire-moves-upward theme here is no mere "secondary" presence at 2.13.1 and beyond, but another factor that tellingly supports and promotes Seneca's all-important emphasis on the ordered yet integrated/interpenetrating world whole.

The interlocutory objection remains (2.14.1) that "All of you, I say, when you give an explanation of shooting stars, say that some portions of the atmosphere *can* draw fire from the heat of the upper region, and can thus be ignited";[60] but in conceding the point, Seneca insists that fire cannot fall (*decidere*) from the celestial region ("nature does not permit it") but "is itself generated in the lower regions [*hic nascitur*]." After the clinical demarcation of the celestial region in 2.13.4, however, the boundary between it and the atmospheric region is more ambiguously drawn in 2.14.2:

> itaque ueri simile est etiam in aëre summo id quod ignis rapiendi naturam habet accendi calore aetheris superpositi. necesse est enim et imus aether habeat aliquid aëri simile, et summus aër non sit dissimilis imo aetheri, quia non fit statim in diuersum ex diuerso transitus; paulatim ista in confinio uim suam miscent, ita ut dubitare possis ad<hoc>[61] aër an iam aether sit.
>
> So, it is probable that, also in the upper atmosphere, something that is capable of catching fire is ignited by the heat of the aether above it. For the lowest part of the aether necessarily has something similar to atmosphere, and the highest part of the atmosphere is necessarily not unlike the lowest level of the aether, because no transition from different to different happens at once. Those neighboring constituencies gradually mingle their properties in such a way that you cannot be sure whether it is still atmosphere or already aether.

After the hard separative tendency of 2.13.3–4, the boundary between the celestial and atmospheric regions proves in 2.14 to be as elusive as the transition point between rainbow colors in Book 1 (cf. 1.3.4). The *ordo rerum* schematizes the whole, but the Senecan eye quickly reverts, as if in reflex response to (overly) clinical division *in partes*, to ambiguity on the margins—a movement from separation to merger that emulates, I propose, the pattern set in the transition in 2.1–11 from Seneca's opening *diuisio* to his unifying discourse on air.[62]

---

60. Reading, with Hine (1996a) 68.290 after Castiglioni (1921) 443–44, *ex loci superioris ardore, et sic accendi* (see for discussion Hine [1981] 260–61). Elsewhere, Seneca explains shooting stars as atmospheric phenomena (e.g., 1.1.9–10, 14.5); when, at 1.15.1, he contemplates "the heat of the upper heavens" (*superioris caeli feruor*) as the cause of σέλα or meteors at the atmospheric level, he does so without endorsing the theory, and as but one of many possibilities (cf. *multis ut aiunt modis*, 1.15.1).

61. So Hine (1996a) 68.303 after Castiglioni (1921) 444; for discussion, Hine (1981) 262–63.

62. See again Chapter Two, Section III.

(C) 2.32–51

This tendency toward merger, with nature's integrated oneness the focus of our perception, is directly relevant to Seneca's treatment of divination in 2.32–51[63]; for basic to that treatment is his characterization of the Etruscan system as relatively blinkered and restricted in scope, at least in comparison with the Stoic view that all events are implicated in the causal nexus that orders the universe.

The Etruscan viewpoint is partial, the Stoic one whole: from the latter perspective, lightning is hardly special in its occurrence, as the Etruscans believe, as if it is produced only, and specifically, to reveal the future (2.32.2); for the Stoics, the predictive potential of lightning is no different from that of any other event in the great causal nexus (cf. 2.32.3–4).[64] But if every event "is a sign of something that will happen" (2.32.4), why, asks an imaginary interlocutor, apparently in defense of the Etruscan position, does augury rely on observation of only a few bird types (2.32.5)? In reply, Seneca asserts the broader viewpoint: *all* living creatures offer predictive signs of future events, whether or not we read those signs (2.32.5). In augural theory omens are valid only if observed and accepted by those to whom they pertain (cf. 2.32.6)[65]—a function of chance (the relevant person observing the occurrence) and of free will (the person acknowledging the omen) that is evidently incompatible with Stoic adherence to the causal nexus. In arguing that "signs also occur that pass unnoticed" (2.32.6), Seneca circumvents this embarrassment by exposing us to omens that apply regardless of observational chance and of any choice as to their acceptance; and that breadth of vision is reinforced

---

63. For the Senecan plan of 2.32–51 conveniently laid out, see Hine (1981) 342–43, with pp. 340–42 for justification of this section's unusual length. Factors include the larger, conducive climate of research in the first century CE (a similar blend of Etruscology and science is found in the elder Pliny at *Nat.* 2.135–46); the rise of Etruscan religion to become "fashionable again in S.'s lifetime" (p. 340); and the consideration that, for Seneca, "Etruscan religion is not merely invested with the authority which was bestowed on it upon its acceptance within the Roman establishment, but it is elevated to the level of a genuine, enlightened religion, grounded on true philosophy." My own analysis of 2.32–51 in Section IV below steers an independent course, but it is hardly incompatible with Hine's approach on pp. 340–42. For basic background on lightning as one of the three divisions of Etruscan divination along with haruspicy and the interpretation/expiation of portents (*ostenta*), see Bouché-Leclercq (1882) 16–17 and Thulin (1906) 1–12 with Bloch (1984) 46–75. On the Etruscan "science fulgurale" in particular, Bouché-Leclercq 32–61 with, conveniently, Bloch 60–68; and for its principles set down in the *libri fulgurales*, see Rasmussen (2003) 44, and cf. the three-fold division into *libri haruspicini, fulgurales* and *rituales* at Cic. *Diu.* 1.72 with Wardle (2006) 282.

64. For analysis of this section, Guillaumont (2006) 186–87 with Wildberger (2006) 341–46, and cf. Armisen-Marchetti (2000) 201 for Seneca's resistance in 2.32 to "une vision bien réductrice de la grandeur divine."

65. Cf. Plin. *Nat.* 28.17, and see Hine (1981) 351–52 with Wardle (2006) 357 on *Diu.* 1.103 "My daughter, I accept the omen."

by the contrasting picture of the Chaldean astrologers who restrict their observations to only the five planets,[66] even though, Seneca asserts (2.32.7–8), our destinies are influenced by *all* stars, the planets as well as the fixed stars. Beyond the philosophical interest of his maneuvers here (to be taken up in Section IV below), the contrast that we observed in Chapter Two between cosmopolitan immersion in the *totum* on the one hand, the partiality of everyday perception on the other, is replayed, with due modification, in this difference between Seneca's panoptic viewpoint and the Etruscans' narrower field of vision in 2.32–51. So in Seneca's treatment, in 2.34.1, of the priority that the Etruscans apparently give to lightning if different classes of sign are contradictory:

> Summam esse uim fulminis iudicant,[67] quia quidquid alia portendunt, interuentus fulminis tollit; quidquid ab hoc portenditur fixum est, nec alterius ostenti significatione mutatur. quidquid exta, quicquid aues minabuntur, secundo fulmine abolebitur; quidquid fulmine denuntiatum est, nec extis nec aue contraria refellitur.

> They conclude that the power of lightning is supreme because the intervention of lightning annuls whatever is portended by other omens. Whatever is foretold by lightning is fixed and unchanged by the meaning of another sign. A favorable bolt will cancel whatever is threatened by entrails or birds; whatever warning is given by lightning is not refuted by any contradictory entrails or bird.

For Seneca, by contrast, the truth is *simplex*, a oneness without gradations ("nothing is truer than the truth," 2.34.2), just as fate is single (*fatum unum est*, 2.34.3) and, "if correctly understood from a first omen, not annulled by a second" (2.34.3).

At issue here is an important point not just of Stoic principle in the localized context, but also of Senecan principle in the *Natural Questions* generally: the oneness of fate in Book 2 naturally belongs within the larger system of oneness—that uninterrupted physical and conceptual unity—that dominates the imaginative world of the *Natural Questions*.

---

66. Five planets, the sun and moon discounted (cf. 7.3.2, 8.3, 13.1, etc.). The *Chaldaei* here denote astrologers generally; see Vottero (1989) 334 n. 10, also relating Seneca's antipathy to the *Chaldaei* to Panaetius frr. 70–74 Van Straaten (1946) 341–45 (see especially fr. 74 = Cic. *Diu.* 2.87–97)—a departure from the more usual Stoic line (see Liebeschuetz [1979] 121, 125, and cf. Section I n. 9 above in this chapter).

67. The Etruscans are presumably the subject of *iudicant*, but later in 2.34 (especially §§2–3) Seneca appears to refer to augural science, not Etruscan divination; see Hine (1981) 364–65 (Seneca "may not be very alert to distinctions between Etruscan haruspicy and Roman augury"), with parallels for lightning as *auspicium optimum/maximum*.

IV: Seneca on Divination in 2.32–51

Our closer inspection of Seneca's chapters on divination takes its starting point
from the proliferation of writings on the subject in the late Republic—a phenomenon partly explained by the exigencies of preserving religious tradition, including the setting down in Latin of the *disciplina Etrusca* as a consequence of the
decline of the Etruscan language.[68] Of these writings, Cicero's *De diuinatione* is of
special relevance for now because of the problematic relationship between the
two books that constitute the work. In Book 1, the positive case for the validity of
divination is presented, along Stoic lines, in the mouth of Quintus Cicero; only
then for Cicero's own *dramatis persona* to offer a strong rebuttal of that case from
a skeptical Academic standpoint in Book 2. How are the two cases for and against
to be weighed against each other? In considering this problem, we shall draw on
De diuinatione partly to contextualize Seneca's own treatment of divination
within a framework of Roman theoretical reflection on the nature and state of
the art; but partly also, in the balance of the two books, to prepare the way for
identifying a comparable balancing of perspectives in the Senecan passage.

In his *De legibus*, which he appears to have left incomplete after 51 BCE,[69]
Cicero, who was himself elevated to the college of augurs in 53 or 52,[70] staunchly
defends (in his own *dramatis persona*) traditional Roman religious practices, divination included:

> Egone? diuinationem, quam Graeci μαντικήν appellant, esse sentio...si
> enim deos esse concedimus, eorumque mente mundum regi, et eosdem
> hominum consulere generi, et posse nobis signa rerum futurarum ostend-
> ere, non uideo cur esse diuinationem negem.
>
> *Leg.* 2.32[71]

> Me? I believe that there is such a thing as divination, which is called *man-
> tike* by the Greeks....For if we accept that the gods exist, and that the
> world is governed by their mind, and that they also give attention to the
> human race and are capable of giving us indications of future events, then
> I see no reason why I should deny the existence of divination.

68. See Rawson (1985) 299, 302–306.

69. Zetzel (1999) xxi; cf. Dyck (2004) 7, dating the work to "the late 50s."

70. For the suggestion that Cicero was nominated in autumn 53 but actually elected in March
52, Linderski (1972) 190–99 = (1995) 240–49; for his enthusiasm for the role, Tucker (1976),
especially 174–75, with Wardle (2006) 7.

71. On the "Stoic premises" here, Dyck (2004) 347.

In *De diuinatione*, however, written probably between late 45 and Caesar's death and published between mid-April and mid-May 44,[72] Cicero strikes a very different note: such practices as reading entrails have no truth to them, but are to be maintained "for the sake of political expediency and shared religious feeling" (2.28; cf. 2.70).[73] How is this apparent *volte-face*[74] to be explained? Few scholars would now adhere to the once-standard theory of the progressive decay of Roman religion, according to which an educated elite in the late Republic and early Empire became increasingly estranged from religious traditions through factors such as the influence of Greek philosophical ideas in an age of rationalism, or disenchantment at the political exploitation of religious practice and belief.[75] Accordingly, one-dimensional readings of Cicero's attack in *De diuinatione* 2 as evidence of this religious decline have given way to more nuanced responses. So, on one approach, Cicero at last reveals in *De diuinatione* 2 his true opinion of divination after bowing to convention in his earlier writings and public speeches;[76] whether he does so purely for the sake of argument or from an earnest desire "to eradicate belief in all forms of divination" and so "to uphold true religion, sharply differentiated from superstition,"[77] his negative stance in *De diuinatione* 2 arguably accentuates the doubt already lurking in *De legibus*.[78] Alternatively, the different natures of *De legibus* and *De diuinatione* have been explained in terms of the *theologia tripertita*, or the three types of theology that were distinguished by Varro and earlier writers; of those three branches, *De legibus* belongs, as a work of political theory, to the *genus ciuile*, *De diuinatione* to the *genus physicum*.[79] Others explain Cicero's change from faith to skepticism by reference to his shift in philosophical affiliation from Antiochus' Old Academy to the Academic Skepticism of

---

72. See Wardle (2006) 37–43, especially 43.

73. Further on this line, Guillaumont (1984) 45–49.

74. Goar (1968) 241 = (1972) 96. For the charge of hypocrisy balanced against the claims of an evolution in Cicero's thought, see Rasmussen (2003) 192–98.

75. For this theory conveniently summarized/critiqued, Liebeschuetz (1979) 7–29 with Brunt (1989) 174 and Feeney (1998) 3–6.

76. Cf. Wardle (2006) 7–8; Timpanaro (1998) lxxix ("Nel *De diuin.* l'esigenza di verità prevale").

77. Goar (1968) 246–47 = (1972) 101–102.

78. Goar (1968) 245 = (1972) 101 ("The scepticism, the inchoate negation, was there all along in *De legibus* II").

79. See Momigliano (1984) 202 with Linderski (1982) 23 = (1995) 469: "In the *De re publica* and *De legibus* Cicero discourses and legislates as a *princeps ciuitatis*; in the *De natura deorum* and *De diuinatione* he presents his views as a philosopher." But for this appeal to the *theologia tripertita* contested, Schofield (1986) 63 n. 30.

Philo and Carneades[80] (a shift coinciding with his unhappy personal circumstances in his last years, including the death of his daughter, Tullia, in February 45);[81] or by reference to his increasing disillusionment at Caesar's exploitation of state religion for political ends.[82] Whatever the true cause (or combination of causes), these various explanations all presuppose that Marcus' voice in *De diuinatione* 2 faithfully reflects the views of Cicero himself—an assumption that itself no longer passes unchallenged.[83]

Yet just how complete or convincing is Cicero's case against divination in *De diuinatione* 2? After all, certain factors appear to undermine his attack, or at least to qualify significant aspects of it. To take just three examples: first, at 1.9, Quintus defines divination as "the foretelling and foreseeing of those events which *are thought* to occur by chance" (*quae* [sc. *diuinatio*] *est earum rerum, quae fortuitae putantur, praedictio atque praesensio*). With *putantur*, Quintus deftly safeguards the Stoic theory from the charge of inconsistency leveled by Carneades (cf. 2.15–19): How is Stoic determinism to be reconciled with a view of divination as "the foreknowledge of things that happen *by chance*" (*fortuitarum rerum . . . praesensio*, 2.19)? In answer, if we accept the alternative Stoic account of chance as "a cause obscure to human understanding," a sense of chance that is "quite neutral with regard to causal determinism,"[84] the meaning of divination as *fortuitarum rerum praesensio* is instantly transformed, its chance element defensible on new criteria. But more pertinent for now: Marcus slyly elides Quintus' *putantur* in repeating the Stoic definition at 2.13 ("I observed [says Marcus] that you defined divination to be 'the foreknowledge and foretelling of things which happen by chance [*quae essent fortuitae*]'") before exploiting that distortion in 2.19: "But if you deny the existence of chance, . . . change

---

80. See Glucker (1988), especially 53 for Cicero's reversion to Skepticism dating to "some time in 45 B.C."

81. See Glucker (1988) 66; Hecht (2003) 145.

82. See Linderski (1982), especially 34–38 = (1995) 480–84; Momigliano (1984) 210 ("The more Caesar was involved in religion, the more Cicero tried to escape it").

83. See especially Beard (1986) 35 (rejection of "any notion of a 'Ciceronian viewpoint' emerging from *De diuinatione*"), 45, and cf. n. 85 below. But for the countercase see now Wardle (2006) 10–14, especially 14: "The burden of proof that Marcus alone, and then only in the theological dialogues, should not be credited with holding the views he expresses lies with those who suggest this."

84. Hankinson (1988) 155; for this Stoic definition of chance as ἄδηλον αἰτίαν ἀνθρωπίνῳ λογισμῷ, *SVF* 2.966, 967, 970, 971 p. 281.8, 12, 15–16, 35–36, 40. Wardle (2006) 122, following Hankinson 155 n. 129, suggests that this definition ultimately goes back to Democritus (cf. D-K 68A70); but for the suggestion that Quintus relies at *Diu.* 1.9 on a Posidonian reformulation of Antipater of Tarsus' (? cf. Pease [1973] 68) definition, see Timpanaro (1998) lxv, xciii.

your definition of divination, which you said was 'the foreknowledge of things that *happen by chance*.'"[85]

Second, beyond the embarrassment that Marcus in effect attacks in Book 2 a definition of divination different from that offered in Book 1,[86] his detection of methodological fault in Quintus' discourse is matched by frailties of his own. "You have indeed defended the Stoic doctrine with accuracy, Quintus," Marcus asserts at 2.8, "and like a Stoic": he presumably refers to Quintus' emphasis on empirical outcomes rather than on causes (cf. 1.86: "You ask *why* each of these things happens. The question is perfectly legitimate, but it is not the point at issue now. The question is *whether* it happens or not"). At one level, Marcus' arguments seem potent enough[87]: how many predictions actually come true? However many do, how to prove that chance played no part in the outcome (cf. 2.52)? And if chance alone is not held responsible for every successful outcome, ambiguous prediction, guesswork, fraud and distortion after the event may account for those other cases. Yet to fault Quintus for his failure to explain causation is not necessarily to demolish his empirical method per se. Quintus himself adduces the parallel of medical remedies, whose healing properties are well known, the exact cause of healing unknown (1.13): quite apart from the consideration that Quintus' case is at least constructive, Marcus' entirely destructive,[88] "are Cicero's objections stronger against divination than they are against any other conjectural τέχνη, medicine included?"[89] Once measured against the shortcomings of its contemporary competitors in the sciences, especially medicine, Quintus' emphasis on outcomes, not causes, may appear far more reasonable than Marcus allows;[90] and given Quintus' disinterest in the *why?* question, much of Marcus' attack may in any case seem fundamentally misdirected, leaving Quintus' empiricist position unassailed.[91]

---

85. I take it that the character Marcus' modification in 2.13 deliberately complicates the relationship of the two books; Cicero *qua* author and Marcus are needlessly conflated (cf. Beard [1986] 35, and see n. 83 above in this chapter) by Pease (1973) 378, for whom Cicero's misquotation at 2.19 of Quintus' words at 1.9 is "doubtless not by intention on his part but through careless joining of somewhat unrelated sources" (cf. similarly Schofield [1986] 62; Timpanaro [1998] xciii).

86. See Schofield (1986) 62.

87. Cf. Kidd (1988) 109 (Quintus' emphasis on outcomes is "not only unPosidonian in its disregard of causes, but nonsense and easily attacked by Cicero in Bk II").

88. On this point, Schofield (1986) 62.

89. Hankinson (1988) 148.

90. For this approach, Hankinson (1988) 148, 157–59.

91. Hankinson (1988) 151. Cf. Denyer (1985), arguing (p. 2) that "[s]ince divination on the Stoic account [Book 1] does not even pretend to be scientific, it is altogether immune from the charge [Book 2] of being no more than pseudo-science."

Thirdly, even if we agree with David Wardle that "Marcus at the very least shows that the Stoic and Peripatetic arguments raised by Quintus can be power-fully countered and probably contradicts them successfully,"[92] Cicero himself offers no conclusion at the end of Book 2; in true Academic fashion, the reader is left to weigh the merits of the two cases for and against divination (cf. 2.150).[93] If Cicero is engaged in a sincere and committed denunciation of divination, why this suspension of judgment at the close? So Mary Beard: "Those who deduce Cicero's personal scepticism from the second book of *De diuinatione* ignore this clear denial of a directed conclusion and neglect to treat the dialogue as a whole, as a balance of arguments for and against divination."[94]

For present purposes our concern is with this balance of arguments, and, still more important, with the different modes of discourse represented by the two arguments. For Malcolm Schofield, Quintus' case for divination amounts to a "rhetoric of anecdote" that relies on "a massive battery of examples drawn from experience, fictional or putatively historical."[95] By contrast, Marcus' coun-tercase applies "the rhetoric of cross-examination" and "appeals constantly to reason"—a rhetorical approach that marks "a Romanization of philosophy as thoroughgoing as Book I's immersion in Roman myth and history."[96] Beard, too, stresses this Romanizing element, but in the context of Cicero's efforts (and real achievement) "in attempting for the first time an active integration between Greek philosophy and traditional Roman practice and thought."[97] In the tensions, limitations and evasions that are visible in and across the two books of *De diuinatione*, Cicero probes "the underlying confrontation between traditional Roman symbolic knowledge of the workings of the world and the developed Hellenizing encyclopaedic rules for comprehending the same phe-nomena"; on this approach, claims Beard, Cicero's treatment of state religion across his philosophical works constitutes not "the argued presentation of an opinion or a view; it constitutes rather the process of formation of a discourse on theology."[98]

---

92. Wardle (2006) 16 and n. 66, building on Repici (1995).

93. On this line, Guillaumont (2006) 325–31, especially 330–31 ("Cicéron, qui a indiqué son choix, mais refuse tout dogmatisme, invite le lecteur à exercer son propre *iudicium*, à se faire une opinion par lui-même").

94. Beard (1986) 35.

95. Schofield (1986) 51, 52.

96. Schofield (1986) 51, 55.

97. (1986) 36.

98. (1986) 41, 46.

Despite pockets of opposition, the balanced approach to *De diuinatione* on offer in the studies of Schofield and Beard has won wide acceptance in later scholarship.[99] For now, however, this approach offers an illuminating precedent for, if not a direct influence on, Seneca's treatment of divination in *Natural Questions* 2. He writes not in a vacuum, I argue, but continues the habit of Roman self-inspection—of exploring the compatibility between Greek philosophical ideas and Roman religious tradition—that is manifested in *De diuinatione*. In Seneca's case, we shall see that the compatibility issue is played out in 2.32–51 in the spirit so well captured by James Allen:

> Though they typically attached great importance to time-hallowed and widely dispersed customs like the practice of divination, *the Stoics felt duty-bound to scrutinize them and to reformulate them in the light of their own canons of sound method.* And their account of divination was in large part an attempt to free it from aetiological pretensions by bringing it into line with the more modest strictures of other less ambitious but more securely grounded arts. This they did principally by reinterpreting it along empirical lines.[100]

My contention is that the Etruscan component in 2.32–51 undergoes precisely this kind of scrutiny and reformulation in alignment with Seneca's Hellenizing, Stoic method. True, Allen's emphasis on a Stoic reformulation of divination along specifically empirical lines is absent in Seneca. The reformulation process that I nevertheless claim for 2.32–51 differs in its particular focus and orientation—a procedure that is conveniently sampled in the following four categories.

(A) Reconciling Prayer and Expiation with a Deterministic View of Fate (2.35–38)

If fate is immutable and omens are encoded in fate, what use can there be in trying to avert them by expiation (2.35.1)? Seneca broaches this familiar question[101] from two opposing standpoints, the first from the perspective of the *rigida secta* that apparently permits no deviations in the flow of fate and therefore dismisses

---

99. For a listing of adherents as well as critics, Wardle (2006) 8 n. 34 with Guillaumont (2006) 21–22 and n. 59.

100. (2001) 161; my emphasis.

101. Cf. Cic. *Diu.* 2.20–21, after Carneades (Timpanaro [1998] lxiii, with his p. 338 n. 33); further parallels in Pease (1973) 378–79. For a convenient overview of Stoic response to the question, see Magris (1990).

expiation as futile (2.35.1–2);[102] and then from the perspective of those who believe that expiation is useful (2.37.1)—the Etruscans, that is, with whom Seneca
subsequently aligns "us Stoics": "For the moment [*interim*], they have this in
common with us, that we, too, think that vows are helpful, without any infringe-
ment of the force and power of fate" (2.37.2).[103]

From this point on, the complexities of Seneca's procedure find important illumination in the techniques that Chrysippus apparently used to combat the so-
called Idle Argument: If fate is fixed and outcomes are predetermined, why
should we bother to make decisions about action?[104] The only surviving attempt
at refutation that is connected to a particular philosopher or school, Chrysippus'
rebuttal is preserved in Cicero's *De fato* 28–30.[105] So in §30:

> Haec ratio a Chrysippo reprehenditur. quaedam enim sunt, inquit, in
> rebus simplicia, quaedam copulata; simplex est: 'Morietur illo die
> Socrates'; huic, siue quid fecerit siue non fecerit, finitus est moriendi
> dies. at si ita fatum est, 'Nascetur Oedipus Laio', non poterit dici: 'siue
> fuerit Laius cum muliere siue non fuerit'; copulata enim res est et confa-
> talis: sic enim appellat quia ita fatum sit, et concubiturum cum uxore
> Laium et ex ea Oedipum procreaturum ... omnes igitur istius generis cap-
> tiones eodem modo refelluntur. 'Siue tu adhibueris medicum siue non

---

102. For Oltramare (1929) 1.86 n. 2, the *rigida secta* represents the old Stoa, but cf. Hine (1981)
367–68 ("no proper evidence for this"). The allusion is perhaps not to a particular phase of, but
to an extreme viewpoint within, Stoicism (cf. Parroni [2002] 518). For an overview of the problem, Armisen-Marchetti (2000) 207–8.

103. I take it that *interim* here introduces a digression that extends down to the end of 2.40,
with 2.41.1 ("The ideas up to this point are shared by the Etruscans and the philosophers")
rounding out Seneca's identification of common ground between the two groups; for full discussion, Hine (1981) 375–77.

104. On Seneca's appropriation of the Idle Argument, and for analysis of 2.34–38 in general,
Wildberger (2006) 321–41.

105. Apart from *Fat.* 30 (= *SVF* 2.956 pp. 277.32–278.6), Bobzien (1998) 181 also cites two
later versions of a Chrysippan rebuttal, the one (which currently concerns us) at *N.Q.* 2.37.3–
38.4, the other in Origen (*C. Cels.* 2.20 = *SVF* 2.957 p. 278.7–40 = Sharples [1991] 92–95 App.
A); see also her coverage (pp. 208–17) of Diogenianus' report of the Chrysippan refutation as
preserved in Eusebius' *Praeparatio euangelica* 6.8.25–38 (= Mras [1982] 325.25–328.4). Bobzien
181 deems it likely that both the argument and Chrysippus' reply belong to his second book on
fate; for Barnes (1985), especially 232–36, Chrysippus is the common and direct source for
both Cicero and Origen (cf. p. 235: "Chrysippus, for those few lines at least, is Cicero's source—
and his source in the precise sense that he is copying, in translation, a passage from Chrysippus'
writings"). For Cicero's *De fato* in planned relation to his *De natura deorum* and *De diuinatione*, see *Diu.* 2.3, 2.19, *Fat.* 1 with Pease (1973) 10 and n. 8 and Wardle (2006) 411 on *Diu.*
1.127; Schofield (1986) 48–51.

adhibueris, conualesces' captiosum; tam enim est fatale medicum adhibere quam conualescere. haec, ut dixi, confatalia ille appellat.

This argument is criticized by Chrysippus. For, he says, there are in actuality two classes of fact, simple and complex. A simple fact is: "Socrates will die on a given day"; in this case, whether he takes some action or takes no action, the day of his death has been determined. But if it is fated that "Laius will have a son Oedipus," it will not be possible to add: "whether Laius mates with a woman or does not mate." For the matter is complex and co-fated—he gives that name to it because he thinks that it is fated for Laius both to have intercourse with his wife and to beget Oedipus by her.... Therefore, all captious arguments of this sort are refuted in the same way. "You will recover whether you call in a doctor or not" is captious; for calling in a doctor is just as much fated as getting better. These connected events, as I said, are termed by Chrysippus co-fated.

It is important to stress that Chrysippus' case as presented here is *only* a refutation of the Idle Argument, and not a defense of free will per se;[106] and that he targets only a particular aspect of the Idle Argument, namely the premise either that "If it is fated that x will happen, then, whether or not you do y, x will happen," or that "If it is fated that x will not happen, then, whether or not you do y, x will not happen." Either version of the premise is false, responds Chrysippus, because, in the counterexamples he gives, action y is inseparable from the outcome x, x and y being *confatalia*, or co-fated occurrents; the limit of his refutation in Cicero is to show that "although all instantiations in the scheme of the Idle Argument may appear sound, as a matter of fact, some [i.e., the two versions of the premise as given above] are not."[107] The further objection remains: If x and y are co-fated, how can those actions depend on our decision? This point is not ignored in ancient responses to Chrysippus,[108] but Cicero makes nothing of it, and understandably so: the point is irrelevant to Chrysippus' immediate task in the *De fato* passage. As Susanne Bobzien observes,

> It is [Chrysippus'] assumption that relations of (causally relevant) necessary condition hold between actions and outcomes, which allowed

---

106. Bobzien (1998) 181.

107. Bobzien (1998) 203. Cf. p. 184 for the full scheme of the Idle Argument laid out: "(P1) If it is fated that *A*, then, whether or not you *Φ*, *A*. (P2) If it is fated that not-*A*, then, whether or not you *Φ*, not-*A*. (P3) Either it is fated that *A* or it is fated that not-*A*. (C) Therefore (with regard to *A*) it is futile (for you) to *Φ*."

108. See Bobzien (1998) 231.

Chrysippus to avert the challenge of the Idle Argument and to uphold his fate-determinism. *The question whether these actions depend on the agent plays an explicit role neither in the argument nor in the refutation*, and the [libertarian] objection is thus irrelevant.[109]

There are indications that Chrysippus did indeed seek to go beyond refutation of the Idle Argument to address the question of how, if all is fated, our decisions for action are not irrelevant.[110] But the key point for now is that Cicero's Chrysippus counters the Idle Argument on grounds that are narrowly limited in scope, with no focus on the problem of whether or not we have freedom of decision and action.

Now to Seneca. Striking parallels exist between his sequence of argument on the relationship of fate and prayer at 2.37.2–38.1 and Chrysippus' refutation of the Idle Argument in Cicero. These parallels persuade Bobzien that the Senecan passage "goes back to Chrysippus' refutation, although the context seems not early Stoic and there is insufficient evidence for the assumption that Seneca drew directly on Chrysippus."[111] Seneca's argument is divisible into six stages:

(i) 2.37.2. Stoic and Etruscan readiness to allow the efficacy of prayer ("For some things have been left undecided by the immortal gods in such a way that they turn to our advantage if prayers are offered to the gods, or if vows are undertaken"). Prayer is not opposed to fate, but is itself also *in* fate.

(ii) 2.37.3. An interlocutory objection, possibly giving voice to the *rigida secta* of 2.35.1: "It will be or it will not be; prayer and vows make no difference."

(iii) Still 2.37.3. Seneca's counterobjection. A third way between the options of "it will be" or "it will not be": it will be, but only if vows are made.[112]

(iv) 2.38.1. The same, persistent interlocutory voice is unremitting: vows, too, are to be included in fate, to the effect that you either will or will not make them.

---

109. (1998) 232; my emphasis.

110. See Bobzien (1998) 232 and n. 128.

111. (1998) 204. Cf. p. 189 n. 29 for differences of Senecan emphasis (including "it will obtain," *futurum est*, as opposed to "it is fated," *fatum est*) that distinguish *N.Q.* 2.36–38 from "classic" formulation of the Idle Argument.

112. Cf. the distinction drawn between unconditional/conditional *fata* (*denuntiatiua* as opposed to *condicionalia*) by Serv. auct. *ad Aen.* 4.696 (Thilo-Hagen 1.582.2–584.22)—a sequence partly represented at *SVF* 2.958 pp. 278.41–279.10, but, as Hine (1981) 370 points out, "there is nothing in the passage itself or elsewhere to prove that it is Stoic, still less that it is Chrysippean."

(v) 2.38.1–2. A Senecan concession that removes decision from his third way: the making (or not making) of vows is included in fate.

(vi) 2.38.3. Such reasoning (2.37.2–38.2) may habitually be used to demonstrate the impossibility of free will, but Seneca promises to reconcile free will and fate "when this matter will be discussed [*cum de ista re agetur*]"; in the meantime, he has explained how, even if fate is unalterable, expiations may yet avert omens because "they are not in conflict with fate but themselves exist in the law of fate" (he thus repeats the thrust of stage (i) above).

After the sparring that takes place in (iii) and (iv), Seneca effectively asserts in (v) the Chrysippan position on co-fated occurrents. We saw above that the limit of Chrysippus' argument in Cicero is to establish the causal relationship between *confatalia*; whether the actions themselves are in their agents' control falls beyond the scope of *De fato* 28–30. So in Seneca: it may appear that in 2.38.3 he all too conveniently postpones addressing the problem of free will by gesturing to a later treatment of that particular issue;[113] but on closer inspection he studiously follows the Chrysippan precedent (at least as portrayed by Cicero) in dealing only with the *confatalia* question. To adapt Bobzien's characterization of Chrysippus: Seneca's goal is to demonstrate that "fate-determinism is compatible with purposeful action [i.e., expiation]. For this he *presupposes* that the actions are in the agents' control; but this point is not at issue in his argumentation" in 2.37.2–38.2.[114] It is introduced as a related but separate issue only in 2.38.3.

For our purposes, Seneca's appeal here to Chrysippus' refutation of the Idle Argument offers a model example of his larger effort in 2.32–51 to rationalize Etruscan divination within Greek terms of argument, or to integrate religious tradition with "a Hellenizing, 'scientific' approach."[115] Hence the powerful effect of the term *aruspex* at 2.38.4—notably, the first and only appearance in Book 2 of a word so charged in its Etruscan identity and origin:[116] "So, then, what use to me," asks Seneca's dogged interlocutor at 2.38.4, "is a diviner

113. On this "not infrequent means of deferring the argument," Parroni (2002) 520, comparing 2.7.2, 46, 53.3; but Vottero (1989) 342 n. 2 finds a probable Senecan allusion to his *Libri moralis philosophiae*, for progress on which cf. *Letters* 106.1–3, 108.1, 109.17 with Griffin (1976) 399 n. G and Vottero (1998a) 204–7 T90–92 and p. 72 (the work dated to the last six months of Seneca's life, from October 64 on).

114. Bobzien (1998) 232.

115. Beard (1986) 36.

116. The word recurs in Seneca only at *Clem.* 1.7.1. For (*h*)*aru/ispex* "assumed to be a loanword from Etruscan," De Vaan (2008) 280; cf. Ernout and Meillet (1967) 290 ("un composé hybride étrusco-latin (?)") with Pfiffig (1975) 45: (*h*)*aruspex* perhaps "eine alte Übersetzung eines etruskisierten Wortes aus *ned*+*Fid*."

[*aruspex*]?[117] For [after fate-determinism wins out in 2.37.2–38.3] it's necessary for me to offer expiation in any case, even if he does not advise it." In response, Seneca validates the role of the *aruspex* by recasting him as "a servant of fate" (*fati minister*), on the analogy of the medical doctor whose ministrations deliver a nevertheless fated cure. A smooth, perhaps too smooth, reconciliation is effected here between the religious and the philosophical positions. For present purposes, however, the persuasiveness (or otherwise) of Seneca's maneuver in 2.38.4—the reconfiguration of the *aruspex* as *fati minister*—matters less than the integrating effort that drives the whole sequence of argument from 2.37.2 onward.

(B) The "Scientific" Classification of Lightning (2.39–40)

Aulus Caecina, Cicero's friend and the distinguished scion of an old Etruscan family from Volaterrae,[118] is Seneca's source for the tripartite classification of lightning that is introduced at 2.39.1. Caecina, educated in the *disciplina Etrusca* by his father (cf. Cic. *Fam.* 6.6.3) in the customary Etruscan way,[119] apparently wrote in Latin the work on which Seneca draws in *Natural Questions* 2 (cf. 2.56.1: "I find this statement in Caecina, a talented man who at one time would have won renown for eloquence, had Cicero not overshadowed him"); his reputation for eloquence suggests that this was a book of high literary quality, and so perhaps well known at Rome.[120] Two features of Seneca's critique of Caecina's classification of lightning are of special relevance for now, the first concerning his differentiation of lightning categories in 2.39. Of the types that he distinguishes at 2.39.1—the *fulgur consiliarium* is directed at those contemplating an action; the *fulgur auctoritatis* occurs after an action, indicating whether the consequences will be good or bad; the *fulgur status* occurs when no action is planned or undertaken, and delivers threats, promises or warnings[121]—Seneca apparently struggles

---

117. *aruspex* here perhaps with derogatory force; cf. Cic. *Diu.* 1.132 *uicanos haruspices* (not necessarily Cicero's words, but arguably part of a Ciceronian paraphrase of Ennius; see Salem [1938] 56, with an update in Wardle [2006] 422), albeit *haruspices* there of "unofficial, private *haruspices*" (Pease [1973] 335), *not* members of the Etruscan elite who advised the Roman senate on prodigies (see on this point Wardle 422 with North [1990] 53 on the different strata of *haruspices*).

118. For bibliography, see Section I n. 11 above in this chapter. I take it that Cicero defended this Caecina's father in his *Pro Caecina* of 69 BCE (so Rawson [1978] 137 n. 43 *contra* Hohti [1975] 419).

119. See Pease (1973) 259 on Cic. *Diu.* 1.92 *principum*; Hohti (1975) 428 and n. 3.

120. Hohti (1975) 428.

121. On this classification, Hine (1981) 379–80 with Bouché-Leclercq (1882) 42, Thulin (1906) 78–81 and Weinstock (1951) 147–49. Cf. Serv. auct. *ad Aen.* 8.524 (Thilo-Hagen 2.273.18–274.1) and Ammian. 23.5.13 with Hine 380: "Ammianus probably [cf. Parroni (2002) xxxvi], and Servius auct. possibly, depend on S."

at 2.39.2 to separate the first and third categories before he finally arrives at two distinctions between them at 2.39.3–4. Why does he dwell in such detail on the difference between the first and third categories? For Hine, Seneca "gives the impression of thinking out loud—perhaps a sign of hasty composition, but possibly a designedly casual way of making the distinction clear."[122] Or, additionally (the various possibilities are not mutually exclusive), does Seneca merely accentuate the extreme generality of Caecina's classifications[123] by going to such lengths to clarify the difference between two of them? Does his ostentatious elaboration at 2.39.2–4 imply a certain lack of definitional rigor on Caecina's part?

Second, Seneca takes Caecina's tripartite division to task in 2.40 for distinguishing not types of lightning but types of meaning (*non sunt fulminum genera, sed significationum*); he subsequently offers a second, more "scientific" classification of lightning types according to their physical nature and effect, beginning with "the type that bores, the type that shatters and the type that burns" (*quod terebrat, quod discutit, quod urit,* 2.40.1; subdivisions of this initial division follow).[124] As Hine points out, scientific writers from Aristotle onward had distinguished types of thunderbolt, and the Roman sources yield a rich variety of classifications, but none of them exactly corresponds to Seneca's here.[125] Does he instead, or in addition, rely on an Etruscological source? His statement at the beginning of the next chapter (2.41.1)—"The ideas up to this point are shared by the Etruscans and the philosophers"—certainly suggests that the Etruscans accepted a division such as that described in 2.40; and Hine for one suspects that "the substance of ch. 40 comes from an Etruscological source."[126] For a further clue to the Etruscan character of 2.40, we turn to a passage of Festus (s.v. *Manubiae*, p. 114.5–14 Lindsay) that yields close parallels with 2.40–41:

> Manubiae Iouis tres creduntur esse, quarum unae sint minimae, quae moneant placataeque sint. alterae quae maiores sint, ac ueniant cum fragore, discutiantque aut diuellant, quae a Ioue sint, et consilio deorum mitti existimentur. tertiae his ampliores, quae cum igne ueniant; et quamquam nullum sine igne fulgur sit, hae propriam differentiam habeant quod aut adurant, aut fuligine deferment, aut accendant; quae statum mutent deorum consilio superiorum.

122. Hine (1981) 380.

123. Hine (1981) 380; cf. Weinstock (1951) 148 for the artificiality of the tripartite division.

124. On this classification, Hine (1981) 382–84 with Bouché-Leclercq (1882) 40–41, Thulin (1906) 56–68 and Weinstock (1951) 127.

125. Hine (1981) 382–83; further parallels in Vottero (1989) 344 n. 1.

126. (1981) 384.

It is believed that Jupiter has three types of thunderbolt.[127] Of these, one is very minor in scale; they give a gentle warning. The second type is larger in scale and arrives with a crash, shattering things or tearing them apart; they are sent by Jupiter, but are thought to be dispatched only after he has taken the gods' advice.[128] The third is still larger in scale than the second type, and comes with fire. Although no lightning flash is without fire, this third category is distinguished by the characteristic that it either causes scorching, or brings disfigurement with soot, or sets something alight. These bolts alter our state of affairs on the advice of the "higher" gods.[129]

Festus here combines two kinds of material—*genera fulminum* in general, Jupiter's *manubiae* in particular—that Seneca keeps separate. After his division of lightning types in 2.40, Seneca moves to the three Jovian *manubiae* in 2.41:

Haec adhuc Etruscis philosophisque communia sunt: in illis dissentiunt, quod fulmina a Ioue iudicant mitti, et tres illi manubias dant. prima, ut aiunt, monet et placata est, et ipsius Iouis consilio mittitur. secundam mittit quidem Iuppiter, sed ex consilii sententia; duodecim enim deos aduocat…tertiam manubiam idem Iuppiter mittit, sed adhibitis in consilium dis quos superiores et inuolutos uocant, quia uastat in quae incidit, et utique mutat statum priuatum publicumque quem inuenit. ignis enim nihil esse quod fuit patitur.

The ideas up to this point are shared by the Etruscans and the philosophers. They disagree on this, namely that the Etruscans adjudge lightning bolts to be sent by Jupiter, and they assign him three *manubiae*. The first, so they say, offers a gentle warning, and is sent on the decision of Jupiter

---

127. On these three types, Bouché-Leclercq (1882) 35–37 with Thulin (1906) 25–32 and Hine (1981) 387. *manubia* is perhaps "a Latinised Etruscan word" (Weinstock [1951] 125; cf. Bouché-Leclercq 35 n. 1); if not, it is possibly derived from *manus* and *habere*, but much uncertainty remains (Weinstock 125 with Hine 390; on its reported etymologies, Maltby [1991] 366 with Ernout and Meillet [1967] 385).

128. This *consilium* is equivalent to the council of twelve gods assembled at *N.Q.* 2.41.1 as quoted below; they are elsewhere known as the *di Consentes* (Hine [1981] 390 with Bouché-Leclercq [1882] 37–38, 97–98, Thulin [1906] 27, 31–32 and Weinstock [1951] 127–29).

129. These "higher" gods otherwise lack sure testimony, but one possibility is that they are precursors of the Roman *Penates*; see Hine (1981) 391 with Bouché-Leclercq (1882) 37, 97, Thulin (1906) 28–31 and Weinstock (1951) 129, and cf. Jannot (2005) 15: "Who are these unnamed gods, whose number is unknown and who have no image? Are they a primitive expression of divinity, older than and superior to Tinia [/Zeus/Jupiter] himself…, or might they be identified as the very fate that dominates individualized gods? Remarkably, decisions concerning the life of humans (or of states) may thus be out of the hands of the most powerful deities."

himself. Jupiter also sends the second type, but on the advice of his council; for he summons the twelve gods.... Jupiter also sends the third type of bolt, but after he has called into council the gods whom the Etruscans call "higher and hidden," because the bolt destroys whatever it strikes, and invariably changes whatever states of affairs, private or public, that it encounters. For fire lets nothing remain as it was.

It might be that Festus draws directly on Seneca here; on balance, however, the differences in detail between the two accounts suggest that both draw on a common source, which for Hine is "very likely Caecina."[130] But we should surely proceed with caution on this last point. After all, given Caecina's apparent division of types not of lightning but of meaning (*non . . . fulminum genera, sed significationum*, 2.40.1), can he really have been Seneca's source for the *genera fulminum* that are so clinically differentiated in 2.40, or for the traces of a similar component (categorization of the burning effects of different bolts) in the Festus passage?

Caecina aside, however, the Festus passage suggests an Etruscan openness to reconciling the religious and philosophical viewpoints. Given that, apart from Caecina and (eventually) Attalus (cf. 2.48.2, 50.1), Seneca cites no other Latin source in 2.32–51, Elizabeth Rawson suspects that "everything here on thunderbolts involving Latin technical terms is from Caecina. And if what 'the Tuscans' say means what Caecina says, he perhaps tried to reconcile religion and philosophy."[131] But our reading above of 2.39–41 suggests another characterization of Caecina: that, *at least as Seneca presents him* (and also in comparison with Attalus later in Book 2), he attempted no such reconciliation. So Stefan Weinstock:

> Seneca's narrative [in 2.39–41] could lead to the conclusion that *Caecina set against the scientific explanation of the Greeks the divinatory one of the Etruscans*. The parallel passage in Festus shows that in fact the Etruscans accepted the scientific explanation but put it into the service of their divination.[132]

Far from serving as a mouthpiece for the Etruscans in general in 2.32–51, Seneca's Caecina here represents, I propose, an Etruscan of a particular stamp, hallowed but nonprogressive, in contrast to those *Etrusci* who apparently do see commonality between the religious and philosophical sides at 2.41.1. In a context where religious

130. (1981) 383; cf. 62.

131. Rawson (1985) 305.

132. Weinstock (1951) 127.

tradition is set in contention, or perhaps rather in constructive dialogue, with philosophical rationalism, this Caecina emerges as a traditionalist resistant to Seneca's
more flexible, integrating effort; this Caecina resembles the stubborn interlocutor
we observed earlier in 2.32–51, as if the former's traditionalism on the Etruscan/re-
ligious front matches the latter's rigidity on the Stoic/philosophical front.

(C) Seneca's Rationalization of Etruscan Belief (2.42–46)

After explicating the nature of thunder, lightning and lightning bolts earlier in *De
rerum natura* 6 (96–378), Lucretius turns on the *disciplina Etrusca*:

> Hoc est igniferi naturam fulminis ipsam
> perspicere et qua ui faciat rem quamque uidere,
> non Tyrrhena retro uoluentem carmina frustra
> indicia occultae diuum perquirere mentis....

6.379–82

> *This* is to understand the true nature of the fiery thunderbolt,
> and to perceive by what power it does each thing,
> and not by unrolling the Tyrrhenian prophecies in vain search
> for signs of the hidden purpose of the gods....

For Lucretius, lightning bolts are evidently no supernatural phenomena; for
(*inter alia*) if Jupiter and the gods hurl their bolts as punishment, why do they not
ensure that only the wicked are struck in a sharp lesson for mankind (*documen
mortalibus acre*, 6.392)? Why are the innocent hit (6.393–95; cf. 2.1103–4)? Why
do the gods waste their efforts by hurling their bolts into desolate places (6.396;
cf. 2.1102)? Why does Jupiter attack the temples and statues of the gods, his own
among them (6.417–20; cf. 2.1101–2)?

The whole series of arguments that Lucretius deploys at 6.379–422 against the
supernatural interpretation of lightning reflects a longstanding tradition extending back to the fifth century.[133] Seneca, too, reflects that skeptical tradition when,
after describing the role played by Jupiter as punisher in the Etruscan system in
2.41 (quoted in Section IV (B) above),[134] he rounds on the folly ("at first sight,

---

133. See Bailey (1947) 1610–11 with Pease (1973) 428 on Cic. *Diu.* 2.44 *frustra, etc.* But for the
specifically Lucretian impact on Book 2, see Althoff (2005), especially 22–30.

134. But since "for the Etruscans lightning was primarily an omen…, and [2.41–46 aside]
there is no other evidence that they also regarded it as a punishment," Seneca's (and Lucretius') attribution of a "punishment view" is perhaps mistaken: Hine (1981) 387–88.

antiquity is in error," 2.42.1) of imagining that Jupiter literally wields punitive bolts;[135] for are we then to attribute to Jupiter's ill will or his poor aim those bolts that strike the innocent or seem to hit pointless and random targets (2.42.1)? Yet, in response to such misgivings, Seneca vindicates the "very wise" Etruscans (*sapientissimi*, 2.42.3) by interpreting allegorically their belief that Jupiter has at his disposal the *manubiae* distinguished in 2.41. So, for the Etruscans, Jupiter neither deliberately targets the innocent nor simply misses when he takes aim at the guilty; through his bolts, he has the overriding objective of instilling in arrogant and corrupt mankind fear of a power that is higher than itself (2.42.3).

On the Stoic side, Seneca defers his full response to the problem of why Jupiter might strike the innocent and pass over the guilty: "You are summoning me to a larger inquiry," he replies to his imaginary interlocutor in 2.46, "which will have to be given its own time and its own place."[136] His provisional answer—Jupiter is responsible not for every specific bolt but for the overall scheme or plan (*ratio*) that systematizes their general occurrence (2.46)—instantly runs into difficulties of its own.[137] But of greater interest for now is the part that this answer plays as a Stoic foil to the Etruscan rationalization at 2.42.3, as if the two sides are set in experimental dialogue with each other, with Seneca acting as a mediator between them, testing or reaching for contact and commonality between the two systems of thought. The Etruscans apparently share the same conception of Jupiter:

> Ne hoc quidem crediderunt, Iouem, qualem in Capitolio et in ceteris aedibus colimus, mittere manu fulmina; sed eundem quem nos Iouem intellegunt, rectorem custodemque uniuersi, animum ac spiritum mundi, operis huius dominum et artificem, cui nomen omne conueniet. uis illum fatum uocare? non errabis...uis illum prouidentiam dicere? recte dic<es>...uis illum naturam uocare? non peccabis...uis illum uocare mundum? non falleris: ipse est enim hoc quod uides totum, partibus suis inditus, et se sustinens et sua. *idem Etruscis quoque uisum est*, et ideo fulmina mitti dixerunt a Ioue quia sine illo nihil geritur.

---

135. For Theophrastan traces also, Mansfeld (1992) 328–31.

136. The work he has in mind, if a specific one (but cf. Parroni [2002] 522), is perhaps his *Libri moralis philosophiae*, not (*pace* Oltramare [1929] 1.94 n. 2 and Corcoran [1971–72] 1.175 n. 1) *De prouidentia* (= *Dialogue* 1); see now Lanzarone (2008) 15–16 with Section IV (A) n. 113 above in this chapter, and cf. Mansfeld (1992) 330 n. 44 ("I am inclined to believe that Seneca also has the concluding chapter of book two in mind").

137. Beginning (Hine [1981] 400) with the problem of why an all-providential god would construct a system with such ill-advised side effects.

Nor did they even believe that Jupiter, such as the one we worship on the Capitol and in the other temples, hurls bolts with his hand. They recognize the same Jupiter we do—the controller and guardian of the universe, the mind and breath of the world, the master and creator of this construction, for whom every name will be suitable. You wish to call him fate? You will not be wrong.... You wish to call him providence? You will be right.... You wish to call him nature? You will not be mistaken.... You wish to call him the world? You will not be wrong; for he himself is all this that you see, implanted in all his parts, and sustaining both himself and all that is his. *The Etruscans had the same concept*, and so they said that lightning bolts are sent by Jupiter because nothing happens without him.

Seneca shows no sign here of accepting any hierarchy among god, fate and nature of the sort that has been (wrongly) attributed to Posidonius on the basis of Cicero and Aetius.[138] The equivalence of names (fate, providence, etc.) is conventional enough in the Stoic tradition,[139] and the hymnic quality of the passage is also paralleled in other philosophical contexts.[140] But the stylistic heightening here may also lend a quasi-ritualistic air to Seneca's configuration of an ordaining force that spans the philosophical and religious domains. He has already identified common ground between the Stoics and Etruscans (cf. *communia*, 2.41.1), but this chapter, 2.45, offers its own experimental quest for commonality in its gradual unfolding of Jupiter's bilateral credentials; the two sides here converge in a Senecan meeting of codes.

(D) Caecina and Attalus (2.48.2–50)

Seneca's report in 2.49 of the definitional names that Caecina assigned to lightning types (e.g., *postulatoria*, or ones "demanding" that sacrifices interrupted or improperly conducted be redone; *peremptalia*, or the "canceling" type that

138. Cf. Aet. *Plac.* 1.28.5 (*DG* p. 324) and Cic. *Diu.* 1.125 ("Therefore, I think we should do as Posidonius does, and trace the whole force and rationale of divination first from god,...secondly from fate, and then from nature") with Wardle (2006) 407–8, Kidd (1988) 414–18 and 426–28 and, especially influential against the hierarchy view, Dragona-Monachou (1974).

139. For convenient exemplification, Kidd (1988) 415 with Wildberger (2006) 37 on "Die Namen Gottes in der stoischen Physik"; Scarpat Bellincioni (1986) 15–16; Dragona-Monachou (1994) 4438–39.

140. See Hine (1981) 397.

removes the threats of prior lightning; Seneca sets out thirteen names in all)[141] amounts to a "rather chaotic"[142] list that is not well coordinated either with the *tria genera* that he also derives from Caecina in 2.39 or with the doctrine of the three *manubiae* in 2.41. Weinstock finds "no visible order in the list, alphabetical or systematic," and only by disregarding the Senecan order does he arrive at four groupings within the thirteen; he traces "this confusing variety" not to "a doctrine…but a practical handbook, another form of the *libri fulgurales*."[143] In contrast to this lack of system stands Attalus'[144] approach at 2.48.2:

> Quae inspicienda sint in fulgure passim et uage dicunt, cum possint sic diuidere quemadmodum ab Attalo philosopho, qui se huic disciplinae dediderat, diuisa sunt: ut inspiciant ubi factum sit, quando, cui, in qua re, quale, quantum.
>
> The Etruscans speak indiscriminately, with no systematic arrangement, about the things to be noted in lightning flashes, although they could classify them as did the philosopher Attalus, who had devoted himself to this area of study. Then they would investigate where the lightning occurred, when, for whom and in what circumstances, what kind it was, and of what size.

Attalus' system, not his own creation,[145] is less convoluted than Caecina's (cf. *simplicior diuisio*, 2.50.1), and reflects the combination of "Etruscan learning and Greek acuteness" that Seneca attributes to Attalus himself (*Attalus noster, uir egregius, qui Etruscorum disciplinam Graeca subtilitate miscuerat*, 2.50.1).[146] Late in Seneca's treatment of divination, can we detect in this Attalus, this skilful blender of Etruscan material and Greek technique, a symbolic embodiment of

---

141. For the types assessed, Weinstock (1951) 149–50 with Hine (1981) 403–10 for annotation on each.

142. Hine (1981) 403.

143. Weinstock (1951) 149, 150. At 2.49.1 he accepts (p. 149 n. 120) *ostentanea*, conjectured by Schmeisser (1872) 27 for MSS *dentanea*, which Hine (1996a) 96.845 prints, albeit with hesitation (cf. [1981] 404–5).

144. Seneca's Stoic teacher, often mentioned by him; see *Letters* 9.7, 63.5, 67.15, etc., with Hine (1981) 402–3 and Inwood (1995) 69 = (2005) 14, and cf. n. 146 below.

145. Weinstock (1951) 150, with convenient tabulation and elucidation of the system on pp. 150–152. Weinstock's scheme is emulated by Hine (1981) 410–11, albeit with one significant modification, for which see Hine 415–16 on 2.51 *nihil significant…perit* and cf. Weinstock 151 n. 136.

146. Cf. Sen. *Suas.* 2.12 for Attalus as "a man of great eloquence, by far the most precise [*subtilissimus*] and most articulate of philosophers seen in your generation."

the blending exercise, or the quest for commonality between the religious and the philosophical standpoints, that we have so far monitored in 2.32–51? On this approach, Attalus contributes to a Roman phenomenon that Weinstock briskly characterizes as follows:

> Since Posidonius, Etruscan divination had become a subject of interest. Etruscan writers contributed the raw material, the Romans treated it in their own fashion: Nigidius Figulus with a curious imagination, Cicero with some philosophical pretensions, Varro in an encyclopaedic spirit; and that is how Attalus came "to mix it with Greek subtlety." *That subtlety may concern the form and interpretation but not the matter itself.* If we can safely say that the Etruscans did not possess his system, we can also add that they did possess all its elements. Posidonius will have interpreted the Etruscan evidence with greater intelligence and imagination, but he certainly did not forge it either.[147]

In his different way, Seneca, too, came to mix the Etruscan raw material with Greek subtlety. In contrast to the Caecina we witness in 2.39 and 2.49, as if a Senecan embodiment of Etruscan tradition, I propose that Attalus *and* Seneca, teacher and pupil, are implicitly conjoined in 2.32–51 as progressive forces, both attuned to an evolving cultural climate in which the Greek-Roman divide is being articulated and contested in the early Empire. In effect, this Attalus—*this* Seneca—conforms to the kind of specialist implicated in Wallace-Hadrill's vision of Roman cultural revolution;[148] in its combination of *Etruscorum disciplina* and *Graeca subtilitas*, Seneca's treatment of divination at 2.32–51 is itself directly relevant to Wallace-Hadrill's thesis.

V: Taking Stock

After filling out his account of lightning's marvelous effects (*mira... opera*, 2.31.1) in 2.52–53, and after completing his second technical/doxographical section in 2.54–58, Seneca is at last prompted by an imaginary interlocutor to offer "something beneficial" (*aliquid salutare*, 2.59.2)—a lesson that focuses not on how lightning occurs, but on dispelling our fear of its dangers.[149] Seneca responds to the call by taking the broader view, as he had in countering the fear of earthquakes

---

147. Weinstock (1951) 152; my emphasis.

148. See Section I above in this chapter.

149. In general on the epilogue, Berno (2003) 209–38 and Limburg (2007) 339–42.

in Book 6: the injunction to despise death neutralizes our fear of lightning by causing us to focus on the certainty of death in general, not on the mere possibility of this, or any other, specific *causa mortis* (2.59.3; cf. 6.32.2–12). In its universalizing emphasis, however, this late salve at the close of Book 2 activates in one direction the Senecan wholeness of viewpoint that is fundamental to the book from its beginning, and that takes programmatic shape in Seneca's disquisition on the unity of air in 2.2–11. By pressing for something useful (*salutare*) at last, the interlocutory voice of 2.59.1 may also inject irony into the proceedings in Book 2, as if Seneca playfully demotes the import of his technical disquisition down to 2.58.[150] Yet, from another angle (and here, perhaps, is the more potent irony), the interlocutor appears either grossly insensitive to, or crudely dismissive of, the continuing training that Book 2 has offered in that most practical of concerns in the *Natural Questions*, seeing the world whole.

Another practical dimension of Book 2 centers on the dialogue that we have observed between competing aspects of the work's hybrid cultural identity: entrenched in the Roman world, the *Natural Questions* is yet so reliant on the Greek meteorological tradition that precedes it. Even if the tradition of philosophical writing in Latin was sufficiently well founded by Seneca's time to give no cause for him to justify, or to draw special attention to, his embarkation on a meteorological work in that language, there are evident signs of cultural contestation. So in Book 5, for example, Seneca's treatment of the Varronian wind compass asserts a vigorously Roman systematization of the winds, many of which are naturalized through a change of nomenclature.[151] While Greek authorities may form a far greater presence than Roman authorities in the *Natural Questions* generally, when the latter do appear they are treated on an equal footing.[152] Roman adventurers are seen on the margins of the empire, as if extending Rome's geographical knowledge in a form of cultural imperialism.[153] Seneca's evocation of Roman legal and political terminology also has its own far-reaching effect:

> [D]escribing the argument in terms of Roman legal or political debate…can be seen as a form of appropriation of Greek philosophy into a Roman context, using Roman forms of argument, and it may be part of a strategy to make the work more appealing to a traditionally minded

---

150. For a similar effect cf. 4b.13.1 and see Chapter Four, Section II; further, Berno (2003) 211–13 and Gauly (2004) 83–84.

151. See Chapter Five, Section IV (B).

152. Hine (2006) 58.

153. See Chapter Six, Section V (B) on Seneca's account at 6.8.3–5 of a Neronian expedition (in 61 CE?) to investigate the Nile's source.

Roman readership who need persuading that this sort of philosophy is important.[154]

In this larger context of Roman self-assertion in the *Natural Questions*, Seneca's experimental alignment of the religious and philosophical positions in 2.32–51 offers another "form of appropriation of Greek philosophy into a Roman context." The contestation played out in Book 2 is neutral in its weighing of the different cultural parts, Etruscan and Greek/Stoic, and concerned more with the process of cultural integration than with asserting any Roman ascendency over, or the "capturing" and redirecting of, Greek methodology. The process is all; and, on the assumption that Book 2 was positioned last in the original ordering of the books, Seneca's treatment of divination stands as a crowning example in the *Natural Questions* of the exercise in cultural integration that is the entire work. Here, perhaps, is the prime justification for the central place, and the extended treatment, that Seneca gives to divination from lightning in this carefully executed book: *fulmen* and *fulguratio* indeed flash forth as striking, and here strikingly symbolic, carriers of meaning in this Senecan interrogation of Greco-Roman cultural cohesion.

---

154. Hine (2006) 56.

Epilogue

I: The Book Order Once More

If we accept that the *Natural Questions* was originally ordered in the sequence 3, 4a, 4b, 5, 6, 7, 1 and 2, and that the work was planned and executed in eight books in all, one important implication of my treatment of comets in Book 7 has yet to be squarely addressed. In asserting his celestial theory of comets, Seneca elevates us to conceptual heights late in Book 7 that are sustained in the cosmic viewpoint that prevails in the preface to Book 1[1]—only for him then to descend from those heights in his coverage first of atmospheric lights in the main body of Book 1, and then of thunder and lightning in Book 2. Does this descent amount to an anticlimax of sorts after our exhilarating ascent *ad caelestia* late in Book 7—an anticlimax despite my claim[2] that "*fulmen* and *fulguratio*...flash forth as striking, *and...strikingly symbolic*, carriers of meaning" in Book 2? After our cosmic travels as recently as the preface to Book 1, does the work as a whole end on a relatively weak note in Seneca's reversion to *sublimia* and, ultimately, in his moralizing exhortation against fear of but one specific danger, lightning, in the last chapter of Book 2? Might he rather have brought the *Natural Questions* to a crescendo-like conclusion by reaching the celestial level only in the final book? One ordering of the books in the MS tradition, the "traditional order,"[3] indeed ends in Book 7. But, quite apart from the strength of the case for the Hine/Codoñer Merino ordering of 3, 4a, 4b, etc.,[4] I argue that the work descends in Books 1 and 2 from the celestial level for another key reason.

The descent to *sublimia* in Books 1 and 2 reproduces, or rather shares in, the state of tension between "higher" and "lower" world perspectives that permeates the entire *Natural Questions*. The attainment of the celestial perspective may be

---

1. See Chapter Seven, Section VII.

2. In conclusion to Chapter Eight, Section V.

3. On which Hine (1981) 4.

4. See my main Introduction on "The Addressee, and the Original Order of the Eight Books."

the work's highest ideal, but Seneca's focus throughout the eight books (and throughout this study) is more on the struggle for elevation than on our ultimate arrival at cosmic consciousness. True, in the case of his own persona the struggle is already overcome, at least in the sense that the preface to Book 3 announces a new freedom of mind and being based on a radical personal transformation late in life. The higher awareness that first takes shape in that preface prefigures the cosmic viewpoint that gradually asserts itself, grows and matures across the eight books: it manifests itself in the way Seneca observes the universal cataclysm at the end of Book 3, for example, or transports Lucilius from bureaucratic restriction in Sicily to the unrestricted majesty of Egypt and the Nile in Book 4a; in the way he surveys the timeless protocols of the winds in Book 5, or asserts his sublime control over nature in his rationalization of earthquakes in Book 6; and, not least, in the way he rises to the celestial appreciation of comets in Book 7. On this approach, the heights attained late in Book 7 and in the preface to Book 1 constitute a summit of sorts in the conceptual landscape of the entire work—a transcendent level, if you will, from which the emancipated mind-set surveys the surrounding meteorological content of the work from a higher, controlling perspective.[5]

Seneca's persona begins, then, by embracing cosmic consciousness in the preface to Book 3 and develops toward the full experience and exercise of it in the course of the *Natural Questions*. He may yet be far from the consummate *sapiens*, but he is nevertheless liberated and detached in ways that Lucilius for one can apparently never be in his Sicilian procuratorship.[6] Seneca is also liberated in ways that distinguish him from the Everyman restricted by the ordinary narrowness of life (cf. *angustias*, 1 pref. 13), and still more from the deviants he condemns in his moralizing outbursts throughout the *Natural Questions*. Yet his persona also models the release that is available to Everyman if our existence is recentered in the cosmic whole. It is this emphasis on our struggle to emerge from the darkness (cf. 1 pref. 2) that requires the *Natural Questions* to descend in Books 1 and 2 from the celestial heights reached in Book 7 and in the preface to Book 1; for while cosmic emancipation is showcased as a Senecan ideal, the work focuses primarily on the effort of ascent, and not on its ultimate attainment. As we saw earlier,[7] Seneca's meteorological theme occupies an intermediate place between *terrena* and *caelestia* (cf. 2.1.1), but it is also intermediate in a more figurative sense: it raises us from ground level and yet trains our eye on phenomena that are unstable, ephemeral and potentially illusory, in contrast to the serene steadiness

---

5. Cf. Chapter Seven, Section VII.

6. Cf. Chapter Three, Section II.

7. Chapter One, Section II.

and permanence of phenomena at the celestial level. In this respect, Seneca's meteorological probings are intrinsically provisional and experimental, progressive rather than definitive; he descends from the heights in Book 7 naturally to return to the intermediate zone, the place of provisionality, that is *the* dominant locus for his entire project.

Two further considerations are also relevant here. First, if the celestial place attained late in Book 7 were reached far earlier in the *Natural Questions*, that rapid arrival would arguably undermine the struggle toward, and the prestige associated with, so high an achievement; and if we arrived at that place at a moment of all-too-clinical neatness—at, say, the work's symbolic center between Books 4b and 5—that positioning would potentially risk appearing too neat, as if our conceptual progress in the *Natural Questions* were being plotted on a graph of simplistic, overly tidy symmetry. Second, we have already seen that, while the supralunary interpretation of comets was not unprecedented before Seneca, Aristotle's influence ensured that the sublunary interpretation held sway in antiquity and far afterward.[8] Could it be that the positioning of Seneca's treatment of comets is meant to arouse expectations that are thwarted as Book 7 proceeds? After the staple meteorological themes that he has covered in idiosyncratic fashion in the earlier books, Seneca would seem to turn conventionally enough in Book 7 to another familiar item in the category of *sublimia*. On this approach, thematic context and generic assumption condition our initial approach to Seneca on comets, only for those expectations to be dramatically overturned when he rejects the conventional Aristotelian/Stoic view (cf. 7.21.1, 22.1) in favor of the supralunary theory. This element of surprise would be intensified still further if Seneca were conspicuously following in the *Natural Questions* an inherited (albeit, for us, a now unverifiable) ordering of his subject matter across the books—in which case his supralunary interpretation would be calculated aggressively to challenge the familiar dynamics of that inherited arrangement. All such conjecture aside, however, any hint of anticlimax in Books 1 and 2 is perhaps better characterized as a resumption of more conventional meteorological progress after Seneca has deliberately disrupted the generic norms in Book 7: the departure he makes in a celestial direction in Book 7 is made all the more striking by juxtaposition with the *sublimia* that prevail once more in Books 1 and 2.

II: Reintegration with Nature

It lies far beyond the scope of this study to capture anything like the full range and complexity of the reception of the *Natural Questions* in later antiquity and

---

8. See Chapter Seven, Section III.

beyond, and in particular to weigh its influence as a work of science in the late medieval and humanistic eras.[9] If in the early modern period "it was still from time to time read for its scientific content,"[10] the transformation that took place in meteorological study through new techniques of experimentation and observation in the seventeenth century rendered Seneca, as Harry Hine nicely puts it, "not part of science, but part of the history of science."[11] For present purposes, however, Seneca's dwindling scientific relevance in the modern era hardly renders the *Natural Questions* obsolete, as if a mere curiosity whose scientific value in the twenty-first century lies largely in its utility as a doxographical resource. The ethical dimension that was stressed from the outset of this study crucially shapes, even one-sidedly exploits, the scientific material toward the nurturing of cosmic consciousness that, I argue, is Seneca's overriding goal in this hybrid work.

As we saw earlier, the recentering of existence in the cosmic whole potentially detaches the self from vulnerabilities at the local level, thereby offering fortification against the vagaries of life in Neronian Rome.[12] Beyond this practical consideration, however, the cosmic dimension in Seneca might also be viewed as a therapeutic exercise for its own sake, and one with suggestive parallels in other epochs. From a modern perspective, for example, his integrating Stoic viewpoint carries shades of an Emersonian sort of reengagement with nature,[13] or of the Romantic/postindustrial rejection of the artificialities and mechanizations of life in favor of our reembracing of *natura ipsa*. Alternatively, the "separation from nature" that modern environmentalism identifies with the ecological crisis[14] finds a loose but tempting Senecan analogy in the unnatural excesses perpetrated by the mullet watchers of 3.17–18, for example, or the ice eaters of 4b.13. The separa-

---

9. See concisely, with extensive further bibliography, Hine (1995) and now (2010c) 124–57; Vottero (1989) 54–69; Stok (2000); Parroni (2002) xxxv–xl and (2004) 315 and 318.

10. Hine (1995) 209.

11. (1995) 211.

12. Chapter One, Section V.

13. Cf., e.g., "The American Scholar," delivered on August 31st, 1837: "The scholar is he of all men whom this spectacle [sc. of nature] most engages. He must settle its value in his mind. What is nature to him? There is never a beginning, there is never an end, to the inexplicable continuity of this web of God, but always circular power returning into itself. Therein it resembles his own spirit, whose beginning, whose ending, he never can find,—*so entire, so boundless*.... To the young mind every thing is individual, stands by itself. By and by, it finds how to join two things and see in them one nature; then three, then three thousand; and so, *tyrannized over by its own unifying instinct*, it goes on tying things together, diminishing anomalies, discovering roots running under ground whereby *contrary and remote things cohere and flower out from one stem*" (cited from Ziff [1982] 85–86; my emphasis).

14. Conveniently on the "separation" theme Lewis (1993), especially 797–99.

tion from nature that is featured in such episodes in the *Natural Questions* is countered by the Senecan effort toward (our) reintegration with nature—a condition of oneness that is rooted in a sense of affinity with the Stoic cosmos as a living being and coherent whole. Hence the enchantment that Seneca describes in consorting with *natura ipsa*[15] bears loose comparison with the "reenchantment of the cosmos as a coherent, integral whole" that "comes from the latest discoveries in the natural sciences" in the modern world.[16] This Senecan reintegration is achieved not so much (or only) by our immersion in technical detail and doxographical accumulation across the eight books, but by the displacement of thought that is effected by our immersion *in nature* to begin with. In this respect, the correctness or plausibility of this theory or that, and the cumulative quality of Seneca's theoretical researches as a whole, matter less than our all-important engagement with nature in the first place. For all its reputation as a work of narrow scope, of outdated science and of limited appeal beyond an audience of specialists, ancient or modern, the *Natural Questions* is in this way a fundamentally accessible and affecting text, and the change of perspective that it promotes is paramount: the work's deepest value lies, perhaps, not in the specialist knowledge that it imparts but in the jolt that it supplies to settled attitudes.

The main thrust of this study has been to argue for Seneca's idiosyncratic *artistic* elaboration of his meteorological theme, and for his development of a distinctive mode of discourse in which examination of the natural world is inseparable from self-examination. The detailed readings offered in the preceding chapters have sought to illuminate the internal dynamics of this Senecan discourse, above all by contextualizing the work within the ancient meteorological and literary influences that inform and provoke Seneca's own special development of his theme. When we step back from the minutiae of close interpretation in a purely Greco-Roman context, however, the *Natural Questions* may yet speak across the ages, exhibiting a form of self-liberation and of cosmic awareness ("to have seen the all with the mind," 3 pref. 10) that is perhaps as pertinent to the crush of so many modern lives as it was to the age of Seneca.

---

15. So, e.g., *Dial.* 8.5.3–4, 12.20.2, *N.Q.* 1 pref. 3–4, 7–8, 11–13.

16. Laszlo (2006) 2, continuing with: "Now, in the first decade of the twenty-first century, innovative scientists at the frontiers of science are rediscovering the integral nature of reality. They lift the private experiences that speak to it from the domain of unverifiable intuition into the realm of interpersonally verifiable public knowledge.

"The emerging vision of reality is more than theory, and it is of interest to more than scientists. It gets us closer than ever before to rending apart the veils of sensory perception and apprehending the true nature of the world. Even in regard to our life and well-being, this is a happy rediscovery: it validates something we have always suspected but in modern times could not express.... *This something is a sense of belonging, of oneness. We are part of each other and of nature; we are not strangers in the universe. We are a coherent part of a coherent world; no more and no less so than a particle, a star, a galaxy*" (my emphasis).

Bibliography

Abbreviations of Journal Titles

A&A	*Antike und Abendland*
A&R	*Atene e Roma*
AC	*L'Antiquité Classique*
AClass	*Acta Classica*
AJP	*American Journal of Philology*
ANRW	*Aufstieg und Niedergang der Römischen Welt*
ASNP	*Annali della Scuola Normale Superiore di Pisa*
BICS	*Bulletin of the Institute of Classical Studies*
C&M	*Classica et Mediaevalia*
CA	*Classical Antiquity*
CB	*Classical Bulletin*
CJ	*Classical Journal*
CPh	*Classical Philology*
CQ	*Classical Quarterly*
CR	*Classical Review*
CW	*Classical World*
G&R	*Greece and Rome*
GIF	*Giornale Italiano di Filologia*
HSCP	*Harvard Studies in Classical Philology*
JHA	*Journal of the History of Astronomy*
JHI	*Journal of the History of Ideas*
JRS	*Journal of Roman Studies*
LCM	*Liverpool Classical Monthly*
LEC	*Les Études Classiques*
MAAR	*Memoirs of the American Academy at Rome*
MD	*Materiali e Discussioni*
MEFR	*Mélanges d'Archéologie et d'Histoire de l'École Française de Rome*
MH	*Museum Helveticum*
MNAW	*Mededelingen der Koninklijke Nederlandse Akademie van Wetenschappen*
PBSR	*Proceedings of the British School at Rome*
PCPhS	*Proceedings of the Cambridge Philological Society*
PP	*La Parola del Passato*
REG	*Revue des Études Grecques*

REL   *Revue des Études Latines*
RFIC   *Rivista di Filologia e di Istruzione Classica*
RFN   *Rivista di Filosofia Neoscolastica*
RhM   *Rheinisches Museum*
RPh   *Revue de Philologie*
SBAW   *Sitzungsberichte der Bayerischen Akademie der Wissenschaften*
SIFC   *Studi Italiani di Filologia Classica*
SJPh   *Southern Journal of Philosophy*
TAPhA   *Transactions of the American Philological Association*

Adams, J. N. *The Latin Sexual Vocabulary*. London, 1982.
———. *The Regional Diversification of Latin 200 BC–AD 600*. Cambridge, 2007.
Ahl, F. *Metaformations: Soundplay and Wordplay in Ovid and Other Classical Poets*. Ithaca, NY, 1985.
Alexander, W. H. "Seneca's *Naturales Quaestiones*: The Text Emended and Explained." *University of California Publications in Classical Philology* 13 (1948): 241–332.
———. "Change of Color in Moribund Fishes (Seneca, *Nat. Quaest.* 3.17–18)." *CW* 48 (1955): 192–93.
Algra, K., Barnes, J., Mansfeld, J., and Schofield, M., eds. *The Cambridge History of Hellenistic Philosophy*. Cambridge, 1999.
Allen, J. *Inference from Signs: Ancient Debates About the Nature of Evidence*. Oxford, 2001.
Althoff, J. "Vom Schicksal einer Metapher: Die Erde als Organismus in Senecas *Naturales Quaestiones*." In Döring et al. 1997: 95–110.
———. "Senecas *Naturales quaestiones*, Buch 2, und Lukrez." In Baier et al. 2005: 9–34.
Ambraseys, N. N., Melville, C. P., and Adams, R. D. *The Seismicity of Egypt, Arabia and the Red Sea: A Historical Review*. Cambridge, 1994.
Anderson, W. S., ed. *P. Ovidii Nasonis Metamorphoses libri XV*. Leipzig and Stuttgart, 1982.
———, ed. *Ovid's Metamorphoses: Books 1–5*. Norman, OK, 1996.
André, J.-M. "Sénèque et l'Égypte: esquisse d'un bilan." *REL* 81 (2003): 172–89.
Andrews, A. C. "The Roman Craze for Surmullets." *CW* 42 (1949): 186–88.
Anonymous. "The 'Sudd' of the White Nile." *Geographical Journal* 15 (1900): 234–39.
———. "Comet May Have Broken in Two." *Science News-Letter* 16 (1929): 114.
———. "Find Bright Comet Splits into Two." *Science News-Letter* 68 (1955): 228.
Antes, J. *Observations on the Manners and Customs of the Egyptians, the Overflowing of the Nile and Its Effects; with Remarks on the Plague, and Other Subjects. Written During a Residence of Twelve Years in Cairo and Its Vicinity*. London, 1800.
Araujo, A. C. "European Public Opinion and the Lisbon Earthquake." *European Review* 14 (2006): 313–19.
Ariew, R. "Theory of Comets at Paris During the Seventeenth Century." *JHI* 53 (1992): 355–72.

Armisen-Marchetti, M. "Imagination et méditation chez Sénèque: l'exemple de la *praemeditatio.*" *REL* 64 (1986): 185–95.

———. *Sapientiae facies: étude sur les images de Sénèque.* Paris, 1989.

———. "Sénèque et la divination." In Parroni 2000b: 193–214.

———. "L'imaginaire analogique et la construction du savoir dans les *Questions Naturelles* de Sénèque." In Courrént and Thomas 2001: 155–74.

———. "Échos du *Songe de Scipion* chez Sénèque: la géographie de la *Consolation à Marcia* 26.6 et des *Questions Naturelles* I praef. 8–13." In Hinojo Andrés and Fernández Corte 2007: 71–79.

Aujac, G. "Stoïcisme et hypothèse géocentrique." *ANRW* 2.36.3 (1989): 1430–53.

Austin, R. G., ed. *P. Vergili Maronis Aeneidos Liber Quartus.* Oxford, 1955.

Axelson, B. *Senecastudien: Kritische Bemerkungen zu Senecas Naturales Quaestiones.* Lund, 1933.

———. *Neue Senecastudien: Textkritische Beiträge zu Senecas Epistulae Morales.* Lund, 1939.

Ayres, L., ed. *The Passionate Intellect: Essays on the Transformation of Classical Traditions Presented to Professor I. G. Kidd. Rutgers University Studies in Classical Humanities* 7. New Brunswick and London, 1995.

Badawy, A. "Historical Seismicity of Egypt." *Acta Geodaetica et Geophysica Hungarica* 34 (1999): 119–35.

Baier, T., Manuwald, G., and Zimmermann, B., eds. *Seneca: Philosophus et Magister. Festschrift für Eckard Lefèvre zum 70. Geburtstag. Paradeigmata* 4. Freiburg im Breisgau and Berlin, 2005.

Bailey, C., ed. *Titi Lucreti Cari De Rerum Natura Libri Sex.* 3 vols. Oxford, 1947.

Bailey, M. E., Clube, S. V. M., and Napier, W. M. *The Origin of Comets.* Oxford, New York, etc., 1990.

Baldacci, O. "Seneca scienziato." *Letterature comparate. Problemi e metodo: studi in onore di Ettore Paratore.* 4 vols. 2.585–595. Bologna, 1981.

Barchiesi, A. "Immovable Delos: *Aeneid* 3.73–98 and the Hymns of Callimachus." *CQ* 44 (1994): 438–43.

———, ed. *Ovidio, Metamorfosi. Vol. I (Libri I–II).* Milan, 2005.

Barnes, J. Review of Reale 1974. *CR* 27 (1977): 40–43.

———. "Cicero's *De Fato* and a Greek Source." In Brunschwig et al. 1985: 229–39.

Baron, M. W. *Kantian Ethics Almost Without Apology.* Ithaca and London, 1995.

Barrenechea, F. "Didactic Aggressions in the Nile Excursus of Lucan's *Bellum Ciuile.*" *AJP* 131 (2010): 259–84.

Barrett, A. A. "Observations of Comets in Greek and Roman Sources Before A.D. 410." *Journal of the Royal Astronomical Society of Canada* 72 (1978): 81–106.

Barton, C. A. *The Sorrows of the Ancient Romans: The Gladiator and the Monster.* Princeton, 1993.

Bartsch, S. "The Philosopher as Narcissus: Vision, Sexuality and Self-Knowledge in Classical Antiquity." In Nelson 2000: 70–97.

————. *The Mirror of the Self: Sexuality, Self-Knowledge, and the Gaze in the Early Roman Empire*. Chicago, 2006.

————, and Wray, D., eds. *Seneca and the Self*. Cambridge, 2009.

Battersby, C. *The Sublime, Terror and Human Difference*. London and New York, 2007.

Beagon, M. *Roman Nature: The Thought of Pliny the Elder*. Oxford, 1992.

————. "Nature and Views of Her Landscapes in Pliny the Elder." In Shipley and Salmon 1996: 284–309.

————. *The Elder Pliny on the Human Animal: Natural History, Book 7*. Oxford, 2005.

————. "Situating Nature's Wonders in Pliny's *Natural History*." In Bispham and Rowe 2007: 19–40.

————. "The Curious Eye of the Elder Pliny." In Gibson and Morello 2011: 71–88.

Beard, M. "Cicero and Divination: The Formation of a Latin Discourse." *JRS* 76 (1986): 33–46.

————. "Religion." In *The Cambridge Ancient History*. 2nd ed. Vol. 9: *The Last Age of the Roman Republic, 146–43 B.C.* 729–68. Cambridge, 1992.

————, and North, J., eds. *Pagan Priests: Religion and Power in the Ancient World*. London, 1990.

————, North, J., and Price, S. *Religions of Rome*. 2 vols. Cambridge, 1998.

Beaujeu, J., ed. *Pline l'ancien: Histoire Naturelle, livre II*. Paris, 1950.

Bedon, R. "Sénèque, *Ad Lucilium*, 91. L'incendie de 64 à Lyon: exploitation littéraire et réalité." In Chevallier and Poignault 1991: 45–61.

Behrends, O., and Sellert, W., eds. *Nomos und Gesetz: Ursprünge und Wirkungen des griechischen Gesetzesdenkens. 6. Symposion der Kommission "Die Funktion des Gesetzes in Geschichte und Gegenwart."* Göttingen, 1995.

Bernard, J. H., trans. *Critique of Judgment by Immanuel Kant*. New York, 1951.

Berno, F. R. "Ostio Quadra allo specchio: riflessioni speculari e speculative su *Nat. Quaest.* 1,16–17." *Athenaeum* 90 (2002): 214–28.

————. *Lo specchio, il vizio e la virtù: studio sulle Naturales Quaestiones di Seneca*. Bologna, 2003.

Berry, D. H., and Erskine, A., eds. *Form and Function in Roman Oratory*. Cambridge, 2010.

Berti, E., ed. *M. Annaei Lucani Bellum Ciuile Liber X*. Florence, 2000.

Bickel, E. "Kant und Seneca. Der bestirnte Himmel über mir und das moralische Gesetz in mir." *RhM* 102 (1959): 289–92.

Bicknell, P. J. "Seneca and Aetius on Anaximander's and Anaximenes' Accounts of Thunder and Lightning." *Latomus* 27 (1968): 181–84.

————. "Neronian Comets and Novae." *Latomus* 28 (1969): 1074–75.

Bispham, E., and Rowe, G., with E. Matthews, eds. *Vita Vigilia Est: Essays in Honour of Barbara Levick*. London, 2007.

Bloch, R. *La divination dans l'antiquité*. Paris, 1984.

Blundell, S. *The Origins of Civilization in Greek and Roman Thought*. London, Sydney and Dover, NH, 1986.

Bobzien, S. *Determinism and Freedom in Stoic Philosophy*. Oxford, 1998.

Bodnár, I. M. *Oenopides of Chius* [*sic*]: *A Survey of the Modern Literature with a Collection of the Ancient Testimonia*. Preprint 327 of the Max Planck Institute for the History of Science. Berlin, 2007.

Boeri, M. D. "Does Cosmic Nature Matter? Some Remarks on the Cosmological Aspects of Stoic Ethics." In Salles 2009: 173–200.

Bollack, M. *La raison de Lucrèce: constitution d'une poétique philosophique avec un essai d'interprétation de la critique lucrétienne*. Paris, 1978.

Bonneau, D. *La crue du Nil: ses descriptions, ses explications, son culte*. Paris, 1964.

Bosworth, B. "Plus ça change…Ancient Historians and their Sources." *CA* 22 (2003): 167–98.

Bouché-Leclercq, A. *Histoire de la divination dans l'antiquité. Tome premier: Introduction. Divination hellénique. (Méthodes.)* Paris, 1879.

――――. *Histoire de la divination dans l'antiquité. Tome quatrième: Divination italique (Étrusque-Latine-Romaine)*. Paris, 1882.

Bourgery, A. *Sénèque prosateur. Études littéraires et grammaticales sur la prose de Sénèque le philosophe*. Paris, 1922.

Boustan, R., and Reed, A. Y., eds. *Heavenly Realms and Earthly Realities in Late Antique Religions*. Cambridge, 2004.

Boyancé, P. "Sur les mystères d'Éleusis." *REG* 75 (1962): 460–82.

Boyer, C. B. *The Rainbow: From Myth to Mathematics*. With New Color Illustrations and Commentary by Robert Greenler. Princeton, 1987 (first published 1959).

Boyle, A. J., ed. *Octavia Attributed to Seneca*. Oxford, 2008.

Bradley, M. *Colour and Meaning in Ancient Rome*. Cambridge, 2009.

Brandt, J. C., and Chapman, R. D. *Introduction to Comets*. 2nd ed. Cambridge, 2004.

Branham, R. B., and Goulet-Cazé, M.-O., eds. *The Cynics: The Cynic Movement in Antiquity and Its Legacy*. Berkeley, Los Angeles and London, 1996.

Bravo Díaz, J. R. "*Spiritus*: estudio de un término científico (*Naturales Quaestiones* de Séneca)." In Ramos Guerreira 1991: 15–28.

Bricault, L., Versluys, M. J., and Meyboom, P. G. P., eds. *Nile into Tiber: Egypt in the Roman World. Proceedings of the IIIrd International Conference of Isis Studies, Faculty of Archaeology, Leiden University, May 11–14 2005*. Leiden and Boston, 2007.

Brink, C. O., ed. *Horace on Poetry III. Epistles Book II: The Letters to Augustus and Florus*. Cambridge, 1982.

Bruns, C. G., ed. *Fontes iuris Romani antiqui*. 7th ed. Tübingen, 1909.

Brunschwig, J. "Introduction: The Beginnings of Hellenistic Epistemology." In Algra et al. 1999: 229–59.

――――, Imbert, C., and Roger, A., eds. *Histoire et structure: à la mémoire de Victor Goldschmidt*. Paris, 1985.

Brunt, P. A. "Philosophy and Religion in the Late Republic." In Griffin and Barnes 1989: 174–98.

Brutsaert, W. *Hydrology: An Introduction.* Cambridge, 2005.

Bruun, P., Hohti, P., Kaimio, J., Michelsen, E., Nielsen, M., and Ruoff-Väänänen, E. *Studies in the Romanization of Etruria.* Rome, 1975.

Budd, M. *The Aesthetic Appreciation of Nature: Essays on the Aesthetics of Nature.* Oxford, 2002.

Burkert, W., ed. *Kleine Schriften zur Geschichte der antiken Philosophie.* Hildesheim, 1969.

Bury, J. B. *The Idea of Progress: An Inquiry into Its Origin and Growth.* London, 1932.

Busa, R., and Zampolli, A. *Concordantiae Senecanae.* Hildesheim, 1975.

Buxbaum, T. *Icehouses.* Princes Risborough, UK, 2002.

Caduff, G. A. *Antike Sintflutsagen.* Göttingen, 1986.

Cailleux, A. "Sénèque et l'esprit scientifique." *LEC* 39 (1971): 475–83.

Callebat, L. "Science et irrationnel. Les *mirabilia aquarum.*" *Euphrosyne* 16 (1988): 155–67.

Calvino, I. "Man, the Sky, and the Elephant." In *The Uses of Literature: Essays.* Trans. P. Creagh. 315–30. San Diego, New York and London, 1986.

Canfora, L. "Seneca e le guerre civili." In Parroni 2000b: 161–77.

Capponi, F. "La scienza e la morale nell'interpretazione della natura." In Rocca 1996: 101–26.

Cardini, R. "Contributo ad una *uexatissima quaestio*: *Maris expers* (Pers. VI 39; nonché Hor. *Sat.* II 8 15, Sen. *Nat. Quaest.* I 16 7, Suet. *Tib.* 45)." In Cardini et al. 1985: 2.693–776.

———, Garin, E., Cesarini Martinelli, L., and Pascucci, G. *Tradizione classica e letteratura umanistica. Per Alessandro Perosa.* 2 vols. Rome, 1985.

Carey, S. *Pliny's Catalogue of Culture: Art and Empire in the Natural History.* Oxford, 2003.

Carratelli, G. P., Del Re, G., Bonacasa, N., and Etman, A., eds. *Roma e l'Egitto nell'antichità classica. Cairo, 6–9 febbraio 1989.* Rome, 1992.

Castiglioni, L. "Studi Anneani—IV. Note critiche al libri delle *Questioni Naturali.*" *RFIC* 49 (1921): 435–55.

Cerutti, S. L., and Richardson, L. "The *retiarius tunicatus* of Suetonius, Juvenal, and Petronius." *AJP* 110 (1989): 589–94.

Cervellera, M. A. "Alcune notazioni su tematica e metafora del potere in Seneca." *Rudiae* 4 (1992): 101–15.

Cesaretti, M. P. *Nerone e l'Egitto: messaggio politico e continuità culturale.* Bologna, 1989.

Chambers, A. B. *Andrew Marvell and Edmund Waller: Seventeenth-Century Praise and Restoration Satire.* University Park and London, 1991.

Champlin, E. *Nero.* Cambridge, MA, and London, 2003.

Chatelain, L. "Théories d'auteurs anciens sur les tremblements de terre." *MEFR* 29 (1909): 87–101.

Chaumartin, F.-R. "Notes critiques sur quelques passages des *Naturales Quaestiones* de Sénèque." *RPh* 67 (1993): 107–17.

———. "La nature dans les *Questions Naturelles* de Sénèque." In Lévy 1996: 177–90.

Chevallier, R., and Poignault, R. eds. *Présence de Sénèque. Collection Caesarodunum* 24. Paris, 1991.

Citroni Marchetti, S. *Plinio il vecchio e la tradizione del moralismo romano.* Pisa, 1991.

———. "Il *sapiens* in pericolo: psicologia del rapporto con gli altri, da Cicerone a Marco Aurelio." *ANRW* 2.36.7 (1994): 4546–98.

Clarke, C. *The Science of Ice Cream. Royal Society of Chemistry Paperbacks.* Cambridge, 2004.

Clarke, K. *Between Geography and History: Hellenistic Constructions of the Roman World.* Oxford, 1999.

Cleary, J. J., and Gurtler, G. M., eds. *Proceedings of the Boston Area Colloquium in Ancient Philosophy* 15. Leiden, Boston and Köln, 2000.

Coccia, M. "Seneca e Alessandro Magno." *Vichiana* 13 (1984): 12–25.

Codoñer (Merino), C., ed. *L. Annaei Senecae Naturales Quaestiones.* 2 vols. Madrid, 1979.

———. "La physique de Sénèque: ordonnance et structure des *Naturales Quaestiones*." *ANRW* II 36.3 (1989): 1779–1822.

Conte, G. B. *Genres and Readers: Lucretius, Love Elegy, Pliny's Encyclopedia.* Trans. G.W. Most. Baltimore and London, 1994.

Cooley, A. E., ed. *Res Gestae Diui Augusti: Text, Translation, and Commentary.* Oxford, 2009.

Cooper, J. M. "Seneca on Moral Theory and Moral Improvement." In Volk and Williams 2006: 43–55.

———, and Procopé, J. F., eds. *Seneca: Moral and Political Essays.* Cambridge, 1995.

Corcoran, T. H. "Roman Fishermen." *CW* 56 (1963): 97–102.

———, ed. *Seneca: Naturales Quaestiones.* 2 vols. Cambridge, MA, and London, 1971–72.

Cornelissen, J. J. *Coniectanea latina.* Deventer, 1870.

Courrént, M., and Thomas, J., eds. *Imaginaire et modes de construction du savoir antique dans les textes scientifiques et techniques. Actes du Colloque international de Perpignan (12 et 13 Mai 2000).* Perpignan, 2001.

Courtney, E., ed. *The Fragmentary Latin Poets.* Oxford, 1993.

Coutant, V., and Eichenlaub, V. L. "The *De Ventis* of Theophrastus: Its Contributions to the Theory of Winds." *Bulletin of the American Meteorological Society* 55 (1974): 1454–62.

———, eds. *Theophrastus: De Ventis.* Notre Dame and London, 1975.

Crawford, M. H., ed. *Roman Statutes: Bulletin of the Institute of Classical Studies Supplement* 64. 2 vols. London, 1996.

Curry, P., and Voss, A., eds. *Seeing with Different Eyes: Essays in Astrology and Divination*. Newcastle, 2007.

Curti, C., and Crimi, C. *Scritti classici e cristiani offerti a Francesco Corsaro*. 2 vols. Catania, 1994.

Dahlmann, H. "Die Verse des 'Vagellius.'" *RhM* 120 (1977): 76–84.

Daiber, H. "The *Meteorology* of Theophrastus in Syriac and Arabic Translation." In Fortenbaugh and Gutas 1992: 166–293.

Dall'Olmo, U. "Latin Terminology Relating to Aurorae, Comets, Meteors and Novae." *JHA* 11 (1980): 10–27.

Daston, L., and Park, K. *Wonders and the Order of Nature 1150–1750*. New York, 2001.

David, E. *Harvest of the Cold Months: The Social History of Ice and Ices*. Edited by J. Norman. New York, 1994.

De Lacy, P. H. "Lucretius and the History of Epicureanism." *TAPhA* 79 (1948): 12–23.

De Nardis, M. "Seneca, Plinio e la spedizione neroniana in Etiopia." *Aegyptus* 69 (1989): 123–52.

De Planhol, X. *L'eau de neige: le tiède et le frais. Histoire et géographie des boissons fraîches*. Paris, 1995.

De Robertis, T., and Resta, G., eds. *Seneca: una vicenda testuale*. Florence, 2004.

De Saint-Denis, E. *Le rôle de la mer dans la poésie latine*. Lyon, 1935.

De Vaan, M. *Etymological Dictionary of Latin and the Other Italic Languages*. Leiden and Boston, 2008.

De Villiers, M. *Windswept: The Story of Wind and Weather*. New York, 2006.

De Vivo, A. *Le parole della scienza: sul trattato de terrae motu di Seneca*. Salerno, 1992a.

———. "Seneca, la citazione virgiliana, la paura del terremoto (*nat.* 6.2.2)," 1992b. In De Vivo and Spina 1992: 119–30.

———. *Costruire la memoria. Ricerche sugli storici latini*. Naples, 1998.

———, and Lo Cascio, E., eds. *Seneca uomo politico e l'età di Claudio e di Nerone. Atti del Convegno internazionale (Capri 25–27 marzo 1999)*. Bari, 2003.

De Vivo, A., and Spina, L., eds. *"Come dice il poeta . . .": Percorsi greci e latini di parole poetiche*. Naples, 1992.

DeBlieu, J. *Wind: How the Flow of Air Has Shaped Life, Myth, and the Land*. Boston and New York, 1998.

Decourt, J.-C., and Lucas, G. *Lyon dans les textes grecs et latins. Travaux de la maison de l'orient* 23. Lyon and Paris, 1993.

Degg, M. R. "A Database of Historical Earthquake Activity in the Middle East." *Transactions of the Institute of British Geographers* 15 (1990): 294–307.

Degl'Innocenti Pierini, R. "Seneca emulo di Ovidio nella rappresentazione del diluvio universale (*Nat. Quaest.* 3, 27, 13 sgg.)." *A&R* 29 (1984): 143–61.

Delatte, L. "Lucilius, l'ami de Sénèque." *LEC* 4 (1935): 367–85, 546–90.

Delehanty, A. T. "Mapping the Aesthetic Mind: John Dennis and Nicolas Boileau." *JHI* 68 (2007): 233–53.

Denyer, N. "The Case Against Divination: An Examination of Cicero's *De Diuinatione*." *PCPhS* 31 (1985): 1–10.

Desanges, J. "Les relations de l'Empire romain avec l'Afrique nilotique et érythréenne, d'Auguste à Probus." *ANRW* II.10.1 (1988): 3–43.

Dickson, P. *The Great American Ice Cream Book*. New York, 1972.

Diels, H. "Seneca und Lucan." *Abhandlungen der kgl. Pr. Akademie der Wissenschaften zu Berlin 1885. Phil. Hist. Kl. III*. (1886): 3–32. Also in Burkert 1969: 379–408.

Diggle, J., ed. *Theophrastus: Characters. Cambridge Classical Texts and Commentaries* 43. Cambridge, 2004.

———, and Goodyear, F. R. D., eds. *The Classical Papers of A. E. Housman*. 3 vols. Cambridge, 1972.

Dillon, J. M., and Long, A. A., eds. *The Question of "Eclecticism": Studies in Later Greek Philosophy*. Berkeley, Los Angeles and London, 1988.

Dingel, J., ed. *Senecas Epigramme und andere Gedichte aus der Anthologia Latina*. Heidelberg, 2007.

Dionigi, I., ed. *L. Anneo Seneca: De otio (dial. viii)*. Brescia, 1983.

Dodds, E. R. Review of Edelstein 1967. *JHI* 29 (1968): 453–57.

———. *The Ancient Concept of Progress and Other Essays on Greek Literature and Belief*. Oxford, 1973.

Domenicucci, P. *Astra Caesarum: astronomia, astrologia e catasterismo da Cesare a Domiziano*. Pisa, 1996.

Donini, P. L. "L'eclettismo impossibile. Seneca e il platonismo medio." In Donini and Gianotti 1979: 149–300.

———, and Gianotti, G. F., eds. *Modelli filosofici e letterari: Lucrezio, Orazio, Seneca*. Bologna, 1979.

Doody, A. "Pliny's *Natural History*: *Enkuklios Paideia* and the Ancient Encyclopedia." *JHI* 70 (2009): 1–21.

———. *Pliny's Encyclopedia: The Reception of the Natural History*. Cambridge, 2010.

Döring, K., Herzhoff, B., and Wöhrle, G., eds. *Antike Naturwissenschaft und ihre Rezeption* 7. Trier, 1997.

Dragona-Monachou, M. "Posidonius' 'Hierarchy' Between God, Fate and Nature and Cicero's *De Diuinatione*." *Philosophia* 4 (1974): 286–301.

———. "Divine Providence in the Philosophy of the Empire." *ANRW* 2.36.7 (1994): 4417–90.

Dunand, F., and Zivie-Coche, C. *Gods and Men in Egypt, 3000 BCE to 395 CE*. Trans. D. Lorton. Ithaca, 2004.

Dunbabin, K. M. D. *Mosaics of the Greek and Roman World*. Cambridge, 1999.

Dupraz, E. "La représentation du volcanisme dans les *Naturales Quaestiones* de Sénèque." In Foulon 2004: 231–58.

Duret, L. "Néron-Phaéton, ou la témérité sublime." *REL* 66 (1988): 139–55.

Dyck, A. R. *A Commentary on Cicero, De Legibus*. Ann Arbor, 2004.

Edelstein, L. *The Idea of Progress in Classical Antiquity*. Baltimore, 1967.

Eden, P. T., ed. *Seneca: Apocolocyntosis*. Cambridge Greek and Latin Classics. Cambridge, 1984.

Edwards, C. *The Politics of Immorality in Ancient Rome*. Cambridge, 1993.

———. "Self-Scrutiny and Self-Transformation in Seneca's *Letters*." *G&R* 44 (1997): 23–38.

Elliott, A. G. "Ovid and the Critics: Seneca, Quintilian, and 'Seriousness.'" *Helios* 12 (1985): 9–20.

Endt, J., ed. *Adnotationes super Lucanum*. Leipzig, 1909.

Ernout, A., ed. *Pline l'Ancien, Histoire Naturelle livre VIII*. Paris, 1952.

———, and Meillet, A. *Dictionnaire étymologique de la langue latine: histoire des mots*. 4th ed. Paris, 1967.

Fahnestock, J. "Accommodating Science: The Rhetorical Life of Scientific Facts." *Written Communication* 3 (1986): 275–96.

Faider, P. "Sénèque en Égypte." *Bulletin de l'Institut français d'archéologie orientale* 30 (1930): 83–87.

Fantham, E. "Dialogues of Displacement: Seneca's Consolations to Helvia and Polybius." In Gaertner 2007: 173–92.

Fedeli, P., ed. *Scienza, cultura, morale in Seneca. Atti del Convegno di Monte Sant'Angelo (27–30 settembre 1999)*. Bari, 2001.

Feeney, D. C. *The Gods in Epic: Poets and Critics of the Classical Tradition*. Oxford, 1991.

———. *Literature and Religion at Rome: Cultures, Contexts, and Beliefs*. Cambridge, 1998.

Fernández, J. A. *Comets: Nature, Dynamics, Origin, and Their Cosmogonical Relevance*. Dordrecht, 2005.

Ferri, R., ed. *Octavia: A Play Attributed to Seneca. Cambridge Classical Texts and Commentaries* 41. Cambridge, 2003.

Fitzgerald, J. T., ed. *Friendship, Flattery, and Frankness of Speech: Studies on Friendship in the New Testament World*. Leiden, 1996.

Flammini, G. "La *praefatio* alle *Naturales Quaestiones* di L. Anneo Seneca." In Santini and Scivoletto 1992: 2.629–59.

Fontana, M. J., Piraino, M. T., and Rizzo, F. P., eds. Φιλίας χάριν. *Miscellanea di studi classici in onore di Eugenio Manni*. 6 vols. Rome, 1980.

Fortenbaugh, W. W., and Gutas, D., eds. *Theophrastus: His Psychological, Doxographical and Scientific Writings. Rutgers University Studies in Classical Humanities* 5. New Brunswick, 1992.

Fortenbaugh, W. W. et al., eds. *Theophrastus of Eresus: Sources for His Life, Writings, Thought and Influence. Part One: Life, Writings, Various Reports, Logic, Physics, Metaphysics, Theology, Mathematics. Philosophia Antiqua* 54. Leiden, New York and Köln, 1992.

Foss, O. "The Pigeon's Neck." *Classica et Mediaevalia F. Blatt septuagenario dedicata*. 140–49. Copenhagen, 1973.

Foucault, M. *The Care of the Self. The History of Sexuality, Vol. 3*. Trans. R. Hurley. New York, 1986.

Foulon, É., ed. *Connaissance et représentations des volcans dans l'antiquité. Actes du Colloque de Clermont-Ferrand Université Blaise Pascal, 19–20 septembre 2002*. Clermont-Ferrand, 2004.

Frazer, J. G. *Pausanias's Description of Greece*. 6 vols. London, 1898.

Frede, D., and Laks, A., eds. *Traditions of Theology: Studies in Hellenistic Theology, Its Background and Aftermath*. Leiden, 2002.

Freeland, C. A. "Scientific Explanation and Empirical Data in Aristotle's *Meteorology*." *Oxford Studies in Ancient Philosophy* 8 (1990): 68–102.

French, R. *Ancient Natural History: Histories of Nature*. London and New York, 1994.

Friedman, J. S. *Out of the Blue: A History of Lightning—Science, Superstition, and Amazing Stories of Survival*. New York, 2008.

Frisinger, H. H. "Early Theories on the Nile Floods." *Weather* 20 (1965): 206–8.

———. "Meteorology Before Aristotle." *Bulletin of the American Meteorological Society* 52 (1971): 1078–80.

———. "Aristotle's Legacy in Meteorology." *Bulletin of the American Meteorological Society* 54 (1973): 198–204.

———. *The History of Meteorology to 1800*. New York, 1977.

Funderburg, A. C. *Chocolate, Strawberry, and Vanilla: A History of American Ice Cream*. Bowling Green, OH, 1995.

Furley, D. "Cosmology." In Algra et al. 1999: 412–51.

Gaertner, J. F., ed. *Writing Exile: The Discourse of Displacement in Greco-Roman Antiquity and Beyond*. Leiden and Boston, 2007.

Galdi, M. "Di una particolare forma di ripetizione nelle *Naturales Quaestiones* di Seneca." *Mouseion* 1 (1923): 118–25.

———. "Seneca e la '*mendax natio*.'" *Mouseion* 2 (1924): 41–46.

Gale, M. R., ed. *Oxford Readings in Classical Studies: Lucretius*. Oxford, 2007.

Garani, M. *Empedocles Rediuiuus: Poetry and Analogy in Lucretius*. New York and London, 2007.

———. "Going with the Wind: Visualizing Volcanic Eruptions in the Pseudo-Vergilian *Aetna*." *BICS* 52 (2009): 103–21.

Garrod, H. W. "Notes on the *Naturales Quaestiones* of Seneca (Continued)." *CQ* 9 (1915): 39–49.

Gauly, B. M. *Senecas Naturales Quaestiones: Naturphilosophie für die römische Kaiserzeit*. Zetemata 122. Munich, 2004.

Geer, R. M. "On the Use of Ice and Snow for Cooling Drinks." *CW* 29 (1935): 61–62.

Gercke, A. *Seneca-Studien*. Leipzig, 1895 (= A. Fleckeisen, ed. *Jahrbücher für classische Philologie*, Supplementband 22 [1896]: 1–334).

———. *L. Annaei Senecae Naturalium Quaestionum libri VIII*. Stuttgart, 1907.

Gergen, K. J. "The Checkmate of Rhetoric (But Can Our Reasons Become Causes?)." 1990. In Simons 1990b: 293–307.

Gibson, R. K., ed. *Ovid: Ars Amatoria Book 3. Cambridge Classical Texts and Commentaries* 40. Cambridge, 2003.

——— . "Elder and Better: The *Naturalis Historia* and the *Letters* of the Younger Pliny." In Gibson and Morello 2011: 187–205.

Gibson, R. K., and Morello, R., eds. *Pliny the Elder: Themes and Contexts*. Leiden and Boston, 2011.

Gigon, O., ed. *Lucrèce: huit exposés suivis de discussions. Entretiens sur l'antiquité classique* 24. Geneva, 1978.

——— . "Senecas *Naturales Quaestiones*." In Grimal 1991: 313–39.

Gilbert, J. *Ovidianae quaestiones criticae et exegeticae*. Meissen, 1896.

Gilbert, O. *Die meteorologischen Theorien des griechischen Altertums*. Leipzig, 1907.

Gillespie, S., and Hardie, P., eds. *The Cambridge Companion to Lucretius*. Cambridge, 2007.

Glucker, J. *Antiochus and the Late Academy*. Göttingen, 1978.

——— . "Cicero's Philosophical Affiliations." In Dillon and Long 1988: 34–69.

Goar, R. J. "The Purpose of *De Diuinatione*." *TAPhA* 99 (1968): 241–48.

——— . *Cicero and the State Religion*. Amsterdam, 1972.

Gosnell, M. *Ice: The Nature, the History, and the Uses of an Astonishing Substance*. New York, 2005.

Goulet-Cazé, M.-O. "Appendix A: A Comprehensive Catalogue of Known Cynic Philosophers." In Branham and Goulet-Cazé 1996: 389–413.

Graham, D. W. "Philosophy on the Nile: Herodotus and Ionian Research." *Apeiron* 36 (2003): 291–310.

——— , ed. *The Texts of Early Greek Philosophy: The Complete Fragments and Selected Testimonies of the Major Presocratics*. 2 vols. Cambridge, 2010.

Grant, E. *A History of Natural Philosophy from the Ancient World to the Nineteenth Century*. Cambridge, 2007.

Graver, M. "Commentary on Inwood." In Cleary and Gurtler 2000: 44–51.

Greenblatt, S. *Renaissance Self-Fashioning: From More to Shakespeare*. Chicago and London, 1980. Reprinted with a new preface, Chicago, 2005.

Griffin, M. T. *Seneca: A Philosopher in Politics*. Oxford, 1976. Reprinted with postscript, 1992.

——— . *Nero: The End of a Dynasty*. London, 1984.

——— , and Barnes, J., eds. *Philosophia Togata I: Essays on Philosophy and Roman Society*. Oxford, 1989.

Grilli, A. "Miscellanea Latina." *Rendiconti dell'Istituto Lombardo, Classe di Lettere e Scienze Morali e Storiche* 97 (1963): 93–170.

Grimal, P. "Encyclopédies antiques." *Cahiers d'histoire mondiale* 9 (1965): 459–82.

——— . "Lucilius en Sicile." In Fontana et al. 1980: 1173–87.

——— , ed. *Sénèque et la prose latine: neuf exposés suivis de discussions. Entretiens sur l'antiquité classique* 36. Geneva, 1991.

Gross, A. G. *The Rhetoric of Science*. Cambridge, MA, and London, 1990.

Gross, N. *Senecas Naturales Quaestiones: Komposition, naturphilosophische Aussagen und ihre Quellen. Palingenesia* 27. Stuttgart, 1989.

Grünthal, G. "The History of Historical Earthquake Research in Germany." *Annals of Geophysics* 47 (2004): 631–43.

Gruppe, O. *Die griechischen Culte und Mythen in ihren Beziehungen zu den orientalischen Religionen.* Leipzig, 1887.

Gudger, E. W. "Pliny's *Historia Naturalis*: The Most Popular Natural History Ever Published." *Isis* 6 (1924): 269–81.

Guidoboni, E., with the collaboration of A. Comastri and G. Traina. *Catalogue of Ancient Earthquakes in the Mediterranean Area up to the 10th Century.* Rome, 1994.

——— , and Ebel, J. E. *Earthquakes and Tsunamis in the Past: A Guide to Techniques in Historical Seismology.* Cambridge, 2009.

Guillaumont, F. *Philosophe et augure. Recherches sur la théorie cicéronienne de la divination. Collection Latomus* 184. Brussels, 1984.

——— . "Sénèque et l'*Etrusca disciplina*." In *Les écrivains et l'Etrusca disciplina de Claude à Trajan. Caesarodunum Supplément* 64 (1995): 1–14.

——— . *Le De Diuinatione de Cicéron et les théories antiques de la divination. Collection Latomus* 298. Brussels, 2006.

Gurval, R. A. "Caesar's Comet: The Politics and Poetics of an Augustan Myth." *MAAR* 42 (1997): 39–71.

Gusfield, J. "The Literary Rhetoric of Science: Comedy and Pathos in Drinking Driver Research." *American Sociological Review* 41 (1976): 16–34.

Guthrie, W. K. C. *A History of Greek Philosophy, I. The Earlier Presocratics and the Pythagoreans.* Cambridge, 1962.

——— . *A History of Greek Philosophy, II. The Presocratic Tradition from Parmenides to Democritus.* Cambridge, 1965.

Haase, F., ed. *L. Annaei Senecae opera quae supersunt.* 3 vols. Leipzig, 1852.

Habinek, T. "Ovid and Empire." In Hardie 2002: 46–61.

——— , and Schiesaro, A., eds. *The Roman Cultural Revolution.* Cambridge, 1997.

Hadot, P. *Philosophy as a Way of Life: Spiritual Exercises from Socrates to Foucault.* Trans. M. Chase. Oxford, 1995.

——— . *The Inner Citadel: The Meditations of Marcus Aurelius.* Trans. M. Chase. Cambridge, MA, and London, 1998.

——— . *The Veil of Isis. An Essay on the History of the Idea of Nature.* Trans. M. Chase. Cambridge, MA, and London, 2006.

Hahm, D. E. *The Origins of Stoic Cosmology.* Columbus, OH, 1977.

Hall, J. J. "Seneca as a Source for Earlier Thought (Especially Meteorology)." *CQ* 27 (1977): 409–36.

Hamblyn, R. *The Invention of Clouds: How an Amateur Meteorologist Forged the Language of the Skies.* New York, 2001.

Hankinson, R. J. "Stoicism, Science and Divination." *Apeiron* 21 (1988): 123–60.

Hannestad, K. "*Sollemne Sacrum Praefecti Aegypti* and Its Historical Background." *C&M* 6 (1944): 41–59.

Hardie, P., ed. *The Cambridge Companion to Ovid*. Cambridge, 2002.

——— . *Lucretian Receptions: History, the Sublime, Knowledge*. Cambridge, 2009a.

——— , ed. *Paradox and the Marvellous in Augustan Literature and Culture*. Oxford, 2009b.

Harley, J. B., and Woodward, D. "The Growth of an Empirical Cartography in Hellenistic Greece." 1987a. In Harley and Woodward 1987b: 148–60.

——— , eds. *The History of Cartography. Vol. I. Cartography in Prehistoric, Ancient, and Medieval Europe and the Mediterranean*. Chicago and London, 1987b.

Hartmann, R. *De Senecae Naturalium Quaestionum libro septimo*. Diss. Münster, 1911.

Häussler, R., ed. *Nachträge zu A. Otto Sprichwörter und sprichwörtliche Redensarten der Römer*. Darmstadt, 1968.

Healy, J. F. *Pliny the Elder on Science and Technology*. Oxford, 1999.

Heath, T. L. *Aristarchus of Samos: The Ancient Copernicus*. Oxford, 1913.

Hecht, J. M. *Doubt: A History. The Great Doubters and Their Legacy of Innovation, from Socrates and Jesus to Thomas Jefferson and Emily Dickinson*. New York, 2003.

Heidarzadeh, T. *A History of Physical Theories of Comets, from Aristotle to Whipple*. *Archimedes* 19. New York, 2008.

Heinonen, S. *Prometheus Revisited: Human Interaction with Nature Through Technology in Seneca. Commentationes Humanarum Litterarum* 115. Helsinki, 2000.

Heintz, J.-G., ed. *Oracles et prophéties dans l'antiquité. Actes du Colloque de Strasbourg 15–17 juin 1995*. Paris, 1997.

Hellman, C. D. *The Comet of 1577: Its Place in the History of Astronomy*. New York, 1944.

——— . "Was Tycho Brahe as Influential as He Thought?" *British Journal for the History of Science* 1 (1963): 295–324.

——— . "The Role of Measurement in the Downfall of a System: Some Examples from Sixteenth Century Comet and Nova Observations." *Vistas in Astronomy* 9 (1967): 43–52.

Hemsing, J. *De Senecae Naturalium Quaestionum libro primo*. Diss. Münster, 1913.

Henderson, J. "Knowing Someone Through Their Books: Pliny on Uncle Pliny (*Epistles* 3.5)." *CPh* 97 (2002): 256–84.

——— . *Morals and Villas in Seneca's Letters: Places to Dwell*. Cambridge, 2003.

——— . "The Nature of Man: Pliny, *Historia Naturalis* as Cosmogram." *MD* 66 (2011): 139–71.

Henry, D., and Walker, B. "Seneca and the *Agamemnon*: Some Thoughts on Tragic Doom." *CPh* 58 (1963): 1–10.

Henry, J. *Aeneidea, or Critical, Exegetical, and Aesthetical Remarks on the Aeneis*. 4 vols. Dublin, 1881; reprinted Hildesheim, 1969.

Henry, M. "L'apparition d'une île: Sénèque et Philostrate, un même témoignage." *AC* 51 (1982): 174–92.

Heydenreich, T. *Tadel und Lob der Seefahrt. Das Nachleben eines antiken Themas in der romanischen Literatur.* Heidelberg, 1970.

Higginbotham, J. *Piscinae: Artificial Fishponds in Roman Italy.* Chapel Hill and London, 1997.

Hine, H. M. "Livy's Judgement on Marius (Seneca, *Natural Questions* 5.18.4; Livy, *Periocha* 80." *LCM* 3 (1978): 83–87.

———. "The Manuscript Tradition of Seneca's *Natural Questions*." *CQ* 30 (1980a): 183–217.

———. "Seneca and Anaxagoras on Snow." *Hermes* 108 (1980b): 503.

———, ed. *An Edition with Commentary of Seneca, Natural Questions, Book 2.* New York, 1981.

———. "*Natural Questions*." In Reynolds 1983: 376–78.

———. "The Date of the Campanian Earthquake: A.D. 62 or A.D. 63, or Both?" *AC* 53 (1984): 266–69.

———. "Seneca's *Natural Questions*—Changing Readerships." In Ayres 1995: 203–11.

———, ed. *L. Annaei Senecae Naturalium Quaestionum libros.* Stuttgart and Leipzig. 1996a.

———. *Studies in the Text of Seneca's Naturales Quaestiones.* Stuttgart and Leipzig, 1996b.

———, ed. *Seneca: Medea.* Warminster, 2000.

———. "Seismology and Vulcanology in Antiquity?" In Tuplin and Rihll 2002: 56–75.

———. "Poetic Influence on Prose: The Case of the Younger Seneca." 2005a. In Reinhardt, Lapidge and Adams 2005: 211–37.

———. Review of Parroni 2002. *CR* 55 (2005b): 545–46.

———. "Rome, the Cosmos, and the Emperor in Seneca's *Natural Questions*." *JRS* 96 (2006): 42–72.

———. "Seneca's *Naturales Quaestiones* 1960–2005 (Part 1)." *Lustrum* 51 (2009): 253–329.

———. "Form and Function of Speech in the Prose Works of the Younger Seneca." 2010a. In Berry and Erskine 2010: 208–24.

———. *Lucius Annaeus Seneca: Natural Questions.* Chicago and London, 2010b.

———. "Seneca's *Naturales Quaestiones* 1960–2005 (Part 2)—with Addenda Covering 2006." *Lustrum* 52 (2010c): 7–160.

Hinojo Andrés, G., and Fernández Corte, J. C., eds. *Munus quaesitum meritis: homenaje a Carmen Codoñer.* Salamanca, 2007.

Hoffer, S. E. *The Anxieties of Pliny the Younger.* Atlanta, GA, 1999.

Hofmann, J. B. *Lateinische Umgangssprache.* 3rd ed. Heidelberg, 1951.

Hohti, P. "Aulus Caecina the Volaterran: Romanization of an Etruscan." In Bruun et al. 1975: 409–33.

Hollis, A. S., ed. *Fragments of Roman Poetry c. 60 BC–AD 20.* Oxford, 2007.

Holmes, N. P. *A Commentary on the Tenth Book of Lucan.* D. Phil. Oxford, 1989.

Hommel, H. "Aristophanes über die Nilschwelle." *RhM* 94 (1951): 315–27.

Horn, C. "Kant und die Stoiker." In Neymeyr et al. 2008: 1081–1103.

Hornblower, S. *A Commentary on Thucydides. Vol. I: Books I–III.* Oxford, 1991.

Hornung, E. *Conceptions of God in Ancient Egypt: The One and the Many.* Trans. J. Baines. London, Melbourne and Henley, 1982.

Housman, A.E. "*Tunica retiarii.*" *CR* 18 (1904): 395–98 = Diggle and Goodyear 1972: 619–22.

———. "*Praefanda.*" *Hermes* 66 (1931): 402–12 = Diggle and Goodyear 1972: 1175–84.

———. "*Fragmenta poetarum.*" *CR* 49 (1935): 166–68 = Diggle and Goodyear 1972: 1244–48.

Howe, N. P. "In Defense of the Encyclopedic Mode: On Pliny's *Preface* to the *Natural History.*" *Latomus* 44 (1985): 561–76.

Huler, S. *Defining the Wind: The Beaufort Scale, and How a 19th-Century Admiral Turned Science into Poetry.* New York, 2004.

Hurley, D. W., ed. *Suetonius: Diuus Claudius.* Cambridge Greek and Latin Classics. Cambridge, 2001.

Hutchinson, G. O. *Latin Literature from Seneca to Juvenal: A Critical Study.* Oxford, 1993.

Huxley, H. H. "Storm and Shipwreck in Roman Literature." *G&R* 21 (1952): 117–24.

Inwood, B. "Seneca in his Philosophical Milieu." *HSCP* 97 (1995): 63–76.

———. "Stoic Ethics." In Algra et al. 1999: 675–705.

———. "God and Human Knowledge in Seneca's *Natural Questions.*" In Cleary and Gurtler 2000: 23–43.

———. "God and Human Knowledge in Seneca's *Natural Questions.*" In Frede and Laks 2002: 119–57.

———. *Reading Seneca: Stoic Philosophy at Rome.* Oxford, 2005.

———. 2009a. "Seneca and Self-Assertion." In Bartsch and Wray 2009: 39–64.

———. 2009b. "Why Physics?" In Salles 2009: 201–23.

Jackson, R. B. *At Empire's Edge: Exploring Rome's Egyptian Frontier.* New Haven and London, 2002.

Jackson, W. T. *Seneca and Kant, or an Exposition of Stoic and Rationalistic Ethics, with a Comparison and Criticism of the Two Systems.* Dayton, OH, 1881.

Jal, P., ed. *Tite-Live Histoire Romaine Tome XXXIII. Livre XLV, Fragments.* Paris, 1979.

Jannot, J.-R. *Religion in Ancient Etruria.* Trans. J. K. Whitehead. Madison, WI, 2005.

Jarvie, I. C., and Agassi, J. "The Problem of the Rationality of Magic." *The British Journal of Sociology* 18 (1967): 55–74 = Wilson 1970: 172–93.

Jashemski, W. F., and Meyer, F. G., eds. *The Natural History of Pompeii.* Cambridge, 2002.

Jayawardhana, R. "Keeping Tabs on Cometary Breakups." *Science* 264 (1994): 907.

Jayo, J. "*Praefanda.* A. E. Housman." *Arion* 9 (2001): 180–200.

Jellinek, E. M. "Drinkers and Alcoholics in Ancient Rome." *Journal of Studies on Alcohol* 37 (1976): 1721–41.

Jervis, J. L. *Cometary Theory in Fifteenth-Century Europe*. Dordrecht, Boston and Lancaster, 1985.

Joly, R. "*Curiositas*." *AC* 30 (1961): 33–44.

Jones, N. F. "Pliny the Younger's Vesuvius *Letters* (6.16 and 6.20)." *CW* 95 (2001): 31–48.

Jónsson, E. M. *Le miroir: naissance d'un genre littéraire*. Paris, 1995.

Jory, E. J. "Associations of Actors in Rome." *Hermes* 98 (1970): 224–53.

Kany-Turpin, J. "La divination augurale romaine, une science des signes?" In Lévy et al. 2003: 61–74.

Kavanagh, B. J. "The Conspirator Aemilius Regulus and Seneca's Aunt's Family." *Historia* 50 (2001): 379–84.

Keller, A. Review of Edelstein 1967. *Technology and Culture* 10 (1969): 87–90.

Kendrick, T. D. *The Lisbon Earthquake*. London, 1956.

Kennedy, G. *The Art of Persuasion in Greece*. Princeton, 1963.

Ker, J. "Nocturnal Writers in Imperial Rome: The Culture of *Lucubratio*." *CPh* 99 (2004): 209–42.

———. *The Deaths of Seneca*. Oxford, 2009.

Keyser, P. T. "On Cometary Theory and Typology from Nechepso-Petosiris Through Apuleius to Servius." *Mnemosyne* 47 (1994): 625–51.

Kidd, I. G. *Posidonius, II: The Commentary. Cambridge Classical Texts and Commentaries* 14A, 14B. Cambridge, 1988.

———. "Theophrastus' Meteorology, Aristotle and Posidonius." In Fortenbaugh and Gutas 1992: 294–306.

———. *Posidonius, III: The Translation of the Fragments. Cambridge Classical Texts and Commentaries* 36. Cambridge, 1999.

Kindstrand, J. F. "Demetrius the Cynic." *Philologus* 124 (1980): 83–98.

Kirk, G. S., Raven, J. E., and Schofield, M., eds. *The Presocratic Philosophers*. 2nd ed. Cambridge, 1983.

Kirschner, P., ed. *Joseph Conrad: Typhoon and Other Stories*. Harmondsworth, 1990.

Kirwan, L. P. "Rome Beyond the Southern Egyptian Frontier." *Geographical Journal* 123 (1957): 13–19.

Kitcher, P. "The Cognitive Functions of Scientific Rhetoric." In Krips et al. 1995: 47–66.

Koeler, G. D., ed. *L. Annaei Senecae Naturalium Quaestionum libri septem*. Göttingen, 1819.

Koestermann, E. *Cornelius Tacitus: Annalen. Band IV: Buch 14–16*. Heidelberg, 1968.

Konstan, D. "Friendship, Frankness and Flattery." In Fitzgerald 1996: 7–19.

Koyré, A. "Du monde de l'à-peu-près' à l'univers de la précision." *Critique* 28 (1948): 806–23.

———. *Études d'histoire de la pensée philosophique.* Paris, 1961.

Krips, H., McGuire, J. E., Melia, T., eds. *Science, Reason, and Rhetoric. Pittsburgh-Konstanz Series in the Philosophy and History of Science 4.* Pittsburgh and Konstanz, 1995.

Kuehn, M. *Kant: A Biography.* Cambridge, 2001.

Kullmann, W. "Antike Vorstufen des modernen Begriffs des Naturgesetzes." In Behrends and Sellert 1995: 36–111.

———. *Naturgesetz in der Vorstellung der Antike, besonders der Stoa. Eine Begriffsuntersuchung.* Stuttgart, 2010.

Küppers, J. "'Kosmosschau' und *uirtus* in den Philosophica Senecas." *A&A* 42 (1996): 57–75.

La Penna, A. "Tra Fetonte e Icaro. Ardimento o amore della scienza?" *Maia* 53 (2001): 535–63.

Labate, M. "Città morte, città future: un tema della poesia augustea." *Maia* 43 (1991): 167–84.

Labhardt, A. "*Curiositas*. Notes sur l'histoire d'un mot et d'une notion." *MH* 17 (1960): 206–24.

Lafond, Y. "Die Katastrophe von 373 v. Chr. und das Verschwinden der Stadt Helike in Achaia." In Olshausen and Sonnabend 1998: 118–23.

Lana, I. *Lucio Anneo Seneca.* Turin, 1955.

———. In discussion after Gigon 1991. In Grimal 1991: 342.

Lanzarone, N., ed. *L. Annaei Senecae Dialogorum liber 1 De prouidentia.* Florence, 2008.

Lapidge, M. "Stoic Cosmology and Roman Literature, First to Third Centuries A.D." *ANRW* II.36.3 (1989): 1379–429.

Lapini, W. "Seneca e il terremoto di Delo: alcuni esempi di confusione tra spostamento geografico e movimento tellurico." *Maia* 47 (1995): 183–200.

Larsen, S. E. "The Lisbon Earthquake and the Scientific Turn in Kant's Philosophy." *European Review* 14 (2006): 359–67.

Laszlo, E. *Science and the Reenchantment of the Cosmos: The Rise of the Integral Vision of Reality.* Rochester, VT, 2006.

Le Blay, F. "Les crocodiles des bords du Nil: Sénèque, *Questions sur la nature*, IVa, II, 12–15." *REL* 85 (2007): 114–30.

Lee, H. D. P., ed. *Aristotle: Meteorologica.* Cambridge, MA, and London, 1952.

Lee, R. L., and Fraser, A. B. *The Rainbow Bridge: Rainbows in Art, Myth, and Science.* University Park, PA, and Bellingham, WA, 2001.

Leitão, D. D. "Senecan Catoptrics and the Passion of Hostius Quadra (Sen. *Nat.* 1)." *MD* 41 (1998): 127–60.

Lévy, C., ed. *Le concept de nature à Rome: la physique. Actes du séminaire de philosophie romaine de l'Université de Paris XII-Val de Marne (1992–1993).* Paris, 1996.

———. "De Chrysippe à Posidonius: variations stoïciennes sur le thème de la divination." In Heintz 1997: 321–43.

————, Besnier, B., and Gigandet, A., eds. *Ars et ratio. Sciences, art et métiers dans la philosophie hellénistique et romaine. Actes du Colloque international organisé à Créteil, Fontenay et Paris du 16 au 18 octobre 1997. Collection Latomus 273.* Brussels, 2003.

Lewis, M. W. "On Human Connectedness with Nature." *New Literary History* 24 (1993): 797–809.

Lewis, N. *Life in Egypt Under Roman Rule.* Oxford, 1983.

Liebeschuetz, J. H. W. G. *Continuity and Change in Roman Religion.* Oxford, 1979.

Limburg, F. J. G. *Aliquid ad Mores: The Prefaces and Epilogues of Seneca's Naturales Quaestiones.* Diss. Leiden, 2007.

————. "The Representation and Role of Badness in Seneca's Moral Teaching: A Case from the *Naturales Quaestiones* (*NQ* 1.16)." In Sluiter and Rosen 2008: 433–49.

Linderski, J. "The Aedileship of Favonius, Curio the Younger and Cicero's Election to the Augurate." *HSCP* 76 (1972): 181–200.

————. "Cicero and Roman Divination." *PP* 37 (1982): 12–38.

————. "Roman Officers in the Year of Pydna." *AJP* 111 (1990): 53–71.

————. *Roman Questions: Selected Papers 1958–1993.* Stuttgart, 1995.

Lloyd, A. B. *Herodotus, Book II: Introduction.* Leiden, 1975.

————. *Herodotus, Book II: Commentary 1–98.* Leiden, 1976.

Lloyd, G. E. R. *Polarity and Analogy: Two Types of Argumentation in Early Greek Thought.* Cambridge, 1966.

————. *Magic, Reason and Experience: Studies in the Origins and Development of Greek Science.* Cambridge, 1979.

Lodge, T. *The Workes of Lucius Annaeus Seneca, Both Morrall and Naturall.* London, 1614.

Long, A. A. "The Stoics on World-Conflagration and Everlasting Recurrence." *SJPh* 23 Supplement (1985): 13–37.

————. *Hellenistic Philosophy: Stoics, Epicureans, Sceptics.* 2nd ed. Berkeley and Los Angeles, 1986.

————. "Cicero's Plato and Aristotle." In Powell 1995: 37–61.

Maass, E., ed. *Commentariorum in Aratum reliquiae.* 2nd ed. Berlin, 1958.

MacDonald, T. L. "Riccioli and Lunar Nomenclature." *Journal of the British Astronomical Association* 77 (1967): 112–17.

Mackail, J. W. "Virgil's Use of the Word *Ingens*." *CR* 26 (1912): 251–55.

MacKendrick, P. *The Philosophical Books of Cicero.* London, 1989.

Mader, G. "Some Observations on the Senecan Götterdämmerung." *AClass* 26 (1983): 61–71.

Magris, A. "'A che serve pregare, se il destino è immutabile?' Un problema del pensiero antico." *Elenchos* 11 (1990): 51–76.

Malaspina, E., ed. *Bibliografia senecana del XX secolo. Pubblicazioni del dipartimento di filologia linguistica e tradizione classica 'Augusto Rostagni' dell'Università di Torino* 23. Bologna, 2005.

Maltby, R. *A Lexicon of Ancient Latin Etymologies*. Leeds, 1991.

Mansfeld, J. *The Pseudo-Hippocratic Tract "Peri hebdomadōn" Ch. 1–11 and Greek Philosophy. Philosophical Texts and Studies* 20. Assen, 1971.

———. "A Theophrastean Excursus on God and Nature and Its Aftermath in Hellenistic Thought." *Phronesis* 37 (1992): 314–35.

Marchesi, I. *The Art of Pliny's Letters: A Poetics of Allusion in the Private Correspondence*. Cambridge, 2008.

Marino, R., ed. *Seneca, Naturales Quaestiones, II*. Pisa and Rome, 1996.

Marsden, B. G. "Cometary Motions." *Celestial Mechanics* 9 (1974): 303–14.

Maso, S. *Lo sguardo della verità: cinque studi su Seneca*. Padua, 1999.

Maurach, G., ed. *Seneca als Philosoph*. Darmstadt, 1975.

Mayer, R. G. "Doctus Seneca." *Mnemosyne* 43 (1990): 395–407.

Mazzoli, G. "Due note anneane, II. L'*inclitum carmen* di Vagellio." *Athenaeum* 46 (1968): 363–68.

———. *Seneca e la poesia*. Milan, 1970.

———. In discussion after Soubiran 1991. In Grimal 1991: 380–81.

McCarty, W. "The Shape of the Mirror: Metaphorical Catoptrics in Classical Literature." *Arethusa* 22 (1989): 161–95.

Merrills, A. Review of Bricault et al. 2007. *CR* 59 (2009): 562–65.

Meyboom, P. G. P. *The Nile Mosaic of Palestrina. Early Evidence of Egyptian Religion in Italy*. Leiden, New York and Köln, 1995.

———, and Versluys, M. J. "The Meaning of Dwarfs in Nilotic Scenes." In Bricault et al. 2007: 170–208.

Migliorini, P. *Scienza e terminologia medica nella letteratura latina di età neroniana: Seneca, Lucano, Persio, Petronio. Studien zur klassischen Philologie* 104. Frankfurt am Main, 1997.

Momigliano, A. "Erodoto e Tucidide sul terremoto di Delo." *SIFC* 8 (1930): 87–89.

———. "The Theological Efforts of the Roman Upper Classes in the First Century B.C." *CPh* 79 (1984): 199–211.

Montanari Caldini, R. "Manilio tra scienza e filosofia. La dottrina delle comete." *Prometheus* 15 (1989): 1–30.

Montiglio, S. "Should the Aspiring Wise Man Travel? A Conflict in Seneca's Thought." *AJP* 127 (2006): 553–86.

Morford, M. P. O. *The Poet Lucan: Studies in Rhetorical Epic*. Oxford, 1967.

Morton Braund, S., ed. *Juvenal: Satires Book 1*. Cambridge Greek and Latin Classics. Cambridge, 1996.

Mosley, A. *Bearing the Heavens: Tycho Brahe and the Astronomical Community of the Late Sixteenth Century*. Cambridge, 2007.

Motto, A. L. "The Idea of Progress in Senecan Thought." *CJ* 79 (1984): 225–40.

———, and Clark, J. R. *Essays on Seneca. Studien zur klassischen Philologie* 79. Frankfurt am Main, 1993.

Mourelatos, A. P. D. "The Ancients' 'Meteorology': Forecasting and Cosmic Natural History." *Rhizai* 2 (2005): 279–91.

Mras, K., *Eusebius Werke*. Vol. 8: *Die Praeparatio Evangelica*. Part 1. 2nd revised ed. by É. Des Places. Berlin, 1982.

Müller, J. "Über die Originalität der *Naturales Quaestiones* Senecas." *Fest-Gruss aus Innsbruck an die XLII. Versammlung deutscher Philologen und Schulmänner in Wien.* Innsbruck, 1893: 1–20.

Murphy, T. *Pliny the Elder's Natural History: The Empire in the Encyclopedia*. Oxford, 2004.

Myerowitz, M. "The Domestication of Desire: Ovid's *Parua Tabella* and the Theater of Love." In Richlin 1992: 131–57.

Naas, V. "Réflexions sur la méthode de travail de Pline l'ancien." *RPh* 70 (1996): 305–32.

———. "Imperialism, *Mirabilia* and Knowledge: Some Paradoxes in the *Naturalis Historia*." In Gibson and Morello 2011: 57–70.

Natali, M. "Tra stoicismo e platonismo: concezione della filosofia e del fine ultimo dell'uomo in Seneca." *RFN* 86 (1994): 427–47.

Nauta, R. R., Van Dam, H.-J., and Smolenaars, J. J. L., eds. *Flavian Poetry*. Leiden and Boston, 2006.

Nelson, R. S., ed. *Visuality Before and Beyond the Renaissance: Seeing as Others Saw*. Cambridge, 2000.

Neymeyr, B., Schmidt, J., and Zimmermann, B., eds. *Stoizismus in der europäischen Philosophie, Literatur, Kunst und Politik: eine Kulturgeschichte von der Antike bis zur Moderne*. Berlin and New York, 2008.

Nicolet, C. *Space, Geography, and Politics in the Early Roman Empire*. Ann Arbor, 1991.

Nielsen, K. "Remarques sur les noms grecs et latins des vents et des régions du ciel." *C&M* 7 (1945): 1–113.

Nightingale, A. W., and Sedley, D., eds. *Ancient Models of Mind: Studies in Human and Divine Rationality*. Cambridge, 2010.

Nisbet, R. G. M., and Hubbard, M. *A Commentary on Horace, Odes, Book I*. Oxford, 1970.

Nisbet, R. G. M., and Rudd, N. *A Commentary on Horace, Odes, Book III*. Oxford, 2004.

Nishimura-Jensen, J. "Unstable Geographies: The Moving Landscape in Apollonius' *Argonautica* and Callimachus' *Hymn to Delos*." *TAPhA* 130 (2000): 287–317.

North, J. "Diviners and Divination at Rome." In Beard and North 1990: 49–71.

Novara, A. *Les idées romaines sur le progrès d'après les écrivains de la République (essai sur le sens latin du progrès)*. 2 vols. Paris, 1982.

Obrist, B. "Wind Diagrams and Medieval Cosmology." *Speculum* 72 (1997): 33–84.

Oeser, E. "Historical Earthquake Theories from Aristotle to Kant." *Historical Earthquakes in Central Europe* 1 (= *Abhandlungen der geologischen Bundesanstalt* 48) (1992): 11–31.

Olshausen, E., and Sonnabend, H., eds. *Stuttgarter Kolloquium zur historischen Geographie des Altertums 6, 1996. "Naturkatastrophen in der antiken Welt."* *Geographica Historica* 10. Stuttgart, 1998.

Oltramare, P. "Le codex Genevensis des *Questions Naturelles* de Sénèque." *RPh* 45 (1921): 5–44.

———, ed. *Sénèque: Questions Naturelles.* 2 vols. Paris, 1929.

Otto, A. *Die Sprichwörter und sprichwörtlichen Redensarten der Römer.* Leipzig, 1890. Reprinted Hildesheim, 1965.

Parroni, P. "Tre congetture alle *Naturales Quaestiones di Seneca.*" In *Dicti studiosus: scritti di filologia offerti a Scevola Mariotti dai suoi allievi.* 103–15. Urbino, 1990.

———. Review of Gross 1989. *RFIC* 120 (1992a): 352–62.

———. "Sul contributo del *Genevensis Lat.* 77 al testo delle *Naturales Quaestiones* di Seneca." *RFIC* 120 (1992b): 165–73.

———. "Osservazioni sul testo delle *Naturales Quaestiones* di Seneca." In Curti and Crimi 1994: 2.537–548.

———. "La nuova edizione teubneriana delle *Naturales Quaestiones* di Seneca." *RFIC* 125 (1997): 113–25.

———. "Le *Naturales Quaestiones* fra scienza e morale," 2000a. In Parroni 2000b: 433–44.

———, ed. *Seneca e il suo tempo. Atti del Convegno internazionale di Roma-Cassino 11- 14 novembre 1998.* Rome, 2000b.

———. "Testo ed esegesi nelle *Naturales Quaestiones.*" In Fedeli 2001: 139–54.

———, ed. *Seneca: Ricerche sulla natura.* Milan, 2002.

———. "Le *Naturales Quaestiones.* Introduzione." In De Robertis and Resta 2004: 313–18.

Parry-Jones, B. "Pagophagia, or Compulsive Ice Consumption: A Historical Perspective." *Psychological Medicine* 22 (1992): 561–71.

Pease, A. S., ed. *M. Tulli Ciceronis De Natura Deorum libri tres.* 2 vols. Cambridge, MA, 1955–58.

———, ed. *M. Tulli Ciceronis De Diuinatione libri duo.* Darmstadt, 1973. Originally published in *University of Illinois Studies in Language and Literature* 6 (1920): 161–500; and 8 (1923): 153–474.

Pecere, O., and Stramaglia, A., eds. *La letteratura di consumo nel mondo greco-latino. Atti del Convegno internazionale, Cassino, 14–17 settembre 1994.* Cassino, 1996.

Pendrick, G. J., ed. *Antiphon the Sophist: The Fragments. Cambridge Classical Texts and Commentaries* 39. Cambridge, 2002.

Pera, M. "The Role and Value of Rhetoric in Science." In Pera and Shea 1991: 29–54.

———, and Shea, W. R., eds. *Persuading Science: The Art of Scientific Rhetoric.* Canton, MA, 1991.

Peterson, W., ed. *M. Fabi Quintiliani Institutionis Oratoriae liber decimus.* Oxford, 1891.

Pfiffig, A. J. *Religio Etrusca.* Graz, 1975.

Pfligersdorffer, G. "Lucan als Dichter des geistigen Widerstandes." *Hermes* 87 (1959): 344–77.

Pisi, G. *La peste in Seneca tra scienza e letteratura.* Rome, 1989.

Porter, J. I. "Lucretius and the Sublime." In Gillespie and Hardie 2007: 167–84.

Postl, B. *Die Bedeutung des Nil in der römischen Literatur mit besonderer Berücksichtigung der wichtigsten griechischen Autoren.* Wien, 1970.

Powell, J. G. F., ed. *Cicero: Cato Maior De Senectute. Cambridge Classical Texts and Commentaries* 28. Cambridge, 1988.

———, ed. *Cicero the Philosopher: Twelve Papers.* Oxford, 1995.

Pownall, F. *Lessons from the Past: The Moral Use of History in Fourth-Century Prose.* Ann Arbor, 2004.

Puhvel, J. "The Origins of Greek *Kosmos* and Latin *Mundus.*" *AJP* 97 (1976): 154–67.

Ramos Guerreira, A., ed. *Mnemosynum C. Codoñer a discipulis oblatum.* Salamanca, 1991.

Ramsey, J. T. "Mithridates, the Banner of Ch'ih-Yu, and the Comet Coin." *HSCP* 99 (1999): 197–253.

———. *A Descriptive Catalogue of Greco-Roman Comets from 500 B.C. to A.D. 400. Syllecta Classica* 17. Iowa City, IA, 2006.

———. "A Catalogue of Greco-Roman Comets from 500 B.C. to A.D. 400." *JHA* 28 (2007): 175–97.

———, and Licht, A. L. *The Comet of 44 B.C. and Caesar's Funeral Games.* Atlanta, GA, 1997.

Rasmussen, S. W. *Public Portents in Republican Rome.* Rome, 2003.

Rauch, M. *Bacchische Themen und Nilbilder auf Campanareliefs.* Rahden-Westfalen, 1999.

Rawson, E. "Caesar, Etruria and the *Disciplina Etrusca.*" *JRS* 68 (1978): 132–52.

———. "The Life and Death of Asclepiades of Bithynia." *CQ* 32 (1982): 358–70.

———. *Intellectual Life in the Late Roman Republic.* London, 1985.

Ray, G. "Reading the Lisbon Earthquake: Adorno, Lyotard, and the Contemporary Sublime." *Yale Journal of Criticism* 17 (2004): 1–18.

Reale, G. *Aristotele: Trattato sul Cosmo per Alessandro.* Naples, 1974.

Reale, G., and Bos, A. P. *Il trattato "Sul cosmo per Alessandro" attribuito ad Aristotele.* 2nd ed. Milan, 1995.

Rehm, A. "Anlage und Buchfolge von Senecas *Naturales Quaestiones.*" *Philologus* 66 (1907): 374–95.

———. "Das siebente Buch der *Naturales Quaestiones* des Seneca und die Kometentheorie des Poseidonios." *SBAW* 1921: 3–40. Reprinted in Maurach 1975: 228–63.

Reinhardt, K. *Poseidonios.* Munich, 1921.

Reinhardt, O., and Oldroyd, D. R. "Kant's Theory of Earthquakes and Volcanic Action." *Annals of Science* 40 (1983): 247–72.

Reinhardt, T., Lapidge, M., and Adams, J. N., eds. *Aspects of the Language of Latin Prose. Proceedings of the British Academy* 129. Oxford, 2005.

Renard, M., and Schilling, R., eds. *Hommages à Jean Bayet. Collection Latomus* 70. Brussels, 1964.

Renehan, R. "The Greek Anthropocentric View of Man." *HSCP* 84 (1981): 239–59.

Reno, E. A. Review of Edelstein 1967. *Review of Metaphysics* 21 (1968): 748.

Repici, L. "Gli Stoici e la divinazione secondo Cicerone." *Hermes* 123 (1995): 175–92.

Reydams-Schils, G. *The Roman Stoics: Self, Responsibility, and Affection.* Chicago and London, 2005.

———. "Seneca's Platonism: The Soul and Its Divine Origin." In Nightingale and Sedley 2010: 196–215.

Reynolds, L. D., ed. *Texts and Transmission: A Survey of the Latin Classics.* Oxford, 1983.

Richardson-Hay, C. "Dinner at Seneca's Table: The Philosophy of Food." *G&R* 56 (2009): 71–96.

Richlin, A. *The Garden of Priapus: Sexuality and Aggression in Roman Humor.* New Haven and London, 1983.

———, ed. *Pornography and Representation in Greece and Rome.* Oxford, 1992.

Rihll, T. E. *Greek Science. Greece & Rome New Surveys in the Classics* 29. Oxford, 1999.

Ringshausen, K. W. *Poseidonios-Asklepiodot-Seneca und ihre Anschauungen über Erdbeben und Vulkane.* Diss. Munich, 1929.

Rocca, S., ed. *L'uomo e la natura. Latina Didaxis XI: Atti del congresso, Bogliasco, 30- 31 marzo 1996.* Genoa, 1996.

Rogers, R. R., and Yau, M. K. *A Short Course in Cloud Physics.* 3rd ed. Boston, 1989.

Rogers, R. S. "The Neronian Comets." *TAPhA* 84 (1953): 237–49.

Roller, M. B. *Constructing Autocracy: Aristocrats and Emperors in Julio-Claudian Rome.* Princeton and Oxford, 2001.

Romm, J. S. *The Edges of the Earth in Ancient Thought: Geography, Exploration, and Fiction.* Princeton, 1992.

Rosenmeyer, T. G. "Seneca and Nature." *Arethusa* 33 (2000): 99–119.

Rossi, P. "Sulle *Naturales Quaestiones* di Seneca: il *De aquis terrestribus* e l'idrologia moderna." *Aufidus* 14 (1991): 147–58.

———. *Geografia generale ed astronomica nelle Naturales Quaestiones di Seneca.* Bari, 1992.

Rudich, V. *Political Dissidence Under Nero: The Price of Dissimulation.* London and New York, 1993.

Rutherford, R. B. *The Meditations of Marcus Aurelius: A Study.* Oxford, 1989.

Salanitro, G. "Scienza e morale nelle *Naturales Quaestiones* di Seneca." *Sileno* 16 (1990): 307–12.

Salem, M. S. "Ennius and the *Isiaci coniectores.*" *JRS* 28 (1938): 56–59.

Salles, R., ed. *God and Cosmos in Stoicism.* Oxford, 2009.

Salvadore, M., ed. *M. Terenti Varronis fragmenta omnia quae extant. Pars I supplementum.* Hildesheim, Zürich and New York, 1999.

Sambursky, S. *Physics of the Stoics.* London, 1959.

Sandys, J., ed. *The Odes of Pindar.* London and New York, 1924.

Santini, C., and Scivoletto, N., eds. *Prefazioni, prologhi, proemi di opere tecnico-scientifiche latine.* 2 vols. Rome, 1992.

Scarpat Bellincioni, M. *Studi senecani e altri scritti*. Brescia, 1986.

Schama, S. *Landscape and Memory*. New York, 1995.

Schechner Genuth, S. *Comets, Popular Culture, and the Birth of Modern Cosmology*. Princeton, 1997.

Schenkeveld, D. M. "Language." In Algra et al. 1999: 177–92, 213–25.

Schepens, G. "Historiographical Problems in Ephorus." In *Historiographia antiqua: Commentationes Lovanienses in honorem W. Peremans septuagenarii editae*. 95–118. Leuven, 1977.

———, and Delcroix, K. "Ancient Paradoxography: Origin, Evolution, Production and Reception." In Pecere and Stramaglia 1996: 373–460.

Schiesaro, A. *The Passions in Play: Thyestes and the Dynamics of Senecan Drama*. Cambridge, 2003.

Schmeisser, G. *Quaestionum de Etrusca disciplina particula*. Diss. Breslau, 1872.

Schofield, M. "Cicero For and Against Divination." *JRS* 76 (1986): 47–65.

Schönberger, O., and Schönberger, E. *L. Annaeus Seneca: naturwissenschaftliche Untersuchungen in acht Büchern*. Würzburg, 1990.

Schrijvers, P. H. "Le regard sur l'invisible: étude sur l'emploi de l'analogie dans l'oeuvre de Lucrèce." In Gigon 1978: 77–114.

———. "The 'Two Cultures' in Lucan: Some Remarks on Lucan's *Pharsalia* and Ancient Sciences of Nature." In Walde 2005: 26–39.

———. "Silius Italicus and the Roman Sublime." In Nauta et al. 2006: 97–111.

———. "A Literary View on the Nile Mosaic at Praeneste," 2007a. In Bricault et al. 2007: 223–39.

———. "Seeing the Invisible: A Study of Lucretius' Use of Analogy in the *De rerum natura*," 2007b. In Gale 2007: 255–88. A translation of Schrijvers 1978.

Scott, J. "The Ethics of the Physics in Seneca's *Natural Questions*." *CB* 75 (1999): 55–68.

Seargent, D. A. J. *The Greatest Comets in History. Broom Stars and Celestial Scimitars*. New York, 2009.

See, T. J. J. "On the Temperature, Secular Cooling and Contraction of the Earth, and on the Theory of Earthquakes Held by the Ancients." *Proceedings of the American Philosophical Society* 46 (1907): 191–299.

Setaioli, A. "Elementi di *sermo cotidianus* nella lingua di Seneca prosatore, I." *SIFC* 52 (1980): 5–47.

———. "Elementi di *sermo cotidianus* nella lingua di Seneca prosatore, II." *SIFC* 53 (1981): 5–49.

———. "Seneca e lo stile." *ANRW* II.32.2 (1985): 776–858.

———. *Seneca e i Greci. Citazioni e traduzioni nelle opere filosofiche*. Bologna, 1988.

———. *Facundus Seneca. Aspetti della lingua e dell'ideologia senecana*. Bologna, 2000.

———. "L'analogie et la similitude comme instruments de démonstration chez Lucrèce." *Pallas* 69 (2005): 117–41.

————. "Seneca and the Divine: Stoic Tradition and Personal Developments." *International Journal of the Classical Tradition* 13 (2007): 333–68.

Shackleton Bailey, D. R. "Notes on Seneca's *Quaestiones Naturales*." *CQ* 73 (1979): 448–56.

Sharples, R. W., ed. *Cicero: On Fate, Boethius: The Consolation of Philosophy IV.5–7, V*. Warminster, 1991.

Shaw, P. *The Sublime*. London and New York, 2006.

Sheikh, H. A. "Roman Expeditions to the Upper Nile." In Carratelli et al. 1992: 157–60.

Sherwin-White, A. N. *The Letters of Pliny: A Historical and Social Commentary*. Oxford, 1966.

Shipley, G., and Salmon, J., eds. *Human Landscapes in Classical Antiquity: Environment and Culture*. London and New York, 1996.

Shute, M. N. "Ancient Imagination and Seismic Disruption." *Yale Review* 69 (1979): 55–71.

Sieberg, A. *Untersuchungen über Erdbeben und Bruchschollenbau im östlichen Mittelmeergebiet*. Jena, 1932.

Sigurdsson, H. "Mount Vesuvius Before the Disaster." In Jashemski and Meyer 2002: 29–36.

Simons, H. W. "Are Scientists Rhetors in Disguise? An Analysis of Discursive Processes Within Scientific Communities." In White 1980: 115–30.

————. "The Rhetoric of Inquiry as an Intellectual Movement," 1990a. In Simons 1990b: 1–31.

————, ed. *The Rhetorical Turn: Invention and Persuasion in the Conduct of Inquiry*. Chicago and London, 1990b.

Sinko, T. "*De Menandri fragmento* 951 K. (Sen. *Nat. Quaest.* IVa praef. 19)." *Eos* 38 (1937): 285–95.

Sluiter, I., and Rosen, R. M., eds. *Kakos: Badness and Anti-Value in Classical Antiquity*. Leiden and Boston, 2008.

Smith, K. F., ed. *The Elegies of Albius Tibullus*. New York, 1913. Reprinted Darmstadt, 1985.

Smith, P. R. "'A Self-Indulgent Misuse of Leisure and Writing'? How Not to Write Philosophy: Did Cicero Get It Right?" In Powell 1995: 301–23.

Solimano, G. *La prepotenza dell'occhio: riflessioni sull'opera di Seneca*. Genoa, 1991.

Solmsen, F. "Cleanthes or Posidonius? The Basis of Stoic Physics." *MNAW* 24 (1961): 265–89.

Solodow, J. B. *The Latin Particle Quidem. American Classical Studies* 4. Boulder, CO, 1978.

————. "Persistence of Virgilian Memories." *LCM* 14 (1989): 119–21.

Sørensen, V. *Seneca: The Humanist at the Court of Nero*. Trans. W. G. Jones. Chicago, 1984.

Soubiran, J. "Sénèque prosateur et poète: convergences métriques." In Grimal 1991: 347–77.

Spencer, D. *The Roman Alexander: Reading a Cultural Myth*. Exeter, 2002.

Stahl, G. "Die 'naturales quaestiones' Senecas. Ein Beitrag zum Spiritualisierungsprozeß der römischen Stoa." *Hermes* 92 (1964): 425–54. Reprinted in Maurach 1975: 264–304.

Stanton, E. A. "The Great Marshes of the White Nile." *Journal of the Royal African Society* 2 (1903): 375–79.

Steinmetz, P. "Zur Erdbebentheorie des Poseidonios." *RhM* 105 (1962): 261–63.

——— . *Die Physik des Theophrastos von Eresos. Palingenesia* 1. Bad Homburg, Berlin and Zürich, 1964.

Stengel, R. *You're Too Kind: A Brief History of Flattery*. New York, 2000.

Stok, F. "La discreta fortuna delle *Naturales Quaestiones*." *GIF* 52 (2000): 349–73.

Strohm, H. "Theophrast und Poseidonios: Drei Interpretationen zur Meteorologie." *Hermes* 81 (1953): 278–95.

——— . "Beiträge zum Verständnis der *Naturales Quaestiones* Senecas." In *Latinität und alte Kirche: Festschrift für Rudolf Hanslik zum 70. Geburtstag*. 309–25. Wien, Köln and Graz, 1977.

Struck, P. T. "A World Full of Signs: Understanding Divination in Ancient Stoicism." In Curry and Voss 2007: 3–20.

Summers, W. C., ed. *Select Letters of Seneca*. London, 1910.

Swetnam-Burland, M. "Egyptian Objects, Roman Contexts: A Taste for Aegyptiaca in Italy." In Bricault et al. 2007: 113–36.

Tandoi, V. "Albinovano Pedone e la retorica giulio-claudia delle conquiste." *SIFC* 36 (1964): 129–68.

Tarrant, R. J., ed. *Seneca: Agamemnon. Cambridge Classical Texts and Commentaries* 18. Cambridge, 1976.

Taub, L. *Ancient Meteorology*. London and New York, 2003.

——— . *Aetna and the Moon: Explaining Nature in Ancient Greece and Rome*. Corvallis, OR, 2008.

Taylor, P., ed. *The Oxford Companion to the Garden*. Oxford, 2006.

Taylor, R. M. "Two Pathic Subcultures in Ancient Rome." *Journal of the History of Sexuality* 7 (1997): 319–71.

——— . *The Moral Mirror of Roman Art*. Cambridge, 2008.

Thomas, R. F., ed. *Virgil: Georgics. Cambridge Greek and Latin Classics*. 2 vols. Cambridge, 1988.

Thompson, D'A. W. "The Greek Winds." *CR* 32 (1918): 49–56.

Thomsen, O. "Seneca the Story-Teller: The Structure and Function, the Humour and Psychology of His Stories." *C&M* 32 (1979–80): 151–97.

Thulin, C. O. *Die Etruskische Disciplin. I: Die Blitzlehre*. Göteborg, 1906.

Timpanaro, S. "La tipologia delle citazioni poetiche in Seneca: alcune considerazioni." *GIF* 36 (1984): 163–82.

——— , ed. *Marco Tullio Cicerone, Della Divinazione*. 4th ed. Milan, 1998.

Toohey, P. G. *Melancholy, Love, and Time:Boundaries of the Self in Ancient Literature*. Ann Arbor, 2004.

Torre, C. "Il banchetto di *luxuria* nell'opera in prosa di Seneca." *Paideia* 52 (1997): 377–96.

Toulmin, S. "Science and the Many Faces of Rhetoric." In Krips et al. 1995: 3–11.

Toynbee, J. M. C. *Animals in Roman Life and Art.* London, 1973.

Traglia, A. "Il valore dossografico del *De terrae motu* di Seneca." *Medioevo e rinascimento: studi in onore di Bruno Nardi.* 2 vols. 2.733–52. Florence, 1955.

Traina, G. "Terremoti e società romana: problemi di mentalità e uso delle informazioni." *ASNP* 15 (1985): 867–87.

Tucker, C. W. "Cicero, *Augur, De Iure Augurali.*" *CW* 70 (1976): 171–77.

Tulin, A. "Xenophanes fr. 18 D.-K. and the Origins of the Idea of Progress." *Hermes* 121 (1993): 129–38.

Tuplin, C. J., and Rihll, T. E., eds. *Science and Mathematics in Ancient Greek Culture.* Oxford, 2002.

Turcan-Deleani, M. "*Frigus amabile.*" In Renard and Schilling 1964: 691–96.

Uglione, R., ed. *L'uomo antico e la natura. Atti del Convegno nazionale di studi, Torino 28–29–30 aprile 1997.* Turin, 1998.

Van Der Horst, P. W. *Chaeremon: Egyptian Priest and Stoic Philosopher.* Leiden, 1984.

Van Nouhuys, T. *The Age of Two-Faced Janus: The Comets of 1577 and 1618 and the Decline of the Aristotelian World View in the Netherlands.* Leiden, Boston and Köln, 1998.

Van Raalte, M. "The Nature of Fire and Its Complications: Theophrastus' *De Igne* 1–10." *BICS* 53 (2010): 47–97.

Van Straaten, M., ed. *Panétius: sa vie, ses écrits et sa doctrine avec une édition des fragments.* Amsterdam, 1946.

Verhagen, F. C. "Worldviews and Metaphors in the Human-Nature Relationship: An Ecolinguistic Exploration Through the Ages." *Language and Ecology* 2 (2008): 1–15.

Versluys, M. J. *Aegyptiaca Romana: Nilotic Scenes and the Roman Views of Egypt.* Leiden and Boston, 2002.

Veyne, P. *Seneca: The Life of a Stoic.* Trans. D. Sullivan. New York and London, 2003.

Vigourt, A. *Les présages impériaux d'Auguste à Domitien.* Paris, 2001.

Viti, A. "Seneca, *Ep.* 91: Liberale e l'incendio di Lione." *Paideia* 52 (1997): 397–406.

Volk, K. "Pious and Impious Approaches to Cosmology in Manilius." *MD* 47 (2001): 85–117.

———. "'Heavenly Steps': Manilius 4.119–121 and Its Background." In Boustan and Reed 2004: 34–46.

———. "Cosmic Disruption in Seneca's *Thyestes*: Two Ways of Looking at an Eclipse." In Volk and Williams 2006: 183–200.

———. *Manilius and His Intellectual Background.* Oxford, 2009.

———, and Williams, G. D., eds. *Seeing Seneca Whole: Perspectives on Philosophy, Poetry and Politics.* Leiden and Boston, 2006.

Vottero, D., ed. *Questioni Naturali di Lucio Anneo Seneca*. Turin, 1989.

——, ed. *L. Anneo Seneca: I frammenti*. Bologna, 1998a.

——. "Seneca e la natura." 1998b. In Uglione 1998: 291–303.

Waiblinger, F. P. *Senecas Naturales Quaestiones: griechische Wissenschaft und römische Form*. Munich, 1977.

Walde, C., ed. *Lucan im 21. Jahrhundert*. Munich and Leipzig, 2005.

Waldherr, G. H. *Erdbeben, das aussergewöhnliche Normale: zur Rezeption seismischer Aktivitäten in literarischen Quellen vom 4. Jahrhundert v. Chr. bis zum 4. Jahrhundert n. Chr. Geographica Historica* 9. Stuttgart, 1997.

Wallace-Hadrill, A. "Pliny the Elder and Man's Unnatural History." *G&R* 37 (1990): 80–96.

——. "*Mutatio Morum*: The Idea of a Cultural Revolution." In Habinek and Schiesaro 1997: 3–22.

——. "Seneca and the Pompeian Earthquake." In De Vivo and Lo Cascio 2003: 177–91.

——. *Rome's Cultural Revolution*. Cambridge, 2008.

Walters, J. "Making a Spectacle: Deviant Men, Invective and Pleasure." *Arethusa* 31 (1998): 355–67.

Wardle, D., ed. *Cicero: On Divination, Book 1*. Oxford, 2006.

Warner, M. *Philosophical Finesse: Studies in the Art of Rational Persuasion*. Oxford, 1989.

Watson, L. *Heaven's Breath: A Natural History of the Wind*. New York, 1984.

Watt, W. S. "Notes on Seneca, *Epistulae* and *Naturales Quaestiones*." *CQ* 44 (1994): 185–98.

——. "Six Notes on the Text of Seneca, *Naturales Quaestiones*." *CQ* 50 (2000): 623–24.

Watterson, B. *The Gods of Ancient Egypt*. London, 1984.

Weber, D. "Ethik und Naturwissenschaft. Die Praefatio zu Senecas *Naturales Quaestiones*." *Zur Philosophie der Antike, WHB Sonderheft*. Vienna, 1995: 73–92.

Wehrli, F., ed. *Die Schule des Aristoteles. Heft 5: Straton von Lampsakos*. Basel, 1950.

Weinstock, S. "*Libri Fulgurales*." *PBSR* 19 (1951): 122–53.

Weissenborn, W., and Müller, H. J., eds. *Titi Livi Ab urbe condita libri*. Vol. 10. *Buch XLV und Fragmente*. 4th ed. Berlin, Dublin and Zürich, 1965.

Wheatley, H. B. *London, Past and Present: Its History, Associations and Traditions. Based on "The Handbook of London" by the Late Peter Cunningham*. 3 vols. London, 1891.

Whipple, F. L. *The Mystery of Comets*. Washington, DC, 1985.

White, A. D. "A History of the Doctrine of Comets." *Papers of the American Historical Association* 2 (1887): 5–43.

White, E. E., ed. *Rhetoric in Transition: Studies in the Nature and Uses of Rhetoric*. University Park, PA, and London, 1980.

Wildberger, J. *Seneca und die Stoa: Der Platz des Menschen in der Welt*. 2 vols. Berlin and New York, 2006.

Wilkinson, L. P. "Lucretius and the Love-Philtre." *CR* 63 (1949): 47–48.

Williams, C. A. *Roman Homosexuality*. 2nd ed. Oxford, 2010.

Williams, G. *Change and Decline: Roman Literature in the Early Empire*. Berkeley and Los Angeles, 1978.

Williams, G. D., ed. *Seneca: De Otio, De Breuitate Vitae*. Cambridge Greek and Latin Classics. Cambridge, 2003.

———. "Interactions: Physics, Morality and Narrative in Seneca, *Natural Questions* 1." *CPh* 100 (2005a): 142–65.

———. "Seneca on Winds: The Art of Anemology in *Natural Questions* 5." *AJP* 126 (2005b): 417–50.

———. "Greco-Roman Seismology and Seneca on Earthquakes in *Natural Questions* 6." *JRS* 96 (2006a): 124–46.

———. "States of Exile, States of Mind: Paradox and Reversal in Seneca's *Consolatio ad Heluiam Matrem*." 2006b. In Volk and Williams 2006: 147–73.

———. "Seneca on Comets and Ancient Cometary Theory in *Natural Questions* 7." *Ramus* 36 (2007): 97–117.

———. "Cold Science: Seneca on Hail and Snow in *Natural Questions* 4B." *PCPhS* 54 (2008a): 209–36.

———. "Reading the Waters: Seneca on the Nile in *Natural Questions*, Book 4a." *CQ* 57 (2008b): 218–42.

Williams, J. *Observations of Comets from 611 B.C. to A.D. 1640 Extracted from the Chinese Annals*. London, 1871.

Williams, R. D., ed. *P. Vergili Maronis Aeneidos liber tertius*. Oxford, 1962.

Wilson, B. R., ed. *Rationality*. Oxford, 1970.

Wimmer, F., ed. *Theophrasti Eresii opera quae supersunt omnia*. Paris, 1866. Reprinted Frankfurt am Main, 1964.

Winterbottom, M. Review of Corcoran 1971–72. *CR* 26 (1976): 46–48.

Woodman, A. J., ed. *Velleius Paterculus: The Tiberian Narrative (2.94–131)*. Cambridge Classical Texts and Commentaries 19. Cambridge, 1977.

———, ed. *Velleius Paterculus: The Caesarian and Augustan Narrative (2.41–93)*. Cambridge Classical Texts and Commentaries 25. Cambridge, 1983.

Yeomans, D. K. *Comets: A Chronological History of Observation, Science, Myth, and Folklore*. New York, 1991.

Zanker, P. *The Power of Images in the Age of Augustus*. Trans. A. Shapiro. Ann Arbor, 1988.

Zeilinga de Boer, J., and Sanders, D. T. *Earthquakes in Human History: The Far-Reaching Effects of Seismic Disruptions*. Princeton and Oxford, 2005.

Zetzel, J. E. G., ed. *Cicero, De Re Publica: Selections*. Cambridge Greek and Latin Classics. Cambridge, 1995.

———, ed. *Cicero: On the Commonwealth and On the Laws*. Cambridge, 1999.

Ziff, L., ed. *Ralph Waldo Emerson: Selected Essays*. Harmondsworth, 1982.

Index of Passages

General Index

Achilles Tatius, astronomer 177
Acoreus in Lucan 119–20
Aeschylus, pupil of Hippocrates of
     Chios 277
Agrippa's global map 52
air
     animating description of 242–45
     internal coherence 61–62, 304
     as material 62, 304
     self-ignition, to cause
          lightning 307–308
     self-motion 180–81, 183, 299, 308
     special force of term *spiritus* 189–91,
          237–38 and n. 87, 247
     as vital elemental force 174–83
Alexander the Great 33–34, 36, 50, 51 n.
     120, 173, 207–208, 209–11, 255
     as antitype of *sapiens* 37
     and Callisthenes 253–54
Allen, James 319
analogy 17, 21, 153–55, 156–57, 164,
     191–92, 233–35, 237–41, 246, 306
     domesticating use of 220–22, 239, 241
     world/body analogy 62 and n. 30,
          127, 128, 174, 179, 190, 241–42
Anaxagoras 133, 134, 135, 155–57, 234 n.
     73, 300, 302, 309
     cometary theory 276, 279, 281 n. 88
     fire-theory of earthquakes 237–38
          and n. 88
     theory of snow's blackness 155
          and n. 66
Anaximander 175 and n. 17, 177 and
     n. 29, 239 n. 92, 300

Anaximenes 65, 175 and n. 18, 231, 239,
     283 n. 94, 300
André, J.-M. 118
anemology tradition 171, 173 and n. 8,
     174–75 and n. 15
Annaeus Fidus 99 and n. 21
anthropocentrism of nature 21, 40, 113,
     268 and n. 34, 290
Antipater of Tarsus 316 n. 84
Apollonius, athlete 99 and n. 21
Apollonius of Myndus 274 n. 53, 277
     and n. 71, 286–89
Arachne 65, 66 n. 42
Araxes 244
Archelaus 231, 240 and nn. 98, 99, 241 n.
     103, 242
Aristarchus of Samos 290 n. 113
Aristophanes of Byzantium 102
Aristotle 28, 146–47, 148, 196, 246
     comets as *sublimia* 273–74, 276,
          279–80, 337
     earthquake theory 240 and n. 100,
          241
     exhalation theory 65 n. 40, 163, 176,
          177, 179 and n. 34, 188, 240 and
          n. 102, 273–74, 299, 300, 301, 309
     on hail 157
     influence in shaping Greek
          meteorological tradition 6 and n. 9
     lightning and thunder 299, 309–11
     rainbow theory 71
     on Thales 232–33
     use of *endoxa* 18 n. 6
     on wind 173, 175–77

Index of Latin Words

Index of Greek Words